MEMOIRS OF MY LIFE

D0451613

MEMOIRS OF MY LIFE

BY

JOHN CHARLES FRÉMONT
Explorer of the American West

INCLUDING THREE JOURNEYS OF WESTERN EXPLORATION

DURING THE YEARS

1842, 1843–1844, 1845–1847

———————

SUPERBLY ILLUSTRATED BY ORIGINAL PORTRAITS, DESCRIPTIVE
PLATES, MAPS, AND, FROM THE MISSOURI RIVER TO THE PACIFIC, BY
A SERIES OF SKETCHES AND DAGUERREOTYPES MADE
DURING THE JOURNEYS.

———————

NEW INTRODUCTION BY CHARLES M. ROBINSON III

Cooper Square Press

First Cooper Square Press edition 2001

This Cooper Square Press paperback edition of *Memoirs of My Life* is an unabridged republication of the edition first published in New York in 1886, with the deletion of three maps, and supplemented with a new introduction by Charles M. Robinson III.

New introduction copyright © 2001 by Charles M. Robinson III

Published by Cooper Square Press
An Imprint of the Rowman & Littlefield Publishing Group
150 Fifth Avenue, Suite 817
New York, New York 10011

Distributed by National Book Network

Library of Congress Cataloging-in-Publication Data

Frémont, John Charles, 1813–1890.
  Memoirs of my life / John Charles Frémont.
    p. cm.
  Originally published: Chicago : Belford, Clarke & Co., 1887.
  ISBN 0-8154-1164-2 (cloth : alk. paper)
    1. Frémont, John Charles, 1813–1890. 2. Explorers— United States— Biography. 3. West (U.S.)— Discovery and exploration. 4. West (U.S.)— Description and travel. 5. California— Discovery and exploration. 6. California— Description and travel. 7. Generals— United States— Biography. 8. Presidential candidates— United States— Biography. I. Title.
  E415.9.F8 F8 2001
  973.6'092— dc21

                                                                2001047018

∞™ The paper used in this publication meets the minimum requirements of American National Standard for Information Sciences— Permanence of Paper for Printed Library Materials, ANSI/NISO Z39.48–1992.
Manufactured in the United States of America.

CONTENTS.

CHAPTER I.

CHAPTER II.

CHAPTER III.

CHAPTER IV.

MY FIRST EXPEDITION, 1842.

CHAPTER V.

CHAPTER VI.

CHAPTER VII.

CHAPTER VIII.

CHAPTER IX.

CHAPTER XIV.

THIRD EXPEDITION, 1845-46.—*Continued.*

CHAPTER XV.

THIRD EXPEDITION, 1845-46.—*Continued.*

CHAPTER OF RESULTS.

LIST OF ILLUSTRATIONS.

MAPS.

INTRODUCTION TO THE
COOPER SQUARE PRESS EDITION.

FREMONT Lake. Fremont Peak. Fremont, Ohio. Fremont, California. All honor John Charles Frémont, explorer extraordinaire of the first half of the nineteenth century. His discoveries in what was then the unknown American West led an admiring public to call him "The Pathfinder." Yet for all the towns, counties, and geographical features named in his honor, Frémont is little remembered in our own time, a fact that to some degree can be attributed to the sterility of late-twentieth-century political correctness. In modern times, men like Frémont, who epitomized American expansionism and empire building, are seen as villains rather than heroes. They are remembered not for what they achieved (often at great personal hardship), but for the negative aspects of their achievements. They have been demonized because of the subsequent subjugation of the American Indian, the destruction of the environment, and a multitude of other sins that they themselves hardly could have foreseen. The great irony is that those who demonize them often sit comfortably in well-salaried, tenured positions in some of the very same regions that these heroes-turned-villains opened for settlement.

In Frémont's time, however, the vast majority of the American people were crowded into the eastern third of the country, hemmed in by Canada to the north, the Gulf of Mexico to the south, the Atlantic Ocean to the east, and the awesome Mississippi–Missouri River system to the west. West of the great rivers was a seemingly endless, featureless void, shown on maps as "the Great American Desert." It had turned back Spaniard and Frenchman in centuries past, and was the realm of the Plains Indian tribes and the mountain man. Through his explorations Frémont revealed the true nature of this desert. He shrank the region into something comprehensible and showed the nation that it might be habitable. This, undoubtedly, was his greatest achievement, and he lived to see the "desert" removed from maps and replaced by inhabited states and territories.

Even in his own time, however, Frémont alternated between fame and obscurity. His life was almost a roller coaster of poverty, wealth, and poverty again, finally leveling out in modest comfort on a government pension. Tainted by what was then the unforgivable sin of illegitimacy, he had to carve his own niche in the world.

Frémont was fortunate in being presented with opportunities for social and educational advancement, but equally fortunate in having the good sense to use them. He was especially gifted in mathematics. This, along with the various social contacts he had acquired, secured him an appointment as assistant engineer for a projected railroad between Charleston, South Carolina, and Cincinnati, Ohio. Much of the region was still untamed wilderness, owned in part by the Cherokee Indians. "Here," he later wrote, "I found the path which I was 'destined to walk.' Through many of the years to come the occupation of my prime of life was to be among Indians and in waste places. . . . The work was laid out and it began here with a remarkable continuity of purpose."

With this experience, and aided by a carefully cultivated association with Secretary of War Joel Poinsett, Frémont secured a commission as second lieutenant in the army, and was assigned to two successive military and scientific expeditions up the Missouri River. Meanwhile, he had caught the attention of Jessie Benton, daughter of Senator Thomas Hart Benton of Missouri, one of the most powerful men in Congress, and one of the architects of American expansionism. On October 19, 1841, after his return from the second Missouri River expedition, Frémont and Jessie eloped. Although she was only sixteen, Senator Benton accepted the situation and became almost a father figure to his son-in-law. With the senator's help Frémont secured command of an expedition into the semi-unknown country beyond South Pass, Wyoming. One of the guides was mountain man Christopher (Kit) Carson. On his return Frémont wrote an account that made them both national celebrities.

Frémont's greatest admirer was his wife. The marriage was a love match that, despite Jessie's social position, reflected frontier values in that she was an equal partner. Indeed, it might be said that she provided the only real stability in his life. In his *Memoirs*, prepared more than forty years later and reprinted here, Frémont wrote of Jessie, "There was a rare union of intelligence to feel the injury of events, and submission to them with silence and discretion; and withal a sweet, and happy, and forbearing temper which has remained proof against the wearing of time."

Jessie herself was a gifted writer with a flair for public relations, but it would be a mistake to believe that she was responsible for her husband's fame. Frémont's goals were already well established; her role was one of encouragement. Secure in the knowledge that her powerful father could make things right—which Benton did—she also fended off interference from the army bureaucracy. It is likewise erroneous to suggest, as some historians have, that Jessie was the true author of his books. As Frémont biographer Ferol Egan has pointed out, her writing style was substantially different. She took his dictation, and made suggestions on words and phrasing, but the work itself is entirely his.

Frémont was typical of the maverick military personality who filled in so many blank spots on the globe. He was a great explorer and leader of expeditions, but otherwise he was a poor soldier. An outsider who had become a hero in spite of the system, he had little use for army protocol. No one can fault him for his part in the Bear Flag Revolt that brought California under American rule. But his egotism would not allow him to step aside as acting military governor and to turn the situation over to a newly arrived and more experienced superior officer, Brigadier General Stephen Watts Kearny. Instead, Frémont became embroiled in a feud between Kearny, backed by the power of the government, and Commodore Robert F. Stockton, an ambitious naval commander. Convicted of three counts of mutiny, Frémont nevertheless was allowed to maintain his military career. Even so, he resigned on the grounds that he should have been acquitted.

Over the next few years Frémont led other expeditions, became wealthy in the California gold rush, served as senator when that state was admitted, and was an outspoken opponent of slavery. His reputation and politics were such that the newly established Republican Party chose him as its candidate for the 1856 presidential election. It was Republican publicists who bestowed on him the sobriquet of "Pathfinder." The Democrats responded with a smear campaign that attacked everything about Frémont, from his birth to his conduct as a soldier and expedition leader. Even so, he stood a very good chance of winning, had it not been for his uncompromising position on slavery, a volatile issue that experienced politicians of the day had learned to avoid. Nevertheless, Frémont's candidacy strengthened the party's viability in the public mind, and cleared the way for the election of Abraham Lincoln four years later.

With the outbreak of the Civil War, Frémont reentered the army. In the spring of 1862, largely in consideration for his past services, he was given command of the Mountain Department in West Virginia, with the rank of major general. Frémont, though, was more explorer than soldier, and had neither the training nor the experience to face his highly skilled Southern opponents. The Mountain Department itself had been created primarily to give him a responsible command, and had little strategic or tactical value. After a lackluster performance, the department was abolished.

Once again, personality conflicts, this time with President Lincoln and the politically powerful Blair family, led to Frémont's resignation. Only fifty years old, he now found that the greatest period of his life was behind him. Upon returning to California, he learned that the custodians of his property there had run up immense debts. This, together with poor investments, wiped out his fortune and reduced him to poverty. A three-year period as territorial governor of Arizona, from 1878 to 1881, brought a regular salary, but for the most part, the family lived on the writings of his wife.

Resurrecting his own writing career, Frémont began working on his memoirs in the hope that the royalties would relieve his financial problems. His inspiration was former President U. S. Grant, who had managed to recoup his own sagging fortunes with the publication of his memoirs. The first volume of Frémont's *Memoirs of My Life* was published in 1887, but sales proved disappointing and the proposed second volume was never written. Grant, the Civil War hero in a world still dominated by Civil War veterans, offered something that the public wanted to read. Frémont, the hero of an earlier era, was out of touch. The pioneers he hoped to reach were gone, and their sons and daughters belonged to the Gilded Age.

Aggravated by ill health, Frémont slipped further into poverty. He received new hope in April 1890, when Congress restored him to the rank of major general, with a pension of $6,000 a year. He had little time to enjoy it. On a trip to New York the seventy-seven-year-old Frémont developed peritonitis and died in his hotel room, attended only by his son and his physician.

Modern historians frequently write off Frémont as a man whose place in history was guaranteed less by his achievements as an explorer than by his good sense in marriage. Between a formidable father-in-law and a beautiful, talented wife, Frémont could hardly avoid fame. There is no question that he owed at least part of his rise to Thomas Hart Benton, just as he depended on other important people to advance his education and early career. Yet one key aspect could only come from Frémont himself—success. Influence might give him command of an expedition, but after that, he was on his own. It was Frémont who organized, led, and inspired. His true greatness was recognized by Christopher (Kit) Carson, himself one of the greatest of all mountain men. Recalling his expeditions with Frémont, Carson wrote:

> *I find it impossible to describe the hardships through which we passed, nor am I capable of doing justice to the credit which he deserves. But his services to his country have been left to the judgment of impartial freemen, and all agree in saying that they were great, and have redounded to his honor, and to that of his country. . . . His perseverance and his willingness to participate in all that was undertaken, no matter whether the duty was rough or easy, are the main causes of his success; and I say, without fear of contradiction, that no one but he could have surmounted so many obstacles, and have succeeded in as many difficult services.*

CHARLES M. ROBINSON III
San Benito, Texas
March 2001

CHARLES M. ROBINSON III is a professor of history at South Texas Community College and author of *The Men Who Wear the Star: The Story of the Texas Rangers, Bad Hand: The Biography of General Ranald S. Mackenzie,* and *A Good Year to Die: The Story of the Great Sioux War.*

FURTHER READING

Carson, Christopher (Kit). *Kit Carson's Autobiography.* Chicago: Lakeside Press, 1935.

DeVoto, Bernard. *Across the Wide Missouri.* Boston: Houghton Mifflin Company, 1947.

Egan, Ferol. *Frémont: Explorer for a Restless Nation.* Reno: University of Nevada Press, 1985.

Smith, Elbert B. *Magnificent Missourian: The Life of Thomas Hart Benton.* Philadelphia: J. B. Lippincott Company, 1958.

SCOPE OF THE WORK.

THE narrative contained in these volumes is personal. It is intended to draw together the more important and interesting parts in the journals of various expeditions made by me in the course of Western exploration, and to give my knowledge of political and military events in which I have myself had part. The principal subjects of which the book will consist, and which, with me, make its *raison d'etre*, are three: the geographical explorations, made in the interest of Western expansion; the presidential campaign of 1856, made in the interest of an undivided country; and the civil war, made in the same interest. Connecting these, and naturally growing out of them, will be given enough of the threads of ordinary life to justify the claim of the work to its title of memoirs: purporting to be the history of one life, but being in reality that of three, because in substance the course of my own life was chiefly determined by its contact with the other two—the events recorded having in this way been created, or directly inspired and influenced, by three different minds, each having the same objects for a principal aim.

The published histories of the various explorations have now passed out of date, and are new to the present generation, to which the region between the Mississippi and the Pacific Ocean presents a different face from that to which these accounts relate.

In the present narrative the descriptions of the regions travelled over will be simply of what would then have met a traveller's eye. The prevailing impression on his mind would have been one of constant surprise that so large a portion of the earth's surface should have so long remained unoccupied and unused. Millions of people now occupy the ground where then he encountered only wild animals and wild men. But nothing of this present condition will be given here.

The slight knowledge which a traveller could glean in journeys that were impelled forward by hunger, and thirst, and imminency of dangers, has in this day been perfected and made thoroughly available. The scant scientific information which was gathered in these travels, and which, as indications or suggestions, had its value at the time, will therefore not have any place in the present narrative. The striking features and general character of the regions traversed, the incidents which made their local coloring, and the hardships belonging to remote and solitary journeys, will be retained, so far as can well be done within the limit of the pages which are intended to embrace narratives covering broad regions of country and half a century of American time. But the emigrants who have since then traversed and changed the face of these regions will doubtless find enough to remind them, and have pleasure in being reminded, of the scenes with which they were once so familiar, and of hardships which they themselves were compelled to face.

Out of these expeditions came the seizure of California in 1846. The third exploring party was merged in a battalion which did its part in wresting that rich territory from Mexico, and the conquest of California will consequently have a prominent place in the narrative of these expeditions.

Concerning the presidential campaign of 1856, in which I was engaged, statements have been made which I wish to correct; and in that of 1864 there were governing facts which have not been made public. These I propose to set out.

Some events of the civil war in which I was directly concerned have been incorrectly stated, and I am not willing to leave the resulting erroneous impressions to crystallize and harden into the semblance of facts.

These subjects, as I have said, make the chief reason for this work.

The general record is being made up. This is being done from different points of view; and, as this view is sometimes distorted by imperfect or prejudiced knowledge, I naturally wish to use the fitting occasion which offers to make my own record. It is not the written but the published fact which stands, and it stands to hold its ground as fact when it can meet every challenge by the testimony of documentary and recorded evidence.

JOHN C. FRÉMONT.

Washington, D. C., May, 1886.

Jessie Benton Frémont

SOME ACCOUNT OF THE PLATES.

BY JESSIE BENTON FRÉMONT.

IN 1853 we were living in Paris, where Mr. Frémont was having his first leisure and rest, and his plan was repose and congenial study for a year or more longer, when there came from my father the information that Congress had ordered three lines to be surveyed with a view to select the best for overland travel and ultimately a railway ; that it had been intended that he, Mr. Frémont, should lead one, but as Congress had not inserted any name in the bill, the then Secretary of War, Mr. Jefferson Davis, had not named Mr. Frémont to any of the three. Captain Gunnison, who had been given the command of the line of surveys intended for Mr. Frémont, was killed by the Indians in the earlier part of his work.

Of the four journeys of exploration already made by Mr. Frémont, three had been under orders of the Government, and one, that of 1848–49, was at his own cost. Finding himself omitted from this culminating work which was based on his own labors, Mr. Frémont organized and made a fifth journey at his own expense.

The instruments were selected in Paris, and on the way through London to his steamer at Liverpool, he found the just published volume of Cosmos, in which Humboldt, speaking of photography, hopes it will be applied in travel, as securing " the truth in Nature." In New York the daguerre apparatus was bought, and a good artist secured, Mr. Carvalho. And though new conditions and difficulties made many embarrassments, yet almost all the plates were beautifully clear, and realized the wish of Humboldt for " truth in representing nature." These plates were afterward made into photographs by Brady in New York. Their long journeying by mule through storms and snows across the Sierras, then the searching tropical damp of the sea voyage back across the Isthmus, left them unharmed and surprisingly clear, and, so far as is known, give the first connected series of views by daguerre of an unknown country, in pictures as truthful as they are beautiful.

During the winter of '55-'56 Mr. Frémont worked constantly at Mr. Brady's studio aiding to fix these daguerre pictures in their more permanent form of photographs. Then at our own house I made a studio of the north drawing-room, where a large bayed window gave the proper light. Here for some months Hamilton worked on these views, reproducing many in oil; he was a pupil of Turner and had great joy in the true cloud effects as well as in the stern mountains and castellated rock formations. The engravings on wood were also made under our home supervision ; by an artist young then, a namesake and grandson of Frank Key, the author of " The Star-Spangled Banner." From these artists their work was passed to artist-engravers of the best school of their art. Darley also contributed his talent. Some pictures he enlarged into india-ink sketches, and from his hand came the figures in many of the plates. This work progressed through the busy year to us of 1856.

Mr. George Childs, of Philadelphia, was to bring out the journals of the various expeditions as a companion book of American travel to the Arctic journeys of Dr. Kane, then being published by the same house. The year of '56 gave no leisure however for writing ; what could be done without too much demand on Mr. Frémont was carried forward, but he alone could write and that was no time for looking back. Private affairs had been so much interfered with and necessarily deranged by the Presidential campaign, that the work proposed to be written and published was unavoidably delayed, and the contract finally cancelled ; Mr. Frémont reimbursing Mr. Childs for all the expenditures made in preparation. The time for writing did not seem to come. Private affairs in California, then our war, and again private business until now. During these thirty years the boxes containing the material for this book were so carefully guarded by me, that all understood they must be saved first in case of fire. When we were leaving for Arizona in '78 the boxes containing the steel plates and wood blocks were placed in Morrell's " Fire-Proof" warehouse, which was destroyed by fire in October of '81. We lost much that was stored in that warehouse, choice books, pictures, and other treasured things, but these materials for the book we had had placed for greater security in the safes below the pavement, where the great fire passed over them and left them completely unharmed.

My father's portrait is another of the illustrations which have gone through the ordeal by fire. When his house here was burned in February of '55, the day chanced to be so cold that the water froze in the hose.

There was no adequate water supply, or good appliances for fire here then, and the firemen could only look on, powerless. Both Houses of Congress had adjourned immediately on hearing of the fire, and a vast throng surrounded the doomed house. My father felt their sympathy, but the volumes of suffocating smoke drove back all who tried to enter, when there came a young friend, our neighbor, and son of an old friend and neighbor, Mr. Frank Key (of " The Star-Spangled Banner "), and in spite of warning cries he plunged into the smoke and fire to save for my father the portrait of my mother, which he thought was in her former room.

When he was seen at a front window a great shout of relief rose. Dropping the picture to outstretched arms he climbed to the lintel of the hospitable door no one was ever to pass again and helping hands and roaring shouts greeted him—singed, scorched, but his eyes alight with joy to have saved the home face to my father. It was a mistake, for the portrait was that of my father in his younger day. It was the one only thing saved from all that house so full of accumulated household treasures from both my mother's and my father's lives and belongings. The library, his own, and his father's, with the great folios of English state trials from which he began to read law and history with his mother, was the keenest felt loss. Many precious private papers were burned, and nearly half the manuscript of the second volume of the Thirty Years' View.

My house was near and my father came to me. Neither of us had slept but he made me lie down and we had talked together as only those who love one another can talk after a calamity. This portrait stood on a dressing table, and we spoke of Barton Key's tender thought and brave effort to save for him what he would most value, and the pity of the mistake. " It is well," my father said, " there is less to leave now—this has made death more easy. *You* will have this picture of me."

I felt the undertone; but never knew until his life was ended that even then he was observing and recording for the guidance of his physician, symptoms which from the first he thought foretold cancer. So wonderful was his calm endurance that Dr. Hall and Dr. May each thought it might be another cause and that an operation might restore his health. For a time it did give relief. Then the disease re-asserted itself. With the certainty now, with the fierce pain eating away his life, my father rewrote the burned manuscript and completed his work. He had exacted silence from his physicians because " my daughters are all young mothers, and must not be subject to the prolonged distress of knowing my condition hopeless."

The last likeness, taken by Brady for me in New York in '57, shows the same energy, will, and directness, but all softened by time and the influence of a mind constantly enlarging and therefore constantly freeing itself from personal views.   And the constant exercise of kindness and protection, so marked in my father's nature and habits, have left a stamp of benignity which proves the tender inner nature lying deeper and stronger than that more commonly known which made his public record of defiant and aggressive leadership, and gives the complete man who was so loved by his friends and family.

The portrait of Mr. Jefferson is from an excellent copy of the original by Stuart, belonging to Mrs. John W. Burke, of Alexandria, Virginia ; the great-granddaughter of Jefferson, and daughter of Mr. Nicholas Trist, the intimate friend of Jackson.   Through another of Jefferson's immediate descendants, Miss Sarah Randolph, who wrote the beautiful "Domestic Life of Jefferson," I am indebted for knowledge of this portrait and the introduction to Mrs. Burke who has so kindly let me use it.

The head of Napoleon is from a collection of authentic Bonaparte souvenirs, a part of which was bequeathed to me by the Count de la Garde, a French gentleman who had made his collection in Paris from the days of the first Consulate.   He was already a man of advanced age when we first knew him there in '52.   His father was a member of the last Cabinet of Louis the 16th, and, as a boy of ten, he had seen the opening of the great revolution.   In 1804 Bonaparte restored to him the remainder of their family estates, and gratitude was added to the sincere admiration he felt for the master-mind that had brought France to order from anarchy.   There was also a previous link of intermarriage which connected his family with that of the Beauharnais, and brought friendly intimacy between Prince Eugène, Queen Hortense, and himself.   From among his rich collection he made up for me an Album of Souvenirs of this historical family, with many autograph letters and various portraits at different epochs of Napoleon, Josephine, Hortense, and her brother Eugène and others.   The portrait here given is of Napoleon as First Consul, date 1804.

The Count de la Garde died in 1861, and it shows how little the most cultivated continental foreigners comprehended our people, when even this charmingly intelligent man provided in his will "that, should the unhappy conditions of the country and disorders arising from revolution make it impossible to trace the Frémont family within a year," then my Album was to go to the Emperor (Napoleon III.), to whom he left all the rest of his Bonaparte collection.

Of course I received at once at my home in New York the letter of the Executor, and there should have been no delay in the bequest being sent to me there after my answer reached Paris.

In place of the Album however came a letter from the Executor, saying the Emperor wished to keep unbroken all souvenirs of his mother, and would

like to have also what the Count de la Garde had intended for me.   That naturally they were of less interest to me, and that in any matter of personal interest to myself *"auprès de votre gouvernement"* the Emperor would lend his aid.

Although I repeated my request for the Album it did not come.   The silence made me uneasy.   I thought of the simple business American plan of asking at Wells and Fargo's Express if they could not get it on my order as a parcel ; explaining the matter and showing them the correspondence. They agreed with me that a quick, silent move which was a business trans- action could not be interfered with.   And in that way my Album was at once secured, and brought to me.   But the year of delay which was to make it lapse to the Emperor was nearly complete.

Other portraits, belonging with events, and given us for this use, will be further spoken of in the book.

Thomas H. Benton

BIOGRAPHICAL SKETCH

OF

SENATOR BENTON,

IN CONNECTION WITH WESTERN EXPANSION.

By JESSIE BENTON FRÉMONT.

When, in the opening of the war of 1812, my Father, under General Jackson, marched from Nashville to defend the lower Mississippi, he made two discoveries which gave new form to his own life and largely moulded the fate of our Western country to its ocean boundary.

The first, on which depended the other, was, that it lay within the power of his own will to regain health and live ; the other, that until then his mind had been one-sided, and that there was a West as well as an East to our country. This march revealed to him the immense possibilities and future power of the then recent "Louisiana purchase;" and his mind gained the needed balance against the exclusively English and seaboard influences to which he had been born and in which he had been trained.

Quick to see and to foresee, and equally steadfast in living up to his convictions, his decision was made then ; to leave inherited lands, family friends, and an already brilliant position in the law, and devote himself to the new West. To its imperial river—the Father of Floods—he became captive, and to it and the lands it drained he gave life-long, faithful, and accumulating service and homage. My father was so proudly and thoroughly American that his departure from all the influences that had created and until then governed his thoughts shows the power of innate force against inherited and educated influence.

Born of English parentage on the English seaboard ; brought up in English and intensely colonial-royalist surroundings ; trained by a scholarly

Englishman to English thought and aims ; and with his profession of the law keeping his mind down to a habit of deference to precedent and safe usage, my father had reached his thirtieth year before he discovered him-self. With the great river and his instinct of what the West must become, came to him the resolve which governed all his after life ; and, by the happy chance which made me the connecting link, this resolve was con-tinued and expanded through that of Mr. Frémont. And so the two lives became one in the work of opening out our Western country to emigration and secure settlement, and in the further acquisition of Pacific territory which " gives us from sea to sea the whole temperate zone," and brings to our Pacific ports, across our continent, that long-contested-for India trade.

In the Park at Saint Louis stands a bronze statue of my father, and upon its pedestal, below the hand which points WEST, are his prophetic words :

> " THERE IS THE EAST;
> THERE LIES THE ROAD TO INDIA ; "

words which, when spoken by him, had made men smile significantly to one another ; too much dwelling on this idea had—they thought—warped his mind. " They who listened said, This man is mad ; now they asked, Hath he a God ? "

Anyone can grasp prepared results. The mind that can see, prepare, and concentrate chaotic and antagonistic conditions, so that a great result becomes inevitable, is rarely the one to wear the laurels of completed suc-cess. Moses led the children of Israel to the Promised land, but he did not enter there and rest. The heat and burden of the day were for him ; the fruit was for those whose doubts and discords had made his heaviest burden.

It is the formation phase of this western expansion of our country, of much that shaped our present national greatness, of which I am able to tell from my own home knowledge—what one might name the fireside history of the great West.

It is only in connection with this side of his long useful public life that I here speak of my father ; but to appreciate his departure from all that had governed his thought and action before he gave in his adhesion to the West, it is needed to know what were those restraining influences from which his own far-sighted mind, and his own will, lifted him into the higher and broader outlook for our future as a completed nation.

His father, English and of reserved and scholarly nature, was out of his element in the new Republic, having come to it from his student-life as pri-vate secretary to Governor Tryon, the last of the royal governors of North Carolina. His natural preference was for settled usages and a life confined to his family and his cherished library. This was in five languages, and he was at home in all five, Greek and Latin and French and Spanish; while the English portion was rich in fine editions of the best works. Shakspere, Don Quixote, and Madame de Sevigné we read in the originals as my grandfather and father had, from this treasure for a new country.

Governor Tryon had also brought over in his suite a chaplain, a man of high character and of the same cultivated mind as my grandfather. In the increasing and angry agitation of the coming separation from the mother-country, these two men, already close friends, found in each other increasing harmony of feeling and mutual support. It soon came to be the strongest earthly support to my grandfather.

He had married into another English family of colonial governors, as my grandmother, Anne Gooch, was the only child of a younger brother of Sir William Gooch, who replaced Lord Dunmore as deputy-governor in his absence from his post in Virginia. New York had a more "loyal" atmosphere than Richmond, and both Lord Dunmore and Governor Tryon were chiefly there during the closing period of English rule. Their official families bore for them the brunt of the rising storm, and, like true men, became only the more devoted to their country, for which they suffered.

With the end of colonial rule came the end of scholarly rest and seclusion for my grandfather. The need for larger provision for many young children turned him westward, and leaving them in their North Carolina home, he led a surveying party of sixteen men, the first to make surveys in Kentucky.

Already his health was giving way under the inroads of pulmonary disease, which at that date was accepted as a death-sentence, and submitted to as inevitable. Doubtless the survey-work in the open air, the change of thoughts, and a new aim in life gained for him a reprieve, and he persevered until he had secured large landed property, but soon after his return to North Carolina died there, asking of his faithful friend, the chaplain, that overlooking care for his family which he could no longer give them. And faithfully was this charge kept.

It is from my father himself that I know what followed.

He was but eight years of age then, and there were six other children. He had not seen his mother during her long illness after his father's death, and when at length he was taken in to her he was struck with awe and terror. In place of the young mother he knew, with bright brown hair crowning her stately head, and health and animation lighting her blue eyes, he saw a thin, white-faced, white-haired woman, who put his hand on that of a baby-girl, and told him that he was now the head of the family, the eldest son, and must be her help in taking care of the others.

" When I came out I rushed into the grove, and there, with cries and tears, *I made war on myself* until I could accept that ghost in place of my own mother."

There the chaplain found him. He had looked for him there, I am sure. Knowing the boy's vitality, his strong affections, and his powerful, self-reliant will, he must have felt that it was only to Nature he would turn in this his first contest with the inevitable.

Coming back from chapel the Sunday following this memorable day, the chaplain led him by the hand through the grove, and taking a little Greek Testament from his pocket, read to him a verse, making him repeat it correctly as he pronounced it after him, then giving him the meaning, and so continuing the oral lesson until they neared the house. It was the Sermon on the Mount, and his first lesson in Greek was the blessing on " they that mourn," with its promise that " they shall be comforted."

These lessons in Greek, and in Latin also, were continued faithfully by the true friend. Fair instruction, of the ordinary kind, was given him at a good college school; but his true education was from the chaplain, from his mother, and through the fine library of his father. From its great folios of " English State Trials " my father had his first law lessons, his mother interesting him in them by choosing the narrative portions, and giving him the needed links of information, then drawing from him his impressions in discussion on the readings. The wise mother made these readings a reward, and prevented any undue influence of such large ideas by encouraging the wholesome out-door life which the four brothers, with horse, dog, and gun, made for themselves.

The moulding influence of this uncommon woman was too life-long and ennobling for her to be omitted from a just account of my father. From her example and her teaching he was trained to industry, to truth, courage, and justice—a good woman's sense of justice, which includes mercy; which causes justice to be thorough by making action follow conviction;— to that moral courage which sustains and defends conviction; above all to the succor and protection of the weak and oppressed. Those who know my father's public life will recognize these underlying forces.

In the brief memoranda for a biographical notice made by himself when nearing his certain and painful death; in recalling what then seemed best worth recording, there comes first the grateful tribute to his Mother. Then, the fact that, when in the Legislature of Tennessee, he had been the author of " a *humane law*, still on her statute-books, giving to slaves the full benefit of jury trial which was the right of white men under the same accusation." This originated in the case of a slave-woman accused of murder, for whom he volunteered as counsel, and defended her successfully on arguments which Maudsly has put in use to-day.

In his young time, in a Southern country, this was a brave outcome of the active sense of justice which a woman had taught him to feel for all women, even those " despised of men."

When he was sixteen they removed to Tennessee, to their large landed property near Nashville, which the father's forethought had secured for his young family. There they commenced cotton-planting. My Father and his three brothers, with the head-negroes, went out one fine night to make a final survey of the ripened crop which lay white and beautiful in the moonlight. The next day found it blackened by frost, and with it withered all the plans founded on its sale. This decided my Father against planting, as " a pursuit of which he could not influence the results."

And he turned to the study of law, keeping at the same time an active supervision of the estate, the family, and the safety of their little colony. For from the southern border of " the Widow Benton's estate," through to the Gulf of Mexico, was unbroken and warlike Indian territory. And leading directly through their lands was the war-trail of neighboring Indian tribes.

He was admitted early to practice, and soon had the friendship of General Jackson among other important settlers. Later, when a member of the General Assembly of the State, he was the author of the Judicial Reform Act, by which the administration of justice was relieved of much delay, expense, and inconvenience to all concerned. This too, came from the home readings and discussions, and was an effort to combine justice with law.

Then came the war of 1812, when, enlisting under Jackson who was major-general of the Tennessee militia, he made the march to the defence of the lower Mississippi which was to radically alter his plan of life, and lead to great good for our whole country.

Doubtless, in leaving North Carolina, his mother had had fresh grief in parting from all the visible memories of her happy time. But she was not of the women who vainly look back, or make their lament aloud; the one blow that struck the color from her life, as from her hair, killed all personal interest in living; leaving her only for duty and protecting love for her children. This, and the many cares of a Southern household of old days, the newer conditions of the large estate, and the obligations of neighborhood in a new country, she was faithful to.

But there came a time when her love and protection could not avail her children. They all grew up apparently full of health and fine promise; but five of the eight died, as their father had died, of rapid consumption. " The Grave of the Three Sisters " is still a known landmark near Nashville, although a great tree has grown up in the enclosure, and partly uprooted its stone walls and the family grave-stones ; the burial-place of their slaves —hard-by, as was the custom—remains comparatively undisturbed.

When my father found himself on the same sad downward road—when constant fever, the hacking cough, and restless nights and days without energy admonished him that his turn had come, he felt despair. " If it had been a battle I would have had a chance, or even in a desperate duel, but for this there was no chance. All was fixed and inevitable."

The war coming then he hailed the occasion to end his life in action rather than in the slow progress of a fatal illness.

As we have seen in our late war, whole neighborhoods of young men went out together, and distinctions of private and officer were only used when on duty. " Sam " Houston was a corporal in the regiment of which my father was colonel, and when they were in the Senate together the ex-President of Texas often signed himself " *Your friend and old subaltern.*"

Some of the young men were not so practised in walking as my Father, and he lent them his horses, himself going on foot. Of course they carried but little baggage, and he supplied the want of fresh clothing by constant baths in the running waters of streams by the way, drying the skin in sunshine. This, with the abundant exercise which opened the pores and threw off fevered conditions, the sleep in open air, the simple regular food, all combined to bring about such changes that hope came to him. His own observations taught him how to follow up these indications of possible health ; and, in brief, seventy years ago my father found for himself the way out of inherited conditions of pulmonary disease by the same means so successfully ordered in our present time—open air, night and day ; abundant perspiration from steady exercise ; bathing and rubbing, always if possible in sunshine ; always, all the sunshine possible ; simple food regularly taken ; and " *to forget yourself in some pursuit.*"

All his life my father needed to keep as close to these rules as circumstances permitted. The continued use of his voice in speaking in public was prepared for by silence for days previous and was almost sure to be followed by flecks of blood from the throat, but his self-control gained him the superb health which was so great a factor in his usefulness.

The English did not come so soon as they were looked for, and when General Jackson returned to Tennessee my father applied for active service, and was commissioned by President Madison a Lieutenant-Colonel of the regular army (39th Infantry) and was sent to Canada on his first duty.

What he saw there of the antagonism of French and English added to his interest in the people of the " Louisiana purchase," whose French settlers were both grieved and angered by their abrupt transfer to their traditional enemy ; for they cared little about other differences where language, laws, and religion were those they were accustomed to hate as "English."

When peace was declared my father resigned from the army and established his new home at Saint Louis. There was no further change. The winter home was in Washington, where his thirty years in the Senate made a home of our own a necessity. But my grandmother remained at the Saint Louis house always ; with her own old servants and some young grandchildren—children of another son whose health could not brave the Saint Louis winters—beautiful and unusually fine children who gave young life about the house before our day, and of whom one has always been like a dear elder sister. When I was in England in '51, my father in writing to me of the death of my only brother, says—"Your cousin Sarah has been constantly with us. Her face, always lovely to me, has been that of an angel."

While in the army my father made the friendship with General James Preston of Virginia which led to what he held to be the crowning good fortune of his life—his marriage to my mother, who was the niece of General Preston. It was his singular good fortune to have both in his mother and his wife friends and sharers in his largest ideas, while every soothing charm of a well-ordered home came as second nature from my mother's influence. To him home brought the strength of peace and repose, and he never suffered the outside public atmosphere of strife to enter there.

" Peace and honor charmed the air."

And in its warmth long-closed memories bloomed anew. Some trouble in tuning a guitar was making one of my sisters impatient, " Bring it to me," spoke my father from his table covered with books and work. We looked on while with strong but light and skilful touch he turned the pegs, and tuned it perfectly, trying a few chords. The sight of " Father playing the guitar " made an outcry from the youngest, but we elder girls felt we must not speak ; when he himself, handing it back, and doubtless seeing some pitying tenderness of look in us, said gently—" I often tuned their guitar for my sisters, and sang with them "—and to one of us, " *You* are like the youngest." Of his brothers we had had many and many a hunting story, and knew their dogs by name, and the gray horse which must have had a troubled life among them, but of the sisters this was all he ever said. But we knew they made the hidden source of his unfailing gentleness to all women. My grandmother lived to past eighty, in fullest clearness of mind sharing and aiding her son's life; and except for his needed absences in Washington they had no separations. They rest together near Saint Louis by the Great River—mother and son—and around them are their children to the third and fourth generations.

Saint Louis was in 1817, when my father established himself there, only a village in numbers, but it had a large and stirring life and great interests which found their outlet and pathway to the sea down the Mississippi. It was like a port on the border of its vast dimly known Indian country, with its business extending deep into Mexico and through to Sonora and the Gulf of California; and across the Rocky Mountains into Oregon to the Pacific Ocean. The armed caravans of merchandise crossing this dangerland encountered not only the perils from savages intent on plunder, but the jealous capricious interferences of Spanish policy; while the small army of hunters and trappers and traders and *voyageurs* belonging with the American Fur Company had in addition to the Indians to meet the covert but powerful hostility of the Hudson Bay Fur Company, and consequent collision with English policy. The whole condition of loss to us and increasing gain and strength to England coming from the joint-occupation of the Columbia; the resulting loss of life and driving out of the American Fur trade; the increasing settlements of English subjects fostered by their government and encouraged to hold the land made the situation my father found governing Saint Louis.

Fresh from his military life he found himself confronting English aggression in another form. The little French town so far in the centre of our continent found itself direct heir to the duel of a century between England and France for the New World and the Asiatic trade, and, France having withdrawn, was meeting the added resentment of English feeling against her late subjects, who now replaced France in that contest. The few years intervening between his arrival among them and his being sent in 1821 to represent them as their first Senator, gave my father time to learn fully their interests, and the sources of information were unusual and each of the highest value.

The venerable General Clarke, who had under Jefferson first explored Oregon and the Columbia, was ending his days quietly but in large usefulness in Saint Louis. He was the chief Superintendent of all western Indians, a post in which his experience and high character gave the best results to the Indians as well as to our Government. Much of what now belongs with the Indian Bureau and Department of the Interior was thus in his control, even the making of treaties. General Clarke had married a connection of my mother's, and there was a family and neighborly intimacy between the two homes. All that one mind can take from that of another who has had the advantage of *seeing*, my father gathered from General Clarke in regard to his exploration. And of the evils growing out of the permitted joint-occupation; a permission fast growing into a right of possession, and already harassing and excluding American settlers.

The headquarters of the Fur Company were with the Chouteaus, an old French family who had come up from New Orleans for this business sixty years before, and remained there; overseeing, themselves and through younger branches, the ramified increasing business which enriched them and gave profitable employment to so many adventurous men. From these all—the heads of the House to the last arrived *voyageur*—my father eagerly and perseveringly gleaned information, and gained grounds for his maturing resolve to carry out Jefferson's plan of overland communication with the Asiatic countries, and to hold for ourselves the port on the Pacific which was its key; and for this to end the impossible condition of combined use of our Oregon territory. Mr. Jefferson had scorned this idea when applied to the Mississippi. He would not even refer to the Senate the treaty containing this provision. What would the English not have made of "*treaty-rights*" for "*free navigation of the Mississippi and access to it through the territories of the United States*" which was their renewed attempt at Ghent in 1814.

From the Père Marquette through to Father de Smet, the missionary priests of the Catholic Church had a great part in opening up our western Indian country, and creating centres of order and good influence wherever they founded their missions. The transfer of Louisiana had been followed by the watchful care of their Church, which did not abandon its Spanish and French people to the new conditions, but sent to them clergy of high dignity and governing minds who made for them new importance and enlarged advantages. Special attention was given to establishments for education. Bishop Du Bourg brought over five Sisters of the Sacred Heart from the famous mother-house in Paris where the daughters of royalty are sent for training. These ladies were of noble families, and their gentle, refined manners, their pure French and accomplishments, gave to the young girls of Saint Louis the same advantages they would have to-day at the Sacré-Cœur in Paris. My father, who comprehended the power of education and promoted it in all forms, was glad to use this rare advantage for his young niece. There was an odd reason for his constant pleasant intercourse with the Bishop aside from public causes.

Those about M. Du Bourg were, like himself, French. He needed to acquire fluent English for all uses, and for use from the pulpit. It was a point of honor among the older French not to learn English—many never did so at all—" *Je suis Français de France et je parle ma langue,*" they would say, ignoring the need for the other language and looking down with reprobation on their descendants born and living contentedly under "foreign" rule, and speaking English. The older people never reacted from the shock of anger and pain which came to them, as their simple annals record, "*on this 9th of July,* 1803, *at 7 p.m.,*" when they learned—

indirectly at first—that " Louisiana has been *sold* by Napoleon to the United States."

To force himself into familiar practice the Bishop therefore secluded himself for a while with the family of an American farmer, where he would hear no French.   Soon he had gained enough to announce a sermon in English, on some occasion of general interest which crowded the Cathedral. My father was there, and as among other languages the Chaplain had taught him a fastidious use of English, his feelings can be imagined when the polished, refined Bishop said to the hushed crowd :

" My friends : *I am right-down glad* to see *such a smart chance of folks* here to-day."

What he thought to say was the paternal gentle " *Mes Amis,*" " I am profoundly happy to see here such an assemblage."

To feel and to act were one thing with my father, and his offered assistance led to an intimacy in which he was as much the gainer in cultivated French as was the Bishop in equivalent English.

By this time my father's thoughts were all converging on the vital importance to our new possession of ridding it of English interference, and through the Bishop, also, he learned much bearing on his main idea.   The missionary priests reported to the Bishop, and their experience swelled the evidence gained through the Fur Company and its employés, that the joint occupation of the Columbia was the virtual loss of that part of our territory ; that our fur trade was already driven out ; that American settlers were harassed—many killed—by Indians friendly with the Hudson Bay Company ; and that our Government was giving no encouragement or protection to our people, while in every way fostering care was given to English settlers who were taking up the land.

What to do ?   " There is all the difference possible between the man who possesses his subject and the man who is possessed by it."

My father became possessed by this Oregon question.   He had that fire of devotion to an idea which transmutes the thought of many into united defined action, and his courage always rose with obstacles.

Oregon was far, unfamiliar, of no distinct interest to the East.

The one man who had foreseen and planned our ownership of its Pacific port, with the resulting gain of overland commerce from Asia peopling our waste lands and enriching the whole country, was not then in power. After his many years of extraordinary services Mr. Jefferson was ending his days in much care from fortune lost while serving his country and neglecting his own interests.   To him, at his mountain home in Virginia, my father made a visit the Christmas of 1824 ; he felt it a pilgrimage.   The commonplace topic of the bad roads was lifted by the mind of genius into a talk which became the link in a chain of national progress ; a talk into which there came an unconscious touch of pain which will find echo in American hearts as unworthy to have been inflicted on that noble mind. From the local road they came to speak of the need for national aid to roads for the spread of our people westward.

My father, having now the vantage-ground of the Senate, was endeavoring to get for those of his constituents whose business led them into Mexican trade as far as to the " Sea of Cortez " (the old name for the Gulf of California), a right of way in Mexico, and consequent protection by both republics. This was meeting opposition on the perennial objection of " creating a precedent." Mr. Jefferson said this objection would be disposed of by a similar road made in the closing year of his administration. He said there could be found in the Library of Congress a manuscript copy of this map bound up in a volume of maps, formerly his own.

" Formerly ! " Could not the representatives of that people who owed so much to him have given him the pitiful price they paid for his library and left it with him, undisturbed, to console the few remaining years of his old age and poverty?

" The sympathies of the American people are instantaneous, and alive to any deeds of merit brought to their notice. But the conscience of the people of this country is not in their own keeping. It is a delegated conscience."

Mr. Jefferson's intention to secure for his country the Asiatic trade by an overland route across our continent so directly governed the three lives written of in this book that I give here to this point some detail, though nothing befitting his foresight and perseverance.

Before the American captain, Captain Gray of Boston, had actually found the mouth of the Columbia, in 1790, Jefferson, then our Minister to France, met in Paris the English traveller Ledyard, who was about to explore the Nile. Mr. Jefferson turned him from this to what both felt to be a fresher and more useful field of discovery. I have listened to such talks; and can fancy the fascination to the born explorer in listening to Jefferson's theory that the snow-clad Rocky Mountains, which shed their waters to the east in such a mighty stream as the Missouri, must have a corresponding water-shed and great river to the west. No explorer had trod its banks, no navigator found its mouth; but where Jefferson thought such a river should be, is the Columbia.

Jefferson obtained for Ledyard the passport which carried him to Saint Petersburg, where he received the permission of the Empress Catherine to traverse her dominions in a high northern latitude to their eastern extremity; then he would cross the sea from Khamschatka, or at Behring's Straits; and, descending the northwest coast of America, come down the river which they were certain must have its head opposite that of the Missouri; ascend it to its source in the Rocky Mountains, and then follow the Missouri to the French settlements of the Upper Mississippi, thence home.

By what petty intrigue, or whose small mind overthrew such a grand plan we cannot know—very small causes aid to determine the fate of great events—but all the large thought of Jefferson, the enterprise of Ledyard, and the intelligent co-operation of the Empress Catherine were defeated when Ledyard, who had already reached Siberia, was overtaken by an order revoking his permission, and conducted back " as a spy " out of Russia.

The Nile exploration was resumed; to end in the early death of the enthusiastic young explorer.

When, as President he had the power, Mr. Jefferson renewed his plan, and projected the Expedition of Lewis and Clarke; and having obtained the consent of Congress, sent them to discover the head and course of the river, whose mouth was then known; giving to Congress in his message the reason that this would " *open overland commercial relations with Asia ;* and enlarge the boundaries of geographical science "—putting as the first motive a North-American road to India, and the introduction of Asiatic trade over that road.   What proud emotion must have filled him when he secured from France our ownership of that vast " Louisiana purchase "— the mouth of the Columbia and the mouth of the Mississippi, and all the lands they drained throughout their mighty length !   When in an English treaty a clause was inserted providing free navigation on the Mississippi and access through our territories to it President Jefferson would not even refer it to the Senate but suppressed it himself.   Here again was the same intention to regain something of the lost power over us, to acquire such hold in Oregon as would enable her to keep the mouth of the Columbia, and add that port on the Pacific to those of Gibraltar, Malta, the Cape of Good Hope, and her other such outposts.

The story of varying intrigues, now bold, now crafty, is long, but it was now with her own children she was dealing, and with men who had *felt* the war of the revolution and that of 1812, and who had not laid their armor by, and were ready to resist any further attempts at dominion. My father was a man grown when the Mississippi and the Columbia were French property and Saint Louis and New Orleans French ports. Although so bred and tutored in English feeling and knowledge, yet there lay all about him the atmosphere of our successful rebellion against unjust abuse of power, and the going to Tennessee had opened his mind to still more American impressions of self-reliance and thought.   The military episode which gave him back health, and revealed to him the future of the West, brought also reliance on his own will.   He had found it could control the issues of life and death; he came back to the new life conscious of

THOMAS JEFFERSON.

an ally within himself on which he could surely rely—his own will. And in his work to make secure our Pacific outlet that will never faltered, but gained strength from opposition, and expanded with the greatness of the object.

In 1813, while this new life was coming to my father, there began, again on the eastern sea-coast, another life which was to be in alliance with his ; to carry forward and enlarge his plans ; and to seize opportunity to bring them to a higher and more grand realization than one life alone could compass.

The renewal of the joint-occupation of the Columbia had effectually dis-couraged American enterprise, and infused new life into the English occu-pation ; their encroachments were continued in various forms, now open, now covert; they even built upon the Columbia River a cordon of forts ostensibly for " defence" against Indians, who were in reality allies of the Hudson Bay Company, and made fur-trading and trapping impossible to Americans.

Every measure proposed by their western friends for protection was met by opposition, curious to read to-day. Even so late as '43 the ignorance, the indifference, the blindness to the value of our Pacific territory—the heedless inattention to the evidence of living history as to England's per-tinacious designs on that coast, is shown in the debates on every bill. On one giving lands to settlers, while a Senator from Ohio (then a very west-ern State), Mr. Tappan, supported the measure and said 50,000 settlers with their 50,000 rifles should be given lands to colonize the banks of the Oregon, there was open expression that this would give offence to England, and the vote to strike out the land-donation clause was very close, 24 to 22.

Allen of Ohio led the vote in favor of lands for colonists.

Yeas : Allen, Benton, Buchanan, Clayton, Fulton, Henderson, King, Linn, McRoberts, Mangum, Merrick, Phelps, Sevier, Smith of Connecticut, Smith of Indiana, Sturgeon, Tappan, Walker, White, Wilcox, Williams, Woodbury, Wright, Young.

Nays : Archer, Bagby, Barrow, Bates, Bayard, Berrien, Calhoun, Choate, Conrad, Crafts, Dayton, Evans, Graham, Huntington, McDuffie, Miller, Porter, Rives, Simmons, Sprague, Tallmadge, Woodbridge.

They could not get the House to act upon the bill, but this vote of the Senate encouraged the West, and they went forward and planted the colony which forced the stand against England that our Congress had been unwilling to make. The debate is too long for this paper, but belongs in the book as part of the ground for the explorations and other acts for our national as well as for our western benefits. It is strange to-day to see how our Government refused its own great property ; on what grounds it left it to England and, with some, how it was scorned and regretted as a possession.

Mr. McDuffie of South Carolina openly regretted we owned it; that it was "worthless except a mere strip along the sea-coast—the rest, mountains almost inaccessible, and lowlands covered with stone and volcanic remains; where rain never falls except during the spring, and even on the coast no rain falls from April to October, and for the remainder of the year there is nothing but rain. Why, sir, of what use will this be for agricultural purposes? I would not for that purpose give a pinch of snuff for the whole territory. I wish to God we did not own it. . . . Who are we to send there? Do you think honest farmers in Pennsylvania, New York, or even Ohio and Missouri, will abandon their farms to go upon any such enterprise as that? God forbid! If any man who is to go to that country under the temptations of this bill was my child—if he was an honest, industrious man, I would say to him, for God's sake do not go there. . . . But if I had a son whose conduct was such as made him a fit subject for Botany Bay, I would say to him in the name of God, go."

And further that England would be offended and forced into war "in defence of her rights and her honor."

Mr. Calhoun was as strongly opposed to the bill as his colleague, though his keen intelligence made him see "the value of the territory and the commercial advantages in communicating with China and Japan which should not be lost." He takes an admirable far-sighted view of this. But he too thinks the danger of war too great, and the possession so remote that we could not meet the difficulty and expense of defending it. He thinks "Time" is our best ally, and "a wise and masterly inactivity."

My father admitted that England would take offence, and that it was her intention to do so whatever we might do. But that was not the question. Had she the *right* to take offence? It was agreed she had not. Then, he was for going forward on our rights, and not taking counsel of fear. "Neither nations nor individuals ever escaped danger by fearing it. They must face it and defy it."

Mr. Nicollet, a French astronomer and savant of distinction, who had already spent some years in his own studies of the river and its Indians, had just finished for our Government a two years' survey of the country between the Missouri and Mississippi; coming to Washington to make up his report, he found in my father an appreciative friend. Mr. Frémont had been the topographical engineer of the surveys, and was now making up its maps. My father found so much to inform and interest him in this Mississippi work, that quickly there grew up close and friendly relations. He communicated to them his earnest feeling of the need for further western surveys in the interest of our emigration to Oregon. The inevitable result of our "conciliatory" policy on the joint-occupation had now reached a point

THERE IS THE EAST
THERE IS THE ROAD TO INDIA

BENTON MONUMENT—ST. LOUIS, MO.

at which one or the other country must be the only holder; a short time later it threatened war, and it was only in '46 that the subject was settled as it stands to-day.   Immediate surveys which should mark out the road for emigration, and at least *imply* government interest and protection, seemed to my father the nearest measure.   Mr. Nicollet entered into the idea with enthusiasm though his health was much worn by unusual discomforts and exposures, but in Mr. Frémont my father found his Ledyard.

Coming home from school in an Easter holiday, I found Mr. Frémont part of my father's "Oregon work."   It was the spring of '41; in October we were married, and in '42 the first expedition was sent out under Mr. Frémont.   Mr. Nicollet died during the summer, regretting he could have no part in this great and useful development of the country which had been part of France.

This first encouragement to the emigration westward fitted into so large a need that it met instant favor, and a second was ordered to connect with it further surveys to the sea-coast of Oregon.   At last my father could feel his idea "moved."   Of his intense interest and pride and joy in these expeditions I knew best; and when it came in my way to be of use to them and protect his life-time work, there was no shadow of hesitation.   Mr. Frémont was at the frontier getting his camp and animals into complete travelling condition when (as with Ledyard) there came an order recalling him to Washington; where he was to explain why he had armed his party with a howitzer; that the howitzer had been charged to him; that it was a scientific and not a military expedition, and should not have been so armed; and that he must return at once to Washington and "explain."

Fortunately I was alone in Saint Louis, my father being out of town. It was before telegraphs; and nearly a week was required to get letters either to the frontier or to Washington.   I was but eighteen, an age at which consequences do not weigh against the present.   The important thing was to save the expedition, and gain time for a good start which should put it beyond interference.   I hurried off a messenger—the mails were slow—to Mr. Frémont, writing that he must start at once and never mind the grass and animals, they could rest and fatten at Bent's Fort; only, go, and leave the rest to my father; that he could not have the reason for haste, but there was reason enough.

To the Colonel of the Topographical Bureau who had given the order of recall I answered more at leisure.   I wrote him exactly what I had done and to him I gave the reason.   That I had not sent forward the order nor let Mr. Frémont know of it because it was given on insufficient knowledge and to obey it would ruin the expedition; that it would require a fortnight to settle the party, leave it, and get to Washington—and indefinite delay there —another fortnight for the return, and by that time the early grass would be past its best and the underfed animals would be thrown into the mountains for the winter; that the country of the Blackfeet and other fierce tribes had to be crossed, and they knew nothing of the rights of science. When my father came he entirely approved my wrongdoing and wrote to Washington that he would be responsible for my act; and that he would call for a court-martial on the point charged against Mr. Frémont. But there was never further question of the wisdom of arming his party sufficiently—in fact it was but a pretext. The precious time had been secured and "they'd have fleet feet who follow" where such purpose leads the advance. I had grown up to and into my father's large purpose; and now that my husband could be of such aid to him in its accomplishment, I had no hesitation in risking for him all consequences. We three understood each other and acted together—then and later—without question or delay.

That expedition led directly to our acquiring California; which was accomplished during the third, and last, of the expeditions made under the Government. My father was a man grown when our western boundary was the Mississippi. In 1821 he commenced in the Senate his championship of a quarter of a century for our new territory on the Pacific. Now with California added he could say in that Senate:

"We own the country from sea to sea—from the Atlantic to the Pacific—and upon a breadth equal to the length of the Mississippi and embracing the whole temperate zone."

The long contest, the opposition, the indifference, the ignorance, the sneering doubts were in the past. From his own hearth had gone forth the one who carried his hopes to fullest execution; and who now after many perils and anxieties was back in safety—even to a seat in the Senate beside him. Who had enabled him to make true his prophetic words carved on the pedestal of his statue in Saint Louis, whose bronze hand points *West:*

"THERE IS THE EAST;
THERE IS THE ROAD TO INDIA."

For with our Pacific ports came to us that Asiatic trade which was the underlying cause of all the wars of France and England for a hundred years. France lost India—Canada—and the vigilant English navy prevented her from protecting Louisiana. Then Napoleon avenged himself and made the master move which checkmated England by giving over to her rebellious colonies the Mississippi and the Columbia.

England was loth to lose her grasp. She tried to get by treaty free navigation of the Mississippi and right of way over our territories in access to it. But Jefferson was President. He would not even lay before the Senate the treaty containing that clause.

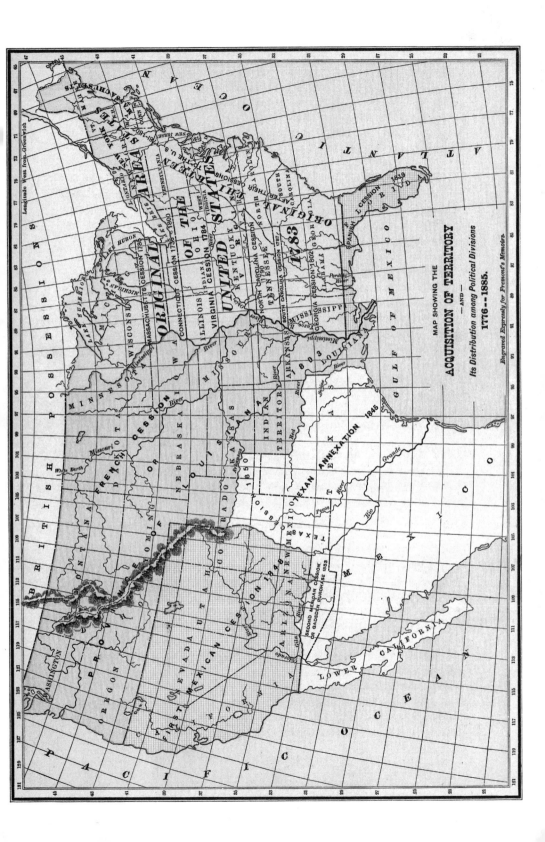

MAP SHOWING THE

ACQUISITION OF TERRITORY

— AND —

Its Distribution among Political Divisions

1776--1885.

Engraved Expressly for Fremont's Memoirs.

England tried then by force to get New Orleans—and failed. Then followed her attempt to colonize and in that way hold Oregon under the permitted joint-occupation, weakly prolonged by our Government until we barely escaped war in regaining our boundary.

There remained the Mexican territory of California with its noble harbor of San Francisco ; surveyed by England as her own.

The issue had narrowed as to who should possess this the finest harbor on the coast.

In the early home readings my father had studied the trial of Warren Hastings, and Clive and India were almost as close to his boyhood as our war is to the boys of to-day. The struggle for India and its trade " greater than that of Tyre and Sidon " made the story of a great war on a background of oriental splendor.

To gain for one's country a great rich land was the glory to be envied by him in those dreams of boyhood when nothing seems impossible.

What mysterious foreshadowing may not have moved him to the long labors that led to a greater and richer addition to his own country ? That enabled America to hold the Golden Gate to the commerce of the Pacific?

With her territory we inherited from France her long contest, and now when the Mexican war opened up a fresh opportunity it was England and America who faced each other.

Two men were in position to use deciding influence, and both understood the crisis and each other, my father in Washington with his established power in the Senate ; Mr. Frémont on the ground where the decisive blow must be given.

The tenacity of purpose, the staying-power of England was impersonated in one of her American descendants, and the partly French blood added French audacity of execution to the other whose life and purpose was interwoven with that of my father.

Long thought and deliberation had ripened hopes and plans : when the signal came the duel of a century was ended by the raising of the American Flag.

MEMOIRS OF MY LIFE.

By JOHN CHARLES FRÉMONT.

CHAPTER I.

1828-33 School days—1833-36 Cruise on U. S. S. Natchez—1836-37 Appointed Professor of Mathematics in the Navy—Assistant Engineer under Captain Williams—Work in Mountains of North and South Carolina—1837-38 Threatened hostilities with Cherokee Indians, etc., etc.

LOOKING back over the years of the life which I am about to transfer to the blank pages before me, I see in its earlier part but few things worthy of note. The lights and shadows of schoolboy life are like April weather. There is much sunshine and the clouds pass quickly. Farther along the shadows darken and lengthen. But the current events which belong to early life make slight impressions and have no consequences. They do not extend their influence into the time when life begins in earnest. Looking back over the misty road I dwell with mixed feelings upon the pictures that rise up in my memory. Not upon all with pleasure.

Yet they are part of myself and represent pleasant scenes and faces that were dear, now dim in the obscurity of years. But on these pages I recur only to those passages in my early life which had some connnection with its after part and were a governing influence in it. Throughout, at different periods it has been my good fortune to be in familiar relations with men who were eminent, each in his own line, all of whom were individualized by character and some distinguished by achievement. Even if insensibly, such associations influence the course of life and give its coloring to it. The early part of mine was desultory. "The path that men are destined to walk" had not been marked out for me. Later events determined this, and meantime I had freedom of choice in preparatory studies.

At sixteen I was a good scholar. My teacher, who became my friend as well, was a Scotch gentleman who had been educated at Edinburgh ; he was thoroughly imbued with classic learning, and lived an inner life among the Greeks and Latins. Under his enthusiastic instruction I became fond as himself of the dead languages, and to me also they became replete with living images. I entered upon the study of Greek with genuine pleasure and excitement. It had a mysterious charm for me as if behind the strange characters belonging to an ancient world I was to find things of wonderful interest. I loved to pore over the volumes of old Greek plays in their beautiful Edinburgh print that were among my teacher's cherished books and the fresh ones that occasionally came to him from Scotland. Filled with the figures of that ancient world into which I had entered they remain stamped as pleasing bits into the recollections of that time, and show how completely my mind was possessed by my work. The years spent in this way gave me habits of study and laid the foundation for a knowledge of modern languages which long afterward became valuable in important events.

Upon the strength of these studies I now entered at once into the junior class at the Charleston college, though far behind it in other branches and especially in mathematics. But this new field interrupted the close relations with my friend and teacher Dr. John Roberton. Many years afterward, in reading the introduction to his translation of Xenophon's Anabasis I had the pleasure to find him speaking of me as " his once beloved and favorite pupil—his prodigious memory and enthusiastic application."

I was fond of study, and in what I had been deficient easily caught up with the class. In the new studies I did not forget the old, but at times I neglected both. While present at class I worked hard, but frequently absented myself for days together. This infraction of college discipline brought me frequent reprimands. During a long time the faculty forbore with me because I was always well prepared at recitation, but at length, after a formal warning neglected, their patience gave way and I was expelled from college for continued disregard of discipline. I was then in the senior class. In this act there was no ill-feeling on either side. My fault was such a neglect of the ordinary college usages and rules as the faculty could not overlook and I knew that I was a transgressor.

A few years afterward the faculty voluntarily revised their decision and conferred on me the degree of Bachelor and Master of Arts, so taking me back into the fold. Meantime I had my compensation. The college authorities had wrapped themselves in their dignity and reluctantly but sternly inflicted on me condign punishment. To me this came like summer wind, that breathed over something sweeter than the " bank whereon the wild thyme blows." I smiled to myself while I listened to words about the disappointment of friends—and the broken career. I was living in a charmed atmosphere and their edict only gave me complete freedom. What the poets dwell on as " the rarest flower of life " had bloomed in my path—only seventeen I was passionately in love. This was what had made me regardless of discipline and careless of consequences. This was the true rebel that carried me off to pleasant days and returned me buoyant at night to hard work in order to catch up with my class next morning. With my memory full of those days, as the recollection rises to the surface I put it down here. This is an autobiography and it would not be true to itself if I left out the bit of sunshine that made the glory of my youth—what Schiller calls " his glorious youth." It is only a few lines, a tribute which as they reappear around me I give to the pleasant companions who made life gay at that time. There will be enough hereafter of grave and hard, conflict and dissension, violence and injury and fraud; but none of these things were known to us, that little circle of sworn friends, who were gathering our spring flowers. We took no thought for the harvest but gathered our cornflowers from the upspringing grain.

I remember, once along the banks of the Des Moines, a botanist with me stooped down and grasped the clustered head of a low flowering plant. Under the broad leaves lay coiled a rattlesnake, close to his hand. Geyer escaped, but it gave him a spasm that made him dig his heels into the ground and jerk his arms nervously about as he threw off the shock.

Always afterward he looked for snakes among his flowers. With ours there were never any. Some thorns perhaps as I had just found, but these go with the sweetest flowers.

Since I was fourteen years old I had been intimate with a creole family who had escaped from the San Domingo massacre. With the mother and grandmother, there were two boys and three girls. The elder of the boys was older than I, the girls all younger. The eldest of the three girls was Cecilia. They were all unusually handsome ; clear brunette complexions, large dark eyes, and abundant blue-black hair.

The grandmother was the head of the family and its autocratrice. She was a tall, stern old woman, with iron-gray hair, over seventy years of age, and held absolute rule over us all, from the mother down. Often when the riot was at the highest or we had kept it up late, her sudden appearance would disperse us like a flock of quail. The house-children would scamper off to bed and the visitors make a prompt escape. The house stood on a corner and there was a room at the rear which is daguerreotyped on my memory. This room opened directly on the street and belonged to us by squatters' right. It was by this door that we were accustomed to make a sudden exit when the grandmother made one too many for us.

But her ill-humor of the moment never lasted until the next time came for us to meet. The severe lines imprinted on her face by trials, after repose had not smoothed away. But often when we were in full flight before her I have seen the lurking smiles break into a pleased laugh that cleared away the sternness.   In a manner I grew up with the children.   Before and after I left college they, but especially one, were the companions with whom I was always happy to spend what time I could seize upon.   The boys and I made a restless trio.

The days went by on wings.   In the summer we ranged about in the woods, or on the now historic islands, gunning or picnicking, the girls sometimes with us ; sometimes in a sailboat on the bay, oftener going over the bar to seaward and not infrequently when the breeze failed us getting dangerously near the breakers on the bar.   I remember as in a picture, seeing the beads of perspiration on the forehead of my friend Henry as he tugged frantically at his oar when we had found ourselves one day in the suck of Drunken Dick, a huge breaker that to our eyes appeared monstrous as he threw his spray close to the boat.   For us it really was pull Dick pull Devil.

Those were the splendid outside days ; days of unreflecting life when I lived in the glow of a passion that now I know extended its refining influence over my whole life.   The recollection of those days has never faded.   I am glad that it was not required of me to come back as an enemy among those scenes.

This holiday time could not last, but it was beautiful, although I was conscious that I could not afford it.   I had not entirely neglected my studies.   Sometimes seized with a temporary remorse for time lost I gathered up my books and overworked myself for awhile, only to relapse with keener zest into the more natural life.

The accidents that lead to events are often hardly noticeable.   A single book sometimes enters fruitfully into character or pursuit.   I had two such. One was a chronicle of men who had made themselves famous by brave and noble deeds, or infamous by cruel and base acts.   With a schoolboy's enthusiasm I read these stories over and over again, with alternate pleasure or indignation.   I please myself in thinking they have sometimes exercised a restraining or inspiring influence.   Dwelling in the memory they were like the ring of Amasis.

The other was a work on practical astronomy, published in the Dutch. The language made it a closed book but for the beautifully clear maps of the stars and many examples of astronomical calculations.   By its aid I became well acquainted with the night skies and familiarized myself with the ordinary observations necessary to determine latitude and longitude. This was the beginning of the astronomical knowledge afterwards so essential to me.

Soon now the day for care and work came.   We were only two, my mother and I.   We had lost my sister.   My brother was away, making his own career, and I had to concern myself for mine.   I was unwilling to leave my mother.   Circumstances had more than usually endeared us to each other and I knew that her life would be solitary without me.   I was accustomed to be much at home and our separations had been slight.   But now it was likely to be for long and the hard part would be for the one left alone.   For me it was very different.   Going out into the excitement of strange scenes and occurrences I would be forced out of myself and for long intervals could forget what I left behind.   For her in the sameness of daily life there would be a blank not easily filled.   But my mother had an experience of sacrifice which with her true womanly nature it had been hard to learn.   Realizing that now the time had come for another, she, but not cheerfully, sent me forward on my way.

The necessity for exertion was making itself felt and the outlook for my future was vague.   But among the few men whom I had come to know as friends there was one whose kindly aid and counsel was often valuable to me, then and afterward.

Mr. Poinsett was one of the distinguished men of the day, of broad and liberal mind, refined by study and much travel.   While Minister to Mexico his cultivated taste led him to interest himself in the luxuriant flora of that country.   Known in a graver way through his public works and service, it has chanced that his name has been kept familiarly present and most popularly known by the scarlet Poinsettia which he contributed to botany.

I knew him after he returned from Mexico, and before and during the time when he was Secretary of War.   By his aid, but not with his approval, I went to the South American coast as teacher on board the U. S. sloop of war Natchez, Captain Zantzinger.   Admiral Farragut was one of the Lieutenants.   The voyage had its advantages.   I saw more of the principal cities and people than a traveller usually does on passing through a country, though nothing of the interior.   But the time spent was long and had no future bearing.   Among the few events that occurred to break the routine of ship life there was one in which I was concerned that I remember with satisfaction.   While lying at Rio de Janeiro a duel had taken place between two of the midshipmen in which one lost his life.   Both were men of high character and had been friends.   The fatal termination of the meeting was deeply regretted, and by no one more than the survivor. A trivial misunderstanding shortly after resulted in another.   The principals on this occasion were Mr. Lovell, of South Carolina, and Mr. Parrott, of Massachusetts.   Decatur Hurst was Lovell's second, and I Parrott's. Lovell was a nephew of Mr. Poinsett and Hurst a nephew of Commodore Decatur.   Hurst and I were friends.   He proposed to put only powder in the pistols for the first fire.   If then another should be insisted on we would give them lead.   In this we incurred some personal risk, but were quite willing to take it for the sake of the persons principally interested in the result.

This being agreed upon, we succeeded in leaving the ship without having attracted any attention to our movements, and crossing the bay quietly landed on the north shore. Leaving the boat, we found a narrow strip of sandy beach about forty yards long between the water and the mountain. In such a place men could hardly miss each other. The few preparations made, we placed our men twelve paces apart and gave the word. Both looked sincerely surprised that they remained standing upright as before. Going up each to his man, we declared the affair over ; the cause of quarrel in our opinion not justifying a second shot. There was some demur, but we insisting carried our men triumphantly back to the ship, nobody hurt and nobody wiser. Hurst and I greatly enjoyed our little *ruse de guerre*.

Of the four men three are dead. Just when Lovell died I do not know. Admiral Parrott died in New York about seven years ago. Hurst too is dead. While on the African coast he was badly wounded in a duel, which ultimately caused his death not long afterward.

When the cruise was over I returned to Charleston. In the meantime Congress had created the post of Professor of Mathematics in the Navy. I applied for a commission and was ordered before an examining board, to be convened shortly at Norfolk. Then came for me another pleasant month, for I was back among my old friends, and the strong motive I had now added to the pleasure I always found in study. All day long I was at my books, and the earliest dawn found me at an upper window against which stood a tall poplar, where the rustling of the glossy leaves made a soothing accompaniment. The surroundings go for a great deal in intellectual work.

My examination was successfully over and I had received, and declined, my appointment.

Just then an opportunity was offered me to go under Captain W. G. Williams, of the U. S. Topographical Corps, as one of the assistant engineers on surveys to be made for a projected railway from Charleston to Cincinnati. I gladly accepted the chance that fell to me, and spent a summer in congenial work among the mountains of South Carolina and Tennessee. There were several parties, each under an able engineer. That to which I belonged was under the direction of Lieutenant White, a graduate of West Point, who knew well how to make our work agreeable. We were engaged in running experimental lines, and the plotting of the field notes sometimes kept us up until midnight. Our quarters were sometimes at a village inn and more frequently at some farmer's house, where milk and honey and many good things were welcome to an appetite sharpened by all day labor on foot and a tramp of several miles backward and forward, morning and evening. It was cheery, wholesome work. The summer weather in the mountains was fine, the cool water abundant, and the streams lined with azaleas.   As often is with flowers of that color the white azaleas were fragrant.   The survey was a kind of picnic with work enough to give it zest, and we were all sorry when it was over.

The surveys being suspended, I returned home and only casually if ever met again the men with whom I had been associated.   General Morrell, with whom many years afterward I lived as neighbor on the Hudson, was the only one I remember to have met.

It had been the policy of President Jefferson, suggested by his acquisition of the Louisiana territory, to remove all the Indian tribes from the Eastern States to the west of the Mississippi.   This policy was adopted and carried forward by Mr. Monroe, and completed under President Jackson.

The last to be removed were the Cherokees who inhabited a district where the States of North Carolina, Tennessee, and Georgia cornered together.   This territory was principally in Georgia, and consisted in greater part of a body of land ceded to the Cherokees by Georgia in 1783.

For the good of the bordering States, and for the welfare of the Indians as well, this was a wise and humane measure.   But the Cherokees were averse to the change.   They were unwilling to leave the homes where they had been domiciled for half a century.

The country was mountainous and the face of it not accurately known. Looking to the contingency of hostilities already threatening with the Indians, Captain Williams was ordered to make a military reconnaissance of the territory they occupied.   I went with him again as one of his assistants.

The accident of this employment curiously began a period of years of like work for me among similar scenes.   Here I found the path which I was " destined to walk."   Through many of the years to come the occupation of my prime of life was to be among Indians and in waste places. Other events which intervened were incidents in this and grew out of it. There were to be no more years wasted in tentative efforts to find a way for myself.   The work was laid out and it began here with a remarkable continuity of purpose.

This was a winter survey made hurriedly.   When we entered the Indian territory we were three together, Archie Campbell, Hull Adams and I.   About dark we reached the Nantahéylè River, at an Indian village. The Indians were having a feast and a carouse and were all drunk.   The squaws hid us in a log out-cabin, half filled with shucked corn.   We did not pass a comfortable night.   The shouts of the drunken Indians and rats running over us kept us awake ; and we were glad when morning came. The night had been cold and our bath-tub was the Nantahéylè River. There was ice along the banks and the water in my hair froze into fretful quills.

With the beginning of the reconnaissance our little party was scattered, each to separate work. The Indians after their usual way of living, occupied the country sparsely. In parts, this was beautifully fertile; broad level valleys, with fine streams and forest land. I had a guide named Laudermilk, a very intelligent, good-tempered man, intimately acquainted with the territory to be surveyed. In true pioneer spirit he had built his cabin at a spot in the woods as much out of the way and isolated as he could well find. He was about thirty years old and his wife twenty. It was comfortable quarters. Occasionally we would spend a night there, making a hard ride through snow to reach it. Sometimes we were alone, making a sketch of some stream, and stopping at night at an Indian cabin. At other times, when the work was in a more uninhabited part of the territory, we had a small party of men, with pack-saddles to carry our tents and provisions.

It was a forest country thinly occupied by Indian farms. At night we slept in half-faced tents, with great fires of hickory logs at our feet. Pigs which ranged during the fall and fattened on chestnuts made our *pièce de resistance* on these occasions.

As it sometimes chanced, I was present at Indian feasts, where all would get wild with excitement and some furious with drink. Bloody frays were a certain accompaniment, slashing with knives, hands badly cut from clutching the blades and ugly body wounds. Their exhibition of brute courage and indifference to pain compelled admiration, with regret for the good material wasted. But these were the exceptional occasions. In their villages and in their ordinary farming life they lived peaceably and comfortably. Many of their farms were much the same as those that are to be met with everywhere on our remote frontier. The depreciating and hurtful influence was the proximity of the whites. One of the pieces of work assigned to me was a reconnaissance of the Hiwassee River. It was over very rough and tangled ground. The first day's work of twenty miles on foot made me so stiff next morning that I moved like a foundered horse, and I suppose I was foundered for the time. In getting over the trunks of fallen trees I had to sit down upon them and lift over first one leg and then the other. But this was only for the first day. That night we had stopped at the log house of an Indian. It was a handsome specimen of forest architecture; a square-built house standing on a steep bank of the Hiwassee, with glass-paned windows. But the striking feature in such surroundings was that all the logs were evenly hewed so that they laid solidly together and presented a smoothly even surface. Its finish, in its own way, made quite an agreeable impression from its unexpectedness in such a place. Below, the river banks fell away, leaving a little valley, in which he had made his cornfield.

In much travel among Indians I have had a fair opportunity to become acquainted with different tribes and learned to appreciate and comprehend the results of the differing influences brought to bear upon them. Here in the Cherokee country, as in different regions afterward, I saw how their differing conditions depended upon their surroundings. In the Great Basin I saw them in the lowest stage of human existence where it was in its simplest elements, differing from that of wild animals only in the greater intelligence of the Indians. Sage bush sheltered them, seeds, bush squirrels and hares, grasshoppers, worms, anything that had life made their food.

Going upward I saw them on the great prairie plains in the higher stages to which the surrounding facilities for a more comfortable and easier life had raised them. Nomadic, following the game and the seasons but living in villages, buffalo and large game gave them good food and clothing, and made for them dry warm lodges. And afterward in the nearer approach to the civilized life to which the intermittent efforts of the Government at agencies and reservations, and the labor of the Protestant and Catholic churches, had brought them.

The efforts of the Protestant churches had been limited by time and extent of territory. The area of their work had been confined chiefly to a part of the country east of the Mississippi, where they found the field yet unoccupied and the influences English and Protestant. The Catholic Church was first in the field in the West. Its area west of the Mississippi extended from the Gulf of Mexico into Canada and along the shores of the Pacific, where, under Spanish rule, their stable policy was best displayed.

The earlier explorers west of the Mississippi were French. Explored, occupied, and owned by France and Spain as this whole country was, inevitably their religion became part of it also, and was carried among the Indians by the missionary priests of that Church. For two centuries this was their undisturbed domain. The policy of the Roman Catholic Church is unchanging and impersonal, and the perpetuity of its institutions seems infused into the extremest details. The policy of its government was the policy of the agent who was part of the government, having the same interest at heart ; and the interest and well-being of the Indians were equally the interest and object of the government and its agent, who was always one of the body politic and religious and whose aim was impersonal, directed solely to the good of his church. All this I have seen exemplified in the missions on the Pacific coast, in the remnant of civilization among the interior tribes, and in the present condition of the missions on the Atlantic side. The results of their work stand out to-day in the great buildings which under their direction were erected by the Indians in California. They made them herdsmen and raised by them hundreds of thousands of horses and cattle. They made them farmers self-supplying, and taught them a foreign language too deeply implanted to be eradicated by long disuse. The remnants of their teachings remain in the grain fields of the Pimas on the Gila River of Arizona and in the orchards of the Sepais in the cañon valleys of the Colorado, to whom the Navajoes come regularly every year to trade for fruit and grain. All this resulted from a singleness of purpose carried into effect by agents inevitably responsible. And they went ahead to occupy and civilize with reliance on the support of their government.

The Protestant churches had the aid of no such strength, and their success, as I have seen it evidenced among the Cherokees and Shawnees and Delaware people, as with later missionary efforts, has been due to individual energy and character.

On the other hand, our Government, itself changing in its personality every few years, administered the details of its general policy through agents to whom change was the normal and expected condition; who had no persistent interest in the Indians and, above all, no responsibility. So there has been no continuous effective policy by the Government except in the removal of the Indians from East to West, and out of the way of the white man, as the tide of population rose.

These results clearly show that the Indians were capable of being civilized and utilized, and they show too how this could be effected more or less by the nature of the policy directed upon them.

Our army is a permanent body, having continuity of existence, and its officers have not only a class responsibility but a responsibility founded in a regard for their individual and personal honor, and the honor of the body to which they belong. These two qualities of permanency and responsibility make the army the best and simplest as well as the safest and least expensive medium through which to control and care for these Indian wards of the nation. We have taken away from them their property and means of support and are bound to a corresponding obligation.

In the fall of 1853, on an overland journey, I spent a day at the Catholic station of Saint Mary's on the Kansas River, among the Pottawatamie Indians. Under the impression of what I saw I wrote then in my notebook as follows:

" *Oct.* 25. Went to Uniontown and nooned. This is a street of log-cabins. Nothing to be had here. Some corn for our animals and a piece of cheese for ourselves. Lots of John Barleycorn which the men about were consuming. Uniontown is called a hundred miles from Kansas."

" *Oct.* 26. High wind and sleet. Clouds scudding across the sky. About two o'clock we reached the pretty little Catholic Mission of

Saint Mary's. The well-built, whitewashed houses, with the cross on the spire showing out above them was already a very grateful sight. On the broad bottoms immediately below are the fields and houses of the Pottawatamie Indians. Met with a hospitable reception from the head of the Mission. A clear sky promises a bright day for to-morrow. Learned here some of the plants which are medicinal among the Indians. Among them *Asarum Canadensis*—jewel-weed—a narcotic; and *Oryngium Aquaticum*, the great remedy of the Pottawatamies for snake-bites."

" *Oct.* 27. White frost covers the ground this morning. Sky clear and air still. With bowls of good coffee and excellent bread made a good breakfast. We already begin to appreciate food. Prepared our luggage, threw into the wagon the provisions obtained here, and at ten o'clock took leave of the hospitable priests and set out. I was never more impressed by the efficiency of well-directed and permanent missionary effort than here at this far-off mission settlement, where the progress and good order strike forcibly as they stand in great contrast with the neighboring white settlement."

In the course of a winter exploration into the Rocky Mountains in 1848-'49 I had been driven southward by stress of weather, and in the spring of the latter year I passed through Arizona. With the treaty of Guadaloupe Hidalgo that Territory had just come under the dominion of the United States. I had gone as far south as the little town of San Pedro, which still was within Mexico. Returning northward down the San Pedro River we passed on the way an abandoned Mission where there was an extensive peach orchard in solitary bloom. The soft pink bloom was startling where the ideas of the place spoke only now of violence and bloodshed. There were large buildings here, and the situation in the river valley was beautiful, but the Apaches had made it too dangerous to live in isolated places.

We followed the river down until it spread out where it entered the plain and lost itself in the ground. At the foot of a steep hill we found grass and water, and next morning continued our journey in a northwesterly direction and struck the Gila near the villages of the Pimas and Maricopas above the Great Bend of the river. I found these Indians still retaining the civilization that had been taught them by the missionary priests and living as farmers in fixed habitations. They raised wheat and corn, watermelons, beans and other vegetables, and grew cotton out of which they made blankets. They lived undisturbed, having no other enemy than the wild Apaches, who seldom dared molest them, and they were friendly to the Mexican or other travellers who at rare intervals passed that way on their road to the Californias.

They received me in a truly friendly and hospitable way, supplying in exchange for a few trifling articles all the provisions that I required. What they particularly valued was a small opaque white bead, of which we had a quantity.

In 1879, while Governor of Arizona, I was travelling between Phœnix and Maricopa, which is on the line of the South Pacific Railway, and again passed by their villages. Our Government had covered the ground they occupied by a reservation. Under the laws of Spain and Mexico, they in their legal and recognized character of citizens living in Pueblos were entitled to the ownership of four square leagues of land. The terms of the treaty confirmed this right; but with its usual disregard of private right our Government had assumed ownership and reserved to them their own lands, as against other trespassers than itself.

The settlements of these Indians stretch along the bottom lands of the Gila above the Great Bend. Their houses are built with wattled sides, the roofs being of the natural long laths of the *seguara*—a tree cactus—and of *ocotillo* a scarlet flowering shrub, plastered with earth. These houses are detached and in this way the village covers considerable space. As we reached the reservation the driver of the stage-coach in which I was travelling drew up his horses at a small adobe house, which had a *ramada* or bush-covered shed in front. An Indian was leaning against one of the posts, and a gray-headed white man came out to the coach. The driver delivered to him a demijohn, and after a word or two he went back into the house and returned with a stout glass of whiskey for the driver. These Indians were then, when I saw them last, deteriorating fast. Their lands are very fertile, and the grain which they raise is of excellent quality. Ten car-loads of wheat raised by the Maricopas, about the time I write of, and sent to San Francisco were sold at $2.20 the hundred, the ruling price at the time being $2.10 to $2.15 the hundred.

If these Indians were under the immediate control of an army officer who would act as their factor and sell their produce and make their necessary purchases to the greatest advantage, aiding their progress in agriculture while at the same time he held them in wholesome restraint, their villages would soon become handsome and industrious settlements.

CHAPTER II.

THE Cherokee survey was over. I remained at home only just long enough to enjoy the pleasure of the return to it, and to rehabituate myself to old scenes. While I was trying to devise and settle upon some plan for the future, my unforgetful friend, Mr. Poinsett, had also been thinking for me. He was now Secretary of War, and, at his request, I was appointed by President Van Buren a second lieutenant in the United States Topographical Corps, and ordered to Washington. Wash-ington was greatly different then from the beautiful capital of to-day. In-stead of many broad, well-paved, and leafy avenues, Pennsylvania Avenue about represented the town. There were not the usual resources of public amusement. It was a lonesome place for a young man knowing but one person in the city, and there was no such attractive spot as the Battery by the sea at Charleston, where a stranger could go and feel the freedom of both eye and thought.

Shut in to narrow limits, the mind is driven in upon itself and loses its elasticity; but the breast expands when, upon some hill-top, the eye ranges over a broad expanse of country, or in face of the ocean. We do not value enough the effect of space for the eye; it reacts on the mind, which unconsciously expands to larger limits and freer range of thought. So I was low in my mind and lonesome until I learned, with great relief, that I was to go upon a distant survey into the West. But that first im-pression of flattened lonesomeness which Washington had given me has remained with me to this day.

About this time, a distinguished French savant had returned from a geographical exploration of the country about the sources of the Missis-sippi, the position of which he first established. That region and its capa-bilities were then but little known, and the results of his journey were of so interesting a nature that they had attracted public notice and comment. Through Mr. Poinsett, Mr. Nicollet was invited to come to Washington, with the object of engaging him to make a complete examination of the great prairie region between the Mississippi and Missouri Rivers, as far north as the British line, and to embody the whole of his labors in a map and general report for public use.

Mr. Nicollet had left France, intending to spend five years in geographical researches in this country. His mind had been drawn to the early discoveries of his countrymen, some of which were being obliterated and others obscured in the lapse of time. He anticipated great pleasure in renewing the memory of these journeys, and in rescuing them all from the obscurity into which they had fallen. A member of the French Academy of Sciences, he was a distinguished man in the circles to which Arago and other savants of equal rank belonged. Not only had he been trained in science, but he was habitually schooled to the social observances which make daily intercourse attractive, and become invaluable where hardships are to be mutually borne and difficulties overcome and hazards met. His mind was of the higher order. A musician as well as a mathematician, it was harmonious and complete.

The Government now arranged with him to extend his surveys south and west of the country which he had already explored. Upon this survey I was ordered to accompany him as his assistant.

It was a great pleasure to me to be assigned to this duty. By this time I had gone through some world-schooling and was able to take a sober view of the realities of life. I had learned to appreciate fully the rare value of the friendly aid which had opened up for me such congenial employment, and I resolved that, if it were in me to do so, I would prove myself worthy of it. The years of healthy exercise which I had spent in open air had hardened my body, and the work I had been engaged in was kindred to that which I was now to have. Field work in a strange region, in association with a man so distinguished, was truly an unexpected good fortune, and I went off from Washington full of agreeable anticipation.

At St. Louis I joined Mr. Nicollet. This was the last large city on the western border, and the fitting-out place for expeditions over the uninhabited country. The small towns along the western bank of the Missouri made for two or three hundred miles a sort of fringe to the prairies. At St. Louis I met for the first time General Robert E. Lee, then a captain in the United States Engineer Corps, charged with improvements of the Mississippi River. He was already an interesting man. His agreeable, friendly manner to me as a younger officer when I was introduced to him, left a more enduring impression than usually goes with casual introductions.

In St. Louis Mr. Nicollet had a pleasant circle of friends among the old French residents. They were proud of him as a distinguished countryman, and were gratified with his employment by the American Government, which in this way recognized his distinction and capacity. His intention, in the prosecution of his larger work to revive the credit due to early French discoverers, was pleasing to their national pride.

His acquaintances he made mine, and I had the pleasure and advantage to share in the amiable intercourse and profuse hospitality which in those days characterized the society of the place. He was a Catholic, and his distinction, together with his refined character, made him always a welcome guest with his clergy. And I may say in the full sense of the word, that I " assisted " often at the agreeable suppers in the refectory. The pleasure of these grew in remembrance afterward, when hard and scanty fare and sometimes starvation and consequent bodily weakness made visions in the mind, and hunger made memory dwell upon them by day and dream of them by night.

Such social evenings followed almost invariably the end of the day's preparations. These were soon now brought to a close with the kindly and efficient aid of the Fur Company's officers. Their personal experience made them know exactly what was needed on the proposed voyage, and both stores and men were selected by them; the men out of those in their own employ. These were principally practised *voyageurs*, accustomed to the experiences and incidental privations of travel in the Indian country.

The aid given by the house of Chouteau was, to this and succeeding expeditions, an advantage which followed them throughout their course to their various posts among the Indian tribes.

Our destination now was a trading post on the west bank of the Mississippi, at the mouth of the St. Peter's, now better known as the Mini-sotah River. This was the residence of Mr. Henry Sibley, who was in charge of the Fur Company's interests in the Mississippi Valley. He gave us a frontier welcome and heartily made his house our headquarters. This was the point of departure at which the expedition began its work. It was on the border line of civilization. On the left or eastern bank of the river were villages and settlements of the whites, and the right was the Indian country which we were about to visit. Fort Snelling was on the high bluff point opposite between the Mini-sotah and the Mississippi. Near by was a Sioux Indian village, and usually its Indians were about the house grounds. Among these I saw the most beautiful Indian girl I have ever met, and it is a tribute to her singular beauty that after so many years I remember still the name of " Ampetu-washtoy "—" the Beautiful day."

The house had much the character of a hunting-lodge. There were many dogs around about, and two large wolfhounds, Lion and Tiger, had the run of the house and their quarters in it. Mr. Sibley was living alone, and these fine dogs made him friendly companions, as he belonged to the men who love dogs and horses. For his other dogs he had built within the enclosure a lookout about fifteen feet high. Around its platform the railing was usually bordered with the heads of dogs resting on their paws and looking wistfully out over the prairie, probably reconnoitering for wolves. Of the two hounds Tiger had betrayed a temper of such ferocity, even against his master, as eventually cost him his life. Lion, though a brother, had, on the contrary, a companionable and affectionate disposition and almost human intelligence, which in his case brought about a separation from his old home.

On the marriage of Mr. Sibley, Lion so far resented the loss of his first place that he left the house, swam across the Mississippi, and went to the Fort, where he ended his days. Always he was glad to meet his master when he came over, keeping close by him and following him to the shore, though all persuasion failed to make him ever recross the river to the home where he had been supplanted; but his life-size portrait still hangs over the fireplace of Mr. Sibley's library. These dogs were of the rare breed of the Irish wolfhound, and their story came up as an incident in a correspondence, stretching from Scotland to Mini-sotah, on the question as to whether it had not become extinct; growing out of my happening to own a dog inheriting much of that strain.

Cut off from the usual resources, Mr. Sibley had naturally to find his in the surroundings. The prominent feature of Indian life entered into his, and hunting became rather an occupation than an amusement. But his hunting was not the tramp of a day to some neighboring lake for wild fowl, or a ride on the prairie to get a stray shot at a wolf. These hunting expeditions involved days' journeys to unfrequented ranges where large game was abundant, or in winter to the neighborhood of one of his trading-posts, where in event of rough weather the stormy days could be passed in shelter. He was fully six feet in height, well and strongly built, and this, together with his skill as a hunter, gave him a hold on the admiration and respect of the Indians.

In all this stir of frontier life Mr. Nicollet felt no interest and took no share; horse and dog were nothing to him. His manner of life had never brought him into their companionship, and the congenial work he now had in charge engrossed his attention and excited his imagination. His mind dwelt continually upon the geography of the country, the Indian names of lakes and rivers and their signification, and upon whatever tradition might retain of former travels by early French explorers.

Some weeks had now been spent in completing that part of the outfit which had been referred to this place. The intervening time had been used to rate the chronometers and make necessary observations of the latitude and longitude of our starting-point.

At length we set out. As our journey was to be over level and un-broken country the camp material was carried in one-horse carts, driven by Canadian voyageurs, the men usually employed by the Fur Company in their business through this region. M. de Montmort, a French gentle-man attached to the legation at Washington, and Mr. Eugene Flandin, a young gentleman belonging to a French family of New York, accompanied the party as friends of Mr. Nicollet. These were pleasant travelling com-panions, and both looked up to Mr. Nicollet with affectionate deference and admiration. No botanist had been allowed to Mr. Nicollet by the Government, but he had for himself employed Mr. Charles Geyer, a bot-anist recently from Germany, of unusual practical knowledge in his pro-fession and of companionable disposition.

The proposed surveys of this northwestern region naturally divided themselves into two: the present one, at this point connecting with Mr. Nicollet's surveys of the upper Mississippi, was to extend westward to the waters of the Missouri Valley; the other, intended for the operations of the succeeding year, was to include the valley of the Missouri River, and the northwestern prairies as far as to the British line.

Our route lay up the Mini-sotah for about a hundred and fifteen miles, to a trading-post at the lower end of the *Traverse des Sioux;* the prairie and river valley being all beautiful and fertile country. We travelled along the southern side of the river, passing on the way several Indian camps, and establishing at night the course of the river by astronomical ob-servations. The *Traverse des Sioux* is a crossing-place about thirty miles long, where the river makes a large rectangular bend, coming down from the northwest and turning abruptly to the northeast; the streams from the southeast, the south, and southwest flowing into a low line of depres-sion to where they gather into a knot at the head of this bend, and into its lowest part as into a bowl. In this great elbow of the river is the Marah-tanka or Big Swan Lake, the summer resort of the Sissiton Sioux. Our way over the crossing lay between the lake and the river. At the end of the *Traverse* we returned to the right shore at the mouth of the Waraju or Cottonwood River, and encamped near the principal village of the Sissitons. Their lodges were pitched in a beautiful situation, under large trees. It needs only the slightest incident to throw an Indian village into a sudden excitement which is startling to a stranger. We were occupied quietly among the Indians, Mr. Nicollet, as usual, surrounded by them, with the aid of the interpreter getting them to lay out the form of the lake and the course of the streams entering the river near by, and, after repeated pronunciations, entering their names in his note-book; Geyer, followed by some Indians, curiously watching him while digging up plants ; and I, more numerously attended, pouring out the quicksilver for the artificial horizon, each in his way busy at work ; when suddenly everything started into motion, the Indians running tumultuously to a little rise which commanded a view of the prairie, all clamor and excitement. The commotion was caused by the appearance of two or three elk on the prairie horizon. Those of us who were strangers, and ignorant of their usages, fancied there must be at least a war-party in sight.

From this point we travelled up the Waraju River and passed a few days in mapping the country around the Pelican Lakes, and among the lower spurs of the *Coteau des Prairies*, a plateau which separates the waters of the Mississippi and Missouri Rivers. This is the single elevation separating the prairies of the two rivers. Approaching it, the blue line which it presents, marked by wooded ravines in contrast with the green prairie which sweeps to its feet, suggested to the *voyageurs* the name they gave it, of the Prairie Coast. At this elevation, about fifteen hundred feet above the sea, the prairie air was invigorating, the country studded with frequent lakes was beautiful, and the repose of a few days was refreshing to men and animals after the warmer and moister air of the lower valley. Throughout this region, the rivers and lakes, and other noticeable features of the country, bear French and Indian names, Sioux or Chippewa, and sometimes Shayan (Cheyenne). Sometimes they perpetuate the memory of an early French discoverer, or rest upon some distinguishing local character of stream or lake ; and sometimes they record a simple incident of chase or war which in their limited history were events.

We now headed for our main object in this direction, the Red Pipe Stone Quarry, which was to be the limit of our western travel; from there we were to turn directly north. All this country had been a battle-ground between the Sioux and Sacs and Foxes. Crossing the high plains over which our journey now lay, we became aware that we were followed by a party of Indians. Guard at night was necessary. But it was no light thing, after a day's work of sketching the country, to stand guard the night through, as it now fell to me among others to do. When we would make the noon halt I promptly took my share of it under the shade of a cart in deep sleep, which the fragrant breeze of the prairie made delightful.

Our exaggerated precautions proved useless, as the suspected hostile party were only friendly Sioux who, knowing nothing about us, were on their side cautiously watching us.

The Indians have a belief that the Spirit of the Red Pipe Stone speaks in thunder and lightning whenever a visit is made to the Quarry. With a singular coincidence such a storm broke upon us as we reached it, and the confirmation of the legend was pleasing to young Renville and the Sioux who had accompanied us.

As we came into the valley the storm broke away in a glow of sunshine on the line of red bluff which extended for about three miles. The day after our arrival the party of Indians we had been watching came in. We spent three friendly days together; they were after the red pipe stone, and we helped them, by using gunpowder, to uncover the rock.

It was in itself a lovely place, made interesting by the mysterious character given to it by Indian tradition, and because of the fact that the existence of such a rock is not known anywhere else. It is on the land of the Sissiton Sioux, but the other Indians make to it annual pilgrimages, as it is from this they make their images and pipes. This famous stone, where we saw it, was in a layer about a foot and a half thick, overlaid by some twenty-six feet of red-colored indurated sand-rock; the color diminishing in intensity from the base to the summit. The water in the little valley had led the buffalo through it in their yearly migration from north to south, and the tradition is that their trail wore away the surface and uncovered the stone.

There was a detached pedestal standing out a few feet away from the bluff, and about twenty-five feet high. It was quite a feat to spring to this from the bluff, as the top was barely a foot square and uneven, and it required a sure foot not to go further. This was a famous place of the country, and nearly all of us, as is the custom in famous places the world over, carved our names in the stone. It speaks for the enduring quality of this rock that the names remain distinct to this day.

When the position had been established and other objects of the visit accomplished, we took up the northern line of march for the *Lac qui parle*, the trading-post and residence of the Renville family.

On our way we passed through and mapped the charming lake country of the *Coteau des Prairies*.

The head of the Renville family, a French Canadian, was a border chief. Between him and the British line was an unoccupied region of some seven hundred miles. Over all the Indian tribes which ranged these plains he had a controlling influence; they obeyed himself and his son, who was a firm-looking man of decided character. Their good will was a passport over this country.

The hospitable reception which is the rule of the country met us here. I take pleasure in emphasizing and dwelling on this, because it is apart from the hospitality of civilized life. There is lively satisfaction on both sides. The advent of strangers in an isolated place brings novelty and excitement, and to the stranger arriving, there is great enjoyment in the change from privations and watchful unrest, to the quiet safety and profusion of plenty in such a frontier home. Our stay here was made very agreeable. We had abundance of milk and fresh meat and vegetables, all seasoned with a traveller's appetite and a hearty welcome.

To gratify us a game of Lacrosse was played with spirit and skill by the Indians. Among the players was a young half-breed of unusual height, who was incomparably the swiftest runner among them. He was a relation of the Renvilles and seemed to have some recognized family authority, for during the play he would seize an Indian by his long hair and hurl him backward to the ground to make room for himself, the other taking it as matter of course.

Some time was spent here in visiting the various lakes near by, fixing their position and gathering information concerning the character of the country and its Indians. This over, and the limit of the present journey attained, we turned our faces eastward and started back to the mouth of the St. Peter's.

While Mr. Nicollet was occupied in making a survey of the Lesueur River, and identifying localities and verifying accounts of preceding travellers, I was sent to make an examination of the Mankato or Blue Earth River, which bore upon the subjects he had in view. The eastern division of the expedition now closed with our return to Mr. Sibley's.

Among the episodes which gave a livelier coloring to the instructive part of this campaign, was a hunting expedition on which I went with Mr. Sibley. With him also went M. Faribault, a favorite companion of his on such occasions. It was a royal hunt. He took with him the whole of Red Dog's village—men, women, and children. The hunting-ground was a number of days' journey to the south, in Ioway, where game was abundant; many deer and some elk. It was in November, when the does are in their best condition. The country was well timbered and watered, stretches of prairie interspersed with clumps and lines of woods.

Early in the morning the chief would indicate the camping-ground for the night, and the men sally out for the hunt. The women, with the camp equipage, would then make direct for the spot pointed out, ordinarily some grove about nine miles distant. Toward nightfall the hunters came in with their game.

The day's tramp gave a lively interest to the principal feature which the camp presented; along the woods bright fires, where fat venison was roasting on sticks before them, or stewing with corn or wild rice in pots hanging from tripods; squaws busy over the cooking and children rolling about over the ground. No sleep is better or more restoring than follows such a dinner, earned by such a day.

On the march one day, a squaw dropped behind, but came into camp a little later than the others, bringing a child a few hours old. By circum-

stance of birth he should have become a mighty hunter, but long before
he reached man's age he had lost birthright, he and his tribe, and I doubt
if he got even the mess of pottage for which Esau bartered his.   During
the hunt we had the experience of a prairie fire.   We were on a detached
excursion, Sibley, Faribault and I.   After midnight we were aroused from a
sound sleep by the crackling noise, and springing to our feet, found ourselves surrounded, without a minute to lose.   Gathering in our animals, we
set fire to the grass near our tent, transferring quickly animals and baggage to the cleared ground.   The fire swept past, and in a few seconds
struck a grove of aspens near by and leaped up the trees, making a wall of
flame that sent a red glow into the sky brighter even than the waves of
fire that rolled over the prairie.   We lost nothing, only tent and belongings a little blackened with the smouldering grass; but the harm was to
the woods and the game.

The work of the year and in this quarter was now finished, and we returned to St. Louis, to prepare for the survey of the more western division
in the succeeding year.

A partial equipment for the expedition to the northwest prairies was
obtained in St. Louis.   Arrangements had previously been made at *Lac
qui parle*, during the preceding journey, for a reinforcement of men to meet
the party at an appointed time on Rivière à Jacques, a tributary to the Missouri River.   At St. Louis five men were engaged, four of them experienced in prairie and mountain travel ; one of them Etienne Provost, known
as *l'homme des montagnes*.   The other man was Louis Zindel, who had
seen service as a non-commissioned officer of Prussian artillery, and was
skilled in making rockets and fireworks.   We left St. Louis early in April,
1839, on board the Antelope, one of the American Fur Company's steam-
boats, which, taking its customary advantage of the annual rise in the Missouri from the snows of the Rocky Mountains, was about starting on its
regular voyage to the trading-posts on the upper waters of the river.

For nearly two months and a half we were struggling against the current of the turbid river, which in that season of high waters was so swift
and strong that sometimes the boat would for moments stand quite still,
seeming to pause to gather strength, until the power of steam asserted itself and she would fight her way into a smooth reach.   In places the river
was so embarrassed with snags that it was difficult to thread a way among
them in face of the swift current and treacherous channel, constantly
changing.   Under these obstacles we usually laid up at night, making fast
to the shore at some convenient place, where the crew could cut a supply
of wood for the next day.   It was a pleasant journey, as little disturbed
as on the ocean.   Once above the settlements of the lower Missouri, there
were no sounds to disturb the stillness but the echoes of the high-pressure

steam-pipe, which travelled far along and around the shores, and the incessant crumbling away of the banks and bars, which the river was steadily undermining and destroying at one place to build up at another. The stillness was an impressive feature, and the constant change in the character of the river shores offered always new interest as we steamed along. At times we travelled by high perpendicular escarpments of light colored rock, a gray and yellow marl, made picturesque by shrubbery or trees ; at others the river opened out into a broad delta-like expanse, as if it were approaching the sea. At length, on the seventieth day we reached Fort Pierre, the chief post of the American Fur Company. This is on the right or western bank of the river, about one thousand and three hundred miles from St. Louis. On the prairie, a few miles away, was a large village of Yankton Sioux. Here we were in the heart of the Indian country and near the great buffalo ranges. Here the Indians were sovereign.

This was to be our starting-point for an expedition northward over the great prairies, to the British line. Some weeks were spent in making the remaining preparations, in establishing the position and writing up journals, and in negociations with the Indians. After the usual courtesies had been exchanged our first visit to their village was arranged. On our way we were met by thirty of the principal chiefs, mounted and advancing in line. A noble-looking set of men showing to the best advantage, their fine shoulders and breasts being partly uncovered. We were conducted by them to the village, where we were received with great ceremony by other chiefs, and all their people gathered to meet us. We were taken into a large and handsome lodge and given something to eat, an observance without which no Indian welcome is complete. The village covered some acres of ground, and the lodges were pitched in regular lines. These were large, of about twenty skins or more. The girls were noticeably well clothed, wearing finely dressed skins nearly white, much embroidered with beads and porcupine quills dyed many colors; and stuffs from the trading-post completed their dress. These were the best formed and best looking Indians of the plains, having the free bearing belonging with their unrestrained life in sunshine and open air. Their mode of life had given them the uniform and smooth development of breast and limb which indicates power, without knots of exaggerated muscle, and the copper-bronze of their skins, burnt in by many suns, increased the statue-like effect. The buffalo and other game being near, gave them abundant food and means to obtain from the trading-posts what to them were luxuries.

Having made the customary and expected presents which ratified the covenants of good will and free passage over their country, we left the village, escorted half-way by the chiefs.

A few days after our visit to the village, one of the chiefs came to the fort, bringing with him a pretty girl of about eighteen, handsomely dressed after the manner I have described. Accompanied by her and the interpreter, he came to the room opening on the court where we were employed over our sketch-books and maps, and formally offered her to Mr. Nicollet as a wife for him. This placed our chief for a moment in an embarrassing position. But, with ready and crafty tact he explained to the chief that he already had one, and that the Great Father would not permit him to have two. At the same time suggesting that the younger chief, designating me, had none. This put me in a worse situation. But being at bay, I promptly replied that I was going far away and not coming back, and did not like to take the girl away from her people; that it might bring bad luck; but that I was greatly pleased with the offer, and to show that I was so, would give the girl a suitable present. Accordingly, an attractive package of scarlet and blue cloths, beads, a mirror, and other trifles was made up, and they left us; the girl quite satisfied with her trousseau, and he with other suitable presents made him. Meantime we had been interested by the composure of the girl's manner, who during the proceedings had been quietly leaning against the door-post, apparently not ill-pleased with the matrimonial conference.

All was now ready. The rating of the chronometers had been verified. Our observations had placed Fort Pierre in latitude, 44°23′28″, longitude, 100°12′30″, and elevation above the sea 1456 feet. Horses, carts, and provisions had been obtained at the fort and six men added to the party; Mr. May, of Kentucky, and a young man from Pembinah had joined us. They were on their way to the British Colony of the Red River of the North. William Dixon and Louison Frenière had been engaged as interpreters and guides. Both of these were half-breeds, well known as fine horsemen and famous hunters, as well as most experienced guides. The party now consisted of nineteen persons, thirty-three horses, and ten carts. With Mr. Nicollet, Mr. Geyer, who was again our botanist, and myself, was an officer of the French army, Captain Belligny, who wished to use so good an occasion to see the Indian country. We reached the eastern shore with all our equipage in good order, and made camp for the night at the foot of the river hills opposite the fort. The hills leading to the prairie plateau, about five hundred feet above the river, were rough and broken into ravines. We had barely reached the upland when the hunters came galloping in, and the shout of *la vache! la vache!* rang through the camp, everyone repeating it, and everyone excited.

A herd of buffalo had been discovered, coming down to water. In a few moments the buffalo horses were saddled and the hunters mounted, each with a smooth-bore, single or double-barrelled gun, a handkerchief

CHEYENNE BELLE.

bound fillet-like around the head, and all in the scantiest clothing. Conspicuous among them were Dixon and Louison. To this latter I then, and thereafter, attached myself.

My horse was a good one, an American, but grass-fed and prairie-bred. Whether he had gained his experience among the whites or Indians I do not know, but he was a good hunter and knew about buffalo, and badger holes as well, and when he did get his foot into one it was not his fault.

Now I was to see the buffalo. This was an event on which my imagination had been dwelling. I was about to realize the tales the mere telling of which was enough to warm the taciturn Renville into enthusiastic expression, and to rouse all the hunter in the excitable Frenière.

The prairie over which we rode was rolling, and we were able to keep well to leeward and out of sight of the herd. Riding silently up a short slope, we came directly upon them. Not a hundred yards below us was the great, compact mass of animals, moving slowly along, feeding as they went, and making the loud incessant grunting noise peculiar to them. There they were.

The moment's pause that we made on the summit of the slope was enough to put the herd in motion. Instantly as we rose the hill, they saw us. There was a sudden halt, a confused wavering movement, and then a headlong rout; the hunters in their midst. How I got down that short hillside I never knew. From the moment I saw the herd I never saw the ground again until all was over. I remember, as the charge was made, seeing the bulls in the rear turn, then take a few bounds forward, and then, turning for a last look, join the headlong flight.

As they broke into the herd the hunters separated. For some instants I saw them as they showed through the clouds of dust, but I scarcely noticed them. I was finding out what it was to be a prairie hunter. We were only some few miles from the river, hardly clear of the breaks of the hills, and in places the ground still rough. But the only things visible to me in our flying course were the buffalo and the dust, and there was tumult in my breast as well as around me. I made repeated ineffectual attempts to steady myself for a shot at a cow after a hard struggle to get up with her, and each time barely escaped a fall. In such work a man must be able to forget his horse, but my horsemanship was not yet equal to such a proof. At the outset, when the hunters had searched over the herd and singled out each his fattest cow, and made his dash upon her, the herd broke into bands which spread over the plain. I clung to that where I found myself, unwilling to give up, until I found that neither horse nor man could bear the strain longer. Our furious speed had carried us far out over the prairies. Only some straggling groups were in sight, loping slowly off, seemingly conscious that the chase was over. I dismounted and reloaded, and sat down on the grass for a while to give us both rest.   I could nowhere see any of my companions, and, except that it lay somewhere to the south of where I was, I had no idea where to look for the camp.   The sun was getting low, and I decided to ride directly west, thinking that I might reach the river hills above the fort while there was light enough for me to find our trail of the morning.   In this way I could not miss the camp, but for the time being I was lost.

My horse was tired and I rode slowly.   He was to be my companion and reliance in a long journey, and I would not press him.   The sun went down, and there was no sign that the river was near.   While it was still light an antelope came circling round me, but I would not fire at him.   His appearance and strange conduct seemed uncanny but companionable, and the echo to my gun might not be a pleasant one.   Long after dark I struck upon a great number of paths, deeply worn, and running along together in a broad roadway.   They were leading directly toward the river, and I supposed, to the fort.   With my anxieties all relieved I was walking contentedly along, when I suddenly recognized that these were buffalo-trails leading to some accustomed great watering-place.   The discovery was something of a shock, but I gathered myself together and walked on.   I had been for some time leading my horse.   Toward midnight I reached the breaks of the river hills at a wooded ravine, and just then I saw a rocket shoot up into the sky, far away to the south.   That was camp, but apparently some fifteen miles distant, impossible for me to reach by the rough way in the night around the ravines.   So I led my horse to the brink of the ravine, and going down I found water, which, à plusieurs reprises, I brought up to him, using my straw hat for a bucket.   Taking off his saddle and bridle, and fastening him by his long lariat to one of the stirrups, I made a pillow of the saddle and slept soundly until morning.   He did not disturb me much, giving an occasional jerk to my pillow, just enough to let me see that all was right.

At the first streak of dawn I saddled up.   I had laid my gun by my side in the direction where I had seen the rocket, and riding along that way, the morning was not far advanced when I saw three men riding toward me at speed.   They did not slacken their pace until they came directly up against me, when the foremost touched me.   It was Louison Frenière.   A reward had been promised by Mr. Nicollet to the first who should touch me, and Louison won it.   And this was the end of my first buffalo hunt.

The camp gathered around all glad to see me.   To be lost on the prairie in an Indian country is a serious accident, involving many chances, and no one was disposed to treat it lightly.   Our party was made up of men experienced in prairie and in mountain travel, exposed always to unforeseen incidents.

AMONG THE BUFFALO.

When Frenière left the camp in search of me he had no hesitation about where to look. In the rolling country over which the hunt lay it would have been merely an accident to find either camp or water. He knew I would not venture the chance, but would strike directly for the river; and so in leaving camp he kept the open ground along the heads of the ravines, confident that he would either find me or my trail. He was sure I would remain on the open ground at the first water I found. He knew, too, as I did not, that from the Fort the valley of the river trended to the northwest, by this increasing the distance I had to travel; still farther increased by a large bend in which the river sweeps off to the westward. On the maps in common use it was nearly north and south, and had it really been so in fact I should have reached the breaks while it was still light enough for me to see the Fort or recognize our crossing-place, and perhaps to find my way to the camp. All the same I had made an experience and it had ended well.

The camp equipage being carried in carts, and not packed upon mules, the gearing up was quickly done; but meanwhile I had time for a fine piece of fat buffalo-meat standing already roasted on a stick before the fire, and a tin cup of good coffee. My horse and I did a fair share of walking on this day's march, and at every unusually good spot of grass I took the bit from his mouth and let him have the chance to recruit from the night before.

We were now on the upland of the *Coteau du Missouri*, here 1,960 feet above the sea. Travelling to the northeastward our camp for the night was made by a fork of the Medicine Bow River, the last running water our line would cross until we should reach the waters of the *Rivière à Jacques* on the eastern slopes of the plateau. On the open plains water is found only in ponds; not always permanent, and not frequent.

From the top of the hill which gives its name to the stream where we had encamped the view was over great stretches of level prairie, fading into the distant horizon, and unbroken except by the many herds of buffalo which made on it dark spots that looked like groves of timber; here and there puffs of dust rising from where the bulls were rolling or fighting. On these high plains the buffalo feed contentedly, and good buffalo grass usually marks the range where they are found. The occasional ponds give them water, and, for them, the rivers are never far away.

This was the Fourth of July. I doubt if any boy in the country found more joy in his fireworks than I did in my midnight rocket with its silent message. Water and wood to-night were abundant, and with plenty in camp and buffalo all around we celebrated our independence of the outside world.

Some days were now occupied in making the crossing of the plateau; our line being fixed by astronomical positions, and the level prairie required no sketching. I spent these days with Frenière among the buffalo. Sometimes when we had gotten too far ahead of our caravan it was an enjoyment to lie in careless ease on the grass by a pond and be refreshed by the breeze which carried with it the fragrance of the prairie. Edged with grasses growing into the clear water, and making a fresh border around them, these resting-spots are rather lakelets than ponds.

The grand simplicity of the prairie is its peculiar beauty, and its occurring events are peculiar and of their own kind. The uniformity is never sameness, and in his exhilaration the voyager feels even the occasional field of red grass waving in the breeze pleasant to his eye. And whatever the object may be—whether horseman, or antelope, or buffalo—that breaks the distant outline of the prairie, the surrounding circumstances are of necessity always such as to give it a special interest. The horseman may prove to be enemy or friend, but the always existing uncertainty has its charm of excitement in the one case, and the joy of the chase in the other. There is always the suspense of the interval needed to verify the strange object; and, long before the common man decides anything, the practised eye has reached certainty. This was the kind of lore in which Frenière was skilled, and with him my prairie education was continued under a master. He was a reckless rider. Never troubling himself about impediments, if the shortest way after his buffalo led through a pond through it he plunged. Going after a band on one of these days we came upon a long stretch of shallow pond that we had not seen, and which was thickly sown with boulders half hidden in tall grass and water. As I started to go around he shouted, " In there—in ! *Tout droit ! faut pas craindre le cheval.*" And in we went, floundering through, happily without breaking bones of ourselves or our horses. It was not the horse that I was afraid of; I did not like that bed of rocks and water.

Crossing the summit level of the plateau we came in sight of the beautiful valley, here about seventy miles broad, of the *Rivière à Jacques*, its scattered wooded line stretching as far as the eye could reach. Descending the slope we saw in the distance ahead moving objects, soon recognized as horsemen; and before these could reach us a clump of lodges came into view. They proved to be the encampment of about a hundred Indians, to whom Dixon and Frenière were known as traders of the Fur Company. After an exchange of friendly greetings our camp was pitched near by. Such a rare meeting is an exciting break in the uneventful Indian life; and the making of presents gave a lively expression to the good feeling with which they received us, and was followed by the usual Indian rejoicing. After a conference in which our line of travel was in-

dicated, the chief offered Mr. Nicollet an escort, the country being uncertain, but the offer was declined. The rendezvous for our expected
reinforcement was not far away, and Indians with us might only prove
the occasion for an attack in the event of meeting an unfriendly band.
They had plenty of good buffalo-meat, and the squaws had gathered in
a quantity of the *pommes des prairies*, or prairie turnips (*Psoralia esculenta*), which is their chief vegetable food, and abundant on the prairie.
They slice and dry this for ordinary and winter use.

Travelling down the slope of the coteau, in a descent of 750 feet
we reached the lake of " The Scattered Small Wood," a handsome but
deceptive bit of water, agreeable to the eye, but with an unpleasant
brackish taste.

About two years ago I received a letter, making of me some inquiries
concerning this beautiful lake country of the Northwest. In writing now
of the region over which I had travelled, I propose to speak of it as
I had seen it, preserving as far as possible its local coloring of the time;
shutting out what I may have seen or learned of the changes years have
wrought. But, since the time of which I am writing, I have not seen this
country. Looking over it, in the solitude where I left it, its broad valleys
and great plains untenanted as I saw and describe them, I think that the
curiosity and interest with which I read this letter, will also be felt by any
who accompany me along these pages. Under this impression, and because the writer of the letter had followed our trail to this point—the
" *Lake of the Scattered Small Wood*"—I give it here:

" IOWA CITY, IA., February 13, 1884.

. . . . " This I write feeling that as you have devoted your life
to engineering and scientific pursuits, it will be at least a gratification
to receive a letter upon such subjects as are connected with what you
have done. It has been my fortune to locate and construct railway lines
for the Chicago & Northwestern Railway in Minnesota and Dakota,
in doing which I have surveyed not less than three thousand miles of line,
and in so doing have passed over a very large extent of the surface of that
region. While doing this work I have been led to inquire into the climate of that remarkable region. I visited many places which you in 1838
discovered and named. Among these are Lakes Benton and Hendricks,
the first about twenty miles north of the famous ' Red Pipe Stone Quarry,'
a very fine sheet of water, along the south shore of which I located the
railroad, and there has sprung up a fine town called Lake Benton. West
of this, in Dakota, and on the west side of the Big Sioux River, is a lake
region, to many of the lakes in which you gave names, and it is to this
locality that I wish to particularly call your attention. These lakes bear

the names of Thompson, Whitewood, Preston, Te-tonka-ha, Abert (now changed to Albert), Poinsett, and Kampeska. The last named is at the head of the Big Sioux, and Poinsett a few miles to the southward.

"When I constructed the Dakota Central Railway in 1879–80, all these lakes excepting Thompson, Poinsett, and Kampeska, were dry; and it took me a long time and no small research to ascertain when they last held water. They had been known to be dry for the twenty-five years preceding 1879, or at least persons who had lived there or in the vicinity for twenty-five years said that the lakes were dry when they came into the locality, and had, with numerous smaller ones, been dry ever since ; and all who knew about them had a theory that they had dried up long since, and that they never would fill again ; but I found old Frenchmen who had seen these lakes full of water in 1843–46, and I, in studying over the matter, found that you had seen and named them in 1836–38, and I would thank you very much if you will take the time and trouble to describe them to me as you saw them then.

"I came very near locating the railroad line through Lake Preston, for the head men of the railroad company believed that it had dried up for all time ; but on my presenting the testimony of certain reliable voyageurs, they allowed me to go around it. It was well that they did, for the winter of 1880-81 gave a snow-fall such as had not been seen since the years 1843-44, and in the spring of 1881 all these lakes filled up, bank full, and have continued so ever since. I had the pleasure of comparing my engineer's levels for elevation above the sea with your barometer determination at Fort Pierre on the Missouri River. Your altitude was 1,450 feet, mine was 1,437, the difference 13 feet. My determination is within the limits of ± 6 feet. The distance over which my levels were taken was 680 miles, and were well checked. I also followed up your trail as you marched from Fort Pierre northeasterly to the ' *Scattered Small Wood Lake.*' I was so successful as to verify your barometer readings in several instances by checking with mine, and in no case found over 15 feet difference between us, and that always in the same relation as at Fort Pierre. Hoping that you will excuse this long letter, and that you may be able to tell me if those lakes were dry when you saw them, or otherwise, and add any other information you see fit,

"I am, truly yours,

"C. W. IRISH, C. E."

The next day we reached the Rivière à Jacques, at the *Talle de Chênes*, a clump of oaks which was the rendezvous where our expected reinforcement was to meet us. The river valley here is about seventy miles wide. Observations made during the four days that we remained at the Talle de

Chênes place it in latitude 45° 16′ 34″, longitude 98° 7″ 45, and the elevation above the sea 1,341 feet.   At the end of this time, no one appearing, the party again took up the line of march, and, following the right bank, on the evening of the 14th encamped near the mouth of Elm River. This river and its forks are well timbered, and for the reason that they furnish firewood and shelter, Indian hunting parties make it their winter crossing-place on the way westward after buffalo on the Missouri plateau.

On the high plains the winter storms are dangerous.   Many tales are told of hunters caught out in a *poudrerie* with no timber near, when it is impossible to see one's way, and every landmark is obliterated or hidden by the driving snow.   At such times the hunter has no other resource than to dig for himself a hole in the snow, leaving only a breathing-place above his head, and to remain in it wrapped in his blankets until the storm passes over ; when, putting on the dry socks and moccasins which he always carries, he makes for the nearest wood.

The buffalo herds, when caught in such storms and no timber in sight, huddle together in compact masses, all on the outside crowding and fighting to get to the inside ; and so, kept warm by the struggling, incessant motion, the snow meanwhile being stamped away under their feet, protect themselves from the fiercest storms.

For several days we travelled up the valley of the *Jacques*, making astronomical stations, and collecting material for Mr. Nicollet's map.   Occasionally, to the same end, I was detached, with Dixon or Frenière, on topographical excursions, which gave me a good general knowledge of the country along the route.   At the *Butte aux Os* (Bone Hill), in latitude 46° 27′ 37″, longitude 98° 8′ elevation above the sea 1,400 feet, we left the *Rivière à Jacques*, or *Chan-sansan*, its valley extending apparently far in a course to west of north, and in a few miles we reached the height of land which separates it from the Shayen River.   This is a tributary to the Red River of the North, and was formerly the home of the Shayens, to-day written Cheyennes.   In the incessant wars between the various tribes of this region the Shayens were driven from their country over the Missouri River south to where they now are.

The summit of the plateau was only 1,460 feet above the sea.   Here we regained the great prairie plains, and here we saw in their magnificent multitudes the grand buffalo herds on their chief range.   They were moving southwestwardly, apparently toward the plains of the upper Missouri.   For three days we were in their midst, travelling through them by day and surrounded by them at night.   We could not avoid them.   Evidently some disturbing cause had set them in motion from the north.   It was necessary to hobble some of our animals and picket them all, and keep them close in to prevent any of them from making off with the buffalo, when they would have been irretrievably lost. Working through the herds it was decided, in order to get more out of their way, to make a temporary halt for a day or two on the *Tampa*, a small stream flowing into the Shayen. On the second day after, Dixon and Frenière came in with three Indians from a party which had been reconnoitring our camp. They belonged to a hunting village of some three hundred lodges, who were out making buffalo-meat and were just about arranging for a grand " *surround.*" It would have been dangerous to risk breaking in upon this, as might easily happen in our ignorance of the locality and their plans. To avert mischief Frenière, on the third day, rode over to the village with a message requesting their chiefs to indicate the time and route for our march. In consequence we were invited to come on to their encampment. Pushing our way through the crowds of buffalo, we were met in the afternoon by two of the chiefs, who escorted us to the village and pointed out the place for our camp. We found the encampment made up of about three hundred lodges of various tribes—Yanktons, Yanktonons, and Sissitons—making about two thousand Indians.

The representations of our guides had insured us a most friendly reception. We were invited to eat in the lodges of different chiefs; the choicest, fattest pieces of buffalo provided for us, and in return they were invited to eat at our camp. The chiefs sat around in a large circle on buffalo robes or blankets, each provided with a deep soup plate and spoon of tin. The first dish was a generous *pot-au-feu*, principally of fat buffalo meat and rice. No one would begin until all the plates were filled. When all was ready the feast began. With the first mouthful each Indian silently laid down his spoon, and each looked at the other. After a pause of bewilderment the interpreter succeeded in having the situation understood. Mr. Nicollet had put among our provisions some Swiss cheese, and to give flavor to the soup a liberal portion of this had been put into the kettles. Until this strange flavor was accounted for the Indians thought they were being poisoned; but, the cheese being shown to them, and explanation made, confidence was restored; and by the aid of several kettles of water well sweetened with molasses, and such other tempting *delicatessen* as could be produced from our stores, the dinner party went on and terminated in great good humor and general satisfaction.

The next day they made their surround. This was their great summer hunt when a provision of meat was made for the year, the winter hunting being in smaller parties. The meat of many fat cows was brought in, and the low scaffolds on which it was laid to be sun-dried were scattered over all the encampment. No such occasion as this was to be found for the use of presents, and the liberal gifts distributed through the village heightened their enjoyment of the feasting and dancing, which was prolonged through the night. Friendly relations established, we continued our journey.

Having laid down the course of the river by astronomical stations, during three days' travel; we crossed to the left bank and directed our road toward the Devil's Lake, which was the ultimate object of the expedition. The Indian name of the lake is *Mini-wakan*, the Enchanted Water; converted by the whites into Devil's Lake.

Our observations placed the river where we left it in latitude 47° 46' 29", longitude 98° 13' 30", and elevation above the sea 1,328 feet; the level of the bordering plateaus being about one hundred and sixty feet above the river.

In our journey along this river, mosquitoes had infested the camp in such swarms and such pertinacity that the animals would quit feeding and come up to the fires to shelter themselves in the smoke. So virulent were they that to eat in any quiet was impossible, and we found it necessary to use the long green veils, which to this end had been recommended to us by the fur traders. Tied around our straw hats the brims kept the veils from our faces, making a space within which the plates could be held; and behind these screens we contrived to eat without having the food uncomfortably flavored by mosquito sauce piquante.

After a short day's march of fourteen miles we made our first camp on this famous war and hunting ground, four miles from the *Mini-wakan.* Early in the day's march we had caught sight of the woods and hills bordering the lake, among them being conspicuous a heart-shaped hill near the southern shore. The next day after an hour's march we pitched our camp at the head of a deep bay not far from this hill. To this the Indians have given the name of the "*Heart of the Enchanted Water*," by the whites translated "Heart of the Devil's Lake."

At a wooded lake of fresh water near last night's camp on the plateau we had found traces of a large encampment which had been recently abandoned. The much-trodden ground and trails all round showed that a large party had been here for several weeks. From many cart-wheel tracks and other signs our guides recognized it as a hunting camp of the *Métis,* or *Bois-Brulés,* of the Red River of the North; and the deep ruts cut by the wheels showed that the carts had received their full load, and that the great hunt of the year was over. It was this continuous and widespread hunt that had put in motion the great herds through which we had passed.

Among other interesting features of the northwest we had heard much from our guides about these people and their buffalo hunts; and to have just missed them by a few days only was quite a disappointment.

The home of the Half-breeds is at Pembina in British North America. They are called indifferently *Métis* or Half-breeds, *Bois-Brulés,* and *Gens libres* or Free People of the North. The Half-breeds themselves are in greater part the descendants of French Canadian traders and others who, in the service of the Fur Company, and principally of the Northwest Company of Montreal, had been stationed at their remote forts, or scattered over the northwest Indian country in gathering furs. These usually took local wives from among the Indian women of the different tribes, and their half Indian children grew up to a natural life of hunting and kindred pursuits, in which their instincts gave them unusual skill.

The Canadian *engagés* of the company who had remained in the country after their term of service had expired were called Free Canadians; and, from their association with the Half-breeds came also the name of *Gens libres*. They were prominently concerned in a singular event which occurred in British America about a quarter of a century before the time of which I am writing. In the rivalry between the Hudson's Bay Company and the Northwest Fur and Trading Company of Montreal, the Half-breeds were used by the Northwest Company in their successful attempts to destroy a Scotch colony which had been planted by the Earl of Selkirk on the Red River of the North at its confluence with the Assiniboine, about forty miles above Lake Winnipeg. The colony was founded upon a grant of land made to the Earl by the Hudson's Bay Company in 1811; and about a hundred immigrants were settled at the Forks in 1812, reaching to some two hundred in 1814. This was called the Kildonan settlement, from a parish in the County of Sutherland which had been the home of the immigrants. In August of 1815 it was entirely broken up by the Northwest Company, and the settlers driven away and dispersed. During the following winter and spring the colony was re-established, and in prosperous condition when it was attacked by a force of Half-breeds, under officers of the Northwest Company, and some twenty unresisting persons killed; including Mr. Semple, the Governor of the Hudson's Bay Company and five of his officers. In the course of this contest there were acts of a savage brutality, not repugnant, perhaps, to the usages of the Indian country where they were perpetrated, but unknown among civilized men. The opposition made to the colony by the Northwest Company was for the declared reason that "Colonization was unfavorable to the Fur Trade:" their policy was to hold the great part of a continent as a game preserve for the benefit solely of their trade.

The colony was revived when the Northwest was merged in the Hudson's Bay Company, and reoccupied its old site at the Forks of Red River; the settlements extending gradually southward along the banks of the river. The grants of land which had been made to the colonists by the Earl of Selkirk held good under the general grant made to him by the Hudson's Bay Company in 1811, and have been so maintained.

Meantime the Half-breeds had been increasing in number; and, as the buffalo have receded before the settlements in British America, they make their hunting expeditions to the plains around the Devil's Lake. With them, the two important events of the year are the buffalo hunts which they come to these plains to make. They bring with them carts built to carry each the meat of ten buffalo, which they make into *pemmican.* This consists of the meat dried by fire or sun, coarsely pounded and mixed with melted fat, and packed into skin sacks. It is of two qualities; the ordinary pemmican of commerce, being the meat without selection, and the finer, in small sacks, consisting of the choicest parts kneaded up with the marrow. Buffalo tongues, pemmican, and robes, constitute chiefly their trade and support.

When making their hunts the party is usually divided; one-half to hunt, the other to guard the camp. Years ago they were much harassed by the Indians of the various tribes who frequented these buffalo grounds as much to fight as to hunt. But as a result of these conflicts with the Half-breeds the Indians were always obliged to go into mourning; and gradually they had learned to fight shy of these people and of late years had ceased to molest them. They are good shots and good riders, and have a prairie-wide reputation for skill in hunting and bravery in fighting.

We remained on the Devil's Lake over a week, during which three stations were made along the southern shore, giving for the most northern latitude 47° 59′ 29″, and for longitude 98° 28′. Our barometer gave for the top of the "Enchanted Hill" 1,766 feet above the sea, for the plateau 1,486 feet, and for the lake 1,476 feet. It is a beautiful sheet of water, the shores being broken into pleasing irregularity by promontories and many islands. As in some other lakes on the plateau, the water is brackish, but there are fish in it; and it is doubtless much freshened by the rains and melting snows of the spring. No outlet was found, but at the southern end there are low grounds by which at the season of high waters the lake may discharge into the Shayen River. This would put it among the sources of the Red River. The most extended view of its waters obtainable from any of the surrounding hills seemed to reach about forty miles in a northwesterly direction. Accompanied by Dixon or Frenière, I was sent off on several detached excursions to make out what I could of the shape and size of the lake. On one of these I went for a day's journey along the western shore, but was unable in the limited time to carry my work to the northern end. Toward nightfall we found near the shore good water and made there our camp in open ground. Nothing disturbed our rest for several hours, when we were roused by a confused heavy trampling and the usual grunting sounds which announced buffalo. We had barely time to get our animals close in and to throw on dry wood and stir up the fire, before the herd was upon us. They were coming to the lake for water, and the near ones being crowded forward by those in the rear and disregarding us, they were nigh going directly over us. By shouting and firing our pieces, we succeeded in getting them to make a little space, in which they kept us as they crowded down into the lake. The brackish, salty water, is what these animals like, and to turn the course of such a herd from water at night would be impossible.

Unwieldy as he looks, the buffalo bull moves with a suddenness and alertness that make him at close quarters a dangerous antagonist. Frenière and I being together one day, we discovered a bull standing in the water of a little lake near the shore, and we rode up to see what he was doing there alone. "He may be sick," said Frenière. As we approached we noticed that he was watching us inquiringly, his head high up, with intention, as a bull in an arena. As we got abreast of him within a few yards, he made two or three quick steps toward us and paused. "*Oho! bonjour camarade,*" Frenière called out, and moved his horse a little away. My attention for an instant was diverted to my *riata,* which was trailing, when the bull made a dash at us. I made an effort to get out of his range, but my horse appeared to think that it was in the order of proceeding for me first to fire. A rough graze to his hind quarters which staggered him made him see that the bull had decided to take this particular affair into his own hands, or horns, and under the forcible impression he covered a rod or two of ground with surprising celerity; the bull meanwhile continuing his course across the prairie without even turning his head to look at us. Concluding that it was not desirable to follow up our brief acquaintance, we too continued our way. A good hunter does not kill merely for the sake of killing.

The outward line of the expedition being closed, our route was now turned eastward across the plateau toward the valley of the Red River of the North. The first night was passed at a small fresh-water lake near the Lake of the Serpents, which is salt; and on August 7th we encamped again on the Shayen-oju. Continuing east, we crossed next day the height of land at an elevation of 1,500 feet above sea level, and a few miles farther came in view of the wide-spread valley of the Red River, its green wooded line extending far away to the north on its way to British America. From this point, travelling southerly, a week was spent in sketching and determining positions among the head-waters of its tributaries; and on August 14th we descended again to the valley of the Shayen and recrossed that river at an elevation of 1,228 feet above the sea, its course not many miles below curving northeast to the Red River. Two days later we reached the Lake of the Four Hills, about a hundred feet above the river. This lake is near the foot of the ascent to the *Ré-*

ipahan, or Head of the Coteau des Prairies. We ascended the slope to the highest point at the head of the Coteau, where the elevation was 2,000 feet above the sea and the width of the Coteau about twenty miles. In its extension to the south it reaches, in about a hundred and fifty miles, a breadth of forty miles; sloping abruptly on the west to the great plains of the *Riviere à Jacques*, and on the east to the prairies of the Mini-sotah River. Here we spent several days in the basin of the beautiful lakes which make the head-waters of the Mini-sotah of the Mississippi River, and the Tchankasndata or Sioux River of the Missouri. The two groups of lakes are near together, occupying apparently the same basin, with a slight rise between; the Mini-sotah group being the northern. They lie in a depression or basin, from 150 to 300 feet below the rim of the Coteau, full of clear living water, often partially wooded; and, having sometimes a sandy beach or shore strewed with boulders, they are singularly charming natural features. These were pleasant camping-grounds—wood was abundant, the water was good, and there were fish in the lakes.

From the lake region we descended 800 or 900 feet to the lower prairies, and took up our march for the residence of our friends the Renvilles.

Some well employed time was devoted here to make examinations of the Big Stone and other lakes, and to making observations and collecting materials to render Mr. Nicollet's projected map of this region as nearly complete as practicable. In all these excursions we had the effective aid of the Renvilles, whose familiar knowledge of the country enabled us to economize both labor and time.

The autumn was far advanced when we took our leave of this post. That year the prairie flowers had been exceptional in luxuriance and beauty. The rich lowlands near the house were radiant with asters and golden-rod, and memory chanced to associate these flowers, as the last thing seen, with the place. Since then I have not been in that country or seen the Renvilles; but still I never see the golden-rod and purple asters in handsome bloom, without thinking of that hospitable refuge on the far northern prairies.

Some additional examinations on the water-shed of the Mini-sotah and along the Mississippi closed the labors of these expeditions; and at nightfall early in November I landed at *Prairie du Chien* in a bark canoe, with a detachment of our party. A steamboat at the landing was firing up and just about starting for St. Louis, but we thought it would be pleasant to rest a day or two and enjoy comfortable quarters while waiting for the next boat. But the next boat was in the spring, for next morning it was snowing hard, and the river was frozen from bank to bank. I had time enough while there to learn two things: one, how to skate; the other, the value of a day.

After some weeks of wagon journey through Illinois, in a severe winter, we reached St. Louis; when, after the party had been cared for, I went on to Washington to assist Mr. Nicollet in working up the material collected in the expeditions.

BIG TIMBER. ARKANSAS RIVER.

CHAPTER III.

THE official report of our return to Washington was duly made. I accompanied Mr. Nicollet in his visit to the President and Mr. Poinsett, by whom he was received with marked cordiality and assured of their great satisfaction in the success of the expedition. It had brought back valuable knowledge concerning a region of great agricultural capacities, little known to the people at large, and which opened to them a new field to occupy. Mr. Poinsett told me of his gratification with the good report which Mr. Nicollet gave him concerning myself; and his kind reception and approval were to me the culminating pleasure of a campaign which had been full of novel interest.

Some pleasant days were spent in welcomes to Mr. Nicollet by his friends in Baltimore, in which I was usually included. Among the agreeable acquaintances made at this time the most interesting to me was Bishop Chanche, of St. Mary's College. Here, as in St. Louis, Mr. Nicollet's relations with the upper clergy were intimate and friendly; and with him I had in this way the advantage of seeing in intimacy men of secluded and dignified lives and large impersonal aims. They received him as the abbots of old welcomed a congenial traveller into their calm retreats when monasteries were seats of learning. The security and peace and orderly comfort made for them a grateful refreshment and relief.

At the college, Mr. Nicollet had his quarters, which were always kept ready for him. He used to take pleasure in showing me in his wardrobes the wealth of linen and other luxuries of his former civilized life; which were all in amusing contrast with that which we had lately been leading, where the chief luxury we could command was a clean skin. It is an uncommon pleasure in a man's life to have such an interior welcome and so real a home in many places as Mr. Nicollet had. The sight of these things usually recalled to him other scenes and events, and led him in confidential intercourse to tell them over to me as they came up in his mind, and so carried my knowledge of him back into his former life.

The loss of friends marks our path through life with crosses which tell us of griefs, as in unfrequented countries a wayside cross or heap of stones marks the spot where some traveller had suddenly come face to face with death on his road. Involuntarily one looks around as if the hidden danger still lurked there. The cross gives a warning impress, and imagination lends its aid to recall the tragedy which had left its shadow on the ground. I had returned to Washington in a condition of happy thoughtlessness, relieved from work, and my mind not burdened with a care. The campaign was over and its objects accomplished. What now remained to be done was merely the giving a definite shape to its results, so interesting that it could not be called labor, but pleasure only. And so I was already enjoying the fruitful repose, in expectation.

But now there came to me the news that our little circle had been broken by the loss of my only brother, who had returned to die at home. So soon as the requirement of immediate duty permitted I obtained leave. The short time which had been given me I spent with my mother. The years had been made lonely by the absence of both, and now still more by the loss of one of us, and I was happy for her sake in the unusual brightness my presence brought with it; and for a while it was almost the old time again.

But the brief leave was soon over, and I returned to Washington. Among Mr. Nicollet's scientific affiliations, one of the most intimate and the most interesting, because of the opposite characters of the two men, was that with Mr. Hassler, the chief of the United States Coast Survey. Both were indurated in science, and so far congenial, but both entirely opposite in complexion of mind and in manner; the one flint, and the other steel, fire flashing out in every argument. Mr. Nicollet was urbane, forbearing, rounding off obstructions in intercourse; polished and persuasive, and careful of the feelings of others. Mr. Hassler was abrupt, full of sharp edges and intolerant of pretentious mediocrity. Going directly to the heart of his subject and in language the most direct, he was almost a distinct species, where the exterior photographed the inner man. What he did, or the manner in which he did it, was absolutely without reference to outside opinion or outside effect. What he intended to do he did in what seemed to him the best way, and that was all. His life had been the pursuit of science, and his occupation now was its application; and for this he was exceptionally qualified, and any interference with his work he resented with indignant promptitude.

To a member of a committee who complained to him of a delay in his report to Congress, with the remark that when he had a report to write he

COLORADO VALLEY.

did it in a day, Mr. Hassler replied: "That is time enough for such reports, but before you could write one of mine, your days would be numbered." He would not allow the prefix of " Honorable," merely because of usage. A cabinet officer who had offended him he addressed: " Mr.,——, the Honorable Secretary, etc." The place was honorable, he conceded—not the man.

All Washington of that date remembers the figure dressed in white flannel, which habitually was driven through the streets in a large foreign-built carriage, commonly called " the ark." In this he was used to go to the field of his operations along the coast, where his surveying parties were occupied. The ark was so arranged that in it on these occasions were always packed some of the essentials for clean and comfortable sleeping and toilet needs ; together with red and white German wines, and some such provision as was good for the health of a man who knew that good food was essential to good brain-work. He was both abstemious and fastidious. When he accepted an invitation to dinner, which was seldom, his habit was to carry with him some bottles of these German wines, as he would drink of no other kind, and only of his own. But his abruptness never degenerated into common rudeness. The thin, intellectual face, and tall, slight figure contradicted any idea of that kind. It was always intellect speaking, not passion ; and withal there was a kindly disposition.

Mr. Nicollet's work was to be done in Washington, which was also Mr. Hassler's headquarters. These two men were naturally happy of the occasion that enabled them to come together, and it was decided that we three should make our bachelor quarters at Mr. Hassler's own house on Capitol Hill. In this arrangement there was some disparity of purse as well as of age. It was interesting to see the manner in which these two proceeded to organize the establishment. Of one thing they were aware, as many otherwise good housekeepers in our country are not, that the essential element in a household for economy and health is the cook. In this, accident favored us. A *chef* recently arrived from France had just been rejected by President Van Buren, on account of the high salary which he considered proportioned to his skill. Somehow he found his way to us. An examination, non-competitive, resulted in showing him regularly trained to his occupation. He was a man of middle age, of imposing presence, and opened the interview by the production of a long sheet of paper with this heading: " *Pour un cuisinier Français il faut une batterie de cuisine,*" and, following this, an enumeration incomprehensible even to Mr. Nicollet. This was the beginning and end of his examination, and made him master of the situation. A man who knew so much about his tools was likely to know how to use them, and he did. For Mr. Nicollet delicate food had become a necessity. His health had been impaired by the discomforts and exposures in his expeditions, seriously so in that to the sources of the Mississippi.   During this he had been long and dangerously ill when off alone with only his guide, and now it pleased him to have this opportunity to nurse his injured health.   The first dinner was a fête to me, to whom for two years the batterie de cuisine had been a chaudière, the camp-kettle of the Canadian voyageur.

It was a summer evening, and, going to the front of the house, we found our new *chef*, in white cap and apron, quietly installed on the porch enjoying the evening air.   Mr. Nicollet was taken aback by the unexpected vision, and in his quiet way suggested to him, " *Mon garçon, c'est pas comme il faut, ceçi.*"   The man on his part was equally surprised, for he said that he had understood that in this country all were on terms of equality.   But he was sensible, and took it, as it was meant, in good part, and our *menage* worked on smoothly, to Mr. Nicollet's great benefit.

Our work was to be done in the Coast Survey building on the hill. Here Mr. Hassler had appropriated to us several rooms; some of which were for the work, and others for our more private use.   I had here with me a congenial companion of my own age, and of the same corps, Lieutenant Scammon, who had been assigned to duty with Mr. Nicollet in working up astronomical observations and the construction of the map.   Both of us had unusual facility in figures.   Like myself, he was a lover of chess, and this engrossed much of our leisure time.   In fact, the time was divided between work and chess.   He was also a man of varied and large reading for one so young, and had the gift of a pleasant and companionable temper; this rounded the circle of my daily associates.

The house on the hill overlooked the Potomac, and the breeze from the valley swept away the summer heat.   Mr. Nicollet profited by the situation and the command of fine instruments to put up an observatory here, where he and I spent many interesting nights in observations.   The night-watches were sometimes long, after the day spent among figures which required care, but there is something in the tranquil movements of the great bodies, endless through space, which impresses patience on those watching.   Mr. Nicollet's mind was fruitful of interesting things, so that the hours never dulled into sleep.   I remember, one night, lying by my lantern when we were engaged in some outside work, a beetle lit on the open book in which I was recording observations made by him from time to time.   I was glad to have something to do, and before the insect flew off I made a sketch of him which happened to be life-like.   Coming to the lantern to read off his instrument, Mr. Nicollet struck at the drawing to brush away the beetle.   He was vexed by the hearty laugh which expressed my pleasure at his testimony to the accuracy of my drawing, and reproached me for the frivolity, which was really light-heartedness that goes soon enough.

To him an astronomical observation was a solemnity, and required such decorous preparation as an Indian makes when he goes where he thinks there are supernatural beings. "*C'est toujours comme ça chez vous,*" he said. "Instead of occupying your mind with these grand objects, you give your attention to insect things." "But," I reply, "that is because my mind is not large enough to get those enormous bodies into it. I try, but I get lost in the size of them ; my mind has not yet got to comprehend them. I can reach a certain distance or a certain size, and then my mind stops and falls back upon itself. I get baffled in the mental effort to imagine a hugeness which the sight is always contradicting. With you it is very different. You have been studying these things so long and so deeply that your mind has become broadened and takes them in comfortably. You have gotten to comprehend this infinity—I not yet. Perhaps if I remain long enough with you I shall." And with the implied compliment his irritation was soothed, and our talk turned into strange and kindred, and always interesting, speculations on discoveries yet to come.

And in this way, or something like it, our nights were often passed.

Mr. Benton was a disciple of Jefferson. He was familiar with all that had been said and done by him concerning the region on the North Pacific, and the subject had been dwelt upon, made personal to him by the explorer, General Clarke. With a mind full of the subject, he wished to confer with Mr. Jefferson, and made a visit to him at his home in the winter of 1825. The ideas in reference to overland communication which had grown up in the mind of Mr. Jefferson were based upon the acquisition of the Louisiana territory. He talked these over with Mr. Benton, and they became his in the way that he assimilated information which he recognized to be good. To such a mind, of which the chief bias was to utilize material, this vast unused region had already presented itself as an object of immediate and accumulating interest. In area it was an empire ; shut off from the new, it opened to the ancient east by one great harbor, at which all the avenues to interior communication concentrated. And this empire, ours of right, was in the hands of an old enemy whose firm grasp was unrelenting.

From the moment he realized the situation, he had resolved to wrest back this region and hold it where it belonged, in the American empire.

In his position of Senator he had now a standpoint from which to work, and thenceforward he devoted his energies to carrying through the plans which these two statesmen had the forecast to initiate. Taking part as he did in all the great questions that came before Congress, the rigorous maintenance of our title to the Columbia was with him continuously the greater question, because the interests of his State demanded it; in this as in all the important passages of his life he certainly earned recognition as exceptionally the man "tenacious of purpose."

The occupation of the Lower Columbia by an American emigration, and the enforcing of our title to its whole valley and the Pacific coast north to the 49th parallel, had already become the aim of his persistent effort before he entered political life.

In 1820, the first proposition made in Congress for the occupation of the Columbia was introduced through Mr. Floyd, who was a member of the House, from Virginia. Mr. Floyd was a near relation of Mrs. Benton. The old "Indian Queen," on what was called by way of distinction "the Avenue," was a headquarters for western and southwestern men. Mr. Floyd and Mr. Benton were staying there ; and with them were Mr. Ramsay Crooks and Mr. Russell Farnham, both concerned in the American Fur Company, and at that time representing its interests at Washington.

Mr. Farnham had recently returned from a visit to the Lower Columbia. Mr. Benton the year before had written and published, in St. Louis, a series of essays in relation to the treaty of 1818, directed to show that the joint occupation must result in possession by England if our own occupation of the river-valley were longer delayed. These essays had been read by Mr. Floyd, and were fully agreed in by him. Mr. Benton had not yet been admitted to his seat in the Senate because of the long debate on the Missouri Compromise, which virtually settled the question of slavery extension.

After reviewing and consulting together over the Oregon situation, Mr. Floyd took up the subject and moved for a committee to consider and report upon it. A select committee of three was granted by the House, which within six days reported a bill "to authorize the occupation of the Columbia River, and to regulate trade and intercourse with the Indian tribes thereon."

"The bill was treated with parliamentary courtesy, which respect for the committee required; it was read twice and committed to a Committee of the Whole House for the next day—most of the members not considering it a serious proceeding."

This act required courage, for at that time the measure met only ridicule or indifference.

"In 1821, when the occupation of the Columbia was first presented to the consideration of Congress, the British minister at Washington, Mr. Canning, *twice* called upon the Secretary of State, Mr. Adams, with a view to arrest the progress of that measure. He went so far as to say that such occupation would *conflict* with his majesty's claims in that quarter."

"Contemporaneously with this interference and threat was the appearance of numerous essays in the *National Intelligencer*, evidently from the pens of persons in the employment of England and Russia, attacking and ridiculing all the claims of the United States to the northwest coast of America. These derive importance from the fact of the repetition of their contents in the halls of Congress. These essays have become a magazine from which gentlemen borrow arms for attacking the interests of their own country."

Nothing further was done in the House that session. But Mr. Benton was admitted to his seat soon afterward, and gave to the measure immediate attention and advocacy. In 1825, shortly after a visit to Mr. Jefferson, Mr. Benton brought into the Senate a bill to authorize the President, Mr. Monroe, to use a detachment of the army and navy to act efficiently in protecting American interests in Oregon.

"Besides the preservation of our own territory on the Pacific, the establishment of a port there for the shelter of our commercial and military marine, the protection of the fur trade, and aid to the whaling-vessels, and the accomplishment of Mr. Jefferson's idea of a commercial communication with Asia through the heart of our own continent" were constantly insisted upon by him as a consequence of planting an American colony at the mouth of the Columbia.

Mr. Dickerson, Senator from New Jersey, was among the strongest opponents of this measure—using the arguments that it would be "highly improper" to "exercise any act of possession or occupation" until 1828, to which time the treaty of 1818 for joint occupation had been prolonged; that the distance was against it, the generally forbidding and undesirable nature of the whole country which, "from the meridian of Council Bluffs extending to the Rocky Mountains, can never be cultivated, and of course never admit of a civilized population."

"The Rocky Mountains and inhospitable regions adjoining them will never admit of a white population." . . . The territory lying between the Rocky Mountains and the western ocean he admits "may be susceptible of a white population," "but its best destiny is to make of it our Indian territory." "As to the Oregon territory, it can never be of any pecuniary advantage to the United States, but it may be the means of promoting the cause of humanity; and this is the best possible disposition, while the worst would be the adoption of the provisions of the present bill. . . . But is this territory of Oregon ever to become a State, a member of this Union? Never. . . . Oregon can never be one of the United States. If we extend our laws to it we must consider it a colony."

"The period never will arrive when it will be proper to adopt the measures proposed by the friends of the present bill; but if ever, this is not the time, because their adoption now would interfere with existing relations between the British Government and ours." "What is the immediate pressure for such a force (a detachment of army and navy) at this time? To protect our ships engaged in the whaling and fishing and in the fur trade, and taking of sea-otters. . . . All the sea-otters we shall ever take upon the coast of the Oregon territory would not pay the expense of marching a single company across the Rocky Mountains."

Mr. Benton, who spoke from knowledge of the subject, maintained his position by facts; but the feeling was against disturbing England, and against protecting our settlers and emigrants. Out of 42 Senators voting, 13 voted with Mr. Benton and 28 against. The friends of Oregon were: Messrs. Barbour, of Virginia; Benton, of Missouri; Bouligny, of Louisiana; Cobb, of Georgia; Hayne, of South Carolina; General Jackson, of Tennessee; Richard Johnson, of Kentucky; Johnston, of Louisiana (brother of Albert Sidney Johnston); Lloyd, of Massachusetts; Mills, of Massachusetts; Noble, of Indiana; Ruggles, of Ohio; Talbot, of Kentucky. Among those voting against was Mr. Van Buren.

In 1828, when the convention for renewal of the Oregon joint occupation was sent in to the Senate, Mr. Benton again made determined opposition to prolonging the English occupation, but he was only one of seven Senators who opposed its ratification.

"Eighteen years afterward, and when we had got to the cry of 'inevitable war,' I had the gratification to see the whole Senate, all Congress, and all the United States, occupy the same ground in relation to this joint occupation on which only seven Senators stood at the time the convention for it was ratified."

Of such kind had been the objections, but such the power of the opposition, in the face of which the friends of Oregon maintained and carried their measures for its rescue.

It will be observed through the progress of the Senate debates that Mr. Benton steadily maintained the 49th parallel as our northern boundary to the Pacific, neither receding from it nor going beyond it; that his aim was to assert our title by American occupation, in order to counteract the English occupation which was in daily progress; that in this he was opposed by the feeble interest of its friends and by the weight of administrations which yielded the delay that England wanted, and which refused to aid or encourage an American emigration; that Senator Benton pursued this course before he entered the Senate, and after, until the treaty of 1846, which placed our boundary on that 49th degree, and established the fact that England had no title to the Columbia Valley south of that line.

I was with Mr. Nicollet in his official visit of duty to the Missouri Senators, Mr. Benton and Mr. Linn. He knew of the comprehending interest which both, especially Mr. Benton, had in the results of the expedition as being directly in the line of western progress. Through the Chouteaus and other leading men in St. Louis, with whom he was on intimate terms, Mr. Nicollet knew of Mr. Benton's unwearied interest in furthering knowledge of our western possessions and bringing them into occupation.

The essential importance to the country of the great band of unoccupied territory which lay between the Mississippi and the Pacific coast had been one of the chief subjects which western members were endeavoring to force upon the early action of Congress. The farming value of the country over which the surveys of Mr. Nicollet extended impressed them still more strongly with the importance of the trans-Missouri region, and gave fresh impulse to their efforts. Oregon was now coming to the forefront among political questions which were tending to embitter party politics. But the presidential elections were absorbing attention, and for a period suspended effort on other questions.

The Democratic party, which had been so strong and masterful under Jackson, was nearing the end of its powerful reign. As foreigners and men of science, Mr. Hassler and Mr. Nicollet had but little interest in passing political affairs. To them the recurring party struggles were in the established order of things. They looked upon their own work as belonging with the material development of the country, disconnected from the political changes which to them meant only a change in the personnel of the Government. National questions which affected the whole country they looked at in their large aspect, and followed with the close attention of thinking and far-sighted men. As for myself, neither then nor afterward had I any interest in merely party contests, but naturally I was deeply interested in their frequent discussion of questions which grew out of the progress of the country. These gave shape and solidity to my own crude ideas. The one question to which I had given any serious thought was outside of politics and above party.

Mr. Poinsett had lived much abroad. His education had been finished in England, and he had travelled in Asia as well as in Europe. He had been our minister to revolutionary Mexico, and to the new South American republics.

In the midst of these surroundings he was able to compare their political elements with the new growth of government which promised a grand future to his own country ; but, looking at it from a distance so great that only the salient points were visible, he saw the dark spot on the sun which was ominous of evil, and under the impressions then made he formed the opinions which determined and guided his political course.

I was one of his devoted adherents. My education and condition of life had left me disinterested and unprejudiced as to the question which was the root of discord, and I had never given thought to its material side. My opinions on this subject grew out of my education, which had inculcated intolerance of oppression in every form and that love of the common country which in America was part of a boy's growth. In this condition of mind when General Jackson's course drew the line in South Carolina, I had joined the party of Mr. Poinsett and gave unwavering allegiance to the Union.

I was now settled down to regular work. There was always in this the interest of a problem to be worked out. There is pleasure in labor which is sure of a result, and this was as sure as the stars which had their part in it.

I have said that our settlement was near the Capitol, and some of the leading subjects of discussion there had special interest for us as being kindred to our own occupation and looking to its continuation.

Members of both Houses occasionally came to see the progress of Mr. Hassler's coast surveys, and usually extended their visit to our rooms. We were not yet at work on the map. There was a mass of astronomical and other observations to be calculated and discussed before a beginning on this could be made. Indeed, the making of such a map is an interesting process. It must be exact. First, the foundations must be laid in observations made in the field ; then the reduction of these observations to latitude and longitude ; afterward the projection of the map, and the laying down upon it of positions fixed by the observations ; then the tracing from the sketch-books of the lines of the rivers, the forms of the lakes, the contours of the hills. Specially is it interesting to those who have laid in the field these various foundations, to see them all brought into final shape— fixing on a small sheet the results of laborious travel over waste regions, and giving to them an enduring place on the world's surface.

Mr. Benton had expected to find the map in progress, and was disappointed to see only the blank projection. But his disappointment gave way to interest of another kind when he saw spread out on the tables the evidences of the material first to be digested. His visit was not simply one of intelligent curiosity, but there was purpose in it, as indeed, I found when afterward I came to know him, there was in all that he did. The character of his mind was to utilize, and what he could not assimilate he did not touch. He knew well to use information and give it point. The results of our journeys between the two great rivers had suggested to him the same work for the broader field beyond the Missouri. His inquiries on this occasion were all of distinct pertinency. They were directed to know about our means and manner of travelling, the nature of the work required to be done, and the instruments employed. In the course of his inquiries he dwelt on the unoccupied country beyond the Missouri and the existing uncertain and incomplete knowledge concerning it. The interview left on me a profound impression and raised excited interest. The ideas suggested remained fixtures in my mind. The thought of penetrating into the recesses of that wilderness region filled me with enthusiasm—I saw visions. Formerly I had been entirely devoted to my intended profession of engineering. The lives of great engineers had been my treasured exemplars. But strict engineering had lost its inspiration in the charm of the new field into which I had entered during the last few years.

In this interview with Mr. Benton my mind had been quick to see a larger field and differing and greater results. It would be travel over a part of the world which still remained the New—the opening up of unknown lands; the making unknown countries known; and the study without books—the learning at first hand from nature herself; the drinking first at her unknown springs—became a source of never-ending delight to me. I felt that it was an unreasonable pleasure to expect that it might happen to me to be among the very few to whom the chance had fallen to work with nature where in all her features there was still aboriginal freshness.

This interview with Mr. Benton was pregnant of results and decisive of my life. In what way it brought these results about, and how important they were, will be seen as we go on.

His visit, returned by Mr. Nicollet and myself, led into others and grew into intimacy. Congress was in session, and at his house I often met western members; all, at that time, being "west" which lay beyond Pennsylvania. Often, on such evenings, we being present, the conversation turned upon our surveys and naturally led to the subjects which so much interested Mr. Benton and his western colleagues. Among those who were more especially his personal and political friends were his fellow-Senator from Missouri, Lewis F. Linn, and Senator Dodge, the elder half-brother of Mr. Linn—a man with such composure of natural dignity, in aspect and manner, that he was known among his friends as "the Sachem." There was great love and unity between the brothers, who were in appearance very different: Senator Dodge, of powerful build and unusual height, his quiet strength of manner indicating the thoughtful, commanding habit of his mind; Senator Linn, of moderate size, but with a beauty as complete as it was remarkable—a head and features resembling the young head of Byron, but made winning by the expression of kind feelings and the play of a quick mind.

In these unpremeditated talks, where unstudied expression gave the color of every man's mind and bits of information found receptive place, plans were of easy digestion. And in this way measures were conceived

and perfected which, by the strength behind them, carried their own fulfilment.   And gradually, as being kindred with our thoughts and present
occupations, they engrossed our minds and settled into practical shape.

The months passed, and carried with them labor done.   Our prelimi-
nary work had been in greater part completed, and we had begun on the
map, Mr. Scammon and I.   Meantime, Mr. Nicollet's health was being
steadily undermined.   He had grown restless, and made frequent visits
away from Washington; I think usually to some quiet retreat among his
friends in Baltimore, where, too, was a physician who had his confidence.
He was not in condition to reduce into shape the materials for his report,
which were varied and interesting and embraced the labor of years of
thought and study following upon most interesting travel.   And, waiting
for the return of nerve and strength which were slow in coming, his writing was delayed.   No second hand can do this like the first.   The impressions made by the visible objects, the pleasure of the first experience and
the anticipations of roused curiosity, the sense of danger threatened and
met, the relief from obstacles overcome, cannot be transfused into a mind
that is cold and unexcited.   The lights and shadows are all lost on the
level plane; and to such physical description, the eye that has not seen cannot bring a mind to feel and comprehend.   And so Mr. Nicollet waited,
hoping for the health that did not return.

In the family of Mr. Benton were four sisters and but one son, Randolph, then twelve years old.   It fell to each of the sisters to have a
marked life; and, as they grew into womanhood, they were separated far
apart, as often happens in this large country of ours.   All of them had
strong, high character, and capacities carefully cultivated; and among them
rare musical talent.   Randolph died when just entering into what promised to be a distinguished life.

Jessie was the second daughter.

I went with the eldest of the sisters to a school concert in Georgetown,
where I saw her.   She was then just in the bloom of her girlish beauty,
and perfect health effervesced in bright talk which the pleasure of seeing
her sister drew out.

Naturally I was attracted.   She made the effect that a rose of rare color
or beautiful picture would have done.   Months passed before, in the vaca-
tion time, I saw her again, at her father's house which already I had come
to frequent.   She was happy in the return to her home, and my first impressions of her were made in the unreserve of family life, where the real
nature most readily expresses itself.   Her beauty had come far enough
down from English ancestry to be now in her that American kind which
is made up largely of mind expressed in the face; but it still showed its
Saxon descent.   At that time of awakening mind the qualities that made

hers could only be seen in flitting shadows across the face, or in the expressions of incipient thought and unused and untried feeling. So in writing here I give what after-knowledge made known to me. Nor would it be possible to disentangle the interwoven threads of memory and confine impressions to the time when they were made. There are features which convey to us a soul so white that they impress with instant pleasure, and of this kind were hers. As, too, in the daily contact there are others from which to receive pleasant words or kindly acts gives the sort of agreeable surprise we feel when suddenly we come upon patches of bright, parti-colored phlox growing on naked rocks. The phlox loves the naked sand or rock, but the difference is in the warmth it finds there. In the human rock there is no heart to replace the sun.

Her qualities were all womanly, and education had curiously preserved the down of a modesty which was innate. There had been no experience of life to brush away the bloom. She had inherited from her father his grasp of mind, comprehending with a tenacious memory; but with it a quickness of perception and instant realization of subjects and scenes in their completed extent which did not belong to his; and with these, warm sympathies—a generous pity for human suffering, and a tenderness and sensibility that made feeling take the place of mind; so compelled was every impulse to pass through these before it could reach the surface to find expression. There was a rare union of intelligence to feel the injury of events, and submission to them with silence and discretion; and withal a sweet, and happy, and forbearing temper which has remained proof against the wearing of time.

Insensibly and imperceptibly, in these frequent meetings, there came a glow into my heart which changed the current and color of daily life and gave beauty to common things. And so it came that there was no room for reason, which found a cold and dull ear that heard, but did not listen.

For the rest, I think I may leave what more I might say to the record as it goes along. I find that, in undertaking to write a life-history which shall truly give the complexion of the minds and events of which I know, I have set for myself a difficult task. To speak of friends who have been dear to me in the intimate relations of life; of events in which I had part, and of the persons concerned in them with me—and it is precisely of these that I have undertaken to write—is hedged with obstacles which oppose my pen at every line. And the occurrences in even a few lives through fifty years are long to give, though the very details, which for various reasons are forced from the page, are just what might prove interesting as making up our human life. Still, I console myself with thinking that this perhaps would be a life-picture that no living man might draw.

And yet I thought to do it.

The winter work of making up charts required the rooms we had been using at the Coast Survey building. This, with the frequent and prolonged absences of Mr. Nicollet, brought about a change in our establishment to smaller but comfortable quarters at the foot of the Capitol. And so there the work was continued through the winter, without event, until the death of President Harrison. For the day of the funeral ceremonies, I cleared our work-room and made it gay with plants and flowers; for from its windows the family of Mr. Benton had consented to view the procession. The death of a President so suddenly following his accession to power was a shock to the community. As yet no President had died in office; and there was sincere personal feeling for General Harrison, who was a brave and amiable man. The funeral pageant was something to see and remember, as an event of the time. I was to take part with my corps in the ceremonies, but I procured leave and went back to be with my friends; for to me the funeral occasion proved, as I had hoped, to be my red-letter day.

All this time Mr. Nicollet's health was not mending. The writing of his report was still delayed.

In the surveys that had been made during his last expedition, the upper part only of some of the larger rivers had been embraced. The Des Moines was one of these; and at his request I was sent, in July, to make such a reconnoissance of its lower course as would nearly complete it. Whether or not this detachment of myself from Washington originated with Mr. Nicollet I do not know, but I was loath to go.

I had again with me on this survey one of my companions of the former expedition in Mr. Charles Geyer, who accompanied me as botanist. I established the course of the river upward from its mouth about two hundred miles, which brought the survey to the Racoon Forks; and Mr. Geyer did all that the season and time allowed for botany. It was here that Geyer found the snake under his flowers. There were many snakes along the river, and botany became a hazardous pursuit. As had been proposed, our examination was confined to the immediate valley of the river, but we frequently ranged into the woods, where deer and wild turkey were abundant; and the survey was a health-giving excursion, but it did not cure the special complaint for which I had been sent there.

The influence of women is a force sometimes dangerous. Mrs. Benton was not friendly to my suit, though to me she always was. She thought her daughter much too young—she was but sixteen—and, beyond this, that the unsettled life of an army officer was unfavorable to making such a home as she wished for her. She had herself, for seven years, delayed to marry Colonel Benton until he resigned from the army.

Mrs. Poinsett and Mrs. Benton were on friendly terms, and Mr. Poinsett was Secretary of War and my friend. The charge of this reconnoissance, in connection with Mr. Nicollet's important work, was an advance for me, and accordingly I was sent. But it did not take long to get through with it. I returned to Washington and set about reducing to shape the new material just collected, in order to add the results to Mr. Nicollet's map.

I was leading a busy, working life; what was immediately at hand and what projected should have been enough to occupy my thoughts and time. A probation of a year had been agreed upon, but, as sometimes happens, the most important events of our individual life come upon us suddenly and unpremeditatedly; and so it was with our marriage, which was on October 19, 1841.

Mr. Nicollet was ill in Baltimore, and we went there to see him at the house of his friend Professor Ducatel. Our visit pleased and roused him. The nervous exhaustion which was a feature of his illness made everything seem a task. He had come to remain late in bed, sometimes doing his writing there and not rising at all during the day. He had formed an ideal to himself for his work, which he was never satisfied to have reached when he got his thoughts on paper.

In reality, the material which his science had enabled him to gather was so interesting that to barely set down the facts in the light of his own knowledge would have made a great work.

In intervals of revived health he came to Washington, coming always to us—to him we were "*mes enfants.*" But he was fixedly morbid about the impediments and discouragements which he fancied in the way of getting out his work.

I was now busily occupied in office-work every day while the light lasted, hurrying to put in good order what remained for me to do in connection with Mr. Nicollet's surveys. As I have said, the discussions among the western members had taken shape; they were agreed that the time had come to put into action their views concerning Oregon.

I knew that Mr. Benton was decided that an expedition ought to be sent to open the way for the emigration through the mountains; and I knew, also, he intended Mr. Nicollett should be at its head, and that I should be his assistant.

This expedition was intended to be "auxiliary and in aid to the emigration to the Lower Columbia;" it was to indicate and describe the line of travel, and the best positions for military posts; and to describe, and fix in position, the South Pass in the Rocky Mountains, at which this initial expedition was to terminate. At this time the South Pass, at the head of the Platte River, was the one most available for our emigration and already used.

With this knowledge, and the hope of having part in such an expedition, I worked unremittingly to have the way cleared of previous work; leaving only the brief evening hours for the new home just begun for me.

I felt I was being drawn into the current of important political events : the object of this expedition was not merely a survey ; beyond that was its bearing on the holding of our territory on the Pacific ; and the contingencies it involved were large.

One stormy evening near Christmas, when we were quietly enjoying the warm glow of firelight, a note was brought in to me from Mr. Hassler. The bearer was a strange figure—a shock of light curly hair standing up thick about his head, and a face so red that we attributed it to a wrong cause instead of to the cold and the nervousness and anxiety which turned his speech into stammering. Under the first impression I went outside with him. I found that he was a German, a skilled topographer, who came to me with this letter from Mr. Hassler requesting employment for him if we had any to give. I brought him in again, and sat him down by the fire while I thought over what might be done to have the pleasure of meeting Mr. Hassler's wish. I found that he was actually without means of support. The failure of an appropriation had thrown him out of his regular work, and the needs of his little family were immediate. He was divided between their want and his own natural pride, and asked of me to go with him to verify their condition, which I did ; and their Christmas was made comfortable.

There were astronomical observations remaining unreduced. That work, I told him, I could get for him. This he said he was not able to do. His profession was topography—in this he excelled, but that was all. The only thing I could devise was to get for him this astronomical work and do it myself, which I could by working in the evenings. It troubled him greatly that I should have to do this for him, but it was the only way I could come in aid ; and so it was done. This was Preuss ; and this was the beginning of our long friendly comradeship. The little service which I was able to render him he amply repaid by years of faithful and valuable service as topographer on my journeys, during which his even temper and patient endurance of hardship earned my warm regard. Preuss had the endurance in working with an aim that so characterizes his nation, and with it a cheerful philosophy of his own which often brightened dark situations. He was of those who were comrades, and part with me, in the life of which I am writing.

Therefore I give them their place, not content to leave them on the page merely as a bodiless name which awakens no interest. I wish to give enough of their personality to individualize them, and make them known as I came to know them, so that hereafter when from time to time they reappear in the narrative, it will be as familiar figures in whom something of the interest of old acquaintance may be felt.

The year which had been so eventful to me was drawing to its close, and the Christmas time which smooths its end was at hand. Mr. Hassler offered us his carriage to make the New Year's visit of ceremony to the President, and to please him we accepted it. But it took some nerve to drive up in the ark among the holiday crowd, who were familiar enough with its Noah, but looked and smiled on the young lady in full dress and officer in uniform. Mrs. Frémont disembarked at her father's to assist in the reception there, and that evening in the intimacy of after-dinner talk there came to me the probability of my being the head of the proposed expedition.

Mr. Nicollet's health did not improve; but was steadily failing. My mind was unwilling to see this. But the larger experience of Mr. Benton made him sure Mr. Nicollet could not again take charge of an expedition.

The evening was passed in considering this contingency, and with the New Year began my joint work with Mr. Benton in behalf of our western territories.

The months immediately following were occupied in preparation. The object of the expedition, as "ordered by the Topographical Bureau with the sanction of the Secretary of War," was simply to explore the country between the Missouri River and the Rocky Mountains; but its real purpose, the objects which were had in view in designing it, were known only to the circle of its friends. It was not until long after that it was avowed to be " in aid of and auxiliary to the Oregon emigration."

General Harrison, as a western and military man, would most probably have entered heartily into the ultimate motive of the expedition. With him Mr. Benton was on friendly terms. President Harrison's Secretary of War, John Bell, of Tennessee, was also a western man. But the death of the President made different conditions. Mr. Tyler threw the weight of his administration against any measure to encourage and aid the emigration to Oregon. His Secretary of War, Mr. Spencer, was from the east, and a lawyer. These were the altered circumstances which required prudence and reserve in avoiding any check to the projected movement to settle the Oregon question by emigration. The amount appropriated was small. In obtaining this it was necessary to use caution, in order to avoid the opposition which for various reasons might be expected. This Mr. Benton's parliamentary experience enabled him to do successfully. But the limited means exacted a close economy in the outfit. With the plan fully settled I went in March to New York to obtain necessary instruments and other essentials. Among these I had made an india-rubber boat, with air-tight compartments, to be used in crossing or examining water-courses. So far as I know, this was the first boat of the kind made or used in such work. When finished it was brought to Washington by Mr. Horace Day, who took much pride in it. It was the early day of india-rubber, when its preparations were not "odorless." Mr. Day himself un-packed it at the house, on a broad gallery opening from the dining-room, saying that there "might be some odor from the chemicals." There was; to such a degree that it was promptly transferred to the stable, but not in time to avoid a long-contested battle between his "chemicals" and the obligatory disinfectants. Notwithstanding, it proved of valuable service, until finally it came to a violent end in the line of its duty.

The unreserve of daily intercourse under his own roof had given me a familiar knowledge of Mr. Benton's plans. Recognizing fully his forceful energy, and the certainty of success this carried with it, I gave henceforward to him and the work confided to me unstinted devotion.

KIT CARSON.

CHAPTER IV.

My first Expedition—Personnel of Party—Meet Kit Carson—Enormous Herds of Buffalo—Incidents of Journey—Meet Bridger—His late Fight with Sioux—Fort Laramie—South Pass Reached—Ascent of the loftiest Peak of Wind River Chain—American Flag Planted—The Pioneer Bee—Object of Expedition so far Successful—Homeward Journey—Running the Cañons, etc., etc.

ALL was now ready. I left Washington for the West on May 2d, Mrs. Frémont remaining at home with her family during my absence.

Arriving at St. Louis, I was received at her home with cordial hospitality by Mrs. Sarah Benton Brant, the favorite niece of Mr. Benton and wife of an old friend and army officer. In all my journeys from St. Louis, and in my visits to it in later years, I have been always welcomed by her with an affectionate regard which I have reciprocated and cherished to the present hour as among the most satisfactory of my recollections.

This expedition, directed as it was toward the opening of the western territory, was pleasing to the people of St. Louis, who furthered my preparations with prompt and willing aid.

For this journey, which would be exposed to serious contingencies, good men and fitting animals were a first necessity. The getting these together —the necessary equipment which it needs experienced foresight to provide —required time; but at the end of several weeks this had been done, and a party of valuable and experienced men selected. Among these I had engaged as hunter Lucien Maxwell, a son-in-law of one of the principal merchants in New Mexico, Mr. Beaubien, and brother-in-law of Christopher Carson, better known as "Kit Carson," who also had his home in Taos. Maxwell was about twenty-eight years of age, about five feet ten inches in height, and strongly built. He was personally known, by trading among them, to the tribes who ranged the country toward New Mexico, accustomed to the life of the prairies, and a resolute man and good hunter. Carson and he were close friends.

My journey from St. Louis was by steamboat up the Missouri to a point near the mouth of the Kansas River, where a few houses were the nucleus of a future town, but then called "Chouteau's" or Kansas Landing.

On the boat I met Kit Carson. He was returning from putting his little daughter in a convent-school at St. Louis. I was pleased with him and his manner of address at this first meeting. He was a man of medium height, broad-shouldered and deep-chested, with a clear steady blue eye and frank speech and address ; quiet and unassuming.

It will be anticipating to speak here of Carson in connection with after-events, but I give one incident to illustrate the simple honesty of his character.

He had gone to Washington with despatches from me in 1847, and was staying at the house of Senator Benton, welcomed there as my friend. Mr. Benton was in the West, but Carson's modesty and gentleness quickly made him a place in the regard of the family, to whom he gave back a lasting attachment. At one time during his stay he was seen to be troubled in mind, and our young friend, Midshipman Beale, being asked to find what had quenched Carson's good spirits, ascertained that he felt it was wrong to be among such ladies when they might not like to associate with him if they knew he had had an Indian wife. " She was a good wife to me. I never came in from hunting that she did not have the warm water ready for my feet." She had died long since, and he was now married to a daughter of Beaubien. But his straightforward nature would not let him rest while there was anything concealed which he thought ought to be known to the family who were receiving him as a friend. It was the child of his Indian wife that he had just placed in the shelter of the St. Louis convent-school when we first met.

I had expected to engage as guide an old mountaineer, Captain Drips, but I was so much pleased with Carson that when he asked to go with me I was glad to take him.

Now, he has become so familiarly known that I will let the narrative tell of the life we had together, out of which grew our enduring friendship.

From the Landing I went ten miles up the Kansas River to the trading-post of Mr. Cyprian Chouteau, where we were already on Indian ground. This was one of the friendly contributions by the St. Louis Chouteaus, which were to come in aid on this and future journeys. We were delayed here some twenty days in fitting men and animals, arms and equipment, into place and good order ; but the time used in this was regained in the strength of the animals, as the spring grass was improving with every day.

This was now to be their only food ; and in a measure regulated the travel, which depended on their condition.

At length we set out. It was like a ship leaving the shore for a long voyage, and carrying with her provision against all needs in her isolation on the ocean.

Bad weather, which interfered with astronomical observations, delayed us several days in the early part of June at this post, which is on the right bank of the Kansas River, about ten miles above the mouth, and six beyond the western boundary of Missouri. The sky cleared off at length, and we were enabled to determine our position—in longitude 94° 25' 46", and latitude 39° 5' 57". The elevation above the sea is about seven hundred feet. Our camp, in the meantime, presented an animated and bustling scene. All were busily occupied in completing the necessary arrangements for our campaign in the wilderness, and profiting by this short delay on the verge of civilization to provide ourselves with all the little essentials to comfort in the nomadic life we were to lead for the ensuing summer months. Gradually, however, everything—the *matériel* of the camp, men, horses, and even mules—settled into its place, and by the 10th we were ready to depart; but, before we mount our horses, I will give a short description of the party with which I performed this service.

I had collected in the neighborhood of St. Louis twenty-one men, principally Creole and Canadian voyageurs, who had become familiar with prairie life in the service of the fur companies in the Indian country. Mr. Charles Preuss, a native of Germany, was my assistant in the topographical part of the survey. Maxwell, as has already been said, had been engaged as hunter; Carson was our guide. The persons engaged in St. Louis were:

Clément Lambert, J. B. L'Esperance, J. B. Lefèvre, Benjamin Potra, Louis Gouin, J. B. Dumés, Basil Lajeunesse, François Tessier, Benjamin Cadotte, Joseph Clément, Daniel Simonds, Leonard Benoit, Michel Morly, Baptiste Bernier, Honoré Ayot, François Latulippe, François Badeau, Louis Ménard, Joseph Ruelle, Moïse Chardonnais, Auguste Janisse, Raphael Proue.

In addition to these, Henry Brant, son of Colonel J. B. Brant, of St Louis, a young man nineteen years of age, and Randolph, a lively boy of twelve, son of Mr. Benton, accompanied me, for the development of mind and body which such an expedition would give. We were all well armed; and mounted, with the exception of eight men, who conducted as many carts, in which were packed our stores, with the baggage and instruments, and which were each drawn by two mules. A few loose horses, and four oxen which had been added to our stock of provisions, completed the train. We set out on the morning of the 10th, which happened to be Friday—a circumstance which our men did not fail to remember and recall during the hardships and vexations of the ensuing journey. Mr. Cyprian Chouteau, to whose kindness during our stay at his house we were much indebted, accompanied us several miles on our way, until we met an Indian whom he had engaged to conduct us on the first thirty or forty miles, where he was to consign us to the ocean of prairie, which, we were told, stretched without interruption almost to the base of the Rocky Mountains.

From the belt of wood which borders the Kansas, in which we had passed several good-looking Indian farms, we suddenly emerged on the prairies, which received us at the outset with some of their striking characteristics; for here and there rode an Indian, and but a few miles distant heavy clouds of smoke were rolling before the fire. In about ten miles we reached the Santa Fé road, along which we continued for a short time and encamped early on a small stream; having travelled about eleven miles. During our journey, it was the customary practice to encamp an hour or two before sunset, when the carts were disposed so as to form a sort of barricade around a circle some eighty yards in diameter. The tents were pitched, and the horses hobbled and turned loose to graze; and but a few minutes elapsed before the cooks of the messes, of which there were four, were busily engaged in preparing the evening meal. At nightfall the horses, mules, and oxen were driven in, and picketed—that is, secured by a halter, of which one end was tied to a small steel-shod picket, and driven into the ground; the halter being twenty or thirty feet long, which enabled them to obtain a little food during the night. When we had reached a part of the country where such a precaution became necessary, the carts being regularly arranged for defending the camp, guard was mounted at eight o'clock, consisting of three men, who were relieved every two hours; the morning watch being horse-guard for the day. At daybreak the camp was roused, the animals turned loose to graze, and breakfast generally over between six and seven o'clock, when we resumed our march, making regularly a halt at noon for one or two hours. Such was usually the order of the day, except when accident of country forced a variation; which, however, happened but rarely. We travelled the next day along the Sante Fé road, which we left in the afternoon, and encamped late in the evening on a small creek, called by the Indians Mishmagwi. Just as we arrived at camp, one of the horses set off at full speed on his return, and was followed by others. Several men were sent in pursuit, and returned with the fugitives about midnight, with the exception of one man, who did not make his appearance until morning. He had lost his way in the darkness of the night, and slept on the prairie. Shortly after midnight it began to rain heavily, and, as our tents were of light and thin cloth, they offered but little obstruction to rain; we were all well soaked, and glad when morning came. We had a rainy march on the 12th, but the weather grew fine as the day advanced. We encamped in a remarkably beautiful situation on the Kansas bluffs, which commanded a fine view of the river valley, here from three to four miles wide. The central portion was occupied by a broad belt of heavy timber, and nearer the hills the prairies were of the richest verdure. One of the oxen was killed here for food.

We reached the ford of the Kansas late in the afternoon of the 14th, where the river was two hundred and thirty yards wide, and commenced immediately preparations for crossing. I had expected to find the river fordable; but it had been swollen by the late rains, and was sweeping by with an angry current, yellow and turbid as the Missouri. Up to this point, the road we had travelled was a remarkably fine one, well beaten, and level—the usual road of a prairie country. By our route, the ford was one hundred miles from the mouth of the Kansas River. Several mounted men led the way into the stream, to swim across. The animals were driven in after them, and in a few minutes all had reached the opposite bank in safety, with the exception of the oxen, which swam some distance down the river, and, returning to the right bank, were not got over until the next morning. In the meantime, the carts had been unloaded and dismantled, and an india-rubber boat, which I had brought with me for the survey of the Platte River, placed in the water. The boat was twenty feet long and five broad, and on it were placed the body and wheels of a cart, with the load belonging to it, and three men with paddles.

The velocity of the current, and the inconvenient freight, rendering it difficult to be managed, Basil Lajeunesse, one of our best swimmers, took in his teeth a line attached to the boat, and swam ahead in order to reach a footing as soon as possible, and assist in drawing her over. In this manner, six passages had been successfully made, and as many carts with their contents, and a greater portion of the party deposited on the left bank; but night was drawing near, and, in our anxiety to have all over before the darkness closed in, I put upon the boat the remaining two carts, with their accompanying load. The man at the helm was timid on water, and, in his alarm, capsized the boat. Carts, barrels, boxes, and bales were in a moment floating down the current; but all the men who were on the shore jumped into the water, without stopping to think if they could swim, and almost everything—even heavy articles, such as guns and lead—was recovered.

Two of the men, who could not swim, came nigh being drowned, and all the sugar belonging to one of the messes wasted its sweets on the muddy waters; but our heaviest loss was a bag of coffee, which contained nearly all our provision. It was a loss which none but a traveller in a strange and inhospitable country can appreciate; and often afterward, when excessive toil and long marching had overcome us with fatigue and weariness, we remembered and mourned over our loss in the Kansas. Carson and Maxwell had been much in the water yesterday, and both, in consequence, were taken ill. The former continuing so, I remained in camp. A number of Kansas Indians visited us to-day. Going up to one of the groups who were scattered among the trees, I found one sitting on the ground, among some of the men, gravely and fluently speaking French, with as much facility and as little embarrassment as any of my own party, who were nearly all of French origin.

On all sides was heard the strange language of his own people, wild, and harmonizing well with their appearance. I listened to him for some time with feelings of strange curiosity and interest. He was now apparently thirty-five years of age; and, on inquiry, I learned that he had been at St. Louis when a boy, and there had learned the French language. From one of the Indian women I obtained a fine cow and calf in exchange for a yoke of oxen. Several of them brought us vegetables, pumpkins, onions, beans, and lettuce. One of them brought butter, and from a half-breed near the river I had the good fortune to obtain some twenty or thirty pounds of coffee. The dense timber in which we had encamped interfered with astronomical observations, and our wet and damaged stores required exposure to the sun. Accordingly the tents were struck early the next morning, and, leaving camp at six o'clock, we moved about seven miles up the river, to a handsome, open prairie, some twenty feet above the water, where the fine grass afforded a luxurious repast to our horses.

During the day we occupied ourselves in making astronomical observations, in order to lay down the country to this place; it being our custom to keep up our map regularly in the field, which we found attended with many advantages. The men were kept busy in drying the provisions, painting the cart-covers, and otherwise completing our equipage, until the afternoon, when powder was distributed to them, and they spent some hours in firing at a mark. We were now fairly in the Indian country, and it began to be time to prepare for the chances of the wilderness.

Friday, June 17th.—The weather yesterday had not permitted us to make the observations I was desirous to obtain here, and I therefore did not move to-day. The people continue their target-firing. In the steep bank of the river here were nests of innumerable swallows, into one of which a large prairie-snake had got about half his body, and was occupied in eating the young birds. The old ones were flying about in great distress, darting at him, and vainly endeavoring to drive him off. A shot wounded him, and, being killed, he was cut open, and eighteen young swallows were found in his body. A sudden storm that burst upon us in the afternoon, cleared away in a brilliant sunset, followed by a clear night, which enabled us to determine our position, in longitude 95° 38′ 05″, and in latitude 39° 06′ 40″.

A party of emigrants to the Columbia River, under the charge of Dr.

White, an agent of the Government in Oregon Territory, were about three weeks in advance of us. They consisted of men, women, and children. There were sixty-four men, and sixteen or seventeen families. They had a considerable number of cattle, and were transporting their household furniture in large heavy wagons. I understood that there had been much sickness among them, and that they had lost several children. One of the party, who had lost his child, and whose wife was very ill, had left them about one hundred miles hence on the prairies ; and as a hunter, who had accompanied them, visited our camp this evening, we availed ourselves of his return to the States to write to our friends.

The morning of the 18th was very unpleasant. A fine rain was falling, with cold wind from the north, and mists made the river-hills look dark and gloomy. We left our camp at seven, journeying along the foot of the hills which border the Kansas Valley, generally about three miles wide, and extremely rich. We halted for dinner, after a march of about thirteen miles, on the banks of one of the many little tributaries to the Kansas, which look like trenches in the prairie, and are usually well timbered. After crossing this stream, I rode off some miles to the left, attracted by the appearance of a cluster of huts near the mouth of the Vermilion. It was a large but deserted Kansas village, scattered in an open wood, along the margin of the stream, on a spot chosen with the customary Indian fondness for beauty of scenery. The Pawnees had attacked it in the early spring. Some of the houses were burnt, and others blackened with smoke, and weeds were already getting possession of the cleared places. Riding up the Vermilion River, I reached the ford in time to meet the carts, and, crossing, encamped on its western side. The weather continued cool, the thermometer being this evening as low as 49° ; but the night was sufficiently clear for astronomical observations, which placed us in longitude 96° 04′ 07″, and latitude 39° 15′ 19″. At sunset the barometer was at 28.845, thermometer 64°.

We breakfasted the next morning at half-past five, and left our encampment early. The morning was cool, the thermometer being at 45°. Quitting the river bottom, the road ran along the uplands, over a rolling country, generally in view of the Kansas, from eight to twelve miles distant. Many large boulders, of a very compact sandstone, of various shades of red, some of them four or five tons in weight, were scattered along the hills ; and many beautiful plants in flower, among which the *Amorpha canescens* was a characteristic, enlivened the green of the prairie. At the heads of the ravines I remarked, occasionally, thickets of *Salix longifolia*, the most common willow of the country. We travelled nineteen miles, and pitched our tents at evening on the head-waters of a small creek, now nearly dry, but having in its bed several fine springs. The barometer indicated a considerable rise in the country—here about fourteen hundred feet above the sea—and the increased elevation appeared already to have some slight influence upon the vegetation. The night was cold, with a heavy dew ; the thermometer at 10 P.M. standing at 46°, barometer 28.483. Our position was in longitude 96° 14′ 49″, and latitude 39° 30′ 40″.

The morning of the twentieth was fine, with a southerly breeze, and a bright sky ; and at seven o'clock we were on the march. The country to-day was rather more broken, rising still, and covered everywhere with frag-ments of siliceous limestone, particularly on the summits, where they were small, and thickly strewed as pebbles on the shore of the sea. In these exposed situations grew but few plants ; though whenever the soil was good and protected from the winds, in the creek bottoms and ravines and on the slopes, they flourished abundantly ; among them the *amorpha* still retaining its characteristic place. We crossed, at 10 A.M., the Big Vermil-ion, which has a rich bottom of about one mile in breadth, one-third of which is occupied by timber. Making our usual halt at noon, after a day's march of twenty-four miles, we reached the Big Blue, and encamped on the uplands of the western side, near a small creek, where was a fine large spring of very cold water. This is a clear and handsome stream, about one hundred and twenty feet wide, running, with a rapid current, through a well-timbered valley. To-day antelope were seen running over the hills, and at evening Carson brought us a fine deer. Longitude of the camp 96° 32′ 35″, latitude 39° 45′ 08″. Thermometer at sunset 75°. A pleasant southerly breeze and fine morning had given place to a gale, with indica-tions of bad weather ; when, after a march of ten miles, we halted to noon on a small creek, where the water stood in deep pools. In the bank of the creek limestone made its appearance in a stratum about one foot thick. In the afternoon, the people seemed to suffer for want of water. The road led along a high dry ridge ; dark lines of timber indicated the heads of streams in the plains below ; but there was no water near, and the day was very oppressive, with a hot wind, and the thermometer at 90°. Along our route the *amorpha* has been in very abundant but variable bloom—in some places, bending beneath the weight of purple clusters ; in others, without a flower. It seems to love best the sunny slopes, with a dark soil and southern exposure. Everywhere the rose is met with, and reminds us of cultivated gardens and civilization. It is scattered over the prairies in small *bosquets*, and, when glittering in the dews and waving in the pleasant breeze of the early morning, is the most beautiful of the prairie flowers. The *artemisia*, absinthe, or prairie sage, as it is variously called, is in-creasing in size, and glitters like silver, as the southern breeze turns up its leaves to the sun. All these plants have their insect habitants, vari-ously colored ; taking generally the hue of the flower on which they live.

The *artemisia* has its small fly accompanying it through every change of elevation and latitude ; and wherever I have seen the *Asclepias tuberosa*, I have always remarked, too, on the flower a large butterfly, so nearly resembling it in color, as to be distinguishable at a little distance only by the motion of its wings. Travelling on the fresh traces of the Oregon emigrants relieves a little the loneliness of the road; and to-night, after a march of twenty-two miles, we halted on a small creek which had been one of their encampments. As we advance westward, the soil appears to be getting more sandy, and the surface-rock, an erratic deposit of sand and gravel, rests here on a bed of coarse yellow and gray and very friable sandstone. Evening closed over with rain and its usual attendant, hordes of mosquitoes, with which we were annoyed for the first time.

June 22d.—We enjoyed at breakfast this morning a luxury, very unusual in this country, in a cup of excellent coffee, with cream from our cow. Being milked at night, cream was thus had in the morning. Our mid-day halt was at Wyeth's Creek, in the bed of which were numerous boulders of dark ferruginous sandstone, mingled with others of the red sandstone already mentioned. Here a pack of cards, lying loose on the grass, marked an encampment of our Oregon emigrants ; and it was at the close of the day when we made our bivouac in the midst of some well-timbered ravines near the Little Blue, twenty-four miles from our camp of the preceding night. Crossing the next morning a number of handsome creeks, with clear water and sandy beds, we reached at 10 A.M. a very beautiful wooded stream, about thirty-five feet wide, called Sandy Creek, and sometimes, as the Ottoes frequently winter there, the Ottoe Fork. The country has become very sandy, and the plants less varied and abundant, with the exception of the *amorpha*, which rivals the grass in quantity, though not so forward as it has been found to the eastward.

At the Big Trees, where we had intended to noon, no water was to be found. The bed of the little creek was perfectly dry, and on the adjacent sandy bottom *cacti*, for the first time, made their appearance. We made here a short delay in search of water ; and, after a hard day's march of twenty-eight miles, encamped at five o'clock on the Little Blue, where our arrival made a scene of the Arabian desert. As fast as they arrived, men and horses rushed into the stream, where they bathed and drank together in common enjoyment. We wěre now in the range of the Pawnees, who were accustomed to infest this part of the country, stealing horses from companies on their way to the mountains, and, when in sufficient force, openly attacking and plundering them, and subjecting them to various kinds of insult. For the first time, therefore, guard was mounted to-night. Our route the next morning lay up the valley, which, bordered by hills with graceful slopes, looked uncommonly green and beautiful. The stream was about fifty feet wide, and three or four deep, fringed by cotton-wood and willow, with frequent groves of oak tenanted by flocks of turkeys. Game here, too, made its appearance in greater plenty. Elk were frequently seen on the hills, and now and then an antelope bounded across our path, or a deer broke from the groves. The road in the afternoon was over the upper prairies, several miles from the river, and we encamped at sunset on one of its small tributaries, where an abundance of prêle (*equisetum*) afforded fine forage to our tired animals. We had travelled thirty-one miles. A heavy bank of black clouds in the west came on us in a storm between nine and ten, preceded by a violent wind. The rain fell in such torrents that it was difficult to breathe facing the wind, the thunder rolled incessantly, and the whole sky was tremulous with lightning; now and then illuminated by a blinding flash, succeeded by pitchy darkness. Carson had the watch from ten to midnight, and to him had been assigned our young *compagnons de voyage* Messrs. Brant and R. Benton. This was their first night on guard, and such an introduction did not augur very auspiciously of the pleasures of the expedition. Many things conspired to render their situation uncomfortable; stories of desperate and bloody Indian fights were rife in the camp; our position was badly chosen, surrounded on all sides by timbered hollows, and occupying an area of several hundred feet, so that necessarily the guards were far apart; and now and then I could hear Randolph, as if relieved by the sound of a voice in the darkness, calling out to the sergeant of the guard to direct his attention to some imaginary alarm; but they stood it out, and took their turn regularly afterward.

The next morning we had a specimen of the false alarms to which all parties in these wild regions are subject. Proceeding up the valley, objects were seen on the opposite hills, which disappeared before a glass could be brought to bear upon them. A man who was a short distance in the rear came spurring up in great haste, shouting, "Indians! Indians!" He had been near enough to see and count them, according to his report, and had made out twenty-seven. I immediately halted, arms were examined and put in order; the usual preparations made; and Kit Carson, springing upon one of the hunting horses, crossed the river, and galloped off into the opposite prairies, to obtain some certain intelligence of their movements.

Mounted on a fine horse, without a saddle, and scouring bareheaded over the prairies, Kit was one of the finest pictures of a horseman I have ever seen. A short time enabled him to discover that the Indian war-party of twenty-seven consisted of six elk, which had been gazing curiously at our caravan as it passed by, and were now scampering off at full speed.

This was our first alarm, and its excitement broke agreeably on the monotony of the day.   At our noon halt, the men were exercised at a target; and in the evening we pitched our tents at a Pawnee encampment of last July.   They had apparently killed buffalo here, as many bones were lying about, and the frames where the hides had been stretched were yet standing.   The road of the day had kept the valley, which is sometimes rich and well timbered, though the country is generally sandy.   Mingled with the usual plants, a thistle (*Carduus leucógraphus*) had for the last day or two made its appearance; and along the river bottom, *tradescantia virginica* and milk plant (*Asclepias syriaca* *), in considerable quantities.

Our march to-day had been twenty-one miles, and the astronomical observations gave us a chronometric longitude of 98° 22′ 12″, and latitude 40° 26′ 50″.   We were moving forward at seven in the morning, and in about five miles reached a fork of the Blue, where the road leaves that river, and crosses over to the Platte.   No water was to be found on the dividing ridge, and the casks were filled, and the animals here allowed a short repose.   The road led across a high and level prairie ridge, where were but few plants, and those principally thistle (*Carduus leucógraphus*), and a kind of dwarf artemisia.   Antelope were seen frequently during the morning, which was very stormy.   Squalls of rain, with thunder and lightning, were around us in every direction; and while we were enveloped in one of them, a flash, which seemed to scorch our eyes as it passed, struck in the prairie within a few hundred feet, sending up a column of dust.

Crossing on the way several Pawnee roads to the Arkansas, we reached, in about twenty-one miles from our halt on the Blue, what is called the coast of the Nebraska, or Platte, River.   This had seemed in the distance a range of high and broken hills; but on a nearer approach were found to be elevations of forty to sixty feet, into which the wind had worked the sand. They were covered with the usual fine grasses of the country, and bordered the eastern side of the ridge on a breadth of about two miles. Change of soil and country appeared here to have produced some change in the vegetation.   *Cacti* were numerous, and all the plants of the region appeared to flourish among the warm hills.   Among them the *amorpha*, in full bloom, was remarkable for its large and luxuriant purple clusters. From the foot of the coast, a distance of two miles across the level bottom brought us to our encampment on the shore of the river, about twenty

---

* " This plant is very odoriferous, and in Canada charms the traveller, especially when passing through woods in the evening.   The French there eat the tender shoots in the spring, as we do asparagus.   The natives make a sugar of the flowers, gathering them in the morning when they are covered with dew, and collect the cotton from the pods to fill their beds.   On account of the silkiness of this cotton, Parkinson calls the plant Virginian silk."—*Loudon's Encyclopedia of Plants.*

The Sioux Indians of the Upper Platte eat the young pods of this plant, boiling them with the meat of the buffalo.

miles below the head of Grand Island, which lay extended before us, covered with dense and heavy woods. From the mouth of the Kansas, according to our reckoning, we had travelled three hundred and twenty-eight miles ; and the geological formation of the country we had passed over consisted of lime and sandstone, covered by the same erratic deposit of sand and gravel which forms the surface rock of the prairies between the Missouri and Mississippi Rivers. Except in some occasional limestone boulders, I had met with no fossils. The elevation of the Platte Valley above the sea is here about two thousand feet. The astronomical observations of the night placed us in longitude 98° 45′ 49″, latitude 40° 41′ 06″.

June 27th.—The animals were somewhat fatigued by their march of yesterday, and, after a short journey of eighteen miles along the river-bottom, I encamped near the head of Grand Island, in longitude, by observation, 99° 05′ 24″, latitude 40° 39′ 32″. The soil here was light but rich, though in some places rather sandy ; and, with the exception of a scattered fringe along the bank, the timber, consisting principally of poplar (*populus monilifera*), elm, and hackberry (*celtis crassifolia*), is confined almost entirely to the islands.

June 28th.—We halted to noon at an open reach of the river, which occupies rather more than a fourth of the valley, here only about four miles broad. The camp had been disposed with the usual precaution, the horses grazing at a little distance attended by the guard, and we were all sitting quietly at our dinner on the grass, when suddenly we heard the startling cry, "*du monde !*" In an instant every man's weapon was in his hand, the horses were driven in, hobbled, and picketed, and horsemen were galloping at full speed in the direction of the new-comers, screaming and yelling with the wildest excitement. "Get ready, my lads !" said the leader of the approaching party to his men, when our wild-looking horsemen were discovered bearing down upon them ; "*Nous allons attraper des coups de baguette.*" They proved to be a small party of fourteen, under the charge of a man named John Lee, and, with their baggage and provisions strapped to their backs, were making their way on foot to the frontier. A brief account of their fortunes will give some idea of navigation in the Nebraska. Sixty days since, they had left the mouth of Laramie's fork, some three hundred miles above, in barges laden with the furs of the American Fur Company. They started with the annual flood, and, drawing but nine inches water, hoped to make a speedy and prosperous voyage to St. Louis ; but, after a lapse of forty days, found themselves only one hundred and thirty miles from their point of departure. They came down rapidly as far as Scott's bluffs, where their difficulties began. Sometimes they came upon places where the water was spread over a great extent, and here they toiled from morning until night, en-

CHEYENNE BRAVE.

deavoring to drag their boat through the sands, making only two or three miles in as many days. Sometimes they would enter an arm of the river, where there appeared a fine channel, and, after descending prosperously for eight or ten miles, would come suddenly upon dry sands, and be compelled to return, dragging their boat for days against the rapid current; and at others they came upon places where the water lay in holes, and, getting out to float off their boat, would fall into water up to their necks, and the next moment tumble over against a sand-bar. Discouraged at length, and finding the Platte growing every day more shallow, they discharged the principal part of their cargoes one hundred and thirty miles below Fort Laramie, which they secured as well as possible, and, leaving a few men to guard them, attempted to continue their voyage, laden with some light furs and their personal baggage. After fifteen or twenty days more struggling in the sands, during which they made but one hundred and forty miles, they sunk their barges, made a *cache* of their remaining furs and property in trees on the bank, and, packing on his back what each man could carry, had commenced, the day before we encountered them, their journey on foot to St. Louis.

We laughed then at their forlorn and vagabond appearance, and in our turn, a month or two afterward, furnished the same occasion for merriment to others. Even their stock of tobacco, that *sine qua non* of a voyageur, without which the night-fire is gloomy, was entirely exhausted. However, we shortened their homeward journey by a small supply from our own provision. They gave us the welcome intelligence that the buffalo were abundant some two days' march in advance, and made us a present of some choice pieces, which were a very acceptable change from our salt pork. In the interchange of news and the renewal of old acquaintanceships we found wherewithal to fill a busy hour; then we mounted our horses, and they shouldered their packs, and we shook hands and parted. Among them I had found an old companion on the northern prairie, a hardened and hardly served veteran of the mountains, who had been as much hacked and scarred as an old *moustache* of Napoleon's "Old Guard." He flourished in the soubriquet of La Tulipe, and his real name I never knew. Finding that he was going to the States only because his company was bound in that direction, and that he was rather more willing to return with me, I took him again into my service. We travelled this day but seventeen miles.

At our evening camp, about sunset, three figures were discovered approaching, which our glasses made out to be Indians. They proved to be Cheyennes—two men and a boy of thirteen. About a month since, they had left their people on the south fork of the river, some three hundred miles to the westward, and, a party of only four in number, had been to the Pawnee villages on a horse-stealing excursion, from which they were returning unsuccessful. They were miserably mounted on wild horses from the Arkansas plains, and had no other weapons than bows and long spears; and had they been discovered by the Pawnees, could not, by any possibility, have escaped. They were mortified by their ill success, and said the Pawnees were cowards who shut up their horses in their lodges at night. I invited them to supper with me, and Randolph and the young Cheyenne, who had been eying each other suspiciously and curiously, soon became intimate friends. After supper we sat down on the grass, and I placed a sheet of paper between us, on which they traced rudely, but with a certain degree of relative truth, the water-courses of the country which lay between us and their villages, and of which I desired to have some information. Their companions, they told us, had taken a nearer route over the hills; but they had mounted one of the summits to spy out the country, whence they had caught a glimpse of our party, and, confident of good treatment at the hands of the whites, hastened to join company. Latitude of the camp, 40° 39′ 51″.

We made the next morning sixteen miles. I remarked that the ground was covered in many places with an efflorescence of salt, and the plants were not numerous. In the bottoms was frequently seen *tradescantia*, and on the dry benches were *carduus*, *cactus*, and *amorpha*. A high wind during the morning had increased to a violent gale from the northwest, which made our afternoon ride cold and unpleasant. We had the welcome sight of two buffaloes on one of the large islands, and encamped at a clump of timber about seven miles from our noon halt, after a day's march of twenty-two miles.

The air was keen the next morning at sunrise, the thermometer standing at 44°, and it was sufficiently cold to make overcoats very comfortable. A few miles brought us into the midst of the buffalo, swarming in immense numbers over the plains, where they had left scarcely a blade of grass standing. Mr. Preuss, who was sketching at a little distance in the rear, had at first noted them as large groves of timber. In the sight of such a mass of life, the traveller feels a strange emotion of grandeur. We had heard from a distance a dull and confused murmuring, and when we came in view of their dark masses there was not one among us who did not feel his heart beat quicker. It was the early part of the day, when the herds are feeding; and everywhere they were in motion. Here and there a huge old bull was rolling in the grass, and clouds of dust rose in the air from various parts of the bands, each the scene of some obstinate fight. Indians and buffalo make the poetry and life of the prairie, and our camp was full of their exhilaration. In place of the quiet monotony of the march, relieved only by the cracking of the whip, and an "*avance donc! enfant de garce!*" shouts and songs resounded from every part of the line, and our evening camp was always the commencement of a feast which terminated only with our departure on the following morning. At any time of the night might be seen pieces of the most delicate and choicest meat, roasting *en appolas*, on sticks around the fire, and the guard were never without company. With pleasant weather and no enemy to fear, an abundance of the most excellent meat, and no scarcity of bread or tobacco, they were enjoying the oasis of a voyageur's life. Three cows were killed to-day. Kit Carson had shot one, and was continuing the chase in the midst of another herd, when his horse fell headlong, but sprang up and joined the flying band. Though considerably hurt, he had the good fortune to break no bones; and Maxwell, who was mounted on a fleet hunter, captured the runaway after a hard chase. He was on the point of shooting him, to avoid the loss of his bridle (a handsomely mounted Spanish one), when he found that his horse was able to come up with him. Animals are frequently lost in this way; and it is necessary to keep close watch over them in the vicinity of the buffalo, in the midst of which they scour off to the plains and are rarely retaken. One of our mules took a sudden freak into his head, and joined a neighboring band to-day. As we were not in a condition to lose horses, I sent several men in pursuit, and remained in camp, in the hope of recovering him; but lost the afternoon to no purpose, as we did not see him again. Astronomical observations placed us in longitude 100° 05′ 47″, latitude 40° 49′ 55″.

July 1st.—Along our road to-day the prairie-bottom was more elevated and dry, and the hills which border the right side of the river higher and more broken and picturesque in the outline. The country, too, was better timbered. As we were riding quietly along the bank a grand herd of buffalo, some seven or eight hundred in number, came crowding up from the river, where they had been to drink, and commenced crossing the plain slowly, eating as they went. The wind was favorable; the coolness of the morning invited to exercise; the ground was apparently good, and the distance across the prairie (two or three miles) gave us a fine opportunity to charge them before they could get among the river-hills. It was too fine a prospect for a chase to be lost; and, halting for a few moments, the hunters were brought up and saddled, and Kit Carson, Maxwell, and I started together. They were now somewhat less than half a mile distant, and we rode easily along until within about three hundred yards, when a sudden agitation, a wavering in the band, and a galloping to and fro of some which were scattered along the skirts, gave us the intimation that we were discovered. We started together at a hand-gallop, riding steadily abreast of each other, and here the interest of the chase became so engrossingly intense that we were sensible to nothing else. We were now closing upon them rapidly, and the front of the mass was already in rapid motion for the hills, and in a few seconds the movement had communicated itself to the whole herd.

A crowd of bulls, as usual, brought up the rear, and every now and then some of them faced about, and then dashed on after the band a short distance, and turned and looked again, as if more than half inclined to stand and fight. In a few moments, however, during which we had been quickening our pace, the rout was universal, and we were going over the ground like a hurricane. When at about thirty yards, we gave the usual shout (the hunter's *pas de charge*) and broke into the herd. We entered on the side, the mass giving way in every direction in their heedless course. Many of the bulls, less active and less fleet than the cows, paying no attention to the ground, and occupied solely with the hunter, were precipitated to the earth with great force, rolling over and over with the violence of the shock, and hardly distinguishable in the dust. We separated on entering, each singling out his game.

My horse was a trained hunter, famous in the West under the name of Proveau, and, with his eyes flashing and the foam flying from his mouth, sprang on after the cow like a tiger. In a few moments he brought me alongside of her, and, rising in the stirrups, I fired at the distance of a yard, the ball entering at the termination of the long hair, and passing near the heart. She fell headlong at the report of the gun, and checking my horse, I looked around for my companions. At a little distance Kit was on the ground, engaged in tying his horse to the horns of a cow which he was preparing to cut up. Among the scattered bands, at some distance below, I caught a glimpse of Maxwell; and while I was looking a light wreath of white smoke curled away from his gun, from which I was too far to hear the report. Nearer, and between me and the hills toward which they were directing their course, was the body of the herd, and giving my horse the rein we dashed after them. A thick cloud of dust hung upon their rear, which filled my mouth and eyes and nearly smothered me. In the midst of this I could see nothing, and the buffalo were not distinguishable until within thirty feet. They crowded together more densely still as I came upon them, and rushed along in such a compact body that I could not obtain an entrance—the horse almost leaping upon them. In a few moments the mass divided to the right and left, the horns clattering with a noise heard above everything else, and my horse darted into the opening. Five or six bulls charged on us as we dashed along the line, but were left far behind ; and, singling out a cow, I gave her my fire, but struck too high. She gave a tremendous leap, and scoured on swifter than before. I reined up my horse, and the band swept on like a torrent,

MOVING CAMP

leaving the place quiet and clear. Our chase had led us into dangerous ground. A prairie-dog village, so thickly settled that there were three or four holes in every twenty yards square, occupied the whole bottom for nearly two miles in length. Looking around, I saw only one of the hunters, nearly out of sight, and the long dark line of our caravan crawling along, three or four miles distant. After a march of twenty-four miles, we encamped at nightfall one mile and a half above the lower end of Brady's Island. The breadth of this arm of the river was eight hundred and eighty yards, and the water nowhere two feet in depth. The island bears the name of a man killed on this spot some years ago. His party had encamped here, three in company, and one of the number went off to hunt, leaving Brady and his companion together. These two had frequently quarrelled, and on the hunter's return he found Brady dead, and was told that he had shot himself accidentally. He was buried here on the bank ; but, as usual, the wolves had torn him out, and some human bones that were lying on the ground we supposed were his. Troops of wolves that were hanging on the skirts of the buffalo kept up an uninterrupted howling during the night, venturing almost into camp. In the morning they were sitting at a short distance, barking, and impatiently waiting our departure to fall upon the bones.

July 2d.—The morning was cool and smoky. Our road led closer to the hills, which here increased in elevation, presenting an outline of conical peaks three hundred to five hundred feet high. Some timber, apparently pine, grow in the ravines, and streaks of clay or sand whiten their slopes. We crossed during the morning a number of hollows, timbered principally with box elder (*acer negundo*), poplar, and elm. Brady's Island is well wooded, and all the river along which our road led to-day may, in general, be called tolerably well timbered. We passed near an encampment of the Oregon emigrants, where they appear to have reposed several days. A variety of household articles were scattered about, and they had probably disburdened themselves here of many things not absolutely necessary. I had left the usual road before the mid-day halt, and in the afternoon, having sent several men in advance to reconnoitre, marched directly for the mouth of the South Fork. On our arrival, the horsemen were sent in and scattered about the river to search the best fording-places, and the carts followed immediately. The stream is here divided by an island into two channels. The southern is four hundred and fifty feet wide, having eighteen or twenty inches water in the deepest places. With the exception of a few dry bars, the bed of the river is generally quicksands, in which the carts began to sink rapidly so soon as the mules halted, so that it was necessary to keep them constantly in motion.

The northern channel, two thousand two hundred and fifty feet wide, was somewhat deeper, having frequently three feet of water in the numerous small channels, with a bed of coarse gravel. The whole breadth of the Nebraska, immediately below the junction, is five thousand three hundred and fifty feet. All our equipage had reached the left bank safely at six o'clock, having to-day made twenty miles. We encamped at the point of land immediately at the junction of the North and South Forks. Between the streams is a low rich prairie, extending from their confluence eighteen miles westwardly to the bordering hills, where it is five and a half miles wide. It is covered with a luxuriant growth of grass, and along the banks is a slight and scattered fringe of cottonwood and willow. In the buffalo trails and wallows I remarked saline efflorescences, to which a rapid evaporation in the great heat of the sun probably contributes, as the soil is entirely unprotected by timber. In the vicinity of these places there was a bluish grass, which the cattle refuse to eat, called by the voyageurs "*herbe salée*" (salt grass). The latitude of the junction is 40° 04′ 47″, and longitude, by chronometer and lunar distances, 100° 49′ 43″. The elevation above the sea is about two thousand seven hundred feet. The hunters came in with a fat cow; and, as we had labored hard, we enjoyed well a supper of roasted ribs and *boudins*, the *chef d'œuvre* of a prairie-cook. Mosquitoes thronged about us this evening; but, by ten o'clock, when the thermometer had fallen to 47°, they had all disappeared.

July 3d.—As this was to be a point in our homeward journey, I made a *cache* (a term used in all this country for what is hidden in the ground) of a barrel of pork. It was impossible to conceal such a proceeding from the sharp eyes of our Cheyenne companions, and I therefore told them to go and see what it was they were burying. They would otherwise have not failed to return and destroy our *cache*, in expectation of some rich booty; but pork they dislike, and never eat. We left our camp at nine, continuing up the South Fork, the prairie-bottom affording us a fair road; but in the long grass we roused myriads of mosquitoes and flies, from which our horses suffered severely. The day was smoky, with a pleasant breeze from the south, and the plains on the opposite side were covered with buffalo. Having travelled twenty-five miles, we encamped at six in the evening; and the men were sent across the river for wood, as there is none here on the left bank. Our fires were partially made of the *bois de vache*, the dry excrement of the buffalo, which, like that of the camel in the Arabian deserts, furnishes to the traveller a very good substitute for wood, burning like turf. Wolves in great numbers surrounded us during the night, crossing and recrossing from the opposite herds to our camp, and howling and trotting about in the river until morning.

July 4th.—The morning was very smoky, the sun shining dimly and red, as in a thick fog. The camp was roused with a salute at daybreak,

and from our scanty store a portion of what our Indian friends called the
"red fire-water" served out to the men. While we were at breakfast a
buffalo calf broke through the camp, followed by a couple of wolves. In
its fright it had probably mistaken us for a band of buffalo. The wolves
were obliged to make a circuit around the camp, so that the calf got a little the start, and strained every nerve to reach a large herd at the foot of
the hills, about two miles distant; but first one, and then another, and another wolf joined in the chase, until its pursuers amounted to twenty or
thirty, and they ran him down before he could reach his friends. There
were a few bulls near the place, and one of them attacked the wolves and
tried to rescue him; but was driven off immediately, and the little animal
fell an easy prey, half devoured before he was dead. We watched the
chase with the interest always felt for the weak; and had there been a saddled horse at hand, he would have fared better. Leaving camp, our road
soon approached the hills, in which strata of a marl like that of the Chimney Rock, hereafter described, make their appearance. It is probably of
this rock that the hills on the right bank of the Platte, a little below the
junction, are composed, and which are worked by the winds and rains into
sharp peaks and cones, giving them, in contrast to the surrounding level
region, something of a picturesque appearance. We crossed this morning
numerous beds of the small creeks which, in the time of rains and melting
snow, pour down from the ridge, bringing down with them always great
quantities of sand and gravel, which have gradually raised their beds four
to ten feet above the level of the prairie which they cross, making each
one of them a miniature Po. Raised in this way above the surrounding
prairie, without any bank, the long yellow and winding line of their beds
resembles a causeway from the hills to the river. Many spots on the
prairie are yellow with sunflower (*helianthus*).

As we were riding slowly along this afternoon, clouds of dust in the
ravines, among the hills to the right, suddenly attracted our attention, and
in a few minutes column after column of buffalo came galloping down,
making directly to the river. By the time the leading herds had reached
the water the prairie was darkened with the dense masses. Immediately
before us, when the bands first came down into the valley, stretched an
unbroken line, the head of which was lost among the river-hills on the opposite side; and still they poured down from the ridge on our right.
From hill to hill, the prairie-bottom was certainly not less than two miles
wide; and, allowing the animals to be ten feet apart, and only ten in a
line, there were already eleven thousand in view. Some idea may thus
be formed of their number when they had occupied the whole plain. In a
short time they surrounded us on every side, extending for several miles
in the rear, and forward as far as the eye could reach; leaving around us,

as we advanced, an open space of only two or three hundred yards. This movement of the buffalo indicated to us the presence of Indians on the North Fork.

I halted earlier than usual, about forty miles from the junction, and all hands were soon busily engaged in preparing a feast to celebrate the day. The kindness of our friends at St. Louis had provided us with a large supply of excellent preserves and rich fruit-cake ; and when these were added to a macaroni-soup and variously prepared dishes of the choicest buffalo meat, crowned with a cup of coffee, and enjoyed with prairie appetite, we felt, as we sat in barbaric luxury around our smoking supper on the grass, a greater sensation of enjoyment than the Roman epicure at his perfumed feast. But most of all it seemed to please our Indian friends, who, in the unrestrained enjoyment of the moment, demanded to know if our " medicine days came often." No restraint was exercised at the hospitable board, and, to the great delight of his elders, our young Indian lad made himself extremely drunk.

Our encampment was within a few miles of the place where the road crosses to the North Fork, and various reasons led me to divide my party at this point. The North Fork was the principal object of my survey ; but I was desirous to ascend the South Branch, with a view of obtaining some astronomical positions, and determining the mouths of its tributaries as far as St. Vrain's Fort, estimated to be some two hundred miles farther up the river and near to Long's Peak. There I hoped to obtain some mules, which I found would be necessary to relieve my horses. In a military point of view, I was desirous to form some opinion of the country relative to the establishment of posts on the line connecting the settlements with the South Pass of the Rocky Mountains, by way of the Arkansas and the South and Laramie Forks of the Platte. Crossing the country northwestwardly, from St. Vrain's Fort to the American Company's Fort at the mouth of Laramie, would give me some acquaintance with the affluents which head in the mountains between the two ; I therefore determined to set out the next morning, accompanied by Mr. Preuss and four men—Maxwell, Bernier, Ayot, and Basil Lajeunesse. Our Cheyennes, whose village lay up this river, also decided to accompany us. The party I left in charge of Clément Lambert, with orders to cross to the North Fork ; and at some convenient place, near to the *Coulée des Frênes*, make a *cache* of everything not absolutely necessary to the further progress of our expedition. From this point, using the most guarded precaution in his march through the country, he was to proceed to the American Company's Fort at the mouth of Laramie's Fork, and await my arrival, which would be prior to the 16th, as on that and the following night would occur some occultations which I was desirous to obtain at that place.

July 5th.—Before breakfast all was ready. We had one led horse in addition to those we rode and a pack-mule, destined to carry our instruments, provisions, and baggage; the last two articles not being of very great weight. The instruments consisted of a sextant, artificial horizon, etc., a barometer, spy-glass, and compass. The chronometer I of course kept on my person. I had ordered the cook to put up for us some flour, coffee, and sugar, and our rifles were to furnish the rest. One blanket, in addition to his saddle and saddle-blanket, furnished the materials for each man's bed, and everyone was provided with a change of linen. All were armed with rifles or double-barrelled guns; and, in addition to these, Maxwell and myself were furnished with excellent pistols. Thus accoutred, we took a parting breakfast with our friends, and set forth.

Our journey the first day afforded nothing of any interest. We shot a buffalo toward sunset, and, having obtained some meat for our evening meal, encamped where a little timber afforded us the means of making a fire. Having disposed our meat on roasting-sticks, we proceeded to unpack our bales in search of coffee and sugar and flour for bread. With the exception of a little parched coffee, unground, we found nothing. Our cook had neglected to put it up, or it had been somehow forgotten. Tired and hungry, with tough bull-meat without salt (for we had not been able to kill a cow) and a little bitter coffee, we sat down in silence to our miserable fare, a very disconsolate party; for yesterday's feast was yet fresh in our memories, and this was our first brush with misfortune. Each man took his blanket, and laid himself down silently; for the worst part of these mishaps is, that they make people ill-humored. To-day we had travelled about thirty-six miles.

July 6th.—Finding that our present excursion would be attended with considerable hardship, and unwilling to expose more persons than necessary, I determined to send Mr. Preuss back to the party. His horse, too, appeared in no condition to support the journey; and accordingly, after breakfast, he took the road across the hills, attended by one of my most trusty men, Bernier. The ridge between the rivers is here about fifteen miles broad, and I expected he would probably strike the fork near their evening camp. At all events, he would not fail to find their trail, and rejoin them the next day.

We continued our journey, seven in number, including the three Cheyennes. Our general course was southwest, up the valley of the river, which was sandy, bordered on the northern side of the valley by a low ridge; and on the south, after seven or eight miles, the river hills became higher. Six miles from our resting-place we crossed the bed of a considerable stream, now entirely dry—a bed of sand. In a grove of willows near the mouth, were the remains of a considerable fort, constructed of trunks of large trees. It was apparently very old, and had probably been the scene of some hostile encounter among the roving tribes. Its solitude formed an impressive contrast to the picture which our imaginations involuntarily drew of the busy scene which had been enacted here. The timber appeared to have been much more extensive formerly than now. There were but few trees, a kind of long-leaved willow, standing; and numerous trunks of large trees were scattered about on the ground. In many similar places I had occasion to remark an apparent progressive decay in the timber. Ten miles farther we reached the mouth of Lodge Pole Creek, a clear and handsome stream, running through a broad valley. In its course through the bottom it has a uniform breadth of twenty-two feet, and six inches in depth. A few willows on the banks strike pleasantly on the eye, by their greenness, in the midst of the hot and barren sands.

The *amorpha* was frequent among the ravines, but the sunflower (*helianthus*) was the characteristic; and flowers of deep warm colors seem most to love the sandy soil. The impression of the country travelled over to-day was one of dry and barren sands. We turned in toward the river at noon, and gave our·horses two hours for food and rest. I had no other thermometer than the one attached to the· barometer, which stood at 89°, the height of the column in the barometer being 26.235 at meridian. The sky was clear with a high wind from the south.. At two, we continued our journey; the wind had moderated, and it became almost unendurably hot, and our animals suffered severely. In the course of the afternoon, the wind rose suddenly, and blew hard from the southwest, with thunder and lightning, and squalls of rain; these were blown against us with violence by the wind; and, halting, we turned our backs to the storm until it blew over. Antelope were tolerably frequent, with a large gray hare; but the former were shy, and the latter hardly worth the delay of stopping to shoot them; so, as evening drew near, we again had recourse to an old bull, and encamped at sunset on an island of the Platte.

We ate our meat with a good relish this evening, for we were all in fine health, and had ridden nearly all of a long summer's day, with a burning sun reflected from the sands. My companions slept rolled up in their blankets, and the Indians lay in the grass near the fire; but my sleeping-place generally had an air of more pretension. Our rifles were tied together near the muzzle, the butts resting on the ground, and a knife laid on the rope, to cut away in case of an alarm. Over this, which made a kind of frame, was thrown a large india-rubber cloth, which we used to cover our packs. This made a tent sufficiently large to receive about half of my bed, and was a place of shelter for my instruments; and as I was careful always to put this part against the wind, I could lie here with a sensation of satisfied enjoyment, and hear the wind blow, and the rain patter close to my head, and know that I should be at least half dry. Certainly, I never slept more soundly. The barometer at sunset was 26.010, thermometer 81°, and cloudy; but a gale from the west sprang up with the setting sun, and in a few minutes swept away every cloud from the sky. The evening was very fine, and I remained up to take some astronomical observations, which made our position in latitude 40° 51′ 17″, and longitude 103° 07′ 00″.

July 7th.—At our camp this morning, at six o'clock, the barometer was at 26.183, thermometer 69°, and clear, with a light wind from the southwest. The past night had been squally, with high winds, and occasionally a few drops of rain. Our cooking did not occupy much time, and we left camp early. Nothing of interest occurred during the morning; the same dreary barrenness, except that a hard marly clay had replaced the sandy soil. Buffalo absolutely covered the plain on both sides the river, and, whenever we ascended the hills, scattered herds gave life to the view in every direction. A small drove of wild horses made their appearance on the low river bottoms, a mile or two to the left, and I sent off one of the Indians (who seemed very eager to catch one) on my led horse, a spirited and fleet animal. The savage manœuvred a little to get the wind of the horses, in which he succeeded—approaching within a hundred yards without being discovered. The chase for a few minutes was animated and interesting. My hunter easily overtook and passed the hindmost of the wild drove, which the Indian did not attempt to *lasso ;* all his efforts being directed to the capture of the leader. But the strength of the horse, weakened by the insufficient nourishment of grass, failed in a race, and all the drove escaped. We halted at noon on the bank of the river, the barometer at the time being 26.192, and the thermometer 103°, with a light air from the south, and clear weather.

In the course of the afternoon, dust rising among the hills at a particular place attracted our attention ; and, riding up, we found a band of eighteen or twenty buffalo bulls engaged in a desperate fight. Though butting and goring were bestowed liberally and without distinction, yet their efforts were evidently directed against one—a huge gaunt old bull, very lean, while his adversaries were all fat and in good order. He appeared very weak, and had already received some wounds, and, while we were looking on, was several times knocked down and badly hurt, and a very few moments would have put an end to him. Of course we took the side of the weaker party, and attacked the herd ; but they were so blind with rage, that they fought on, utterly regardless of our presence, although on foot and on horseback we were firing in open view within twenty yards of them. But this did not last long. In a very few seconds we created a commotion among them. One or two which were knocked over by the balls, jumped up and ran off into the hills; and they began to retreat slowly along a broad ravine to the river, fighting furiously as they went. By the time they had reached the bottom, we had pretty well dispersed them, and the old bull hobbled off to lie down somewhere. One of his enemies remained on the ground where we had first fired upon them, and we stopped there for a short time to cut from him some meat for our supper. We had neglected to secure our horses, thinking it an unnecessary precaution in their fatigued condition; but our mule took it into his head to start, and away he went, followed at full speed by the pack-horse, with all the baggage and instruments on his back. They were recovered and brought back, after a chase of a mile. Fortunately everything was well secured, so that nothing, not even the barometer, was in the least injured.

The sun was getting low, and some narrow lines of timber four or five miles distant promised us a pleasant camp, where, with plenty of wood for fire, and comfortable shelter, and rich grass for our animals, we should find clear cool springs, instead of the warm water of the Platte. On our arrival, we found the bed of a stream fifty to one hundred feet wide, sunk some thirty feet below the level of the prairie, with perpendicular banks, bordered by a fringe of green cottonwood, but not a drop of water. There were several small forks to the stream, all in the same condition. With the exception of the Platte bottom, the country seemed to be of a clay formation, dry, and perfectly devoid of any moisture, and baked hard by the sun. Turning off toward the river, we reached the bank in about a mile, and were delighted to find an old tree, with thick foliage and spreading branches, where we encamped. At sunset the barometer was at 25.950, thermometer 81°, with a strong wind from S. 20° E., and the sky partially covered with heavy masses of cloud, which settled a little toward the horizon by ten o'clock, leaving it sufficiently clear for astronomical observations, which placed us in latitude 40° 33′ 26″, and longitude 103° 30′ 37″.

July 8th.—The morning was very pleasant. The breeze was fresh from S. 50° E. with few clouds; the barometer at six o'clock standing at 25.970, and the thermometer at 70°. Since leaving the forks, our route had passed over a country alternately clay and sand, each presenting the same naked waste. On leaving camp this morning, we struck again a sandy region, in which the vegetation appeared somewhat more vigorous than that which we had observed for the last few days; and on the opposite side of the river were some tolerably large groves of timber.

Journeying along, we came suddenly upon a place where the ground was covered with horses' tracks, which had been made since the rain, and indicated the immediate presence of Indians in our neighborhood. The buffalo, too, which the day before had been so numerous, were nowhere in sight—another sure indication that there were people near. Riding on, we discovered the carcass of a buffalo recently killed—perhaps the day before. We scanned the horizon carefully with the glass, but no living object was to be seen. For the next mile or two, the ground was dotted with buffalo carcasses, which showed that the Indians had made a sur- round here, and were in considerable force. We went on quickly and cautiously, keeping the river bottom, and carefully avoiding the hills ; but we met with no interruption and began to grow careless again. We had already lost one of our horses, and here Basil's mule showed symptoms of giving out, and finally refused to advance, being what the Canadians call *resté*. He therefore dismounted, and drove her along before him; but this was a very slow way of travelling. We had inadvertently got about half a mile in advance, but our Cheyennes, who were generally a mile or two in the rear, remained with him. There were some dark-look- ing objects among the hills, about two miles to the left, here low and un- dulating, which we had seen for a little time, and supposed to be buffalo coming in to water ; but, happening to look behind, Maxwell saw the Cheyennes whipping up furiously, and another glance at the dark objects showed them at once to be Indians coming up at speed.

Had we been well mounted, and disencumbered of instruments, we might have set them at defiance ; but as it was, we were fairly caught. It was too late to rejoin our friends, and we endeavored to gain a clump of timber about half a mile ahead ; but the instruments and the tired state of our horses did not allow us to go faster than a steady canter, and they were gaining on us fast. At first they did not appear to be more than fifteen or twenty in number, but group after group darted into view at the top of the hills, until all the little eminences seemed in motion, and, in a few minutes from the time they were first discovered, two or three hun- dred, naked to the breech-cloth, were sweeping across the prairie. In a few hundred yards we discovered that the timber we were endeavoring to make was on the opposite side of the river ; and before we could reach the bank, down came the Indians upon us.

I am inclined to think that in a few seconds more the leading man, and, perhaps, some of his companions, would have rolled in the dust ; for we had jerked the covers from our guns, and our fingers were on the triggers ; men in such cases generally act from instinct, and a charge from three hundred naked savages is a circumstance not well calculated to pro- mote a cool exercise of judgment. Just as he was about to fire, Max- well recognized the leading Indian, and shouted to him in the Indian language, " You're a fool, God damn you, don't you know me ? " The sound of his own language seemed to shock the savage, and, swerving his horse a little, he passed us like an arrow. He wheeled, as I rode out toward him, and gave me his hand, striking his breast and exclaiming "Arapahó!" They proved to be a village of that nation among whom Maxwell had resided as a trader a year or two previously, and recognized him accordingly. We were soon in the midst of the band, answering as well as we could a multitude of questions; of which the very first was, of what tribe were our Indian companions who were coming in the rear? They seemed disappointed to know that they were Cheyennes, for they had fully anticipated a grand dance around a Pawnee scalp that night.

The chief showed us his village at a grove on the river six miles ahead, and pointed out a band of buffalo, on the other side of the Platte immediately opposite us, which he said they were going to surround. They had seen the band early in the morning from their village, and had been making a large circuit, to avoid giving them the wind, when they discovered us. In a few minutes the women came galloping up, astride on their horses, and naked from the knees down, and the hips up. They followed the men, to assist in cutting up and carrying off the meat.

The wind was blowing directly across the river, and the chief requested us to halt where we were for a while, in order to avoid raising the herd. We therefore unsaddled our horses, and sat down on the bank to view the scene; and our new acquaintances rode a few hundred yards lower down, and began crossing the river. Scores of wild-looking dogs followed, looking like troops of wolves, and having, in fact, but very little of the dog in their composition. Some of them remained with us, and I checked one of the men, whom I found aiming at one, which he was about to kill for a wolf. The day had become very hot. The air was clear, with a very slight breeze; and now, at twelve o'clock, while the barometer stood at 25.920, the attached thermometer was at 108°. Our Cheyennes had learned that with the Arapaho village were about twenty lodges of their own, including their own families; they therefore immediately commenced making their toilette. After bathing in the river, they invested themselves in some handsome calico shirts, which I afterward learned they had stolen from my own men, and spent some time in arranging their hair and painting themselves with some vermilion I had given them. While they were engaged in this satisfactory manner, one of their half-wild horses, to which the crowd of prancing animals which had just passed had recalled the freedom of her existence among the wild droves on the prairie, suddenly dashed into the hills at the top of her speed. She was their pack-horse, and had on her back all the worldly wealth of our poor Cheyennes, all their accoutrements, and all the little articles which they had picked up among us, with some few presents I had given them. The loss which they seemed to regret most were their spears and shields, and some tobacco which they had received from me. However, they bore it all with the philosophy of an Indian, and laughingly continued their toilette. They appeared, however, a little mortified at the thought of returning to the village in such a sorry plight. "Our people will laugh at us," said one of them, "returning to the village on foot, instead of driving back a drove of Pawnee horses." He demanded to know if I loved my sorrel hunter very much; to which I replied he was the object of my most intense affection. Far from being able to give, I was myself in want of horses; and any suggestion of parting with the few I had valuable, was met with a peremptory refusal. In the meantime the slaughter was about to commence on the other side. So soon as they reached it, the Indians separated into two bodies. One party proceeded directly across the prairie toward the hills in an extended line, while the other went up the river; and instantly as they had given the wind to the herd, the chase commenced. The buffalo started for the hills, but were intercepted and driven back toward the river, broken and running in every direction. The clouds of dust soon covered the whole scene, preventing us from having any but an occasional view. It had a very singular appearance to us at a distance, especially when looking with the glass. We were too far to hear the report of the guns, or any sound; and at every instant through the clouds of dust which the sun made luminous, we could see for a moment two or three buffalo dashing along, and close behind them an Indian with his long spear, or other weapon, and instantly again they disappeared. The apparent silence, and the dimly seen figures flitting by with such rapidity, gave it a kind of dreamy effect, and seemed more like a picture than a scene of real life. It had been a large herd when the *cerne* commenced, probably three or four hundred in number; but, though I watched them closely, I did not see one emerge from the fatal cloud where the work of destruction was going on. After remaining here about an hour, we resumed our journey in the direction of the village.

Gradually, as we rode on, Indian after Indian came dropping along, laden with meat; and by the time we had neared the lodges, the backward road was covered with the returning horsemen. It was a pleasant contrast with the desert road we had been travelling. Several had joined company with us, and one of the chiefs invited us to his lodge. The village consisted of about one hundred and twenty-five lodges, of which twenty were Cheyennes; the latter pitched a little apart from the Arapahoes. They were disposed in a scattering manner on both sides of a broad irregular street, about one hundred and fifty feet wide, and running along the river. As we rode along, I remarked near some of the lodges a kind of tripod frame, formed of three slender poles of birch, scraped very clean, to which were affixed the shield and spear, with some other weapons of a chief. All were scrupulously clean, the spear-head was burnished bright, and the shield white and stainless. It reminded me of the days of feudal chivalry ; and when, as I rode by, I yielded to the passing impulse, and touched one of the spotless shields with the muzzle of my gun, I almost expected a grim warrior to start from the lodge and resent my challenge. The master of the lodge spread out a robe for me to sit upon, and the squaws set before us a large wooden dish of buffalo meat. He had lit his pipe in the meanwhile, and when it had been passed around, we commenced our dinner while he continued to smoke. Gradually five or six other chiefs came in, and took their seats in silence. When we had finished, our host asked a number of questions relative to the object of our journey, of which I made no concealment; telling him simply that I had made a visit to see the country, preparatory to the establishment of military posts on the way to the mountains. Although this was information of the highest interest to them, and by no means calculated to please them, it excited no expression of surprise, and in no way altered the grave courtesy of their demeanor. The others listened and smoked. I remarked that in taking the pipe for the first time, each had turned the stem upward, with a rapid glance, as in offering to the Great Spirit, before he put it in his mouth. A storm had been gathering for the past hour, and some pattering drops on the lodge warned us that we had some miles to go to our camp. Some Indian had given Maxwell a bundle of dried meat, which was very acceptable, as we had nothing ; and springing upon our horses, we rode off at dusk in the face of a cold shower and driving wind. We found our companions under some densely foliaged old trees, about three miles up the river. Under one of them lay the trunk of a large cottonwood, to leeward of which the men had kindled a fire, and we sat here and roasted our meat in tolerable shelter. Nearly opposite was the mouth of one of the most considerable affluents of the South Fork, *la Fourche aux Castors* (Beaver Fork), heading off in the ridge to the southeast.

July 9th.—This morning we caught the first faint glimpse of the Rocky Mountains, about sixty miles distant. Though a tolerably bright day, there was a slight mist, and we were just able to discern the snowy summit of "Long's Peak" ("*les deux oreilles*" of the Canadians), showing like a small cloud near the horizon. I found it easily distinguishable, there being a perceptible difference in its appearance from the white clouds that were floating about the sky. I was pleased to find that among the traders and voyagers the name of "Long's Peak" had been adopted and become familiar in the country. In the ravines near this place, a light brown sandstone made its first appearance. About eight, we discerned several persons on horseback a mile or two ahead, on the opposite side of the river. They turned in toward the river, and we rode down to meet them. We found them to be two white men, and a mulatto named Jim Beckwith, who had left St. Louis when a boy, and gone to live with the Crow Indians. He had distinguished himself among them by some acts of daring bravery, and had risen to the rank of a chief, but had now, for some years, left them. They were in search of a band of horses that had gone off from a camp some miles above, in charge of Mr. Chabonard. Two of them continued down the river, in search of the horses, and the American turned back with us, and we rode on toward the camp. About eight miles from our sleeping-place we reached Bijou's Fork, an affluent of the right bank. Where we crossed it, a short distance from the Platte, it has a sandy bed about four hundred yards broad ; the water in various small streams, a few inches deep. Seven miles farther brought us to a camp of some four or five whites (New Englanders, I believe), who had accompanied Captain Wyeth to the Columbia River, and were independent trappers. All had their squaws with them, and I was really surprised at the number of little fat buffalo-fed boys that were tumbling about the camp, all apparently of the same age, about three or four years old. They were encamped on a rich bottom, covered with a profusion of fine grass, and had a large number of fine-looking horses and mules. We rested with them a few minutes, and in about two miles arrived at Chabonard's camp, on an island in the Platte. On the heights above, we met the first Spaniard I had seen in the country. Mr. Chabonard was in the service of Bent and St. Vrain's company, and had left their fort some forty or fifty miles above, in the spring, with boats laden with the furs of the last year's trade. He had met the same fortune as the voyagers on the North Fork, and, finding it impossible to proceed, had taken up his summer's residence on this island, which he had named St. Helena. The river hills appeared to be composed entirely of sand, and the Platte had lost the muddy character of its waters, and here was tolerably clear. From the mouth of the South Fork, I had found it occasionally broken up by small islands ; and at the time of our journey, which was at a season of the year when the waters were at a favorable stage, it was not navigable for anything drawing six inches water. The current was very swift—the bed of the stream a coarse gravel.

From the place at which we had encountered the Arapahoes, the Platte had been tolerably well fringed with timber, and the island here had a fine grove of very large cottonwoods, under whose broad shade the tents were pitched. There was a large drove of horses in the opposite prairie bottom ; smoke was rising from the scattered fires, and the encampment had quite a patriarchal air. Mr. Chabonard received us hospitably. One of the people was sent to gather mint, with the aid of which he concocted very good julep ; and some boiled buffalo tongue, and coffee with the luxury of sugar, were soon set before us. The people in his employ were generally

Spaniards, and among them I saw a young Spanish woman from Taos, whom I found to be Beckwith's wife.

July 10*th.*—We parted with our hospitable host after breakfast the next morning, and reached St. Vrain's Fort, about forty-five miles from St. Helena, late in the evening. This post is situated on the South Fork of the Platte, immediately under the mountains, about seventeen miles east of Long's Peak. It is on the right bank, on the verge of the upland prairie, about forty feet above the river, of which the immediate valley is about six hundred yards wide. The stream is divided into various branches by small islands, among which it runs with a swift current. The bed of the river is sand and gravel, the water very clear, and here may be called a mountain stream. This region appears to be entirely free from the limestones and marls which give to the Lower Platte its yellow and dirty color. The Black Hills lie between the stream and the mountains, whose snowy peaks glitter a few miles beyond. At the fort we found Mr. St. Vrain, who received us with much kindness and hospitality. Maxwell had spent the last two or three years between this and the village of Taos ; and here he was at home, and among his friends. Spaniards frequently come over in search of employment; and several came in shortly after our arrival. They usually obtain about six dollars a month, generally paid to them in goods. They are very useful in a camp, in taking care of horses and mules ; and I engaged one, who proved to be an active, laborious man, and was of very considerable service to me. The elevation of the Platte here is five thousand four hundred feet above the sea. The neighboring mountains did not appear to enter far the region of perpetual snow, which was generally confined to the northern side of the peaks. On the southern, I remarked very little. Here it appeared, so far as I could judge in the distance, to descend but a few hundred feet below the summits.

I regretted that time did not permit me to visit them ; but the proper object of my survey lay among the mountains farther north ; and I looked forward to an exploration of their snowy recesses with great pleasure. The piney region of the mountains to the south was enveloped in smoke, and I was informed had been on fire several months. Pike's Peak is said to be visible from this place, about one hundred miles to the southward ; but the smoky state of the atmosphere prevented my seeing it. The weather continued overcast during my stay here, so that I failed in determining the latitude, but obtained good observations for time on the mornings of the 11th and 12th. An assumed latitude of 40° 22′ 30″ from the evening position of the 12th, enabled me to obtain, for a tolerably correct longitude, 105° 12′ 12″.

July 12*th.*—The kindness of Mr. St. Vrain had enabled me to obtain a couple of horses and three good mules ; and with a further addition to our party of the Spaniard whom I had hired, and two others, who were go-ing to obtain service at Laramie's Fork, we resumed our journey at ten, on the morning of the 12th. We had been able to procure nothing at the post in the way of provision. An expected supply from Taos had not yet arrived, and a few pounds of coffee was all that could be spared to us. In addition to this, we had dried meat enough for the first day ; on the next, we expected to find buffalo. From this post, according to the estimate of the country, the fort at the mouth of Laramie's Fork, which was our next point of destination, was nearly due north, distant about one hundred and twenty-five miles.

For a short distance, our road lay down the valley of the Platte, which resembled a garden in the splendor of fields of varied flowers which filled the air with fragrance. The only timber I noticed consisted of poplar, birch, cottonwood, and willow. In something less than three miles, we crossed Thompson's Creek, one of the affluents to the left bank of the South Fork—a fine stream, about sixty-five feet wide, and three feet deep. Journeying on, the low dark line of the Black Hills lying between us and the mountains to the left, in about ten miles from the fort we reached *Cache à la Poudre,* where we halted to noon. This is a very beautiful mountain stream, about one hundred feet wide, flowing with a full swift current over a rocky bed. We halted under the shade of some cotton-woods, with which the stream is wooded scatteringly. In the upper part of its course, it runs amid the wildest mountain scenery, and, breaking through the Black Hills, falls into the Platte, about ten miles below this place. In the course of our late journey, I had managed to become the possessor of a very untractable mule—a perfect vixen—and her I had turned over to my Spaniard. It occupied us about half an hour to-day to get the saddle upon her ; but, once on her back, José could not be dis-mounted, realizing the accounts given of Mexican horses and horseman-ship ; and we continued our route in the afternoon.

At evening we encamped on Crow (?) Creek, having travelled about twenty-eight miles. None of the party were well acquainted with the coun-try, and I had great difficulty in ascertaining what were the names of the streams we crossed between the North and South Forks of the Platte. This I supposed to be Crow Creek. It is what is called a salt stream, and the water stands in pools having no continuous course. A fine-grained sandstone made its appearance in the banks. The observations of the night placed us in latitude 40° 42', longitude 104° 57' 49". The barometer at sunset was 25.231 ; attached thermometer at 66°. Sky clear, except in the east, with a light wind from the north.

July 13th.—There being no wood here, we used last night the *bois de vache,* which is very plentiful. At our camp this morning the barometer

was at 25.235 ; the attached thermometer 60°.   A few clouds were moving through a deep-blue sky, with a light wind from the west.   After a ride
of twelve miles, in a northerly direction, over a plain covered with innumerable quantities of *cacti,* we reached a small creek in which there was
water, and where several herds of buffalo were scattered about among the
ravines, which always afford good pasturage.   We seem now to be passing along the base of a plateau of the Black Hills, in which the formation
consists of marls, some of them white and laminated ; the country to the
left rising suddenly, and falling off gradually and uniformly to the right.
In five or six miles of a northeasterly course, we struck a high ridge,
broken into conical peaks, on whose summits large boulders were gathered in heaps.   The magnetic direction of the ridge is northwest and
southeast, the glittering white of its precipitous sides making it visible for
many miles to the south.   It is composed of a soft earthy limestone and
marls, resembling that hereafter described in the neighborhood of the
Chimney rock, on the North Fork of the Platte, easily worked by the
winds and rains, and sometimes moulded into very fantastic shapes.   At
the foot of the northern slope was the bed of a creek, some forty feet
wide, coming, by frequent falls, from the bench above.   It was shut in by
high perpendicular banks, in which were strata of white laminated marl.
Its bed was perfectly dry, and the leading feature of the whole region is
one of remarkable aridity, and perfect freedom from moisture.   In about
six miles we crossed the bed of another dry creek ; and, continuing our
ride over a high level prairie, a little before sundown we came suddenly
upon a beautiful creek, which revived us with a feeling of delighted surprise by the pleasant contrast of the deep verdure of its banks with the
parched desert we had passed.   We had suffered much to-day, both men
and horses, for want of water ; having met with it but once in our uninterrupted march of forty miles, and an exclusive meat diet creates much
thirst.

"*Las bestias tienen mucha hambre,*" said the young Spaniard, inquiringly; "*y la gente tambien,*" said I : "*amigo,* we'll camp here."   A stream
of good and clear water ran winding about through the little valley, and a
herd of buffalo were quietly feeding a little distance below.   It was quite
a hunter's paradise ; and while some ran down toward the band to kill
one for supper, others collected *bois de vache* for a fire, there being no
wood ; and I amused myself with hunting for plants among the grass.

It will be seen, by occasional remarks on the geological formation, that
the constituents of the soil in these regions are good, and every day
served to strengthen the impression in my mind, confirmed by subsequent
observation, that the barren appearance of the country is due almost entirely to the extreme dryness of the climate.   Along our route the country

had seemed to increase constantly in elevation. According to the indication of the barometer, we were at our encampment five thousand four hundred and forty feet above the sea.

The evening was very clear, with a fresh breeze from the south, 50° east. The barometer at sunset was 24.862, the thermometer attached showing 68°. I supposed this to be a fork of Lodge Pole Creek, so far as I could determine from our uncertain means of information. Astronomical observations gave for the camp a longitude of 104° 39′ 37″, and latitude 41° 08′ 31″.

July 14th.—The wind continued fresh from the same quarter in the morning; the day being clear, with the exception of a few clouds in the horizon. At our camp at six o'clock the height of the barometer was 24.830, the attached thermometer 61°. Our course this morning was directly north by compass, the variation being 15° or 16° easterly. A ride of four miles brought us to Lodge Pole Creek, which we had seen at its mouth on the South Fork; crossing on the way two dry streams, in eighteen miles from our encampment of the past night, we reached a high bleak ridge, composed entirely of the same earthy limestone and marl previously described. I had never seen anything which impressed so strongly on my mind a feeling of desolation. The valley, through which ran the waters of Horse Creek, lay in view to the north, but too far to have any influence on the immediate view. On the peak of the ridge where I was standing, some six or seven hundred feet above the river, the wind was high and bleak; the barren and arid country seemed as if it had been swept by fires, and in every direction the same dull ash-colored hue, derived from the formation, met the eye. On the summits were some stunted pines, many of them dead, all wearing the same ashen hue of desolation. We left the place with pleasure; and, after we had descended several hundred feet, halted in one of the ravines, which, at the distance of every mile or two, cut the flanks of the ridge with little rushing streams, wearing something of a mountain character. We had already begun to exchange the comparatively barren lands for those of a more fertile character. Though the sandstone formed the broken banks of the creek, yet they were covered with a thin grass; and the fifty or sixty feet which formed the bottom land of the little stream were clothed with very luxuriant grass, among which I remarked willow and cherry (*Cerasus virginiana*); and a quantity of gooseberry and currant bushes occupied the greater part.

The creek was three or four feet broad, and about six inches deep, with a swift current of clear water, and tolerably cool. We had struck it too low down to find the cold water, which we should have enjoyed nearer to its sources. At two P.M. the barometer was at 25.050, the attached thermometer 104°. A day of hot sunshine, with clouds, and a moderate breeze from the south. Continuing down the stream, in about four miles we reached its mouth, at one of the main branches of Horse Creek. Looking back upon the ridge, whose direction appeared to be a little to the north of east, we saw it seamed at frequent intervals with the dark lines of wooded streams, affluents of the river that flowed so far as we could see along its base. We crossed, in the space of twelve miles from our noon halt, three or four forks of Horse Creek, and encamped at sunset on the most easterly.

The fork on which we encamped appeared to have followed an easterly direction up to this place; but here it makes a very sudden bend to the north, passing between two ranges of precipitous hills, called, as I was informed, Goshen's Hole. There is somewhere in or near this locality a place so called, but I am not certain that it was the place of our encampment. Looking back upon the spot, at the distance of a few miles to the northward, the hills appear to shut in the prairie, through which runs the creek, with a semi-circular sweep, which might very naturally be called a hole in the hills. The geological composition of the ridge is the same which constitutes the rock of the Court-house and Chimney, on the North Fork, which appeared to me a continuation of this ridge. The winds and rains work this formation into a variety of singular forms. The pass into Goshen's Hole is about two miles wide, and the hill on the western side imitates, in an extraordinary manner, a massive fortified place, with a remarkable fulness of detail. The rock is marl and earthy limestone, white, without the least appearance of vegetation, and much resembles masonry at a little distance; and here it sweeps around a level area two or three hundred yards in diameter, and in the form of a half-moon, terminating on either extremity in enormous bastions. Along the whole line of the parapets appear domes and slender minarets, forty or fifty feet high, giving it every appearance of an old fortified town.

On the waters of White River, where this formation exists in great extent, it presents appearances which excite the admiration of the solitary voyageur, and form a frequent theme of their conversation when speaking of the wonders of the country. Sometimes it offers the perfectly illusive appearance of a large city, with numerous streets and magnificent buildings, among which the Canadians never fail to see their *cabaret;* and sometimes it takes the form of a solitary house, with many large chambers, into which they drive their horses at night, and sleep in these natural defences perfectly secure from any attack of prowling savages. Before reaching our camp at Goshen's Hole, in crossing the immense detritus at the foot of the Castle Rock, we were involved amid winding passages cut by the waters of the hill; and where, with a breadth scarcely large enough

FORT LARAMIE.

for the passage of a horse, the walls rise thirty and forty feet perpendicularly. This formation supplies the discoloration of the Platte. At sunset, the height of the mercurial column was 25.500, the attached thermometer 80°, and wind moderate from S. 38° E. Clouds covered the sky with the rise of the moon, but I succeeded in obtaining the usual astronomical observations, which placed us in latitude 41° 40′ 13″, and longitude 104° 24′ 36″.

July 15*th.*—At six this morning the barometer was at 25.515, the thermometer 72°; the day was fine, with some clouds looking dark on the south, with a fresh breeze from the same quarter. We found that in our journey across the country we had kept too much to the eastward. This morning, accordingly, we travelled by compass some 15° or 20° to the west of north, and struck the Platte some thirteen miles below Fort Laramie. The day was extremely hot, and among the hills the wind seemed to have just issued from an oven. Our horses were much distressed, as we had travelled hard, and it was with some difficulty that they were all brought to the Platte; which we reached at one o'clock. In riding in toward the river, we found the trail of our carts, which appeared to have passed a day or two since.

After having allowed our animals two hours for food and repose, we resumed our journey, and toward the close of the day came in sight of Laramie's Fork. Issuing from the river hills, we came first in view of Fort Platte, a post belonging to Messrs. Sybille, Adams & Co., situated immediately in the point of land at the junction of Laramie with the Platte. Like the post we had visited on the South Fork, it was built of earth, and still unfinished, being enclosed with walls (or rather houses) on three of the sides, and open on the fourth to the river. A few hundred yards brought us in view of the post of the American Fur Company, called Fort John, or Laramie. This was a large post, having more the air of military construction than the fort at the mouth of the river. It is on the left bank, on a rising ground some twenty-five feet above the water; and its lofty walls, white-washed and picketed, with the large bastions at the angles, gave it quite an imposing appearance in the uncertain light of evening. A cluster of lodges, which the language told us belonged to Sioux Indians, was pitched under the walls, and, with the fine background of the Black Hills and the prominent peak of Laramie Mountain, strongly drawn in the clear light of the western sky where the sun had already set, the whole formed at the moment a strikingly beautiful picture. From the company at St. Louis I had letters for Mr. Boudeau, the gentleman in charge of the post, by whom I was received with great hospitality and an efficient kindness, which was invaluable to me during my stay in the country. I found our people encamped on the bank, a short distance above the fort.

All were well : and in the enjoyment of a bountiful supper, which coffee and bread made luxurious to us, we soon forgot the fatigues of the last ten days.

July 16*th.*—I found that, during my absence, the situation of affairs had undergone some change ; and the usual quiet and somewhat monotonous regularity of the camp had given place to excitement and alarm. The circumstances which occasioned this change will be found narrated in the following extract from the journal of Mr. Preuss, which commences with the day of our separation on the South Fork of the Platte.

"*July* 6*th.*—We crossed the plateau or high land between the two forks in about six hours. I let my horse go as slow as he liked, to indemnify us both for the previous hardship ; and about noon we reached the North Fork. There was no sign that our party had passed ; we rode, therefore, to some pine-trees, unsaddled the horses, and stretched our limbs on the grass, awaiting the arrival of our company. After remaining here two hours, my companion became impatient, mounted his horse again, and rode off down the river to see if he could discover our people. I felt so *marode* yet, that it was a horrible idea to me to bestride that saddle again ; so I lay still. I knew they could not come any other way, and then my companion, one of the best men of the company, would not abandon me. The sun went down ; he did not come. Uneasy I did not feel, but very hungry ; I had no provisions, but I could make a fire ; and, as I espied two doves in a tree, I tried to kill one ; but it needs a better marks man than myself to kill a little bird with a rifle. I made a large fire, however, lighted my pipe—this true friend of mine in every emergency—lay down, and let my thoughts wander to the far east. It was not many minutes after when I heard the tramp of a horse, and my faithful companion was by my side. He had found the party, who had been delayed by making their *cache*, about seven miles below. To the good supper which he brought with him I did ample justice. He had forgotten salt, and I tried the soldier's substitute in time of war, and used gunpowder ; but it answered badly—bitter enough, but no flavor of kitchen salt. I slept well ; and was only disturbed by two owls, which were attracted by the fire, and took their place in the tree under which we slept. Their music seemed as disagreeable to my companion as to myself; he fired his rifle twice, and then they let us alone.

"*July* 7*th.*—At about ten o'clock, the party arrived ; and we continued our journey through a country which offered but little to interest the traveller. The soil was much more sandy than in the valley below the confluence of the forks, and the face of the country no longer presented the refreshing green which had hitherto characterized it. The rich grass was now found only in dispersed spots, on low grounds, and on the bottom land of the streams. A long drought, joined to extreme heat, had so parched the upper prairies, that they were in many places bald or covered only with a thin growth of yellow and poor grass. The nature of the soil renders it extremely susceptible to the vicissitudes of the climate. Between the forks, and from their junction to the Black Hills, the formation consists of marl and a soft earthy limestone, with granitic sandstone. Such a formation cannot give rise to a sterile soil ; and on our return in September, when the country had been watered by frequent rains, the valley of the Platte looked like a garden : so rich was the verdure of the grasses, and so luxuriant the bloom of abundant flowers. The wild sage begins to make its appearance, and timber is so scarce that we generally made our fires of the *bois de vache.* With the exception of now and then an isolated tree or two, standing like a light-house on the river bank, there is none whatever to be seen.

" *July 8th.*—Our road to-day was a solitary one. No game made its appearance—not even a buffalo or a stray antelope ; and nothing occurred to break the monotony until about five o'clock, when the caravan made a sudden halt. There was a galloping in of scouts and horsemen from every side—a hurrying to and fro in noisy confusion ; rifles were taken from their cover ; bullet-pouches examined : in short, there was the cry of ' Indians ' heard again. I had become so much accustomed to these alarms, that now they made but little impression on me ; and before I had time to become excited the new-comers were ascertained to be whites. It was a large party of traders and trappers, conducted by Mr. Bridger, a man well known in the history of the country. As the sun was low, and there was a fine grass patch not far ahead, they turned back and encamped for the night with us.

" Mr. Bridger was invited to supper ; and, after the *table-cloth* was removed, we listened with eager interest to an account of their adventures. What they had met we would be likely to encounter ; the chances which had befallen them would probably happen to us ; and we looked upon their life as a picture of our own. He informed us that the condition of the country had become exceedingly dangerous. The Sioux, who had been badly disposed, had broken out into open hostility, and in the preceding autumn his party had encountered them in a severe engagement, in which a number of lives had been lost on both sides. United with the Cheyenne and Gros Ventre Indians, they were scouring the upper country in war parties of great force, and were at this time in the neighborhood of the *Red Buttes*, a famous landmark, which was directly on our path. They had declared war upon every living thing which should be found westward of that point ; though their main object was to attack a large camp of whites and Snake Indians who had a rendezvous in the Sweet Water

Valley.   Availing himself of his intimate knowledge of the country, he had reached Laramie by an unusual route through the Black Hills, and avoided coming into contact with any of the scattered parties.

" This gentleman offered his services to accompany us so far as the head of the Sweet Water ; but the absence of our leader, which was deeply regretted by us all, rendered it impossible for us to enter upon such arrangement.   In a camp consisting of men whose lives had been spent in this country, I expected to find every one prepared for occurrences of this nature ; but, to my great surprise, I found, on the contrary, that this news had thrown them all into the greatest consternation, and on every side I heard only one exclamation, '*Il n'y aura pas de vie pour nous.*'   All the night scattered groups were assembled around the fires, smoking their pipes, and listening with the greatest eagerness to exaggerated details of Indian hostilities ; and in the morning I found the camp dispirited, and agitated by a variety of conflicting opinions.   A majority of the people were strongly disposed to return ; but Clément Lambert, with some five or six others, professed their determination to follow Mr. Frémont to the uttermost limit of his journey.   The others yielded to their remonstrances, and, somewhat ashamed of their cowardice, concluded to advance at least so far as Laramie Fork, eastward of which they were aware no danger was to be apprehended.

" Notwithstanding the confusion and excitement, we were very early on the road, as the days were extremely hot, and we were anxious to profit by the freshness of the morning.   The soft marly formation, over which we were now journeying, frequently offers to the traveller views of remarkable and picturesque beauty.   To several of these localities, where the winds and the rain have worked the bluffs into curious shapes, the voyageurs have given names according to some fancied resemblance.   One of these, called the *Court-house,* we passed about six miles from our encampment of last night, and toward noon came in sight of the celebrated *Chimney Rock.* It looks, at this distance of about thirty miles, like what it is called—the long chimney of a steam-factory establishment, or a shot-tower in Baltimore.   Nothing occurred to interrupt the quiet of the day, and we encamped on the river after a march of twenty-four miles.   Buffalo had become very scarce, and but one cow had been killed, of which the meat had been cut into thin slices and hung around the carts to dry.

" *July 10th.*—We continued along the same fine plainly beaten road, which the smooth surface of the country afforded us for a distance of six hundred and thirty miles, from the frontiers of Missouri to the Laramie Fork.   In the course of the day we met some whites, who were following along in the train of Mr. Bridger ; and, after a day's journey of twenty-four miles, encamped about sunset at the Chimney Rock, of which

CHIMNEY ROCK.

the accompanying sketch will render any description unnecessary. It consists of marl and earthy limestone, and the weather is rapidly diminishing its height, which is now not more than two hundred feet above the river. Travellers who visited it some years since placed its height at upward of five hundred feet.

"*July* 11*th*.—The valley of the North Fork is of a variable breadth, from one to four, and sometimes six miles. Fifteen miles from the Chimney Rock we reached one of those places where the river strikes the bluffs, and forces the road to make a considerable circuit over the uplands. This presented an escarpment on the river of about nine hundred yards in length, and is familiarly known as Scott's Bluffs. We had made a journey of thirty miles before we again struck the river, at a place where some scanty grass afforded an insufficient pasturage to our animals. About twenty miles from the Chimney Rock we had found a very beautiful spring of excellent and cold water; but it was in such a deep ravine, and so small, that the animals could not profit by it, and we therefore halted only a few minutes, and found a resting-place ten miles farther on. The plain between Scott's Bluffs and Chimney Rock was almost entirely covered with drift-wood, consisting principally of cedar, which, we were informed, had been supplied from the Black Hills, in a flood five or six years since.

"*July* 12*th*.—Nine miles from our encampment of yesterday we crossed Horse Creek, a shallow stream of clear water, about seventy yards wide, falling into the Platte on the right bank. It was lightly timbered, and great quantities of drift-wood were piled up on the banks, appearing to be supplied by the creek from above. After a journey of twenty-six miles, we encamped on a rich bottom which afforded fine grass to our animals. Buffalo have entirely disappeared and we live now upon the dried meat, which is exceedingly poor food. The marl and earthy limestone which constituted the formation for several days past had changed during the day into a compact white or grayish-white limestone, sometimes containing hornstone; and at the place of our encampment this evening some strata in the river-hills cropped out to the height of thirty or forty feet, consisting of a fine-grained granitic sandstone, one of the strata closely resembling gneiss.

"*July* 13*th*.—To-day, about four o'clock, we reached Fort Laramie, where we were cordially received; we pitched our camp a little above the fort, on the bank of Laramie River, in which the pure and clear water of the mountain-stream looked refreshingly cool, and made a pleasant contrast to the muddy, yellow waters of the Platte."

I walked up to visit our friends at the fort, which is a quadrangular structure, built of clay, after the fashion of the Mexicans, who are generally employed in building them.   The walls are about fifteen feet high, surmounted with a wooden palisade, and form a portion of ranges of houses which entirely surround a yard of about one hundred and thirty feet square.   Every apartment has its door and window—all, of course, opening on the inside.   There are two entrances, opposite each other and midway the wall, one of which is a large and public entrance, the other smaller and more private—a sort of postern gate.   Over the great entrance is a square tower with loop-holes, and, like the rest of the work, built of earth.   At two of the angles, and diagonally opposite each other, are large square bastions, so arranged as to sweep the four faces of the walls.

This post belongs to the American Fur Company, and, at the time of our visit, was in charge of Mr. Boudeau.   Two of the company's clerks, Messrs. Galpin and Kellogg, were with him, and he had in the fort about sixteen men.   As usual, these had found wives among the Indian squaws; and, with the usual accompaniment of children, the place had quite a populous appearance.   It is hardly necessary to say that the object of the establishment is trade with the neighboring tribes, who, in the course of the year, generally make two or three visits to the fort.   In addition to this, traders, with a small outfit, are constantly kept among them.   The articles of trade consist, on the one side, almost entirely of buffalo-robes; and, on the other, of blankets, calicoes, guns, powder, and lead, with such cheap ornaments as glass-beads, looking-glasses, rings, vermilion for painting, tobacco, and principally, and in spite of the prohibition, of spirits, brought into the country in the form of alcohol and diluted with water before sold.

While mentioning this fact, it is but justice to the American Fur Company to state that, throughout the country, I have always found them strenuously opposed to the introduction of spirituous liquors.   But, in the present state of things, when the country is supplied with alcohol, when a keg of it will purchase from an Indian everything he possesses—his furs, his lodge, his horses, and even his wife and children—and when any vagabond who has money enough to purchase a mule can go into a village and trade against them successfully, without withdrawing entirely from the trade it is impossible for them to discontinue its use.   In their opposition to this practice the company is sustained, not only by their obligation to the laws of the country and the welfare of the Indians, but clearly, also, on grounds of policy; for, with heavy and expensive outfits, they contend at manifestly great disadvantage against the numerous independent and unlicensed traders who enter the country from various avenues, from the United States and from Mexico, having no other stock in trade than some kegs of liquor, which they sell at the modest price of thirty-six dollars the gallon.   The difference between the regular trader and the *coureur des bois* (as the French call the itinerant or peddling traders), with respect to the sale of spirits, is here, as it always has been, fixed and permanent, and growing out of the nature of their trade. The regular trader looks ahead, and has an interest in the preservation of the Indians and in the regular pursuit of their business, and the preservation of their arms, horses, and everything necessary to their future and permanent success in hunting; the *coureur des bois* has no permanent interest, and gets what he can and for what he can, from every Indian he meets even at the risk of disabling him from doing anything more at hunting.

The fort had a very cool and clean appearance. The great entrance in which I found the gentlemen assembled, and which was floored, and about fifteen feet long, made a pleasant, shaded seat, through which the breeze swept constantly; for this country is famous for high winds. In the course of conversation I learned the following particulars, which will explain the condition of the country.

For several years the Cheyennes and Sioux had gradually become more and more hostile to the whites, and in the latter part of August, 1841, had had a rather severe engagement with a party of sixty men under the command of Mr. Frapp, of St. Louis. The Indians lost eight or ten warriors, and the whites had their leader and four men killed. This fight took place on the waters of Snake River; and it was this party, on their return under Mr. Bridger, which had spread so much alarm among my people. In the course of the spring, two other small parties had been cut off by the Sioux —one on their return from the Crow nation, and the other among the Black Hills. The emigrants to Oregon and Mr. Bridger's party met here, a few days before our arrival. Division and misunderstandings had grown up among the emigrants; they were already somewhat disheartened by the fatigue of their long and wearisome journey, and the feet of their cattle had become so much worn as to be scarcely able to travel. In this situation they were not likely to find encouragement in the hostile attitude of the Indians, and the new and unexpected difficulties which sprang up before them. They were told that the country was entirely swept of grass, and that few or no buffalo were to be found on their line of route; and, with their weakened animals, it would be impossible for them to transport their heavy wagons over the mountain.

Under these circumstances, they disposed of their wagons and cattle at the forts; selling them at the prices they had paid in the States, and taking in exchange coffee and sugar at one dollar a pound and miserable worn-out horses which died before they reached the mountains. Mr. Boudeau informed me that he had purchased thirty, and the lower fort eighty, head of fine cattle, some of them of the Durham breed.

Mr. Fitzpatrick, whose name and high reputation are familiar to all who interest themselves in the history of this country, had reached Laramie in company with Mr. Bridger; and the emigrants were fortunate enough to obtain his services to guide them as far as the British post of Fort Hall, about two hundred and fifty miles beyond the South Pass of the mountains. They had started for this post on July 4th, and, immediately after their departure, a war party of three hundred and fifty braves set out upon their trail. As their principal chief or partisan had lost some relations in the recent fight, and had sworn to kill the first whites on his path, it was supposed that their intention was to attack the party should a favorable opportunity offer; or, if they were foiled in their principal object by the vigilance of Mr. Fitzpatrick, content themselves with stealing horses and cutting off stragglers.

These had been gone but a few days previous to our arrival.

The effect of the engagement with Mr. Frapp had been greatly to irritate the hostile spirit of the savages; and immediately subsequent to that event the Gros Ventre Indians had united with the Oglallahs and Cheyennes, and taken the field in great force—so far as I could ascertain, to the amount of eight hundred lodges. Their object was to make an attack on a camp of Snake and Crow Indians and a body of about one hundred whites, who had made a rendezvous somewhere in the Green River Valley or on the Sweet Water. After spending some time in buffalo-hunting in the neighborhood of the Medicine Bow Mountain, they were to cross over to the Green River waters, and return to Laramie by way of the South Pass and the Sweet Water Valley. According to the calculation of the Indians, Mr. Boudeau informed me they were somewhere near the head of the Sweet Water.

I subsequently learned that the party led by Mr. Fitzpatrick were overtaken by their pursuers near Rock Independence, in the valley of the Sweet Water; but his skill and resolution saved them from surprise, and, small as his force was, they did not venture to attack him openly. Here they lost one of their party by an accident, and, continuing up the valley, they came suddenly upon the large village. From these they met with a doubtful reception. Long residence and familiar acquaintance had given to Mr. Fitzpatrick great personal influence among them, and a portion of them were disposed to let him pass quietly; but by far the greater number were inclined to hostile measures, and the chiefs spent the whole of one night, during which they kept the little party in the midst of them, in council, debating the question of attacking them the next day; but the influence of "The Broken Hand," as they called Mr. Fitzpatrick (one of his hands having been shattered by the bursting of a gun), at length prevailed, and obtained for them an unmolested passage; but they sternly assured him that this path was no longer open, and that any party of whites which should hereafter be found upon it would meet with certain destruction.

From all that I have been able to learn, I have no doubt that the emigrants owe their lives to Mr. Fitzpatrick.

Thus it would appear that the country was swarming with scattered war parties; and when I heard, during the day, the various contradictory and exaggerated rumors which were incessantly repeated to them, I was not surprised that so much alarm prevailed among my men. Carson, one of the best and most experienced mountaineers, fully supported the opinion given by Bridger of the dangerous state of the country, and openly expressed his conviction that we could not escape without some sharp encounters with the Indians. In addition to this, he made his will; and among the circumstances which were constantly occurring to increase their alarm, this was the most unfortunate; and I found that a number of my party had become so much intimidated that they had requested to be discharged at this place. I dined to-day at Fort Platte, which has been mentioned as situated at the junction of Laramie River with the Nebraska. Here I heard a confirmation of the statements given above. The party of warriors which had started a few days since on the trail of the emigrants was expected back in fourteen days, to join the village with which their families and the old men had remained. The arrival of the latter was hourly expected; and some Indians have just come in who had left them on the Laramie Fork, about twenty miles above. Mr. Bissonette, one of the traders belonging to Fort Platte, urged the propriety of taking with me an interpreter and two or three old men of the village, in which case he thought there would be little or no hazard in encountering any of the war parties. The principal danger was in being attacked before they should know who we were.

These Indians had a confused idea of the numbers and power of our people, and dreaded to bring upon themselves the military force of the United States. Mr. Bissonette who spoke the language fluently, offered his services to accompany me so far as the Red Buttes. He was desirous to join the large party on its return, for purposes of trade, and it would suit his views, as well as my own, to go with us to the Buttes; beyond which point it would be impossible to prevail on a Sioux to venture, on account of their fear of the Crows. From Fort Laramie to the Red Buttes, by the ordinary road, is one hundred and thirty-five miles; and, though only on the threshold of danger, it seemed better to secure the services of an interpreter for the partial distance than to have none at all.

So far as frequent interruption from the Indians would allow, we occupied ourselves in making some astronomical calculations and bringing up the general map to this stage of our journey; but the tent was generally occupied by a succession of our ceremonious visitors. Some came for presents, and others for information of our object in coming to the country;

now and then one would dart up to the tent on horseback, jerk the trappings from his horse, and stand silently at the door, holding him by the halter, signifying his desire to trade him.   Occasionally a savage would stalk in with an invitation to a feast of honor—a dog-feast—and deliberately sit down and wait quietly until I was ready to accompany him.   I went to one; the women and children were sitting outside the lodge, and we took our seats on buffalo-robes spread around.   The dog was in a large pot over the fire, in the middle of the lodge, and immediately on our arrival was dished up in large wooden bowls, one of which was handed to each. The flesh appeared very glutinous, with something of the flavor and appearance of mutton.   Feeling something move behind me, I looked round and found that I had taken my seat among a litter of fat young puppies. Had I been nice in such matters the prejudices of civilization might have interfered with my tranquillity ; but, fortunately, I am not of delicate nerves, and continued quietly to empty my platter.

The weather was cloudy at evening, with a moderate south wind, and the thermometer, at six o'clock, 85°.   I was disappointed in my hope of obtaining an observation of an occultation which took place about midnight. The moon brought with her heavy banks of clouds, through which she scarcely made her appearance during the night.

The morning of the 18th was cloudy and calm, the thermometer at six o'clock at 64°.   About nine, with a moderate wind from the west, a storm of rain came on, accompanied by sharp thunder and lightning, which lasted about an hour.   During the day the expected village arrived, consisting principally of old men, women, and children.   They had a considerable number of horses, and large troops of dogs.   Their lodges were pitched near the fort, and our camp was constantly crowded with Indians, of all sizes, from morning until night, at which time some of the soldiers generally came to drive them all off to the village.   My tent was the only place which they respected.   Here only came the chiefs and men of distinction, and generally one of them remained to drive away the women and children.   The numerous strange instruments, applied to still stranger uses, excited awe and admiration among them, and those which I used in talking with the sun and stars they looked upon with especial reverence as mysterious things of " great medicine."   Of the three barometers which I had brought with me thus far successfully, I found that two were out of order, and spent the greater part of the 19th in repairing them—an operation of no small difficulty in the midst of the incessant interruptions to which I was subjected.   We had the misfortune to break here a large thermometer, graduated to show fifths of a degree, which I used to ascertain the temperature of boiling water, and with which I had promised myself some interesting experiments in the mountains.   We had but one remaining on which the graduation extended sufficiently high; and this was too small for exact observations. During our stay here the men had been engaged in making numerous repairs, arranging pack-saddles, and otherwise preparing for the chances of a rough road and mountain travel. All things of this nature being ready, I gathered them around me in the evening, and told them that " I had determined to proceed the next day. They were all well armed. I had engaged the services of Mr. Bissonette as interpreter, and had taken, in the circumstances, every possible means to insure our safety. In the rumors we had heard I believed there was much exaggeration, and then they were men accustomed to this kind of life and to the country; and that these were the dangers of every-day occurrence, and to be expected in the ordinary course of their service. They had heard of the unsettled condition of the country before leaving St. Louis, and therefore could not make it a reason for breaking their engagements. Still, I was unwilling to take with me, on a service of some certain danger, men on whom I could not rely; and as I had understood that there were among them some who were disposed to cowardice, and anxious to return, they had but to come forward at once, and state their desire, and they would be discharged with the amount due to them for the time they had served." To their honor be it said, there was but one among them who had the face to come forward and avail himself of the permission. I asked him some few questions, in order to expose him to the ridicule of the men, and let him go. The day after our departure he engaged himself to one of the forts, and set off with a party for the Upper Missouri. I did not think that the situation of the country justified me in taking our young companions, Messrs. Brant and Benton, along with us. In case of misfortune it would have been thought, at the least, an act of great imprudence, and therefore, though reluctantly, I determined to leave them. Randolph had been the life of the camp, and the *petit garçon* was much regretted by the men, to whom his buoyant spirits had afforded great amusement. They all, however, agreed in the propriety of leaving him at the fort, because, as they said, he might cost the lives of some of the men in a fight with the Indians.

July 21*st.*—A portion of our baggage, with our field-notes and observations, and several instruments, were left at the fort. One of the gentlemen, Mr. Galpin, took charge of a barometer, which he engaged to observe during my absence; and I intrusted to Randolph, by way of occupation, the regular winding up of two of my chronometers, which were among the instruments left. Our observations showed that the chronometer which I retained for the continuation of our voyage had preserved its rate in a most satisfactory manner. As deduced from it, the longitude of Fort Laramie is 7*h.* 01′ 21″, and from lunar distance 7*h.* 01′ 29″; giving for the adopted longitude 104° 47′ 43″. Comparing the barometrical observations made during our stay here, with those of Dr. G. Engelman at St. Louis, we find for the elevation of the fort above the Gulf of Mexico four thousand four hundred and seventy feet. The winter climate here is remarkably mild for the latitude; but rainy weather is frequent, and the place is celebrated for winds, of which the prevailing one is west. An east wind in summer, and a south wind in winter, are said to be always accompanied with rain.

We were ready to depart; the tents were struck, the mules geared up, and our horses saddled, and we walked up to the fort to take the *stirrup-cup* with our friends in an excellent home-brewed preparation. While thus pleasantly engaged, seated in one of the little cool chambers, at the door of which a man had been stationed to prevent all intrusion from the Indians, a number of chiefs, several of them powerful, fine-looking men, forced their way into the room in spite of all opposition. Handing me the following letter, they took their seats in silence:

"FORT PLATTE, Juillet 1, 1842.

"M. FRÉMONT : Les chefs s'étant assemblés présentement me disent de vous avertir de ne point vous mettre en route, avant que le parti de jeunes gens qui est en dehors, soient de retour. De plus, ils me disent qu'ils sont très certains qu'ils feront feu à la première rencontre. Ils doivent être de retour dans sept à huit jours. Excusez si je vous fais ces observations, mais il me semble qu'il est de mon devoir de vous avertir du danger. Même de plus, les chefs sont les porteurs de ce billet, qui vous défendent de partir avant le retour des guerriers.

"Je suis votre obéissant serviteur,
"JOSEPH BISSONETTE,
"Par L. B. CHARTRAIN

"*Les noms de quelques chefs*—Le Chapeau de Loutre, le Casseur de Flèches, la Nuit Noire, la Queue de Bœuf."

"FORT PLATTE, July 1, 1842.

"MR. FRÉMONT : The chiefs having assembled in council, have just told me to warn you not to set out before the party of young men which is now out shall have returned. Furthermore, they tell me that they are very sure they will fire upon you as soon as they meet you. They are expected back in seven or eight days. Excuse me for making these observations, but it seems my duty to warn you of danger. Moreover, the chiefs who prohibit your setting out before the return of the warriors are the bearers of this note.

"I am, your obedient servant,
"JOSEPH BISSONETTE,
"By L. B. CHARTRAIN.

"*Names of some of the chiefs*—The Otter Hat, the Breaker of Arrows, the Black Night, the Bull's Tail."

After reading this, I mentioned its purport to my companions; and, seeing that all were fully possessed of its contents, one of the Indians rose up, and, having first shaken hands with me, spoke as follows:

"You have come among us at a bad time. Some of our people have been killed, and our young men, who are gone to the mountains, are eager to avenge the blood of their relations, which has been shed by the whites. Our young men are bad, and if they meet you they will believe that you are carrying goods and ammunition to their enemies, and will fire upon you. You have told us that this will make war. We know that our great father has many soldiers and big guns, and we are anxious to have our lives. We love the whites, and are desirous of peace. Thinking of all these things we have determined to keep you here until our warriors return. We are glad to see you among us. Our father is rich, and we expected that you would have brought presents to us—horses and guns and blankets. But we are glad to see you. We look upon your coming as the light which goes before the sun; for you will tell our great father that you have seen us, and that we are naked and poor, and have nothing to eat; and he will send us all these things." He was followed by the others to the same effect.

The observations of the savage appeared reasonable; but I was aware that they had in view only the present object of detaining me, and were unwilling I should go farther into the country. In reply, I asked them, through the interpretation of Mr. Boudeau, to select two or three of their number to accompany us until we should meet their people—they should spread their robes in my tent and eat at my table, and on our return I would give them presents in reward of their services. They declined, saying that there were no young men left in the village, and that they were too old to travel so many days on horseback, and preferred now to smoke their pipes in the lodge, and let the warriors go on the war-path. Besides, they had no power over the young men, and were afraid to interfere with them. In my turn I addressed them: "You say that you love the whites; why have you killed so many already this spring? You say that you love the whites, and are full of many expressions of friendship to us; but you are not willing to undergo the fatigue of a few days' ride to save our lives. We do not believe what you have said, and will not listen to you. Whatever a chief among us tells his soldiers to do, is done. We are the soldiers of the great chief, your father. He has told us to come here and see this country, and all the Indians, his children. Why should we not go? Before we came, we heard that you had killed his people, and ceased to be his children; but we came among you peaceably, holding out our hands. Now we find that the stories we heard are not lies, and that you are no longer his friends and children. We have thrown away our bodies, and will not turn back. When you told us that your young men would kill us, you did not know that our hearts were strong, and you did not see the rifles which my young men carry in their hands. We are few, and you are many, and may kill us all; but there will be much crying in your villages, for many of your young men will stay behind, and forget to return with your warriors from the mountains. Do you think that our great chief will let his soldiers die and forget to cover their graves? Before the snows melt again, his warriors will sweep away your villages as the fire does the prairie in the autumn. See! I have pulled down my *white houses*, and my people are ready; when the sun is ten paces higher we shall be on the march. If you have anything to tell us, you will say it soon." I broke up the conference, as I could do nothing with these people; and, being resolved to proceed, nothing was to be gained by delay. Accompanied by our hospitable friends, we returned to the camp. We had mounted our horses, and our parting salutations had been exchanged, when one of the chiefs (the Bull's Tail) arrived to tell me that they had determined to send a young man with us; and if I would point out the place of our evening camp, he should join us there. "The young man is poor," said he; "he has no horse, and expects you to give him one." I described to him the place where I intended to encamp, and, shaking hands, in a few minutes we were among the hills, and this last habitation of whites shut out from our view.

The road led over an interesting plateau between the north fork of the Platte on the right, and Laramie River on the left. At the distance of ten miles from the fort we entered the sandy bed of a creek, a kind of defile, shaded by precipitous rocks, down which we wound our way for several hundred yards to a place where, on the left bank, a very large spring gushes with considerable noise and force out of the limestone rock. It is called "The Warm Spring," and furnishes to the hitherto dry bed of the creek a considerable rivulet. On the opposite side, a little below the spring, is a lofty limestone escarpment, partially shaded by a grove of large trees, whose green foliage, in contrast with the whiteness of the rock, renders this a picturesque locality. The rock is fossiliferous, and, so far as I was able to determine the character of the fossils, belongs to the carboniferous limestone of the Missouri River, and is probably the western limit of that formation. Beyond this point I met with no fossils of any description.

I was desirous to visit the Platte near the point where it leaves the Black Hills, and therefore followed this stream, for two or three miles, to the mouth; where I encamped on a spot which afforded good grass and *prêle* (*equisetum*) for our animals. Our tents having been found too thin to protect ourselves and the instruments from the rains, which in this ele-

SUNSET. UPPER WATERS COLORADO.

vated country are attended with cold and unpleasant weather, I had procured from the Indians at Laramie a tolerably large lodge, about eighteen
feet in diameter, and twenty feet in height.   Such a lodge, when properly
pitched, is, from its conical form, almost perfectly secure against the violent winds which are frequent in this region, and, with a fire in the centre,
is a dry and warm shelter in bad weather.   By raising the lower part so
as to permit the breeze to pass freely, it is converted into a pleasant summer residence, with the extraordinary advantage of being entirely free from
mosquitoes, one of which I have never seen in an Indian lodge.   While
we were engaged very unskilfully in erecting this, the interpreter, Mr.
Bissonette, arrived, accompanied by the Indian and his wife.   She laughed
at our awkwardness, and offered her assistance, of which we were frequently afterward obliged to avail ourselves, before the men acquired sufficient expertness to pitch it without difficulty.   From this place we had a
fine view of the gorge where the Platte issues from the Black Hills, changing its character abruptly from a mountain stream into a river of the plains.
Immediately around us the valley of the stream was tolerably open ; and
at the distance of a few miles, where the river had cut its way through the
hills, was the narrow cleft, on one side of which a lofty precipice of bright
red rock rose vertically above the low hills which lay between us.

July 22d.—In the morning, while breakfast was being prepared, I visited
this place with my favorite man, Basil Lajeunesse.   Entering so far as
there was footing for the mules, we dismounted, and, tying our animals,
continued our way on foot.   Like the whole country, the scenery of the
river had undergone an entire change, and was in this place the most
beautiful I had ever seen.   The breadth of the stream, generally near that
of its valley, was from two to three hundred feet, with a swift current,
occasionally broken by rapids, and the water perfectly clear.   On either
side rose the red precipices, vertical, and sometimes overhanging, two and
four hundred feet in height, crowned with green summits, on which were
scattered a few pines.   At the foot of the rocks was the usual detritus,
formed of masses fallen from above.   Among the pines that grew here,
and on the occasional banks, were the cherry (*Cerasus virginiana*), currants, and grains de bœuf (*Shepherdia argentea*).   Viewed in the sunshine
of a pleasant morning, the scenery was of a most striking and romantic
beauty, which arose from the picturesque disposition of the objects, and the
vivid contrast of colors.   I thought with much pleasure of our approaching descent in the canoe through such interesting places ; and, in the expectation of being able at that time to give to them a full examination, did
not now dwell so much as might have been desirable upon the geological
formations along the line of the river, where they are developed with great
clearness.   The upper portion of the red strata consists of very compact

clay, in which are occasionally seen embedded large pebbles.   Below was a stratum of compact red sandstone, changing a little above the river into a very hard silicious limestone.   There is a small but handsome open prairie immediately below this place, on the left bank of the river, which would be a good locality for a military post.   There are some open groves of cotton-wood on the Platte.   The small stream which comes in at this place is well timbered with pine, and good building-rock is abundant.

If it is in contemplation to keep open the communications with Oregon Territory, a show of military force in this country is absolutely necessary ; and a combination of advantages renders the neighborhood of Fort Lara-mie the most suitable place, on the line of the Platte, for the establishment of a military post.   It is connected with the mouth of the Platte and the Upper Missouri by excellent roads, which are in frequent use, and would not in any way interfere with the range of the buffalo, on which the neigh-boring Indians mainly depend for support.   It would render any posts on the Lower Platte unnecessary ; the ordinary communication between it and the Missouri being sufficient to control the intermediate Indians.   It would operate effectually to prevent any such coalitions as are now formed among the Gros Ventres, Sioux, Cheyennes, and other Indians, and would keep the Oregon road through the valley of the Sweet Water and the South Pass of the mountains constantly open.   A glance at the map which ac-companies this chapter will show that it lies at the foot of a broken and mountainous region, along which, by the establishment of small posts in the neighborhood of St. Vrain's Fort, on the South Fork of the Platte, and Bent's Fort, on the Arkansas, a line of communication would be formed, by good *wagon* roads, with our southern military posts, which would en-tirely command the mountain passes, hold some of the most troublesome tribes in check, and protect and facilitate our intercourse with the neigh-boring Spanish settlements.   The valleys of the rivers on which they would be situated are fertile ; the country, which supports immense herds of buffalo, is admirably adapted to grazing ; and herds of cattle might be maintained by the posts, or obtained from the Spanish country, which al-ready supplies a portion of their provisions to the trading-posts mentioned above.

Just as we were leaving the camp this morning, our Indian came up and stated his intention of not proceeding any farther until he had seen the horse which I intended to give him.   I felt strongly tempted to drive him out of the camp ; but his presence appeared to give confidence to my men, and the interpreter thought it absolutely necessary.   I was, there-fore, obliged to do what he requested, and pointed out the animal, with which he seemed satisfied, and we continued our journey.   I had imagined that Mr. Bissonette's long residence had made him acquainted with the country, and, according to his advice, proceeded directly forward, without attempting to regain the usual road. He afterward informed me that he had rarely ever lost sight of the fort ; but the effect of the mistake was to involve us for a day or two among the hills, where, although we lost no time, we encountered an exceedingly rough road.

To the south, along our line of march to-day, the main chain of the Black or Laramie Hills rises precipitously. Time did not permit me to visit them ; but, from comparative information, the ridge is composed of the coarse sandstone or conglomerate hereafter described. It appears to enter the region of clouds, which are arrested in their course, and lie in masses along the summits. An inverted cone of black cloud (cumulus) rested during all the forenoon on the lofty peak of Laramie Mountain, which I estimated to be about two thousand feet above the fort, or six thousand five hundred above the sea. We halted to noon on the *Fourche Amère*, so called from being timbered principally with the *liard amère* (a species of poplar), with which the valley of the little stream is tolerably well wooded, and which, with large expansive summits, grows to the height of sixty or seventy feet.

The bed of the creek is sand and gravel, the water dispersed over the broad bed in several shallow streams. We found here, on the right bank, in the shade of the trees, a fine spring of very cold water. It will be re-marked that I do not mention, in this portion of the journey, the tempera-ture of the air, sand, springs, etc.—an omission which will be explained in the course of the narrative. In my search for plants I was well rewarded at this place.

CHAPTER V.

With the change in the geological formation on leaving Fort Laramie the whole face of the country has entirely altered its appearance. Eastward of that meridian the principal objects which strike the eye of a traveller are the absence of timber, and the immense expanse of prairie, covered with the verdure of rich grasses, and highly adapted for pasturage. Wherever they are not disturbed by the vicinity of man, large herds of buffalo give animation to this country. Westward of Laramie River the region is sandy and apparently sterile; and the place of the grass is usurped by the *artemisia* and other odoriferous plants, to whose growth the sandy soil and dry air of this elevated region seem highly favorable.

One of the prominent characteristics in the face of the country is the extraordinary abundance of the *artemisias*. They grow everywhere—on the hills, and over the river bottoms, in tough, twisted, wiry clumps; and, wherever the beaten track was left, they rendered the progress of the carts rough and slow. As the country increased in elevation on our advance to the west, they increased in size; and the whole air is strongly impregnated and saturated with the odor of camphor and spirits of turpentine which belongs to this plant. This climate has been found very favorable to the restoration of health, particularly in cases of consumption; and possibly the respiration of air so highly impregnated by aromatic plants may have some influence.

Our dried meat had given out, and we began to be in want of food; but one of the hunters killed an antelope this evening, which afforded some relief, although it did not go far among so many hungry men. At eight o'clock at night, after a march of twenty-seven miles, we reached our proposed encampment on the *Fer-à-Cheval*, or Horse-shoe Creek. Here we found good grass, with a great quantity of *prêle*, which furnished good food for our tired animals. This creek is well timbered, principally with *liard amère*, and, with the exception of Deer Creek, which we had not yet reached, is the largest affluent of the right bank between Laramie and the mouth of the Sweet Water.

July 23d.—The present year had been one of unparalleled drought, and throughout the country the water had been almost dried up. By availing themselves of the annual rise, the traders had invariably succeeded in carrying their furs to the Missouri; but this season, as has already been mentioned, on both forks of the Platte they had entirely failed. The greater number of the springs, and many of the streams, which made halting-places for the voyageurs, had been dried up. Everywhere the soil looked parched and burnt; the scanty yellow grass crisped under the foot, and even the hardiest plants were destroyed by want of moisture. I think it necessary to mention this fact, because to the rapid evaporation in such an elevated region, nearly five thousand feet above the sea, almost wholly unprotected by timber, should be attributed much of the sterile appearance of the country, in the destruction of vegetation, and the numerous saline efflorescences which covered the ground. Such I afterward found to be the case.

I was informed that the roving villages of Indians and travellers had never met with difficulty in finding an abundance of grass for their horses; and now it was after great search that we were able to find a scanty patch of grass, sufficient to keep them from sinking; and in the course of a day or two they began to suffer very much. We found none to-day at noon; and in the course of our search on the Platte, came to a grove of cotton-wood where some Indian village had recently encamped. Boughs of the cotton-wood, yet green, covered the ground, which the Indians had cut down to feed their horses upon. It is only in the winter that recourse is had to this means of sustaining them; and their resort to it at this time was a striking evidence of the state of the country. We followed their example, and turned our horses into a grove of young poplars. This began to present itself as a very serious evil, for on our animals depended altogether the further prosecution of our journey.

Shortly after we had left this place, the scouts came galloping in with the alarm of Indians. We turned in immediately toward the river, which here had a steep high bank, where we formed with the carts a very close barricade, resting on the river, within which the animals were strongly hobbled and picketed. The guns were discharged and reloaded, and men thrown forward, under cover of the bank, in the direction by which the Indians were expected. Our interpreter, who, with the Indian, had gone to meet them, came in, in about ten minutes, accompanied by two Sioux. They looked sulky, and we could obtain from them only some confused

information.   We learned that they belonged to the party which had been
on the trail of the emigrants, whom they had overtaken at Rock Independence, on the Sweet Water.   Here the party had disagreed, and came nigh
fighting among themselves.   One portion were desirous of attacking the
whites, but the others were opposed to it; and finally they had broken up
into small bands, and dispersed over the country.   The greater portion of
them had gone over into the territory of the Crows, and intended to return by way of the Wind River Valley, in the hope of being able to fall
upon some small parties of Crow Indians.   The remainder were returning
down the Platte, in scattered parties of ten and twenty; and those whom
we had encountered belonged to the party who had advocated an attack on
the emigrants.   Several of the men suggested shooting them on the spot;
but I promptly discountenanced any such proceeding.   They further informed me that buffalo were very scarce, and little or no grass to be found.
There had been no rain, and innumerable quantities of grasshoppers had
destroyed the grass.   This insect had been so numerous since leaving
Fort Laramie, that the ground seemed alive with them; and in walking,
a little moving cloud preceded our footsteps.   This was bad news.   No
grass, no buffalo—food for neither horse nor man.   I gave them some
plugs of tobacco, and they went off, apparently well satisfied to be
clear of us; for my men did not look upon them very lovingly, and
they glanced suspiciously at our warlike preparations, and the little ring
of rifles which surrounded them.   They were evidently in a bad humor,
and shot one of their horses when they had left us a short distance.

We continued our march, and, after a journey of about twenty-one
miles, encamped on the Platte.   During the day I had occasionally remarked among the hills the *Psoralea esculenta*, the bread-root of the Indians.   The Sioux use this root very extensively, and I have frequently
met with it among them, cut into thin slices and dried.   In the course of
the evening we were visited by six Indians, who told us that a larger party
was encamped a few miles above.   Astronomical observations placed us in
longitude 104° 59' 59", and latitude 42° 39' 25".

We made the next day twenty-two miles, and encamped on the right
bank of the Platte, where a handsome meadow afforded tolerably good
grass.   There were the remains of an old fort here, thrown up in some
sudden emergency, and on the opposite side was a picturesque bluff of
ferruginous sandstone.   There was a handsome grove a little above, and
scattered groups of trees bordered the river.   Buffalo made their appearance this afternoon, and the hunters came in, shortly after we had encamped, with three fine cows.   The night was fine, and observations gave
for the latitude of the camp, 42° 47' 40".

July 25th.—We made but thirteen miles this day, and encamped about noon in a pleasant grove on the right bank. Low scaffolds were erected, upon which the meat was laid, cut up into thin strips, and small fires kindled below. Our object was to profit by the vicinity of the buffalo, to lay in a stock of provisions for ten or fifteen days. In the course of the afternoon the hunters brought in five or six cows, and all hands were kept busily employed in preparing the meat, to the drying of which the guard attended during the night. Our people had recovered their gayety, and the busy figures around the blazing fires gave a picturesque air to the camp. A very serious accident occurred this morning, in the breaking of one of the barometers. These had been the object of my constant solicitude, and, as I had intended them principally for mountain service, I had used them as seldom as possible; taking them always down at night and on the occurrence of storms, in order to lessen the chances of being broken. I was reduced to one, a standard barometer of Troughton's construction. This I determined to preserve, if possible. The latitude is $42° 51' 35''$, and by a mean of the results from chronometer and lunar distances, the adopted longitude of this camp is $105° 50' 45''$.

July 26th.—Early this morning we were again in motion. We had a stock of provisions for fifteen days carefully stored away in the carts, and this I resolved should only be encroached upon when our rifles should fail to procure us present support. I determined to reach the mountains, if it were in any way possible. In the meantime buffalo were plenty. In six miles from our encampment (which, by way of distinction, we shall call Dried Meat Camp) we crossed a handsome stream, called *La Fourche Boisée*. It is well timbered, and, among the flowers in bloom on its banks, I remarked several *asters*.

Five miles farther we made our noon halt, on the banks of the Platte, in the shade of some cotton-woods. There were here, as generally now along the river, thickets of *hippophaæ*, the *grains de bœuf* of the country. They were of two kinds—one bearing a red berry (the *Shepherdia argentea* of Nuttall); the other a yellow berry, of which the Tartars are said to make a kind of rob.

By a meridian observation, the latitude of the place was $42° 50' 08''$. It was my daily practice to take observations of the sun's meridian altitude; and why they are not given will appear in the sequel. Eight miles farther we reached the mouth of Deer Creek, where we encamped. Here was an abundance of rich grass, and our animals were compensated for past privations. This stream was at this time twenty feet broad, and well timbered with cotton-wood of an uncommon size. It is the largest tributary of the Platte between the mouth of the Sweet Water and the Laramie. Our astronomical obsevations gave for the mouth of the stream a longitude of $106° 08' 24''$, and latitude $42° 52' 24''$.

July 27th.—Nothing worthy of mention occurred on this day ; we travelled later than usual, having spent some time in searching for grass, crossing and recrossing the river before we could find a sufficient quantity for our animals.   Toward dusk, we encamped among some artemisia bushes, two and three feet in height, where some scattered patches of short, tough grass afforded a scanty supply.   In crossing, we had occasion to observe that the river was frequently too deep to be forded, though we always succeeded in finding a place where the water did not enter the carts.   The stream continued very clear, with two or three hundred feet breadth of water, and the sandy bed and banks were frequently covered with large round pebbles.   We had travelled this day twenty-seven miles. The main chain of the Black Hills was here only about seven miles to the south, on the right bank of the river, rising abruptly to the height of eight and twelve hundred feet.   Patches of green grass in the ravines on the steep sides marked the presence of springs, and the summits were clad with pines.

July 28th.—In two miles from our encampment we reached the place where the regular road crosses the Platte.   There was two hundred feet breadth of water at this time in the bed, which has a variable width of eight to fifteen hundred feet.   The channels were generally three feet deep, and there were large angular rocks on the bottom, which made the ford in some places a little difficult.   Even at its low stages this river cannot be crossed at random, and this has always been used as the best ford. The low stage of the waters the present year had made it fordable in almost any part of its course, where access could be had to its bed.

For the satisfaction of travellers, I will endeavor to give some description of the nature of the road from Laramie to this point.   The nature of the soil may be inferred from its geological formation.   The limestone at the eastern limit of this section is succeeded by limestone without fossils, a great variety of sandstone, consisting principally of red sandstone and fine conglomerates.   The red sandstone is argillaceous, with compact white gypsum or alabaster, very beautiful.   The other sandstones are gray, yellow, and ferruginous, sometimes very coarse.   The apparent sterility of the country must therefore be sought for in other causes than the nature of the soil.   The face of the country cannot with propriety be called hilly.   It is a succession of long ridges, made by the numerous streams which come down from the neighboring mountain range.   The ridges have an undulating surface, with some such appearance as the ocean presents in an ordinary breeze.

The road which is now generally followed through this region is, therefore, a very good one, without any difficult ascents to overcome. The principal obstructions are near the river, where the transient waters of heavy rains have made deep ravines with steep banks, which render frequent circuits necessary. It will be remembered that wagons pass this road only once or twice a year, which is by no means sufficient to break down the stubborn roots of the innumerable artemisia bushes. A partial absence of these is often the only indication of the track; and the roughness produced by their roots in many places gives the road the character of one newly opened in a wooded country. This is usually considered the worst part of the road east of the mountains; and, as it passes through an open prairie region, may be much improved, so as to avoid the greater part of the inequalities it now presents.

From the mouth of the Kansas to the Green River valley, west of the Rocky Mountains, there is no such thing as a mountain road on the line of communication.

We continued our way, and about four miles beyond the ford Indians were discovered again; and I halted while a party were sent forward to ascertain who they were. In a short time they returned, accompanied by a number of Indians of the Oglallah band of Sioux. From them we received some interesting information. They had formed part of the great village, which they informed us had broken up, and was on its way home. The greater part of the village, including the Arapahoes, Cheyennes, and Oglallahs, had crossed the Platte eight or ten miles below the mouth of the Sweet Water, and were now behind the mountains to the south of us, intending to regain the Platte by way of Deer Creek. They had taken this unusual route in search of grass and game. They gave us a very discouraging picture of the country. The great drought, and the plague of grasshoppers, had swept it so that scarce a blade of grass was to be seen, and there was not a buffalo to be found in the whole region. Their people, they further said, had been nearly starved to death, and we would find their road marked by lodges which they had thrown away in order to move more rapidly, and by the carcasses of the horses which they had eaten, or which had perished by starvation. Such was the prospect before us.

When he had finished the interpretation of these things, Mr. Bissonette immediately rode up to me, and urgently advised that I should entirely abandon the further prosecution of my exploration. "*Le meilleur avis que je pourrais vous donner, c'est de virer de suite.*" "The best advice I can give you, is to turn back at once." It was his own intention to return, as we had now reached the point to which he had engaged to attend me. In reply, I called up my men, and communicated to them fully the information I had just received. I then expressed to them my fixed determination to proceed to the end of the enterprise on which I had been sent; but as the situation of the country gave me some reason to apprehend that it might be attended with an unfortunate result to some of us, I would leave it optional with them to continue with me or to return.

Among them were some five or six who I knew would remain. We had still ten days' provisions ; and, should no game be found, when this stock was expended, we had our horses and mules, which we could eat when other means of subsistence failed. But not a man flinched from the undertaking. " We'll eat the mules," said Basil Lajeunesse ; and thereupon we shook hands with our interpreter and his Indians, and parted. With them I sent back one of my men, Dumés, whom the effects of an old wound in the leg rendered incapable of continuing the journey on foot, and his horse seemed on the point of giving out. Having resolved to disencumber ourselves immediately of everything not absolutely necessary to our future operations, I turned directly in toward the river, and encamped on the left bank, a little above the place where our council had been held, and where a thick grove of willows offered a suitable spot for the object I had in view.

The carts having been discharged, the covers and wheels were taken off, and, with the frames, carried into some low places among the willows, and concealed in the dense foliage in such a manner that the glitter of the iron-work might not attract the observation of some straggling Indian. In the sand, which had been blown up into waves among the willows, a large hole was then dug, ten feet square and six deep. In the meantime all our effects had been spread out upon the ground, and whatever was designed to be carried along with us separated and laid aside, and the remaining part carried to the hole and carefully covered up. As much as possible, all traces of our proceedings were obliterated, and it wanted but a rain to render our *cache* safe beyond discovery. All the men were now set at work to arrange the pack-saddles and make up the packs.

The day was very warm and calm, and the sky entirely clear, except where, as usual along the summits of the mountainous ridge opposite, the clouds had congregated in masses. Our lodge had been planted, and, on account of the heat, the ground-pins had been taken out, and the lower part slightly raised. Near to it was standing the barometer, which swung in a tripod frame ; and within the lodge, where a small fire had been built, Mr. Preuss was occupied in observing the temperature of boiling water. At this instant, and without any warning, until it was within fifty yards, a violent gust of wind dashed down the lodge, burying under it Mr. Preuss and about a dozen men who had attempted to keep it from being carried away. I succeeded in saving the barometer, which the lodge was carrying off with itself, but the thermometer was broken. We had no others of a high graduation, none of those which remained going higher than 135° Fahrenheit. Our astronomical observations gave to this place, which we named *Cache* Camp, a longitude of 106° 38′ 26″, latitude 42° 50′ 53″.

July 29th.—All our arrangements having been completed, we left the encampment at seven o'clock this morning. In this vicinity the ordinary road leaves the Platte, and crosses over to the Sweet Water River, which it strikes near Rock Independence. Instead of following this road, I had determined to keep the immediate valley of the Platte so far as the mouth of the Sweet Water, in the expectation of finding better grass. To this I was further prompted by the nature of my instructions. To Mr. Carson was assigned the office of guide, as we had now reached a part of the country with which, or a great part of which, long residence had made him familiar. In a few miles we reached the Red Buttes, a famous landmark in this country, whose geological composition is red sandstone, limestone, and calcareous sandstone and pudding-stone.

The river here cuts its way through a ridge; on the eastern side of it are the lofty escarpments of red argillaceous sandstone which are called the Red Buttes. In this passage the stream is not much compressed or pent up, there being a bank of considerable though variable breadth on either side. Immediately on entering, we discovered a band of buffalo. The hunters failed to kill any of them; the leading hunter being thrown into a ravine, which occasioned some delay, and in the meantime the herd clambered up the steep face of the ridge. It is sometimes wonderful to see these apparently clumsy animals make their way up and down the most rugged and broken precipices. We halted to noon before we had cleared this passage, at a spot twelve miles distant from *Cache* Camp, where we found an abundance of grass. So far, the account of the Indians was found to be false. On the banks were willow and cherry-trees. The cherries were not yet ripe, but in the thickets were numerous fresh tracks of the grizzly bear, which are very fond of this fruit. The soil here is red, the composition being derived from the red sandstone. About seven miles brought us through the ridge, in which the course of the river is north and south. Here the valley opens out broadly, and high walls of the red formation present themselves among the hills to the east. We crossed here a pretty little creek, an affluent of the right bank. It is well timbered with cotton-wood in this vicinity, and the absinthe has lost its shrublike character, and becomes small trees six and eight feet in height, and sometimes eight inches in diameter. Two or three miles above this creek we made our encampment, having travelled to-day twenty-five miles. Our animals fared well here, as there is an abundance of grass. The river bed is made up of pebbles, and in the bank, at the level of the water, is a conglomerate of coarse pebbles about the size of ostrich-eggs, and which I remarked in the banks of the Laramie Fork. It is overlaid by a soil of mixed clay and sand, six feet thick. By astronomical observations our position is in longitude 106° 54′ 32″, and latitude 42° 38′.

July 30th.—After travelling about twelve miles this morning, we reached a place where the Indian village had crossed the river. Here were the poles of discarded lodges and skeletons of horses lying about. Mr. Carson, who had never been higher up than this point on the river, which has the character of being exceedingly rugged, and walled in by precipices above, thought it advisable to camp near this place, where we were certain of obtaining grass, and to-morrow make our crossing among the rugged hills to the Sweet Water River. Accordingly, we turned back and descended the river to an island near by, which was about twenty acres in size, covered with a luxuriant growth of grass. The formation here I found highly interesting. Immediately at this island the river is again shut up in the rugged hills, which come down to it from the main ridge in a succession of spurs three or four hundred feet high, and alternated with green, level *prairillons* or meadows, bordered on the river banks with thickets of willow, and having many plants to interest the traveller. The island lies between two of the ridges, three or four hundred yards apart, of which that on the right bank is composed entirely of red argillaceous sandstone, with thin layers of fibrous gypsum. On the left bank, the ridge is composed entirely of silicious pudding-stone, the pebbles in the numerous strata increasing in size from the top to the bottom, where they are as large as a man's head. So far as I was able to determine, these strata incline to the northeast, with a dip of about fifteen degrees. This pudding-stone, or conglomerate formation, I was enabled to trace through an extended range of country, from a few miles east of the meridian of Fort Laramie to where I found it superposed on the granite of the Rocky Mountains, in longitude 109°. From its appearance, the main chain of the Laramie Mountain is composed of this rock; and in a number of places I found isolated hills, which served to mark a former level, which had been probably swept away.

These conglomerates are very friable, and easily decomposed; and I am inclined to think this formation is the source from which was derived the great deposit of sand and gravel which forms the surface rock of the prairie country west of the Mississippi.

Crossing the ridge of red sandstone, and traversing the little prairie which lies to the southward of it, we made in the afternoon an excursion to a place which we have called the Hot Spring Gate. This place has much the appearance of a gate, by which the Platte passes through a ridge composed of a white and calcareous sandstone. The length of the passage is about four hundred yards, with a smooth, green prairie on either side. Through this place the stream flows with a quiet current, unbroken by any rapid, and is about seventy yards wide between the walls, which rise perpendicularly from the water. To that on the right bank, which is the lower, the barometer gave a height of three hundred and sixty feet. Annexed is a view of this place, which will be more particularly described hereafter, as we passed through it on our return.

We saw here numerous herds of mountain sheep, and frequently heard the volley of rattling stones which accompanied their rapid descent down the steep hills. This was the first place at which we had killed any of these animals; and, in consequence of this circumstance, and of the abundance of these sheep or goats (for they are called by each name), we gave to our encampment the name of Goat Island. Their flesh is much esteemed by the hunters, and has very much the flavor of the Alleghany Mountain sheep. I have seen a horn of this animal three feet long and seventeen inches in circumference at the base, weighing eleven pounds. But two or three of these were killed by our party at this place, and of these the horns were small. The use of these horns seems to be to protect the animal's head in pitching down precipices to avoid pursuing wolves—their only safety being in places where they cannot be followed. The bones are very strong and solid, the marrow occupying but a very small portion of the bone in the leg, about the thickness of a rye straw. The hair is short, resembling the winter color of our common deer, which it nearly approaches in size and appearance. Except in the horns, it has no resemblance whatever to the goat. The longitude of this place, resulting from chronometer and lunar distances, and an occultation of ε Arietis, is 107° 13′ 29″, and the latitude 42° 33′ 27″. One of our horses, which had given out, we left to recover strength on the island, intending to take her, perhaps, on our return.

July 31*st.*—This morning we left the course of the Platte, to cross over to the Sweet Water. Our way, for a few miles, lay up the sandy bed of a dry creek, in which I found several interesting plants. Leaving this, we wound our way to the summit of the hills, of which the peaks are here eight hundred feet above the Platte, bare and rocky. A long and gradual slope led from these hills to the Sweet Water, which we reached in fifteen miles from Goat Island. I made an early encampment here, in order to give the hunters an opportunity to procure a supply from several bands of buffalo which made their appearance in the valley near by. The stream here is about sixty feet wide, and at this time twelve to eighteen inches deep, with a very moderate current.

The adjoining prairies are sandy, but the immediate river bottom is a good soil, which afforded an abundance of soft green grass to our horses, and where I found a variety of interesting plants, which made their appearance for the first time. A rain to-night made it unpleasantly cold; and there was no tree here to enable us to pitch our single tent, the poles of which had been left at *Cache Camp.* We had, therefore no shelter except what was to be found under cover of the absinthe bushes, which grew in many thick patches, one or two, and sometimes three feet high.

August 1st.—The hunters went ahead this morning, as buffalo appeared tolerably abundant, and I was desirous to secure a small stock of provisions; we moved about seven miles up the valley, and encamped one mile below Rock Independence. This is an isolated granite rock, about six hundred and fifty yards long, and forty in height. Except in a depression of the summit, where a little soil supports a scanty growth of shrubs, with a solitary dwarf pine, it is entirely bare. Everywhere within six or eight feet of the ground, where the surface is sufficiently smooth, and in some places sixty or eighty feet above, the rock is inscribed with the names of travellers. Many a name famous in the history of this country, and some well known to science, are to be found mixed among those of the traders and of travellers for pleasure and curiosity, and of missionaries among the savages. Some of these have been washed away by the rain, but the greater number are still very legible. The position of this rock is in longitude 107° 26', latitude 42° 29' 36''. We remained at our camp of August 1st until noon of the next day, occupied in drying meat. By observation, the longitude of the place is 107° 25' 23'', latitude 42° 29' 56''.

August 2d.—Five miles above Rock Independence we came to a place called the Devil's Gate, where the Sweet Water cuts through the point of a granite ridge. The length of the passage is about three hundred yards, and the width thirty-five yards. The walls of rock are vertical, and about four hundred feet in height; and the stream in the gate is almost entirely choked up by masses which have fallen from above. In the wall, on the right bank, is a dike of trap-rock, cutting through a fine-grained gray granite. Near the point of this ridge crop out some strata of the valley formation, consisting of a grayish micaceous sandstone, and fine-grained conglomerate, and marl. We encamped eight miles above the Devil's Gate, of which a view is given in the accompanying plate. There was no timber of any kind on the river, but good fires were made of drift-wood, aided by the *bois de vache*.

We had to-night no shelter from the rain, which commenced, with squalls of wind about sunset. The country here is exceedingly picturesque. On either side of the valley, which is four or five miles broad, the mountains rise to the height of twelve and fifteen hundred or two thousand feet. On the south side, the range appears to be timbered, and to-night is luminous with fires—probably the work of the Indians, who have just passed through the valley. On the north, broken and granite masses rise abruptly from the greensward of the river, terminating in a line of broken summits.   Except in the crevices of the rock, and here and there on a ledge or bench of the mountain, where a few hardy pines have clustered together, these are perfectly bare and destitute of vegetation.

Among these masses, where there are sometimes isolated hills and ridges, green valleys open in upon the river, which sweeps the base of these mountains for thirty-six miles.   Everywhere its deep verdure and profusion of beautiful flowers is in pleasing contrast with the sterile grandeur of the rock and the barrenness of the sandy plain, which, from the right bank of the river, sweeps up to the mountain range that forms its southern boundary.   The great evaporation on the sandy soil of this elevated plain, and the saline efflorescences which whiten the ground, and shine like lakes reflecting the sun, make a soil wholly unfit for cultivation.

August 3d.—We were early on the road the next morning, travelling along the upland part of the valley, which is overgrown with artemisia. Scattered about on the plain are occasional small isolated hills.   One of these, which I examined, about fifty feet high, consisted of white clay and marl, in nearly horizontal strata.   Several bands of buffalo made their appearance to-day, with herds of antelope ; and a grizzly bear—the only one we encountered during the journey—was seen scrambling up among the rocks.   As we passed over a slight rise near the river, we caught the first view of the Wind River Mountains, appearing, at this distance of about seventy miles, to be a low and dark mountainous ridge.   The view dissipated in a moment the pictures which had been created in our minds, by many descriptions of travellers, who have compared these mountains to the Alps in Switzerland, and speak of the glittering peaks which rise in icy majesty amidst the eternal glaciers nine or ten thousand feet into the region of eternal snows.   The nakedness of the river was relieved by groves of willows, where we encamped at night, after a march of twenty-six miles ; and numerous bright-colored flowers had made the river bottom look gay as a garden.   We found here a horse, which had been abandoned by the Indians because his hoofs had been so much worn that he was unable to travel ; and, during the night, a dog came into the camp.

August 4th.—Our camp was at the foot of the granite mountains, which we climbed this morning to take some barometrical heights ; and here among the rocks was seen the first magpie.   On our return, we saw one at the mouth of the Platte River.   We left here one of our horses, which was unable to proceed farther.   A few miles from the encampment we left the river, which makes a bend to the south, and, traversing an undulating country, consisting of a grayish micaceous sandstone and fine-grained conglomerates, struck it again, and encamped, after a journey of twenty-five miles.   Astronomical observations placed us in latitude 42° 32′ 30″, and longitude 108° 30′ 13″.

August 5th.—The morning was dark, with a driving rain, and disa-greeably cold. We continued our route as usual; but the weather be-came so bad that we were glad to avail ourselves of the shelter offered by a small island, about ten miles above our last encampment, which was cov-ered with a dense growth of willows. There was fine grass for our ani-mals, and the timber afforded us comfortable protection and good fires. In the afternoon the sun broke through the clouds for a short time, and the barometer at 5 P.M. was at 23.713, the thermometer 60°, with the wind strong from the northwest. We availed ourselves of the fine weather to make excursions in the neighborhood. The river, at this place, is bor-dered by hills of the valley formation. They are of moderate height; one of the highest peaks on the right bank being, according to the barometer, one hundred and eighty feet above the river. On the left bank they are higher. They consist of a fine white clayey sandstone, a white calcareous sandstone, and coarse sandstone or pudding-stone.

August 6th.—It continued steadily raining all the day; but, notwith-standing, we left our encampment in the afternoon. Our animals had been much refreshed by their repose, and an abundance of rich, soft grass, which had been much improved by the rains. In about three miles we reached the entrance of a cañon, where the Sweet Water issues upon the more open valley we had passed over. Immediately at the entrance, and super-imposed directly upon the granite, are strata of compact, calcareous sand-stone and chert, alternating with fine white and reddish-white, and fine gray and red sandstones. These strata dip to the eastward at an angle of about eighteen degrees, and form the western limit of the sand and lime-stone formations on the line of our route. Here we entered among the primitive rocks. The usual road passes to the right of this place; but we wound, or rather scrambled, our way up the narrow valley for several hours. Wildness and disorder were the character of this scenery. The river had been swollen by the late rains, and came rushing through with an impetuous current, three or four feet deep, and generally twenty yards broad. The valley was sometimes the breadth of the stream, and some-times opened into little green meadows, sixty yards wide, with open groves of aspen. The stream was bordered throughout with aspen, beech, and willow; and tall pines grew on the sides and summits of the crags. On both sides the granite rocks rose precipitously to the height of three hun-dred and five hundred feet, terminating in jagged and broken-pointed peaks; and fragments of fallen rock lay piled up at the foot of the preci-pices. Gneiss, mica slate, and a white granite, were among the varieties I noticed. Here were many old traces of beaver on the stream; remnants of dams, near which were lying trees which they had cut down, one and two feet in diameter. The hills entirely shut up the river at the end of

BUFFALO ESCAPING FROM PRAIRIE-FIRES

about five miles, and we turned up a ravine that led to a high prairie, which seemed to be the general level of the country. Hence, to the summit of the ridge, there is a regular and very gradual rise. Blocks of granite were piled up at the heads of the ravines, and small bare knolls of mica slate and milky quartz protruded at frequent intervals on the prairie, which was whitened in occasional spots with small salt lakes, where the water had evaporated, and left the bed covered with a shining incrustation of salt. The evening was very cold, a northwest wind driving a fine rain in our faces ; and at nightfall we descended to a little stream, on which we encamped, about two miles from the Sweet Water. Here had recently been a very large camp of Snake and Crow Indians ; and some large poles lying about afforded the means of pitching a tent, and making other places of shelter. Our fires to-night were made principally of the dry branches of the artemisia, which covered the slopes. It burns quickly, with a clear oily flame, and makes a hot fire. The hills here are composed of hard, compact mica slate, with veins of quartz.

August 7th.—We left our encampment with the rising sun. As we rose from the bed of the creek, the *snow* line of the mountains stretched grandly before us, the white peaks glittering in the sun. They had been hidden in the dark weather of the last few days, and it had been *snowing* on them, while it *rained* in the plains. We crossed a ridge, and again struck the Sweet Water—here a beautiful, swift stream, with a more open valley, timbered with beech and cotton-wood. It now began to lose itself in the many small forks which make its head ; and we continued up the main stream until near noon, when we left it a few miles, to make our noon halt on a small creek among the hills, from which the stream issues by a small opening. Within was a beautiful grassy spot, covered with an open grove of large beech-trees, among which I found several plants that I had not previously seen.

The afternoon was cloudy, with squalls of rain ; but the weather became fine at sunset, when we again encamped on the Sweet Water, within a few miles of the South Pass. The country over which we have passed to-day consists principally of the compact mica slate, which crops out on all the ridges, making the uplands very rocky and slaty. In the escarpments which border the creeks, it is seen alternating with a light-colored granite, at an inclination of 45° ; the beds varying in thickness from two or three feet to six or eight hundred. At a distance, the granite frequently has the appearance of irregular lumps of clay, hardened by exposure. A variety of *asters* may now be numbered among the characteristic plants, and the artemisia continues in full glory ; but *cacti* have become rare, and mosses begin to dispute the hills with them. The evening was damp and unpleasant ; the thermometer, at 10 o'clock, being at 36°, and the grass wet with a heavy dew. Our astronomical observations placed this encampment in longitude 109° 21′ 32″, and latitude 42° 27′ 15″.

Early in the morning we resumed our journey, the weather still cloudy, with occasional rain. Our general course was west, as I had determined to cross the dividing ridge by a bridle-path over the broken country more immediately at the foot of the mountains, and return by the wagon road, two and a half miles to the south of the point where the trail crosses.

About six miles from our encampment brought us to the summit. The ascent had been so gradual that, with all the intimate knowledge possessed by Carson, who had made this country his home for seventeen years, we were obliged to watch very closely to find the place at which we had reached the culminating point. This was between two low hills, rising on either hand fifty or sixty feet. When I looked back at them, from the foot of the immediate slope on the western plain, their summits appeared to be about one hundred and twenty feet above. From the impression on my mind at this time, and subsequently on our return, I should compare the elevation which we surmounted immediately at the pass, to the ascent of the Capitol Hill from the Avenue, at Washington. It is difficult for me to fix positively the breadth of this pass. From the broken ground where it commences, at the foot of the Wind River chain, the view to the southeast is over a champaign country, broken, at the distance of nineteen miles, by the Table Rock; which, with the other isolated hills in its vicinity, seems to stand on a comparative plain. This I judged to be its termination, the ridge recovering its rugged character with the Table Rock. It will be seen that it in no manner resembles the places to which the term is commonly applied—nothing of the gorge-like character and winding ascents of the Alleghany passes in America; nothing of the Great St. Bernard and Simplon Passes in Europe. Approaching it from the mouth of the Sweet Water, a sandy plain, one hundred and twenty miles long, conducts, by a gradual and regular ascent, to the summit, about seven thousand feet above the sea; and the traveller, without being reminded of any change by toilsome ascents, suddenly finds himself on the waters which flow to the Pacific Ocean. By the route we had travelled, the distance from Fort Laramie is three hundred and twenty miles, or nine hundred and fifty from the mouth of the Kansas.

Continuing our march, we reached, in eight miles from the pass, the Little Sandy, one of the tributaries of the Colorado, or Green River of the Gulf of California. The weather had grown fine during the morning, and we remained here the rest of the day, to dry our baggage and take some astronomical observations. The stream was about forty feet wide, and two or three deep, with clear water and a full swift current, over a sandy bed. It was timbered with a growth of low, bushy and dense willows, among which were little verdant spots, which gave our animals fine grass, and where I found a number of interesting plants. Among the neighboring hills I noticed fragments of granite containing magnetic iron. Longitude of the camp was 109° 37' 59", and latitude 42° 27' 34."

August 9th.—We made our noon halt to-day on Big Sandy, another tributary of Green River. The face of the country traversed was of a brown sand of granite materials, the *detritus* of the neighboring mountains. Strata of the milky quartz cropped out, and blocks of granite were scattered about containing magnetic iron. On Sandy Creek the formation was of parti-colored sand, exhibited in escarpments fifty to eighty feet high. In the afternoon we had a severe storm of hail, and encamped at sunset on the first New Fork. Within the space of a few miles, the Wind Mountains supply a number of tributaries to Green River, which are all called the New Forks. Near our camp were two remarkable isolated hills, one of them sufficiently large to merit the name of mountain. They are called the Two Buttes, and will serve to identify the place of our encampment, which the observations of the evening placed in longitude 109° 58' 11", and latitude 42° 42' 46". On the right bank of the stream, opposite to the large hill, the strata which are displayed consist of decomposing granite, which supplies the brown sand of which the face of the country is composed to a considerable depth.

August 10th.—The air at sunrise is clear and pure, and the morning extremely cold, but beautiful. A lofty snow-peak of the mountain is glittering in the first rays of the sun, which has not yet reached us. The long mountain wall to the east, rising two thousand feet abruptly from the plain, behind which we see the peaks, is still dark, and cuts clear against the glowing sky. A fog, just risen from the river, lies along the base of the mountain. A little before sunrise the thermometer was at 35°, and at sunrise 33°. Water froze last night, and fires are very comfortable. The scenery becomes hourly more interesting and grand, and the view here is truly magnificent; but, indeed, it needs something to repay the long prairie journey of a thousand miles. The sun has just shot above the wall, and makes a magical change. The whole valley is glowing and bright, and all the mountain peaks are gleaming like silver. Though these snow-mountains are not the Alps, they have their own character of grandeur and magnificence, and will doubtless find pens and pencils to do them justice. In the scene before us, we feel how much wood improves a view. The pines on the mountain seemed to give it much additional beauty. I was agreeably disappointed in the character of the streams on this side of the ridge. Instead of the creeks which description had led me to expect, I find bold broad streams, with three or four feet water and a rapid current.   The fork on which we are encamped is upward of a hundred feet wide, timbered with groves or thickets of the low willow.

We were now approaching the loftiest part of the Wind River chain ; and I left the valley a few miles from our encampment, intending to penetrate the mountains as far as possible with the whole party.   We were soon involved in very broken ground, among long ridges covered with fragments of granite.   Winding our way up a long ravine, we came unexpectedly in view of a most beautiful lake, set like a gem in the mountains.   The sheet of water lay transversely across the direction we had been pursuing ; and, descending the steep, rocky ridge, where it was necessary to lead our horses, we followed its banks to the southern extremity.   Here a view of the utmost magnificence and grandeur burst upon our eyes.   With nothing between us and their feet to lessen the effect of the whole height, a grand bed of snow-capped mountains rose before us, pile upon pile, glowing in the bright light of an August day.   Immediately below them lay the lake, between two ridges, covered with dark pines which swept down from the main chain to the spot where we stood.   Here, where the lake glittered in the open sunlight, its banks of yellow sand and the light foliage of aspengroves contrasted well with the gloomy pines.   " Never before," said Preuss, " in this country or in Europe, have I seen such magnificent, grand rocks."

I was so much pleased with the beauty of the place that I determined to make the main camp here, where our animals would find good pasturage, and explore the mountains with a small party of men.   Proceeding a little farther, we came suddenly upon the outlet of the lake, where it found its way through a narrow passage between low hills.   Dark pines, which overhung the stream, and masses of rock, where the water foamed along, gave it much romantic beauty.   Where we crossed, which was immediately at the outlet, it is two hundred and fifty feet wide, and so deep that with difficulty we were able to ford it.   Its bed was an accumulation of rocks, boulders, and broad slabs, and large angular fragments, among which the animals fell repeatedly.

The current was very swift, and the water cold and of a crystal purity. In crossing this stream, I met with a great misfortune in having my barometer broken.   It was the only one.   A great part of the interest of the journey for me was in the exploration of these mountains, of which so much had been said that was doubtful and contradictory ; and now their snowy peaks rose majestically before me, and the only means of giving them authentically to science, the object of my anxious solicitude by night and day, was destroyed.   We had brought this barometer in safety a thousand miles, and broke it almost among the snow of the mountains.   The loss was felt by the whole camp—all had seen my anxiety, and aided me in preserving it. The height of these mountains, considered by the hunt-ers and traders the highest in the whole range, had been a theme of con-stant discussion among them; and all had looked forward with pleasure to the moment when the instrument, which they believed to be true as the sun, should stand upon the summits and decide their disputes. Their grief was only inferior to my own.

This lake is about three miles long, and of very irregular width, and apparently great depth, and is the head-water of the third New Fork, a tributary to Green River, the Colorado of the West. On the map and in the narrative I have called it Mountain Lake. I encamped on the north side, about three hundred and fifty yards from the outlet. This was the most western point at which I obtained astronomical observations, by which this place, called Bernier's encampment, is made in 110° 08′ 03″ west lon-gitude from Greenwich, and latitude 42° 49′ 49″. The mountain peaks, as laid down, were fixed by bearings from this and other astronomical points. We had no other compass than the small ones used in sketching the coun-try; but from an azimuth, in which one of them was used, the variation of the compass is 18° east. The correction made in our field-work by the astronomical observations indicates that this is a very correct observation.

As soon as the camp was formed, I set about endeavoring to repair my barometer. As I have already said, this was a standard cistern-barometer of Troughton's construction. The glass cistern had been broken about midway; but as the instrument had been kept in a proper position, no air had found its way into the tube, the end of which had always remained covered. I had with me a number of vials of tolerably thick glass, some of which were of the same diameter as the cistern, and I spent the day in slowly working on these, endeavoring to cut them of the requisite length; but, as my instrument was a very rough file, I invariably broke them. A groove was cut in one of the trees, where the barometer was placed during the night, to be out of the way of any possible danger, and in the morning I commenced again. Among the powder-horns in the camp I found one which was very transparent, so that its contents could be almost as plainly seen as through glass. This I boiled and stretched on a piece of wood to the requisite diameter, and scraped it very thin in order to increase to the utmost its transparency. I then secured it firmly in its place on the instru-ment, with strong glue made from a buffalo, and filled it with mercury properly heated. A piece of skin which had covered one of the vials furnished a good pocket, which was well secured with strong thread and glue, and then the brass cover was screwed to its place. The instrument was left some time to dry; and when I reversed it, a few hours after, I had the satisfaction to find it in perfect order, its indications being about the same as on the other side of the lake before it had been broken. Our success in this little incident diffused pleasure throughout the camp ; and we immediately set about our preparations for ascending the mountains.

As will be seen on reference to a map, on this short mountain chain are the head-waters of four great rivers of the continent ; namely, the Colorado, Columbia, Missouri, and Platte Rivers. It had been my design, after having ascended the mountains, to continue our route on the western side of the range, and, crossing through a pass at the northwestern end of the chain, about thirty miles from our present camp, return along the eastern slope, across the heads of the Yellowstone River, and join on the line to our station of August 7th, immediately at the foot of the ridge. In this way I should be enabled to include the whole chain, and its numerous waters, in my survey; but various considerations induced me, very reluctantly, to abandon this plan.

I was desirous to keep strictly within the scope of my instructions, and it would have required ten or fifteen additional days for the accomplishment of this object; our animals had become very much worn out with the length of the journey ; game was very scarce ; and, though it does not appear in the course of the narrative (as I have avoided dwelling upon trifling incidents not connected with the objects of the expedition), the spirits of the men had been much exhausted by the hardships and privations to which they had been subjected. Our provisions had well-nigh all disappeared. Bread had been long out of the question ; and of all our stock, we had remaining two or three pounds of coffee and a small quantity of macaroni, which had been husbanded with great care for the mountain expedition we were about to undertake. Our daily meal consisted of dry buffalo-meat, cooked in tallow ; and, as we had not dried this with Indian skill, part of it was spoiled ; and what remained of good was as hard as wood, having much the taste and appearance of so many pieces of bark. Even of this, our stock was rapidly diminishing in a camp which was capable of consuming two buffaloes in every twenty-four hours. These animals had entirely disappeared ; and it was not probable that we should fall in with them again until we returned to the Sweet Water.

Our arrangements for the ascent were rapidly completed. We were in a hostile country, which rendered the greatest vigilance and circumspection necessary. The pass at the north end of the mountain was generally infested by Blackfeet ; and immediately opposite was one of their forts, on the edge of a little thicket, two or three hundred feet from our encampment. We were posted in a grove of beech, on the margin of the lake and a few hundred feet long, with a narrow *prairillon* on the inner side, bordered by the rocky ridge. In the upper end of this grove we cleared a circular space about forty feet in diameter, and, with the felled timber and interwoven branches, surrounded it with a breastwork five feet in height.

A gap was left for a gate on the inner side, by which the animals were to be driven in and secured, while the men slept around the little work. It was half hidden by the foliage; and, garrisoned by twelve resolute men, would have set at defiance any band of savages which might chance to discover them in the interval of our absence. Fifteen of the best mules, with fourteen men, were selected for the mountain party. Our provisions consisted of dried meat for two days, with our little stock of coffee and some macaroni. In addition to the barometer and a thermometer, I took with me a sextant and spyglass, and we had, of course, our compasses. In charge of the camp I left Bernier, one of my most trustworthy men, who possessed the most determined courage.

·*August* 12*th*.—Early in the morning we left the camp, fifteen in number, well armed, of course, and mounted on our best mules. A pack-animal carried our provisions, with a coffee-pot and kettle, and three or four tin cups. Every man had a blanket strapped over his saddle, to serve for his bed, and the instruments were carried by turns on their backs. We entered directly on rough and rocky ground; and, just after crossing the ridge, had the good fortune to shoot an antelope. We heard the roar and had a glimpse of a waterfall as we rode along; and, crossing in our way two fine streams, tributary to the Colorado, in about two hours' ride we reached the top of the first row or range of the mountains. Here, again, a view of the most romantic beauty met our eyes. It seemed as if, from the vast expanse of uninteresting prairie we had passed over, nature had collected all her beauties together in one chosen place. We were overlooking a deep valley, which was entirely occupied by three lakes, and from the brink the surrounding ridges rose precipitously five hundred and a thousand feet, covered with the dark green of the balsam-pine, relieved on the border of the lake with the light foliage of the aspen. They all communicated with each other; and the green of the waters, common to mountain lakes of great depth, showed that it would be impossible to cross them. The surprise manifested by our guides when these impassable obstacles suddenly barred our progress proved that they were among the hidden treasures of the place, unknown even to the wandering trappers of the region. Descending the hill, we proceeded to make our way along the margin to the southern extremity. A narrow strip of angular fragments of rock sometimes afforded a rough pathway for our mules, but generally we rode along the shelving side, occasionally scrambling up, at a considerable risk of tumbling back into the lake.

The slope was frequently sixty degrees; the pines grew densely together, and the ground was covered with the branches and trunks of trees. The air was fragrant with the odor of the pines; and I realized, this delightful morning, the pleasure of breathing that mountain air which makes a constant theme of the hunter's praise, and which now made us feel as if we had all been drinking some exhilarating gas. The depths of this unexplored forest were a place to delight the heart of a botanist. There was a rich undergrowth of plants, and numerous gay-colored flowers in brilliant bloom. We reached the outlet at length, where some freshly barked willows that lay in the water showed that the beaver had been recently at work. There were some small brown squirrels jumping about in the pines, and a couple of large mallard ducks swimming about in the stream.

The hills on this southern end were low, and the lake looked like a mimic sea as the waves broke on the sandy beach in the force of a strong breeze. There was a pretty open spot, with fine grass for our mules; and we made our noon halt on the beach, under the shade of some large hemlocks. We resumed our journey after a halt of about an hour, making our way up the ridge on the western side of the lake. In search of smoother ground, we rode a little inland; and, passing through groves of aspen, soon found ourselves again among the pines. Emerging from these, we struck the summit of the ridge above the upper end of the lake.

We had reached a very elevated point, and in the valley below, and among the hills, were a number of lakes at different levels; some two or three hundred feet above others, with which they communicated by foaming torrents. Even to our great height, the roar of the cataracts came up, and we could see them leaping down in lines of snowy foam. From this scene of busy waters we turned abruptly into the stillness of a forest, where we rode among the open bolls of the pines, over a lawn of verdant grass having strikingly the air of cultivated grounds. This led us, after a time, among masses of rock which had no vegetable earth but in hollows and crevices, though still the pine-forest continued. Toward evening we reached a defile, or rather a hole in the mountains, entirely shut in by dark pine-covered rocks.

A small stream, with a scarcely perceptible current, flowed through a level bottom of perhaps eighty yards' width, where the grass was saturated with water. Into this the mules were turned, and were neither hobbled nor picketed during the night, as the fine pasturage took away all temptation to stray; and we made our bivouac in the pines. The surrounding masses were all of granite. While supper was being prepared I set out on an excursion in the neighborhood, accompanied by one of my men. We wandered about among the crags and ravines until dark, richly repaid for our walk by a fine collection of plants, many of them in full bloom. Ascending a peak to find the place of our camp, we saw that the little defile in which we lay communicated with the long green valley of some stream, which, here locked up in the mountains, far away to the south found its way in a dense forest to the plains.

Looking along its upward course, it seemed to conduct, by a smooth gradual slope, directly toward the peak, which, from long consultation as we approached the mountain, we had decided to be the highest of the range. Pleased with the discovery of so fine a road for the next day, we hastened down to the camp, where we arrived just in time for supper. Our table service was rather scant; and we held the meat in our hands, and clean rocks made good plates on which we spread our macaroni. Among all the strange places on which we had occasion to encamp during our long journey, none have left so vivid an impression on my mind as the camp of this evening. The disorder of the masses which surrounded us; the little hole through which we saw the stars overhead; the dark pines where we slept; and the rocks lit up with the glow of our fires—made a night-picture of very wild beauty.

August 13*th.*—The morning was bright and pleasant, just cool enough to make exercise agreeable, and we soon entered the defile I had seen the preceding day. It was smoothly carpeted with a soft grass, and scattered over with groups of flowers of which yellow was the predominant color. Sometimes we were forced, by an occasional difficult pass, to pick our way on a narrow ledge along the side of the defile, and the mules were frequently on their knees; but these obstructions were rare, and we journeyed on in the sweet morning air, delighted at our good fortune in having found such a beautiful entrance to the mountains. This road continued for about three miles, when we suddenly reached its termination in one of the grand views which, at every turn, meet the traveller in this magnificent region. Here the defile up which we had travelled opened out into a small lawn, where, in a little lake, the stream had its source.

There were some fine *asters* in bloom, but all the flowering plants appeared to seek the shelter of the rocks, and to be of lower growth than below, as if they loved the warmth of the soil and kept out of the way of the winds. Immediately at our feet a precipitous descent led to a confusion of defiles, and before us rose the mountains as we have represented them in the annexed view. It is not by the splendor of far-off views, which have lent such a glory to the Alps, that these impress the mind; but by a gigantic disorder of enormous masses, and a savage sublimity of naked rock, in wonderful contrast with innumerable green spots of a rich floral beauty shut up in their stern recesses. Their wildness seems well suited to the character of the people who inhabit the country.

I determined to leave our animals here, and make the rest of our way on foot. The peak appeared so near that there was no doubt of our returning before night, and a few men were left in charge of the mules with our provisions and blankets. We took with us nothing but our arms and instruments, and, as the day had become warm, the greater part left their coats. Having made an early dinner, we started again. We were soon involved in the most rugged precipices, nearing the central chain very slowly, and rising but little. The first ridge hid a succession of others; and when, with great fatigue and difficulty, we had climbed up five hundred feet, it was but to make an equal descent on the other side; all these intervening places were filled with small deep lakes, which met the eye in every direction, descending from one level to another, sometimes under bridges formed by huge fragments of granite, beneath which was heard the roar of the water. These constantly obstructed our path, forcing us to make long *détours;* frequently obliged to retrace our steps, and frequently falling among the rocks. Maxwell was precipitated toward the face of a precipice, and saved himself from going over by throwing himself flat on the ground. We clambered on, always expecting with every ridge that we crossed to reach the foot of the peaks, and always disappointed, until about four o'clock, when, pretty well worn out, we reached the shore of a little lake, in which there was a rocky island, and from which we obtained the view given here. We remained here a short time to rest, and continued on around the lake, which had in some places a beach of white sand, and in others was bound with rocks, over which the way was difficult and dangerous, as the water from innumerable springs made them very slippery.

By the time we had reached the farther side of the lake, we found ourselves all exceedingly fatigued, and, much to the satisfaction of the whole party, we encamped. The spot we had chosen was a broad flat rock, in some measure protected from the winds by the surrounding crags, and the trunks of fallen pines afforded us bright fires. Near by was a foaming torrent, which tumbled into the little lake about one hundred and fifty feet below us, and which, by way of distinction, we have called Island Lake. We had reached the upper limit of the piny region; as, above this point, no tree was to be seen, and patches of snow lay everywhere around us on the cold sides of the rocks. The flora of the region we had traversed since leaving our mules was extremely rich, and, among the characteristic plants, the scarlet flowers of the *Dodecatheon dentatum* everywhere met the eye in great abundance. A small green ravine, on the edge of which we were encamped, was filled with a profusion of alpine plants in brilliant bloom. From barometrical observations, made during our three days' sojourn at this place, its elevation above the Gulf of Mexico is ten thousand feet. During the day, we had seen no sign of animal life; but among the rocks here we heard what was supposed to be the bleat of a young goat, which we searched for with hungry activity, and found to proceed from a small animal of a gray color, with short ears and no tail—probably the Siberian squirrel. We saw a considerable number of them, and, with the exception

WIND RIVER CHAIN.

of a small bird like a sparrow, it is the only inhabitant of this elevated part of the mountains. On our return we saw, below this lake, large flocks of the mountain goat. We had nothing to eat to-night. Lajeunesse, with several others, took their guns and sallied out in search of a goat; but returned unsuccessful. At sunset the barometer stood at 20.522; the attached thermometer, 50°. Here we had the misfortune to break our thermometer, having now only that attached to the barometer. I was taken ill shortly after we had encamped, and continued so until late in the night, with violent headache and vomiting. This was probably caused by the excessive fatigue I had undergone, and want of food, and perhaps, also, in some measure, by the rarity of the air. The night was cold, as a violent gale from the north had sprung up at sunset, which entirely blew away the heat of the fires. The cold, and our granite beds, had not been favorable to sleep, and we were glad to see the face of the sun in the morning. Not being delayed by any preparations for breakfast, we set out immediately.

On every side as we advanced was heard the roar of water, and of a torrent, which we followed up a short distance, until it expanded into a lake about one mile in length. On the northern side of the lake was a bank of ice, or rather of snow covered with a crust of ice. Carson had been our guide into the mountains, and, agreeably to his advice, we left this little valley and took to the ridges again; which we found extremely broken, and where we were again involved among precipices. Here were ice-fields; among which we were all dispersed, seeking each the best path to ascend the peak. Preuss attempted to walk along the upper edge of one of these fields, which sloped away at an angle of about twenty degrees; but his feet slipped from under him, and he went plunging down the plane. A few hundred feet below, at the bottom, were some fragments of sharp rock, on which he landed; and, though he turned a couple of somersets, fortunately received no injury beyond a few bruises. Two of the men, Clément Lambert and Descoteaux, had been taken ill, and lay down on the rocks a short distance below; and at this point I was attacked with headache and giddiness, accompanied by vomiting, as on the day before. Finding myself unable to proceed, I sent the barometer over to Preuss, who was in a gap two or three hundred yards distant, desiring him to reach the peak, if possible, and take an observation there. He found himself unable to proceed farther in that direction, and took an observation where the barometer stood at 19.401; attached thermometer 50°, in the gap. Carson, who had gone over to him, succeeded in reaching one of the snowy summits of the main ridge, whence he saw the peak toward which all our efforts had been directed, towering eight or ten hundred feet into the air above him. In the meantime, finding myself grow rather worse than better, and doubtful how far my strength would carry me, I sent

Basil Lajeunesse, with four men, back to the place where the mules had been left.

We were now better acquainted with the topography of the country, and I directed him to bring back with him, if it were in any way possible, four or five mules, with provisions and blankets. With me were Maxwell and Ayot ; and after we had remained nearly an hour on the rock, it became so unpleasantly cold, though the day was bright, that we set out on our return to the camp, at which we all arrived safely, straggling in one after the other. I continued ill during the afternoon, but became better toward sundown, when my recovery was completed by the appearance of Basil and four men, all mounted. The men who had gone with him had been too much fatigued to return, and were relieved by those in charge of the horses ; but in his powers of endurance Basil resembled more a mountain goat than a man. They brought blankets and provisions, and we enjoyed well our dried meat and a cup of good coffee. We rolled ourselves up in our blankets, and, with our feet turned to a blazing fire, slept soundly until morning.

August 15*th.*—It had been supposed that we had finished with the mountains ; and the evening before it had been arranged that Carson should set out at daylight, and return to breakfast at the Camp of the Mules, taking with him all but four or five men, who were to stay with me and bring back the mules and instruments. Accordingly, at the break of day they set out. With Preuss and myself remained Basil Lajeunesse, Clément Lambert, Janisse, and Descoteaux. When we had secured strength for the day by a hearty breakfast, we covered what remained, which was enough for one meal, with rocks, in order that it might be safe from any marauding bird ; and, saddling our mules, turned our faces once more toward the peaks. This time we determined to proceed quietly and cautiously, deliberately resolved to accomplish our object if it were within the compass of human means. We were of opinion that a long defile which lay to the left of yesterday's route would lead us to the foot of the main peak. Our mules had been refreshed by the fine grass in the little ravine at the Island Camp, and we intended to ride up the defile as far as possible in order to husband our strength for the main ascent. Though this was a fine passage, still it was a defile of the most rugged mountains known, and we had many a rough and steep slippery place to cross before reaching the end. In this place the sun rarely shone ; snow lay along the border of the small stream which flowed through it, and occasional icy passages made the footing of the mules very insecure, and the rocks and ground were moist with the trickling waters in this spring of mighty rivers. We soon had the satisfaction to find ourselves riding along the huge wall which forms the central summits of the chain. There at last it rose by our sides, a nearly perpendicular wall of granite, terminating, from two to three thousand feet above our heads, in a serrated line of broken, jagged cones. We rode on until we came almost immediately below the main peak, which I denominated the Snow Peak, as it exhibited more snow to the eye than any of the neighboring summits. Here were three small lakes of a green color, each of perhaps a thousand yards in diameter, and apparently very deep. These lay in a kind of chasm; and, according to the barometer, we had attained but a few hundred feet above the Island Lake. The barometer here stood at 20.450, attached thermometer, 70°.

We managed to get our mules up to a little bench about a hundred feet above the lakes, where there was a patch of good grass, and turned them loose to graze. During our rough ride to this place, they had exhibited a wonderful surefootedness. Parts of the defile were filled with angular, sharp fragments of rock, three or four and eight or ten feet cube; and among these they had worked their way, leaping from one narrow point to another, rarely making a false step, and giving us no occasion to dismount. Having divested ourselves of every unnecessary encumbrance, we commenced the ascent. This time, like experienced travellers, we did not press ourselves, but climbed leisurely, sitting down so soon as we found breath beginning to fail. At intervals we reached places where a number of springs gushed from the rocks, and about one thousand eight hundred feet above the lakes came to the snow-line. From this point our progress was uninterrupted climbing. Hitherto I had worn a pair of thick moccasons, with soles of *parflèche;* but here I put on a light thin pair, which I had brought for the purpose, as now the use of our toes became necessary to a further advance. I availed myself of a sort of comb of the mountain, which stood against the wall like a buttress, and which the wind and the solar radiation, joined to the steepness of the smooth rock, had kept almost entirely free from snow. Up this I made my way rapidly. Our cautious method of advancing in the outset had spared my strength; and, with the exception of a slight disposition to headache, I felt no remains of yesterday's illness. In a few minutes we reached a point where the buttress was overhanging, and there was no other way of surmounting the difficulty than by passing around one side of it, which was the face of a vertical precipice of several hundred feet.

Putting hands and feet in the crevices between the blocks, I succeeded in getting over it, and, when I reached the top, found my companions in a small valley below. Descending to them, we continued climbing, and in a short time reached the crest. I sprang upon the summit, and another step would have precipitated me into an immense snow-field five hundred feet below. To the edge of this field was a sheer icy precipice; and then, with a gradual fall, the field sloped off for about a mile, until it struck the foot of another lower ridge. I stood on a narrow crest, about three feet in width, with an inclination of about 20° N., 51° E. As soon as I had gratified the first feelings of curiosity I descended, and each man ascended in his turn ; for I would only allow one at a time to mount the unstable and precarious slab, which it seemed a breath would hurl into the abyss below. We mounted the barometer in the snow of the summit, and, fixing a ramrod in a crevice, unfurled the national flag to wave in the breeze where never flag waved before. During our morning's ascent we had met no sign of animal life, except the small sparrow-like bird already mentioned. A stillness the most profound and a terrible solitude forced themselves constantly on the mind as the great features of the place. Here, on the summit, where the stillness was absolute, unbroken by any sound, and the solitude complete, we thought ourselves beyond the region of animated life ; but, while we were sitting on the rock, a solitary bee (*bromus, the humble bee*) came winging his flight from the eastern valley, and lit on the knee of one of the men.

It was a strange place, the icy rock and the highest peak of the Rocky Mountains, for a lover of warm sunshine and flowers ; and we pleased ourselves with the idea that he was the first of his species to cross the mountain barrier—a solitary pioneer to foretell the advance of civilization. I believe that a moment's thought would have made us let him continue his way unharmed ; but we carried out the law of this country, where all animated nature seems at war, and, seizing him immediately, put him in at least a fit place—in the leaves of a large book, among the flowers we had collected on our way. The barometer stood at 18.293, the attached thermometer at 44°; giving for the elevation of this summit thirteen thousand five hundred and seventy feet above the Gulf of Mexico, which may be called the highest flight of the bee. It is certainly the highest known flight of that insect. From the description given by Mackenzie of the mountains where he crossed them, with that of a French officer still farther to the north, and Colonel Long's measurements to the south, joined to the opinion of the oldest traders of the country, it is presumed that this is the highest peak of the Rocky Mountains. The day was sunny and bright, but a slight shining mist hung over the lower plains, which interfered with our view of the surrounding country. On one side we overlooked innumerable lakes and streams, the spring of the Colorado of the Gulf of California ; and on the other was the Wind River Valley, where were the heads of the Yellowstone branch of the Missouri ; far to the north we just could discover the snowy heads of the *Trois Tetons*, where were the sources of the Missouri and Columbia Rivers ; and at the southern extremity of the ridge the peaks were plainly visible, among which were some of the

CENTRAL CHAIN OF WIND RIVER MOUNTAINS.—FREMONT PEAK.

springs of the Nebraska or Platte River. Around us the whole scene had one main striking feature, which was that of terrible convulsion. Parallel to its length, the ridge was split into chasms and fissures ; between which rose the thin lofty walls, terminated with slender minarets and columns, which is correctly represented in the view from the camp on Island Lake. According to the barometer, the little crest of the wall on which we stood was three thousand five hundred and seventy feet above that place, and two thousand seven hundred and eighty above the little lakes at the bottom, immediately at our feet. Our camp at the Two Hills (an astronomical station) bore S. 3° E., which, with a bearing afterward obtained from a fixed position, enabled us to locate the peak. The bearing of the *Trois Tetons* was N. 50° W., and the direction of the central ridge of the Wind River Mountains S. 39° E. The summit rock was gneiss, succeeded by sienitic gneiss. Sienite and feldspar succeeded in our descent to the snow-line, where we found a feldspathic granite. I had remarked that the noise produced by the explosion of our pistols had the usual degree of loudness, but was not in the least prolonged, expiring almost instantaneously. Having now made what observations our means afforded, we proceeded to descend. We had accomplished an object of laudable ambition, and beyond the strict order of our instructions. We had climbed the loftiest peak of the Rocky Mountains, and looked down upon the snow a thousand feet below, and, standing where never human foot had stood before, felt the exultation of first explorers.* It was about two o'clock when we left the summit; and when we reached the bottom the sun had already sunk behind the wall, and the day was drawing to a close. It would have been pleasant to have lingered here and on the summit longer ; but we hurried away as rapidly as the ground would permit, for it was an object to regain our party as soon as possible, not knowing what accident the next hour might bring forth.

We reached our cache of provisions at nightfall. Here was not the inn which awaits the tired traveller on his return from Mont Blanc, or the orange groves of South America, with their refreshing juices and soft fragrant air ; but we found our little cache of dried meat and coffee undisturbed. Though the moon was bright, the road was full of precipices, and the fatigue of the day had been great. We therefore abandoned the idea of rejoining our friends, and lay down on the rock, and, in spite of the cold, slept soundly.

---

* I received, under date of March 8, 1884, a letter from Mr. H. G. Nickerson, a member of the Eighth Legislative Assembly, Wyoming Territory, informing me that their Legislature had just passed an act to create the county of Frémont ; embracing within its limits the head-waters of Wind River and the Peak, the ascent of which, in 1842, is told in the preceding pages.

J. C. F.

August 16*th*.—We left our encampment with the daylight. We saw on our way large flocks of the mountain goat looking down on us from the cliffs. At the crack of a rifle they would bound off among the rocks, and in a few minutes make their appearance on some lofty peak, some hundred or a thousand feet above. It is needless to attempt any further description of the country ; the portion over which we travelled this morning was rough as imagination could picture it, and to us seemed equally beautiful. A concourse of lakes and rushing waters, mountains of rocks naked and destitute of vegetable earth, dells and ravines of the most exquisite beauty, all kept green and fresh by the great moisture in the air, and sown with brilliant flowers, and everywhere thrown around all the glory of most magnificent scenes—these constitute the features of the place, and impress themselves vividly on the mind of the traveller. It was not until eleven o'clock that we reached the place where our animals had been left when we first attempted the mountains on foot. Near one of the still burning fires we found a piece of meat, which our friends had thrown away, and which furnished us a mouthful—a very scanty breakfast. We continued directly on, and reached our camp on the mountain lake at dusk. We found all well. Nothing had occurred to interrupt the quiet since our departure, and the fine grass and good cool water had done much to re-establish our animals. All heard with great delight the order to turn our faces homeward ; and toward sundown of the 17th we encamped again at the Two Buttes.

In the course of this afternoon's march the barometer was broken past remedy. I regretted it, as I was desirous to compare it again with Dr. Engelman's barometers at St. Louis, to which mine were referred ; but it had done its part well, and my objects were mainly fulfilled. It had touched the highest point of its destiny, and would never be put to a less noble use—as the Scandinavians mean, when, after drinking the health of the bride, the glass is thrown over the shoulder and shattered that it may never be used again.

August 19*th*.—We left our camp on Little Sandy River at about seven in the morning, and traversed the same sandy, undulating country. The air was filled with the turpentine scent of the various artemisias, which are now in bloom, and, numerous as they are, give much gayety to the landscape of the plains. At ten o'clock we stood exactly on the divide in the pass, where the wagon road crosses, and, descending immediately upon the Sweet Water, halted to take a meridian observation of the sun. The latitude was 42° 24′ 32″.

In the course of the afternoon we saw buffalo again, and at our evening halt on the Sweet Water the roasted ribs again made their appearance around the fires ; and with them, good humor, and laughter, and song

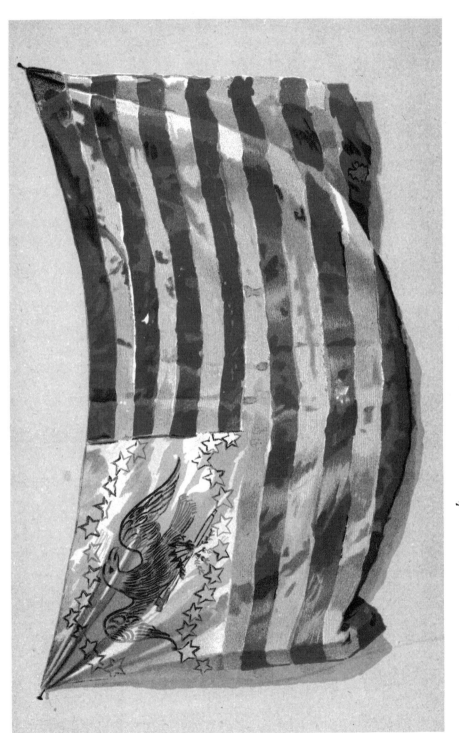

FRÉMONTS ROCKY-MOUNTAIN FLAG.

Raised on highest Peak of Wind-River Chain
August, 15th 1842.

were restored to the camp. Our coffee had been expended, but we now made a kind of tea from the roots of the wild cherry-tree.

August 23d.—Yesterday evening we reached our encampment at Rock Independence, where I took some astronomical observations. Here, not unmindful of the custom of early travellers and explorers in our country, I engraved on this rock of the Far West a symbol of the Christian faith. Among the thickly inscribed names I made on the hard granite the impression of a large cross, which I covered with a black preparation of india-rubber well calculated to resist the influence of wind and rain. It stands amidst the names of many who have long since found their way to the grave, and for whom the huge rock is a giant gravestone.

One George Weymouth was sent out to Maine by the Earl of Southampton, Lord Arundel, and others; and in the narrative of their discoveries he says: "The next day we ascended in our pinnace that part of the river which lies more to the westward, carrying with us a cross—a thing never omitted by any Christian traveller—which we erected at the ultimate end of our route." This was in the year 1605; and in 1842 I obeyed the feeling of early travellers, and left the impression of the cross deeply engraved on the vast rock one thousand miles beyond the Mississippi, to which discoverers have given the national name of *Rock Independence.*

In obedience to my instructions to survey the River Platte if possible, I had determined to make an attempt at this place. The india-rubber boat was filled with air, placed in the water, and loaded with what was necessary for our operations; and I embarked with Preuss and a party of men. When we had dragged our boat for a mile or two over the sands, I abandoned the impossible undertaking, and waited for the arrival of the party, when we packed up our boat and equipage, and at nine o'clock were again moving along on our land journey. We continued along the valley on the right bank of the Sweet Water, where the formation, as already described, consists of a grayish, micaceous sandstone, and fine-grained conglomerate, and marl. We passed over a ridge which borders or constitutes the river hills of the Platte, consisting of huge blocks, sixty or eighty feet cube, of decomposing granite. The cement which united them was probably of easier decomposition, and has disappeared and left them isolate, and separated by small spaces. Numerous horns of the mountain goat were lying among the rocks; and in the ravines were cedars, whose trunks were of extraordinary size. From this ridge we descended to a small open plain at the mouth of the Sweet Water, which rushed with a rapid current into the Platte, here flowing along in a broad, tranquil, and apparently deep stream, which seemed, from its turbid appearance, to be considerably swollen. I obtained here some astronomical observations, and the afternoon was spent in getting our boat ready for navigation the next day.

August 24th.—We started before sunrise, intending to breakfast at Goat Island. I had directed the land party, in charge of Bernier, to proceed to that place, where they were to remain, should they find no note to apprise them of our having passed. In the event of receiving this information, they were to continue their route, passing by certain places which had been designated. Preuss accompanied me, and with us were five of my best men, viz.: Lambert, Basil Lajeunesse, Honoré Ayot, Benoist, and Descoteaux. Here appeared no scarcity of water, and we took on board, with various instruments and baggage, provisions for ten or twelve days. We paddled down the river rapidly, for our little craft was light as a duck on the water; and the sun had been some time risen, when we heard before us a hollow roar, which we supposed to be that of a fall, of which we had heard a vague rumor, but whose exact locality no one had been able to describe to us. We were approaching a ridge, through which the river passes by a place called " cañon " (pronounced *kanyon*), a Spanish word, signifying a piece of artillery, the barrel of a gun, or any kind of tube; and which, in this country, has been adopted to describe the passage of a river between perpendicular rocks of great height, which frequently approach each other so closely overhead as to form a kind of tunnel over the stream, which foams along below, half choked up by fallen fragments. Between the mouth of the Sweet Water and Goat Island there is probably a fall of three hundred feet, and that was principally made in the cañons before us; as, without them, the water was comparatively smooth. As we neared the ridge the river made a sudden turn, and swept squarely down against one of the walls of the cañon with a great velocity, and so steep a descent that it had to the eye the appearance of an inclined plane. When we launched into this, the men jumped overboard to check the velocity of the boat, but were soon in water up to their necks, and our boat ran on; but we succeeded in bringing her to a small point of rocks on the right, at the mouth of the cañon. Here was a kind of elevated sand-beach, not many yards square, backed by the rocks, and around the point the river swept at a right angle. Trunks of trees deposited on jutting points twenty or thirty feet above, and other marks, showed that the water here frequently rose to a considerable height. The ridge was of the same decomposing granite already mentioned, and the water had worked the surface, in many places, into a wavy surface of ridges and holes.

We ascended the rocks to reconnoitre the river, and from the summit the passage appeared to be a continued cataract foaming over many obstructions and broken by a number of small falls. We saw nowhere a fall answering to that which had been described to us as having twenty or twenty-five feet; but still concluded this to be the place in question, as, in the season of floods, the rush of the river against the wall would produce a great rise, and the waters, reflected squarely off, would descend through the passage in a sheet of foam having every appearance of a large fall.

Eighteen years previous to this time, as I have subsequently learned from himself, Mr. Fitzpatrick, somewhere above on this river, had embarked with a valuable cargo of beaver. Unacquainted with the stream, which he believed would conduct him safely to the Missouri, he came unexpectedly into this cañon, where he was wrecked, with the total loss of his furs. It would have been a work of great time and labor to pack our baggage across the ridge, and I determined to run the cañon. We all again embarked, and at first attempted to check the way of the boat; but the water swept through with so much violence that we narrowly escaped being swamped, and were obliged to let her go in the full force of the current, and trust to the skill of the boatmen. The dangerous places in this cañon were where huge rocks had fallen from above, and hemmed in the already narrow pass of the river to an open space of three or four and five feet. These obstructions raised the water considerably above, which was sometimes precipitated over in a fall; and at other places, where this dam was too high, rushed through the contracted opening with tremendous violence. Had our boat been made of wood, in passing the narrows she would have been staved; but her elasticity preserved her unhurt from every shock, and she seemed fairly to leap over the falls.

In this way we passed three cataracts in succession, where, perhaps, one hundred feet of smooth water intervened; and finally, with a shout of pleasure at our success, issued from our tunnel into the open day beyond. We were so delighted with the performance of our boat, and so confident in her powers, that we would not have hesitated to leap a fall of ten feet with her. We put to shore for breakfast at some willows on the right bank, immediately below the mouth of the cañon; for it was now eight oclock, and we had been working since daylight, and were all wet, fatigued, and hungry. While the men were preparing breakfast, I went out to reconnoitre. The view was very limited. The course of the river was smooth, so far as I could see; on both sides were broken hills; and but a mile or two below was another high ridge. The rock at the mouth of the cañon was still the decomposing granite, with great quantities of mica, which made a very glittering sand.

We re-embarked at nine o'clock, and in about twenty minutes reached the next cañon. Landing on a rocky shore at its commencement, we ascended the ridge to reconnoitre. Portage was out of the question. So far as we could see, the jagged rocks pointed out the course of the cañon, on a winding line of seven or eight miles. It was simply a narrow, dark chasm in the rock; and here the perpendicular faces were much higher than in the previous pass, being at this end two to three hundred, and farther down, as we afterward ascertained, five hundred feet in vertical height. Our previous success had made us bold, and we determined again to run the cañon. Everything was secured as firmly as possible; and, having divested ourselves of the greater part of our clothing, we pushed into the stream. To save our chronometer from accident, Preuss took it and attempted to proceed along the shore on the masses of rock, which in places were piled up on either side; but after he had walked about five minutes everything like shore disappeared, and the vertical wall came squarely down into the water. He therefore waited until we came up.

An ugly pass lay before us. We had made fast to the stern of the boat a strong rope about fifty feet long; and three of the men clambered along among the rocks, and with this rope let her down slowly through the pass. In several places high rocks lay scattered about in the channel; and in the narrows it required all our strength and skill to avoid staving the boat on the sharp points. In one of these the boat proved a little too broad, and stuck fast for an instant, while the water flew over us; fortunately it was but for an instant, as our united strength forced her immediately through. The water swept overboard only a sextant and a pair of saddle-bags. I caught the sextant as it passed by me; but the saddlebags became the prey of the whirlpools. We reached the place where Preuss was standing, took him on board, and, with the aid of the boat, put the men with the rope on the succeeding pile of rocks. We found the passage much worse than the previous one, and our position was rather a bad one. To go back was impossible; before us, the cataract was a sheet of foam; and, shut up in the chasm by the rocks, which in some places seemed almost to meet overhead, the roar of the water was deafening.

We pushed off again; but after making a little distance the force of the current became too great for the men on shore, and two of them let go the rope. Lajeunesse, the third man, hung on, and was jerked head-foremost into the river from a rock about twelve feet high; and down the boat shot like an arrow, Basil following us in the rapid current and exerting all his strength to keep in mid-channel—his head only seen occasionally like a black spot in the white foam. How far we went, I do not exactly know; but we succeeded in turning the boat into an eddy below. "'Cré Dieu," said Basil Lajeunesse, as he arrived immediately after us, "je crois bien que j'ai nagé un demi-mile." He had owed his life to his skill as a swimmer; and I determined to take him and the two others on board, and trust to skill and fortune to reach the other end in safety.

We placed ourselves on our knees, with the short paddles in our hands, the most skilful boatman being at the bow; and again we commenced our rapid descent. We cleared rock after rock, and shot past fall after fall, our little boat seeming to play with the cataract. We became flushed with success and familiar with the danger; and, yielding to the excitement of the occasion, broke forth together into a Canadian boat-song. Singing, or rather shouting, we dashed along; and were, I believe, in the midst of the chorus, when the boat struck a concealed rock immediately at the foot of a fall, which whirled her over in an instant. Three of my men could not swim, and my first feeling was to assist them and save some of our effects; but a sharp concussion or two convinced me that I had not yet saved myself. A few strokes brought me into an eddy, and I landed on a pile of rocks on the left side. Looking around, I saw that Preuss had gained the shore on the same side, about twenty yards below; and a little climbing and swimming soon brought him to my side. On the opposite side, against the wall, lay the boat, bottom up; and Lambert was in the act of saving Descoteaux, whom he had grasped by the hair, and who could not swim; "*Lâche pas,*" said he, as I afterward learned, "*lâche pas, cher frère.*" "*Crains pas,*" was the reply, "*je m'en vais mourir avant de te lâcher.*" Such was the reply of courage and generosity in this danger.

For a hundred yards below, the current was covered with floating books and boxes, bales of blankets, and scattered articles of clothing; and so strong and boiling was the stream that even our heavy instruments, which were all in cases, kept on the surface, and the sextant, circle, and the long black box of the telescope were in view at once. For a moment, I felt somewhat disheartened. All our books—almost every record of the journey—our journals and registers of astronomical and barometrical observations—had been lost in a moment. But it was no time to indulge in regrets; and I immediately set about endeavoring to save something from the wreck. Making ourselves understood as well as possible by signs (for nothing could be heard in the roar of waters), we commenced our operations. Of everything on board, the only article that had been saved was my double-barrelled gun, which Descoteaux had caught and clung to with drowning tenacity. The men continued down the river on the left bank. Preuss and myself descended on the side we were on; and Lajeunesse, with a paddle in his hand, jumped on the boat alone, and continued down the cañon. She was now light, and cleared every bad place with much less difficulty. In a short time he was joined by Lambert; and the search was continued for about a mile and a half, which was as far as the boat could proceed in the pass.

Here the walls were about five hundred feet high, and the fragments of rocks from above had choked the river into a hollow pass, but one or two feet above the surface.   Through this and the interstices of the rock, the water found its way.   Favored beyond our expectations, all of our registers had been recovered, with the exception of one of my journals, which contained the notes and incidents of travel, and topographical descriptions, a number of scattered astronomical observations, principally meridian altitudes of the sun, and our barometrical register west of Laramie.   Fortunately, our other journals contained duplicates of the most important barometrical observations which had been taken in the mountains.   These, with a few scattered notes, were all that had been preserved of our meteorological observations.   In addition to these, we saved the circle; and these, with a few blankets, constituted everything that had been rescued from the waters.

The day was running rapidly away, and it was necessary to reach Goat Island, whither the party had preceded us, before night.   In this uncertain country, the traveller is so much in the power of chance, that we became somewhat uneasy in regard to them.   Should anything have occurred, in the brief interval of our separation, to prevent our rejoining them, our situation would be rather a desperate one.   We had not a morsel of provisions—our arms and ammunition were gone—and we were entirely at the mercy of any straggling party of savages, and not a little in danger of starvation.   We therefore set out at once in two parties ; Mr. Preuss and myself on the left, and the men on the opposite side of the river.   Climbing out of the cañon, we found ourselves in a very broken country, where we were not yet able to recognize any locality.   In the course of our descent through the cañon, the rock, which at the upper end was of the decomposing granite, changed into a varied sandstone formation.   The hills and points of the ridges were covered with fragments of a yellow sandstone, of which the strata were sometimes displayed in the broken ravines which interrupted our course, and made our walk extremely fatiguing.

At one point of the cañon the red argillaceous sandstone rose in a wall of five hundred feet, surmounted by a stratum of white sandstone ; and in an opposite ravine a column of red sandstone rose, in form like a steeple, about one hundred and fifty feet high.   The scenery was extremely picturesque, and, notwithstanding our forlorn condition, we were frequently obliged to stop and admire it.   Our progress was not very rapid.   We had emerged from the water half naked, and, on arriving at the top of the precipice, I found myself with only one moccasin.   The fragments of rock made walking painful, and I was frequently obliged to stop and pull out the thorns of the *cactus*, here the prevailing plant, and with which a few minutes' walk covered the bottom of my feet.   From this ridge the river emerged into a smiling prairie, and, descending to the bank for water, we were joined by Benoist.   The rest of the party were out of sight, having taken a more inland route. We crossed the river repeatedly—sometimes able to ford it, and sometimes swimming—climbed over the ridges of two more cañons, and toward evening reached the cut, which we here named the Hot Spring gate.

On our previous visit in July, we had not entered this pass, reserving it for our descent in the boat; and when we entered it this evening Mr. Preuss was a few hundred feet in advance. Heated with the long march, he came suddenly upon a fine bold spring gushing from the rock, about ten feet above the river. Eager to enjoy the crystal water, he threw himself down for a hasty draught, and took a mouthful of water almost boiling hot. He said nothing to Benoist, who laid himself down to drink; but the steam from the hot water arrested his eagerness, and he escaped the hot draught. We had no thermometer to ascertain the temperature, but I could hold my hand in the water just long enough to count two seconds. There are eight or ten of these springs, discharging themselves by streams large enough to be called runs. A loud hollow noise was heard from the rock, which I supposed to be produced by the fall of the water. The strata immediately where they issue is a fine white and calcareous sandstone, covered with an incrustation of common salt.

Leaving this Thermopylæ of the West, in a short walk we reached the red ridge which has been described as lying just above Goat Island. Ascending this, we found some fresh tracks and a button, which showed that the other men had already arrived. A shout from the man who first reached the top of the ridge, responded to from below, informed us that our friends were all on the island; and we were soon among them. We found some pieces of buffalo standing around the fire for us, and managed to get some dry clothes among the people. A sudden storm of rain drove us into the best shelter we could find, where we slept soundly, after one of the most fatiguing days I have ever experienced.

August 25th.—Early this morning Lajeunesse was sent to the wreck for the articles which had been saved, and about noon we left the island. The mare which he had left here in July had much improved in condition, and she served us well again for some time, but was finally abandoned at a subsequent part of the journey. At ten in the morning of the 26th we reached Cache camp, where we found everything undisturbed. We disinterred our deposit, arranged our carts which had been left here on the way out, and, travelling a few miles in the afternoon, encamped for the night at the ford of the Platte.

August 27th.—At midday we halted at the place where we had taken dinner on July 27th. The country which, when we passed up, looked as if the hard winter frosts had passed over it, had now assumed a new face, so much of vernal freshness had been given to it by the late rains. The

Platte was exceedingly low—a mere line of water among the sandbars. We reached Fort Laramie on the last day of August, after an absence of forty-two days, and had the pleasure to find our friends all well. The fortieth day had been fixed for our return; and the quick eyes of the Indians, who were on the lookout for us, discovered our flag as we wound among the hills. The fort saluted us with repeated discharges of its single piece, which we returned with scattered volleys of our small arms, and felt the joy of a home-reception in getting back to this remote station, which seemed so far off as we went out.

On the morning of September 3d we bade adieu to our kind friends at the fort, and continued our homeward journey down the Platte, which was glorious with the autumnal splendor of innumerable flowers in full and brilliant bloom. On the warm sands, among the *helianthi*, one of the characteristic plants, we saw great numbers of rattlesnakes, of which five or six were killed in the morning's ride. We occupied ourselves in improving our previous survey of the river; and, as the weather was fine, astronomical observations were generally made at night and at noon.

We halted for a short time on the afternoon of the 5th with a village of Sioux Indians, some of whose chiefs we had met at Laramie. The water in the Platte was extremely low; in many places, the large expanse of sands, with some occasional stunted trees on the banks, gave it the air of the sea-coast; the bed of the river being merely a succession of sandbars, among which the channel was divided into rivulets a few inches deep. We crossed and recrossed with our carts repeatedly and at our pleasure; and, whenever an obstruction barred our way, in the shape of precipitous bluffs that came down upon the river, we turned directly into it, and made our way along the sandy bed, with no other inconvenience than the frequent quicksands, which greatly fatigued our animals. Disinterring on the way the *cache* which had been made by our party when they ascended the river, we reached without accident, on the evening of September 12th, our old encampment of July 2d at the junction of the forks. Our *cache* of the barrel of pork was found undisturbed, and proved a seasonable addition to our stock of provisions. At this place I had determined to make another attempt to descend the Platte by water, and accordingly spent two days in the construction of a bull-boat. Men were sent out on the evening of our arrival, the necessary number of bulls killed, and their skins brought to the camp. Four of the best of them were strongly sewed together with buffalo sinew, and stretched over a basket-frame of willow. The seams were then covered with ashes and tallow, and the boat left exposed to the sun for the greater part of one day, which was sufficient to dry and contract the skin, and make the whole work solid and strong. It had a rounded bow, was eight feet long and five broad, and drew with four men about four inches of water. On the morning of the 15th we embarked in our hide-boat, Mr. Preuss and myself, with two men. We dragged her over the sands for three or four miles, and then left her on a bar, and abandoned entirely all further attempts to navigate this river. The names given by the Indians are always remarkably appropriate; and certainly none was ever more so than that which they have given to this stream—"the Nebraska, or Shallow River." Walking steadily the remainder of the day, a little before dark we overtook our people at their evening camp, about twenty-one miles below the junction. The next morning we crossed the Platte, and continued our way down the river bottom on the left bank, where we found an excellent, plainly beaten road.

On the 18th we reached Grand Island, which is fifty-two miles long, with an average breadth of one mile and three-quarters. It has on it some small eminences, and is sufficiently elevated to be secure from the annual floods of the river. As has been already remarked, it is well timbered, with an excellent soil, and recommends itself to notice as the best point for a military position on the Lower Platte.

On the 22d we arrived at the village of the Grand Pawnees, on the right bank of the river, about thirty miles above the mouth of the Loup Fork. They were gathering in their corn, and we obtained from them a very welcome supply of vegetables.

The morning of the 24th we reached the Loup Fork of the Platte. At the place where we forded it, this stream was four hundred and thirty yards broad, with a swift current of *clear* water; in this respect, differing from the Platte, which has a yellow, muddy color, derived from the limestone and marl formation, of which we have previously spoken. The ford was difficult, as the water was so deep that it came into the body of the carts, and we reached the opposite bank after repeated attempts, ascending and descending the bed of the river in order to avail ourselves of the bars. We encamped on the left bank of the fork, in the point of land at its junction with the Platte. During the two days that we remained here for astronomical observations, the bad weather permitted us to obtain but one good observation for the latitude—a meridian altitude of the sun, which gave for the latitude of the mouth of the Loup Fork, 41° 22′ 11″.

Five or six days previously, I had sent forward Lambert, with two men, to Bellevue, with directions to ask from Mr. Pierre Sarpy, the gentleman in charge of the American Company's establishment at that place, the aid of his carpenters in constructing a boat, in which I proposed to descend the Missouri. On the afternoon of the 27th we met one of the men, who had been despatched by Mr. Sarpy with a welcome supply of provisions and a very kind note, which gave us the very gratifying intelligence that our boat was in rapid progress. On the evening of the 30th we encamped in an almost impenetrable undergrowth on the left bank of the Platte, in the point of land at its confluence with the Missouri—three hundred and fifteen miles, according to our reckoning, from the junction of the forks, and five hundred and twenty from Fort Laramie.

From the junction we had found the bed of the Platte occupied with numerous islands, many of them very large, and all well timbered; possessing, as well as the bottom lands of the river, a very excellent soil. With the exception of some scattered groves on the banks, the bottoms are generally without timber. A portion of these consist of low grounds, covered with a profusion of fine grasses, and are probably inundated in the spring; the remaining part is high prairie, entirely beyond the influence of the floods. The breadth of the river is usually three quarters of a mile, except where it is enlarged by islands. That portion of its course which is occupied by Grand Island, has an average breadth, from shore to shore, of two and a half miles. The breadth of the valley, with the various accidents of ground—springs, timber, and whatever I have thought interesting to travellers and settlers—I indicated on one of the maps which accompanied the report I made of this journey.

October 1st.—I rose this morning long before daylight, and heard, with a feeling of pleasure, the tinkling of cow-bells at the settlements on the opposite side of the Missouri. Early in the day we reached Mr. Sarpy's residence; and, in the security and comfort of his hospitable mansion, felt the pleasure of being again within the pale of civilization. We found our boat on the stocks; a few days sufficed to complete her; and in the afternoon of the 4th we embarked on the Missouri. All our equipage—horses, carts, and the *matériel* of the camp—had been sold at public auction at Bellevue. The strength of my party enabled me to man the boat with ten oars, relieved every hour; and we descended rapidly. Early on the morning of the 10th, we halted to make some astronomical observations at the mouth of the Kansas, exactly four months since we had left the trading-post of Mr. Cyprian Chouteau, on the same river, ten miles above. On our descent to this place, we had employed ourselves in surveying and sketching the Missouri, making astronomical observations regularly at night and at midday, whenever the weather permitted. These operations on the river were continued until our arrival at the city of St. Louis, Missouri, on the 17th. At St. Louis the sale of our remaining effects was made; and, leaving that city by steamboat on the 18th, I reached the city of Washington on October 29th.

I found the family well.

The winter was busily occupied in preparing my report of the expedition. To Mr. Preuss was assigned the labor of the maps. In addition to the general map of the country explored, a series of maps representing,

JESSIE BENTON FRÉMONT.

each a day's journey, a guide-book in atlas form, was prepared for the use of the emigration. This was the suggestion of Mr. Benton. Upon each of the maps the places were indicated for camps where grass and water and wood would be found.

The distinguished botanist, Professor Torrey, kindly undertook the description of the plants collected during the journey. To me fell the labor of the various computations and the writing of the report.

The third life alluded to in the "scope" of this narrative came now in for its portion of work.

I write more easily by dictation. Writing myself I have too much time to think and dwell upon words as well as ideas. In dictation there is not time for this and then, too, I see the face of my second mind, and get there at times the slight dissent confirming my own doubt, or the pleased expression which represents the popular impression of a mind new to the subject. This invites discussion : a form of discussion impossible except with a mind and purpose in harmony with one's own and on the same level; therefore the labor of amanuensis, commencing at this early time, has remained with Mrs. Frémont.

The report was called for by the Senate, and on the motion of Mr. Linn it was printed for the use of the Senate, and a number of extra copies ordered.

In support of his motion, Mr. Linn said:

" The object of the expedition was to examine and report upon the rivers and country between the frontiers of Missouri and the base of the Rocky Mountains : and especially to examine the character, and ascertain the latitude and longitude of the South Pass, the great crossing-place in those mountains on the way to the Oregon. All the objects of the expedition have been accomplished, and in a way to be beneficial to science and instructive to the general reader as well as useful to the Government. Supplied with the best astronomical and barometrical instruments, well qualified to use them, and accompanied by twenty-five voyageurs enlisted for the purpose at St. Louis, and trained to all the hardships and dangers of the prairies and the mountains, Mr. Frémont left the mouth of the Kansas, on the frontiers of Missouri, on June 10th, and in the incredibly short space of four months returned to the same point without an accident to a man, and with a vast mass of useful observations and many hundred specimens in botany and geology.

" In executing his instructions, Mr. Frémont proceeded up the Kansas River far enough to ascertain its character, and then crossed over to the Great Platte and pursued that river to its source in the mountains, where the Sweet Water (a head-branch of the Platte) issues from the neighborhood of the South Pass. He reached the pass on August 8th, and described it as a wide and low depression of the mountains, where the ascent is as easy as that of the hill on which this Capitol stands, and where a plainly beaten wagon-road leads to the Oregon through the valley of Lewis River, a fork of the Columbia.

"He went through the pass and saw the head-waters of the Colorado of the Gulf of California; and, leaving the valleys, to indulge a laudable curiosity and to make some useful observations, and attended by four of his men, he climbed the loftiest peak of the Rocky Mountains, until then untrodden by any known human being; and on August 15th looked down upon ice and snow some thousand feet below, and traced in the distance the valleys of the rivers which, taking their rise in the same elevated ridge, flow in opposite directions to the Pacific Ocean and to the Mississippi. From that ultimate point he returned by the valley of the Great Platte, following the stream in its whole course, and solving all questions in relation to its navigability and the character of the country through which it flows.

"The results of all these observations Mr. Frémont has condensed into a brief report—enough to make a document of ninety or one hundred pages; and believing that this document would be of general interest to the whole country, and beneficial to science as well as useful to the Government, I move the printing of the extra number which has been named.

"This report proves conclusively that the country for several hundred miles from the frontier of Missouri is exceedingly beautiful and fertile; alternate woodland and prairie, and certain portions well supplied with water. It also proves that the valley of the River Platte has a very rich soil, affording great facilities for emigrants to the west of the Rocky Mountains."

This was the first act done with the, apparent, support of the Government in aid to the Oregon emigration.

Upon this subject Mr. Benton says:

"Connected with this emigration, and auxiliary to it, was the first expedition of Lieutenant Frémont to the Rocky Mountains, and undertaken and completed in the summer of 1842—upon its outside view the conception of the Government, but in fact conceived without its knowledge, and executed upon solicited orders, of which the design was unknown."

In the meantime the second expedition had been planned.

Pending the discussion at Washington of the Ashburton Treaty some propositions concerning Oregon which had been suggested between the negotiators were submitted to the Senators from Missouri, and by them promptly rejected. These suggestions of "a conventional divisional line" forewarned them of a basis of settlement that admitted doubt upon the clear title of the United States to the Valley of the Columbia, which they had resolved to maintain against the field. The divisional line meant the north bank of the Columbia for the boundary, with equal rights of navigation in the river and to the harbor at its mouth.

The proposition to surrender simply inspired promptness in the measures projected to commit the Government to their views and render any compromise impossible; and the plans for extending the exploration into Oregon were hurried forward.

A policy of delay suggested in the President's message required that before any title to lands be given to emigrants in Oregon Territory, "the respective claims of the two Governments should be settled."

The answer to this open proposition for delay, in deference to the claims of England, was made by Senator Linn, of Missouri, who introduced a bill to encourage and protect emigration by stockading the line of travel and providing for grants of land.

This bill gave the key-note to the emigration; though the bill passed the Senate it was not acted on in the House, but the emigrants assumed it to mean government protection.

It was fair to set out distinctly the distorted and absurdly erroneous views entertained concerning the country we had to examine, as a reason for the explorations that brought to common knowledge the inexhaustible riches of the vast region which, through years of obstacle, its friends had struggled to reclaim from the possession of a foreign power. The necessity must be looked at from conditions existing at the time, not by the light thrown back upon them by the conditions of to-day.

The following extract from the *Athenæum*, London, reviewing, in March, 1844, the first report, shows the undetermined conditions which also existed on the other side of the water at the time. It concludes: "It is said that Lieutenant Frémont has been appointed to the survey of the Oregon Territory. We are heartily glad of it. He will be sure to do his work well, and if our topographical engineers labor in the same style and spirit, we may reckon on obtaining, through their joint efforts, an accurate knowledge of that country, so that we may be able to calculate, on safe grounds, the exact amount of blood and treasure which may be prudently expended in the conquest of it."

The second expedition was to connect with the first expedition at the South Pass, but to approach the mountains on a different line. It was intended to examine the broad region south of the Columbia River, lying between the Rocky Mountains and the Pacific Ocean. In this way the two expeditions would give a connected survey of the interior and western half of the continent.

Early in the spring of 1843, I left Washington with the whole family, Mr. Benton having preceded us to Missouri. Mr. Preuss and Jacob Dodson were with us.   Jacob was only eighteen, but strong and active, and nearly six feet in height.   He was of the good colored people of the district, born free, but with the feeling of belonging with a family and giving to it unchanging service.   Others of his people held life-time service in the family of Mr. Benton, and it was the ambition of this boy to go with me. About noon the stage-coach was climbing up one of the Pennsylvania mountains—when reaching the summit it capsized.   The driver, too confident of his skill, and disregarding the shouts of the wagoner, attempted to pass one of those huge wagons with its string of horses, with the result of overturning us into a gully, the coach lighting on its roof.   Jacob, who was on the box, was at the horses' heads before the coach reached the gully, and the wagoner's men prevented further harm from frightened animals.

Inside the coach all was so silent that the first thought was that all had been hurt, but as they were drawn out one by one, Mrs. Benton was found to be the only one injured.   She had received a hurt on the head which stunned her, and made rest necessary, so that we remained over until next day.

Preuss, who had gotten out to enjoy a walk up the mountain in the company of his pipe, was not to be consoled because he had not been part of the disaster ; it was necessary to remind him that his being away had saved the precious barometer, which he never left out of his care.

Chance had given us a good place for the overset.   The "wagon-stand" near by stood on the stony, bleak mountain-side ; it was one of the by-gone, old-fashioned, Pennsylvania taverns, and the abundant game hanging about gave it now the appearance of a rough hunting-lodge. The landlady, who had seen the coach go over, tried to comfort us by loading her table with every good thing she had, or her housewifely skill could prepare.   The buckwheat cakes were half an inch thick and porous like a sponge, capable of absorbing enough of the good mountain butter to support a man for a day ; with honey from the buckwheat fields, and maple-syrup from the forest.   The venison steaks were excellent, broiled over wood-coals.   It was the native abundance of that day.

One may forget many things but it would not be easy to efface from a traveller's memory this contrast to many an after time ; before a year had passed Preuss and I had recalled the stone house in the mountains with its big fires and lavish abundance of good food.

Mrs. Frémont was to remain in St. Louis during my absence, which was not to be for more than about eight months.

Experience enabled me to make my preparations quickly.   Among the men engaged at St. Louis for this journey were six who had been with me in the first : Alexis Ayot, François Badeau, Baptiste Bernier, Basil Lajeunesse, Louis Ménard and Raphael Proue ; all good men ; together with Louis Zindel, Prussian artillerist, who was one of the party under Mr. Nicollet in his second expedition.

As I expected to be much among Indians who had for many years a known character for audacious bravery and treachery, I applied to Colonel S. W. Kearny, commanding Third Military Division, for a howitzer, which he furnished me from the arsenal at St. Louis.

I had obtained for guide Mr. Thomas Fitzpatrick, well known in the mountains. He was known to be a brave man and had lived through rough experiences in the Indian country. On one occasion, surrounded by Blackfeet in the Wind River Mountains, all his party had been killed except himself, but the peril and excitement of the three days among the rocks while the Indians were searching for him had turned his thick hair entirely white. He was still young, and it made a contrast to the healthy ruddy color of his face.

On May 17th I arrived at the little town of Kansas, near the junction of the Kansas River with the Missouri. Maxwell, who will be remembered as having accompanied me in 1842, joined the camp here to accompany me as far as the upper Arkansas. Carson joined me as we reached the mountains at a little Mexican pueblo on the Arkansas River.

In setting out on this journey I made the acquaintance of Major Cummins, who had long been Indian Agent among the Delawares and other Indians, and a friend of long-standing to Senator Benton and valued by him. He was a large, fine-looking man, advanced now in years, but staunch in person as in character. His house was always open to me with a frontier welcome, which means much; and the introduction he gave me to the Shawnee and Delaware Indians gained me their confidence and proved most valuable to me for years afterward.

While engaged in completing my outfit I received from Mrs. Frémont a letter which urged me to set out upon the journey forthwith and make at Bents' Fort the waiting for the grass to get its full strength.

Satisfied that there was reason for such urgency I started on the morning of the 29th, twelve days only after reaching Kansas, and made my first encampment on the verge of the great prairies four miles beyond the frontier.

It was not until my return that I learned the reason why this sudden move was required of me.

I had requested Mrs. Frémont to open all my letters, using her discretion in regard to forwarding any of them while I remained on the frontier. But there came an official order from the head of my corps, Colonel Abert, directing me to return to Washington in order to explain why, in addition to ordinary arms, I had taken a howitzer with me: that it was a scientific expedition—not military—and not to be armed as such.

The flimsiness of this excuse for breaking up the expedition after it had been planned and ordered and in movement, was so apparent to Mrs. Frémont, as also was the true reason for it, that she did not hesitate to suppress the order, and write me the letter which caused me to make an immediate start. She did not communicate this proceeding to Colonel Abert until I was far beyond the reach of recall. Mr. Benton was not in St. Louis, and she took council with no one. She acted entirely on her own knowledge, which was full, concerning the expedition, and existing reasons for opposing it.

I never knew where the order originated. It came through Colonel Abert. He was a quiet man, not likely to disturb an expedition gotten up, apparently, under his own direction and, so far as he knew, originating with himself. It was not probable that I would have been recalled from the Missouri frontier to Washington, fifteen hundred miles of water and stage-coach travelling, to explain why I had taken an arm that simply served to increase the means of defence for a small party very certain to encounter Indian hostility, and which involved very trifling expense.

On his return to St. Louis Mr. Benton approved Mrs. Frémont's action, and so wrote to Washington, at the same time asking an explanation, but there the subject rested.

I mention it here to show the compliance of the administration with the English situation in Oregon.

CHAPTER VI.

My Second Expedition—Personnel of Party—Osages make a Charge—Ceremonious Arapahoes—Prairie-dog Village—Kit joins us again—Godey Engaged—Yampah River—An Attack by Arapahoes—Preuss objects to Kooyah—Our Rubber Boat.

My party consisted principally of Creole and Canadian French, and Americans, amounting in all to thirty-nine men; among whom will be recognized several of those who were with me in my first expedition, and who have been favorably brought to notice. Mr. Thomas Fitzpatrick, whom many years of hardship and exposure in the Western territories had rendered familiar with a portion of the country it was designed to explore, had been selected as our guide; and Mr. Charles Preuss, who had been my assistant in the previous journey, was again associated with me in the same capacity on the present expedition. Mr. Theodore Talbot, of Washington City, had been attached to the party, with a view to advancement in his profession; and at St. Louis I had been joined by Mr. Frederick Dwight, a gentleman of Springfield, Mass., who availed himself of our overland journey to visit the Sandwich Islands and China, by way of Fort Vancouver.

The men engaged for the service were: Alexis Ayot, François Badeau, Oliver Beaulieu, Baptiste Bernier, John A. Campbell, John G. Campbell, Manuel Chapman, Ransom Clark, Philibert Courteau, Michel Crélis, William Creuss, Clinton Deforest, Baptiste Derosier, Basil Lajeunesse, François Lajeunesse, Henry Lee, Louis Ménard, Louis Montreuil, Samuel Neil, Alexis Pera, François Pera, James Power, Raphael Proue, Oscar Sarpy, Baptiste Tabeau, Charles Taplin, Baptiste Tesson, Auguste Vasquez, Joseph Verrot, Patrick White, Tiery Wright, and Louis Zindel. Two Delaware Indians—a fine-looking old man and his son—were engaged to accompany the expedition as hunters, through the kindness of Major Cummins, the excellent Indian Agent.

The party was armed generally with Hall's carbines, which, with a brass twelve-pound howitzer, had been furnished to me by Colonel Kearny. Three men were specially detailed for the management of this piece, under the charge of Zindel, who had been nineteen years a non-commissioned officer of artillery in the Prussian army, and regularly instructed in the duties of his profession. The camp-equipage and provisions were transported in twelve carts, drawn each by two mules; and a light covered wagon, mounted on good springs, had been provided for the safer carriage of the instruments. These were: One refracting telescope, by Frauenhofer; one reflecting circle, by Gambey; two sextants, by Troughton; one pocket chronometer, No. 837, by Goffe, Falmouth; one pocket chronometer, No. 739, by Brockbank; one syphon barometer, by Bunten, Paris; one cistern barometer, by Frye & Shaw, New York; six thermometers, and a number of small compasses.

To make the exploration as useful as possible, I determined, in conformity to my general instructions, to vary the route to the Rocky Mountains from that followed in the year 1842. The route then was up the Valley of the Great Platte River to the South Pass, in north latitude 42°; the route now determined on was up the Valley of the Kansas River and to the head of the Arkansas, and to some pass in the mountains, if any could be found, at the sources of that river.

By making this deviation from the former route, the problem of a new road to Oregon and California, in a climate more genial, might be solved; and a better knowledge obtained of an important river, and the country it drained; while the great object of the expedition would find its point of commencement at the termination of the former, which was at that great gate in the ridge of the Rocky Mountains called the South Pass.

Resuming our journey on the 31st, after the delay of a day to complete our equipment and furnish ourselves with some of the comforts of civilized life, we encamped in the evening at Elm Grove, in company with several emigrant wagons, constituting a party which was proceeding to Upper California under the direction of Mr. J. B. Childs, of Missouri. The wagons were variously freighted with goods, furniture, and farming utensils, containing among other things an entire set of machinery for a mill which Mr. Childs designed erecting on the waters of the Sacramento River, emptying into the Bay of San Francisco.

We were joined here by Mr. William Gilpin, of Missouri, who, intending this year to visit the settlements in Oregon, had been invited to accompany us, and proved a useful and agreeable addition to the party. From this encampment, our route until June 3d was nearly the same as that described to you in 1842. Trains of wagons were almost constantly in sight, giving to the road a populous and animated appearance, although the greater portion of the emigrants were collected at the crossing, or already on their march beyond the Kansas River.

Leaving at the ford the usual emigrant road to the mountains, we continued our route along the southern side of the Kansas, where we found the country much more broken than on the northern side of the river, and where our progress was much delayed by the numerous small streams, which obliged us to make frequent bridges.   On the morning of the 4th we crossed a handsome stream, called by the Indians Otter Creek, about one hundred and thirty feet wide, where a flat stratum of limestone, which forms the bed, made an excellent ford.   We met here a small party of Kansas and Delaware Indians, the latter returning from a hunting and trapping expedition on the upper waters of the river ; and on the heights above were five or six Kansas women, engaged in digging prairie pota-toes (*Psoralea esculenta*).   On the afternoon of the 6th, while busily en-gaged in crossing a wooded stream, we were thrown into a little confu-sion by the sudden arrival of Maxwell, who entered the camp at full speed at the head of a war party of Osage Indians, with gay red blankets, and heads shaved to the scalp-lock.   They had run him a distance of about nine miles, from a creek on which we had encamped the day previous, and to which he had returned in search of a runaway horse belonging to Mr. Dwight, which had taken the homeward road, carrying with him saddle, bridle, and holster-pistols.   The Osages were probably ignorant of our strength, and, when they charged into the camp, drove off a num-ber of our best horses ; but we were fortunately well-mounted, and after a hard chase of seven or eight miles succeeded in recovering them all.

This accident, which occasioned delay and trouble, and threatened danger and loss, and broke down some good horses at the start, and ac-tually endangered the expedition, was a first-fruit of having gentlemen in company—very estimable, to be sure, but who are not trained to the care and vigilance and self-dependence which such an expedition required, and who are not subject to the orders which enforce attention and exertion.

We arrived on the 8th at the mouth of the Smoky-hill Fork, which is the principal southern branch of the Kansas ; forming here, by its junction with the Republican, or northern branch, the main Kansas River.   Neither stream was fordable, and the necessity of making a raft, together with bad weather, detained us here until the morning of the 11th, when we resumed our journey along the Republican Fork.   By our observations the junc-tion of the streams is in latitude 39° 03′ 38″, longitude 96° 24′ 56″, and at an elevation of nine hundred and twenty-six feet above the Gulf of Mexico. For several days we continued to travel along the Republican, through a country beautifully watered with numerous streams, handsomely timbered ; and rarely an incident occurred to vary the general resemblance which one day on the prairies here bears to another, and which scarcely require a particular description.   Now and then we caught a glimpse of a small herd of elk ; and occasionally a band of antelopes, whose curiosity sometimes brought them within rifle range, would circle round us, and then scour off into the prairies. As we advanced on our road these became more frequent; but as we journeyed on the line usually followed by the trapping and hunting parties of the Kansas and Delaware Indians, game of every kind continued very shy and wild. The bottoms which form the immediate valley of the main river were generally about three miles wide; having a rich soil of black vegetable mould, and, for a prairie country, well interspersed with wood. The country was everywhere covered with a considerable variety of grasses—occasionally poor and thin, but far more frequently luxuriant and rich. We had been gradually and regularly ascending in our progress westward, and on the evening of the 14th, when we encamped on a little creek in the valley of the Republican, two hundred and sixty-five miles by our travelling road from the mouth of the Kansas, we were at an elevation of one thousand five hundred and twenty feet. That part of the river where we were now encamped is called by the Indians the *Big Timber.* Hitherto our route had been laborious and extremely slow, the unusually wet spring and constant rain having so saturated the whole country that it was necessary to bridge every water-course, and, for days together, our usual march averaged only five or six miles. Finding that at such a rate of travel it would be impossible to comply with my instructions, I determined at this place to divide the party, and, leaving Mr. Fitzpatrick with twenty-five men in charge of the provisions and heavier baggage of the camp, to proceed myself in advance, with a light party of fifteen men, taking with me the howitzer and the light wagon which carried the instruments.

Accordingly, on the morning of the 16th the parties separated; and, bearing a little out from the river, with a view of heading some of the numerous affluents, after a few hours' travel over somewhat broken ground we entered upon an extensive and high level prairie, on which we encamped toward evening at a little stream where a single dry cotton-wood afforded the necessary fuel for preparing supper. Among a variety of grasses which to-day made their first appearance, I noticed bunch grass (*festuca*) and buffalo grass (*Sesleria dactyloides*). Amorpha canescens (*lead plant*) continued the characteristic plant of the country, and a narrow-leaved *lathyrus* occurred during the morning in beautiful patches. *Sida coccinea* occurred frequently, with a *psoralea*, near *Psoralea floribunda*, and a number of plants not hitherto met, just verging into bloom. The water on which we had encamped belonged to Solomon's Fork of the Smoky-hill River, along whose tributaries we continued to travel for several days.

The country afforded us an excellent road, the route being generally over high and very level prairies; and we met with no other delay than being frequently obliged to bridge one of the numerous streams, which were well timbered with ash, elm, cotton-wood, and a very large oak—the latter being, occasionally, five or six feet in diameter, with a spreading summit. *Sida coccinea* is very frequent in vermilion-colored patches on the high and low prairie; and I remarked that it has a very pleasant perfume.

The wild sensitive plant (*Schrankia angustata*) occurs frequently, generally on the dry prairies, in valleys of streams, and frequently on the broken prairie bank. I remark that the leaflets close instantly to a very light touch. *Amorpha*, with the same *psoralea*, and a dwarf species of *lupinus*, are the characteristic plants.

On the 19th, in the afternoon, we crossed the Pawnee road to the Arkansas, and, travelling a few miles onward, the prevailing quiet of the prairies was suddenly broken by the appearence of five or six buffalo bulls, forming a vanguard of immense herds, among which we were travelling a few days afterward. Prairie dogs were seen for the first time during the day; and we had the good fortune to obtain an antelope for supper. Our elevation had now increased to one thousand nine hundred feet. *Sida coccinea* was a characteristic on the creek bottoms, and buffalo grass is becoming abundant on the higher parts of the ridges.

June 21st.—During the forenoon we travelled up a branch of the creek on which we had encamped, in a broken country, where, however, the dividing ridges always afforded a good road. Plants were few; and with the short sward of the buffalo grass, which now prevailed everywhere, giving to the prairies a smooth and mossy appearance, were mingled frequent patches of a beautiful red grass (*Aristida pallens*), which had made its appearance only within the last few days.

We halted to noon at a solitary cotton-wood in a hollow, near which was killed the first buffalo, a large old bull.

Antelope appeared in bands during the day. Crossing here to the affluents of the Republican, we encamped on a fork about forty feet wide and one foot deep, flowing with a swift current over a sandy bed, and well wooded with ash-leaved maple (*Negundo fraxinifolium*), elm, cotton-wood, and a few white oaks. We were visited in the evening by a very violent storm, accompanied by wind, lightning, and thunder; a cold rain falling in torrents. According to the barometer our elevation was two thousand one hundred and thirty feet above the Gulf.

At noon on the 23d we descended into the valley of a principal fork of the Republican, a beautiful stream forty feet wide and four feet deep, with a dense border of wood, consisting principally of varieties of ash. It was musical with the notes of many birds, which, from the vast expanse of silent prairie around, seemed all to have collected here. We continued during the afternoon our route along the river, which was populous with prairie dogs (the bottoms being entirely occupied with their villages), and late in the evening encamped on its banks.

The prevailing timber is a blue-foliaged ash (*fraxinus*, near *F. Americana*) and ash-leaved maple. With these were *Fraxinus Americana*, cotton-wood, and long-leaved willow. We gave to this stream the name of Prairie Dog River. Elevation two thousand three hundred and fifty feet. Our road on the 25th lay over high smooth ridges, three thousand one hundred feet above the sea; buffalo in great numbers, absolutely covering the face of the country. At evening we encamped within a few miles of the main Republican, on a little creek where the air was fragrant with the perfume of *Artemisia filifolia*, which we here saw for the first time, and which was now in bloom. Shortly after leaving our encampment on the 26th, we found suddenly that the nature of the country had entirely changed. Bare sand-hills everywhere surrounded us in the undulating ground along which we were moving; and the plants peculiar to a sandy soil made their appearance in abundance. A few miles farther we entered the valley of a large stream, afterward known to be the Republican Fork of the Kansas, whose shallow waters, with a depth of only a few inches, were spread out over a bed of yellowish-white sand six hundred yards wide.

With the exception of one or two distant and detached groves, no timber of any kind was to be seen; and the features of the country assumed a desert character, with which the broad river, struggling for existence among quicksands along the treeless banks, was strikingly in keeping. On the opposite side the broken ridges assumed almost a mountainous appearance; and, fording the stream, we continued on our course among these ridges, and encamped late in the evening at a little pond of very bad water, from which we drove away a herd of buffalo that were standing in and about it.

Our encampment this evening was three thousand five hundred feet above the sea. We travelled now for several days through a broken and dry sandy region, about four thousand feet above the sea, where there were no running streams; and some anxiety was constantly felt on account of the uncertainty of water, which was only to be found in small lakes that occurred occasionally among the hills. The discovery of these always brought pleasure to the camp, as around them were generally green flats, which afforded abundant pasturage for our animals; and here were usually collected herds of the buffalo, which now were scattered over all the country in countless numbers.

The soil of bare and hot sands supported a varied and exuberant growth of plants, which were much further advanced than we had previously found them, and whose showy bloom somewhat relieved the appear-

ance of general sterility.   Crossing the summit of an elevated and continuous range of rolling hills, on the afternoon of June 30th we found ourselves
overlooking a broad and misty valley where, about ten miles distant, and
one thousand feet below us, the South Fork of the Platte was rolling mag-
nificently along, swollen with the waters of the melting snows.   It was in
strong and refreshing contrast with the parched country from which we had
just issued ; and when at night the broad expanse of water grew indistinct,
it almost seemed that we had pitched our tents on the shore of the sea.

Travelling along up the valley of the river, here four thousand feet
above the sea, in the afternoon of July 1st we caught a far and uncertain
view of a faint blue mass in the west, as the sun sank behind it ; and from
our camp in the morning, at the mouth of Bijou, Long's Peak and the
neighboring mountains stood out into the sky, grand and luminously white,
covered to their bases with glittering snow.

On the evening of the 3d, as we were journeying along the partially
overflowed bottoms of the Platte, where our passage stirred up swarms of
mosquitoes, we came unexpectedly upon an Indian, who was perched on a
bluff, curiously watching the movements of our caravan.   He belonged to
a village of Oglallah Sioux, who had lost all their animals in the severity
of the preceding winter, and were now on their way up the Bijou Fork to
beg horses from the Arapahoes, who were hunting buffalo at the head of
that river.   Several came into our camp at noon ; and as they were hungry, as usual, they were provided with buffalo meat, of which the hunters
had brought in an abundant supply.

About noon on July 4th we arrived at the fort, where Mr. St. Vrain
received us with his customary kindness and invited us to join him in a
feast which had been prepared in honor of the day.

Our animals were very much worn out, and our stock of provisions entirely exhausted when we arrived at the fort ; but I was disappointed in
my hope of obtaining relief, as I found it in a very impoverished condition ;
and we were able to procure only a little unbolted Mexican flour and some
salt, with a few pounds of powder and lead.

As regarded provisions, it did not much matter in a country where
rarely the day passed without seeing some kind of game, and where it was
frequently abundant.   It was a rare thing to lie down hungry, and we had
already learned to think bread a luxury ; but we could not proceed without
animals, and our own were not capable of prosecuting the journey beyond
the mountains without relief.

I had been informed that a large number of mules had recently arrived
at Taos from Upper California ; and as our friend Maxwell was about to
continue his journey to that place, where a portion of his family resided,
I engaged him to purchase for me ten or twelve mules, with the under-

standing that he should pack them with provisions and other necessaries, and meet me at the mouth of the *Fontaine qui bouit,* on the Arkansas River, to which point I would be led in the course of the survey.

Agreeably to his own request, and in the conviction that his habits of life and education had not qualified him to endure the hard life of a voyageur, I discharged here one of my party, Oscar Sarpy, having furnished him with arms and means of transportation to Fort Laramie, where he would be in the line of caravans returning to the States.

At daybreak on July 6th Maxwell was on his way to Taos; and a few hours after we also had recommenced our journey up the Platte, which was continuously timbered with cotton-wood and willow, on a generally sandy soil. Passing on the way the remains of two abandoned forts (one of which, however, was still in good condition), we reached, in ten miles, Fort Lancaster, the trading establishment of Mr. Lupton. His post was beginning to assume the appearance of a comfortable farm: stock, hogs, and cattle, were ranging about on the prairie; there were different kinds of poultry; and there was the wreck of a promising garden in which a considerable variety of vegetables had been in a flourishing condition, but it had been almost entirely ruined by the recent high waters. I remained to spend with him an agreeable hour, and set off in a cold storm of rain, which was accompanied with violent thunder and lightning. We encamped immediately on the river, sixteen miles from St. Vrain's. Several Arapahoes, on their way to the village which was encamped a few miles above us, passed by the camp in the course of the afternoon. Night set in stormy and cold, with heavy and continuous rain which lasted until morning.

July 7th.—We made this morning an early start, continuing to travel up the Platte; and in a few miles frequent bands of horses and mules, scattered for several miles round about, indicated our approach to the Arapaho village, which we found encamped in a beautiful bottom, and consisting of about one hundred and sixty lodges. It appeared extremely populous, with a great number of children; a circumstance which indicated a regular supply of the means of subsistence. The chiefs, who were gathered together at the farther end of the village, received us (as probably strangers are always received to whom they desire to show respect or regard) by throwing their arms around our necks and embracing us.

It required some skill in horsemanship to keep the saddle during the performance of this ceremony, as our American horses exhibited for them the same fear they have for a bear or any other wild animal. Having very few goods with me, I was only able to make them a meagre present, accounting for the poverty of the gift by explaining that my goods had been left with the wagons in charge of Mr. Fitzpatrick, who was well known to them as the White-Head, or the Broken Hand. I saw here, as

I had remarked in an Arapaho village the preceding year, near the lodges of the chiefs, tall tripods of white poles supporting their spears and shields, which showed it to be a regular custom.

Though disappointed in obtaining the presents which had been evidently expected, they behaved very courteously, and after a little conversation I left them, and, continuing on up the river, halted to noon on the bluff, as the bottoms were almost inundated; continuing in the afternoon our route along the mountains, which were dark, misty, and shrouded— threatening a storm; the snow-peaks sometimes glittering through the clouds beyond the first ridge.

We surprised a grizzly bear sauntering along the river; which, raising himself upon his hind legs, took a deliberate survey of us that did not appear very satisfactory to him, and he scrambled into the river and swam to the opposite side. We halted for the night a little above Cherry Creek; the evening cloudy, with many mosquitoes.

Some indifferent observations placed the camp in latitude 39° 43′ 53″, and chronometric longitude 105° 24′ 34″.

July 8th.—We continued to-day to travel up the Platte; the morning pleasant, with a prospect of fairer weather. During the forenoon our way lay over a more broken country, with a gravelly and sandy surface; although the immediate bottom of the river was a good soil, of a dark sandy mould, resting upon a stratum of large pebbles, or rolled stones, as at Laramie Fork. On our right, and apparently very near, but probably eight or ten miles distant, and two or three thousand feet above us, ran the first range of the mountains, like a dark corniced line, in clear contrast with the great snowy chain which, immediately beyond, rose glittering five thousand feet above them.

We caught this morning a view of Pike's Peak; but it appeared for a moment only, as clouds rose early over the mountains, and shrouded them in mist and rain all the day. In the first range were visible, as at the Red Buttes on the North Fork, very lofty escarpments of red rock. While travelling through this region, I remarked that always in the morning the lofty peaks were visible and bright, but very soon small white clouds began to settle around them—brewing thicker and darker as the day advanced, until the afternoon, when the thunder began to roll; and invariably at evening we had more or less of a thunder-storm.

At eleven o'clock, and twenty-one miles from St. Vrain's Fort, we reached a point in this Southern Fork of the Platte where the stream is divided into three forks; two of these (one of them being much the largest) issuing directly from the mountains on the west, and forming, with the easternmost branch, a river of the plains. The elevation of this point is about five thousand five hundred feet above the sea; this river falling two thousand eight hundred feet in a distance of three hundred and sixteen miles, to its junction with the North Fork of the Platte. In this estimate the elevation of the junction is assumed as given by our barometrical observations in 1842.

On the easternmost branch, up which we took our way, we first came among the pines growing on the top of a very high bank, and where we halted on it to noon ; quaking asp (*Populus tremuloides*) was mixed with the cotton-wood, and there were excellent grass and rushes for the animals.

During the morning we came across many beautiful flowers, which we had not hitherto met. Among them, the common blue flowering flax made its first appearance; and a tall and handsome species of *gilia*, with slender scarlet flowers, which appeared yesterday for the first time, was very frequent to-day.

We had found very little game since leaving the fort, and provisions began to get unpleasantly scant, as we had no meat for several days ; but toward sundown, when we had already made up our minds to sleep another night without supper, Lajeunesse had the good fortune to kill a fine deer, which he found feeding in a hollow near by ; and as the rain began to fall, threatening an unpleasant night, we hurried to secure a comfortable camp in the timber.

To-night the camp fires, girdled with *appolas* of fine venison, looked cheerful in spite of the stormy weather.

July 9th.—On account of the low state of our provisions and the scarcity of game, I determined to vary our route, and proceed several camps to the eastward, in the hope of falling in with the buffalo. This route along the dividing grounds between the South Fork of the Platte and the Arkansas, would also afford some additional geographical information. This morning, therefore, we turned to the eastward, along the upper waters of the stream on which we had encamped, entering a country of picturesque and varied scenery ; broken into rocky hills of singular shapes ; little valleys, with pure crystal water, here leaping swiftly along, and there losing itself in the sands; green spots of luxuriant grass, flowers of all colors, and timber of different kinds—everything to give it a varied beauty, except game.

To one of these remarkably shaped hills, having on the summit a circular flat rock, two or three hundred yards in circumference, some one gave the name of Pound-cake rock, which it has been permitted to retain, as our hungry people seemed to think it a very agreeable comparison. In the afternoon a buffalo bull was killed, and we encamped on a small stream, near the road which runs from St. Vrain's fort to the Arkansas.

July 10th.—Snow fell heavily on the mountains during the night, and Pike's Peak this morning is luminous and grand, covered from the summit, as low down as we can see, with glittering white. Leaving the encampment at six o'clock, we continued our easterly course over a rolling country, near to the high ridges, which are generally rough and rocky with a coarse conglomerate displayed in masses, and covered with pines. This rock is very friable, and it is undoubtedly from its decomposition that the prairies derive their sandy and gravelly formation.

In six miles we crossed a head-water of the Kioway River, on which we found a strong fort and *corrál* that had been built in the spring, and halted to noon on the principal branch of the river. During the morning our route led over a dark vegetable mould mixed with sand and gravel, the characteristic plant being *esparcette* (*Onobrychis sativa*), a species of clover which is much used in certain parts of Germany for pasturage of stock—principally hogs. It is sown on rocky, waste ground, which would otherwise be useless, and grows very luxuriantly, requiring only a renewal of the seed about once in fifteen years. Its abundance here greatly adds to the pastoral value of this region.

A species of antennaria in flower was very common along the line of road, and the creeks were timbered with willow and pine. We encamped on Bijou's fork, the water of which, unlike the clear streams we had previously crossed, is of a whitish color, and the soil of the bottom a very hard, tough clay. There was a prairie-dog village on the bottom, and, in the endeavor to unearth one of the little animals, we labored ineffectually in the tough clay until dark. After descending with a slight inclination, until it had gone the depth of two feet, the hole suddenly turned at a sharp angle in another direction for one more foot in depth, when it again turned, taking an ascending direction to the next nearest hole. I have no doubt that all their little habitations communicate with each other.

The greater part of the people were sick to-day, and I was inclined to attribute their indisposition to the meat of the bull which had been killed the previous day.

July 11*th.*—There were no indications of buffalo having been recently in the neighborhood; and, unwilling to travel farther eastward, I turned this morning to the southward, up the valley of Bijou. *Esparcette* occurred universally, and among the plants on the river I noticed, for the first time during this journey, a few small bushes of the *absinthe* of the voyageurs, which is commonly used for fire-wood (*Artemisia tridentata*).

Yesterday and to-day the road has been ornamented with the showy bloom of a beautiful *lupinus*, a characteristic in many parts of the mountain region, on which were generally great numbers of an insect with very bright colors (*Litta vesicatoria*).

As we were riding quietly along, eagerly searching every hollow in search of game, we discovered, at a little distance in the prairie, a large grizzly bear so busily engaged in digging roots that he did not perceive us until we were galloping down a little hill fifty yards from him, when he charged upon us with such sudden energy that several of us came near losing our saddles.   Being wounded, he commenced retreating to a rocky piny ridge near by, from which we were not able to cut him off, and we entered the timber with him.   The way was very much blocked up with fallen timber ; and we kept up a running fight for some time, animated by the bear charging among the horses.   He did not fall until after he had received six rifle balls.   He was miserably poor, and added nothing to our stock of provisions.

We followed the stream to its head in a broken ridge, which, according to the barometer, was about seven thousand five hundred feet above the sea.   This is a piny elevation into which the prairies are gathered, and from which the waters flow in almost every direction to the Arkansas, Platte, and Kansas Rivers ; the latter stream having here its remotest sources.   Although somewhat rocky and broken, and covered with pines, in comparison with the neighboring mountains it scarcely forms an interruption to the great prairie plains which sweep up to their bases.

The annexed view of Pike's Peak from this camp, at the distance of forty miles, represents very correctly the manner in which this mountain barrier presents itself to travellers on the plains, which sweep almost directly to its bases ; an immense and comparatively smooth and grassy prairie, in very strong contrast with the black masses of timber, and the glittering snow above them.   This is the picture which has been left upon my mind, and its general features are given in the accompanying view.

With occasional exceptions, comparatively so very small as not to require mention, these prairies are everywhere covered with a close and vigorous growth of a great variety of grasses, among which the most abundant is the buffalo-grass (*Sesleria dactyloides.*)   Between the Platte and Arkansas Rivers, that part of this region which forms the basin drained by the waters of the Kansas, with which our operations made us more particularly acquainted, is based upon a formation of calcareous rocks.

The soil of all this country is excellent, admirably adapted to agricultural purposes, and would support a large agricultural and pastoral population.   The plain is watered by many streams.   Throughout its western half these are shallow with sandy beds, becoming deeper as they reach the richer lands approaching the Missouri River ; they generally have bottom lands bordered by bluffs varying from fifty to five hundred feet in height.   In all this region the timber is entirely confined to the streams.   In the eastern half, where the soil is a deep, rich vegetable mould, retentive of rain and moisture, it is of vigorous growth, and of many different kinds ; and throughout the western half it consists entirely of various

VIEW OF PIKE'S PEAK.

species of cotton-wood, which deserves to be called the tree of the desert —growing in sandy soils, where no other tree will grow ; pointing out the existence of water, and furnishing to the traveller fuel, and food for his animals. Add to this that the western border of the plain is occupied by the Sioux, Arapaho, and Cheyenne nations, and its eastern limits by the Pawnees and other half-civilized tribes for whom the intermediate country is a war ground ; and a tolerably correct idea can be formed of the appearance and condition of the country.

Descending a somewhat precipitous and rocky hill-side among the pines, which rarely appear elsewhere than on the ridge, we encamped at its foot, where there were several springs, which make one of the extreme sources of the Smoky Hill Fork of the Kansas. From this place the view extended over the Arkansas Valley, and the Spanish peaks in the south beyond.

As the greater part of the men continued sick, I encamped here for the day, and ascertained conclusively, from experiments on myself, that their illness was caused by the meat of the buffalo bull.

On the summit of the ridge, near the camp, were several rock-built forts, which in front were very difficult of approach, and in the rear were protected by a precipice entirely beyond the reach of a rifle ball. The evening was tolerably clear, with a temperature at sunset of 63°. Elevation of the camp, seven thousand three hundred feet.

Turning the next day to the southwest, we reached, in the course of the morning, the wagon road to the settlements on the Arkansas River, and encamped in the afternoon on the *Fontaine-qui-bouit* (or Boiling Spring) River, where it was fifty feet wide, with a swift current. I afterward found that the spring and river owe their names to the bubbling of the effervescing gas in the former, and not to the temperature of the water which is cold. During the morning a tall species of *gilia*, with a slender white flower, was characteristic ; and in the latter part of the day, another variety of *esparcette* (wild clover), having the flower white, was equally so. We had a fine sunset of golden brown ; and in the evening, a very bright moon, with the near mountains, made a beautiful scene. Thermometer, at sunset, was 69°, and our elevation above the sea five thousand eight hundred feet.

July 13*th.*—The morning was clear, with a northwesterly breeze, and the thermometer at sunrise at 46°. There were no clouds along the mountains, and the morning sun showed very clearly their rugged character.

We resumed our journey very early down the river, following an extremely good lodge-trail, which issues by the head of this stream from the bayou Salade, a high mountain valley behind Pike's Peak. The soil along the road was sandy and gravelly, and the river well timbered.

We halted at noon under the shade of some fine large cotton-woods, our animals luxuriating on rushes (*Equisetum hyemale*), which, along this river, were remarkably abundant. A variety of cactus made its appearance, and among several strange plants were numerous and beautiful clusters of a plant resembling *mirabilis jalapa*, with a handsome convolvulus I had not hitherto seen (*calystegia*).

In the afternoon we passed near the encampment of a hunter named Maurice, who had been out on the plains in pursuit of buffalo calves, a number of which I saw among some domestic cattle near his lodge. Shortly afterward, a party of mountaineers galloped up to us—fine-looking and hardy men, dressed in skins and mounted on good, fat horses; among them were several Connecticut men, a portion of Wyeth's party, whom I had seen the year before, and others were men from the western States.

Continuing down the river, we encamped at noon on the 14th at its mouth, on the Arkansas River. A short distance above our encampment, on the left bank of the Arkansas, is a *pueblo* (as the Mexicans call their civilized Indian villages), where a number of mountaineers, who had married Spanish women in the valley of Taos, had collected together and occupied themselves in farming, carrying on at the same time a desultory Indian trade. They were principally Americans, and treated us with all the rude hospitality their situation admitted; but as all commercial intercourse with New Mexico was now interrupted, in consequence of Mexican decrees to that effect, there was nothing to be had in the way of provisions. They had, however, a fine stock of cattle, and furnished us an abundance of excellent milk. I learned here that Maxwell, in company with two other men, had started for Taos on the morning of the 9th, but that he would probably fall into the hands of the Utah Indians, commonly called *Spanish Utes*.

As Maxwell had no knowledge of their being in the vicinity when he crossed the Arkansas, his chance of escape was very doubtful; but I did not entertain much apprehension for his life, having great confidence in his prudence and courage. I was further informed that there had been a popular tumult among the *pueblos*, or civilized Indians residing near Taos, against the "*foreigners*" of that place, in which they had plundered their houses and ill-treated their families. Among those whose property had been destroyed was Mr. Beaubien, father-in-law of Maxwell, from whom I had expected to obtain supplies, and who had been obliged to make his escape to Santa Fé.

By this position of affairs our expectation of obtaining supplies from Taos was cut off. I had here the satisfaction to meet our good buffalo hunter of 1842, Christopher Carson, whose services I considered myself

THE SPANISH PEAKS.

fortunate to secure again ; and as a reinforcement of mules was absolutely necessary, I despatched him immediately, with an account of our necessities, to Mr. Charles Bent, whose principal post is on the Arkansas River, about seventy-five miles below *Fontaine-qui-bouit.*

He was directed to proceed from that post by the nearest route across the country, and meet me with what animals he should be able to obtain at St. Vrain's Fort. I also admitted into the party Charles Towns—a native of St. Louis, a serviceable man, with many of the qualities of a good voyageur.

According to our observations the latitude of the mouth of the river is 38° 15′ 23″ ; its longitude 104° 58′ 30″ ; and its elevation above the sea four thousand eight hundred and eighty feet.

On the morning of the 16th, the time for Maxwell's arrival having expired, we resumed our journey, leaving for him a note in which it was stated that I would wait for him at St. Vrain's Fort until the morning of the 26th, in the event that he should succeed in his commission. Our direction was up the Boiling Spring River, it being my intention to visit the celebrated springs from which the river takes its name, and which are on its upper waters at the foot of Pike's Peak.

Our animals fared well while we were on this stream, there being everywhere a great abundance of *prêle. Ipomea leptophylla*, in bloom, was a characteristic plant along the river, generally in large bunches, with two to five flowers on each. Beautiful clusters of the plant resembling *Mirabilis jalapa* were numerous, and *Glycyrrhiza lepidota* was a characteristic of the bottoms. Currants, nearly ripe, were abundant, and among the shrubs which covered the bottom was a very luxuriant growth of chenopodiaceous shrubs four to six feet high.

On the afternoon of the 17th we entered among the broken ridges at the foot of the mountains, where the river made several forks. Leaving the camp to follow slowly, I rode ahead in the afternoon in search of the springs. In the meantime the clouds, which had been gathered all the afternoon over the mountains, began to roll down their sides ; and a storm so violent burst upon me that it appeared I had entered the storehouse of the thunder-storms.

I continued, however, to ride along up the river until about sunset, and was beginning to be doubtful of finding the springs before the next day, when I came suddenly upon a large, smooth rock, about twenty yards in diameter, where the water from several springs was bubbling and boiling up in the midst of a white incrustation with which it had covered a portion of the rock. As this did not correspond with a description given me by the hunters, I did not stop to taste the water, but, dismounting, walked a little way up the river, and, passing through a narrow thicket of shrubbery bordering the stream, stepped directly upon a huge white rock, at the foot of which the river, already become a torrent, foamed along, broken by a small fall.

A deer which had been drinking at the spring was startled by my approach, and, springing across the river, bounded off up the mountain. In the upper part of the rock, which had apparently been formed by deposition, was a beautiful white basin, overhung by currant bushes, in which the cold, clear water bubbled up, kept in constant motion by the escaping gas, and overflowing the rock, which it had almost entirely covered with a smooth crust of glistening white. I had all day refrained from drinking, reserving myself for the spring; and as I could not well be more wet than the rain had already made me, I lay down by the side of the basin, and drank heartily of the delightful water.

The accompanying sketch is only a rude one, but it will give some idea of the character of the scenery and the beauty of this spot, immediately at the foot of lofty mountains, beautifully timbered, which sweep closely round, shutting up the little valley in a kind of cove. As it was beginning to grow dark, I rode quickly down the river, on which I found the camp a few miles below.

The morning of the 18th was beautiful and clear, and, all the people being anxious to drink of these famous waters, we encamped immediately at the springs, and spent there a very pleasant day. On the opposite side of the river is another locality of springs, which are entirely of the same nature.

The water has a very agreeable taste, which Mr. Preuss found very much to resemble that of the famous Selters Springs, in the Grand Duchy Nassau, a country famous for wine and mineral waters; and it is almost of entirely of the same character, though still more agreeable than that of the famous Beer Springs, near Bear River of the Great Salt Lake.

The following is an analysis of an incrustation with which the water had covered a piece of wood lying on the rock:

Carbonate of lime	92.25
Carbonate of magnesia	1.21
Sulphate of lime ⎫	
Chloride of calcium ⎬	0.23
Chloride of magnesia ⎭	
Silica	1.50
Vegetable matter	0.20
Moisture and loss	4.61
	100.00

At eleven o'clock, when the temperature of the air was 73°, that of the water in this was 60.5°; and that of the upper spring, which issued from

UPPER ARKANSAS PRAIRIES NEAR RIVER HILLS.

WEST ROCKY MOUNTAINS BORDERING GREAT COLORADO VALLEY.

the flat rock, more exposed to the sun, was 69°. At sunset, when the temperature of the air was 66°, that of the lower spring was 58°, and that of the upper 61°.

July 19*th.*—A beautiful and clear morning, with a slight breeze from the northwest; the temperature of the air at sunrise being 57.5°. At this time the temperature of the lower spring was 57.8°, and that of the upper 54.3°.

The trees in the neighborhood were birch, willow, pine, and an oak resembling *Quercus alba.* In the shrubbery along the river are currant bushes (*ribes*), of which the fruit has a singular piny flavor; and on the mountain side, in a red, gravelly soil, is a remarkable coniferous tree (perhaps an *abies*), having the leaves singularly long, broad, and scattered, with bushes of *Spiræa ariæfolia.* By our observations this place is six thousand three hundred and fifty feet above the sea, in latitude 38° 52′ 10″, and longitude 105° 22′ 45″.

Resuming our journey on this morning, we descended the river in order to reach the mouth of the eastern fork, which I proposed to ascend. The left bank of the river here is very much broken. There is a handsome little bottom on the right, and both banks are exceedingly picturesque— strata of red rock, in nearly perpendicular walls, crossing the valley from north to south.

About three miles below the springs, on the right bank of the river, is a nearly perpendicular limestone rock, presenting a uniformly unbroken surface, twenty to forty feet high, containing very great numbers of a large univalve shell, which appears to belong to the genus *inoceramus*, and in the appendix is designated by the No. 42.

In contact with this, to the westward, was another stratum of limestone, containing fossil shells of a different character; and still higher up on the stream were parallel strata, consisting of a compact, somewhat crystalline limestone, and argillaceous bituminous limestone in thin layers. During the morning we travelled up the eastern fork of the *Fontaine-qui-bouit* River, our road being roughened by frequent deep gullies timbered with pine, and halted to noon on a small branch of this stream, timbered principally with the narrow-leaved cotton-wood (*Populus angustifolia*), called by the Canadians *Liard amère.*

On a hill near by were two remarkable columns of a grayish-white conglomerate rock, one of which was about twenty feet high, and two feet in diameter. They are surmounted by slabs of a dark ferruginous conglomerate, forming black caps, and adding very much to their columnar effect at a distance. This rock is very destructible by the action of the weather, and the hill, of which they formerly constituted a part, is entirely abraded.

A shaft of the gun-carriage was broken in the afternoon; and we made an early halt, the stream being from twelve to twenty feet wide, with clear water.   As usual, the clouds had gathered to a storm over the mountains, and we had a showery evening.   At sunset the thermometer stood at 62°, and our elevation above the sea was six thousand five hundred and thirty feet.

July 20th.—This morning (as we generally found the mornings under these mountains) was very clear and beautiful, and the air cool and pleasant, with the thermometer at 44°.   We continued our march up the stream, between pine hills on the one hand, and the main Black Hills on the other, along a green sloping bottom, toward the ridge which separates the waters of the Platte from those of the Arkansas.

As we approached the dividing ridge, the whole valley was radiant with flowers ; blue, yellow, pink, white, scarlet, and purple vied with each other in splendor.   Esparcette was one of the highly characteristic plants, and a bright-looking flower (*Gaillardia aristata*) was very frequent ; but the most abundant plant along our road to-day was *Geranium maculatum*, which is the characteristic plant on this portion of the dividing grounds.

Crossing to the waters of the Platte, fields of blue flax added to the magnificence of this mountain garden ; this was occasionally four feet in height, which was a luxuriance of growth that I rarely saw this almost universal plant attain throughout the journey.   Continuing down a branch of the Platte, among high and very steep timbered hills, covered with fragments of rock, toward evening we issued from the piny region, and made a late encampment near Poundcake Rock, on that fork of the river which we had ascended on July 8th.   Our animals enjoyed the abundant rushes this evening, as the flies were so bad among the pines that they had been much harassed.

A deer was killed here this evening ; and again the evening was overcast, and a collection of brilliant red clouds in the west was followed by the customary squall of rain.

Achillea millefolium (milfoil) was among the characteristic plants of the river bottoms to-day.   This was one of the most common plants during the whole of our journey, occurring in almost every variety of situation. I noticed it on the lowlands of the rivers, near the coast of the Pacific, and near to the snow among the mountains of the Sierra Nevada.

During this excursion we had surveyed to its head one of the two principal branches of the Upper Arkansas, seventy-five miles in length, and entirely completed our survey of the South Fork of the Platte to the extreme sources of that portion of the river which belongs to the plains and heads in the broken hills of the Arkansas dividing ridge at the foot of the mountains.   That portion of its waters which were collected among these mountains it was hoped to explore on our homeward voyage.

Reaching St. Vrain's Fort on the morning of the 23d, we found Mr. Fitz-

UTAH INDIAN

patrick and his party in good order and excellent health, and with him my true and reliable friend, Kit Carson, who had brought ten good mules with the necessary pack-saddles.

Mr. Fitzpatrick, who had often endured every extremity of want during the course of his mountain life, and knew well the value of provisions in this country, had watched over our stock with jealous vigilance; and there was an abundance of flour, rice, sugar, and coffee in the camp; and again we fared luxuriously. Meat was, however, very scarce; and two very small pigs, which we obtained at the fort, did not go far among forty men. Mr. Fitzpatrick had been here a week, during which time his men had been occupied in refitting the camp; and the repose had been very beneficial to his animals, which were now in tolerably good condition.

I had been able to obtain no certain information in regard to the character of the passes in this portion of the Rocky Mountain range, which had always been represented as impracticable for carriages, but the exploration of which was incidentally contemplated with the view of finding some convenient point of passage for the road of emigration, which would enable it to reach, on a more direct line, the usual ford of the Great Colorado—a place considered as determined by the nature of the country beyond that river. It is singular that, immediately at the foot of the mountains, I could find no one sufficiently acquainted with them to guide us to the plains at their western base; but the race of trappers who formerly lived in their recesses has almost entirely disappeared—dwindled to a few scattered individuals—some one or two of whom are regularly killed in the course of each year by the Indians.

It will be remembered that, in the previous year, I brought with me to their village, near this post, and hospitably treated on the way, several Cheyenne Indians whom I had met on the Lower Platte. Shortly after their arrival here, these were out with a party of Indians (themselves the principal men), which discovered a few trappers in the neighboring mountains, whom they immediately murdered, although one of them had been nearly thirty years in the country, and was perfectly well known, as he had grown gray among them.

Through this portion of the mountains, also, are the customary roads of the war-parties going out against the Utah and Shoshonee Indians; and occasionally parties from the Crow nation make their way down to the southward along this chain, in the expectation of surprising some straggling lodges of their enemies. Shortly before our arrival, one of their parties had attacked an Arapaho village in the vicinity, which they had found unexpectedly strong; and their assault was turned into a rapid flight, and a hot pursuit, in which they had been compelled to abandon the animals they had ridden, and escape on their war-horses.

Into this uncertain and dangerous region small parties of three or four trappers who now could collect together rarely ventured; and consequently it was seldom visited and little known.   Having determined to try the passage by a pass through a spur of the mountains made by the *Cáche-à-la-Poudre* River, which rises in the high bed of mountains around Long's Peak, I thought it advisable to avoid any encumbrance which would occasion detention, and accordingly again separated the party into two divisions—one of which, under the command of Mr. Fitzpatrick, was directed to cross the plains to the mouth of Laramie River, and, continuing thence its route along the usual emigrant road, meet me at Fort Hall, a post belonging to the Hudson Bay Company, and situated on Snake River, as it is commonly called in the Oregon Territory, although better known to us as Lewis' Fork of the Columbia.   The latter name is there restricted to one of the upper forks of the river.

Our Delaware Indians having determined to return to their homes, it became necessary to provide this party with a good hunter; and I accordingly engaged in that capacity Alexander Godey, a young man about twenty-five years of age, who had been in this country six or seven years, all of which time he had been actively employed in hunting for the support of the posts, or in solitary trading expeditions among the Indians.

In courage and professional skill he was a formidable rival to Carson, and constantly afterwards was among the best and most efficient of the party, and in difficult situations was of incalculable value.   Hiram Powers, one of the men belonging to Mr. Fitzpatrick's party, was discharged at this place.

A French engagé at Lupton's Fort had been shot in the back on July 4th, and died during our absence to the Arkansas.   The wife of the murdered man, an Indian woman of the Snake nation, desirous, like Naomi of old, to return to her people, requested and obtained permission to travel with my party to the neighborhood of Bear River, where she expected to meet with some of their villages.   Happier than the Jewish widow, she carried with her two children, pretty little half-breeds, who added much to the liveliness of the camp.   Her baggage was carried on five or six pack-horses; and I gave her a small tent, for which I no longer had any use, as I had procured a lodge at the fort.

For my own party I selected the following men, a number of whom old associations rendered agreeable to me:

Charles Preuss, Christopher Carson, Basil Lajeunesse, François Badeau, Jean Baptiste Bernier, Louis Menard, Raphael Proue, Jacob Dodson, Louis Zindel, Henry Lee, Jean Baptiste Derosier, François Lajeunesse, and Auguste Vasquez.

By observation the latitude of the post is 40° 16′ 33″, and its longitude

105° 12′ 23″, depending, with all the other longitudes along this portion of the line, upon a subsequent occultation of September 13, 1843, to which they are referred by the chronometer.

Its distance from Kansas Landing, by the road we travelled (which, it will be remembered, was very winding along the Lower Kansas River), was seven hundred and fifty miles. The rate of the chronometer, determined by observations at this place for the interval of our absence, during this month, was 33.72″, which you will hereafter see did not sensibly change during the ensuing month, and remained nearly constant during the remainder of our journey across the continent. This was the rate used in referring to St. Vrain's Fort, the longitude between that place and the mouth of the *Fontaine-qui-bouit.*

Our various barometrical observations, which are better worthy of confidence than the isolated determination of 1842, give, for the elevation of the fort above the sea, four thousand nine hundred and thirty feet. The barometer here used was also a better one, and less liable to derangement.

At the end of two days, which was allowed to my animals for necessary repose, all the arrangements had been completed, and on the afternoon of the 26th we resumed our respective routes. Some little trouble was experienced in crossing the Platte, the waters of which were still kept up by rains and melting snow ; and, having travelled only about four miles, we encamped in the evening on Thompson's Creek, where we were very much disturbed by mosquitoes.

The following days we continued our march westward over comparative plains, and, fording the *Cáche-à-la-Poudre* on the morning of the 28th, entered the Black Hills, and nooned on this stream in the mountains beyond them. Passing over a fine large bottom in the afternoon, we reached a place where the river was shut up in the hills ; and, ascending a ravine, made a laborious and very difficult passage around by a gap, striking the river again about dusk. A little labor, however, would remove this difficulty, and render the road to this point a very excellent one. The evening closed in dark, with rain, and the mountains looked gloomy.

July 29th.—Leaving our encampment about seven in the morning, we travelled until three in the afternoon along the river, which, for this distance of about six miles, runs directly through a spur of the main mountains.

We were compelled by the nature of the ground to cross the river eight or nine times at difficult, deep, and rocky fords, the stream running with great force, swollen by the rains—a true mountain torrent, only forty or fifty feet wide. It was a mountain valley of the narrowest kind—almost a chasm ; and the scenery very wild and beautiful.

Towering mountains rose round about ; their sides sometimes dark with forests of pine, and sometimes with lofty precipices, washed by the river ;

while below, as if they indemnified themselves in luxuriance for the scanty space, the green river bottom was covered with a wilderness of flowers, their tall spikes sometimes rising above our heads as we rode among them. A profusion of blossoms on a white flowering vine (*Clematis lasianthi*), which was abundant along the river, contrasted handsomely with the green foliage of the trees. The mountain appeared to be composed of a greenish gray and red granite, which in some places appeared to be in a state of decomposition, making a red soil.

The stream was wooded with cotton-wood, box-elder, and cherry, with currant and service-berry bushes. After a somewhat laborious day, during which it had rained incessantly, we encamped near the end of the pass at the mouth of a small creek, in sight of the great Laramie Plains.

It continued to rain heavily, and at evening the mountains were hid in mists; but there was no lack of wood, and the large fires we made to dry our clothes were very comfortable; and at night the hunters came in with a fine deer. Rough and difficult as we found the pass to-day, an excellent road may be made with a little labor. Elevation of the camp five thousand five hundred and forty feet, and distance from St. Vrain's Fort fifty-six miles.

July 30th.—The day was bright again; the thermometer at sunrise 52°; and leaving our encampment at eight o'clock, in about half a mile we crossed the *Câche-à-la-Poudre* River for the last time; and, entering a smoother country, we travelled along a kind of *vallon*, bounded on the right by red buttes and precipices, while to the left a high rolling country extended to a range of the Black Hills, beyond which rose the great mountains around Long's Peak.

By the great quantity of snow visible among them, it had probably snowed heavily thére the previous day, while it had rained on us in the valley.

We halted at noon on a small branch; and in the afternoon travelled over a high country, gradually ascending toward a range of *buttes*, or high hills covered with pines, which forms the dividing ridge between the waters we had left and those of Laramie River.

Late in the evening we encamped at a spring of cold water, near the summit of the ridge, having increased our elevation to seven thousand five hundred and twenty feet. During the day we had travelled twenty-four miles. By some indifferent observations our latitude is 41° 02′ 19″. A species of *hedeome* was characteristic along the whole day's route.

Emerging from the mountains, we entered a region of bright, fair weather. In my experience in this country I was forcibly impressed with the different character of the climate on opposite sides of the Rocky Mountain range. The vast prairie plain on the east is like the ocean; the rain and clouds from the constantly evaporating snow of the mountains rushing down into the heated air of the plains, on which you will have occasion to remark the frequent storms of rain we encountered during our journey.

July 31*st.*—The morning was clear; temperature 48°. A fine rolling road, among piny and grassy hills, brought us this morning into a large trail where an Indian village had recently passed. The weather was pleasant and cool; we were disturbed by neither mosquitoes nor flies; and the country was certainly extremely beautiful.

The slopes and broad ravines were absolutely covered with fields of flowers of the most exquisitely beautiful colors. Among those which had not hitherto made their appearance, and which here were characteristic, was a new *delphinium*, of a green and lustrous metallic-blue color, mingled with compact fields of several bright-colored varieties of *astragalus*, which were crowded together in splendid profusion. This trail conducted us through a remarkable defile to a little timbered creek, up which we wound our way, passing by a singular and massive wall of dark-red granite.

The formation of the country is a red feldspathic granite, overlying a decomposing mass of the same rock, forming the soil of all this region, which everywhere is red and gravelly, and appears to be of a great floral fertility.

As we emerged on a small tributary of the Laramie River, coming in sight of its principal stream, the flora became perfectly magnificent; and we congratulated ourselves, as we rode along our pleasant road, that we had substituted this for the uninteresting country between Laramie Hills and the Sweet Water Valley. We had no meat for supper last night, or breakfast this morning, and were glad to see Carson come in at noon with a good antelope.

A meridian observation of the sun placed us in latitude 41° 04′ 06.″ In the evening we encamped on the Laramie River, which is here very thinly timbered with scattered groups of cotton-wood at considerable intervals. From our camp we are able to distinguish the gorges in which are the sources of Câche-à-la-Poudre and Laramie Rivers; and the Medicine Bow Mountain, toward the point of which we are directing our course this after-noon, has been in sight the greater part of the day.

By observation the latitude was 41° 15′ 02″, and longitude 106° 16′ 54″. The same beautiful flora continued till about four in the afternoon, when it suddenly disappeared with the red soil, which became sandy and of a whit-ish-gray color. The evening was tolerably clear; temperature at sunset 64°. The day's journey was thirty miles.

August 1*st.*—The morning was calm and clear, with sunrise tempera-ture at 42°. We travelled to-day over a plain, or open rolling country, at the foot of the Medicine Bow Mountain; the soil in the morning being sandy, with fragments of rock abundant; and in the afternoon, when we approached closer to the mountain, so stony that we made but little way.

The beautiful plants of yesterday reappeared occasionally; flax in bloom occurred during the morning, and esparcette in luxuriant abundance was a characteristic of the stony ground in the afternoon. The camp was roused into a little excitement by a chase after a buffalo bull, and an encounter with a war-party of Sioux and Cheyenne Indians about thirty strong. Hares and antelope were seen during the day, and one of the latter was killed. The Laramie Peak was in sight this afternoon. The evening was clear, with scattered clouds: temperature 62°. The day's journey was twenty-six miles.

August 2d.—Temperature at sunrise 52°, and scenery and weather made our road to-day delightful. The neighboring mountain is thickly studded with pines, intermingled with the brighter foliage of aspens, and occasional spots like lawns between the patches of snow among the pines, and here and there on the heights. Our route below lay over a comparative plain covered with the same brilliant vegetation, and the day was clear and pleasantly cool.

During the morning we crossed many streams, clear and rocky, and broad grassy valleys, of a strong black soil washed down from the mountains and producing excellent pasturage. These were timbered with the red willow and long-leaved cotton-wood, mingled with aspen, as we approached the mountain more nearly toward noon. *Esparcette* was a characteristic, and flax occurred frequently in bloom. We halted at noon on the most western fork of Laramie River—a handsome stream about sixty feet wide and two feet deep, with clear water and a swift current over a bed composed entirely of bowlders or roll-stones. There was a large open bottom here, on which were many lodge-poles lying about; and in the edge of the surrounding timber were three strong forts that appeared to have been recently occupied.

At this place I became first acquainted with the *yampah* (*Anethum graveolens*), which I found our Snake woman engaged in digging in the low-timbered bottom of the creek. Among the Indians along the Rocky Mountains, and more particularly among the Shoshonee or Snake Indians, in whose territory it is very abundant, this is considered the best among the roots used for food. To us it was an interesting plant—a little link between the savage and civilized life. Here, among the Indians, its root is a common article of food, which they take pleasure in offering to strangers; while with us, in a considerable portion of America and Europe, the seeds are used to flavor soup. It grows more abundantly and in greater luxuriance on one of the neighboring tributaries of the Colorado than in any other part of this region; and on that stream, to which the Snakes are

UTAH INDIAN.

accustomed to resort every year to procure a supply of their favorite plant, they have bestowed the name of *Yampah* River. Among the trappers it is generally known as Little Snake River; but in this and other instances where it illustrated the history of the people inhabiting the country, I have preferred to retain on the map the aboriginal name.

By a meridional observation the latitude is 41° 45' 59".

In the afternoon we took our way directly across the spurs from the point of the mountain, where we had several ridges to cross; and, although the road was not rendered bad by the nature of the ground, it was made extremely rough by the stiff, tough bushes of *Artemisia tridentata,*[*] in this country commonly called sage.

This shrub now began to make its appearance in compact fields; and we were about to quit for a long time this country of excellent pasturage and brilliant flowers.

Ten or twelve buffalo bulls were seen during the afternoon; and we were surprised by the appearance of a large red ox. We gathered around him as if he had been an old acquaintance, with all our domestic feelings as much awakened as if we had come in sight of an old farm-house. He had probably made his escape from some party of emigrants on Green River; and, with a vivid remembrance of some old green field, he was pursuing the straightest course for the frontier that the country admitted. We carried him along with us as a prize; and when it was found in the morning that he had wandered off, I would not let him be pursued, for I would rather have gone through a starving time of three entire days than let him be killed after he had successfully run the gauntlet so far among the Indians.

I have been told by Mr. Bent's people of an ox, born and raised at St. Vrain's Fort, which made his escape from them at Elm Grove, near the frontier, having come in that year with the wagons. They were on their way out, and saw occasionally places where he had eaten and lain down to rest; but did not see him for about seven hundred miles, when they overtook him on the road, travelling along to the fort, having unaccountably escaped Indians and every other mischance.

We encamped at evening on the principal fork of Medicine Bow River, near to an isolated mountain called the Medicine *Butte*, which appeared to be about eighteen hundred feet above the plain, from which it rises abruptly, and was still white, nearly to its base, with a great quantity of snow. The streams were timbered with the long-leaved cotton-wood and red willow; and during the afternoon a species of onion was very abundant.

---

[*] The greater portion of our subsequent journey was through a region where this shrub constituted the tree of the country; and as it will often be mentioned in occasional descriptions, the word *artemisia* only will be used, without the specific name.

I obtained here an immersion of the first satellite of Jupiter, which, corresponding very nearly with the chronometer, placed us in longitude 106° 47′ 25″. The latitude, by observation, was 41° 37′ 16″; elevation above the sea seven thousand eight hundred feet, and distance from St. Vrain's Fort one hundred and forty-seven miles.

August 3d.—There was a white frost last night; the morning is clear and cool. We were early on the road, having breakfasted before sunrise, and in a few miles' travel entered the pass of the Medicine *Butte*, through which led a broad trail which had been recently travelled by a very large party. Immediately in the pass the road was broken by ravines, and we were obliged to clear a way through groves of aspens, which generally made their appearance when we reached elevated regions. According to the barometer this was eight thousand three hundred feet; and while we were detained in opening a road, I obtained a meridional observation of the sun, which gave 41° 35′ 48″ for the latitude of the pass. The Medicine *Butte* is isolated by a small tributary of the North Fork of the Platte, but the mountains approach each other very nearly, the stream running at their feet. On the south they are smooth, with occasional streaks of pine; but the butte itself is ragged, with escarpments of red feldspathic granite, and dark with pines; the snow reaching from the summit to within a few hundred feet of the trail.

The granite here was more compact and durable than that in the formation which we had passed through a few days before to the eastward of Laramie. Continuing our way over a plain on the west side of the pass, where the road was terribly rough with artemisia, we made our evening encampment on the creek, where it took a northern direction, unfavorable to the course we were pursuing.

Bands of buffalo were discovered as we came down upon the plain; and Carson brought into the camp a cow which had the fat on the fleece two inches thick. Even in this country of rich pasturage and abundant game it is rare that the hunter chances upon a finer animal. Our voyage had already been long, but this was the first good buffalo meat we had obtained. We travelled to-day twenty-six miles.

August 4th.—The morning was clear and calm; and, leaving the creek, we travelled toward the North Fork of the Platte, over a plain which was rendered rough and broken by ravines. With the exception of some thin grasses the sandy soil here was occupied almost exclusively by artemisia, with its usual turpentine odor. We had expected to meet with some difficulty in crossing the river, but happened to strike it where there was a very excellent ford, and halted at noon on the left bank, two hundred miles from St. Vrain's Fort.

The hunters brought in pack-animals loaded with fine meat. According to our imperfect knowledge of the country there should have been a small affluent to this stream a few miles higher up; and in the afternoon we continued our way among the river hills, in the expectation of encamping upon it in the evening. The ground proved to be so exceedingly difficult, broken up into hills, terminating in escarpments and broad ravines five or six hundred feet deep, with sides so precipitous that we could scarcely find a place to descend, that, toward sunset, I turned directly in toward the river, and, after nightfall, entered a sort of ravine. We were obliged to feel our way and clear a road in the darkness, the surface being much broken, and the progress of the carriages being greatly obstructed by the artemisia, which had a luxuriant growth of four to six feet in height.

We had scrambled along this gully for several hours, during which we had knocked off the carriage-lamps, broken a thermometer and several small articles, when, fearing to lose something of more importance, I halted for the night at ten o'clock. Our animals were turned down toward the river, that they might pick up what little grass they could find; and after a little search some water was found in a small ravine, and improved by digging.

We lighted up the ravine with fires of artemisia, and about midnight sat down to a supper which we were hungry enough to find delightful, although the buffalo meat was crusted with sand and the coffee was bitter with the wormwood taste of the artemisia leaves.

A successful day's hunt had kept our hunters occupied until late, and they slept out, but rejoined us at daybreak, when, finding ourselves only about a mile from the river, we followed the ravine down, and camped in a cotton-wood grove on a beautiful grassy bottom, where our animals indemnified themselves for the scanty fare of the past night. It was quite a pretty and pleasant place; a narrow strip of prairie about five hundred yards long terminated at the ravine where we entered by high precipitous hills closing in upon the river, and at the upper end by a ridge of low, rolling hills.

In the precipitous bluffs were displayed a succession of strata containing fossil vegetable remains and several beds of coal. In some of the beds the coal did not appear to be perfectly mineralized; and in some of the seams it was compact and remarkably lustrous. In these latter places there were, also, thin layers of a very fine white salts, in powder.

As we had a large supply of meat in the camp, which it was necessary to dry, and the surrounding country appeared to be well stocked with buffalo, which it was probable, after a day or two, we would not see again until our return to the Mississippi waters, I determined to make here a provision of dried meat, which would be necessary for our subsistence in the region we were about entering, which was said to be nearly destitute of game. Scaffolds were accordingly soon erected, fires made, and the meat cut into thin slices to be dried; and all were busily occupied, when the camp was thrown into a sudden tumult by a charge from about seventy mounted Indians, over the low hills at the upper end of the little bottom.

Fortunately, the guard, who was between them and our animals, had caught a glimpse of an Indian's head, as he raised himself in his stirrups to look over the hill, a moment before he made the charge, and succeeded in turning the band into the camp, as the Indians charged into the bottom with the usual yell. Before they reached us, the grove on the verge of the little bottom was occupied by our people, and the Indians brought to a sudden halt, which they made in time to save themselves from a howitzer shot, which would, undoubtedly, have been very effective in such a compact body, and further proceedings were interrupted by their signs for peace. They proved to be a war-party of Arapaho and Cheyenne Indians, and informed us that they had charged upon the camp under the belief that we were hostile Indians, and had discovered their mistake only at the moment of the attack—an excuse which policy required us to receive as true, though under the full conviction that the display of our little howitzer and our favorable position in the grove, certainly saved our horses, and probably ourselves, from their marauding intentions. They had been on a war-party, and had been defeated, and were, consequently, in a state of mind which aggravates their innate thirst for plunder and blood. Their excuse, however, was taken in good part, and the usual evidences of friendship interchanged. The pipe went round, provisions were spread, and the tobacco and goods furnished the customary presents, which they look for even from traders, and much more from Government authorities.

They were returning from an expedition against the Shoshonee Indians, one of whose villages they had surprised, at Bridger's Fort, on Ham's Fork of Green River (in the absence of the men, who were engaged in an antelope surround), and succeeded in carrying off their horses, and taking several scalps. News of the attack reached the Snakes immediately, who pursued and overtook them, and recovered their horses; and, in the running fight which ensued, the Arapahoes had lost several men killed, and a number wounded, who were coming on more slowly with a party in the rear. Nearly all the horses they had brought off were the property of the whites at the fort. After remaining until nearly sunset, they took their departure; and the excitement which their arrival had afforded subsided into our usual quiet, a little enlivened by the vigilance rendered necessary by the neighborhood of our uncertain visitors. At noon the thermometer was at 75°, at sunset 70°, and the evening clear.

UTAH INDIAN.

Elevation above the sea, six thousand eight hundred and twenty feet; latitude 41° 36′ 00″; longitude 107° 22′ 27″.

August 6th.—At sunrise the thermometer was 46°, the morning being clear and calm. We travelled to-day over an extremely rugged country, barren and uninteresting—nothing to be seen but artemisia bushes; and, in the evening, found a grassy spot among the hills, kept green by several springs, where we encamped late. Within a few hundred yards was a very pretty little stream of clear cool water, whose green banks looked refreshing among the dry rocky hills. The hunters brought in a fat mountain sheep (*Ovis montana*).

Our road the next day was through a continued and dense field of artemisia, which now entirely covered the country in such a luxuriant growth that it was difficult and laborious for a man on foot to force his way through, and nearly impracticable for our light carriages. The region through which we were travelling was a high plateau, constituting the dividing ridge between the waters of the Atlantic and Pacific Oceans, and extending to a considerable distance southward, from the neighborhood of the Table rock, at the southern side of the South Pass. Though broken up into rugged and rocky hills of a dry and barren nature, it has nothing of a mountainous character; the small streams which occasionally occur belonging neither to the Platte nor the Colorado, but losing themselves either in the sand or in small lakes.

From an eminence, in the afternoon, a mountainous range became visible in the north, in which were recognized some rocky peaks belonging to the range of the Sweet Water Valley; and, determining to abandon any further attempt to struggle through this almost impracticable country, we turned our course directly north, toward a pass in the valley of the Sweet Water River. A shaft of the gun-carriage was broken during the afternoon, causing a considerable delay; and it was late in an unpleasant evening before we succeeded in finding a very poor encampment, where there was a little water in a deep trench of a creek, and some scanty grass among the shrubs. All the game here consisted in a few straggling buffalo bulls, and during the day there had been but very little grass, except in some green spots where it had collected around springs or shallow lakes. Within fifty miles of the Sweet Water, the country changed into a vast saline plain, in many places extremely level, occasionally resembling the flat sandy beds of shallow lakes. Here the vegetation consisted of a shrubby growth, among which were several varieties of *chenopodiaceous* plants; but the characteristic shrub was *Fremontia vermicularis*, with smaller saline shrubs growing with singular luxuriance, and in many places holding exclusive possession of the ground.

On the evening of the 8th, we encamped on one of these fresh water lakes, which the traveller considers himself fortunate to find ; and the next day, in latitude by observation 42° 20′ 06″, halted to noon immediately at the foot of the southern side of the range which walls in the Sweet Water Valley, on the head of a small tributary to that river.

Continuing in the afternoon our course down the stream, which here cuts directly through the ridge, forming a very practicable pass, we entered the valley ; and, after a march of about nine miles, encamped on our familiar river, endeared to us by the acquaintance of the previous expedition ; the night having already closed in with a cold rain-storm. Our camp was about twenty miles above the Devil's Gate, which we had been able to see in coming down the plain ; and, in the course of the night, the clouds broke away around Jupiter for a short time, during which we obtained an immersion of the first satellite, the result of which agreed very nearly with the chronometer, giving for the mean longitude 107° 50′ 07″ ; elevation above the sea, six thousand and forty feet ; and distance from St. Vrain's Fort, by the road we had just travelled, three hundred and fifteen miles.

Here passes the road to Oregon ; and the broad, smooth highway, where the numerous heavy wagons of the emigrants had entirely beaten and crushed the artemisia, was a happy exchange to our poor animals for the sharp rocks and tough shrubs among which they had been toiling so long ; and we moved up the valley rapidly and pleasantly. With very little deviation from our route of the preceding year, we continued up the valley ; and, on the evening of the 12th, encamped on the Sweet Water, at a point where the road turns off to cross to the plains of Green River. The increased coolness of the weather indicated that we had attained a great elevation, which the barometer here placed at seven thousand two hundred and twenty feet ; and during the night water froze in the lodge.

The morning of the 13th was clear and cold, there being a white frost ; and the thermometer, a little before sunrise, standing at 26.5°. Leaving this encampment (our last on the waters which flow toward the rising sun) we took our way along the upland, toward the dividing ridge which separates the Atlantic from the Pacific waters, and crossed it by a road some miles further south than the one we had followed on our return in 1842. We crossed very near the Table Mountain, at the southern extremity of the South Pass, which is near twenty miles in width and already traversed by several different roads.

Selecting as well as I could, in the scarcely distinguishable ascent, what might be considered the dividing ridge in this remarkable depression in the mountain, I took a barometrical observation, which gave seven thousand four hundred and ninety feet for the elevation above the Gulf of Mexico. On my visit of the preceding year, I estimated the elevation of this pass at about seven thousand feet ; a correct observation with a good barometer enables me now to give it with more precision.   Its importance, as the great gate through which commerce and travelling may hereafter pass between the valley of the Mississippi and the North Pacific, justifies a precise notice of its locality and distance from leading points, in addition to this statement of its elevation.   Its latitude at the point where we crossed is 42° 24′ 32″ ; its longitude, 109° 26′ 00″; its distance from the mouth of the Kansas, by the common travelling route, nine hundred and sixty-two miles ; from the mouth of the Great Platte, along the valley of that river, according to our previous survey, eight hundred and eighty-two miles; and its distance from St. Louis about four hundred miles more by the Kansas, and about seven hundred by the Great Platte route—these additions being steamboat conveyance in both instances.   From this pass to the mouth of the Oregon is about one thousand six hundred miles by the common travelling route; so that, under a general point of view, it may be assumed to be about half-way between the Mississippi and the Pacific Ocean on the common travelling route.

Following a hollow of slight and easy descent, in which was very soon formed a little tributary to the Gulf of California (for the waters which flow west from the South Pass go to this gulf), we made our usual halt four miles from the pass, in latitude by observation 42° 19′ 53″.   Entering here the valley of Green River—the great Colorado of the West—and inclining very much to the southward along the streams which form the Sandy River, the road led for several days over dry and level uninteresting plains; to which a low, scrubby growth of artemisia gave a uniform dull, grayish color ; and on the evening of the 15th we encamped in the Mexican Territory, on the left bank of the Green River, sixty-nine miles from the South Pass, in longitude 110° 05′ 05″, and latitude 41° 53′ 54″, distant one thousand and thirty-one miles from the mouth of the Kansas.   This is the emigrant road to Oregon, which bears much to the southward to avoid the mountains about the western heads of Green River—the *Rio Verde* of the Spaniards.

August 16*th.*—Crossing the river, here about four hundred feet wide, by a very good ford, we continued to descend for seven or eight miles on a pleasant road along the right bank of the stream, of which the islands and shores are handsomely timbered with cotton-wood.   The refreshing appearance of the broad river, with its timbered shores and green-wooded islands, in contrast to its dry sandy plains, probably obtained for it the name of Green River, which was bestowed on it by the Spaniards, who first came into this country to trade some twenty-five years ago.   It was then familiarly known as the Seeds-kedée-agie, or Prairie Hen (*tetrao uro-phasianus*) River ; a name which is received from the Crows, to whom its upper waters belong, and on which this bird is still very abundant.

By the Shoshonee and Utah Indians, to whom belongs, for a considerable distance below, the country where we were now travelling, it was called the Bitter-root River, from the great abundance in its valley of a plant which affords them one of their favorite roots.   Lower down, from Brown's hole to the southward, the river runs through lofty chasms, walled in by precipices of *red* rock ; and even among the wilder tribes who inhabit that portion of its course I have heard it called, by Indian refugees from the Californian settlements, the Rio *Colorado.*

We halted to noon at the upper end of a large bottom, near some old houses, which had been a trading-post, in latitude 41° 46′ 54″.   At this place the elevation of the river above the sea is six thousand two hundred and thirty feet; that of Lewis' Fork of the Columbia at Fort Hall is, according to our subsequent observations, four thousand five hundred feet. The descent of each stream is rapid, but that of the Colorado is but little known, and that little derived from vague report.   Three hundred miles of its lower part, as it approaches the Gulf of California, is reported to be smooth and tranquil ; but its upper part is manifestly broken into many falls and rapids.   From many descriptions of trappers, it is probable that in its foaming course among its lofty precipices it presents many scenes of wild grandeur ; and though offering many temptations, and often discussed, no trappers have been found bold enough to undertake a voyage which has so certain a prospect of a fatal termination.   The Indians have strange stories of beautiful valleys abounding with beaver, shut up among inaccessible walls of rock in the lower course of the river ; and to which the neighboring Indians, in their occasional wars with the Spaniards, and among themselves, drive their herds of cattle and flocks of sheep, leaving them to pasture in perfect security.

The road here leaves the river, which bends considerably to the east ; and in the afternoon we resumed our westerly course, passing over a somewhat high and broken country ; and about sunset, after a day's travel of twenty-six miles, reached Black's Fork of the Green River—a shallow stream, with a somewhat sluggish current, about one hundred and twenty feet wide, timbered principally with willow, and here and there an occasional large tree.

At three in the morning I obtained an observation of an emersion of the first satellite of Jupiter, with other observations.   The heavy wagons have so completely pulverized the soil that clouds of fine light dust are raised by the slightest wind, making the road sometimes very disagreeable.

August 17*th.*—Leaving our encampment at six in the morning, we travelled along the bottom, which is about two miles wide, bordered by low hills, in which the strata contained handsome and very distinct vegetable fossils.   In a gully a short distance farther up the river, and under-

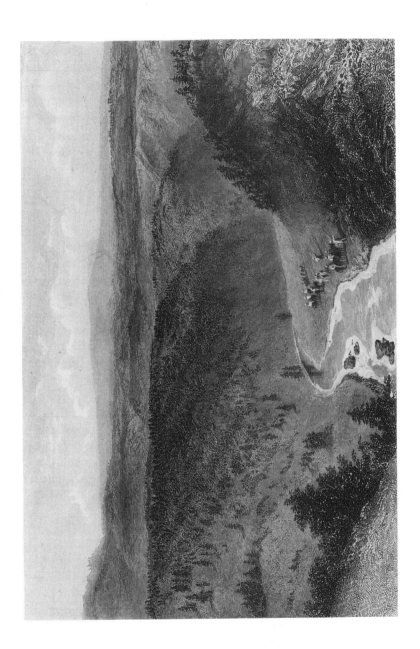

UNCUMPAGRE RIVER. WEST SLOPE ROCKY MOUNTAINS.

lying these, was exposed a stratum of an impure or argillaceous limestone. Crossing on the way Black's Fork, where it is one foot deep and forty wide, with clear water and a pebbly bed, in nine miles we reached Ham's Fork, a tributary to the former stream, having now about sixty feet breadth and a few inches' depth of water. It is wooded with thickets of red willow, and in the bottom is a tolerably strong growth of grass. The road here makes a traverse of twelve miles across a bend of the river.

Passing on the way some remarkable hills, two or three hundred feet high, with frequent and nearly vertical escarpments of a green stone, consisting of an argillaceous carbonate of lime, alternating with strata of an iron-brown limestone, and worked into picturesque forms by wind and rain, at two in the afternoon we reached the river again; having made to-day twenty-one miles. Since crossing the great dividing ridge of the Rocky Mountains, plants have been very few in variety, the country being covered principally with artemisia.

August 18*th*.—We passed on the road this morning the grave of one of the emigrants, being the second we had seen since falling into their trail; and halted to noon on the river a short distance above.

The Shoshonee woman took leave of us here, expecting to find some of her relations at Bridger's Fort, which is only a mile or two distant, on a fork of this stream. In the evening we encamped on a salt creek, about fifteen feet wide, having to-day travelled thirty-two miles.

I obtained an emersion of the first satellite under favorable circumstances, the night being still and clear.

One of our mules died here, and in this portion of our journey we lost six or seven of our animals. The grass which the country had lately afforded was very poor and insufficient; and animals which have been accustomed to grain become soon weak, and unable to labor, when reduced to no other nourishment than grass. The American horses (as those are usually called which are brought to this country from the States) are not of any serviceable value until after they have remained a winter in the country, and become accustomed to live entirely on grass.

August 19*th*.—Desirous to avoid every delay not absolutely necessary, I sent on Carson in advance to Fort Hall this morning, to make arrangements for a small supply of provisions. A few miles from our encampment the road entered a high ridge, which the trappers called the "little mountain," connecting the Utah with the Wind River chain; and in one of the hills near which we passed I remarked strata of a conglomerate formation, fragments of which were scattered over the surface. We crossed a ridge of this conglomerate, the road passing near a grove of low cedar, and descended upon one of the heads of Ham's Fork, called Muddy, where we made our midday halt.

In the river hills at this place I discovered strata of fossiliferous rock having an *oolitic structure*, which, in connection with the neighboring strata, authorizes us to believe that here, on the west side of the Rocky Mountains, we find repeated the modern formations of Great Britain and Europe, which have hitherto been wanting to complete the system of North American geology.

In the afternoon we continued our road, and, searching among the hills a few miles up the stream, and on the same bank, I discovered among alternating beds of coal and clay a stratum of white indurated clay containing very clear and beautiful impressions of vegetable remains. This was the most interesting fossil locality I had met in the country, and I deeply regretted that time did not permit me to remain a day or two in the vicinity; but I could not anticipate the delays to which I might be exposed in the course of our journey—or, rather, I knew that they were many and inevitable—and after remaining here only about an hour, I hurried off, loaded with as many specimens as I could conveniently carry.

Coal made its appearance occasionally in the hills during the afternoon, and was displayed in rabbit-burrows in a kind of gap, through which we passed over some high hills, and we descended to make our encampment on the same stream, where we found but very poor grass.

In the evening a fine cow with her calf, which had strayed off from some emigrant party, were found several miles from the road and brought into camp; and as she gave an abundance of milk, we enjoyed to-night an excellent cup of coffee. We travelled to-day twenty-eight miles, and, as has been usual since crossing the Green River, the road has been very dusty and the weather smoky and oppressively hot. Artemisia was characteristic among the few plants.

August 20th.—We continued to travel up the creek by a very gradual ascent and a very excellent grassy road, passing on the way several small forks of the stream. The hills here are higher, presenting escarpments of parti-colored and apparently clay rocks—purple, dark-red, and yellow—containing strata of sandstone and limestone with shells, with a bed of cemented pebbles, the whole overlaid by beds of limestone. The alternation of red and yellow gives a bright appearance to the hills, one of which was called by our people the Rainbow Hill; and the character of the country became more agreeable, and travelling far more pleasant, as now we found timber and very good grass. Gradually ascending, we reached the lower level of a bed of white limestone, lying upon a white clay, on the upper line of which the whole road is abundantly supplied with beautiful cool springs, gushing out a foot in breadth and several inches deep, directly from the hill-side.

At noon we halted at the last main fork of the creek, at an elevation of seven thousand two hundred feet, and in latitude, by observation, 41° 39′ 45″; and in the afternoon continued on the same excellent road, up the left or northern fork of the stream, toward its head, in a pass which the barometer placed at eight thousand two hundred and thirty feet above the sea. This is a connecting ridge between the Utah or Bear River Mountains and the Wind River chain of the Rocky Mountains, separating the waters of the Gulf of California on the east, and those on the west belonging more directly to the Pacific, from a vast interior basin whose rivers are collected into numerous lakes having no outlet to the ocean. From the summit of this pass, the highest which the road crosses between the Mississippi and the western ocean, our view was over a very mountainous region, whose rugged appearance was greatly increased by the smoky weather, through which the broken ridges were dark and dimly seen. The ascent to the summit of the gap was occasionally steeper than the national road in the Alleghanies; and the descent, by way of a spur on the western side, is rather precipitous, but the pass may still be called a good one. Some thickets of willow in the hollows below deceived us into the expectation of finding a camp at our usual hour at the foot of the mountain; but we found them without water, and continued down a ravine, and encamped about dark at a place where the springs again began to make their appearance, but where our animals fared badly; the stock of the emigrants having grazed the grass as completely as if we were again in the midst of the buffalo.

August 21*st.*—An hour's travel this morning brought us into the fertile and picturesque valley of Bear River, the principal tributary to the Great Salt Lake. The stream is here two hundred feet wide, fringed with willows and occasional groups of hawthorns. We were now entering a region which for us possessed a strange and extraordinary interest. We were upon the waters of the famous lake which forms a salient point among the remarkable geographical features of the country, and around which the vague and superstitious accounts of the trappers had thrown a delightful obscurity, which we anticipated pleasure in dispelling, but which, in the meantime, left a crowded field for the exercise of our imagination.

In our occasional conversations with the few old hunters who had visited the region, it had been a subject of frequent speculation; and the wonders which they related were not the less agreeable because they were highly exaggerated and impossible.

Hitherto this lake had been seen only by trappers who were wandering through the country in search of new beaver streams, caring very little for geography; its islands had never been visited; and none were to be found who had entirely made the circuit of its shores; and no instrumental observations, or geographical survey of any description, had ever been made anywhere in the neighboring region. It was generally supposed that it had no visible outlet; but among the trappers, including those in my own camp, were many who believed that somewhere on its surface was a terrible whirlpool, through which its waters found their way to the ocean by some subterranean communication.

All these things had made a frequent subject of discussion in our desultory conversations around the fires at night; and my own mind had become tolerably well filled with their indefinite pictures, and insensibly colored with their romantic descriptions, which, in the pleasure of excitement, I was well disposed to believe, and half expected to realize.

Where we descended into this beautiful valley it is three to four miles in breadth, perfectly level, and bounded by mountainous ridges, one above another, rising suddenly from the plain.

The emigrant road passes along a portion of the river, which in its character of level bottoms, inclosed between abrupt mountains, presents a type of the streams of this region.

We continued our road down the river, and at night encamped with a family of emigrants—two men, women, and several children—who appeared to be bringing up the rear of the great caravan. I was struck with the fine appearance of their cattle, some six or eight yoke of oxen, which really looked as well as if they had been all the summer at work on some good farm. It was strange to see one small family travelling alone through such a country, so remote from civilization. Some nine years since, such a security might have been a fatal one; but since their disastrous defeats in the country a little north, the Blackfeet have ceased to visit these waters. Indians, however, are very uncertain in their localities; and the friendly feelings, also, of those now inhabiting it may be changed.

According to barometrical observation at noon, the elevation of the valley was six thousand four hundred feet above the sea; and our encampment at night in latitude 42° 03' 47'', and longitude 111° 10' 53'', by observation —the day's journey having been twenty-six miles. This encampment was therefore within the territorial limit of the United States; our travelling, from the time we entered the valley of the Green River, on August 15th, having been to the south of the forty-second degree of north latitude, and consequently on Mexican territory; and this is the route all the emigrants now travel to Oregon.

The temperature at sunset was 65°; and at evening there was a distant thunder-storm, with a light breeze from the north.

Antelope and elk were seen during the day on the opposite prairie; and there were ducks and geese in the river.

The next morning, in about three miles from our encampment, we reached Smith's Fork, a stream of clear water, about fifty feet in breadth.

It is timbered with cotton-wood, willow, and aspen, and makes a beautiful débouchement through a pass about six hundred yards wide, between remarkable mountain hills, rising abruptly on either side, and forming gigantic columns to the gate by which it enters Bear River Valley. The bottoms, which below Smith's Fork had been two miles wide, narrowed, as we advanced, to a gap five hundred yards wide ; and during the greater part of the day we had a winding route, the river making very sharp and sudden bends, the mountains steep and rocky, and the valley occasionally so narrow as only to leave space for a passage through.

We made our halt at noon in a fertile bottom, where the common blue flax was growing abundantly, a few miles below the mouth of Thomas' Fork, one of the larger tributaries of the river.

Crossing, in the afternoon, the point of a narrow spur, we descended into a beautiful bottom, formed by a lateral valley, which presented a picture of home beauty that went directly to our hearts. The edge of the wood, for several miles along the river, was dotted with the white covers of emigrant wagons, collected in groups at different camps, where the smokes were rising lazily from the fires, around which the women were occupied in preparing the evening meal, and the children playing in the grass ; and herds of cattle, grazing about in the bottom, had an air of quiet security and civilized comfort that made a rare sight for the traveller in such a remote wilderness.

In common with all the emigration, they had been reposing for several days in this delightful valley, in order to recruit their animals on its luxuriant pasturage after their long journey, and prepare them for the hard travel along the comparatively sterile banks of the Upper Columbia. At the lower end of this extensive bottom the river passes through an open cañon where there were high vertical rocks to the water's edge, and the road here turns up a broad valley to the right. It was already near sunset ; but, hoping to reach the river again before night, we continued our march along the valley, finding the road tolerably good, until we arrived at a point where it crosses the ridge by an ascent of a mile in length, which was so very steep and difficult for the gun and carriage that we did not reach the summit until dark.

It was absolutely necessary to descend into the valley for water and grass, and we were obliged to grope our way in the darkness down a very steep, bad mountain, reaching the river at about ten o'clock. It was late before our animals were gathered into camp, several of those which were very weak being necessarily left to pass the night on the ridge ; and we sat down again to a midnight supper. The road, in the morning, presented an animated appearance. We found that we had encamped near a large party of emigrants, and a few miles below another body was already in motion. Here the valley had resumed its usual breadth, and the river swept off along the mountains on the western side, the road continuing directly on.

In about an hour's travel we met several Shoshonee Indians, who informed us that they belonged to a large village which had just come into the valley from the mountains to the westward, where they had been hunting antelope, and gathering service-berries. Glad at the opportunity of seeing one of their villages, and in the hope of purchasing from them a few horses, I turned immediately off into the plain toward their encampment, which was situated on a small stream near the river.

We had approached within something more than a mile of the village, when suddenly a single horseman emerged from it at full speed, followed by another, and another, in rapid succession; and then party after party poured into the plain, until, when the foremost rider reached us, all the whole intervening plain was occupied by a mass of horsemen, which came charging down upon us with guns and naked swords, lances, and bows and arrows—Indians entirely naked, and warriors fully dressed for war, with the long red streamers of their war bonnets reaching nearly to the ground —all mingled together in the bravery of savage warfare. They had been thrown into a sudden tumult by the appearance of our flag, which, among these people, is regarded as an emblem of hostility; it being usually borne by the Sioux, and the neighboring mountain Indians, when they come here to war; and we had accordingly been mistaken for a body of their enemies. A few words from the chief quieted the excitement; and the whole band, increasing every moment in number, escorted us to their encampment, where the chief pointed out a place for us to encamp near his own lodge, and made known our purpose in visiting the village.

In a very short time we purchased eight horses, for which we gave in exchange blankets, red and blue cloth, beads, knives, and tobacco, and the usual other articles of Indian traffic. We obtained from them also a considerable quantity of berries of different kinds, among which service-berries were the most abundant; and several kinds of roots and seeds, which we could eat with pleasure, as any kind of vegetable food was gratifying to us.

I ate here, for the first time, the *kooyah*, or *tobacco root* (*Valeriana edulis*), the principal edible root among the Indians who inhabit the upper waters of the streams on the western side of the mountains. It has a very strong and remarkably peculiar taste and odor, which I can compare to no other vegetable that I am acquainted with, and which to some persons is extremely offensive. It was characterized by Mr. Preuss as the most horrid food he had ever put in his mouth; and when, in the evening, one of the chiefs sent his wife to me with a portion which she had prepared as a delicacy to regale us, the odor immediately drove him out of the lodge;

and frequently afterward he used to beg that when those who liked it had taken what they desired, it might be sent away.   To others, however, the taste is rather an agreeable one, and I was afterward always glad when it formed an addition to our scanty meals.   It is full of nutriment ; and in its unprepared state is said by the Indians to have very strong poisonous qualities, of which it is deprived by a peculiar process, being baked in the ground for about two days.

The morning of the 24th was disagreeably cool, with an easterly wind and very smoky weather.   We made a late start from the village, and re-gaining the road (on which, during all the day, were scattered the emi-grant wagons), we continued on down the valley of the river, bordered by high and mountainous hills, on which fires are seen at the summit.

The soil appears generally good, although, with the grasses, many of the plants are dried up, probably on account of the great heat and want of rain.   The common blue flax of cultivation, now almost entirely in seed— only a scattered flower here and there remaining—is the most characteris-tic plant of the Bear River Valley.   When we encamped at night on the right bank of the river, it was growing as in a sown field.   We had trav-elled during the day twenty-two miles, encamping in latitude (by observa-tion) 42° 36′ 56″, chronometric longitude 111° 42′ 05″.

In our neighborhood, the mountains appeared extremely rugged, giv-ing still greater value to this beautiful natural pass.

August 25th.—This was a cloudless but smoky autumn morning, with a cold wind from the southeast, and a temperature of forty-five degrees at sunrise.   In a few miles I noticed, where a little stream crossed the road, fragments of *scoriated basalt* scattered about—the first volcanic rock we had seen, and which now became a characteristic rock along our future road.   In about six miles' travel from our encampment, we reached one of the points in our journey to which we had always looked forward with great interest—the famous *Beer Springs*.   It is a basin of mineral waters inclosed by the mountains, which sweep around a circular bend of Bear River here, at its most northern point, and which from a northern, in the course of a few miles acquires a southern direction toward the GREAT SALT LAKE.

A pretty little stream of clear water enters the upper part of the basin from an open valley in the mountains, and, passing through the bottom, discharges into Bear River.   Crossing this stream, we descended a mile below, and made our encampment in a grove of cedar immediately at the Beer Springs, which, on account of the effervescing gas and acid taste, have received their name from the voyageurs and trappers of the country, who, in the midst of their rude and hard lives, are fond of finding some fancied resemblance to the luxuries they rarely have the fortune to enjoy.

Although somewhat disappointed in the expectations which various descriptions had led me to form of unusual beauty of situation and scenery, I found it altogether a place of very great interest; and a traveller for the first time in a volcanic region remains in a constant excitement, and at every step is arrested by something remarkable and new. There is a confusion of interesting objects gathered together in a small space. Around the place of encampment the Beer Springs were numerous; but, as far as we could ascertain, were entirely confined to that locality in the bottom. In the bed of the river, in front, for a space of several hundred yards, they were very abundant, the effervescing gas rising up and agitating the water in countless bubbling columns. In the vicinity round about were numerous springs of an entirely different and equally marked mineral character.

In a rather picturesque spot, about thirteen hundred yards below our encampment, and immediately on the river bank, is the most remarkable spring of the place. In an opening on the rock, a white column of scattered water is thrown up, in form like a *jet d'eau*, to a variable height of about three feet, and, though it is maintained in a constant supply, its greatest height is attained only at regular intervals, according to the action of the force below. It is accompanied by a subterranean noise, which, together with the motion of the water, makes very much the impression of a steamboat in motion; and, without knowing that it had been already previously so called, we gave to it the name of the *Steamboat Spring.* The rock through which it is forced is slightly raised in a convex manner, and gathered at the opening into an urn-mouthed form, and is evidently formed by continued deposition from the water, and colored bright red by oxide of iron.

An analysis of this deposited rock, which I subjoin, will give you some idea of the properties of the water, which, with the exception of the Beer Springs, is the mineral water of the place.* It is a hot spring, and the water has a pungent and disagreeable metallic taste, leaving a burning effect on the tongue. Within perhaps two yards of the *jet d'eau* is a small hole of about an inch in diameter, through which, at regular intervals, escapes a blast of hot air with a light wreath of smoke, accompanied by a regular noise. This hole had been noticed by Dr. Wislizenus, a gentleman who several years since passed by this place, and who remarked,

* ANALYSIS.

Carbonate of lime	92.55
Carbonate of magnesia	0.42
Oxide of iron	1.05
Silica ⎫	
Alumina ⎬	5.98
Water and loss ⎭	
	100.00

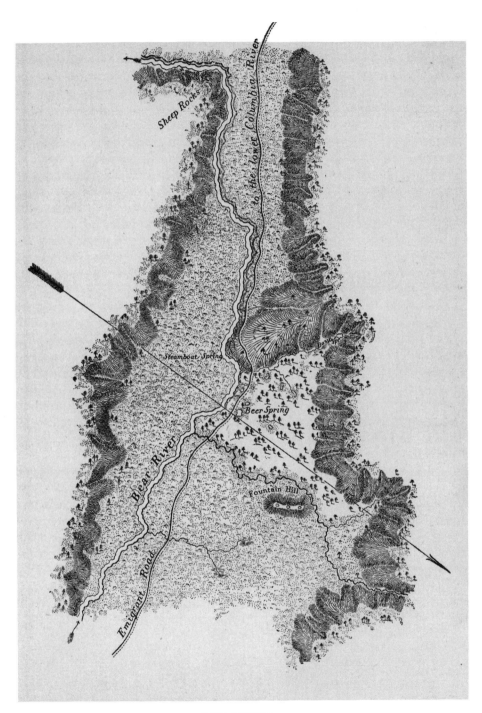

BEER SPRINGS.

with very nice observation, that smelling the gas which issued from the orifice produced a sensation of giddiness and nausea.

Mr. Preuss and myself repeated the observation, and were so well satisfied with its correctness, that we did not find it pleasant to continue the experiment, as the sensation of giddiness which it produced was certainly strong and decided. A huge emigrant wagon, with a large and diversified family, had overtaken us and halted to noon at our encampment; and, while we were sitting at the spring, a band of boys and girls, with two or three young men came up, one of whom I asked to stoop down and smell the gas, desirous to satisfy myself further of its effects. But his natural caution had been awakened by the singular and suspicious features of the place, and he declined my proposal decidedly, adding a few indistinct remarks about the devil, whom he seemed to consider the *genius loci.* The ceaseless motion and the play of the fountain, the red rock, and the green trees near, make this a picturesque spot.

A short distance above the spring, and near the foot of the same spur, is a very remarkable yellow-colored rock, soft and friable, consisting principally of carbonate of lime and oxide of iron, of regular structure, which is probably a fossil coral. The rocky bank along the shore between the Steamboat Spring and our encampment, along which is dispersed the water from the hills, is composed entirely of strata of a calcareous *tufa*, with the remains of moss and reed-like grasses, which is probably the formation of springs.

The *Beer* or *Soda Springs*, which have given name to this locality, are agreeable, but less highly flavored than the *Boiling Springs* at the foot of Pike's Peak, which are of the same character. They are very numerous, and half hidden by tufts of grass, which we amused ourselves in removing and searching about for more highly impregnated springs. They are some of them deep and of various sizes—sometimes several yards in diameter, and kept in constant motion by columns of escaping gas. By analysis, one quart of the water contains as follows:

	Grains.
Sulphate of magnesia	12.10
Sulphate of lime	2.12
Carbonate of lime	3.86
Carbonate of magnesia	3.22
Chloride of calcium	1.33
Chloride of magnesium	1.12
Chloride of sodium	2.24
Vegetable extractive matter, etc.	0.85
	26.84

The carbonic acid, originally contained in the water, had mainly escaped before it was subjected to analysis; and it was not therefore taken into consideration.

In the afternoon I wandered about among the cedars, which occupy the greater part of the bottom toward the mountains. The soil here has a dry and calcined appearance; in some places, the open grounds are covered with saline efflorescences, and there are a number of regularly shaped and very remarkable hills, which are formed of a succession of convex strata that have been deposited by the waters of extinct springs, the orifices of which are found on their summits, some of them having the form of funnel-shaped cones.

Others of these remarkably shaped hills are of a red-colored earth, entirely bare, and composed principally of carbonate of lime, with oxide of iron, formed in the same manner. Walking near one of them, on the summit of which the springs were dry, my attention was attracted by an underground noise, around which I circled repeatedly, until I found the spot from beneath which it came; and, removing the red earth, discovered a hidden spring, which was boiling up from below, with the same disagreeable metallic taste as the Steamboat Spring.

Continuing up the bottom, and crossing the little stream which has been already mentioned, I visited several remarkable red and white hills, which had attracted my attention from the road in the morning. These are immediately upon the stream, and, like those already mentioned, are formed by the deposition of successive strata from the springs. On their summits, the orifices through which the waters had been discharged were so large that they resembled miniature craters, being some of them several feet in diameter, circular, and regularly formed as if by art. At a former time, when these dried-up fountains were all in motion, they must have made a beautiful display on a grand scale; and nearly all this basin appears to me to have been formed under their action, and should be called the *place of fountains.*

At the foot of one of these hills, or rather on its side near the base, are several of these small limestone columns, about one foot in diameter at the base, and tapering upward to a height of three or four feet; and on the summit the water is boiling up and bubbling over, constantly adding to the height of the little obelisks. In some, the water only boils up, no longer overflowing, and has here the same taste as the Steamboat Spring. The observer will remark a gradual subsidence in the water which formerly supplied the fountains, as on all the summits of the hills the springs are now dry, and are found only low down upon their sides or on the surrounding plain.

A little higher up the creek, its banks are formed by strata of a very heavy and hard scoriaceous basalt, having a bright metallic lustre when broken. The mountains overlooking the plain are of an entirely different geological character. Continuing on, I walked to the summit of one of them, where the principal rock was a granular quartz. Descending the mountains, and returning toward the camp along the base of the ridge which skirts the plain, I found at the foot of a mountain spur, and issuing from a compact rock of a dark-blue color, a great number of springs having the same pungent and disagreeably metallic taste already mentioned, the water of which was collected into a very remarkable basin, whose singularity, perhaps, made it appear to me very beautiful. It is large—perhaps fifty yards in circumference; and in it the water is contained at an elevation of several feet above the surrounding ground by a wall of calcareous *tufa*, composed principally of the remains of mosses, three or four, and sometimes ten feet high. The water within is very clear and pure, and three or four feet deep, where it could be conveniently measured near the wall; and, at a considerably lower level, is another pond or basin of very clear water, and apparently of considerable depth, from the bottom of which the gas was escaping in bubbling columns at many places. This water was collected into a small stream which, in a few hundred yards, sank under ground, reappearing among the rocks between the two great springs near the river, which it entered by a little fall.

Late in the afternoon I set out on my return to the camp, and, crossing in the way a large field of a salt that was several inches deep, found on my arrival that our emigrant friends, who had been encamped in company with us, had resumed their journey, and the road had again assumed its solitary character.

The temperature of the largest of the *Beer* Springs at our encampment was 65° at sunset, that of the air being 62.5°. Our barometric observation gave five thousand eight hundred and forty feet for the elevation above the Gulf, being about five hundred feet lower than the Boiling Springs, which are of a similar nature, at the foot of Pike's Peak. The astronomical observations gave for our latitude 42° 39′ 57″, and 111° 46′ 00″ for the longitude. The night was very still and cloudless, and I sat up for an observation of the first satellite of Jupiter, the emersion of which took place about midnight; but fell asleep at the telescope, awaking just a few minutes after the appearance of the star.

The morning of the 26th was calm, and the sky without clouds, but smoky; and the temperature at sunrise 28.5°. At the same time, the temperature of the large Beer Spring, where we encamped, was 56°; that of the Steamboat Spring 87°; and that of the steam-hole near it, 81.5°. In the course of the morning the last wagons of the emigration passed by, and we were again left in our place in the rear.

Remaining in camp until nearly eleven o'clock, we travelled a short distance down the river, and halted to noon on the bank at a point where the road quits the valley of Bear River, and, crossing a ridge which divides the Great Basin from the Pacific waters, reaches Fort Hall by way of the Portneuf River in a distance of probably fifty miles, or two and a half days' journey for wagons.

An examination of the great lake which is the outlet of this river, and the principal feature of geographical interest in the basin, was one of the main objects contemplated in the general plan of our survey ; and I accordingly determined at this place to leave the road, and, after having completed a reconnoissance of the lake, regain it subsequently at Fort Hall. But our little stock of provisions had again become extremely low ; we had only dried-meat sufficient for one meal, and our supply of flour and other comforts was entirely exhausted. I therefore immediately despatched one of the party, Henry Lee, with a note to Carson, at Fort Hall, directing him to load a pack-horse with whatever could be obtained there in the way of provisions, and endeavor to overtake me on the river.

In the meantime, we had picked up along the road two tolerably well-grown calves, which would have become food for wolves, and which had probably been left by some of the earlier emigrants, none of those we had met having made any claim to them ; and on these I mainly relied for support during our circuit to the lake.

In sweeping around the point of the mountain which runs down into the bend, the river here passes between perpendicular walls of basalt, which always fix the attention, from the regular form in which it occurs and its perfect distinctness from the surrounding rocks among which it has been placed. The mountain, which is rugged and steep, and, by our measurement, one thousand four hundred feet above the river directly opposite the place of our halt, is called the *Sheep Rock*—probably because a flock of the common mountain sheep (*Ovis montana*) had been seen on the craggy point.

As we were about resuming our march in the afternoon I was attracted by the singular appearance of an isolated hill with a concave summit, in the plain, about two miles from the river, and turned off toward it while the camp proceeded on its way to the southward in search of the lake. I found the thin and stony soil of the plain entirely underlaid by the basalt which forms the river walls ; and when I reached the neighborhood of the hill, the surface of the plain was rent into frequent fissures and chasms of the same scoriated volcanic rock, from forty to sixty feet deep, but which there was not sufficient light to penetrate entirely, and which I had not time to descend. Arrived at the summit of the hill, I found that it terminated in a very perfect crater, of an oval or nearly circular form, three hundred and sixty paces in circumference, and sixty feet at the greatest depth. The walls, which were perfectly vertical and disposed like masonry in a very regular manner, were composed of a brown-colored scoriaceous

UTAH BOY.

lava, evidently the production of a modern volcano, and having all the appearance of the lighter scoriaceous lavas of Mount Ætna, Vesuvius, and other volcanoes. The faces of the walls were reddened and glazed by the fire, in which they had been melted, and which had left them contorted and twisted by its violent action.

Our route during the afternoon was a little rough, being (in the direction we had taken) over a volcanic plain, where our progress was sometimes obstructed by fissures, and black beds, composed of fragments of the rock. On both sides the mountains appeared very broken, but tolerably well timbered.

August 26th.—Crossing a point of ridge which makes in to the river, we fell upon it again before sunset, and encamped on the right bank, opposite to the encampment of three lodges of Snake Indians. They visited us during the evening, and we obtained from them a small quantity of roots of different kinds in exchange for goods. Among them was a sweet root of very pleasant flavor, having somewhat the taste of preserved quince. My endeavors to become acquainted with the plants which furnish to the Indians a portion of their support were only gradually successful, and after long and persevering attention; and even after obtaining, I did not succeed in preserving them until they could be satisfactorily determined.

In this portion of the journey I found this particular root cut up into such small pieces that it was only to be identified by its taste, when the bulb was met with in perfect form among the Indians lower down on the Columbia, among whom it is the highly celebrated kamás. It was long afterwards, on our return through Upper California, that I found the plant itself in bloom, which I supposed to furnish the kamás root (*Camassia esculenta*). The root-diet had a rather mournful effect at the commencement, and one of the calves was killed this evening for food. The animals fared well on rushes.

August 27th.—The morning was cloudy, with appearance of rain, and the thermometer at sunrise at 29°. Making an unusually early start, we crossed the river at a good ford; and, following for about three hours a trail which led along the bottom, we entered a labyrinth of hills below the main ridge and halted to noon in the ravine of a pretty little stream, timbered with cotton-wood of large size, ash-leaved maple, with cherry and other shrubby trees. The hazy weather, which had prevented any very extended views since entering the Green River Valley, began now to disappear. There was a slight rain in the earlier part of the day, and at noon, when the thermometer had risen to 79.5°, we had a bright sun, with blue sky and scattered *cumuli*. According to the barometer our halt here among the hills was at an elevation of five thousand three hundred and twenty feet.

Crossing a dividing ridge in the afternoon, we followed down another little Bear River tributary to the point where it emerged on an open green flat among the hills, timbered with groves and bordered with cane thickets, but without water. A pretty little rivulet, coming out of the hill-side and over-hung by tall flowering plants of a species I had not hitherto seen, furnished us with a good camping-place. The evening was cloudy, the temperature at sunset 69°, and the elevation five thousand one hundred and forty feet.

Among the plants occurring along the line of road during the day, *épinettes des prairies* (*Grindelia squarrosa*) was in considerable abundance, and is among the very few plants remaining in bloom—the whole country having now an autumnal appearance, in the crisped and yellow plants and dried-up grasses. Many cranes were seen during the day, with a few antelope, very shy and wild.

August 28th.—During the night we had a thunder-storm, with moderate rain, which has made the air this morning very clear, the thermometer being at 55°. Leaving our encampment at the *Cane Spring* and quitting the trail on which we had been travelling, and which would probably have afforded us a good road to the lake, we crossed some very deep ravines, and in about an hour's travelling again reached the river. We were now in a valley five or six miles wide, between mountain ranges which, about thirty miles below, appeared to close up and terminate the valley, leaving for the river only a very narrow pass, or cañon, behind which we imagined that we should find the broad waters of the lake.

We made the usual halt at the mouth of a small clear stream, having a slightly mineral taste (perhaps of salt), four thousand seven hundred and sixty feet above the gulf. In the afternoon we climbed a very steep sandy hill; and after a slow and winding day's march of twenty-seven miles encamped at a slough on the river. There were great quantities of geese and ducks, of which only a few were shot, the Indians having probably made them very wild. The men employed themselves in fishing, but caught nothing. A skunk (*Mephitis Americana*) which was killed in the afternoon made a supper for one of the messes. The river is bordered occasionally with fields of cane, which we regarded as an indication of our approach to a lake country. We had frequent showers of rain during the night, with thunder.

August 29th.—The thermometer at sunrise was 54°, with air from the northwest, and dark rainy clouds moving on the horizon; rain-squalls and bright sunshine by intervals. I rode ahead with Basil to explore the country, and, continuing about three miles along the river, turned directly off on a trail running toward three marked gaps in the bordering range, where the mountains appeared cut through to their bases, toward which the river plain rose gradually.

Putting our horses into a gallop on some fresh tracks which showed very plainly in the wet path, we came suddenly upon a small party of Shoshonee Indians who had fallen into the trail from the north. We could only communicate by signs; but they made us understand that the road through the chain was a very excellent one, leading into a broad valley which ran to the southward. We halted to noon at what may be called the gate of the pass; on either side of which were huge mountains of rock, between which stole a little pure-water stream, with a margin just sufficiently large for our passage. From the river the plain had gradually risen to an altitude of five thousand five hundred feet, and by meridian observation the latitude of the entrance was 42°.

In the interval of our usual halt several of us wandered along up the stream to examine the pass more at leisure. Within the gate the rocks receded a little back, leaving a very narrow, but most beautiful valley, through which the little stream wound its way, hidden by different kinds of trees and shrubs—aspen, maple, willow, cherry, and elder; a fine verdure of smooth, short grass spread over the remaining space to the bare sides of the rocky walls. These were of a blue limestone, which constitutes the mountain here; and opening directly on the grassy bottom were several curious caves, which appeared to be inhabited by root-diggers. On one side was gathered a heap of leaves for a bed, and they were dry, open and pleasant. On the roofs of the caves I remarked bituminous exudations from the rock.

The trail was an excellent one for pack-horses; but as it sometimes crossed a shelving point, to avoid the shrubbery we were obliged in several places to open a road for the carriage through the wood. A squaw on horseback, accompanied by five or six dogs, entered the pass in the afternoon, but was too much terrified at finding herself in such unexpected company to make any pause for conversation, and hurried off at a good pace—being of course no further disturbed than by an accelerating shout. She was well and showily dressed, and was probably going to a village encamped somewhere near, and evidently did not belong to the tribe of *Root-diggers*.

We had now entered a country inhabited by these people; and as in the course of our voyage we shall frequently meet with them in various stages of existence, it will be well to remark that, scattered over the great region west of the Rocky Mountains and south of the Great Snake River, are numerous Indians whose subsistence is almost solely derived from roots and seeds, and such small animals as chance and great good fortune sometimes bring within their reach. They are miserably poor, armed only with bows and arrows, or clubs; and as the country they inhabit is almost destitute of game, they have no means of obtaining better

arms. In the northern part of the region just mentioned they live generally in solitary families; and farther to the south they are gathered
together in villages.

Those who live together in villages, strengthened by association, are
in exclusive possession of the more genial and richer parts of the country,
while the others are driven to the ruder mountains and to the more inhospitable parts of the country. But simply observing, in accompanying us
along our road, will give to the reader a better knowledge of these people
than I could give in any other than a very lengthened description.

Roots, seeds, and grass, every vegetable that affords any nourishment,
and every living animal thing, insect or worm, they eat. Nearly approaching to the lower animal creation, their sole employment is to obtain food ;
and they are constantly occupied in a struggle to support existence.

In the annexed view will be found a sketch of the *Standing Rock*—the
most remarkable feature of the pass, where a huge rock, fallen from the
cliffs above, and standing perpendicularly near the middle of the valley,
presents itself like a watch-tower in the pass. It will give a tolerably correct idea of the character of the scenery in this country, where generally
the mountains rise abruptly up from comparatively unbroken plains and
level valleys ; but it will entirely fail in representing the picturesque beauty
of this delightful place, where a green valley, full of foliage and a hundred
yards wide, contrasts with naked crags that spire up into a blue line of
pinnacles three thousand feet above, sometimes crested with cedar and
pine, and sometimes ragged and bare.

The detention that we met with in opening the road, and perhaps a will-
ingness to linger on the way, made the afternoon's travel short ; and about
two miles from the entrance we passed through another gate, and encamped
on the stream at the junction of a little fork from the southward, around
which the mountains stooped more gently down, forming a small open cove.

As it was still early in the afternoon, Basil and myself in one direction,
and Mr. Preuss in another, set out to explore the country, and ascended
different neighboring peaks in the hope of seeing some indications of the
lake ; but though our elevation afforded magnificent views, the eye ranging
over a long extent of Bear River, with the broad and fertile *Cache Valley*,
in the direction of our search was only to be seen a bed of apparently
impracticable mountains. Among these the trail we had been following
turned sharply to the northward, and it began to be doubtful if it would
not lead us away from the object of our destination ; but I nevertheless
determined to keep it, in the belief that it would eventually bring us right.
A squall of rain drove us out of the mountain, and it was late when we
reached the camp. The evening closed in with frequent showers of rain
with some lightning and thunder.

STANDING ROCK.

August 30th.—We had constant thunder-storms during the night, but in the morning the clouds were sinking to the horizon, and the air was clear and cold, with the thermometer at sunrise at 39°. Elevation by barometer five thousand five hundred and eighty feet. We were in motion early, continuing up the little stream without encountering any ascent where a horse would not easily gallop, and, crossing a slight dividing ground at the summit, descended upon a small stream, along which we continued on the same excellent road. In riding through the pass numerous cranes were seen ; and prairie hens, or grouse (*Bonasia umbellus*), which lately had been rare, were very abundant.

This little affluent brought us to a larger stream, down which we travelled through a more open bottom, on a level road where heavily-laden wagons could pass without obstacle. The hills on the right grew lower, and, on entering a more open country, we discovered a Shoshonee village ; and being desirous to obtain information and purchase from them some roots and berries, we halted on the river, which was lightly wooded with cherry, willow, maple, service-berry, and aspen.

A meridian observation of the sun which I obtained here gave 42° 14′ 22″ for our latitude, and the barometer indicated a height of five thousand one hundred and seventy feet. A number of Indians came immediately over to visit us, and several men were sent to the village with goods, tobacco, knives, cloth, vermilion, and the usual trinkets, to exchange for provisions. But they had no game of any kind ; and it was difficult to obtain any roots from them, as they were miserably poor and had but little to spare from their winter stock of provisions. Several of the Indians drew aside their blankets, showing me their lean and bony figures ; and I would not any longer tempt them with a display of our merchandise to part with their wretched subsistence, when they gave as a reason that it would expose them to temporary starvation.

A great portion of the region inhabited by this nation formerly abounded in game ; the buffalo ranging about in herds, as we had found them on the eastern waters, and the plains dotted with scattered bands of antelope ; but so rapidly have they disappeared within a few years, that now, as we journeyed along, an occasional buffalo-skull and a few wild antelope were all that remained of the abundance which had covered the country with animal life.

The extraordinary rapidity with which the buffalo is disappearing from our territories will not appear surprising when we remember the great scale on which their destruction is yearly carried on. With inconsiderable exceptions, the business of the American trading-posts is carried on in their skins ; every year the Indian villages make new lodges, for which the skin of the buffalo furnishes the material ; and in that portion of the country where they are still found, the Indians derive their entire support from them, and slaughter them with a thoughtless and abominable extravagance. Like the Indians themselves, they have been a characteristic of the great West; and as, like them, they are visibly diminishing, it will be interesting to throw a glance backward through the last twenty years, and give some account of their former distribution through the country and the limit of their western range.

The information is derived principally from Mr. Fitzpatrick, supported by my own personal knowledge and acquaintance with the country. Our knowledge does not go farther back than the spring of 1824, at which time the buffalo were spread in immense numbers over the Green River and Bear River Valleys, and through all the country lying between the Colorado, or Green River of the Gulf of California, and Lewis' Fork of the Columbia River; the meridian of Fort Hall then forming the western limit of their range.

The buffalo then remained for many years in that country, and frequently moved down the valley of the Columbia, on both sides of the river, as far as the *Fishing Falls*. Below this point they never descended in any numbers. About the year 1834 or 1835 they began to diminish very rapidly, and continued to decrease until 1838 or 1840, when, with the country we have just described, they entirely abandoned all the waters of the Pacific north of Lewis' Fork of the Columbia. At that time the Flathead Indians were in the habit of finding their buffalo on the heads of Salmon River and other streams of the Columbia; but now they never meet with them farther west than the three forks of the Missouri, or the plains of the Yellowstone River.

In the course of our journey it will be remarked that the buffalo have not so entirely abandoned the waters of the Pacific, in the Rocky Mountain region south of the Sweet Water, as in the country north of the Great Pass. This partial distribution can only be accounted for in the great pastoral beauty of that country, which bears marks of having long been one of their favorite haunts, and by the fact that the white hunters have more frequented the northern than the southern region—it being north of the South Pass that the hunters, trappers, and traders have had their rendezvous for many years past; and from that section also the greater portion of the beaver and rich furs were taken, although always the most dangerous, as well as the most profitable, hunting-ground.

In that region lying between the Green or Colorado River and the head-waters of the Rio del Norte, over the *Yampah, Kooyah, White*, and *Grand* Rivers—all of which are the waters of the Colorado—the buffalo never extended so far to the westward as they did on the waters of the Columbia; and only in one or two instances have they been known to descend as far west as the mouth of White River.

In travelling through the country west of the Rocky Mountains, observations readily led me to the impression that the buffalo had, for the first time, crossed that range to the waters of the Pacific only a few years prior to the period we are considering; and in this opinion I am sustained by Mr. Fitzpatrick and the older trappers in that country.

In the region west of the Rocky Mountains we never meet with any of the ancient vestiges which, throughout all the country lying upon their eastern waters, are found in the *great highways*, continuous for hundreds of miles, always several inches, and sometimes several feet in depth, which the buffalo have made in crossing from one river to another, or in traversing the mountain ranges. The Snake Indians, more particularly those low down upon Lewis' Fork, have always been very grateful to the American trappers for the great kindness (as they frequently expressed it) which they did to them, in driving the buffalo so low down the Columbia River.

The extraordinary abundance of the buffalo on the east side of the Rocky Mountains, and their extraordinary diminution, will be made clearly evident from the following statement: At any time between the years 1824 and 1836 a traveller might start from any given point, south or north, in the Rocky Mountain range, journeying by the most direct route to the Missouri River; and during the whole distance his road would be always among large bands of buffalo, which would never be out of his view until he arrived almost within sight of the abodes of civilization.

At this time the buffalo occupy but a very limited space, principally along the eastern base of the Rocky Mountains, sometimes extending at their southern extremity to a considerable distance into the plains between the Platte and Arkansas Rivers, and along the eastern frontier of New Mexico as far south as Texas.

The following statement, which I owe to the kindness of Mr. Sanford, a partner in the American Fur Company, will further illustrate this subject, by extensive knowledge acquired during several years of travel through the region inhabited by the buffalo:

"The total amount of robes annually traded by ourselves and others will not be found to differ much from the following statement:

	Robes.
American Fur Company	70,000
Hudson's Bay Company	10,000
All other companies, probably	10,000
Making a total of	90,000

as an average annual return for the last eight or ten years.

" In the northwest the Hudson's Bay Company purchase from the Indians but a very small number—their only market being Canada, to which the cost of transportation nearly equals the produce of the furs; and it is only within a very recent period that they have received buffalo-robes in trade; and out of the great number of buffalo annually killed throughout the extensive regions inhabited by the Comanches and other kindred tribes no robes whatever are furnished for trade. During only four months of the year (from November until March) the skins are good for dressing, those obtained in the remaining eight months being valueless to traders; and the hides of bulls are never taken off or dressed as robes at any season. Probably not more than one-third of the skins are taken from the animals killed, even when they are in good season, the labor of preparing and dressing the robes being very great; and it is seldom that a lodge trades more than twenty skins in a year. It is during the summer months, and in the early part of autumn, that the greatest number of buffalo are killed, and yet at this time a skin is never taken for the purpose of trade."

From these data, which are certainly limited, and decidedly within bounds, the reader is left to draw his own inference of the immense number annually killed.

In 1842 I found the Sioux Indians of the Upper Platte *démontés*, as their French traders expressed it, with the failure of the buffalo; and in the following year large villages from the Upper Missouri came over to the mountains at the heads of the Platte in search of them. The rapidly progressive failure of their principal, and almost their only means of subsistence, has created great alarm among them; and at this time there are only two modes presented to them by which they see a good prospect for escaping starvation: one of these is to rob the settlements along the frontier of the States; and the other is to form a league between the various tribes of the Sioux nation, the Cheyennes, and Arapahoes, and make war against the Crow nation, in order to take from them their country, which is now the best buffalo country in the West. This plan they now have in consideration; and it would probably be a war of extermination, as the Crows have long been advised of this state of affairs, and say that they are perfectly prepared. These are the best warriors in the Rocky Mountains, and are now allied with the Snake Indians; and it is probable that their combination would extend itself to the Utahs, who have long been engaged in war against the Sioux. It is in this section of country that my observation formerly led me to recommend the establishment of a military post.

The further course of our narrative will give fuller and more detailed information of the present disposition of the buffalo in the country we visited.

Among the roots we obtained here I could distinguish only five or six different kinds ; and the supply of the Indians whom we met consisted principally of yampah (*Anethum graveolens*), tobacco root (*Valeriana*), and a large root of a species of thistle (*Circium Virginianum*), which now is occasionally abundant, and is a very agreeably flavored vegetable.

We had been detained so long at the village that in the afternoon we made only five miles, and encamped on the same river after a day's journey of nineteen miles. The Indians informed us that we should reach the big salt water after having slept twice and travelling in a southerly direction. The stream had here entered a nearly level plain or valley, of good soil, eight or ten miles broad, to which no termination was to be seen, and lying between ranges of mountains which, on the right, were grassy and smooth, unbroken by rock, and lower than on the left, where they were rocky and bald, increasing in height to the southward.

On the creek were fringes of young willows, older trees being rarely found on the plains, where the Indians burn the surface to produce better grass. Several magpies (*Pica Hudsonica*) were seen on the creek this afternoon ; and a rattlesnake was killed here, the first which had been seen since leaving the eastern plains. Our camp to-night had such a hungry appearance that I suffered the little cow to be killed, and divided the roots and berries among the people. A number of Indians from the village encamped near.

The weather the next morning was clear, the thermometer at sunrise at 44.5°, and, continuing down the valley, in about five miles we followed the little creek of our encampment to its junction with a larger stream, called *Roseaux*, or Reed River. Immediately opposite, on the right, the range was gathered into its highest peak, sloping gradually low, and running off to a point apparently some forty or fifty miles below. Between this (now become the valley stream) and the foot of the mountains we journeyed along a handsome sloping level, which frequent springs from the hills made occasionally miry, and halted to noon at a swampy spring, where there were good grass and abundant rushes. Here the river was forty feet wide, with a considerable current ; and the valley a mile and a half in breadth ; the soil being generally good, of a dark color, and apparently well adapted to cultivation.

The day had become bright and pleasant, with the thermometer at 71°. By observation our latitude was 41° 59′ 31″, and the elevation above the sea four thousand six hundred and seventy feet. On our left, this afternoon, the range at long intervals formed itself into peaks, appearing to terminate about forty miles below, in a rocky cape ; beyond which several others were faintly visible ; and we were disappointed when at every little rise we did not see the lake. Toward evening our way was somewhat obstructed by fields of artemisia, which began to make their appearance here, and we encamped on the Roseaux, the water of which had acquired a decidedly salt taste, nearly opposite to a cañon gap in the mountains, through which the Bear River enters this valley.

As we encamped, the night set in dark and cold, with heavy rain; and the artemisia, which was here our only wood, was so wet that it would not burn. A poor, nearly starved dog, with a wound in his side from a ball, came to the camp, and remained with us until the winter, when he met a very unexpected fate.

September 1st.—The morning was squally and cold; the sky scattered over with clouds; and the night had been so uncomfortable that we were not on the road until eight o'clock. Travelling between Roseaux and Bear Rivers, we continued to descend the valley, which gradually expanded, as we advanced, into a level plain of good soil, about twenty-five miles in breadth, between mountains three thousand and four thousand feet high, rising suddenly to the clouds, which all day rested upon the peaks. These gleamed out in the occasional sunlight, mantled with the snow which had fallen upon them, while it rained on us in the valley below, of which the elevation here was about four thousand five hundred feet above the sea.

The country before us plainly indicated that we were approaching the lake, though as the ground where we were travelling afforded no elevated point, nothing of it as yet could be seen; and at a great distance ahead were several isolated mountains, resembling islands, which they were afterward found to be. On this upper plain the grass was everywhere dead; and among the shrubs with which it was almost exclusively occupied (artemisia being the most abundant) frequently occurred handsome clusters of several species of *dieteria* in bloom. *Purshia tridentata* was among the frequent shrubs.

Descending to the bottoms of Bear River we found good grass for the animals, and encamped about three hundred yards above the mouth of Roseaux, which here makes its junction, without communicating any of its salty taste to the main stream, of which the water remains perfectly pure. On the river are only willow thickets (*Salix longifolia*), and in the bottoms the abundant plants are canes, solidago, and helianthi, and along the banks of Roseaux are fields of *Malva rotundifolia*. At sunset the thermometer was at 54.5°, and the evening clear and calm; but I deferred making any use of it until one o'clock in the morning, when I endeavored to obtain an emersion of the first satellite; but it was lost in a bank of clouds, which also rendered our usual observations indifferent.

Among the useful things which formed a portion of our equipage was an India-rubber boat, eighteen feet long, made somewhat in the form of a bark canoe of the northern lakes. The sides were formed by two air-tight cylinders, eighteen inches in diameter, connected with others forming the bow and stern. To lessen the danger from accidents to the boat, these were divided into four different compartments, and the interior space was sufficiently large to contain five or six persons, and a considerable weight of baggage. The Roseaux being too deep to be forded, our boat was filled with air, and in about one hour all the equipage of the camp, carriage and gun included, ferried across.

Thinking that perhaps in the course of the day we might reach the outlet at the lake, I got into the boat with Basil Lajeunesse, and paddled down Bear River, intending at night to rejoin the party, which in the meantime proceeded on its way. The river was from sixty to one hundred yards broad, and the water so deep that, even on the comparatively shallow points, we could not reach the bottom within fifteen feet. On either side were alternately low bottoms and willow points, with an occasional high prairie; and for five or six hours we followed slowly the winding course of the river, which crept along with a sluggish current among frequent *détours* several miles around, sometimes running for a considerable distance directly up the valley.

As we were stealing quietly down the stream, trying in vain to get a shot at a strange large bird that was numerous among the willows, but very shy, we came unexpectedly upon several families of *Root Diggers*, who were encamped among the rushes on the shore, and appeared very busy about several weirs or nets which had been rudely made of canes and rushes for the purpose of catching fish. They were very much startled at our appearance, but we soon established an acquaintance; and finding that they had some roots, I promised to send some men with goods to trade with them. They had the usual very large heads, remarkable among the Digger tribe, with matted hair, and were almost entirely naked; looking very poor and miserable, as if their lives had been spent in the rushes where they were, beyond which they seemed to have very little knowledge of anything. From the few words we could comprehend their language was that of the Snake Indians.

Our boat moved so heavily, that we had made very little progress; and, finding that it would be impossible to overtake the camp, as soon as we were sufficiently far below the Indians, we put to the shore near a high prairie bank, hauled up the boat, and *cached* our effects in the willows. Ascending the bank, we found that our desultory labor had brought us only a few miles in a direct line; and, going out into the prairie, after a search we found the trail of the camp, which was now nowhere in sight, but had followed the general course of the river in a large circular sweep which it makes at this place. The sun was about three hours high when we found the trail; and as our people had passed early in the day, we had the prospect of a vigorous walk before us.

Immediately where we landed, the high arable plain on which we had been travelling for several days past, terminated in extensive low flats, very generally occupied by salt marshes, or beds of shallow lakes, whence the water had in most places evaporated, leaving their hard surface encrusted with a shining white residuum, and absolutely covered with very small *univalve* shells. As we advanced, the whole country around us assumed this appearance; and there was no other vegetation than the shrubby chenopodiaceous and other apparently saline plants, which were confined to the rising grounds.

Here and there on the river bank, which was raised like a levee above the flats through which it ran, was a narrow border of grass, and short, black-burned willows; the stream being very deep and sluggish, and sometimes six hundred to eight hundred feet wide. After a rapid walk of about fifteen miles, we caught sight of the camp-fires among clumps of willows just as the sun had sunk behind the mountains on the west side of the valley, filling the clear sky with a golden yellow. These last rays, to us so precious, could not have revealed a more welcome sight. To the traveller, and the hunter, a camp fire in the lonely wilderness is always cheering; and to ourselves, in our present situation, after a hard march in a region of novelty, approaching the *debouches* of a river, in a lake of almost fabulous reputation, it was doubly so.

A plentiful supper of aquatic birds, and the interest of the scene, soon dissipated fatigue; and I obtained during the night emersions of the second, third, and fourth satellites of Jupiter, with observations for time and latitude.

UTAH INDIAN.

CHAPTER VII.

In the Vicinity of Salt Lake—Weber's Fork—Living on Roots—The Unknown Sea—
Fried Worms for Food—Meet Mr. Fitzpatrick—Three Buttes—A Melancholy
and Strange Looking Country—Mr. Payette's Hospitality—Cayuse Indians—A
Perilous Search for Water—Big Trees—The Devil's Hole—Submerged Forests.

September 3d.—The morning was clear, with a light air from the north,
and the thermometer at sunrise at 45.5°. At three in the morning Basil
was sent back with several men and horses for the boat, which, in a direct
course across the flats, was not ten miles distant; and in the meantime
there was a pretty spot of grass here for the animals. The ground was
so low that we could not get high enough to see across the river on account of the willows; but we were evidently in the vicinity of the lake, and
the water-fowl made this morning a noise like thunder. A pelican (*Pele-
canus onocrotalus*) was killed as he passed by, and many geese and ducks
flew over the camp. On the dry salt marsh here is scarce any other plant
than *Salicornia herbacea*.

In the afternoon the men returned with the boat, bringing with them a
small quantity of roots, and some meat, which the Indians had told them
was bear-meat.

Descending the river for about three miles in the afternoon, we found
a bar to any further travelling in that direction—the stream being spread
out in several branches and covering the low grounds with water, where
the miry nature of the bottom did not permit any further advance. We were
evidently on the border of the lake, although the rushes and canes which
covered the marshes prevented any view; and we accordingly encamped
at the little delta which forms the mouth of Bear River, a long arm of the
lake stretching up to the north between us and the opposite mountains.
The river was bordered with a fringe of willows and canes, among which
were interspersed a few plants; and scattered about on the marsh was a
species of *uniola*, closely allied to *U. spicata* of our sea-coast. The whole
morass was animated with multitudes of water-fowl, which appeared to be
very wild—rising for the space of a mile round about at the sound of a gun,
with a noise like distant thunder. Several of the people waded out into the
marshes, and we had to-night a delicious supper of ducks, geese, and plover.

Although the moon was bright the night was otherwise favorable; and

I obtained this evening an emersion of the first satellite, with the usual observations. A mean result, depending on various observations made during our stay in the neighborhood, places the mouth of the river in longitude 112° 19′ 30″ west from Greenwich; latitude 41° 30′ 22″; and, according to the barometer, in elevation four thousand two hundred feet above the Gulf of Mexico. The night was clear, with considerable dew, which I had remarked every night since September first.

The next morning, while we were preparing to start, Carson rode into the camp with flour and a few other articles of light provision, sufficient for two or three days—a scanty but very acceptable supply. Mr. Fitzpatrick had not yet arrived, and provisions were very scarce and difficult to be had at Fort Hall, which had been entirely exhausted by the necessities of the emigrants. He brought me also a letter from Mr. Dwight, who, in company with several emigrants, had reached that place in advance of Mr. Fitzpatrick, and was about continuing his journey to Vancouver.

Returning about five miles up the river, we were occupied until nearly sunset in crossing to the left bank—the stream, which in the last five or six miles of its course is very much narrower than above, being very deep immediately at the banks, and we had great difficulty in getting our animals over. The people with the baggage were easily crossed in the boat, and we encamped on the left bank where we crossed the river. At sunset the thermometer was at 75°, and there was some rain during the night, with a thunder-storm at a distance.

September 5th.—Before us was evidently the bed of the lake, being a great salt marsh perfectly level and bare, whitened in places by saline efflorescences, with here and there a pool of water, and having the appearance of a very level sea-shore at low tide. Immediately along the river was a very narrow strip of vegetation, consisting of willows, helianthi, roses, flowering vines, and grass; bordered on the verge of the great marsh by a fringe of singular plants which appear to be a shrubby salicornia, or a genus allied to it.

About twelve miles to the southward was one of those isolated mountains, now appearing to be a kind of peninsula; and toward this we accordingly directed our course, as it probably afforded a good view of the lake; but the deepening mud as we advanced forced us to return toward the river and gain the higher ground at the foot of the eastern mountains. Here we halted for a few minutes at noon, on a beautiful little stream of pure and remarkably clear water, with a bed of rock *in situ*, on which was an abundant water-plant with a white blossom. There was good grass in the bottoms; and, amid a rather luxuriant growth, its banks were bordered with a large showy plant (*Eupatorium purpureum*), which I here saw for the first time. We named the stream *Clear Creek*.

We continued our way along the mountain, having found here a broad plainly beaten trail, over what was apparently the shore of the lake in the spring; the ground being high and firm, and the soil excellent and covered with vegetation, among which a leguminous plant (*Glycyrrhiza lepidota*) was a characteristic. The ridge here rises abruptly to the height of about four thousand feet, its face being very prominently marked with a massive stratum of rose-colored granular quartz, which is evidently an altered sedimentary rock—the lines of deposition being very distinct. It is rocky and steep, divided into several mountains, and the rain in the valley appears to be always snow on their summits at this season. Near a remarkable rocky point of the mountain, at a large spring of pure water, were several hackberry trees (*celtis*), probably a new species, the berries still green; and a short distance farther, thickets of sumach (*rhus*).

On the plain here I noticed blackbirds and grouse. In about seven miles from Clear Creek the trail brought us to a place at the foot of the mountain where there issued, with considerable force, ten or twelve hot springs, highly impregnated with salt. In one of these the thermometer stood at 136°, and in another at 132.5°; and the water, which spread in pools over the low ground, was colored red.

At this place the trail we had been following turned to the left, apparently with the view of entering a gorge in the mountain, from which issued the principal fork of a large and comparatively well-timbered stream, called Weber's Fork. We accordingly turned off toward the lake and encamped on this river, which was one hundred to one hundred and fifty feet wide, with high banks, and very clear, pure water, without the slightest indication of salt.

September 6th.—Leaving the encampment early, we again directed our course for the peninsular *butte*, across a low shrubby plain, crossing in the way a slough-like creek with miry banks, and wooded with thickets of thorn (*cratægus*) which were loaded with berries. This time we reached the butte without any difficulty, and, ascending to the summit, immediately at our feet beheld the object of our anxious search—the waters of the inland Sea stretching in still and solitary grandeur far beyond the limit of our

---

* An analysis of the red earthy matter deposited in the bed of the stream from the springs gives the following result :

Peroxide of iron	33.50
Carbonate of magnesia	2.40
Carbonate of lime	50.43
Sulphate of lime	2.00
Chloride of sodium	3.45
Silica and alumina	3.00
Water and loss	5.22
	100.00

vision.   It was one of the great points of the exploration; and as we looked eagerly over the lake in the first emotions of excited pleasure, I am doubtful if the followers of Balboa felt more enthusiasm when, from the heights of the Andes, they saw for the first time the great Western Ocean.   It was certainly a magnificent object, and a noble *terminus* to this part of our expedition; and to travellers so long shut up among mountain ranges a sudden view over the expanse of silent waters had in it something sublime.   Several large islands raised their high rocky heads out of the waves; but whether or not they were timbered was still left to our imagination, as the distance was too great to determine if the dark hues upon them were woodland or naked rock.

During the day the clouds had been gathering black over the mountains to the westward, and while we were looking a storm burst down with sudden fury upon the lake and entirely hid the islands from our view.   So far as we could see, along the shores there was not a solitary tree, and but little appearance of grass; and on Weber's Fork, a few miles below our last encampment, the timber was gathered into groves, and then disappeared entirely.   As this appeared to be the nearest point to the lake where a suitable camp could be found, we directed our course to one of the groves, where we found a handsome encampment, with good grass and an abundance of rushes (*Equisetum hyemale*).   At sunset the thermometer was at 55°; the evening clear and calm, with some cumuli.

September 7th.—The morning was calm and clear, with a temperature at sunrise of 39.5°.   The day was spent in active preparation for our intended voyage on the lake.   On the edge of the stream a favorable spot was selected in a grove, and, felling the timber, we made a strong *corral*, or horse-pen, for the animals, and a little fort for the people who were to remain.   We were now probably in the country of the Utah Indians, though none reside upon the lake.   The india-rubber boat was repaired with prepared cloth and gum, and filled with air, in readiness for the next day.

The provisions which Carson had brought with him being now exhausted, and our stock reduced to a small quantity of roots, I determined to retain with me only a sufficient number of men for the execution of our design; and accordingly seven were sent to Fort Hall under the guidance of François Lajeunesse, who, having been for many years a trapper in the country, was considered an experienced mountaineer.   Though they were provided with good horses, and the road was a remarkably plain one of only four days' journey for a horseman, they became bewildered (as we afterward learned), and, losing their way, wandered about the country in parties of one or two, reaching the fort about a week afterward.   Some straggled in of themselves and the others were brought in by Indians who had picked them up on Snake River, about sixty miles below the fort, travelling along the emigrant road in full march for the Lower Columbia.   The leader of this adventurous party was François.

Hourly barometrical observations were made during the day, and, after departure of the party for Fort Hall, we occupied ourselves in continuing our little preparations and in becoming acquainted with the country in the vicinity.   The bottoms along the river were timbered with several kinds of willow, hawthorn, and fine cotton-wood trees (*Populus canadensis*) with remarkably large leaves, and sixty feet in height by measurement.

We formed now but a small family.   With Mr. Preuss and myself, Carson, Bernier, and Basil Lajeunesse had been selected for the boat expedition—the first ever attempted on this interior sea ; and Badeau, with Derosier and Jacob (the colored man), were to be left in charge of the camp. We were favored with most delightful weather.

To-night there was a brilliant sunset of golden orange and green, which left the western sky clear and beautifully pure ; but clouds in the east made me lose an occultation.   The summer frogs were singing around us, and the evening was very pleasant, with a temperature of 60°—a night of a more southern autumn.   For our supper we had *yampah*, the most agreeably flavored of the roots, seasoned by a small fat duck which had come in the way of Jacob's rifle.   Around our fire to-night were many speculations on what to-morrow would bring forth, and in our busy conjectures we fancied that we should find everyone of the large islands a tangled wilderness of trees and shrubbery, teeming with game of every description that the neighboring region afforded and which the foot of a white man or Indian had never violated.

Frequently, during the day, clouds had rested on the summits of their lofty mountains, and we believed that we should find clear streams and springs of fresh water ; and we indulged in anticipations of the luxurious repasts with which we were to indemnify ourselves for past privations. Neither, in our discussions, were the whirlpool and other mysterious dangers forgotten which Indian and hunters' stories attributed to this unexplored lake.

The men had discovered that, instead of being strongly sewed (like that of the preceding year, which so triumphantly rode the cañons of the Upper Great Platte), our present boat was only pasted together in a very insecure manner, the maker having been allowed so little time in the construction that he was obliged to crowd the labor of two months into several days.   The insecurity of the boat was sensibly felt by us ; and, mingled with the enthusiasm and excitement that we all felt at the prospect of an undertaking which had never before been accomplished, was a certain impression of danger, sufficient to give a serious character to our conversation.

The momentary view which had been had of the lake the day before, its great extent and rugged islands, dimly seen amidst the dark waters in the obscurity of the sudden storm, were well calculated to heighten the idea of undefined danger with which the lake was generally associated.

September 8th.—A calm, clear day, with a sunrise temperature of 41°. In view of our present enterprise, a part of the equipment of the boat had been made to consist in three air-tight bags, about three feet long, and capable each of containing five gallons. These had been filled with water the night before, and were now placed in the boat, with our blankets and instruments, consisting of a sextant, telescope, spy-glass, thermometer, and barometer.

We left the camp at sunrise, and had a very pleasant voyage down the river, in which there was generally eight or ten feet of water, deepening as we neared the mouth in the latter part of the day. In the course of the morning we discovered that two of the cylinders leaked so much as to require one man constantly at the bellows to keep them sufficiently full of air to support the boat.

Although we had made a very early start, we loitered so much on the way—stopping every now and then, and floating silently along to get a shot at a goose or a duck—that it was late in the day when we reached the outlet. The river here divided into several branches, filled with fluvials, and so very shallow that it was with difficulty we could get the boat along, being obliged to get out and wade. We encamped on a low point among rushes and young willows, where there was a quantity of drift-wood which served for our fires.

The evening was mild and clear; we made a pleasant bed of the young willows; and geese and ducks enough had been killed for an abundant supper at night, and for breakfast next morning. The stillness of the night was enlivened by millions of water-fowl. Latitude (by observation) 41° 11′ 26″; and longitude 112° 11′ 30″.

September 9th.—The day was clear and calm; the thermometer at sunrise at 49°. As is usual with the trappers on the eve of any enterprise, our people had made dreams, and theirs happened to be a bad one—one which always preceded evil—and consequently they looked very gloomy this morning; but we hurried through our breakfast, in order to make an early start and have all the day before us for our adventure.

The channel in a short distance became so shallow that our navigation was at an end, being merely a sheet of soft mud, with a few inches of water, and sometimes none at all, forming the low-water shore of the lake. All this place was absolutely covered with flocks of screaming plover. We took off our clothes, and, getting overboard, commenced dragging the boat—making, by this operation, a very curious trail, and a very disagreeable smell in stirring up the mud, as we sank above the knee at every step. The water here was still fresh, with only an insipid and disagreeable taste, probably derived from the bed of fetid mud.   After proceeding in this way about a mile we came to a small black ridge on the bottom, beyond which the water became suddenly salt, beginning gradually to deepen, and the bottom was sandy and firm.   It was a remarkable division, separating the fresh water of the rivers from the briny water of the lake, which was entirely *saturated* with common salt.   Pushing our little vessel across the narrow boundary, we sprang on board, and at length were afloat on the waters of the unknown sea.

We did not steer for the mountainous islands, but directed our course toward a lower one which it had been decided we should first visit, the summit of which was formed like the crater at the upper end of Bear River Valley.   So long as we could touch the bottom with our paddles, we were very gay ; but gradually, as the water deepened, we became more still in our frail bateau of gum cloth distended with air, and with pasted seams. Although the day was very calm, there was a considerable swell on the lake ; and there were white patches of foam on the surface, which were slowly moving to the southward, indicating the set of a current in that direction and recalling the recollection of the whirlpool stories.   The water continued to deepen as we advanced ; the lake becoming almost transparently clear, of an extremely beautiful bright-green color ; and the spray, which was thrown into the boat and over our clothes, was directly converted into a crust of common salt, which covered also our hands and arms.

" Captain," said Carson, who for some time had been looking suspiciously at some whitening appearances outside the nearest islands, " what are those yonder?—won't you just take a look with the glass ? " We ceased paddling for a moment, and found them to be the caps of the waves that were beginning to break under the force of a strong breeze that was coming up the lake.   The form of the boat seemed to be an admirable one, and it rode on the waves like a water bird ; but, at the same time, it was extremely slow in its progress.   When we were a little more than half-way across the reach, two of the divisions between the cylinders gave way, and it required the constant use of the bellows to keep in a sufficient quantity of air.   For a long time we scarcely seemed to approach our island, but gradually we worked across the rougher sea of the open channel into the smoother water under the lee of the island, and began to discover that what we took for a long row of pelicans ranged on the beach, were only low cliffs whitened with salt by the spray of the waves ; and about noon we reached the shore, the transparency of the water enabling us to see the bottom at a considerable depth.

It was a handsome broad beach where we landed, behind which the hill, into which the island was gathered, rose somewhat abruptly; and a point of rock at one end enclosed it in a sheltering way; and as there was an abundance of drift-wood along the shore, it offered us a pleasant encampment. We did not suffer our fragile boat to touch the sharp rocks; but, getting overboard, discharged the baggage, and, lifting it gently out of the water, carried it to the upper part of the beach, which was composed of very small fragments of rock.

Among the successive banks of the beach, formed by the action of the waves, our attention, as we approached the island, had been attracted by one ten to twenty feet in breadth, of a dark-brown color. Being more closely examined, this was found to be composed, to the depth of seven or eight, and twelve inches, entirely of the *larvæ* of insects, or, in common language, of the skins of worms, about the size of a grain of oats, which had been washed up by the waters of the lake.

Alluding to this subject some months afterward, when travelling through a more southern portion of this region in company with Mr. Joseph Walker, an old hunter, I was informed by him that, wandering with a party of men in a mountain country east of the great Californian range, he surprised a party of several Indian families encamped near a small salt lake, who abandoned their lodges at his approach, leaving everything behind them. Being in a starving condition, they were delighted to find in the abandoned lodges a number of skin bags, containing a quantity of what appeared to be fish, dried and pounded. On this they made a hearty supper; and were gathering around an abundant breakfast the next morning, when Mr. Walker discovered that it was with these, or a similar worm, that the bags had been filled. The stomachs of the stout trappers were not proof against their prejudices, and the repulsive food was suddenly rejected. Mr. Walker had further opportunities of seeing these worms used as an article of food; and I am inclined to think they are the same as those we saw, and appear to be a product of the salt lakes.

Mr. Walker was associated with Captain Bonneville in his expedition to the Rocky Mountains; and had since that time remained in the country, generally residing in some one of the Snake villages, when not engaged in one of his numerous trapping expeditions, in which he is celebrated as one of the best and bravest leaders who have ever been in the country.

The cliffs and masses of rock along the shore were whitened by an incrustation of salt where the waves dashed up against them; and the evaporating water, which had been left in holes and hollows on the surface of the rocks was covered with a crust of salt about one-eighth of an inch in thickness. It appeared strange that, in the midst of this grand reservoir, one of our greatest wants lately had been salt. Exposed to be more per-

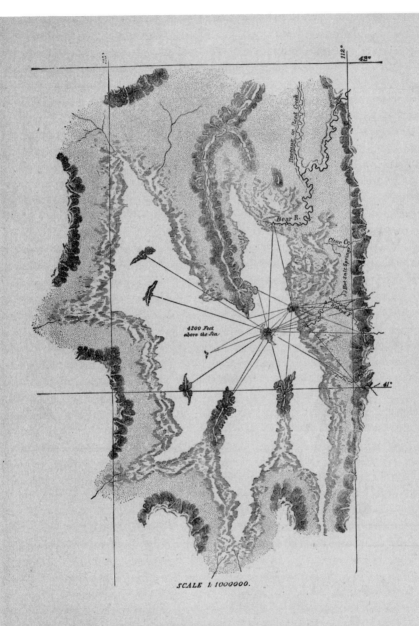

112°   43°

Tonaque or Real Creek

Bear R.

Clear Cr.

Hot Salt Spring

4200 Feet
above the Sea

41°

SCALE 1: 1000000.

THE GREAT SALT LAKE.

fectly dried in the sun, this became very white and fine, having the usual flavor of very excellent common salt, without any foreign taste ; but only a little was collected for present use, as there was in it a number of small black insects.

Carrying with us the barometer and other instruments, in the afternoon we ascended to the highest point of the island—a bare rocky peak, eight hundred feet above the lake. Standing on the summit we enjoyed an extended view of the lake, inclosed in a basin of rugged mountains, which sometimes left marshy flats and extensive bottoms between them and the shore, and in other places came directly down into the water with bold and precipitous bluffs. Following with our glasses the irregular shores, we searched for some indications of a communication with other bodies of water, or the entrance of other rivers ; but the distance was so great that we could make out nothing with certainty. To the southward several peninsular mountains, three thousand or four thousand feet high, entered the lake, appearing, so far as the distance and our position enabled us to determine, to be connected, by flats and low ridges, with the mountains in the rear.

At the season of high waters in the spring, it is probable that all the marshes and low grounds are overflowed, and the surface of the lake considerably greater. In several places the view was of unlimited extent— here and there a rocky islet appearing above the water at a great distance ; and beyond, everything was vague and undefined. As we looked over the vast expanse of water spread out beneath us, and strained our eyes along the silent shores over which hung so much doubt and uncertainty, and which were so full of interest to us, I could hardly repress the almost irresistible desire to continue our exploration ; but the lengthening snow on the mountains was a plain indication of the advancing season, and our frail linen boat appeared so insecure that I was unwilling to trust our lives to the uncertainties of the lake. I therefore unwillingly resolved to terminate our survey here, and remain satisfied for the present with what we had been able to add to the unknown geography of the region. We felt pleasure also in remembering that we were the first who, in the traditionary annals of the country, had visited the islands, and broken, with the cheerful sound of human voices, the long solitude of the place.

From the point where we were standing, the ground fell off on every side to the water, giving us a perfect view of the island, which is twelve or thirteen miles in circumference, being simply a rocky hill, on which there is neither water nor trees of any kind ; although at a distance the *Fremontia vermicularis*, which was in great abundance, might easily be mistaken for woods. The plant seemed here to delight in a congenial air, growing in extraordinary luxuriance seven to eight feet high, and was very abundant on the upper parts of the island, where it was almost the only plant. This is eminently a saline shrub ; its leaves have a very salt taste ; and it luxuriates in saline soils, where it is usually a characteristic. It is widely diffused over all this country. A chenopodiaceous shrub, which is a new species of OBIONE (O. rigida, *Torr. & Frem.*), was equally characteristic of the lower parts of the island. These two are the striking plants on the island, and belong to a class of plants which form a prominent feature in the vegetation of this country. On the lower parts of the island also a prickly pear of very large size was frequent. On the shore, near the water, was a woolly species of *phaca ;* and a new species of umbelliferous plant (*leptotæmia*) was scattered about in very considerable abundance. These constituted all the vegetation that now appeared upon the island.

I accidentally left on the summit the brass cover to the object end of my spy-glass ; and as it will probably remain there undisturbed by Indians, it will furnish matter of speculation to some future traveller. In our excursions about the island we did not meet with any kind of animal; a magpie, and another larger bird, probably attracted by the smoke of our fire, paid us a visit from the shore, and were the only living things seen during our stay. The rock constituting the cliffs along the shore where we were encamped is a talcous rock or stealite, with brown spar.

At sunset the temperature was 70°. We had arrived just in time to obtain a meridian altitude of the sun, and other observations were obtained this evening, which place our camp in latitude 41° 10' 42", and longitude 112° 21' 05" from Greenwich. From a discussion of the barometrical observations made during our stay on the shores of the lake, we have adopted four thousand two hundred feet for its elevation above the Gulf of Mexico. In the first disappointment we felt from the dissipation of our dream of the fertile islands, I called this *Disappointment Island.*

Out of the drift-wood we made ourselves pleasant little lodges, open to the water, and, after having kindled large fires to excite the wonder of any straggling savage on the lake shores, lay down, for the first time in a long journey, in perfect security, no one thinking about his arms. The evening was extremely bright and pleasant,; but the wind rose during the night, and the waves began to break heavily on the shore, making our island tremble. I had not expected in our inland journey to hear the roar of an ocean surf ; and the strangeness of our situation and the excitement we felt in the associated interests of the place made this one of the most interesting nights I remember during our long expedition.

In the morning the surf was breaking heavily on the shore, and we were up early. The lake was dark and agitated, and we hurried through our scanty breakfast, and embarked—having first filled one of the buckets with water from the lake, of which it was intended to make salt. The sun had risen by the time we were ready to start; and it was blowing a strong gale of wind, almost directly off the shore, and raising a considerable sea in which our boat strained very much. It roughened as we got away from the island, and it required all the efforts of the men to make any head against the wind and sea, the gale rising with the sun, and there was danger of being blown into one of the open reaches beyond the island. At the distance of half a mile from the beach the depth of water was sixteen feet, with a clay bottom; but as the working of the boat was very severe labor and during the operation of sounding it was necessary to cease paddling, during which the boat lost considerable way, I was unwilling to discourage the men, and reluctantly gave up my intention of ascertaining the depth, and the character of the bed. There was a general shout in the boat when we found ourselves in one fathom, and we soon after landed on a low point of mud immediately under the *butte* of the peninsula, where we unloaded the boat and carried the baggage about a quarter of a mile to firmer ground.

We arrived just in time for meridian observation, and carried the barometer to the summit of the butte, which is five hundred feet above the lake. Mr. Preuss set off on foot for the camp, which was about nine miles distant, Basil accompanying him to bring back horses for the boat and baggage.

The rude-looking shelter we raised on the shore, our scattered baggage, and boat lying on the beach made quite a picture; and we called this the *Fisherman's camp.* *Lynosiris graveolens,* and another new species of OBIONE (*O. confertifolia—Torr. & Frem.*), were growing on the low grounds, with interspersed spots of an unwholesome salt grass, on a saline clay soil, with a few other plants.

The horses arrived late in the afternoon, by which time the gale had increased to such a height that a man could scarcely stand before it; and we were obliged to pack our baggage hastily, as the rising water of the lake had already reached the point where we were halted. Looking back as we rode off, we found the place of recent encampment entirely covered.

The low plain through which we rode to the camp was covered with a compact growth of shrubs of extraordinary size and luxurance. The soil was sandy and saline; flat places, resembling the beds of ponds, that were bare of vegetation and covered with powdery white salts, being interspersed among the shrubs.

Artemisia tridentata was very abundant, but the plants were principally saline; a large and vigorous chenopodiaceous shrub, five to eight feet high, being characteristic, with *Fremontia vermicularis,* and a shrubby plant which seems to be a new *salicornia.* We reached the camp in time to escape a thunder-storm which blackened the sky, and were received with a discharge of the howitzer by the people, who, having been unable to see anything of us on the lake, had begun to feel some uneasiness.

September 11th.—To-day we remained at this camp, in order to obtain some further observations and to boil down the water which had been brought from the lake for a supply of salt. Roughly evaporated over the fire, the five gallons of water yielded fourteen pints of very fine-grained and very white salt, of which the whole lake may be regarded as a saturated solution. A portion of the salt thus obtained has been subjected to analysis—giving, in one hundred parts, the following proportions :

ANALYSIS OF THE SALT.

Chloride of sodium (common salt)	97.80
Chloride of calcium	0.61
Chloride of magnesia	0.24
Sulphate of soda	0.23
Sulphate of lime	1.12
	100.00

A small stream entering the *Utah Lake,* south of the Spanish Fork, is the first water of that lake which our road of 1844 crosses in coming up from the southward.

When I was on this stream with Mr. Walker in that year he informed me that on the upper part of the river are immense beds of rock-salt of very great thickness, which he had frequently visited. Farther to the southward the rivers which are affluent to the Colorado, such as the Rio Virgen and Gila River, near their mouths are impregnated with salt by the cliffs of rock-salt between which they pass. These mines occur in the same ridge in which, about one hundred and twenty miles to the northward, and subsequently in their more immediate neighborhood, we discovered the fossils belonging to the oolitic period, and they are probably connected with that formation, and are the source from which the Great Lake obtains its salt. Had we remained longer, we should have found them in its bed, and in the mountains around its shores.

By observation the latitude of this camp is 41° 15′ 50″, and longitude 112° 06′ 43″.

The observations made during our stay give for the rate of the chronometer 31″.72, corresponding almost exactly with the rate obtained at St. Vrain's Fort. Barometrical observations were made hourly during the day. This morning we breakfasted on yampah, and had only kamás for supper ; but a cup of good coffee still distinguished us from our *Digger* acquaintances.

September 12*th.*—The morning was clear and calm, with a temperature at sunrise of 33°.   We resumed our journey late in the day, returning by nearly the same route which we had travelled in coming to the lake ; and, avoiding the passage of Hawthorn Creek, struck the hills a little below the hot salt springs.   The flat plain we had here passed over consisted alternately of tolerably good sandy soil and of saline plats.

We encamped early on Clear Creek, at the foot of the high ridge ; one of the peaks of which we ascertained by measurement to be four thousand two hundred and ten feet above the lake, or about eight thousand four hundred feet above the sea.   Behind these front peaks the ridge rises toward the Bear River Mountains, which are probably as high as the Wind River chain.   This creek is here unusually well timbered with a variety of trees.

Among them were birch (*betula*), the narrow-leaved poplar (*Populus angustifolia*), several kinds of willow (*salix*), hawthorn (*cratægus*), alder (*Alnus viridis*), and *cerasus*, with an oak allied to *Quercus alba*, but very distinct from that of any other species in the United States.

We had to-night a supper of sea-gulls, which Carson killed near the lake.   Although cool, the thermometer standing at 47°, mosquitoes were sufficiently numerous to be troublesome this evening.

September 13*th.*—Continuing up the river valley, we crossed several small streams ; the mountains on the right appearing to consist of the blue limestone which we had observed in the same ridge to the northward, alternating here with a granular quartz already mentioned.   One of these streams, which forms a smaller lake near the river, was broken up into several channels ; and the irrigated bottom of fertile soil was covered with innumerable flowers, among which were purple fields of *Eupatorium purpureum*, with helianthi, a handsome solidago (*S. Canadensis*), and a variety of other plants in bloom.

Continuing along the foot of the hills, in the afternoon we found five or six hot springs gushing out together, beneath a conglomerate, consisting principally of fragments of a grayish-blue limestone, efflorescing a salt upon the surface.   The temperature of these springs was 134°, and the rocks in the bed were colored with a red deposit, and there was common salt crystallized on the margin.   There was also a white incrustation upon leaves and roots, consisting principally of carbonate of lime.

There were rushes seen along the road this afternoon, and the soil under the hills was very black, and apparently very good; but at this time the grass is entirely dried up.

We encamped on Bear River, immediately below a cut-off, the cañon by which the river enters this valley bearing north by compass.   The night was mild, with a very clear sky ; and I obtained a very excellent observation of an occultation of Tau¹ Arietis, with other observations. Both immersion and emersion of the star were observed; but, as our observations have shown, the phase at the bright limb generally gives incorrect longitudes, and we have adopted the result obtained from the emersion at the dark limb, without allowing any weight to the immersion. According to these observations the longitude is 112° 05′ 12″, and the latitude 41° 42′ 43.″ All the longitudes on the line of our outward journey, between St. Vrain's Fort and the Dalles of the Columbia, which were not directly determined by satellites, have been chronometrically referred to this place.

The people to-day were rather low-spirited, hunger making them very quiet and peaceable; and there was rarely an oath to be heard in the camp —not even a solitary *enfant de garce.* It was time for the men with an expected supply of provisions from Fitzpatrick to be in the neighborhood; and the gun was fired at evening to give them notice of our locality, but met with no response.

September 14th.—About four miles from this encampment the trail led us down to the river, where we unexpectedly found an excellent ford—the stream being widened by an island, and not yet disengaged from the hills at the foot of the range. We encamped on a little creek where we had made a noon halt in descending the river. The night was very clear and pleasant, the sunset temperature being 67°.

The people this evening looked so forlorn that I gave them permission to kill a fat young horse which I had purchased with goods from the Snake Indians, and they were very soon restored to gayety and good humor. Mr. Preuss and myself could not yet overcome some remains of civilized prejudices, and preferred to starve a little longer—feeling as much saddened as if a crime had been committed.

The next day we continued up the valley, the soil being sometimes very black and good, occasionally gravelly, and occasionally a kind of naked salt plains.

We found on the way this morning a small encampment of two families of Snake Indians, from whom we purchased a small quantity of *kooyah.* They had piles of seeds, of three different kinds, spread out upon pieces of buffalo robe; and the squaws had just gathered about a bushel of the roots of a thistle (*Circium Virginianum*). They were about the ordinary size of carrots, and, as I have previously mentioned, are sweet and well flavored, requiring only a long preparation. They had a band of twelve or fifteen horses, and appeared to be growing in the sunshine with about as little labor as the plants they were eating.

Shortly afterward we met an Indian on horseback who had killed an antelope, which we purchased from him for a little powder and some balls.

We crossed the Roseaux, and encamped on the left bank; halting early for the pleasure of enjoying a wholesome and abundant supper, and were pleasantly engaged in protracting our unusual comfort, when Tabeau galloped into the camp with news that Mr. Fitzpatrick was encamped close by us with a good supply of provisions—flour, rice, and dried meat, and even a little butter.

Excitement to-night made us all wakeful; and after a breakfast before sunrise the next morning, we were again on the road, and, continuing up the valley, crossed some high points of hills and halted to noon on the same stream, near several lodges of Snake Indians, from whom we purchased about a bushel of service-berries, partially dried. By the gift of a knife I prevailed upon a little boy to show me the *kooyah* plant, which proved to be *Valeriana edulis.* The root, which constitutes the *kooyah*, is large, of a very bright yellow color, with the characteristic odor, but not so fully developed as in the prepared substance. It loves the rich moist soil of river bottoms, which was the locality in which I always afterward found it. It was now entirely out of bloom; according to my observation flowering in the months of May and June.

In the afternoon we entered a long ravine leading to a pass in the dividing ridge between the waters of Bear River and the Snake River, or Lewis' Fork of the Columbia; our way being very much impeded, and almost entirely blocked up, by compact fields of luxuriant artemisia. Taking leave at this point of the waters of Bear River, and of the geographical basin which encloses the system of rivers and creeks which belong to the Great Salt Lake, and which so richly deserves a future detailed and ample exploration, I can say of it, in general terms, that the bottoms of this river (Bear) and of some of the creeks which I saw, form a natural resting and recruiting station for travellers, now, and in all time to come. The bottoms are extensive, water excellent, timber sufficient, the soil good and well adapted to the grains and grasses suited to such an elevated region.

A military post and a civilized settlement would be of great value here; and cattle and horses would do well where grass and salt so much abound.

The lake will furnish exhaustless supplies of salt. All the mountain sides here are covered with a valuable nutritious grass, called bunch grass, from the form in which it grows, which has a second growth in the fall. The beasts of the Indians were fat upon it; our own found it a good subsistence; and its quantity will sustain any amount of cattle and make this truly a bucolic region.

We met here an Indian family on horseback, which had been out to gather service-berries, and were returning loaded. This tree was scattered about on the hills, and the upper part of the pass was timbered with aspen (*Populus trem.*); the common blue flowering flax occurring among the plants.

The approach to the pass was very steep ; and the summit about six thousand three hundred feet above the sea—probably only an uncertain approximation, as at the time of observation it was blowing a violent gale of wind from the northwest, with *cumuli* scattered in masses over the sky, the day otherwise bright and clear.

We descended by a steep slope into a broad open valley—good soil—from four to five miles wide; coming down immediately upon one of the head-waters of the Pannack River, which here loses itself in swampy ground. The appearance of the country here is not very interesting. On either side is a regular range of mountains of the usual character, with a little timber, tolerably rocky on the right, and higher and more smooth on the left, with still higher peaks looking out above the range. The valley afforded a good level road ; but it was late when it brought us to water, and we encamped at dark.

The northwest wind had blown up very cold weather, and the artemisia, which was our fire-wood to-night, did not happen to be very abundant. This plant loves a dry, sandy soil, and cannot grow in the good bottoms where it is rich and moist ; but on every little eminence, where water does not rest long, it maintains absolute possession.

Elevation above the sea about five thousand one hundred feet.

At night scattered fires glimmered along the mountains, pointing out camps of the Indians ; and we contrasted the comparative security in which we travelled through this country with the guarded vigilance we were compelled to exert among the Sioux and other Indians on the eastern side of the Rocky Mountains.

At sunset the thermometer was at 50°, and at midnight at 30°.

September 17th.—The morning sky was calm and clear, the temperature at daylight being 25°, and at sunrise 20°. There is throughout this mountain country a remarkable difference between the morning and mid-day temperatures, which at this season was very generally 40° or 50°, and occasionally greater ; and frequently, after a very frosty morning, the heat in a few hours would render the thinnest clothing agreeable.

About noon we reached the main fork. The Pannack River was before us ; the valley being here one and a half mile wide, fertile, and bordered by smooth hills, not over five hundred feet high, partly covered with cedar ; a high ridge in which there is a prominent peak rising behind those on the left. We continued to descend this stream, and found on it at night a warm and comfortable camp. Flax occurred so frequently during the day as to be almost a characteristic, and the soil appeared excellent. The opposite hills on the right are broken here into a great variety of shapes.

The evening was gusty, with a temperature at sunset of 59°. I ob-

UTAH INDIANS.

tained, about midnight, an observation of an emersion of the first satellite ; the night being calm and very clear, the stars remarkably bright, and the thermometer at 30°.   Longitude, from mean of satellite and chronometer, 112° 29′ 52″ ; and latitude, by observation, 42° 44′ 40″.

September 18*th.*—The day clear and calm, with a temperature of 25° at sunrise.   After travelling seven or eight miles we emerged on the plains of the Columbia, in sight of the famous " *Three Buttes,*" a well-known landmark in the country, distant about forty-five miles.

The French word *butte*, which so often occurs in this narrative, is retained from the familiar language of the country, and identifies the objects to which it refers.   It is naturalized in the region of the Rocky Mountains ; and even if desirable to render it in English, I know of no word which would be its precise equivalent.   It is applied to the detached hills and ridges which rise abruptly and reach too high to be called hills or ridges, and not high enough to be called mountains.   *Knob,* as applied in the Western States, is their most descriptive term in English.   *Cerro* is the Spanish term ; but no translation or paraphrase would preserve the identity of these picturesque landmarks, familiar to the traveller, and often seen at a great distance.

Covered as far as could be seen with artemisia, the dark and ugly appearance of this plain obtained for it the name of the *Sage Desert ;* and we were agreeably surprised on reaching the Portneuf River to see a beautiful green valley with scattered timber spread out beneath us on which, about four miles distant, were glistening the white walls of the fort.   The Portneuf runs along the upland plain nearly to its mouth, and an abrupt descent of perhaps two hundred feet brought us down immediately upon the stream, which at the ford is one hundred yards wide and three feet deep, with clear water, a swift current, and gravelly bed ; but a little higher up the breadth was only about thirty-five yards, with apparently deep water.

In the bottom I remarked a very great number of springs and sloughs, with remarkably clear water and gravel beds.   At sunset we encamped with Mr. Talbot and our friends who came on to Fort Hall when we went to the lake, and whom we had the satisfaction to find all well, neither party having met with any mischance in the interval of our separation.   They, too, had had their share of fatigue and scanty provisions, as there had been very little game left on the trail of the populous emigration ; and Mr. Fitzpatrick had rigidly husbanded our stock of flour and light provisions, in view of the approaching winter and the long journey before us.

September 19*th.*—This morning the sky was very dark and gloomy, and at daylight it began snowing thickly, and continued all day, with cold, disagreeable weather.   At sunrise the temperature was 43°.   I rode up to the fort, and purchased from Mr. Grant (the officer in charge of the post) several very indifferent horses, and five oxen in very fine order, which were received at the camp with great satisfaction ; and one being killed at evening, the usual gayety and good humor were at once restored.   Night came in stormy.

September 20th.—We had a night of snow and rain, and the thermometer at sunrise was at 34°; the morning was dark, with a steady rain, and there was still an inch of snow on the ground, with an abundance on the neighboring hills and mountains.   The sudden change in the weather was hard for our animals, which trembled and shivered in the cold—sometimes taking refuge in the timber, and now and then coming out and raking the snow off the ground for a little grass, or eating the young willows.

September 21st.—Ice made tolerably thick during the night, and in the morning the weather cleared up very bright, with a temperature at sunrise of 29°; and I obtained a meridian observation for latitude at the fort, with observations for time.   The sky was again covered in the afternoon, and the thermometer at sunset 48°.

September 22d.—The morning was cloudy and unpleasant, and at sunrise a cold rain commenced, with a temperature of 41°.

The early approach of winter and the difficulty of supporting a large party determined me to send back a number of the men who had become satisfied that they were not fitted for the laborious service and frequent privation to which they were necessarily exposed, and which there was reason to believe would become more severe in the further extension of the voyage.   I accordingly called them together, and, informing them of my intention to continue our journey during the ensuing winter, in the course of which they would probably be exposed to considerable hardship, succeeded in prevailing upon a number of them to return voluntarily. These were : Charles De Forrest, Henry Lee, J. Campbell, William Creuss, A. Vasquez, A. Pera, Patrick White, B. Tesson, M. Creely, François Lajeunesse, Basil Lajeunesse.

Among these I regretted very much to lose Basil Lajeunesse, one of the best men in my party, who was obliged, by the condition of his family, to be at home in the coming winter. · Our preparations having been completed in the interval of our stay here, both parties were ready this morning to resume their respective routes.

Except that there is a greater quantity of wood used in its construction, Fort Hall very much resembles the other trading-posts which have been already described, and would be another excellent post of relief for the emigrant.   It is in the low, rich bottom of the valley, apparently twenty miles long, formed by the confluence of Portneuf River with Lewis' Fork of the Columbia, which it enters about nine miles below the fort, and narrowing gradually to the mouth of the Pannack River, where it has a breadth of only two or three miles. Allowing fifty miles for the road from the *Beer Springs* of Bear River to Fort Hall, its distance along the *travelled* road from the town of Westport, on the frontier of Missouri, by way of Fort Laramie and the great South Pass, is one thousand three hundred and twenty-three miles. Beyond this place, on the line of road along the *barren* valley of the Upper Columbia, there does not occur, for a distance of nearly three hundred miles to the westward, a fertile spot of ground sufficiently large to produce the necessary quantity of grain, or pasturage enough to allow even a temporary repose to the emigrants.

On their recent passage they had been able to obtain, at very high prices and in insufficient quantity, only such assistance as could be afforded by a small and remote trading-post—and that a foreign one—which, in the supply of its own wants, had necessarily drawn around it some of the resources of civilization, but which obtained nearly all its supplies from the distant depot of Vancouver, by a difficult water-carriage of two hundred and fifty miles up the Columbia River and a land-carriage by pack-horses of six hundred miles.

An American military post sufficiently strong to give to their road a perfect security against the Indian tribes, who are unsettled in locality and very *uncertain* in their disposition, and which, with the necessary facilities for the repair of their equipage, would be able to afford them relief in stock and grain from the produce of the post, would be of extraordinary value to the emigration. Such a post (and all others which may be established on the line to Oregon) would naturally form the *nucleus* of a settlement at which supplies and repose would be obtained by the emigrant or trading caravans which may hereafter traverse these elevated and, in many places, desolate and inhospitable regions.

I subjoin an analysis of the soil in the river bottom near Fort Hall, which will be of assistance in forming some correct idea of its general character in the neighboring country. I characterize it as good land, but the analysis will show its precise properties.

ANALYSIS OF SOIL.

Silica	68.55
Alumina	7.45
Carbonate of lime	8.51
Carbonate of magnesia	5.09
Oxide of iron	1.40
Organic vegetable matter	4.74
Water and loss	4.26
	100.00

Our observations place this post in longitude 112° 29′ 54″, latitude 43° 01′ 30″, and in elevation above the sea four thousand five hundred feet.

Taking leave of the homeward party, we resumed our journey down the valley, the weather being very cold and the rain coming in hard gusts which the wind blew directly in our faces. We forded the Portneuf in a storm of rain, the water in the river being frequently up to the axles, and about one hundred and ten yards wide.

After the gust the weather improved a little, and we encamped about three miles below, at the mouth of the Pannack River, on Lewis' Fork, which here has a breadth of about one hundred and twenty yards. The temperature at sunset was 42°; the sky partially covered with dark, rainy clouds.

September 23d.—The temperature at sunrise was 32°, the morning dark and snow falling steadily and thickly, with a light air from the southward. I profited of being obliged to remain in camp to take hourly barometrical observations from sunrise to midnight. The wind at eleven o'clock set in from the northward in heavy gusts, and the snow changed into rain. In the afternoon, when the sky brightened, the rain had washed all the snow from the bottoms; but the neighboring mountains, from summit to foot, were luminously white—an inauspicious commencement of the autumn, of which this was the first day.

September 24th.—The thermometer at sunrise was at 35° and a blue sky in the west promised a fine day. The river bottoms here are narrow and swampy, with frequent sloughs; and after crossing the Pannack the road continued along the uplands, rendered very slippery by the soil of wet clay, and entirely covered with artemisia bushes, among which occur frequent fragments of obsidian.

At noon we encamped in a grove of willows, at the upper end of a group of islands, about half a mile above the *American Falls* of Snake River. Among the willows here were some bushes of Lewis and Clarke's currant (*Ribes aureum*). The river here enters between low mural banks, which consist of a fine vesicular trap-rock, the intermediate portions being compact and crystalline. Gradually becoming higher in its downward course, these banks of scoriated volcanic rock form, with occasional interruptions, its characteristic feature along the whole line to the Dalles of the Lower Columbia, resembling a chasm which had been rent through the country and which the river had afterward taken for its bed. The immediate valley of the river is a high plain, covered with black rocks and artemisias.

In the south is a bordering range of mountains which, although not very high, are broken and covered with snow; and at a great distance to the north is seen the high, snowy line of the Salmon River Mountains, in front of which stand out prominently in the plain the three isolated rugged-looking little mountains commonly known as the *Three Buttes*. Between the river and the distant Salmon River range the plain is represented by Mr. Fitzpatrick as so entirely broken up and rent into chasms as to be impracticable even for a man on foot. By measurement the river above is eight hundred and seventy feet wide, immediately contracted at the fall in the form of a lock, by jutting piles of scoriaceous basalt, over which the foaming river must present a grand appearance at the time of high water. The evening was clear and pleasant, with dew; and at sunset the temperature was 54°. By observation the latitude is 42° 47′ 05″, and the longitude 112° 40′ 13″.

September 25*th*.—Thermometer at sunrise 47°. The day came in clear, with a strong gale from the south, which commenced at eleven of the last night.

The road to-day led along the river, which is full of rapids and small falls. Grass is very scanty; and along the rugged banks are scattered cedars, with an abundance of rocks and sage. We travelled fourteen miles and encamped in the afternoon near the river, on a rocky creek, the bed of which was entirely occupied with bowlders of a very large size. For the last three or four miles the right bank of the river has a palisaded appearance. One of the oxen was killed here for food. The thermometer at evening was at 55°, the sky almost overcast, and the barometer indicated an elevation of four thousand four hundred feet.

September 26*th*.—Rain during the night, and the temperature at sunrise 42°. Travelling along the river, in about four miles we reached a picturesque stream to which we gave the name of Fall Creek. It is remarkable for the many falls which occur in a short distance; and its bed is composed of a calcareous tufa, or vegetable rock, composed principally of the remains of reeds and mosses, resembling that at the *Basin Spring* on Bear River.

The road along the river bluffs had been occasionally very bad; and imagining that some rough obstacles rendered such a detour necessary, we followed for several miles a plain wagon road leading up this stream until we reached a point whence it could be seen making directly toward a low place in the range on the south side of the valley, and we became immediately aware that we were on a trail formed by a party of wagons, in company with which we had encamped at Elm Grove, near the frontier of Missouri, and which were proceeding to Upper California under the direction of Mr. Jos. Childs. At the time of their departure, no practicable passes were known in the Southern Rocky Mountains within the territory of the United States; and the probable apprehension of difficulty in attempting to pass near the settled frontier of New Mexico, together with the desert character of the unexplored region beyond, had induced them to take a more northern and circuitous route by way of the Sweet Water Pass and Fort Hall. They had still between them and the Valley of the Sacramento a great mass of mountains, forming the *Sierra Nevada*, here commonly known as the *Great California Mountain*, and which were at this time considered as presenting an impracticable barrier to wheeled carriages.

Various considerations had suggested to them a division of the party ; and a greater portion of the camp, including the wagons with the mill and other stores, were now proceeding under the guidance of Mr. Joseph Walker, who had engaged to conduct them, by a long sweep to the south-ward, around what is called the *point of the mountain ;* and, crossing through a pass known only to himself, gain the banks of the Sacramento by the Valley of the San Joaquin. It was a long and hazardous journey for a party in which there were women and children. Sixty days was the shortest period of time in which they could reach the point of the moun-tain, and their route lay through a country inhabited by wild and badly disposed Indians and very poor in game ; but the leader was a man pos-sessing great and intimate knowledge of the Indians, with an extraordi-nary firmness and decision of character.

In the meantime Mr. Childs had passed down the Columbia with a party of ten or twelve men, with the intention of reaching the settlements on the Sacramento by a more direct course which indefinite information from hunters had indicated in the direction of the head-waters of the *Rivière aux Malheurs ;* and, having obtained there a re-enforcement of animals and a supply of provisions, meet the wagons, before they should have reached the point of the mountain, at a place which had been previously agreed upon. In the course of our narrative we shall be able to give some in-formation of the fortune which attended the movements of these adven-turous travellers.

Having discovered our error, we immediately regained the line along the river, which the road quitted about noon, and encamped at five o'clock on a stream called Raft River (*Rivière aux Cajeux*), having travelled only thirteen miles. In the north, the Salmon River Mountains are visi-ble at a very far distance ; and on the left, the ridge in which Raft River heads is about twenty miles distant, rocky, and tolerably high. Ther-mometer at sunset 44°, with a partially clouded sky, and a sharp wind from the southwest.

September 27th.—It was now no longer possible, as in our previous journey, to travel regularly every day and find at any moment a conven-ient place for repose at noon, or a camp at night ; but the halting-places were now generally fixed along the road, by the nature of the country, at places where, with water, there was a little scanty grass.

Since leaving the American Falls the road had frequently been very bad; the many short, steep ascents exhausting the strength of our worn-out animals, requiring always at such places the assistance of the men to get up each cart, one by one; and our progress with twelve or fourteen wheeled carriages, though light and made for the purpose, in such a rocky country was extremely slow; and I again determined to gain time by a division of the camp. Accordingly, to-day the parties again separated, constituted very much as before—Mr. Fitzpatrick remaining in charge of the heavier baggage.

The morning was calm and clear, with a white frost, and the temperature at sunrise 24°.

To-day the country had a very forbidding appearance; and after travelling twenty miles over a slightly undulating plain, we encamped at a considerable spring, called Swamp Creek, rising in low grounds near the point of a spur from the mountain.

Returning with a small party in a starving condition from the westward twelve or fourteen years since, Carson had met here three or four buffalo bulls, two of which were killed. They were among the pioneers which had made the experiment of colonizing in the Valley of the Columbia, and which had failed, as heretofore stated.

At sunset the thermometer was at 46°, and the evening was overcast, with a cold wind from the southeast, and to-night we had only sage for fire-wood. Mingled with the artemisia was a shrubby and thorny chenopodiaceous plant.

September 28th.—Thermometer at sunrise 40°. The wind rose early to a gale from the west, with a very cold, driving rain; and after an uncomfortable day's ride of twenty-five miles we were glad when at evening we found a sheltered camp, where there was an abundance of wood, at some elevated rocky islands covered with cedar, near the commencement of another long cañon of the river.

With the exception of a short detention at a deep little stream called Goose Creek, and some occasional rocky places, we had to-day a very good road; but the country has a barren appearance, sandy, and densely covered with the artemisias from the banks of the river to the foot of the mountains.

Here I remarked among the sage-bushes, green bunches of what is called the second growth of grass. The river to-day has had a smooth appearance, free from rapids, with a low, sandy hill-slope bordering the bottoms, in which there is a little good soil. Thermometer at sunset 45°, blowing a gale, and disagreeably cold.

September 29th.—The thermometer at sunrise 36°, with a bright sun, and appearance of finer weather.

The road for several miles was *extremely* rocky, and consequently bad; but entering after this a sandy country it became very good, with no other interruption than the sage-bushes which covered the river plain so far as the eye could reach, and, with their uniform tint of dark gray, gave to the country a gloomy and sombre appearance. All the day the course of the river has been between walls of the black volcanic rock, a dark line of the escarpment on the opposite side pointing out its course, and sweeping along in foam at places where the mountains which border the valley present always on the left two ranges, the lower one a spur of the higher; and, on the opposite side, the Salmon River Mountains are visible at a great distance. Having made twenty-four miles, we encamped about five o'clock on Rock Creek; a stream having considerable water, a swift current, and wooded with willow.

September 30*th.*—Thermometer at sunrise, 28°. In its progress toward the river this creek soon enters a chasm of the volcanic rock, which in places along the wall presents a columnar appearance; and the road becomes extremely rocky whenever it passes near its banks. It is only about twenty feet wide where the road crosses it, with a deep bed and steep banks, covered with rocky fragments, with willows and a little grass on its narrow bottom. The soil appears to be full of calcareous matter, with which the rocks are incrusted. The fragments of rock which had been removed by the emigrants in making a road where we ascended from the bed of this creek were whitened with lime; and during the afternoon's march I remarked in the soil a considerable quantity of calcareous concretions.

Toward evening the sages became more sparse, and the clear spaces were occupied by tufts of green grass. The river still continued its course through a trough or open cañon; and toward sunset we followed the trail of several wagons which had turned in toward Snake River, and encamped, as they had done, on the top of the escarpment. There was no grass here, the soil among the sage being entirely naked; but there is occasionally a little bottom along the river, which a short ravine of rocks at rare intervals leaves accessible; and by one of these we drove our animals down and found some tolerably good grass bordering the water.

Immediately opposite to us a subterranean river bursts out directly from the face of the escarpment, and falls in white foam to the river below. The accompanying view gives a sketch of this remarkable fall, with a representation of the mural precipices which enclose the main river and form its characteristic feature along a great portion of its course. A melancholy and strange-looking country—one of fracture, and violence, and fire.

We had brought with us, when we separated from the camp, a large gaunt ox, in appearance very poor; but, being killed to-night, to the great

LOST ON THE PRAIRIE.

joy of the people, he was found to be remarkably fat. As usual at such oc-currences the evening was devoted to gayety and feasting ; abundant fare now made an epoch among us ; and in this laborious life, in such a country as this, our men had but little else to enjoy.

The temperature at sunset was 65°, with a clear sky and very high wind. By the observation of the evening the encampment was in longitude 114° 25′ 04″, and in latitude 42° 38′ 44″.

October 1st.—The morning clear, with wind from the west, and the ther-mometer at 55°. We descended to the bottom, taking with us the boat, for the purpose of visiting the fall in the opposite cliffs ; and while it was being filled with air we occupied ourselves in measuring the river, which is one thousand seven hundred and eighty-six feet in breadth, with banks two hundred feet high. We were surprised, on our arrival at the opposite side, to find a beautiful basin of clear water, formed by the falling river, around which the rocks were whitened by some saline incrustation. Here the Indians had constructed wicker dams, although I was informed that the salmon do not ascend the river so far ; and its character below would apparently render it impracticable.

The ascent of the steep hill-side was rendered a little difficult by a dense growth of shrubs and fields of cane ; and there were frequent hidden crevices among the rocks, where the water was heard rushing below ; but we succeeded in reaching the main stream, which, issuing from between strata of the trap-rock in two principal branches, produced almost imme-diately a torrent twenty-two feet wide and white with foam. It is a pict-uresque spot of singular beauty, overshaded by bushes, from under which the torrent glances, tumbling into the white basin below, where the clear water contrasted beautifully with the muddy stream of the river. Its outlet was covered with a rank growth of canes, and a variety of unusual plants, and nettles (*urtica canabina*), which, before they were noticed, had set our hands and arms on fire. The temperature of the spring was 58°, while that of the river was 51°. The perpendicular height of the place at which this stream issues is forty-five feet above the river, and one hundred and fifty-two feet below the summit of the precipice, making nearly two hun-dred feet for the height of the wall. On the hill-side here was obtained specimens consisting principally of fragments of the shells of small crus-tacea, and which was probably formed by deposition from these springs proceeding from some lake or river in the highlands above.

We resumed our journey at noon, the day being hot and bright ; and, after a march of seventeen miles, encamped at sunset on the river, near several lodges of Snake Indians.

Our encampment was about one mile below the *Fishing Falls*, a series of cataracts with very inclined planes, which are probably so named because they form a barrier to the ascent of the salmon ; and the great fisheries, from which the inhabitants of this barren region almost entirely derive a subsistence, commence at this place.

These appeared to be unusually gay savages, fond of loud laughter ; and, in their apparent good-nature and merry character, struck me as being entirely different from the Indians we had been accustomed to see.   From several who visited our camp in the evening we purchased, in exchange for goods, dried salmon.   At this season they are not very fat, but we were easily pleased.   The Indians made us comprehend that when the salmon came up the river in the spring they are so abundant that they merely throw in their spears at random, certain of bringing out a fish.

These poor people are but slightly provided with winter clothing ; there is but little game to furnish skins for the purpose ; and of a little animal which seemed to be the most numerous, it required twenty skins to make a covering to the knees.   But they are still a joyous, talkative race, who grow fat and become poor with the salmon, which at least never fail them —the dried being used in the absence of the fresh.   We are encamped immediately on the river-bank, and with the salmon jumping up out of the water, and Indians paddling about in boats made of rushes, or laughing around the fires, the camp to-night has quite a lively appearance.

The river at this place is more open than for some distance above ; and, for the time, the black precipices have disappeared, and no calcareous matter is visible in the soil.   The thermometer at sunset, 74° ; clear and calm.

October 2d.—The sunrise temperature was 48° ; the weather clear and calm.   Shortly after leaving the encampment we crossed a stream of clear water with a variable breadth of ten to twenty-five yards, broken by rapids, and lightly wooded with willow, and having a little grass on its small bottom land.

The barrenness of the country is in fine contrast to-day with the mingled beauty and grandeur of the river, which is more open than hitherto, with a constant succession of falls and rapids.   Over the edge of the black cliffs, and out from their faces, are falling numberless streams and springs ; and all the line of the river is in motion with the play of the water.   In about seven miles we reached the most beautiful and picturesque fall I had seen on the river.

On the opposite side, the vertical fall is perhaps eighteen feet high ; and nearer, the sheet of foaming water is divided and broken into cataracts, where several little islands on the brink and in the river above give it much picturesque beauty, and make it one of those places the traveller turns again and again to fix in his memory.   There were several lodges of Indians here, from whom we traded salmon.

Below this place the river makes a remarkable bend; and the road, ascending the ridge, gave us a fine view of the river below, intersected at many places by numerous fish-dams. In the north, about fifty miles distant, were some high snowy peaks of the Salmon River Mountains; and in the northeast the last peak of the range was visible, at the distance of perhaps one hundred miles or more. The river hills consist of very broken masses of sand, covered everywhere with the same interminable fields of sage, and occasionally the road is very heavy.

We now very frequently saw Indians, who were strung along the river at every little rapid where fish are to be caught, and the cry *haggai, haggai* (fish), was constantly heard whenever we passed near their huts or met them in the road. Very many of them were oddly and partially dressed in overcoat, shirt, waistcoat, or pantaloons, or whatever article of clothing they had been able to procure in trade from the emigrants; for we had now entirely quitted the country where hawks' bells, beads, and vermilion were the current coin, and found that here only useful articles, and chiefly clothing, were in great request. These, however, are eagerly sought after, and for a few trifling pieces of clothing travellers may procure food sufficient to carry them to the Columbia.

We made a long stretch across the upper plain, and encamped on the bluff, where the grass was very green and good; the soil of the upper plains containing a considerable proportion of calcareous matter. This green freshness of the grass was very remarkable for the season of the year. Again we heard the roar of a fall in the river below, where the water in an unbroken volume goes over a descent of several feet. The night is clear, and the weather continues very warm and pleasant, with a sunset temperature of 70°.

October 3d.—The morning was pleasant, with a temperature at sunrise of 42°. The road was broken by ravines among the hills, and in one of these, which made the bed of a dry creek, I found a fragmentary stratum, or brecciated conglomerate, consisting of flinty slate-pebbles, with fragments of limestone containing fossil shells.

On the left the mountains are visible at a distance of twenty or thirty miles, appearing smooth and rather low; but at intervals higher peaks look out from beyond, and indicate that the main ridge, which we are leaving with the course of the river, and which forms the northern boundary of the Great Basin, still maintains its elevation.

About two o'clock we arrived at the ford where the road crosses to the right bank of Snake River.

An Indian was hired to conduct us through the ford, which proved impracticable for us, the water sweeping away the howitzer and nearly drowning the mules, which we were obliged to extricate by cutting them out of the harness. The river here is expanded into a little bay in which there are two islands, across which is the road of the ford; and the emigrants had passed by placing two of their heavy wagons abreast of each other, so as to oppose a considerable mass against the body of water.

The Indians informed us that one of the men, in attempting to turn some cattle which had taken a wrong direction, was carried off by the current and drowned. Since their passage the water had risen considerably; but, fortunately, we had a resource in the boat, which was filled with air and launched; and at seven o'clock we were safely encamped on the opposite bank, the animals swimming across, and the carriage, howitzer, and baggage of the camp being carried over in the boat.

At the place where we crossed, above the islands, the river had narrowed to a breadth of one thousand and forty-nine feet by measurement, the greater portion of which was from six to eight feet deep. We were obliged to make our camp where we landed, among the Indian lodges, which are semicircular huts made of willow, thatched over with straw, and open to the sunny south. By observation, the latitude of our encampment on the right bank of the river was 42° 55′ 58″; chronometric longitude 115° 04′ 46″, and the travelled distance from Fort Hall two hundred and eight miles.

October 4th.—Calm, pleasant day, with the thermometer at sunrise at 47°. Leaving the river at a considerable distance to the left, and following up the bed of a rocky creek, with occasional holes of water, in about six miles we ascended, by a long and rather steep hill, to a plain six hundred feet above the river, over which we continued to travel during the day, having a broken ridge two thousand or three thousand feet high on the right. The plain terminates, where we ascended, in an escarpment of vesicular trap-rock, which supplies the fragments of the creek below. The sky clouded over, with a strong wind from the northwest, with a few drops of rain and occasional sunlight, threatening a change.

Artemisia still covers the plain, but *Purshia tridentata* makes its appearance here on the hill-sides, and on bottoms of the creeks—quite a tree in size, and larger than the artemisia. We crossed several hollows with a little water in them and improved grass; and, turning off from the road in the afternoon in search of water, travelled about three miles up the bed of a willow creek, toward the mountain, and found a good encampment, with wood and grass, and little ponds of water in the bed of the creek; which must be of more importance at other seasons, as we found there several old fixtures for fishing. There were many holes on the creek prairie, which had been made by the diggers in search of roots.

Wind increased to a violent gale from the northwest, with a temperature at sunset of 57°.

October 5th.—The morning was calm and clear, and at sunrise the thermometer was at 32°.   The road to-day was occasionally extremely rocky, with hard volcanic fragments, and our travelling very slow.   In about nine miles the road brought us to a group of smoking hot springs, with a temperature of 164°.

There were a few helianthi in bloom, with some other low plants, and the place was green roundabout ; the ground warm, and the air pleasant, with a summer atmosphere that was very grateful in a day of high and cold searching wind.   The rocks were covered with a white and red incrustation ; and the water has on the tongue the same unpleasant effect as that of the Basin Spring on Bear River.   They form several branches, and bubble up with force enough to raise the small pebbles several inches.

The following is an analysis of the deposite with which the rocks are incrusted :

ANALYSIS.

Silica.	72.55
Carbonate of lime	14.60
Carbonate of magnesia	1.20
Oxide of iron	4.65
Alumina	0.70
Chloride of sodium, etc. } Sulphate of soda } Sulphate of lime, etc. }	1.10
Organic vegetable matter } Water and loss }	5.20
	100.00

These springs are near the foot of the ridge (a dark and rugged-looking mountain), in which some of the nearer rocks have a reddish appearance, and probably consist of a reddish-brown trap, fragments of which were scattered along the road after leaving the spring.   The road was now about to cross the point of this mountain, which we judged to be a spur from the Salmon River range.

We crossed a small creek, and encamped about sunset on a stream which is probably Lake River.   This is a small stream, some five or six feet broad, with a swift current, wooded principally with willows and some few cotton-woods.   Along the banks were canes, rose-bushes, and clematis, with Purshia tridentata and artemisias on the upper bottom.   The sombre appearance of the country is somewhat relieved in coming unexpectedly from the dark rocks upon these green and wooded water-courses, sunk in chasms ; and, in the spring, the contrasted effect must make them beautiful.

The thermometer at sunset 47°, and the night threatening snow.

October 6th.—The morning warm, the thermometer 46° at sunrise, and sky entirely clouded.   After travelling about three miles over an extremely rocky road, the volcanic fragments began to disappear; and, entering among the hills at the point of the mountain, we found ourselves suddenly in a granite country. Here the character of the vegetation was very much changed; the artemisia disappeared almost entirely, showing only at intervals toward the close of the day, and was replaced by Purshia tridentata, with flowering shrubs and small fields of *dieteria divaricata*, which gave bloom and gayety to the hills. These were everywhere covered with a fresh and green short grass, like that of the early spring. This is the fall or second growth, the dried grass having been burnt off by the Indians; and wherever the fire has passed, the bright-green color is universal.

The soil among the hills is altogether different from that of the river plain, being in many places black, in others sandy and gravelly, but of a firm and good character, appearing to result from the decomposition of the granite rocks, which is proceeding rapidly.

In quitting for a time the artemisia (sage) through which we had been so long voyaging, and the sombre appearance of which is so discouraging, I have to remark that I have been informed that in Mexico wheat is grown upon the ground which produces this shrub; which, if true, relieves the soil from the character of sterility imputed to it. Be this as it may, there is no dispute about the grass, which is almost universal on the hills and mountains, and always nutritious, even in its dry state.

We passed on the way masses of granite on the slope of a spur, which was very much weathered and abraded. This is a white feldspathic granite, with small scales of black mica; smoky quartz in which there are garnets appear to constitute this portion of the mountain.

The road at noon reached a broken ridge, on which were scattered many bowlders or blocks of granite; and, passing very small streams, where, with a little more than the usual timber, was sometimes gathered a little wilderness of plants, we encamped on a small stream, after a march of twenty-two miles, in company with a few Indians.

Temperature at sunset, 51°; and the night was partially clear, with a few stars visible through drifting white clouds. The Indians made an unsuccessful attempt to steal a few horses from us—a thing of course with them, and to prevent which the traveller is on perpetual watch.

October 7th.—The day was bright, clear, and pleasant, with a temperature of 45°; and we breakfasted at sunrise, the birds singing in the trees as merrily as if we were in the midst of summer. On the upper edge of the hills, on the opposite side of the creek, the black volcanic rock reappears; and ascending these, the road passed through a basin, around which the hills swept in such a manner as to give it the appearance of an old crater. Here were strata and broken beds of black scoriated rock, and hills composed of the same, on the summit of one of which there was an opening resembling a rent.

We travelled to-day through a country resembling that of yesterday, where, although the surface was hilly, the road was good, being firm and entirely free from rocks and artemisia. To our left, below, was the great sage plain; and on the right were the near mountains, which presented a smoothly broken character, or rather a surface waved into numberless hills. The road was occasionally enlivened by meeting Indians, and the day was extremely beautiful and pleasant; and we were pleased to be free from the sage, even for a day. When we had travelled about eight miles we were nearly opposite to the highest portion of the mountains on the left side of the Smoke River Valley; and, continuing on a few miles beyond, we came suddenly in sight of the broad, green line of the Valley of the *Rivière Boisée* (wooded river), black near the gorge where it debouches into the plains, with high precipices of basalt, between walls of which it passes on emerging from the mountains. Following with the eye its upward course, it appears to be shut in among lofty mountains, confining its valley in a very rugged country.

Descending the hills, after travelling a few miles along the high plain, the road brought us down upon the bottoms of the river, which is a beautiful rapid stream, with clear mountain water, and, as the name indicates, well wooded with some varieties of timber—among which are handsome cotton-woods. Such a stream had become quite a novelty in this country, and we were delighted this afternoon to make a pleasant camp under fine old trees again.

There were several Indian encampments scattered along the river; and a number of their inhabitants, in the course of the evening, came to the camp on horseback with dried and fresh fish to trade. The evening was clear, and the temperature at sunset 57°.

At the time of the first occupation of this region by parties engaged in the fur trade, a small party of men, under the command of —— Reid, constituting all the garrison of a little fort on this river, were surprised and massacred by the Indians; and to this event the stream owes its occasional name of *Reid's River.*

On the 8th we travelled about twenty-six miles, the ridge on the right having scattered pines on the upper parts; and, continuing the next day our road along the river bottom, after a day's travel of twenty-four miles we encamped in the evening on the right bank of the river, a mile above the mouth, and early the next morning arrived at Fort *Boisé.* This is a simple dwelling-house on the right bank of Snake River, about a mile below the mouth of Rivière Boisée; and on our arrival we were received with an agreeable hospitality by Mr. Payette, an officer of the Hudson

Bay Company, in charge of the fort; all of whose garrison consisted in a Canadian *engagé*.

Here the road recrossess the river, which is broad and deep; but, with our good boat, aided by two canoes which were found at the place, the camp was very soon transferred to the left bank. Here we found ourselves again surrounded by the sage; artemisia tridentata, and the different shrubs which during our voyage had always made their appearance abundantly on saline soils, being here the prevailing and almost the only plants. Among them the surface was covered with the usual saline efflorescences, which here consist almost entirely of carbonate of soda, with a small portion of chloride of sodium.

Mr. Payette had made but slight attempts at cultivation, his efforts being limited to raising a few vegetables, in which he succeeded tolerably well; the post being principally supported by salmon. He was very hospitable and kind to us, and we made a sensible impression upon all his comestibles; but our principal inroad was into the dairy, which was abundantly supplied, stock appearing to thrive extremely well; and we had an unusual luxury in a present of fresh butter, which was, however, by no means equal to that of Fort Hall—probably from some accidental cause. During the day we remained here there were considerable numbers of miserable half-naked Indians around the fort, who had arrived from the neighboring mountains. During the summer, the only subsistence of these people is derived from the salmon, of which they are not provident enough to lay up a sufficient store for the winter, during which many of them die from absolute starvation.

Many little accounts and scattered histories, together with an acquaintance which I gradually acquired of their modes of life, had left the aboriginal inhabitants of this vast region pictured in my mind as a race of people whose great and constant occupation was the means of procuring a subsistence; and though want of space and other reasons will prevent me from detailing the many incidents which made these things familiar to me, this great feature among the characteristics of the country will gradually be forced upon the mind of the reader.

Pointing to a group of Indians who had just arrived from the mountains on the left side of the valley, and who were regarding our usual appliances of civilization with an air of bewildered curiosity, Mr. Payette informed me that, every year since his arrival at this post, he had unsuccessfully endeavored to induce these people to lay up a store of salmon for their winter provision. While the summer weather and the salmon lasted, they lived contentedly and happily, scattered along the different streams where the fish were to be found; and as soon as the winter snows began to fall, little smokes would be seen rising among the mountains, where they would be

found in miserable groups, starving out the winter ; and sometimes, according to the general belief, reduced to the horror of cannibalism—the strong,
of course, preying on the weak.   Certain it is they are driven to any extremity for food, and eat every insect, and every creeping thing, however
loathsome and repulsive.   Snails, lizards, ants—all are devoured with the
readiness and greediness of mere animals.

In common with all the other Indians we had encountered since reaching the Pacific waters, these people use the Shoshonee or Snake language,
which, as will be remarked in the course of the narrative, is the universal
language over a very extensive region.

On the evening of the 10th I obtained, with the usual observations, a
very excellent emersion of the first satellite, agreeing very nearly with the
chronometer.   From these observations the longitude of the fort is 116°
47′ 00″, latitude 43° 49′ 22″, and elevation above the sea two thousand
one hundred feet.

Sitting by the fire on the river-bank, and waiting for the immersion of
the satellite, which did not take place until after midnight, we heard the
monotonous song of the Indians, with which they accompany a certain
game of which they are very fond.   Of the poetry we could not judge, but
the music was miserable.

October 11th.—The morning was clear, with a light breeze from the
east, and a temperature at sunrise of 33°.   A part of a bullock purchased
at the fort, together with the boat to assist him in crossing, was left here
for Mr. Fitzpatrick, and at eleven o'clock we resumed our journey ; and
directly leaving the river, and crossing the artemisia plain, in several ascents we reached the foot of a ridge where the road entered a dry, sandy
hollow, up which it continued to the head ; and, crossing a dividing ridge,
entered a similar one.

We met here two poor emigrants (Irishmen) who had lost their horses
two days since—probably stolen by the Indians—and were returning to
the fort in hopes to hear something of them there.   They had recently
had nothing to eat ; and I halted to unpack an animal, and gave them meat
for their dinner.   In this hollow the artemisia is partially displaced on the
hill-sides by grass ; and descending it, about sunset we reached the
Rivière aux Malheurs (the unfortunate or unlucky river), a considerable
stream, with an average breadth of fifty feet and, at this time, eighteen
inches' depth of water.

The bottom lands were generally one and a half mile broad, covered
principally with long dry grass ; and we had difficulty to find sufficient
good grass for the camp.   With the exception of a bad place of a few hundred yards long, which occurred in rounding a point of hill to reach the
ford of the river, the road during the day had been very good.

October 12*th.*—The morning was clear and calm, and the thermometer at sunrise 23°.   My attention was attracted by a smoke on the right side of the river, a little below the ford, where I found on the low bank, near the water, a considerable number of hot springs, in which the temperature of the water was 193°.   The ground, which was too hot for the naked foot, was covered above and below the springs with an incrustation of common salt, very white and good, and fine-grained.

Leading for five miles up a broad dry branch of the Malheurs River, the road entered a sandy hollow where the surface was rendered firm by the admixture of other rock, being good and level until arriving near the head of the ravine, where it became a little rocky, and we met with a number of sharp ascents over an undulating surface.   Crossing here a dividing ridge, it became an excellent road of gradual descent down a very marked hollow ; in which, after ten miles, willows began to appear in the dry bed of a head of the *Rivière aux Bouleaux* (Birch River) ; and descending seven miles we found, at its junction with another branch, a little water, not very good or abundant, but sufficient in case of necessity for a camp.

Crossing Birch River we continued for about four miles across a point of hill, the country on the left being entirely mountainous, with no level spot to be seen ; whence we descended to Snake River—here a fine-looking stream, with a large body of water and a smooth current, although we hear the roar and see below us the commencement of rapids where it enters among the hills.   It forms here a deep bay, with a low sand-island in the midst ; and its course among the mountains is agreeably exchanged for the black volcanic rock.   The weather during the day had been very bright and extremely hot ; but, as usual, so soon as the sun went down, it was necessary to put on overcoats.

I obtained this evening an observation of an emersion of the first satellite, and our observations place this encampment in latitude 44° 17′ 36″, and longitude 116° 56′ 45″, which is the mean of the results from the satellite and chronometer ; the elevation above the sea, one thousand eight hundred and eighty feet.   At this encampment the grass is scanty and poor.

October 13*th.*—The morning was bright, with the temperature at sunrise 28°.   The horses had strayed off during the night, probably in search of grass ; and, after a considerable delay, we had succeeded in finding all but two, when, about nine o'clock, we heard the sound of an Indian song and drum approaching ; and, shortly after, three Cayuse Indians appeared in sight, bringing with them the two animals.   They belonged to a party which had been on a buffalo-hunt in the neighborhood of the Rocky Mountains, and were hurrying home in advance.   We presented them with some tobacco and other things, with which they appeared well satisfied, and, moderating their pace, travelled in company with us.

We were now about to leave the valley of the great southern branch of the Columbia River, to which the absence of timber and the scarcity of water give the appearance of a desert, to enter a mountainous region where the soil is good and in which the face of the country is covered with nutritious grasses and dense forest—land embracing many varieties of trees peculiar to the country, and on which the timber exhibits a luxuriance of growth unknown to the eastern part of the continent and to Europe.

This mountainous region connects itself in the southward and westward with the elevated country belonging to the Cascade or California range; and, as will be remarked in the course of the narrative, forms the eastern limit of the fertile and timbered lands along the desert and mountainous region included within the Great Basin—a term which I apply to the intermediate region between the Rocky Mountains and the next range, containing many lakes, with their own system of rivers and creeks (of which the Great Salt Lake is the principal), and which have no connection with the ocean or the great rivers which flow into it. This Great Basin is yet to be adequately explored.

And here, on quitting the banks of a sterile river to enter on arable mountains, the remark may be made that, on this western slope of our continent, the usual order of distribution of good and bad soil is often reversed—the river and creek bottoms being often sterile and darkened with the gloomy and barren artemisia; while the mountain is often fertile and covered with rich grass, pleasant to the eye and good for flocks and herds.

Leaving entirely the Snake River, which is said henceforth to pursue its course through cañons, amidst rocky and impracticable mountains where there is no possibility of travelling with animals, we ascended a long and somewhat steep hill; and, crossing the dividing ridge, came down into the Valley of *Burnt River*, which here looks like a hole among the hills. The average breadth of the stream here is thirty feet; it is well fringed with the usual small trees; and the soil in the bottoms is good, with better grass than we had lately been accustomed to see.

We now travelled through a very mountainous country; the stream running rather in a ravine than a valley, and the road is decidedly bad and dangerous for single wagons, frequently crossing the stream where the water is sometimes deep; all the day the animals were fatigued in climbing up and descending a succession of steep ascents, to avoid the precipitous hill-sides; and the common trail, which leads along the mountainside at places where the river strikes the base, is sometimes bad even for a horseman.

The mountains along this day's journey were composed, near the river, of a slaty calcareous rock in a metamorphic condition. It appears originally to have been a slaty sedimentary limestone, but its present condition indicates that it has been altered and has become partially crystalline—probably from the proximity of volcanic rocks. But though travelling was slow and fatiguing to the animals, we were delighted with the appearance of the country, which was green and refreshing after our tedious journey down the parched Valley of Snake River.

The mountains were covered with good bunch-grass (*festuca*); the water of the streams was cold and pure; their bottoms were handsomely wooded with various kinds of trees; and huge and lofty and picturesque precipices were displayed where the river cut through the mountains.

We found in the evening some good grass and rushes; and encamped among large timber, principally birch, which had been recently burnt and blackened, and almost destroyed by fire. The night was calm and tolerably clear, with the thermometer at sunset at 59°. Our journey to-day was about twenty miles.

October 14*th.*—The day was clear and calm, with a temperature at sunrise of 46°. After travelling about three miles up the valley, we found the river shut up by precipices in a kind of cañon, and the road makes a circuit over the mountains. In the afternoon we reached the river again, by another little ravine; and, after travelling along it for a few miles, left it enclosed among rude mountains; and, ascending a smaller branch, encamped on it about five o'clock, very much elevated above the valley.

The view was everywhere limited by mountains, on which were no longer seen the black and barren rocks, but a fertile soil, with excellent grass, and partly well covered with pine. I have never seen a wagon-road equally bad, in the same space, as this of yesterday and to-day. I noticed where one wagon had been overturned twice, in a very short distance; and it was surprising to me that those wagons which were in the rear, and could not have had much assistance, got through at all. Still, there is no mud; and the road has one advantage in being perfectly firm. The day had been warm and very pleasant, and the night was perfectly clear.

October 15*th.*—The thermometer at daylight was 42°, and at sunrise 40°; clouds, which were scattered over all the sky, disappeared with the rising sun. The trail did not much improve until we had crossed the dividing grounds between the *Brulé* (Burnt) and Powder Rivers.

The rock displayed on the mountains as we approached the summit was a compact trap, decomposing on the exposed surfaces, and apparently an altered argillaceous sandstone, containing small crystalline nodules of anolcime, apparently filling cavities originally existing. From the summit here the whole horizon shows high mountains; no high plain or level is to be seen; and on the left, from south around by the west to north, the mountains are black with pines; while through the remaining space to the eastward they are bald, with the exception of some scattered pines.

CAMP, OCTOBER 14.—SNAKE RIVER.

We are now entering a region where all the elevated parts are covered with dense and heavy forests. From the dividing grounds we descended by a mountain road to Powder River, on an old bed of which we encamped. Descending from the summit, we enjoyed a picturesque view of high rocky mountains on the right, illuminated by the setting sun.

From the heights we had looked in vain for a well-known landmark on Powder River, which had been described to me by Mr. Payette as *l'arbre seul* (the lone tree); and, on arriving at the river, we found a fine tall pine stretched on the ground, which had been felled by some inconsiderate emigrant axe. It had been a beacon on the road for many years past.

Our Cayuses had become impatient to reach their homes, and travelled on ahead to-day; and this afternoon we were visited by several Indians who belonged to the tribes on the Columbia. They were on horseback, and were out on a hunting excursion, but had obtained no better game than a large gray hare, of which each had some six or seven hanging to his saddle.

We were also visited by an Indian who had his lodge and family in the mountain to the left. He was in want of ammunition, and brought with him a beaver-skin to exchange, which he valued at six charges of powder and ball. I learned from him that there are very few of these animals remaining in this part of the country.

The temperature at sunset was 61°, and the evening clear. I obtained, with other observations, an immersion and emersion of the third satellite. Elevation, three thousand one hundred feet.

October 16th.—For several weeks the weather in the daytime has been very beautiful, clear, and warm; but the nights, in comparison, are very cold. During the night there was ice a quarter of an inch thick in the lodge; and at daylight the thermometer was at 16°, and the same at sunrise—the weather being calm and clear. The annual vegetation now is nearly gone, almost all the plants being out of bloom.

Last night two of our horses had run off again, which delayed us until noon; and we made to-day but a short journey of thirteen miles, the road being very good, and encamped in a fine bottom of Powder River.

The thermometer at sunset was at 61°, with an easterly wind and partially clear sky; and the day has been quite pleasant and warm, though more cloudy than yesterday; and the sun was frequently faint, but it grew finer and clearer toward evening.

October 17th.—Thermometer at sunrise, 25°. The weather at daylight was fine, and the sky without a cloud; but these came up, or were formed with the sun, and at seven were thick over all the sky. Just now this appears to be the regular course—clear and brilliant during the night, and cloudy during the day.

There is snow yet visible in the neighboring mountains, which yesterday extended along our route to the left in a lofty and dark-blue range, having much the appearance of the Wind River Mountains. It is probable that they have received their name of the *Blue Mountains* from the dark-blue appearance given to them by the pines.

We travelled this morning across the affluents to Powder River, the road being good, firm, and level; and the country became constantly more pleasant and interesting. The soil appeared to be very deep, and is black and extremely good, as well among the hollows of the hills on the elevated plats as on the river bottoms; the vegetation being such as is usually found in good ground.

The following analytical result shows the precise qualities of this soil, and will justify to science the character of fertility which the eye attributes to it:

ANALYSIS OF POWDER RIVER SOIL.

Silica..	72.30
Alumina..	6.25
Carbonate of lime...	6.86
Carbonate of magnesia...	4.62
Oxide of iron..	1.20
Organic matter...	4.50
Water and loss...	4.27
	100.00

From the waters of this stream the road ascended by a good and moderate ascent to a dividing ridge, but immediately entered upon ground covered with fragments of an altered siliceous slate, which are in many places large and render the road racking to a carriage.

In this rock the planes of deposition are distinctly preserved, and the metamorphism is evidently due to the proximity of volcanic rocks. On either side, the mountains here are densely covered with tall and handsome trees; and mingled with the green of a variety of pines is the yellow of the European larch (*Pinus larix*), which loses its leaves in the fall. From its present color we were enabled to see that it forms a large proportion of the forests on the mountains, and is here a magnificent tree, attaining sometimes the height of two hundred feet, which I believe is elsewhere unknown.

About two in the afternoon we reached a high point of the dividing ridge, from which we obtained a good view of the *Grand Rond*—a beautiful level basin, or mountain valley, covered with good grass on a rich soil, abundantly watered, and surrounded by high and well-timbered mountains; and its name descriptive of its form—the great circle. It is a place —one of the few we have seen in our journey so far—where a farmer would delight to establish himself, if he were content to live in the seclusion which it imposes. It is about twenty miles in diameter, and may in time form a superb county. Probably with the view of avoiding a circuit, the wagons had directly descended into the *Rond* by the face of a hill so very rocky and continuously steep as to be apparently impracticable ; and, following down on their trail, we encamped on one of the branches of the Grand Rond River, immediately at the foot of the hill. I had remarked, in descending, some very white spots glistening on the plain, and, going out in that direction after we had encamped, I found them to be the bed of a dry salt lake, or marsh, very firm and bare, which was covered thickly with a fine white powder containing a large quantity of carbonate of soda (thirty-three in one hundred parts).

The old grass had been lately burnt off from the surrounding hills, and, wherever the fire had passed, there was a recent growth of strong, green, and vigorous grass ; and the soil of the level prairie, which sweeps directly up to the foot of the surrounding mountains, appears to be very rich, producing flax spontaneously and luxuriantly in various places.

ANALYSIS OF THE GRAND ROND SOIL.

Silica	70.81
Alumina.	10.97
Lime and magnesia..	1.38
Oxide of iron..	2.21
Vegetable matter, partly decomposed..	8.16
Water and loss...	5.46
Phosphate of lime...	1.01
	100.00

The elevation of this encampment is two thousand nine hundred and forty feet above the sea.

October 18*th.*—It began to rain an hour before sunrise, and continued until ten o'clock ; the sky entirely overcast, and the temperature at sunrise 48°.

We resumed our journey somewhat later than usual, travelling in a nearly north direction across this beautiful valley ; and about noon reached a place on one of the principal streams, where I had determined to leave the emigrant trail, in the expectation of finding a more direct and better road across the Blue Mountains. At this place the emigrants appeared to have held some consultation as to their further route, and finally turned directly off to the left ; reaching the foot of the mountain in about three miles, and ascending it by a hill as steep and difficult as that by which we had yesterday descended to the Rond.

Quitting, therefore, this road, which, after a very rough crossing. issue

from the mountains by the heads of the *Umatilah* River, we continued our
northern course across the valley, following an Indian trail which had been
indicated to me by Mr. Payette, and encamped at the northern extremity
of the Grand Rond; on a slough-like stream of very deep water, without
any apparent current.   There are some pines here on the low hills at the
creek; and in the northwest corner of the Rond is a very heavy body of
timber, which descends into the plain.

The clouds, which had rested very low along the mountain sides during the day, rose gradually up in the afternoon; and in the evening the
sky was almost entirely clear, with a temperature at sunset of 47°.   Some
indifferent observations placed the camp in longitude 117° 28′ 26″, latitude
45° 26′ 47″; and the elevation was two thousand six hundred feet above
the sea.

October 19*th.*—This morning the mountains were hidden by fog: there
was a heavy dew during the night, in which the exposed thermometer at
daylight stood at 32°, and at sunrise the temperature was 35°.

We passed out of the Grand Rond by a fine road along the creek,
which, for a short distance, runs in a kind of rocky chasm.   Crossing a
low point, which was a little rocky, the trail conducted into the open valley
of the stream—a handsome place for farms; the soil, even of the hills,
being rich and black.   Passing through a point of pines, which bore evidences of being much frequented by the Indians and in which the trees
were sometimes apparently two hundred feet high and three to seven feet
in diameter, we halted for a few minutes in the afternoon at the foot of the
Blue Mountains, on a branch of the Grand Rond River, at an elevation of
two thousand seven hundred feet.

Resuming our journey we commenced the ascent of the mountain
through an open pine-forest of large and stately trees, among which the
balsam-pine made its appearance; the road being good, with the exception
of one steep ascent with a corresponding descent, which might both have
been easily avoided by opening a way for a short distance through the
timber.

It would have been well had we encamped on the stream where we
had halted below, as the night overtook us on the mountain, and we were
obliged to encamp without water and tie up the animals to the trees for
the night.   We had halted on a smooth, open place of a narrow ridge
which descended very rapidly to a ravine, or piny hollow, at a considerable distance below; and it was quite a pretty spot, had there been water
near.   But the fires at night look very cheerless after a day's march when
there is no preparation for supper going on; and, after sitting some time
around the blazing logs, Mr. Preuss and Carson, with several others, volunteered to take the india-rubber buckets and go down into the ravine in

GETTING WATER, DEEP RAVINE OF SIERRA NEVADA.

search of water. It was a very difficult way, in the darkness, down the slippery side of the steep mountain, and harder still to climb about half a mile up again ; but they found the water, and the cup of coffee, which it enabled us to make, and bread were only enjoyed with greater pleasure.

At sunset the temperature was 46° ; the evening remarkably clear ; and I obtained an emersion of the first satellite, which does not give a good result, although the observation was a very good one. The chronometric longitude was 117° 28' 34", latitude 45° 38' 07", and we had ascended to an elevation of three thousand eight hundred and thirty feet. It appeared to have snowed yesterday on the mountains, their summits showing very white to-day.

October 20*th.*—There was a heavy white frost during the night, and at sunrise the temperature was 37°.

The animals had eaten nothing during the night ; and we made an early start, continuing our route among the pines, which were more dense than yesterday, and still retained their magnificent size.

The larches cluster together in masses on the sides of the mountains, and their yellow foliage contrasts handsomely with the green of the balsam and other pines. After a few miles we ceased to see any pines, and the timber consisted of several varieties of spruce, larch, and balsam-pine, which have a regularly conical figure. These trees appeared from sixty to nearly two hundred feet in height; the usual circumference being ten to twelve feet, and in the pines sometimes twenty-one feet. In open places near the summit these trees became less high and more branching, the conical form having a greater base.

The instrument carriage occasioned much delay, it being frequently necessary to fell trees and remove the fallen timber. The trail we were following led up a long spur, with a very gradual and gentle rise.

At the end of three miles we halted at an open place near the summit, from which we enjoyed a fine view over the mountainous country where we had lately travelled, to take a barometrical observation at the height of four thousand seven hundred and sixty feet.

After travelling occasionally through open places in the forest we were obliged to cut a way through a dense body of timber, from which we emerged on an open mountain side, where we found a number of small springs, and encamped after a day's journey of ten miles. Our elevation here was five thousand feet.

October 21*st.*—There was a very heavy white frost during the night, and the thermometer at sunrise was 30°.

We continued to travel through the forest, in which the road was rendered difficult by fallen trunks, and obstructed by many small trees which it was necessary to cut down. But these are only accidental difficulties, which could easily be removed, and a very excellent road may be had through this pass, with no other than very moderate ascents or declivities.

A laborious day, which had advanced us only six miles on our road, brought us in the afternoon to an opening in the forest, in which there was a fine mountain meadow, with good grass and a large clear-water stream; one of the head branches of the *Umatilah* River.

During this day's journey the barometer was broken, and the elevations above the sea, hereafter given, depend upon the temperature of boiling water. Some of the white spruces which I measured to-day were twelve feet in circumference, and one of the larches ten; but eight feet was the average circumference of those measured along the road.

I held in my hand a tape-line as I walked along, in order to form some correct idea of the size of the timber. Their height appeared to be from one hundred to one hundred and eighty, and perhaps two hundred feet, and the trunks of the larches were sometimes one hundred feet without a limb; but the white spruces were generally covered with branches nearly to the root. All these trees have their branches, particularly the lower ones, declining.

October 22d.—The white frost this morning was like snow on the ground; the ice was a quarter of an inch thick on the creek, and the thermometer at sunrise was at 20°. But in a few hours the day became warm and pleasant, and our road over the mountains was delightful and full of enjoyment.

The trail passed sometimes through very thick young timber, in which there was much cutting to be done; but after travelling a few miles the mountains became more bald, and we reached a point from which there was a very extensive view in the northwest. We were here on the western verge of the Blue Mountains, long spurs of which, very precipitous on either side, extended down into the valley, the waters of the mountain roaring between them.

On our right was a mountain plateau covered with a dense forest; and to the westward, immediately below us, was the great *Nez Percé* (pierced nose) prairie, in which dark lines of timber indicated the course of many affluents to a considerable stream that was seen pursuing its way across the plain toward what appeared to be the Columbia River. This I knew to be the Walahwalah River, and occasional spots along its banks, which resembled clearings, were supposed to be the mission or Indian settlements; but the weather was smoky and unfavorable to far views with the glass.

The rock displayed here in the escarpments is a compact amorphous trap, which appears to constitute the mass of the Blue Mountains in this latitude; and all the region of country through which we have travelled since leaving the Snake River has been the seat of violent and extensive igneous action.

Along the Burnt River Valley the strata are evidently sedimentary rocks, altered by the intrusion of volcanic products, which in some instances have penetrated and essentially changed their original condition. Along our line of route, from this point to the California Mountains, there seems but little essential change. All our specimens of sedimentary rocks show them to be much altered, and volcanic productions appear to prevail throughout the whole intervening distance.

The road now led along the mountain-side, around heads of the precipitous ravines ; and, keeping men ahead to clear a road, we passed alternately through bodies of timber and small open prairies, and encamped in a large meadow, in view of the great prairie below.

At sunset the thermometer was at 40°, and the night was very clear and bright. Water was only to be had here by descending a bad ravine, into which we drove our animals, and had much trouble with them, in a very close growth of small pines. Mr. Preuss had walked ahead, and did not get into camp this evening. The trees here maintained their size, and one of the black spruces measured fifteen feet in circumference. In the neighborhood of the camp pines have reappeared here among the timber.

October 23*d.*—The morning was very clear ; there had been a heavy white frost during the night, and at sunrise the thermometer was at 31°.

After cutting through two thick bodies of timber, in which I noticed some small trees of *hemlock* spruce (*perusse*), the forest became more open, and we had no longer any trouble to clear a way. The pines here were eleven or twelve feet in circumference and about one hundred and ten feet high, and appeared to love the open grounds.

The trail now led along one of the long spurs of the mountain, descending gradually toward the plain ; and, after travelling a few miles, we emerged finally from the forest, in full view of the plain below, and saw the snowy mass of Mount Hood, standing high out above the surrounding country, at a distance of one hundred and eighty miles.

The road along the ridge was excellent, and the grass very green and good ; the old grass having been burnt off early in the autumn. About four o'clock in the afternoon we reached a little bottom on the Walahwalah River, where we found Mr. Preuss, who yesterday had reached this place, and found himself too far in advance of the camp to return. The stream here has just issued from the narrow ravines, which are walled with precipices, in which the rock has a brown and more burnt appearance than above.

At sunset the thermometer was at 48° ; and our position was in longitude 118° 00′ 39″, and in latitude 45° 53′ 35″.

The morning was clear, with a temperature at sunrise of 24°.   Crossing the river, we travelled over a hilly country with good bunch grass ; the river bottom, which generally contains the best soil in other countries, being here a sterile level of rock and pebbles.   We had found the soil in the Blue Mountains to be of excellent quality, and it appeared also to be good here among the lower hills.   Reaching a little eminence, over which the trail passed, we had an extensive view along the course of the river, which was divided and spread over its bottom in a net-work of water, receiving several other tributaries from the mountains.

There was a band of several hundred horses grazing on the hills about two miles ahead ; and as we advanced on the road we met other bands, which Indians were driving out to pasture also on the hills.   True to its general character, the reverse of other countries, the hills and mountains here were rich in grass, the bottoms barren and sterile.

In six miles we crossed a principal fork, below which the scattered water of the river was gathered into one channel; and, passing on the way several unfinished houses, and some cleared patches where corn and potatoes were cultivated, we reached, in about eight miles farther, the missionary establishment of Dr. Whitman, which consisted at this time of one *adobe* house—*i.e.*, built of unburnt bricks, as in Mexico.

I found Dr. Whitman absent on a visit to the *Dalles* of the Columbia ; but had the pleasure to see a fine-looking large family of emigrants—men, women, and children—in robust health, all indemnifying themselves for previous scanty fare in a hearty consumption of potatoes, which are produced here of a remarkably good quality.   We were disappointed in our expectation of obtaining corn-meal or flour at this station, the mill belonging to the mission having been lately burnt down ; but an abundant supply of excellent potatoes banished regrets, and furnished a grateful substitute for bread.

A small town of Nez Percé Indians gave an inhabited, and even a populous appearance to the station ; and, after remaining about an hour, we continued our route, and encamped on the river about four miles below, passing on the way an emigrant encampment.

Temperature at sunset, 49°.

October 25th.—The weather was pleasant, with a sunrise temperature of 36°.   Our road to-day had in it nothing of interest ; and the country offered to the eye only a sandy, undulating plain, through which a scantily timbered river takes its course.

We halted about three miles above the mouth, on account of grass ; and the next morning arrived at the Nez Percé Fort, one of the trading establishments of the Hudson Bay Company, a few hundred yards above the junction of the Walahwalah with the Columbia River.   Here we had the first view of this river, and found it about one thousand two hundred yards wide, and presenting the appearance of a fine navigable stream.

We made our camp in a little grove of willows on the Walahwalah, which are the only trees to be seen in the neighborhood ; but were obliged to send the animals back to the encampment we had left, as there was scarcely a blade of grass to be found. The post is on the bank of the Columbia, on a plain of bare sands, from which the air was literally filled with clouds of dust and sand during one of the few days we remained here—this place being one of the several points on the river which are distinguished for prevailing high winds, which come from the sea. The appearance of the post and country was without interest, except that we here saw, for the first time, the great river on which the course of events for the last half-century has been directing attention and conferring historical fame.

The river is, indeed, a noble object, and has here attained its full magnitude. About nine miles above, and in sight from the heights about the post, is the junction of the two great forks which constitute the main stream —that on which we had been travelling from Fort Hall, and known by the names of Lewis' Fork, Shoshonee, and Snake River ; and the North Fork, which has retained the name of Columbia, as being the main stream.

We did not go up to the junction, being pressed for time ; but the union of two large streams, coming, one from the southeast and the other from the northeast, and meeting in what may be treated as the geographical centre of the Oregon Valley, thence doubling the volume of water to the ocean while opening two great lines of communication with the interior continent, constitutes a feature in the map of the country which cannot be overlooked ; and it was probably in reference to this junction of waters and these lines of communication that this post was established. They are important lines, and, from the structure of the country, must forever remain so—one of them leading to the South Pass and to the valley of the Mississippi, the other to the pass at the head of the Athabasca River and to the countries drained by the waters of the Hudson Bay.

The British fur companies now use both lines ; the Americans, in their emigration to Oregon, have begun to follow the one which leads toward the United States. Bateaus from tide-water ascend to the junction, and thence high up the North Fork, or Columbia. Land conveyance only is used upon the line of Lewis' Fork. To the emigrants to Oregon the Nez Percé is a point of interest, as being, to those who choose it, the termination of their overland journey. The broad expanse of the river here invites them to embark on its bosom ; and the lofty trees of the forest furnish the means of doing so.

From the South Pass to this place is about one thousand miles ; and as it is about the same distance from that Pass to the Missouri River at the mouth of the Kansas, it may be assumed that two thousand miles is the *necessary* land travel in crossing from the United States to the Pacific Ocean on this line.   From the mouth of the Great Platte it would be about one hundred miles less.

Mr. McKinley, the commander of the post, received us with great civility; and both to myself, and the heads of the emigrants who were there at the time, extended his hospitality in a comfortable dinner to which he invited us.

By a meridional altitude of the sun, the only observation that the weather permitted us to obtain, the mouth of the Walahwalah River is in latitude 46° 03′ 46″; and, by the road we had travelled, six hundred and twelve miles from Fort Hall.

At the time of our arrival, a considerable body of the emigrants, under the direction of Mr. Applegate, a man of considerable resolution and energy, had nearly completed the building of a number of Mackinaw boats, in which they proposed to continue their further voyage down the Columbia.

I had seen, in descending the Walahwalah River, a fine drove of several hundred cattle, which they had exchanged for Californian cattle, to be received at Vancouver, and which are considered a very inferior breed. The other portion of the emigration had preferred to complete their journey by land along the banks of the Columbia, taking their stock and wagons with them.

Having reinforced our animals with eight fresh horses, hired from the post, and increased our stock of provisions with dried salmon, potatoes, and a little beef, we resumed our journey down the left bank of the Columbia, being guided on our road by an intelligent Indian boy, whom I had engaged to accompany us as far as the Dalles.

The sketch of a rock which we passed in the course of the morning is annexed, to show the manner in which the basaltic rock, which constitutes the geological formation of the Columbia Valley, now presents itself. From an elevated point over which the road led, we obtained another far view of Mount Hood, one hundred and fifty miles distant.   We obtained on the river bank an observation of the sun at noon, which gave for the latitude 45° 58′ 08″.

The country to-day was very unprepossessing, and our road bad; and as we toiled slowly along through deep loose sands, and over fragments of black volcanic rock, our laborious travelling was strongly contrasted with the rapid progress of Mr. Applegate's fleet of boats, which suddenly came gliding swiftly down the broad river, which here chanced to be tranquil and smooth.   At evening we encamped on the river bank, where there was very little grass, and less timber.   We frequently met Indians

HILL OF COLUMNAR BASALT ON THE COLUMBIA RIVER.

on the road, and they were collected at every favorable spot along the river.

October 29th.—The road continued along the river, and in the course of the day Mount St. Helens, another snowy peak of the Cascade Range, was visible. We crossed the Umàtilah River at a fall near its mouth. This stream is of the same class as the Walahwalah River, with a bed of volcanic rock, in places split into fissures. Our encampment was similar to that of yesterday; there was very little grass, and no wood. The Indians brought us some pieces for sale, which were purchased to make our fires.

October 31st.—By observation, our camp is in latitude 45° 50′ 05″, and longitude 119° 22′ 18″.

The night has been cold, and we have white frost this morning, with a temperature at daylight of 25°, and at sunrise of 24°. The early morning was very clear, and the stars bright; but, as usual, since we are on the Columbia, clouds formed immediately with the rising sun. The day continued fine, the East being covered with scattered clouds, but the West remaining clear, showing the remarkable cone-like peak of Mount Hood brightly drawn against the sky. This was in view all day in the southwest, but no other peaks of the range were visible. Our road was a bad one, of very loose deep sand.

We met on the way a party of Indians unusually well dressed, wearing clothes of civilized texture and form. They appeared intelligent, and, in our slight intercourse, impressed me with the belief that they possessed some aptitude for acquiring languages.

We continued to travel along the river, the stream being interspersed with many sand-bars (it being the season of low water) and with many islands, and an apparently good navigation. Small willows were the only wood; rock and sand the prominent geological feature. The rock of this section is a very compact and tough basalt, occurring in strata which have the appearance of being broken into fragments, assuming the form of columnar hills, and appearing always in escarpments, with the broken fragments strewed at the base and over the adjoining country.

We made a late encampment on the river, and used to-night *Purshia tridentata* for fire-wood. Among the rocks which formed the bank, was very good green grass. Latitude 45° 44′ 23″, longitude 119° 45′ 09″.

November 1st.—Mount Hood is glowing in the sunlight this morning, and the air is pleasant, with a temperature of 38°. We continued down the river, and, passing through a pretty, green valley bounded by high precipitous rock, encamped at the lower end.

On the right shore, the banks of the Columbia are very high and steep; the river is one thousand six hundred and ninety feet broad, and dark bluffs of rock give it a picturesque appearance.

November 2d.—The river here entered among bluffs, leaving no longer room for a road; and we accordingly left it, and took a more inland way among the river hills, on which we had no sooner entered, than we found a great improvement in the country. The sand had disappeared, and the soil was good, and covered with excellent grass, although the surface was broken into high hills, with uncommonly deep valleys.

At noon we crossed John Day's River, a clear and beautiful stream, with a swift current and a bed of rolled stones. It is sunk in a deep valley, which is characteristic of all the streams in this region; and the hill we descended to reach it, well deserves the name of mountain. Some of the emigrants had encamped on the river, and others at the summit of the farther hill, the ascent of which had probably cost their wagons a day's labor; and others again had halted for the night a few miles beyond, where they had slept without water.

We also encamped in a grassy hollow without water; but as we had been forewarned of this privation by the guide, the animals had all been watered at the river, and we had brought with us a sufficient quantity for the night.

November 3d.—After two hours' ride through a fertile, hilly country, covered as all the upland here appears to be with good green grass, we descended again into the river bottom, along which we resumed our sterile road, and in about four miles reached the ford of the Fall River (*Rivière aux Chutes*), a considerable tributary to the Columbia. We had heard, on reaching the Nez Percé Fort, a repetition of the account in regard to the unsettled character of the Columbia Indians at the present time; and to our little party they had at various points manifested a not very friendly disposition, in several attempts to steal our horses. At this place I expected to find a badly-disposed band, who had plundered a party of fourteen emigrant men a few days before, and taken away their horses; and accordingly we made the necessary preparations for our security, but happily met with no difficulty.

The river was high, divided into several arms, with a rocky island at its outlet into the Columbia, which at this place it rivalled in size, and apparently deserved its highly characteristic name, which is received from one of its many falls some forty miles up the river. It entered the Columbia with a roar of falls and rapids, and is probably a favorite fishing station among the Indians, with whom both banks of the river were populous; but they scarcely paid any attention to us.

The ford was very difficult at this time, and, had they entertained any bad intentions, they were offered a good opportunity to carry them out, as I rode directly into the river, and during the crossing the howitzer was occasionally several feet under water, and a number of the men appeared

CROSSING THE FORD AT FALL RIVER.

to be more often below than above. Our guide was well acquainted with the ford, and we succeeded in getting everything safe over to the left bank. We delayed here only a short time to put the gun in order, and ascending a long mountain hill, left both rivers, and resumed our route again among the interior hills.

The roar of the *Falls of the Columbia* is heard from the heights, where we halted a few moments to enjoy a fine view of the river below. In the season of high water it would be a very interesting object to visit, in order to witness what is related of the annual submerging of the fall under the waters which back up from the basin below, constituting a great natural lock at this place. But time had become an object of serious consideration, and the Falls, in their present state, had been seen and described by many.

After a day's journey of seventeen miles, we encamped among the hills on a little clear stream, where, as usual, the Indians immediately gathered round us. Among them was a very old man, almost blind from age, with long and very white hair. I happened, of my own accord, to give this old man a present of tobacco, and was struck with the impression which my unpropitiated notice made on the Indians, who appeared in a remarkable manner acquainted with the real value of goods, and to understand the equivalents of trade.

At evening one of them spoke a few words to his people, and, telling me that we need entertain no uneasiness in regard to our animals, as none of them would be disturbed, they went all quietly away. In the morning when they again came to the camp, I expressed to them the gratification we felt at their reasonable conduct, making them a present of some large knives and a few smaller articles.

November 4th.—The road continued among the hills, and, reaching an eminence, we saw before us, in a little green valley watered by a clear stream, a tolerably large valley through which the trail passed.

In comparison with the Indians of the Rocky Mountains and the great eastern plain, these are disagreeably dirty in their habits. Their huts were crowded with half-naked women and children, and the atmosphere within anything but pleasant to persons who had just been riding in the fresh morning air. We were somewhat amused with the scanty dress of one woman, who, in common with the others, rushed out of the huts on our arrival, and who, in default of other covering, used a child for a fig-leaf.

The road in about half an hour passed near an elevated point, from which we overlooked the valley of the Columbia for many miles, and saw in the distance several houses surrounded by fields, which a chief, who had accompanied us from the village, pointed out to us as the Methodist Missionary Station.

In a few miles we descended to the river, which we reached at one of its remarkably interesting features, known as the *Dalles of the Columbia*. The whole volume of the river at this place passed between the walls of a chasm, which has the appearance of having been rent through the basaltic strata which form the valley rock of the region.   At the narrowest place we found the breadth, by measurement, fifty-eight yards, and the average height of the walls above the water twenty-five feet; forming a trough between the rocks—whence the name, probably applied by a Canadian voyageur.

The mass of water in the present low state of the river, passed swiftly between, deep and black, and curled into many small whirlpools and counter-currents, but unbroken by foam and so still that scarcely the sound of a ripple was heard.   The rock, for a considerable distance from the river, was worn over a large portion of its surface into circular holes and well-like cavities by the abrasion of the river, which, at the season of high waters, is spread out over the adjoining bottoms.

In the recent passage through this chasm, an unfortunate event had occurred to Mr. Applegate's party, in the loss of one of their boats, which had been carried under water in the midst of the Dalles, and two of Mr. Applegate's children and one man drowned.   This misfortune was attributed only to want of skill in the steersman, as at this season there is no impediment to navigation; although the place is entirely impassable at high water, when boats pass safely over the great falls above, in the submerged state in which they then find themselves.

The basalt here is precisely the same as that which constitutes the rock of the valley higher up the Columbia, being very compact, with a few round cavities.

We passed rapidly three or four miles down the level valley, and encamped near the mission.   The character of the forest growth here changed, and we found ourselves, with pleasure, again among oaks and other forest-trees of the East, to which we had long been strangers; and the hospitable and kind reception with which we were welcomed among our country-people at the mission, aided the momentary illusion of home.

Two good-looking wooden dwelling-houses and a large school-house, with stables, barn and garden, and large cleared fields between the houses and the river bank, on which were scattered the wooden huts of an Indian village, gave to the valley the cheerful and busy air of civilization, and had in our eyes an appearance of abundant and enviable comfort.

Our land journey found here its western termination.   The delay involved in getting our camp to the right bank of the Columbia, and in opening a road through the continuous forest to Vancouver, rendered a journey along the river impracticable; and on this side the usual road across the mountain required strong and fresh animals, there being an interval of

"USED A CHILD FOR A FIG LEAF."

three days in which they could obtain no food. I therefore wrote immediately to Mr. Fitzpatrick, directing him to abandon the carts at the Walahwalah Missionary Station, and, as soon as the necessary pack-saddles could be made, which his party required, meet me at the Dalles, from which point I proposed to commence our homeward journey.

The day after our arrival being Sunday, no business could be done at the mission; but on Monday Mr. Perkins assisted me in procuring from the Indians a large canoe, in which I designed to complete our journey to Vancouver, where I expected to obtain the necessary supply of provisions and stores for our winter journey. Three Indians from the family to whom the canoe belonged were engaged to assist in working her during the voyage, and, with them, our water party consisted of Mr. Preuss and myself, with Bernier and Jacob Dodson.

In charge of the party which was to remain at the Dalles I left Carson, with instructions to occupy the people in making pack-saddles and refitting their equipage. The village from which we were to take the canoe was on the right bank of the river, about ten miles below, at the mouth of the Tinanens Creek; and while Mr. Preuss proceeded down the river with the instruments in a little canoe paddled by two Indians, Mr. Perkins accompanied me with the remainder of the party by land. The last of the emigrants had just left the Dalles at the time of our arrival, travelling some by water and others by land, making ark-like rafts, on which they had embarked their families and household, with their large wagons and other furniture, while their stock were driven along the shore.

For about five miles below the Dalles, the river is narrow and probably very deep; but during this distance, it is somewhat open with grassy bottoms on the left. Entering, then, among the lower mountains of the Cascade range, it assumes a general character, and high and steep rocky hills shut it in on either side, rising abruptly in places to the height of one thousand five hundred feet above the water, and gradually acquiring a more mountainous character as the river approaches the Cascades.

After an hour's travel, when the sun was nearly down, we searched along the shore for a pleasant place, and halted to prepare supper. We had been well supplied by our friends at the mission with delicious salted salmon, which had been taken at the fattest season; also with potatoes, bread, coffee, and sugar.

We were delighted at a change in our mode of travelling and living. The canoe sailed smoothly down the river; at night we encamped upon the shore, and a plentiful supply of comfortable provisions supplied the first of wants. We enjoyed the contrast which it presented to our late toilsome marchings, our night watchings, and our frequent privation of food. We were a motley group, but all happy: three unknown Indians;

Jacob, a colored man ; Mr. Preuss, a German ; Bernier, creole French, and myself.

Being now upon the ground explored by the South Sea expedition under Captain Wilkes, and having accomplished the object of uniting my survey with his, and thus presenting a connected exploration from the Mississippi to the Pacific, and the winter being at hand, I deemed it necessary to economize time by voyaging in the night, as is customary here, to avoid the high winds, which rise with the morning, and decline with the day.

Accordingly, after an hour's halt, we again embarked, and resumed our pleasant voyage down the river. The wind rose to a gale after several hours ; but the moon was very bright, and the wind was fair, and the canoe glanced rapidly down the stream, the waves breaking into foam alongside ; and our night voyage, as the wind bore us rapidly along between the dark mountains, was wild and interesting. About midnight we put to the shore on a rocky beach, behind which was a dark-looking pine forest. We built up large fires among the rocks, which were in large masses round about ; and, arranging our blankets in the most sheltered places we could find, passed a delightful night.

After an early breakfast, at daylight we resumed our journey, the weather being clear and beautiful, and the river smooth and still. On either side the mountains are all pine-timbered, rocky, and high. We were now approaching one of the marked features of the Lower Columbia, where the river forms a great *cascade*, with a series of rapids, in breaking through the range of mountains to which the lofty peaks of Mount Hood and St. Helens belong, and which rise as great pillars of snow on either side of the passage.

The main branch of the *Sacramento* River, and the *Tlamath*, issue in cascades from this range ; and the Columbia, breaking through it in a succession of cascades, gives the idea of cascades to the whole range ; and hence the name of the CASCADE RANGE, which it bears, and distinguishes it from the Coast Range lower down. In making a short turn to the south, the river forms the cascades in breaking over a point of agglomerated masses of rock, leaving a handsome bay to the right, with several rocky pine-covered islands, and the mountains sweep at a distance around a cove where several small streams enter the bay.

In less than an hour we halted on the left bank, about five minutes' walk above the cascades, where there were several Indian huts, and where our guides signified it was customary to hire Indians to assist in making the *portage*. When travelling with a boat as light as a canoe, which may easily be carried on the shoulders of the Indians, this is much the better side of the river for the portage, as the ground here is very good and

SHOOTING RAPIDS OF LOWER COLUMBIA

level, being a handsome bottom, which I remarked was covered (*as was now always the case along the river*) with a growth of green and fresh-looking grass.

It was long before we could come to an understanding with the Indians; but at length, when they had first received the price of their assistance in goods, they went vigorously to work; and in a shorter time than had been occupied in making our arrangements, the canoe, instruments, and baggage, were carried through (a distance of about half a mile) to the bank below the main cascade, where we again embarked, the water being white with foam among ugly rocks, and boiling into a thousand whirlpools. The boat passed with great rapidity, crossing and recrossing in the eddies of the current.

After passing through about two miles of broken water, we ran some wild-looking rapids, which are called the Lower Rapids, being the last on the river, which below is tranquil and smooth—a broad, magnificent stream. On a low broad point on the right bank of the river, at the lower end of these rapids, were pitched many tents of the emigrants, who were waiting here for their friends from above, or for boats and provisions which were expected from Vancouver.

In our passage down the rapids, I had noticed their camps along the shore, or transporting their goods across the portage. This portage makes a head of navigation, ascending the river. It is about two miles in length; and above, to the Dalles, is forty-five miles of smooth and good navigation.

We glided on without further interruption between very rocky and high steep mountains, which sweep along the river valley at a little distance, covered with forests of pine, and showing occasionally lofty escarpments of red rock. Nearer, the shore is bordered by steep escarped hills, and huge vertical rocks, from which the waters of the mountain reach the river in a variety of beautiful falls, sometimes several hundred feet in height; occasionally along the river occurred pretty bottoms, covered with the greenest verdure of the spring. To a professional farmer, however, it does not offer many places of sufficient extent to be valuable for agriculture; and after passing a few miles below the Dalles, I had scarcely seen a place on the south shore where wagons could get to the river. The beauty of the scenery was heightened by the continuance of very delightful weather, resembling the Indian summer of the Atlantic.

A few miles below the cascades we passed a singular isolated hill; and in the course of the next six miles occurred five very pretty falls from the heights on the left bank, one of them being of a very picturesque character; and toward sunset we reached a remarkable point of rocks, distinguished, on account of prevailing high winds, and the delay it frequently occasions to the canoe navigation, by the name of *Cape Horn.* It borders the river in a high wall of rock, which comes boldly down into deep water; and in violent gales down the river, and from the opposite shore, which is the prevailing direction of strong winds, the water is dashed against it with considerable violence. It appears to form a serious obstacle to canoe travelling; and I was informed by Mr. Perkins, that in a voyage up the river he had been detained two weeks at this place, and was finally obliged to return to Vancouver.

The winds of this region deserve a particular study. They blow in currents, which show them to be governed by fixed laws; and it is a problem how far they may come from the mountains, or from the ocean, through the breaks in the mountains which let out the river.

The hills here had lost something of their rocky appearance, and had already begun to decline. As the sun went down, we searched along the river for an inviting spot; and, finding a clean rocky beach, where some large dry trees were lying on the ground, we ran our boat to the shore; and, after another comfortable supper, ploughed our way along the river in darkness.

Heavy clouds covered the sky this evening, and the wind began to sweep in gusts among the trees, as if bad weather were coming. As we advanced, the hills on both sides grew constantly lower; on the right, retreating from the shore, and forming a somewhat extensive bottom of intermingled prairie and wooded land. In the course of a few hours, and opposite to a small stream coming in from the north, called the *Tea Prairie* River, the highlands on the left declined to the plains, and three or four miles below disappeared entirely on both sides, and the river entered the low country.

The river had gradually expanded; and when we emerged from the highlands, the opposite shores were so distant as to appear indistinct in the uncertainty of the light. About ten o'clock our pilots halted, apparently to confer about the course; and, after a little hesitation, pulled directly across an open expansion of the river, where the waves were somewhat rough for a canoe, the wind blowing very fresh. Much to our surprise, a few minutes afterward we ran aground. Backing off our boat, we made repeated trials at various places to cross what appeared to be a point of shifting sandbars, where we had attempted to shorten the way by a cut-off. Finally, one of our Indians got into the water, and waded about until he found a channel sufficiently deep, through which we wound along after him, and in a few minutes again entered the deep water below.

As we paddled rapidly down the river, we heard the noise of a saw-mill at work on the right bank; and, letting our boat float quietly down, we listened with pleasure to the unusual sounds; and before midnight en-

NIGHT ON THE LOWER COLUMBIA.

camped on the bank of the river, about a mile above Fort Vancouver. Our fine, dry weather had given place to a dark, cloudy night. At midnight it began to rain; and we found ourselves suddenly in the gloomy and humid season which, in the narrow region lying between the Pacific and the Cascade Mountains, and for a considerable distance along the coast, supplies the place of winter.

In the morning, the first object that attracted my attention was the bark Columbia, lying at anchor near the landing. She was about to start on her voyage to England, and was now ready for sea; being detained only in waiting the arrival of the express batteaus, which descend the Columbia and its north fork with the overland mail from Canada and Hudson's Bay, which had been delayed beyond their usual time.

I immediately waited upon Dr. McLaughlin, the executive officer of the Hudson Bay Company in the territory west of the Rocky Mountains, who received me with the courtesy and hospitality for which he has been eminently distinguished, and which makes a forcible and delightful impression on a traveller from the long wilderness from which we had issued. I was immediately supplied by him with the necessary stores and provisions to refit and support my party in our contemplated winter journey to the States; and also with a Mackinaw boat and canoes, manned with Canadian and Iroquois voyageurs and Indians, for their transportation to the Dalles of the Columbia.

In addition to his efficient kindness in furnishing me with these necessary supplies, I received from.him a warm and gratifying sympathy in the suffering which his great experience led him to anticipate for us in our homeward journey, and a letter of recommendation and credit for any officers of the Hudson Bay Company into whose posts we might be driven by unexpected misfortune.

Of course the future supplies for my party were paid for, bills on the Government of the United States being readily taken ; but every hospitable attention was extended to me, and I accepted an invitation to take a room in the fort, " *and to make myself at home while I stayed.*"

I found many American emigrants at the fort; others had already crossed the river into their land of promise—the Walahmette Valley. Others were daily arriving; and all of them had been furnished with shelter, so far as it could be afforded by the buildings connected with the establishment. Necessary clothing and provisions (the latter to be afterward returned in kind from the produce of their labor) were also furnished. This friendly assistance was of very great value to the emigrants, whose families were otherwise exposed to much suffering in the winter rains, which had now commenced; at the same time that they were in want of all the common necessaries of life.

Those who had taken a water conveyance at the Nez Percé Fort, continued to arrive safely, with no other accident than has been already mentioned. The party which had passed over the Cascade Mountains were reported to have lost a number of their animals ; and those who had driven their stock down the Columbia, had brought them safely in, and found for them a ready and very profitable market, and were already proposing to return to the States in the spring for another supply.

In the space of two days our preparations had been completed, and we were ready to set out on our return. It would have been very gratifying to have gone down to the Pacific, and, solely in the interest and in the love of geography, to have seen the ocean on the western as well as on the eastern side of the continent, so as to give a satisfactory completeness to the geographical picture which had been formed in our minds ; but the rainy season had now regularly set in, and the air was filled with fogs and rain, which left no beauty in any scenery, and obstructed observations.

The object of my instructions had been entirely fulfilled in having connected our reconnoissance with the surveys of Captain Wilkes ; and although it would have been agreeable and satisfactory to terminate here also our ruder astronomical observations, I was not, for such a reason, justified to make a delay in waiting for favorable weather.

Near sunset of the 10th, the boats left the fort, and encamped after making only a few miles. Our flotilla consisted of a Mackinaw barge and three canoes—one of them that in which we had descended the river ; and a party in all of twenty men.

One of the emigrants, Mr. Peter H. Burnet, of Missouri, who had left his family and property at the Dalles, availed himself of the opportunity afforded by the return of our boats to bring them down to Vancouver. This gentleman, as well as the Messrs. Applegate, and others of the emigrants whom I saw, possessed intelligence and character, with the moral and intellectual stamina, as well as the enterprise, which give solidity and respectability to the foundation of colonies.

November 11*th*.—The morning was rainy and misty. We did not move with the practised celerity of my own camp ; and it was near nine o'clock when our motley crew had finished their breakfast and were ready to start. Once afloat, however, they worked steadily and well, and we advanced at a good rate up the river ; and in the afternoon a breeze sprung up, which enabled us to add a sail to the oars. At evening we encamped on a warm-looking beach, on the right bank, at the foot of the high river-hill, immediately at the lower end of Cape Horn.

On the opposite shore is said to be a singular hole in the mountain, from which the Indians believe comes the wind producing these gales. It is called the Devil's Hole ; and the Indians, I was told, have been resolving to send down one of their slaves to explore the region below. At dark, the wind shifted into its stormy quarter, gradually increasing to a gale from the southwest; and the sky becoming clear, I obtained a good observation of an emersion of the first satellite; the result of which, being an absolute observation, I have adopted for the longitude of the place.

November 12th.—The wind during the night had increased to so much violence, that the broad river this morning was angry and white; the waves breaking with considerable force against this rocky wall of the cape. Our old Iroquois pilot was unwilling to risk the boats around the point, and I was not disposed to hazard the stores of our voyage for the delay of a day. Further observations were obtained during the day, giving for the latitude of the place 45° 33′ 09″; and the longitude, obtained from the satellite, is 122° 6′ 15″.

November 13th.—We had a day of disagreeable and cold rain; and, late in the afternoon, began to approach the rapids of the cascades. There is here a high-timbered island on the left shore, below which, in descending, I had remarked in a bluff on the river the extremities of trunks and trees appearing to be imbedded in the rock.

Landing here this afternoon, I found in the lower part of the escarpment a stratum of coal and forest-trees, imbedded between strata of altered clay containing the remains of vegetables, the leaves of which indicate that the plants were dicotyledonous. Among these, the stems of some of the ferns are not mineralized, but merely charred, retaining still their vegetable structure and substance; and in this condition a portion also of the trees remain. The indurated appearance and compactness of the strata, as well, perhaps, as the mineralized condition of the coal, are probably due to igneous action. Some portions of the coal precisely resemble in aspect the cannel coal of England, and, with the accompanying fossils, have been referred to the tertiary formation.

These strata appear to rest upon a mass of agglomerated rock, being but a few feet above the water of the river; and over them is the escarpment of perhaps eighty feet, rising gradually in the rear toward the mountains. The wet and cold evening, and near approach of night, prevented me from making any other than a very slight examination.

The current was now very swift, and we were obliged to *cordelle* the boat along the left shore, where the bank was covered with large masses of rocks. Night overtook us at the upper end of the island, a short distance below the cascades, and we halted on the open point. In the meantime, the lighter canoes, paddled altogether by Indians, had passed ahead, and were out of sight. With them was the lodge, which was the only shelter we had, with most of the bedding and provisions. We shouted, and fired guns; but all to no purpose, as it was impossible for them to hear above the roar of the river ; and we remained all night without shelter, the rain pouring down all the time. The old voyageurs did not appear to mind it much, but covered themselves up as well as they could, and lay down on the sand-beach, where they remained quiet until morning. The rest of us spent a rather miserable night; and, to add to our discomfort, the incessant rain extinguished our fires ; and we were glad when at last daylight appeared, and we again embarked.

Crossing to the right bank, we *cordelled* the boat along the shore, there being no longer any use for the paddles, and put into a little bay below the upper rapids. Here we found the lodge pitched, and about twenty Indians sitting around a blazing fire within, making a luxurious breakfast with salmon, bread, butter, sugar, coffee, and other provisions. In the forest on the edge of the high bluff overlooking the river, is an Indian grave-yard, consisting of a collection of tombs, in each of which were the scattered bones of many skeletons. The tombs were made of boards, which were ornamented with many figures of men and animals of the natural size— from their appearance, constituting the armorial device by which, among Indians, the chiefs are usually known.

The masses of rock displayed along the shores of the ravine in the neighborhood of the cascades, are clearly volcanic products. Between this cove, which I called Grave-yard Bay, and another spot of smooth water above, on the right, called Lüders Bay, sheltered by a jutting point of huge rocky masses at the foot of the cascades, the shore along the intervening rapids is lined with precipices of distinct strata of red and variously colored lavas in inclined positions.

The masses of rock forming the point at Lüders Bay consist of a porous trap, or basalt—a volcanic product of a modern period. The rocks belong to agglomerated masses, which form the immediate ground of the cascades, and have been already mentioned as constituting a bed of cemented conglomerate rocks appearing at various places along the river. Here they are scattered along the shores, and through the bed of the river, wearing the character of convulsion, which forms the impressive and prominent feature of the river at this place.

Wherever we came in contact with the rocks of these mountains, we found them volcanic, which is probably the character of the range ; and at this time, two of the great snowy cones, Mount Regnier and St. Helens, were in action. On the 23d of the preceding November, St. Helens had scattered its ashes, like a light fall of snow, over the Dalles of the Columbia, fifty miles distant. A specimen of these ashes was given to me by Mr. Brewer, one of the clergymen at the Dalles.

The lofty range of the Cascade Mountains forms a distinct boundary between the opposite climates of the regions along its western and eastern bases.   On the west, they present a barrier to the clouds of fog and rain which roll up from the Pacific Ocean and beat against their rugged sides, forming the rainy season of the winter in the country along the coast.   Into the brighter skies of the region along their eastern base, this rainy winter never penetrates ; and at the Dalles of the Columbia the rainy season is unknown, the brief winter being limited to a period of about two months, during which the earth is covered with the slight snows of a climate remarkably mild for so high a latitude.   The Cascade range has an average distance of about one hundred and thirty miles from the sea-coast.   It extends far both north and south of the Columbia, and is indicated to the distant observer, both in course and position, by the lofty volcanic peaks which rise out of it, and which are visible to an immense distance.

During several days of constant rain, it kept our whole force laboriously employed in getting our barge and canoes to the upper end of the cascades. The portage-ground was occupied by emigrant families ; their thin and insufficient clothing, bare-headed and bare-footed children, attesting the length of their journey, and showing that they had, in many instances, set out without a due preparation of what was indispensable.

A gentleman named Lüders, a botanist from the city of Hamburg, arrived at the bay I have called by his name while we were occupied in bringing up the boats.   I was delighted to meet at such a place a man of kindred pursuits ; but we had only the pleasure of a brief conversation, as his canoe, under the guidance of two Indians, was about to run the rapids ; and I could not enjoy the satisfaction of regaling him with a breakfast, which, after his recent journey, would have been an extraordinary luxury.   All of his few instruments and baggage were in the canoe, and he hurried around by land to meet it at the Grave-yard Bay ; but he was scarcely out of sight, when, by the carelessness of the Indians, the boat was drawn into the midst of the rapids, and glanced down the river, bottom up, with the loss of everything it contained.   In the natural concern I felt for his misfortune, I gave to the little cove the name of Lüders Bay.

November 15*th.*—We continued to-day our work at the portage.

About noon the two barges of the express from Montreal arrived at the upper portage landing, which, for large boats, is on the right bank of the river.   They were a fine-looking crew, and among them I remarked a fresh-looking woman and her daughter, emigrants from Canada.   It was satisfactory to see the order and speed with which these experienced watermen effected the portage, and passed their boats over the cascades.   They had arrived at noon, and in the evening they expected to reach Vancouver. These batteaus carry the express of the Hudson Bay Company to the high-est navigable point of the north fork of the Columbia, whence it is carried by an overland party to Lake Winipec, where it is divided—part going to

Montreal, and part to Hudson Bay.   Thus a regular communication is kept up between three very remote points.

The Canadian emigrant was much chagrined at the change of climate, and informed me that, only a few miles above, they had left a country of bright blue sky and a shining sun.   The next morning the upper parts of the mountains which directly overlook the cascades were white with the freshly fallen snow, while it continued to rain steadily below.

Late in the afternoon we finished the portage, and embarking again, moved a little distance up the right bank, in order to clear the smaller rapids of the cascades, and have a smooth river for the next morning. Though we made but a few miles, the weather improved immediately ; and though the rainy country and the cloudy mountains were close behind, before us was the bright sky ; so distinctly is climate here marked by a mountain boundary.

November 17th.—We had to-day an opportunity to complete the sketch of that portion of the river down which we had come by night, and of which I will not give a particular description, which the small scale of our map would not illustrate.   Many places occur along the river where the stumps, or rather portions of the trunks of pine-trees, are standing along the shore, and in the water, where they may be seen at a considerable depth below the surface, in the beautifully clear water.   These collections of dead trees are called on the Columbia the *submerged forest*, and are supposed to have been created by the effects of some convulsion which formed the cascades, and which, by damming up the river, placed these trees under water and destroyed them.   But I venture to presume that the cascades are older than the trees ; and as these submerged forests occur at five or six places along the river, I had an opportunity to satisfy myself that they have been formed by immense land-slides from the mountains, which here closely shut in the river, and which brought down with them into the river the pines of the mountain.   At one place, on the right bank, I remarked a place where a portion of one of these slides seemed to have planted itself with all the evergreen foliage, and the vegetation of the neighboring hill, directly amidst the falling and yellow leaves of the river-trees.   It occurred to me that this would have been a beautiful illustration to the eye of a botanist.

Following the course of a slide, which was very plainly marked along the mountain, I found that in the interior parts the trees were in their usual erect position ; but, at the extremity of the slide, they were rocked about and thrown into a confusion of inclinations.

About four o'clock in the afternoon we passed a sandy bar in the river, whence we had an unexpected view of Mount Hood, bearing directly south by compass.

During the day we used oar and sail, and at night had again a delightful camping ground, and a dry place to sleep upon.

November 18*th.*—The day again was pleasant and bright. At ten o'clock we passed a rock island, on the right shore of the river, which the Indians use as a burial ground; and, halting for a short time, about an hour afterward, at the village of our Indian friends, early in the afternoon we arrived again at the Dalles.

Carson had removed the camp up the river a little nearer to the hills, where the animals had better grass. We found everything in good order, and arrived just in time to partake of an excellent roast of California beef. My friend, Mr. Gilpin, had arrived in advance of the party. His object in visiting this country had been to obtain correct information of the Walahmette settlements; and he had reached this point in his journey, highly pleased with the country over which he had travelled, and with invigorated health. On the following day he continued his journey, in our returning boats, to Vancouver.

The camp was now occupied in making the necessary preparations for our homeward journey, which, though homeward, contemplated a new route, and a great circuit to the south and southeast, and the exploration of the Great Basin between the Rocky Mountains and the *Sierra Nevada.*

Three principal objects were indicated by report, or by maps, as being on this route; the character or existence of which I wished to ascertain, and which I assumed as landmarks, or leading points, on the projected line of return. The first of these points was the *Tlamath* Lake, on the table-land between the head of Fall River, which comes to the Columbia, and the Sacramento, which goes to the bay of San Francisco; and from which lake a river of the same name makes its way westwardly direct to the ocean.

This lake and river are often called *Klamet,* but I have chosen to write its name according to the Indian pronunciation. The position of this lake, on the line of inland communication between Oregon and California; its proximity to the demarcation boundary of latitude 42°; its imputed double character of lake, or meadow, according to the season of the year; and the hostile and warlike character attributed to the Indians about it—all made it a desirable object to visit and examine.

From this lake our course was intended to be about southeast to a reported lake called Mary's, at some days' journey in the Great Basin; and thence, still on southeast, to the reputed *Buenaventura* River, which has had a place in so many maps, and countenanced the belief of the existence of a great river flowing from the Rocky Mountains to the bay of San Francisco. From the Buenaventura the next point was intended to be in that section of the Rocky Mountains which includes the heads of Arkansas

River, and of the opposite waters of the Californian Gulf; and thence down the Arkansas to Bent's Fort, and home.

This was our projected line of return—a great part of it absolutely new to geographical, botanical, and geological science—and the subject of reports in relation to lakes, rivers, deserts, and savages hardly above the condition of mere wild animals, which inflamed desire to know what this *terra incognita* really contained.   It was a serious enterprise, at the commencement of winter, to undertake the traverse of such a region, and with a party consisting only of twenty-five persons, and they of many nations— American, French, German, Canadian, Indian, and colored—and most of them young, several being under twenty-one years of age.

All knew that a strange country was to be explored, and dangers and hardships to be encountered; but no one blenched at the prospect.   On the contrary, courage and confidence animated the whole party.   Cheerfulness, readiness, subordination, prompt obedience, characterized all; nor did any extremity of peril and privation, to which we were afterward exposed, ever belie, or derogate from, the fine spirit of this brave and generous commencement.

The course of the narrative will show at what point, and for what reasons, we were prevented from the complete execution of this plan, after having made considerable progress upon it, and how we were forced by desert plains and mountain ranges, and deep snows, far to the south and near to the Pacific Ocean, and along the western base of the Sierra Nevada; where, indeed, a new and ample field of exploration opened itself before us.   For the present, we must follow the narrative, which will first lead us south along the valley of Fall River, and the eastern base of the Cascade range, to the Tlamath Lake, from which, or its margin, three rivers go in three directions—one west, to the ocean; another north, to the Columbia; the third south, to California.

For the support of the party, I had provided at Vancouver a supply of provisions for not less than three months, consisting principally of flour, peas and tallow—the latter being used in cooking; and, in addition to this, I had purchased at the mission some California cattle, which were to be driven on the hoof.

We had one hundred and four mules and horses—part of the latter procured from the Indians about the mission; and for the sustenance of which our reliance was upon the grass which we should find, and the soft porous wood which was to be its substitute when there was none.

Mr. Fitzpatrick, with Mr. Talbot and the remainder of our party, arrived on the 21st; and the camp was now closely engaged in the labor of preparation.   Mr. Perkins succeeded in obtaining as guide to the Tlamath Lake two Indians—one of whom had been there, and bore the marks of several wounds he had received from some of the Indians in the neighborhood; and the other went along for company. In order to enable us to obtain horses, he despatched messengers to the various Indian villages in the neighborhood, informing them that we were desirous to purchase, and appointing a day for them to bring them in.

We made, in the meantime, several excursions in the vicinity. Mr. Perkins walked with Mr. Preuss and myself to the heights, about nine miles distant on the opposite side of the river, whence, in fine weather, an extensive view may be had over the mountains, including seven great peaks of the Cascade range; but clouds, on this occasion, destroyed the anticipated pleasure, and we obtained bearings only to three that were visible: Mount Regnier, St. Helens, and Mount Hood. On the heights, about one mile south of the mission, a very fine view may be had of Mount Hood and St. Helens. In order to determine their positions with as much accuracy as possible, the angular distances of the peaks were measured with the sextant, at different fixed points from which they could be seen.

The Indians brought in their horses at the appointed time, and we succeeded in obtaining a number in exchange for goods; but they were relatively much higher here, where goods are plenty and at moderate prices, than we had found them in the more eastern part of our voyage. Several of the Indians inquired very anxiously to know if we had any *dollars;* and the horses we procured were much fewer in number than I had desired, and of thin, inferior quality; the oldest and poorest being those that were sold to us. These horses, as our journey gave constant occasion to remark, are valuable for hardihood and great endurance.

November 24th.—At this place one of the men was discharged; and at the request of Mr. Perkins, a Chinook Indian, a lad of nineteen, who was extremely desirous to " see the whites," and make some acquaintance with our institutions, was received into the party, under my especial charge, with the understanding that I would again return him to his friends. He had lived for some time in the household of Mr. Perkins, and spoke a few words of the English language.

November 25th.—We were all up early, in the excitement of turning toward home. The stars were brilliant, and the morning cold—the thermometer at daylight 26°.

Our preparations had been finally completed, and to-day we commenced our journey. The little wagon which had hitherto carried the instruments, I judged it necessary to abandon; and it was accordingly presented to the mission. In all our long travelling, it had never been overturned or injured by any accident of the road; and the only things broken were the glass lamps, and one of the front panels, which had been kicked out by an unruly Indian horse. The howitzer was the only wheeled carriage now remaining.   We started about noon, when the weather had become disagreeably cold, with flurries of snow.   Our friend, Mr. Perkins, whose kindness had been active and efficient during our stay, accompanied us several miles on our road; when he bade us farewell, and consigned us to the care of our guides.

Ascending to the uplands beyond the southern fork of the *Tinanens* Creek, we found the snow lying on the ground in frequent patches, although the pasture appeared good, and the new short grass was fresh and green. We travelled over high, hilly land, and encamped on a little branch of Tinanens Creek, where there were good grass and timber.   The southern bank was covered with snow, which was scattered over the bottom, and the little creek, its borders lined with ice, had a chilly and wintry look.

A number of Indians had accompanied us so far on our road, and remained with us during the night.   Two bad-looking fellows, who were detected in stealing, were tied and laid before the fire, and guard mounted over them during the night.   The night was cold and partially clear.

November 26th.—The morning was cloudy and misty, and but a few stars visible.   During the night water froze in the tents, and at sunrise the thermometer was at 20°.   Left camp at ten o'clock, the road leading along tributaries of the Tinanens, and being, so far, very good.   We turned to the right at a fork of the trail, ascending by a steep ascent along a spur to the dividing grounds between this stream and the waters of Fall River. The creeks we had passed were timbered principally with oak and other deciduous trees.   Snow lies everywhere here on the ground, and we had a slight fall during the morning; but toward noon the gray sky yielded to a bright sun.

This morning we had a grand view of St. Helens and Regnier; the latter appeared of a conical form, and very lofty, leading the eye far up into the sky.   The line of the timbered country is very distinctly marked here, the bare hills making with it a remarkable contrast.   The summit of the ridge commanded a fine view of the Taih Prairie, and the stream running through it, which is a tributary to the Fall River, the chasm of which is visible to the right.   A steep descent of a mountain hill brought us down into the valley, and we encamped on the stream after dark, guided by the light of fires, which some naked Indians belonging to a village on the opposite side were kindling for us on the bank.   This is a large branch of the Fall River.   There was a broad band of thick ice some fifteen feet wide on either bank, and the river current is swift and bold.

The night was cold and clear, and we made our astronomical observation this evening with the thermometer at 20°.

In anticipation of coming hardship, and to spare our horses, there was much walking done to-day; and Mr. Fitzpatrick and myself made the day's

PASS IN THE SIERRA MOJADA.

journey on foot. Somewhere near the mouth of this stream, are the falls from which the river takes its name.

November 27th.—A fine view of Mount Hood this morning; a rose-colored mass of snow, bearing S. 85° W. by compass. The sky is clear, and the air cold; the thermometer 2.5° below zero; the trees and bushes glittering white, and the rapid stream filled with floating ice.

Stiletsi and *the White Crane*, two Indian chiefs who had accompanied us thus far, took their leave, and we resumed our journey at ten o'clock. We ascended by a steep hill from the river bottom, which is sandy, to a volcanic plain, around which lofty hills sweep in a regular form. It is cut up by gullies of basaltic rock, escarpments of which appear everywhere in the hills. This plain is called the Taih Prairie, and is sprinkled with some scattered pines.

The country is now far more interesting to a traveller than the route along the Snake and Columbia Rivers. To our right we had always the mountains, from the midst of whose dark pine forests the isolated snowy peaks were looking out like giants. They served us for grand beacons to show the rate at which we advanced in our journey. Mount Hood was already becoming an old acquaintance, and, when we ascended the prairie, we obtained a bearing to Mount Jefferson, S. 23° W.

The Indian superstition has peopled these lofty peaks with evil spirits, and they have never yet known the tread of a human foot. Sternly drawn against the sky, they look so high and steep, so snowy and rocky, that it would appear almost impossible to climb them; but still a trial would have its attractions for the adventurous traveller.

A small trail takes off through the prairie, toward a low point in the range, and perhaps there is here a pass into the Walahmette Valley. Crossing the plain, we descended by a rocky hill into the bend of a tributary of Fall River, and made an early encampment. The water was in holes and frozen over, and we were obliged to cut through the ice for the animals to drink. An ox, which was rather troublesome to drive, was killed here for food.

The evening was fine, the sky being very clear, and I obtained an immersion of the third satellite, with a good observation of an emersion of the first; the latter of which gives for the longitude, 121° 02' 43"; the latitude, by observation, being 45° 06' 45". The night was cold—the thermometer during the observations standing at 9°.

November 28th.—The sky was clear in the morning, but suddenly clouded over, and at sunrise began to snow, with the thermometer at 18°.

We traversed a broken high country partly timbered with pine, and about noon crossed a mountainous ridge, in which, from the rock occasionally displayed, the formation consists of compact lava.   Frequent tracks of elk were visible in the snow.   On our right, in the afternoon, a high plain, partially covered with pine, extended about ten miles to the foot of the Cascade Mountains.

At evening we encamped in a basin narrowly surrounded by rocky hills, after a day's journey of twenty-one miles.   The surrounding rocks are either volcanic products, or highly altered by volcanic action, consisting of quartz and reddish-colored siliceous masses.

November 29*th.*—We emerged from the basin, by a narrow pass, upon a considerable branch of Fall River, running to the eastward through a narrow valley.   The trail, descending this stream, brought us to a locality of hot springs, which were on either bank.   Those on the left, which were formed into deep, handsome basins, would have been delightful baths if the outer air had not been so keen, the thermometer in these being at 89°.   There were others, on the opposite side, at the foot of an escarpment, in which the temperature of the water was 134°.   These waters deposited around the spring a brecciated mass of quartz and feldspar, much of it of a reddish color.

We crossed the stream here, and ascended again to a high plain, from an elevated point of which we obtained a view of six of the great peaks— Mount Jefferson, followed to the southward by two others of the same class ; and succeeding, at a still greater distance to the southward, were three other lower peaks, clustering together in a branch ridge.   These, like the great peaks, were snowy masses, secondary only to them ; and, from the best examination our time permitted, we are inclined to believe that the range to which they belong is a branch from the great chain which here bears to the westward.   The trail during the remainder of the day followed near to the large stream on the left, which was continuously walled in between high rocky banks.   We halted for the night on a little by-stream.

November 30*th.*—Our journey to-day was short.   Passing over a high plain, on which were scattered cedars, with frequent beds of volcanic rock in fragments, interspersed among the grassy grounds, we arrived suddenly on the verge of the steep and rocky descent to the valley of the stream we had been following and which here ran directly across our path, emerging from the mountains on the right.   You will remark that the country is abundantly watered with large streams which pour down from the neighboring range.

These streams are characterized by the narrow and chasm-like valleys in which they run, generally sunk a thousand feet below the plain.   At the verge of this plain they frequently commence in vertical precipices of basaltic rock, and which leave only casual places at which they can be entered by horses. The road across the country, which would otherwise be very good, is rendered impracticable for wagons by these streams. There is another trail among the mountains, usually followed in the summer, which the snows now compelled us to avoid ; and I have reason to believe that this, passing nearer the heads of these streams, would afford a much better road.

At such places, the gun-carriage was unlimbered, and separately descended by hand. Continuing a few miles up the left bank of the river, we encamped early in an open bottom among the pines, a short distance below a lodge of Indians. Here, along the river, the bluffs present escarpments seven or eight hundred feet in height, containing strata of a very fine porcelain clay, overlaid, at the height of about five hundred feet, by a massive stratum of compact basalt one hundred feet in thickness, which again is succeeded above by other strata of volcanic rocks.

The clay strata are variously colored, some of them very nearly as white as chalk, and very fine-grained. Specimens brought from these have been subjected to microscopical examination by Professor Bailey, of West Point, and are considered by him to constitute one of the most remarkable deposits of fluviatile infusoria on record. While they abound in genera and species which are common in fresh water, but which rarely thrive where the water is even brackish, not one decidedly marine form is to be found among them ; and their fresh-water origin is therefore beyond a doubt. It is equally certain that they lived and died at the situation where they were found, as they could scarcely have been transported by running waters without an admixture of sandy particles ; from which, however, they are remarkably free.

Fossil infusoria of a fresh-water origin had been previously detected by Mr. Bailey in specimens brought by Mr. James D. Dana from the tertiary formation of Oregon. Most of the species in those specimens differed so much from those now living and known, that he was led to infer that they might belong to extinct species, and considered them also as affording proof of an alternation, in the formation from which they were obtained, of fresh and salt water deposits, which, common enough in Europe, had not hitherto been noticed in the United States. Coming evidently from a locality entirely different, our specimens * show very few species in common with those brought by Mr. Dana, but bear a much closer resemblance to those inhabiting the Northeastern States. It is possible that they are from a more recent deposit; but the presence of a few remarkable

---

* The specimens obtained at this locality are designated in the appendix by the Nos. 53, 54, 55, 56, 57, 58, 59, 60. The results obtained by Mr. Bailey in his examination of specimens from the infusorial strata, with a plate exhibiting some of the most interesting forms, will be found embodied in the Appendix.

forms, which are common to the two localities, renders it more probable that there is no great difference in their age.

I obtained here a good observation of an emersion of the second satellite; but clouds, which rapidly overspread the sky, prevented the usual number of observations. Those which we succeeded in obtaining are, however, good; and give for the latitude of the place 44° 35′ 23″, and for the longitude from the satellite 121° 10′ 25″.

CHAPTER VIII.

Talmath Lake—Thermometer at Zero—Lake Abert—Celebrating Christmas Morning—Almost the Missing Link—A Gloomy New Year's Eve—Extraordinary Hot Springs—Pyramid Lake—The *Nut Pine*—Brandy a Good Medicine—Majesty of the Mountains.

December 1st.—A short distance above our encampment we crossed this river, which was thickly lined along its banks with ice. In common with all these mountain streams, the water was very clear, and the current swift. It was not everywhere fordable, and the water was three or four feet deep at our crossing, and perhaps a hundred feet wide. As was frequently the case at such places, one of the mules got his pack, consisting of sugar, thoroughly wet, and turned into molasses.

One of the guides informed me that this was a "salmon water," and pointed out several ingeniously contrived places to catch the fish; among the trees in the bottom I saw an immense pine, about twelve feet in diameter. A steep ascent from the opposite bank delayed us again; and as, by the information of our guides, grass would soon become very scarce, we encamped on the height of land, in a marshy place among the pines, where there was an abundance of grass.

We found here a single Nez Percé family, who had a very handsome horse in their drove, which we endeavored to obtain in exchange for a good cow; but the man "had two hearts," or rather, he had one and his wife had another; she wanted the cow, but he loved the horse too much to part with it. These people attach great value to cattle, with which they are endeavoring to supply themselves.

December 2d.—In the first rays of the sun the mountain peaks this morning presented a beautiful appearance, the snow being entirely covered with a hue of rosy gold. We travelled to-day over a very stony, elevated plain, about which were scattered cedar and pine, and encamped on another large branch of Fall River. We were gradually ascending to a more elevated region, which would have been indicated by the rapidly increasing quantities of snow and ice, had we not known it by other means. A mule which was packed with our cooking utensils wandered off among the pines unperceived, and several men were sent back to search for it.

December 3d.—Leaving Mr. Fitzpatrick with the party, I went ahead with the howitzer and a few men, in order to gain time, as our progress with the gun was necessarily slower.   The country continued the same— very stony, with cedar and pine ; and we rode on until dark, when we en- camped on a hill-side covered with snow, which we used to-night for water, as we were unable to reach any stream.

December 4th.—Our animals had taken the back track, although a great number were hobbled ; and we were consequently delayed until noon. Shortly after we had left this encampment the mountain trail from the Dalles joined that on which we were travelling.   After passing for several miles over an artemisia plain, the trail entered a beautiful pine forest, through which we travelled for several hours ; and about four o'clock de- scended into the valley of another large branch, on the bottom of which were spaces of open pines, with occasional meadows of good grass, in one of which we encamped.   The stream is very swift and deep, and about forty feet wide, and nearly half frozen over.   Among the timber here are larches one hundred and forty feet high and over three feet in diameter. We had to-night the rare sight of a lunar rainbow.

December 5th.—To-day the country was all pine forest, and beautiful weather made our journey delightful.   It was too warm at noon for winter clothes ; and the snow, which lay everywhere in patches through the for- est, was melting rapidly.

After a few hours' ride we came upon a fine stream in the midst of the forest, which proved to be the principal branch of Fall River.   It was oc- casionally two hundred feet wide—sometimes narrowed to fifty feet; the waters very clear, and frequently deep.   We ascended along the river, which sometimes presented sheets of foaming cascades, its banks occa- sionally blackened with masses of scoriated rock, and found a good en- campment on the verge of an open bottom, which had been an old camp- ing-ground of the Cayuse Indians.   A great number of deer-horns were lying about, indicating game in the neighborhood.   The timber was uni- formly large ; some of the pines measuring twenty-two feet in circumfer- ence at the ground, and twelve to thirteen feet at six feet above.

In all our journeying we had never travelled through a country where the rivers were so abounding in falls, and the name of this stream is singu- larly characteristic.   At every place where we come in the neighborhood of the river is heard the roaring of falls.   The rock along the banks of the stream, and the ledge over which it falls, is a scoriated basalt, with a bright metallic fracture.   The stream goes over in one clear pitch, succeeded by a foaming cataract of several hundred yards.   In the little bottom above the falls a small stream discharges into an *entonnoir*, and disappears below.

We had made an early encampment, and in the course of the evening Mr. Fitzpatrick joined us here with the lost mule.   Our lodge-poles were nearly worn out, and we found here a handsome set leaning against one of the trees, very white, and cleanly scraped. Had the owners been here, we would have purchased them ; but as they were not, we merely left the old ones in their place, with a small quantity of tobacco.

December 6th.—The morning was frosty and clear. We continued up the stream on undulating forest ground, over which there was scattered much fallen timber. We met here a village of Nez Percé Indians, who appeared to be coming down from the mountains and had with them fine bands of horses. With them were a few Snake Indians of the root-digging species.

From the forest we emerged into an open valley ten or twelve miles wide, through which the stream was flowing tranquilly, upward of two hundred feet broad, with occasional islands, and bordered with fine broad bottoms. Crossing the river, which here issues from a great mountain ridge on the right, we continued up the southern and smaller branch, over a level country, consisting of fine meadow land alternating with pine forests, and encamped on it early in the evening. A warm sunshine made the day pleasant.

December 7th.—To-day we had good travelling ground ; the trail leading sometimes over rather sandy soils in the pine forest, and sometimes over meadow land along the stream. The great beauty of the country in summer constantly suggested itself to our imaginations ; and even now we found it beautiful, as we rode along these meadows, from half a mile to two miles wide. The rich soil and excellent water, surrounded by noble forests, make a picture that would delight the eye of a farmer ; and I regret that the very small scale of the map would not allow us to give some representation of these features of the country.

I observed to-night an occultation of η *Geminorum ;* which, although at the bright limb of the moon, appears to give a very good result, that has been adopted for the longitude. The occultation, observations of satellites, and our position deduced from daily surveys with the compass agree remarkably well together, and mutually support and strengthen each other. The latitude of the camp is 43° 30′ 36″ ; and longitude, deduced from the occultation, 121° 33′ 50″.

December 8th.—To-day we crossed the last branch of the Fall River, issuing, like all the others we had crossed, in a southwesterly direction from the mountains. Our direction was a little east of south, the trail leading constantly through pine forests.

The soil was generally bare, consisting, in greater part, of a yellowish-white pumice-stone, producing varieties of magnificent pines, but not a blade of grass ; and to-night our horses were obliged to do without food, and use snow for water. These pines are remarkable for the red color of the boles ; and among them occurs a species, of which the Indians had informed me when leaving the Dalles. The unusual size of the cone (sixteen or eighteen inches long) had attracted their attention ; and they pointed it out to me among the curiosities of the country. They are more remarkable for their large diameter than their height, which usually averages only about one hundred and twenty feet. The leaflets are short—only two or three inches long, and five in a sheath ; the bark of a red color.

December 9th.—The trail leads always through splendid pine forests. Crossing dividing grounds by a very fine road, we descended very gently toward the south. The weather was pleasant, and we halted late. The soil was very much like that of yesterday ; and on the surface of a hill, near our encampment, were displayed beds of pumice-stone ; but the soil produced no grass, and again the animals fared badly.

December 10th.—The country began to improve ; and about eleven o'clock we reached a spring of cold water on the edge of a savannah, or grassy meadow, which our guides informed us was an arm of the Tlamath Lake ; and a few miles further we entered upon an extensive meadow, or lake of grass, surrounded by timbered mountains. This was the Tlamath Lake. It was a picturesque and beautiful spot, and rendered more attractive to us by the abundant and excellent grass, which our animals, after travelling through pine forests, so much needed ; but the broad sheet of water which constitutes a lake was not to be seen. Overlooking it, immediately west, were several snowy knobs, belonging to what we have considered a branch of the Cascade range. A low point covered with pines made out into the lake, which afforded us a good place for an encampment, and for the security of our horses, which were guarded in view on the open meadow.

The character of courage and hostility attributed to the Indians of this quarter induced more than usual precaution ; and, seeing smokes rising from the middle of the lake (or savannah) and along the opposite shores, I directed the howitzer to be fired. It was the first time our guides had seen it discharged ; and the bursting of the shell at a distance, which was something like the second fire of the gun, amazed and bewildered them with delight. It inspired them with triumphant feelings ; but on the camps at a distance the effect was different, for the smokes in the lake and on the shores immediately disappeared.

The point on which we were encamped forms, with the opposite eastern shore, a narrow neck, connecting the body of the lake with a deep cove or bay which receives the principal affluent stream, and over the greater part of which the water (or rather ice) was at this time dispersed in shallow pools. Among the grass, and scattered over the prairie lake, appeared to be similar marshes. It is simply a shallow basin, which, for a short period at the time of melting snows, is covered with water from the neighboring mountains; but this probably soon runs off, and leaves for the remainder of the year a green savannah, through the midst of which the river Tlamath, which flows to the ocean, winds its way to the outlet on the southwestern side.

December 11*th.*—No Indians made their appearance, and I determined to pay them a visit. Accordingly, the people were gathered together, and we rode out toward the village in the middle of the lake, which one of our guides had previously visited. It could not be directly approached, as a large part of the lake appeared a marsh; and there were sheets of ice among the grass, on which our horses could not keep their footing. We therefore followed the guide for a considerable distance along the forest; and then turned off toward the village, which we soon began to see was a few large huts, on the top of which were collected the Indians. When we had arrived within half a mile of the village, two persons were seen advancing to meet us; and, to please the fancy of our guides, we ranged ourselves into a long line, riding abreast, while they galloped ahead to meet the strangers.

We were surprised, on riding up, to find one of them a woman, having never before known a squaw to take any part in the business of war. They were the village chief and his wife, who, in excitement and alarm at the unusual event and appearance, had come out to meet their fate together. The chief was a very prepossessing Indian, with very handsome features, and a singularly soft and agreeable voice—so remarkable as to attract general notice.

The huts were grouped together on the bank of the river, which from being spread out in a shallow marsh at the upper end of the lake, was collected here into a single stream. They were large round huts, perhaps twenty feet in diameter, with rounded tops, on which was the door by which they descended into the interior. Within, they were supported by posts and beams.

Almost like plants, these people seem to have adapted themselves to the soil, and to be growing on what the immediate locality afforded. Their only subsistence at this time appeared to be a small fish, great quantities of which, had been smoked and dried, were suspended on strings about the lodge. Heaps of straw were lying around; and their residence in the midst of grass and rushes had taught them a peculiar skill in converting this material to useful purposes. Their shoes were made of straw or grass, which seemed well adapted for a snowy country; and the women wore on their head a closely-woven basket, which made a very good cap. Among other things, were parti-colored mats about four feet square, which we purchased to lay on the snow under our blankets, and to use for table-cloths.

Numbers of singular-looking dogs, resembling wolves, were sitting on the tops of the huts ; and of these we purchased a young one, which, after its birthplace, was named Tlamath.

The language spoken by these Indians is different from that of the Shoshonee and Columbia River tribes ; and otherwise than by signs they cannot understand each other.   They made us comprehend that they were at war with the Modoc who lived to the southward and to the eastward ; but I could obtain from them no certain information.

The river on which they live enters the Cascade Mountains on the western side of the lake, and breaks through them by a passage imprac- ticable for travellers ; but over the mountains, to the northward, are passes which present no other obstacle than in the almost impenetrable forests. Unlike any Indians we had previously seen, these wore shells in their noses.   We returned to our camp after remaining here an hour or two, accompanied by a number of Indians.

In order to recruit a little the strength of our animals, and obtain some acquaintance with the locality, we remained here for the remainder of the day.   By observation, the latitude of the camp was 42° 56′ 51″ ; and the diameter of the lake, or meadow, as has been intimated, about twenty miles. It is a picturesque and beautiful spot ; and, under the hand of cultivation, might become a little paradise.   Game is found in the forest ; timbered and snowy mountains skirt it, and fertility characterizes it.   Situated near the heads of three rivers, and on the line of inland communication with California, and near to Indians noted for treachery, it will naturally, in the progress of the settlement of Oregon, become a point for military occupa- tion and settlement.

From Tlamath Lake, the further continuation of our voyage assumed a character of discovery and exploration, which, from the Indians here, we could obtain no information to direct, and where the imaginary maps of the country, instead of assisting, exposed us to suffering and defeat.   In our journey across the desert, Mary's Lake, and the famous Buenaventura River, were two points on which I relied to recruit the animals, and repose the party.

Forming, agreeably to the best maps in my possession, a connected water-line from the Rocky Mountains to the Pacific Ocean, I felt no other anxiety than to pass safely across the intervening desert to the banks of the Buenaventura, where, in the softer climate of a more southern latitude, our horses might find grass to sustain them, and ourselves be sheltered from the rigors of winter and from the inhospitable desert.

The guides who had conducted us thus far on our journey, were about to return ; and I endeavored in vain to obtain others to lead us, even for a few days, in the direction (east) which we wished to go.   The chief to whom I applied alleged the want of horses, and the snow on the mountains across which our course would carry us, and the sickness of his family, as reasons for refusing to go with us.

December 12*th.*—This morning the camp was thronged with Tlamath Indians from the southeastern shore of the lake ; but, knowing the treacherous disposition, which is a remarkable characteristic of the Indians south of the Columbia, the camp was kept constantly on its guard. I was not unmindful of the disasters which Smith and other travellers had met with in this country, and therefore was equally vigilant in guarding against treachery and violence.

According to the best information I had been able to obtain from the Indians, in a few days' travelling we should reach another large water, probably a lake, which they indicated exactly in the course we were about to pursue.

We struck our tents at ten o'clock, and crossed the lake in a nearly east direction, where it has the least extension—the breadth of the arm being here only about a mile and a half. There were ponds of ice, with but little grass for the greater part of the way ; and it was difficult to get the pack-animals across, which fell frequently, and could not get up with their loads, unassisted. The morning was very unpleasant, snow falling at intervals in large flakes, and the sky dark.

In about two hours we succeeded in getting the animals over ; and, after travelling another hour along the eastern shore of the lake, we turned up into a cove where there was a sheltered place among the timber, with good grass, and encamped. The Indians who had accompanied us so far, returned to their village on the southeastern shore. Among the pines here, I noticed some five or six feet in diameter.

December 13*th.*—The night has been cold ; the peaks around the lake gleam out brightly in the morning sun, and the thermometer is at zero. We continued up the hollow formed by a small affluent to the lake, and immediately entered an open pine forest on the mountain. The way here was sometimes obstructed by fallen trees, and the snow was four to twelve inches deep. The mules at the gun pulled heavily, and walking was a little laborious.

In the midst of the wood we heard the sound of galloping horses, and were agreeably surprised by the unexpected arrival of our Tlamath chief with several Indians. He seemed to have found his conduct inhospitable in letting the strangers depart without a guide through the snow, and had come, with a few others, to pilot us a day or two on the way. After travelling in an easterly direction through the forest, for about four hours, we reached a considerable stream, with a border of good grass ; and here, by the advice of our guides, we encamped. It is about thirty feet wide, and two to four feet deep; the water clear, with some current; and, according to the information of our Indians, is the principal affluent to the lake, and the head-water of the Tlamath River.

A very clear sky enabled me to obtain here to-night good observations, including an emersion of the first satellite of Jupiter, which gave for the longitude 121° 20′ 42″, and for the latitude 42° 51′ 26″. This emersion coincides remarkably well with the result obtained from an occultation at the encampment of December 7 to 8, 1843; from which place the line of our survey gives an easting of thirteen miles. The day's journey was twelve miles.

December 14th.—Our road was over a broad mountain, and we rode seven hours in a thick snow-storm, always through pine-forests, when we came down upon the head-waters of another stream, on which there was grass. The snow lay deep on the ground, and only the high swamp grass appeared above.

The Indians were thinly clad, and I had remarked during the day that they suffered from the cold. This evening they told me that the snow was getting too deep on the mountain, and I could not induce them to go any farther. The stream we had struck issued from the mountain in an easterly direction, turning to the southward a short distance below; and, drawing its course upon the ground, they made us comprehend that it pursued its way for a long distance in that direction, uniting with many other streams, and gradually becoming a great river.

Without the subsequent information, which confirmed the opinion, we became immediately satisfied that this water formed the principal stream of the *Sacramento* River; and, consequently, that this main affluent of the Bay of San Francisco had its source within the limits of the United States, and opposite a tributary to the Columbia, and near the head of the Tlamath River, which goes to the ocean north of 42°, and within the United States.

December 15th.—A present consisting of useful goods afforded much satisfaction to our guides; and, showing them the national flag, I explained that it was a symbol of our nation; and they engaged always to receive it in a friendly manner. The chief pointed out a course, by following which we would arrive at the big water, where no more snow was to be found.

Travelling in a direction North 60° East by compass, which the Indians informed me would avoid a bad mountain to the right, we crossed the Sacramento where it turned to the southward, and entered a grassy level plain—a smaller Grand Rond; from the lower end of which the river issued into an inviting country of low rolling hills. Crossing a hard frozen swamp on the farther side of the Rond, we entered again the pine forest, in which very deep snow made our travelling slow and laborious. We were slowly but gradually ascending a mountain; and, after a hard journey of seven hours, we came to some naked places among the timber, where a few tufts of grass showed above the snow, on the side of a hollow; and here we encamped. Our cow, which every day got poorer, was killed here, but the meat was rather tough.

December 16th.—We travelled this morning through snow about three feet deep, which, being crusted, very much cut the feet of our animals. The mountain still gradually rose; we crossed several spring heads covered with quaking asp, otherwise it was all pine forest. The air was dark with falling snow, which everywhere weighed down the trees. The depths of the forest were profoundly still; and below, we scarce felt a breath of the wind which whirled the snow through their branches.

I found that it required some exertion of constancy to adhere steadily to one course through the woods, when we were uncertain how far the forest extended, or what lay beyond; and on account of our animals it would be bad to spend another night on the mountain. Toward noon the forest looked clear ahead, appearing suddenly to terminate; and beyond a certain point we could see no trees. Riding rapidly ahead to this spot, we found ourselves on the verge of a vertical and rocky wall of the mountain.

At our feet—more than a thousand feet below—we looked into a green prairie country, in which a beautiful lake, some twenty miles in length, was spread along the foot of the mountains, its shores bordered with green grass. Just then the sun broke out among the clouds, and illuminated the country below, while around us the storm raged fiercely. Not a particle of ice was to be seen on the lake, or snow on its borders, and all was like summer or spring. The glow of the sun in the valley below brightened up our hearts with sudden pleasure; and we made the woods ring with joyful shouts to those behind; and gradually, as each came up, he stopped to enjoy the unexpected scene. Shivering on snow three feet deep, and stiffening in a cold north wind, we exclaimed at once that the names of Summer Lake and Winter Ridge should be applied to these two proximate places of such sudden and violent contrast.

We were now immediately on the verge of the forest land, in which we had been travelling so many days; and, looking forward to the east, scarce a tree was to be seen. Viewed from our elevation, the face of the country exhibited only rocks and grass, and presented a region in which the artemisia became the principal wood, furnishing to its scattered inhabitants fuel for their fires, building material for their huts, and shelter for the small game which ministers to their hunger and nakedness. Broadly marked by the boundary of the mountain wall, and immediately below us, were the first waters of that Great Interior Basin which has the Wahsatch and Bear

River Mountains for its eastern, and the Sierra Nevada for its western rim ; and the edge of which we had entered upward of three months before at the Great Salt Lake.

When we had sufficiently admired the scene below, we began to think about descending, which here was impossible, and we turned toward the north, travelling always along the rocky wall. We continued on for four or five miles, making ineffectual attempts at several places ; and at length succeeded in getting down at one which was extremely difficult of descent. Night had closed in before the foremost reached the bottom, and it was dark before we all found ourselves together in the valley. There were three or four half-dead dry cedar-trees on the shore, and those who first arrived kindled bright fires to light on the others.

One of the mules rolled over and over two or three hundred feet into a ravine, but recovered himself, without any other injury than to his pack ; and the howitzer was left mid-way the mountain until morning. By observation, the latitude of this encampment is 42° 57′ 22″. It delayed us until near noon the next day to recover ourselves, and put everything in order ; and we made only a short camp along the western shore of the lake, which, in the summer temperature we enjoyed to-day, justified the name we had given it.

Our course would have taken us to the other shore, and over the highlands beyond ; but I distrusted the appearance of the country, and decided to follow a plainly beaten Indian trail leading along this side of the lake. We were now in a country where the scarcity of water and of grass makes travelling dangerous, and great caution was necessary.

December 18*th.*—We continued on the trail along the narrow strip of land between the lake and the high rocky wall, from which we had looked down two days before. Almost every half-mile we crossed a little spring, or stream of pure cold water ; and the grass was certainly as fresh and green as in the early spring. From the white efflorescence along the shore of the lake, we were enabled to judge that the water was impure, like that of lakes we subsequently found ; but the mud prevented us from approaching it.

We encamped near the eastern point of the lake, where there appeared between the hills a broad and low connecting hollow with the country beyond. From a rocky hill in the rear, I could see, marked out by a line of yellow dried grass, the bed of a stream which probably connected the lake with other waters in the spring.

The observed latitude of this encampment is 42° 42′ 37″.

December 19*th.*—After two hours' ride in an easterly direction through a low country, the high ridge with pine forests still to our right, and a rocky and bald but lower one on the left, we reached a considerable fresh-water stream, which issues from the piny mountains. So far as we had been able to judge, between this stream and the lake we had crossed dividing grounds ; and there did not appear to be any connection, as might be inferred from the impure condition of the lake water.

The rapid stream of pure water, roaring along between banks overhung with aspens and willows, was a refreshing and unexpected sight ; and we followed down the course of the stream which brought us soon into a marsh, or dry lake, formed by the expanding waters of the stream. It was covered with high reeds and rushes, and large patches of ground had been turned up by the squaws in digging for roots, as if a farmer had been preparing the land for grain.

I could not succeed in finding the plant for which they had been digging. There were frequent trails, and fresh tracks of Indians ; and, from the abundant signs visible, the black-tailed hare appears to be numerous here. It was evident that, in other seasons, this place was a sheet of water. Crossing this marsh toward the eastern hills, and passing over a bordering plain of heavy sands, covered with artemisia, we encamped before sundown on the creek, which here was very small, having lost its water in the marshy grounds. We found here tolerably good grass. The wind to-night was high, and we had no longer our huge pine fires, but were driven to our old resource of small dried willows and artemisia. About twelve miles ahead, the valley appears to be closed in by a high dark-looking ridge.

December 20th.—Travelling for a few hours down the stream this morning, we turned a point of the hill on our left, and came suddenly in sight of another and much larger lake, which, along its eastern shore, was closely bordered by the high black ridge which walled it in by a precipitous face on this side. Throughout this region the face of the country is characterized by these precipices of black volcanic rock, generally enclosing the valleys of streams, and frequently terminating the hills.

Often in the course of our journey we would be tempted to continue our road up the gentle ascent of a sloping hill, which, at the summit, would terminate abruptly in a black precipice. Spread out over a length of twenty miles, the lake, when we first came in view, presented a handsome sheet of water ; and I gave to it the name of Lake Abert, in honor of the chief of the corps to which I belonged.

The fresh-water stream we had followed emptied into the lake by a little fall ; and I was doubtful for a moment whether to go on, or encamp at this place. The miry ground in the neighborhood of the lake did not allow us to examine the water conveniently, and, being now on the borders of a desert country, we were moving cautiously. It was, however, still early in the day, and I continued on, trusting either that the water would be drinkable, or that we should find some little spring from the hill-side. We were following an Indian trail which led along the steep rocky precipice ; a black ridge along the western shore holding out no prospect whatever. The white efflorescences which lined the shore like a bank of snow, and the disagreeable odor which filled the air as soon as we came near, informed us too plainly that the water belonged to one of those fetid salt lakes which are common in this region.

We continued until late in the evening to work along the rocky shore, but, as often afterward, the dry inhospitable rock deceived us ; and, halting on the lake, we kindled up fires to guide those who were straggling along behind. We tried the water, but it was impossible to drink it, and most of the people to-night lay down without eating ; but some of us, who had always a great reluctance to close the day without supper, dug holes along the shore, and obtained water, which, being filtered, was sufficiently palatable to be used, but still retained much of its nauseating taste. There was very little grass for the animals, the shore being lined with a luxuriant growth of chenopodiaceous-shrubs, which burned with a quick bright flame, and made our firewood.

The next morning we had scarcely travelled two hours along the shore when we reached a place where the mountains made a bay, leaving at their feet a low bottom around the lake. Here we found numerous hillocks covered with rushes, in the midst of which were deep holes, or springs, of pure water ; and the bottom was covered with grass, which, although of a bad and unwholesome quality, and mixed with saline efflorescences, was still abundant, and made a good halting-place to recruit our animals ; and we accordingly encamped here for the remainder of the day.

I rode ahead several miles to ascertain if there was any appearance of a water-course entering the lake, but found none, the hills preserving their dry character, and the shore of the lake sprinkled with the same white powdery substance, and covered with the same shrubs. There were flocks of ducks on the lake, and frequent tracks of Indians along the shore, where the grass had been recently burned by their fires.

We ascended the bordering mountain, in order to obtain a more perfect view of the lake in sketching its figure ; hills sweep entirely around its basin, from which the waters have no outlet.

December 22*d.*—To-day we left this forbidding lake Impassable rocky ridges barred our progress to the eastward, and I accordingly bore off toward the south, over an extensive sage plain. At a considerable distance ahead, and a little on our left, was a range of snowy mountains, and the country declined gradually toward the foot of a high and nearer ridge immediately before us, which presented the feature of black precipices, now becoming common to the country.

On the summit of the ridge, snow was visible; and there being every indication of a stream at its base, we rode on until after dark, but were unable to reach it, and halted among the sage bushes on the open plain, without either grass or water. The two india-rubber bags had been filled with water in the morning, which afforded sufficient for the camp; and rain in the night-formed pools, which relieved the thirst of the animals. Where we encamped on the bleak sandy plain, the Indians had made huts or circular enclosures, about four feet high and twelve feet broad, of artemisia bushes. Whether these had been forts or houses, or what they had been doing in such a desert place, we could not ascertain.

December 23d.—The weather is mild; the thermometer at daylight 38°; the wind having been from the southward for several days. The country has a very forbidding appearance, presenting to the eye nothing but sage and barren ridges. We rode up toward the mountain, along the foot of which we found a lake, which we could not approach on account of the mud; and, passing around its southern end, ascended the slope at the foot of the ridge, where in some hollows we had discovered bushes and small trees—in such situations a sure sign of water.

We found here several springs, and the hill-side was well sprinkled with a species of *festuca*—a better grass than we had found for many days. Our elevated position gave us a good view over the country, but we discovered nothing very encouraging. Southward, about ten miles distant, was another small lake, toward which a broad trail led along the ridge; and this appearing to afford the most practicable route, I determined to continue our journey in that direction.

December 24th.—We found the water of the lake tolerably pure, and encamped at the farther end. There were some good grass and canes along the shore, and the vegetation at this place consisted principally of chenopodiaceous shrubs.

December 25th.—We were roused on Christmas morning, by a discharge from the small arms and howitzer, with which our people saluted the day; and the name of which we bestowed on the lake. It was the first time, perhaps, in this remote and desolate region, in which it had been so commemorated.

Always, on days of religious or national commemoration, our voyageurs expect some unusual allowance; and, having nothing else, I gave to them each a little brandy (which was carefully guarded as one of the most useful articles a traveller can carry) with some coffee and sugar, which here, where every eatable was a luxury, was sufficient to make them a feast. The day was sunny and warm, and, resuming our journey, we crossed some slight dividing grounds into a similar basin, walled in on the right by a lofty mountain ridge. The plainly beaten trail still continued, and occasionally we passed camping-grounds of the Indians, which indicated to me that we were on one of the great thoroughfares of the country.

In the afternoon I attempted to travel in a more eastern direction ; but, after a few laborious miles, was beaten back into the basin by an impassable country. There were fresh Indian tracks about the valley, and last night a horse was stolen. We encamped on the valley bottom, where there was some cream-like water in ponds, colored by a clay soil and frozen over. Chenopodiaceous shrubs constituted the growth, and made again our firewood. The animals were driven to the hill, where there was tolerably good grass.

December 26th.—Our general course was again south. The country consists of larger or smaller basins, into which the mountain waters run down, forming small lakes ; they present a perfect level, from which the mountains rise immediately and abruptly. Between the successive basins, the dividing grounds are usually very slight ; and it is probable that, in the seasons of high water, many of these basins are in communication. At such times there is evidently an abundance of water, though now we find scarcely more than the dry beds.

On either side, the mountains, though not very high, appear to be rocky and sterile. The basin in which we were travelling declined toward the southwest corner, where the mountains indicated a narrow outlet ; and, turning round a rocky point or cape, we continued up a lateral branch valley, in which we encamped at night on a rapid, pretty little stream of fresh water, which we found unexpectedly among the sage near the ridge, on the right side of the valley. It was bordered with grassy bottoms and clumps of willows, the water partially frozen. This stream belongs to the basin we had left. By a partial observation to-night, our camp was found to be directly on the forty-second parallel. To-night a horse belonging to Carson, one of the best we had in the camp, was stolen by the Indians.

December 27th.—We continued up the valley of the stream, the principal branch of which here issues from the bed of high mountains. We turned up a branch to the left, and fell into an Indian trail, which conducted us by a good road over open bottoms along the creek, where the snow was five or six inches deep. Gradually ascending, the trail led through a good broad pass in the mountain, where we found the snow about one foot deep.

There were some remarkably large cedars in the pass which were covered with an unusual quantity of frost, which we supposed might possibly indicate the neighborhood of water ; and as, in the arbitrary position of Mary's Lake, we were already beginning to look for it, this circumstance contributed to our hope of finding it near. Descending from the mountain we reached another basin, on the flat lake-bed of which we found no water, and encamped among the sage on the bordering plain, where the snow was still about one foot deep. Among this the grass was remarkably green, and to-night the animals fared tolerably well.

December 28th.—The snow being deep, I had determined, if any more horses were stolen, to follow the tracks of the Indians into the mountains, and put a temporary check to their sly operations; but it did not occur again.

Our road this morning lay down a level valley, bordered by steep mountainous ridges, rising very abruptly from the plain. Artemisia was the principal plant, mingled with Fremontia and the chenopodiaceous shrubs. The artemisia was here extremely large, being sometimes a foot in diameter and eight feet high.

Riding quietly along over the snow, we came suddenly upon smokes rising among these bushes; and, galloping up, we found two huts open at the top, and loosely built of sage, which appeared to have been deserted at the instant; and, looking hastily around, we saw several Indians on the crest of the ridge near by, and several others scrambling up the side. We had come upon them so suddenly, that they had been well-nigh surprised in their lodges. A sage fire was burning in the middle; a few baskets made of straw were lying about, with one or two rabbit skins; and there was a little grass scattered about, on which they had been lying. "Tabibo—bo!" they shouted from the hills—a word which, in the Snake language, signifies *white*—and remained looking at us from behind the rocks.

Carson and Godey rode toward the hill, but the men ran off like deer. They had been so much pressed, that a woman with two children had dropped behind a sage bush near the lodge, and when Carson accidentally stumbled upon her, she immediately began screaming in the extremity of fear, and shut her eyes fast, to avoid seeing him. She was brought back to the lodge, and we endeavored in vain to open a communication with the men. By dint of presents, and friendly demonstrations, she was brought to calmness; and we found that they belonged to the Snake nation, speaking the language of that people.

Eight or ten appeared to live together, under the same little shelter; and they seemed to have no other subsistence than the roots or seeds they might have stored up, and the hares which live in the sage, and which they are enabled to track through the snow, and are very skilful in killing. Their skins afford them a little scanty covering. Herding together among bushes, and crouching almost naked over a little sage fire, using their instinct only to procure food, these may be considered, among human beings, the nearest approach to the mere animal creation. We have reason to believe that these had never before seen the face of a white man.

The day had been pleasant, but about two o'clock it began to blow; and crossing a slight dividing ground we encamped on the sheltered side of a hill where there was good bunch grass, having made a day's journey of twenty-four miles. The night closed in, threatening snow; but the large sage bushes made bright fires.

December 29th.—The morning mild, and at four o'clock it commenced snowing. We took our way across a plain, thickly covered with snow, toward a range of hills in the southeast. The sky soon became so dark with snow, that little could be seen of the surrounding country; and we reached the summit of the hills in a heavy snow-storm. On the side we had approached, this had appeared to be only a ridge of low hills; and we were surprised to find ourselves on the summit of a bed of broken mountains, which, as far as the weather would permit us to see, declined rapidly to some low country ahead, presenting a dreary and savage character; and for a moment I looked around in doubt on the wild and inhospitable prospect, scarcely knowing what road to take which might conduct us to some place of shelter for the night.

Noticing among the hills the head of a grassy hollow, I determined to follow it, in the hope that it would conduct us to a stream. We followed a winding descent for several miles, the hollow gradually broadening into little meadows, and becoming the bed of a stream as we advanced; and toward night, we were agreeably surprised by the appearance of a willow grove, where we found a sheltered camp, with water and excellent and abundant grass. The grass, which was covered by the snow on the bottom, was long and green, and the face of the mountain had a more favorable character in its vegetation, being smoother, and covered with good bunch grass.

The snow was deep, and the night very cold. A broad trail had entered the valley from the right, and a short distance below the camp were the tracks where a considerable party of Indians had passed on horseback, who had turned out to the left, apparently with the view of crossing the mountains to the eastward. These Indians were probably Modocs.

December 30th.—After following the stream for a few hours in a southeasterly direction it entered a cañon where we could not follow; but determined not to leave the stream, we searched a passage below, where we could regain it, and entered a regular narrow valley. The water had now more the appearance of a flowing creek; several times we passed groves of willows, and we began to feel ourselves out of all difficulty. From our position it was reasonable to conclude that this stream would find its outlet in Mary's Lake, and conduct us into a better country.

We had descended rapidly, and here we found very little snow. On both sides the mountains showed often stupendous and curious looking rocks, which at several places so narrowed the valley, that scarcely a pass was left for the camp. It was a singular place to travel through—shut up in the earth, a sort of chasm, the little strip of grass under our feet, the rough walls of bare rock on either hand, and the narrow strip of sky above. The grass to-night was abundant, and we encamped in high spirits.

December 31*st.*—After an hour's ride this morning our hopes were once more destroyed. The valley opened out, and before us again lay one of the dry basins. After some search, we discovered a high water outlet, which brought us in a few miles, and by a descent of several hundred feet, into another long broad basin, in which we found the bed of a stream, and obtained sufficient water by cutting the ice. The grass on the bottoms was salt and unpalatable.

Here we concluded the year 1843, and our new year's eve was rather a gloomy one. The result of our journey began to be very uncertain ; the country was singularly unfavorable to travel ; the grasses being frequently of a very unwholesome character, and the hoofs of our animals were so worn and cut by the rocks, that many of them were lame, and could scarcely be got along.

New Year's Day, 1844.—We continued down the valley, between a dry-looking black ridge on the left, and a more snowy and high one on the right. Our road was bad, along the bottom being broken by gullies and impeded by sage, and sandy on the hills, where there is not a blade of grass, nor does any appear on the mountains. The soil in many places consists of a fine powdery sand, covered with a saline efflorescence ; and the general character of the country is desert. During the day we directed our course toward a black cape, at the foot of which a column of smoke indicated hot springs.

January 2*d.*—We were on the road early, the face of the country hidden by falling snow. We travelled along the bed of the stream, in some places dry, in others covered with ice ; the travelling being very bad, through deep fine sand, rendered tenacious by a mixture of clay. The weather cleared up a little at noon, and we reached the hot springs of which we had seen the vapor the day before. There was a large field of the usual salt grass here peculiar to such places. The country otherwise is a perfect barren, without a blade of grass, the only plants being some dwarf Fremontias. We passed the rocky cape, a jagged broken point, bare and torn.

The rocks are volcanic, and the hills here have a burnt appearance— cinders and coal occasionally appearing as at a blacksmith's forge. We crossed the large dry bed of a muddy lake in a southeasterly direction, and encamped at night without water and without grass, among sage bushes covered with snow. The heavy road made several mules give out to-day; and a horse, which had made the journey from the States successfully thus far, was left on the trail.

January 3d.—A fog, so dense that we could not see a hundred yards, covered the country, and the men that were sent out after the horses were bewildered and lost; and we were consequently detained at camp until late in the day.

Our situation had now become a serious one. We had reached and run over the position where, according to the best maps in my possession, we should have found Mary's Lake, or River. We were evidently on the verge of the desert which had been reported to us; and the appearance of the country was so forbidding, that I was afraid to enter it, and determined to bear away to the southward, keeping close along the mountains, in the full expectation of reaching the Buenaventura River.

This morning I put every man in the camp on foot—myself, of course, among the rest—and in this manner lightened, by distribution, the loads of the animals. We travelled seven or eight miles along the ridge bordering the valley, and encamped where there were a few bunches of grass on the bed of a hill torrent, without water. There were some large artemisias; but the principal plants are chenopodiaceous shrubs. The rock composing the mountains is here changed suddenly into white granite. The fog showed the tops of the hills at sunset, and stars enough for observations in the early evening, and then closed over us as before. Latitude by observation, 40° 48′ 15″.

January 4th.—The fog to-day was still more dense, and the people again were bewildered. We travelled a few miles around the western point of the ridge, and encamped where there were a few tufts of grass, but no water. Our animals now were in a very alarming state, and there was increased anxiety in the camp.

January 5th.—Same dense fog continued, and one of the mules died in camp this morning. I have had occasion to remark in such conditions as these, that animals which are about to die leave the band, and coming into the camp, lie down about the fires. We moved to a place where there was a little better grass, about two miles distant. Taplin, one of our best men, who had gone out on a scouting excursion, ascended a mountain near by, and to his great surprise emerged into a region of bright sunshine, in which the upper parts of the mountain were glowing, while below all was obscured in the darkest fog.

January 6th.—The fog continued the same, and with Mr. Preuss and Carson, I ascended the mountain to sketch the leading features of the country, as some indication of our future route, while Mr. Fitzpatrick explored the country below. In a very short distance we had ascended above the mist, but the view obtained was not very gratifying. The fog

PYRAMID LAKE.

had partially cleared off from below when we reached the summit; and in the southwest corner of a basin communicating with that in which we had encamped, we saw a lofty column of smoke, sixteen miles distant, indicating the presence of hot springs. There, also, appeared to be the outlet of those draining channels of the country; and as such places afforded always more or less grass, I determined to steer in that direction. The ridge we had ascended, appeared to be composed of fragments of white granite. We saw here traces of sheep and antelope.

Entering the neighboring valley, and crossing the bed of another lake, after a hard day's travel over ground of yielding mud and sand, we reached the springs, where we found an abundance of grass, which, though only tolerably good, made this place, with reference to the past, a refreshing and agreeable spot.

This is the most extraordinary locality of hot springs we had met during the journey. The basin of the largest one has a circumference of several hundred feet; but there is at one extremity a circular space of about fifteen feet in diameter, entirely occupied by the boiling water. It boils up at irregular intervals, and with much noise. The water is clear, and the spring deep; a pole about sixteen feet long was easily immersed in the centre, but we had no means of forming a good idea of the depth. It was surrounded on the margin with a border of *green* grass, and near the shore the temperature of the water was 206°. We had no means of ascertaining that of the centre, where the heat was greatest; but, by dispersing the water with a pole, the temperature at the margin was increased to 208°, and in the centre it was doubtless higher. By driving the pole toward the bottom, the water was made to boil up with increased force and noise. There are several other interesting places where water and smoke or gas escape, but they would require a long description. The water is impregnated with common salt, but not so much so as to render it unfit for general cooking; and a mixture of snow made it pleasant to drink.

In the immediate neighborhood the valley bottom is covered almost exclusively with chenopodiaceous shrubs, of greater luxuriance, and larger growth, than we have seen them in any preceding part of the journey.

I obtained this evening some astronomical observations.

Our situation now required caution. Including those which gave out from the injured condition of their feet, and those stolen by Indians, we had lost, since leaving the Dalles of the Columbia, fifteen animals; and of these, nine had been left in the last few days. I therefore determined, until we should reach a country of water and vegetation, to feel our way ahead, by having the line of route explored some fifteen or twenty miles in advance, and only to leave a present encampment when the succeeding one was known.

Taking with me Godey and Carson, I made to-day a thorough exploration of the neighboring valleys, and found in a ravine in the bordering mountains a good camping-place, where was water in springs, and a sufficient quantity of grass for a night. Overshading the springs were some trees of the sweet cotton-wood, which, after a long interval of absence, we saw again with pleasure, regarding them as harbingers of a better country. To us they were eloquent of green prairies and buffalo.

We found here a broad and plainly marked trail, on which there were tracks of horses, and we appeared to have regained one of the thoroughfares which pass by the watering-places of the country. On the western mountains of the valley, with which this of the boiling spring communicates, we remarked scattered cedars—probably an indication that we were on the borders of the timbered region extending to the Pacific. We reached the camp at sunset, after a day's ride of about forty miles. The horses we rode were in good order, being of some that were kept for emergencies, and rarely used.

Mr. Preuss had ascended one of the mountains, and occupied the day in sketching the country; and Mr. Fitzpatrick had found, a few miles distant, a hollow of excellent grass and pure water, to which the animals were driven, as I remained another day to give them an opportunity to recruit their strength. Indians appear to be everywhere prowling about like wild animals, and there is a fresh trail across the snow in the valley near.

Latitude of the boiling springs, 40° 39' 46".

On the 9th we crossed over to the cotton-wood camp. Among the shrubs on the hills were a few bushes of *ephedra occidentalis*, which we afterward found frequently along our road, and, as usual, the lowlands were occupied with artemisia. While the party proceeded to this place, Carson and myself reconnoitered the road in advance, and found another good encampment for the following day.

January 10th.—We continued our reconnoissance ahead, pursuing a south direction in the basin along the ridge; the camp following slowly after. On a large trail there is never any doubt of finding suitable places for encampments. We reached the end of the basin, where we found, in a hollow of the mountain which enclosed it, an abundance of good bunch grass. Leaving a signal for the party to encamp, we continued our way up the hollow, intending to see what lay beyond the mountain. The hollow was several miles long, forming a good pass, the snow deepening to about a foot as we neared the summit. Beyond, a defile between the mountains descended rapidly about two thousand feet; and, filling up all the lower space, was a sheet of green water, some twenty miles broad. It broke upon our eyes like the ocean.

The neighboring peaks rose high above us, and we ascended one of

SIERRA MOJADA

them to obtain a better view. The waves were curling in the breeze, and their dark-green color showed it to be a body of deep water. For a long time we sat enjoying the view, for we had become fatigued with mountains, and the free expanse of moving waves was very grateful. It was set like a gem in the mountains, which, from our position, seemed to enclose it almost entirely. At the western end it communicated with the line of basins we had left a few days since; and on the opposite side it swept a ridge of snowy mountains, the foot of the great Sierra. Its position at first inclined us to believe it Mary's Lake, but the rugged mountains were so entirely discordant with descriptions of its low rushy shores and open country, that we concluded it some unknown body of water, which it afterward proved to be.

On our road down, the next day, we saw herds of mountain sheep, and encamped on a little stream at the mouth of the defile, about a mile from the margin of the water, to which we hurried down immediately. The water is so slightly salt, that, at first, we thought it fresh, and would be pleasant to drink when no other could be had. The shore was rocky—a handsome beach, which reminded us of the sea. On some large *granite* boulders that were scattered about the shore, I remarked a coating of a calcareous substance, in some places a few inches, and in others a foot in thickness. Near our camp, the hills, which were of primitive rock, were also covered with this substance, which was in too great quantity on the mountains along the shore of the lake to have been deposited by water, and has the appearance of having been spread over the rocks in mass.*

Where we had halted, appeared to be a favorite camping-place for Indians.

January 13*th.*—We followed again a broad Indian trail along the shore of the lake to the southward. For a short space we had room enough in the bottom; but after travelling a short distance, the water swept the foot of precipitous mountains, the peaks of which are about three thousand feet above the lake. The trail wound along the base of these precipices, against which the water dashed below, by a way nearly impracticable for the howitzer. During a greater part of the morning the lake was nearly hid by a

---

* The label attached to a specimen of this rock was lost; but I append an analysis of that which, from memory, I judge to be the specimen.

Carbonate of lime	77.31
Carbonate of magnesia..	5.25
Oxide of iron...	1.60
Alumina..	1.05
Silica...	8.55
Organic matter, water, and loss	6.24
	100.00

snow-storm, and the waves broke on the narrow beach in a long line of foaming surf, five or six feet high.

The day was unpleasantly cold, the wind driving the snow sharp against our faces; and, having advanced only about twelve miles, we encamped in a bottom formed by a ravine, covered with good grass, which was fresh and green.

We did not get the howitzer into camp, but were obliged to leave it on the rocks until morning. We saw several flocks of sheep, but did not succeed in killing any. Ducks were riding on the waves, and several large fish were seen. The mountain-sides were crusted with the calcareous cement previously mentioned.

There were chenopodiaceous and other shrubs along the beach; and, at the foot of the rocks, an abundance of *Ephedra occidentalis*, whose dark-green color makes them evergreens among the shrubby growth of the lake. Toward evening the snow began to fall heavily, and the country had a wintry appearance.

The next morning the snow was rapidly melting under a warm sun. Part of the morning was occupied in bringing up the gun; and, making only nine miles, we encamped on the shore, opposite a very remarkable rock in the lake, which had attracted our attention for many miles. It rose, according to our estimate, six hundred feet above the water; and, from the point we viewed it, presented a pretty exact outline of the great pyramid of Cheops.

The accompanying view presents it as we saw it. Like other rocks along the shore, it seemed to be incrusted with calcareous cement. This striking feature suggested a name for the lake; and I called it Pyramid Lake; and though it may be deemed by some a fanciful resemblance, I can undertake to say that the future traveller will find a much more striking resemblance between this rock and the pyramids of Egypt, than there is between them and the object from which they take their name.

The elevation of this lake above the sea is four thousand eight hundred and ninety feet, being nearly seven hundred feet higher than the Great Salt Lake, from which it lies nearly west, and distant about eight degrees of longitude. The position and elevation of this lake make it an object of geographical interest. It is the nearest lake to the western rim, as the Great Salt Lake is to the eastern rim, of the Great Basin which lies between the base of the Rocky Mountains and the Sierra Nevada; and the extent and character of which, its whole circumference and contents, it is so desirable to know.

The last of the cattle which had been driven from the Dalles was killed here for food, and was still in good condition.

January 15*th.*—A few poor-looking Indians made their appearance this morning, and we succeeded in getting one into the camp. He was naked, with the exception of a tunic of hare-skins. He told us that there was a river at the end of the lake, but that he lived in the rocks near by. From the few words our people could understand, he spoke a dialect of the Snake language; but we were not able to understand enough to know whether the river ran in or out, or what was its course; consequently, there still remained a chance that this might be Mary's Lake.

Groves of large cotton-wood, which we could see at the mouth of the river, indicated that it was a stream of considerable size; and, at all events, we had the pleasure to know that now we were in a country where human beings could live. Accompanied by the Indian, we resumed our road, passing on the way several caves in the rock where there were baskets and seeds; but the people had disappeared. We saw also horse-tracks along the shore.

Early in the afternoon, when we were approaching the groves at the mouth of the river, three or four Indians met us on the trail. We had an explanatory conversation in signs, and then moved on together toward the village, which the chief said was encamped on the bottom.

Reaching the groves, we found the *inlet* of a large fresh water stream, and all at once were satisfied that it was neither Mary's River, nor the waters of the Sacramento, but that we had discovered a large interior lake, which the Indians informed us had no outlet. It is about thirty-five miles long; and by the mark of the water-line along the shores, the spring level is about twelve feet above its present waters. The chief commenced speaking in a loud voice as we approached; and parties of Indians armed with bows and arrows issued from the thickets.

We selected a strong place for our encampment, a grassy bottom, nearly enclosed by the river, and furnished with abundant firewood. The village, a collection of straw huts, was a few hundred yards higher up. An Indian brought in a large fish to trade, which we had the inexpressible satisfaction to find was a salmon-trout; we gathered round him eagerly. The Indians were amused with our delight, and immediately brought in numbers; so that the camp was soon stocked. Their flavor was excellent—superior, in fact, to that of any fish I have ever known. They were of extraordinary size—about as large as the Columbia River salmon—generally from two to four feet in length. From the information of Mr. Walker, who passed among some lakes lying more to the eastward, this fish is common to the streams of the inland lakes. He subsequently informed me that he had obtained them weighing six pounds when cleaned and the head taken off; which corresponds very well with the size of those obtained at this place. They doubtless formed the subsistence of these people, who hold the fishery in exclusive possession.

I remarked that one of them gave a fish to the Indian we had first seen, which he carried off to his family. To them it was probably a feast; being of the Digger tribe, and having no share in the fishery, living generally on seeds and roots. Although this was a time of the year when the fish have not yet become fat, they were excellent, and we could only imagine what they are at the proper season. These Indians were very fat, and appeared to live an easy and happy life. They crowded into the camp more than was consistent with our safety, retaining always their arms; and, as they made some unsatisfactory demonstrations, they were given to understand that they would not be permitted to come armed into the camp; and strong guards were kept with the horses. Strict vigilance was maintained among the people, and one third at a time were kept on guard during the night. There is no reason to doubt that these dispositions, uniformly preserved, conducted our party securely through Indians famed for treachery.

In the meantime, such a salmon-trout feast as is seldom seen was going on in our camp; and every variety of manner in which fish could be prepared—boiled, fried, and roasted in the ashes—was put into requisition; and every few minutes an Indian would be seen running off to spear a fresh one.

Whether these Indians had seen whites before, we could not be certain; but they were evidently in communication with others who had, as one of them had some brass buttons, and we noticed several other articles of civilized manufacture. We could obtain from them but little information respecting the country. They made on the ground a drawing of the river, which they represented as issuing from another lake in the mountains three or four days distant, in a direction a little west of south; beyond which, they drew a mountain; and further still, two rivers; on one of which they told us that people like ourselves travelled. Whether they alluded to the settlements on the Sacramento, or to a party from the United States which had crossed the Sierra about three degrees to the southward, a few years before, I am unable to determine.

I tried unsuccessfully to prevail on some of them to guide us for a few days on the road, but they only looked at each other and laughed.

The latitude of our encampment, which may be considered the mouth of the inlet, is 39° 51′ 13″ by our observations.

January 16th.—This morning we continued our journey along this beautiful stream, which we naturally called the Salmon Trout River. Large trails led up on either side; the stream was handsomely timbered with large cotton-woods; and the waters were very clear and pure. We were travelling along the mountains of the great Sierra, which rose on our right, covered with snow; but below, the temperature was mild and pleasant. We saw a number of dams which the Indians had constructed to catch fish. After having made about eighteen miles, we encamped under some large cotton-woods on the river bottom, where there was tolerably good grass.

January 17*th.*—This morning we left the river, which here issues from the mountains on the west. With every stream I now expected to see the great Buenaventura; and Carson hurried eagerly to search, on everyone we reached, for beaver cuttings, which he always maintained we should find only on waters that ran to the Pacific; and the absence of such signs was to him a sure indication that the water had no outlet from the great basin.

We followed the Indian trail through a tolerably level country, with small sage bushes, which brought us, after twenty miles journey, to another large stream timbered with cotton-wood, and flowing also out of the mountains, but running more directly to the eastward.

On the way we surprised a family of Indians in the hills; but the man ran up the mountain with rapidity; and the woman was so terrified, and kept up such a continued screaming, that we could do nothing with her, and were obliged to let her go.

January 18*th.*—There were Indian lodges and fish-dams on the stream. There were no beaver cuttings on the river; but below, it turned round to the right; and hoping that it would prove a branch of the Buenaventura, we followed it down for about three hours, and encamped.

I rode out with Mr. Fitzpatrick and Carson to reconnoitre the country, which had evidently been alarmed by the news of our appearance. This stream joined with the open valley of another to the eastward; but which way the main water ran, it was impossible to tell. Columns of smoke rose over the country at scattered intervals—signals by which the Indians here, as elsewhere, communicate to each other that enemies are in the country. It is a signal of ancient and very universal application among barbarians.

Examining into the condition of the animals when I returned into the camp, I found their feet so much cut up by the rocks, and so many of them lame, that it was evidently impossible that they could cross the country to the Rocky Mountains. Every piece of iron that could be used for the purpose had been converted into nails, and we could make no further use of the shoes we had remaining. I therefore determined to abandon my eastern course, and to cross the Sierra Nevada into the Valley of the Sacramento, wherever a practical pass could be found. My decision was heard with joy by the people, and diffused new life throughout the camp.

Latitude by observation 39° 24′ 16″.

January 19*th.*—A great number of smokes are still visible this morning, attesting at once the alarm which our appearance had spread among these people, and their ignorance of us. If they knew the whites, they would understand that their only object in coming among them was to trade, which required peace and friendship; but they have nothing to trade—consequently nothing to attract the white man: hence their fear and flight.

At daybreak we had a heavy snow; but sat out, and, returning up the stream, went out of our way in a circuit over a little mountain, and encamped on the same stream a few miles above, in latitude 39° 19′ 21″ by observation.

January 20th.—To-day we continued up the stream, and encamped on it close to the mountains. The freshly-fallen snow was covered with the tracks of Indians, who had descended from the upper waters, probably called down by the smokes in the plain.

We ascended a peak of the range, which commanded a view of the stream behind the first ridge, where it was winding its course through a somewhat open valley, and I sometimes regret that I did not make the trial to cross here; but while we had fair weather below, the mountains were darkened with falling snow, and, feeling unwilling to encounter them, we turned away again to the southward. In that direction we travelled the next day over a tolerably level country, having always the high mountains on the west. There was but little snow or rock on the ground; and, after having travelled twenty-four miles, we encamped again on another large stream, running off to the northward and eastward, to meet that we had left. It ran through broad bottoms having a fine meadow-land appearance.

Latitude 39° 01′ 53″.

January 22d.—We travelled up the stream for about fourteen miles to the foot of the mountains, from which one branch issued in the southwest, the other flowing from south-southeast along their base. Leaving the camp below, we ascended the range through which the first stream passed, in a cañon; on the western side was a circular valley, about fifteen miles long, through which the stream wound its way, issuing from a gorge in the main mountain, which rose abruptly beyond.

The valley looked yellow with faded grass; and the trail we had followed was visible, making toward the gorge, and this was evidently a pass; but again, while all was bright sunshine on the ridge, and on the valley where we were, the snow was falling heavily in the mountains. I determined to go still to the southward, and encamped on the stream near the forks; the animals being fatigued, and the grass tolerably good.

The rock of the ridge we had ascended is a compact lava, assuming a granitic appearance and structure, and containing, in some places, small nodules of obsidian. So far as composition and aspect are concerned, the rock in other parts of the ridge appears to be granite ; but it is probable that this is only a compact form of lava of recent origin.

By observation, the elevation of the encampment was five thousand and twenty feet ; and the latitude 38° 49′ 54″.

January 23d.—We moved along the course of the other branch toward the southeast, the country affording a fine road ; and, passing some slight dividing grounds, descended toward the valley of another stream. There was a somewhat rough-looking mountain ahead, which it appeared to issue from, or to enter—we could not tell which ; and as the course of the valley and the inclination of the ground had a favorable direction, we were sanguine to find here a branch of the Buenaventura ; but were again disappointed, finding it an inland water, on which we encamped after a day's journey of twenty-four miles.

It was evident that, from the time we descended into the plain at Summer Lake, we had been flanking the great range of mountains which divided the Great Basin from the waters of the Pacific ; and that the continued succession, and almost connection, of lakes and rivers which we encountered, were the drainings of that range. Its rains, springs, and snows, would sufficiently account for these lakes and streams, numerous as they were.

January 24th.—A man was discovered running toward the camp as we were about to start this morning, who proved to be an Indian of rather advanced age—a sort of forlorn hope, who seemed to have been worked up into the resolution of visiting the strangers who were passing through the country. He seized the hand of the first man he met as he came up, out of breath, and held on as if to assure himself of protection. He brought with him in a little skin bag a few pounds of the seeds of a pine-tree, which to-day we saw for the first time, and which Dr. Torrey has described as a new species, under the name of *pinus monophyllus;* in popular language, it might be called the *nut pine.* We purchased them all from him. The nut is oily, of very agreeable flavor, and must be very nutritious, as it constitutes the principal subsistence of the tribes among which we were now travelling. By a present of scarlet cloth, and other striking articles, we prevailed upon this man to be our guide for two days' journey. As clearly as possible by signs, we made him understand our object ; and he engaged to conduct us in sight of a good pass which he knew.

Here we ceased to hear the Shoshonee language ; that of this man being perfectly unintelligible. Several Indians, who had been waiting to see what reception he would meet with, now came into camp ; and, accompanied by the new-comers, we resumed our journey.

The road led us up the creek, which here becomes a rather rapid mountain stream fifty feet wide, between dark-looking hills without snow ; but immediately beyond them rose snowy mountains on either side, timbered principally with the nut pine. On the lower grounds, the general height of this tree is twelve to twenty feet, and eight inches the greatest diameter; it is rather branching, and has a peculiar and singular but pleasant odor. We followed the river for only a short distance along a rocky trail, and crossed it at a dam which the Indians made us comprehend had been built to catch salmon trout. The snow and ice were heaped up against it three or four feet deep entirely across the stream.

Leaving here the stream, which runs through impassable cañons, we continued our road over a very broken country, passing through a low gap between the snowy mountains. The rock which occurs immediately in the pass has the appearance of impure sandstone, containing scales of black mica. This may be only a stratified lava; on issuing from the gap, the compact lava, and other volcanic products usual in the country, again occurred.

We descended from the gap into a wide valley, or rather basin, and encamped on a small tributary to the last stream, on which there was very good grass. It was covered with such thick ice, that it required some labor with pick-axes to make holes for the animals to drink. The banks are lightly wooded with willow, and on the upper bottoms are sage and Fremontia, with *Ephedra occidentalis*, which begins to occur more frequently.

The day has been a summer one, warm and pleasant; no snow on the trail, which, as we are all on foot, makes travelling more agreeable. The hunters went into the neighboring mountains, but found no game. We have five Indians in camp to-night.

January 25th.—The morning was cold and bright, and as the sun rose the day became beautiful. A party of twelve Indians came down from the mountains to trade pine-nuts, of which each one carried a little bag. These seemed now to be the staple of the country; and whenever we met an Indian, his friendly salutation consisted in offering a few nuts to eat and to trade; their only arms were bows and flint-pointed arrows.

It appeared that in almost all the valleys the neighboring bands were at war with each other; and we had some difficulty in prevailing on our guides to accompany us on this day's journey, being at war with the people on the other side of a large snowy mountain which lay before us.

The general level of the country appeared to be getting higher, and we were gradually entering the heart of the mountains. Accompanied by all the Indians, we ascended a long ridge and reached a pure spring at the edge of the timber, where the Indians had waylaid and killed an antelope, and where the greater part of them left us. Our pacific conduct had quieted their alarms, and though at war among each other yet all confided in us, thanks to the combined effects of power and kindness—for our arms inspired respect, and our little presents and good treatment conciliated their confidence.   Here we suddenly entered snow six inches deep, and the ground was a little rocky with volcanic fragments, the mountain appearing to be composed of such rock.   The timber consists principally of nut-pines (*Pinus monophyllus*), which here are of a larger size—twelve to fifteen inches in diameter ; heaps of cones lying on the ground where the Indians had gathered the seeds.

The snow deepened gradually as we advanced.   Our guides wore out their moccasons, and putting one of them on a horse, we enjoyed the unusual sight of an Indian who could not ride.   He could not even guide the animal, and appeared to have no knowledge of horses.   The snow was three or four feet deep on the summit of the pass; and from this point the guide pointed out our future road, declining to go any farther.

Below us was a little valley, and beyond this the mountains rose higher still, one ridge above another, presenting a rude and rocky outline. We descended rapidly to the valley ; the snow impeded us but little ; yet it was dark when we reached the foot of the mountain.

The day had been so warm that our moccasons were wet with melting snow ; but here, as soon as the sun begins to decline, the air gets suddenly cold, and we had great difficulty to keep our feet from freezing—our moccasons being frozen perfectly stiff.

After a hard day's march of twenty-seven miles we reached the river, some time after dark, and found the snow about a foot deep on the bottom —the river being entirely frozen over.   We found a comfortable camp where there were dry willows abundant, and we soon had blazing fires.

A little brandy, which I husbanded with great care, remained ; and I do not know any medicine more salutary, or any drink (except coffee) more agreeable, than this in a cold night after a hard day's march.   Mr. Preuss questioned whether the famed nectar even possessed so exquisite a flavor.   All felt it to be a reviving cordial.

The next morning, when the sun had not yet risen over the mountains, the thermometer was two degrees below zero ; but the sky was bright and pure, and the weather changed rapidly into a pleasant day of summer.   I remained encamped, in order to examine the country and allow the animals a day of rest, the grass being good and abundant under the snow.

The river is fifty to eighty feet wide, with a lively current and very clear water.   It forked a little above our camp, one of its branches coming directly from the south.   At its head appeared to be a handsome pass ; and from the neighboring heights we could see, beyond, a comparatively low and open country, which was supposed to form the valley of the Buenaventura.   The other branch issued from a nearer pass, in a direction S.

75° W., forking at the foot of the mountain, and receiving part of its waters from a little lake.

I was in advance of the camp when our last guides had left us ; but, so far as could be understood, this was the pass which they had indicated, and, in company with Carson, to-day I set out to explore it. Entering the range we continued in a northwesterly direction up the valley, which here bent to the right. It was a pretty, open bottom, locked between lofty mountains, which supplied frequent streams as we advanced. On the lower part they were covered with nut-pine trees, and above with masses of pine, which we easily recognized from the darker color of the foliage. From the fresh trails which occurred frequently during the morning, deer appeared to be remarkably numerous in the mountain.

We had now entirely left the desert country, and were on the verge of a region which, extending westward to the shores of the Pacific, abounds in large game, and is covered with a singular luxuriance of vegetable life.

The little stream grew rapidly smaller, and in about twelve miles we had reached its head, the last water coming immediately out of the mountain on the right ; and this spot was selected for our next encampment. The grass showed well in sunny places ; but in colder situations the snow was deep, and began to occur in banks, through which the horses found some difficulty in breaking a way.

To the left the open valley continued in a southwesterly direction, with a scarcely perceptible ascent, forming a beautiful pass ; the exploration of which we deferred until the next day, and returned to the camp.

To-day an Indian passed through the valley on his way into the mountains, where he showed us was his lodge. We comprehended nothing of his language ; and, though he appeared to have no fear, passing along in full view of the camp, he was indisposed to hold any communication with us, but showed the way he was going, and pointed for us to go on our road.

By observation, the latitude of this encampment was 38° 18' 01", and the elevation above the sea six thousand three hundred and ten feet.

January 27th.—Leaving the camp to follow slowly, with directions to Carson to encamp at the place agreed on, Mr. Fitzpatrick and myself continued the reconnoissance. Arriving at the head of the stream, we began to enter the pass—passing occasionally through open groves of large pine-trees, on the warm side of the defile, where the snow had melted away, occasionally exposing a large Indian trail. Continuing along a narrow meadow, we reached in a few miles the gate of the pass, where there was a narrow strip of prairie, about fifty yards wide, between walls of granite rock. On either side rose the mountains, forming on the left a rugged mass, or nucleus, wholly covered with deep snow, presenting a glittering and icy surface. At the time, we supposed this to be the point into which they were gathered between the two great rivers, and from which the waters flowed off to the bay. This was the icy and cold side of the pass, and the rays of the sun hardly touched the snow. On the left, the mountains rose into peaks; but they were lower and secondary, and the country had a somewhat more open and lighter character. On the right were several hot springs, which appeared remarkable in such a place. In going through, we felt impressed by the majesty of the mountain, along the huge wall of which we were riding. Here there was no snow; but immediately beyond was a deep bank, through which we dragged our horses with considerable effort.

We then immediately struck upon a stream, which gathered itself rapidly, and descended quickly; and the valley did not preserve the open character of the other side, appearing below to form a cañon. We therefore climbed one of the peaks on the right, leaving our horses below; but we were so much shut up, that we did not obtain an extensive view, and what we saw was not very satisfactory, and awakened considerable doubt. The valley of the stream pursued a northwesterly direction, appearing below to turn sharply to the right, beyond which further view was cut off.

It was, nevertheless, resolved to continue our road the next day down this valley, which we trusted still would prove that of the middle stream between the two great rivers. Toward the summit of this peak the fields of snow were four or five feet deep on the northern side; and we saw several large hares, which had on their winter color, being white as the snow around them.

The winter day is short in the mountains, the sun having but a small space of sky to travel over in the visible part above our horizon; and the moment his rays are gone the air is keenly cold. The interest of our work had detained us long, and it was after nightfall when we reached the camp.

CHAPTER IX.

Men exhausted by Snow and Cold—The Sierra Nevada—A dreary Outlook—Cutting Our Way through Snow—Three Degrees below Zero top of Sierra Nevada—*Menu:* Pea-Soup, Mule and Dog—An Unlooked-for Icy Bath—Mule Soup—Severe Suffering—Mr. Preuss Lost and Found—Hearty Reception by Captain Sutter—Sutter's Fort and Farm.

January 28th.—To-day we went through the pass with all the camp, and, after a hard day's journey of twelve miles, encamped on a high point where the snow had been blown off, and the exposed grass afforded a scanty pasture for the animals. Snow and broken country together made our travelling difficult; we were often compelled to make large circuits, and ascend the highest and most exposed ridges, in order to avoid snow, which in other places was banked up to a great depth.

During the day a few Indians were seen circling around us on snow-shoes, and skimming along like birds; but we could not bring them within speaking distance.

Godey, who was a little distance from the camp, had sat down to tie his moccasins, when he heard a low whistle near, and looking up, saw two Indians half-hiding behind a rock about forty yards distant; they would not allow him to approach, but breaking into a laugh, skimmed off over the snow, seeming to have no idea of the power of fire-arms, and thinking themselves perfectly safe when beyond arm's length.

To-night we did not succeed in getting the howitzer into camp. This was the most laborious day we had yet passed through; the steep ascents and deep snow exhausting both men and animals. Our single chronometer had stopped during the day, and its error in time occasioned the loss of an eclipse of a satellite this evening. It had not preserved the rate with which we started from the Dalles, and this will account for the absence of longitudes along this interval of our journey.

January 29th.—From this height we could see, at a considerable distance below, yellow spots in the valley, which indicated that there was not much snow. One of these places we expected to reach to-night; and some time being required to bring up the gun, I went ahead with Mr. Fitzpatrick and a few men, leaving the camp to follow in charge of Mr. Preuss.

We followed a trail down a hollow where the Indians had descended, the snow being so deep that we never came near the ground; but this only made our descent the easier, and when we reached a little affluent to the river at the bottom, we suddenly found ourselves in presence of eight or ten Indians. They seemed to be watching our motions, and like the others, at first were indisposed to let us approach, ranging themselves like birds on a fallen log on the hill-side above our heads, where, being out of reach, they thought themselves safe. Our friendly demeanor reconciled them, and when we got near enough, they immediately stretched out to us handfuls of pine-nuts, which seemed an exercise of hospitality. We made them a few presents, and telling us that their village was a few miles below, they went on to let their people know what we were.

The principal stream still running through an impracticable cañon, we ascended a very steep hill, which proved afterward the last and fatal obstacle to our little howitzer, which was finally abandoned at this place. We passed through a small meadow a few miles below, crossing the river, which depth, swift current, and rock made it difficult to ford; and after a few more miles of very difficult trail, issued into a larger prairie bottom, at the farther end of which we encamped, in a position rendered strong by rocks and trees. The lower parts of the mountain were covered with the nut-pine.

Several Indians appeared on the hill-side, reconnoitring the camp, and were induced to come in; others came in during the afternoon; and in the evening we held a council. They immediately made it clear that the water on which we were also belonged to the Great Basin, in the edge of which we had been since December 17th; and it became evident that we had still the great ridge on the left to cross before we could reach the Pacific waters.

We explained to the Indians that we were endeavoring to find a passage across the mountains into the country of the whites, whom we were going to see; and told them that we wished them to bring us a guide, to whom we would give presents of scarlet cloth and other articles, which were shown to them. They looked at the reward we offered, and conferred with each other, but pointed to the snow on the mountain, and drew their hands across their necks, and raised them above their heads, to show the depth; and signified that it was impossible for us to get through. They made signs that we must go to the southward, over a pass through a lower range, which they pointed out; there, they said, at the end of one day's travel, we would find people who lived near a pass in the great mountain; and to that point they engaged to furnish us a guide. They appeared to have a confused idea, from report, of whites who lived on the other side of the mountain; and once, they told us, about two years ago, a party of twelve men, like ourselves, had ascended their river, and crossed to the other waters.   They pointed out to us where they had crossed ; but then, they said, it was summer time ; now it would be impossible.

I believe that this was a party led by Mr. Chiles, one of the only two men whom I know to have passed through the California mountains from the interior of the Basin—Walker being the other ; and both were engaged upward of twenty days, in the summer time, in getting over. Chiles's destination was the Bay of San Francisco, to which he descended by the Stanislaus River ; and Walker subsequently informed me that, like myself, descending to the southward on a more eastern line, day after day he was searching for the Buenaventura, thinking that he had found it with every new stream, until, like me, he abandoned all idea of its existence, and turning abruptly to the right, crossed the great chain.   These were both Western men, animated with the spirit of exploratory enterprise which characterizes that people.

The Indians brought in during the evening an abundant supply of pine-nuts, which we traded from them.   When roasted, their pleasant flavor made them an agreeable addition to our now scanty store of provisions, which were reduced to a very low ebb.   Our principal stock was in peas, which it is not necessary to say contain scarcely any nutriment.   We had still a little flour left, some coffee, and a quantity of sugar, which I reserved as a defence against starvation.

The Indians informed us that at certain seasons they have fish in their waters, which we supposed to be salmon-trout ; for the remainder of the year they live upon the pine-nuts, which form their great winter subsistence—a portion being always at hand, shut up in the natural storehouse of the cones.   At present they were presented to us as a whole people living upon this simple vegetable.

The other division of the party did not come in to-night, but encamped in the upper meadow, and arrived the next morning.   They had not succeeded in getting the howitzer beyond the place mentioned, and where it had been left by Mr. Preuss in obedience to my orders ; and, in anticipation of the snow-banks and snow-fields still ahead, foreseeing the inevitable detention to which it would subject us, I reluctantly determined to leave it there for the time.   It was of the kind invented by the French for the mountain part of their war in Algiers ; and the distance it had come with us, proved how well it was adapted to its purpose.   We left it, to the great sorrow of the whole party, who were grieved to part with a companion which had made the whole distance from St. Louis, and commanded respect for us on some critical occasions, and which might be needed for the same purpose again.

January 30th.—Our guide, who was a young man, joined us this

TALK WITH INDIANS OF EASTERN SLOPE SIERRA NEVADA.

morning; and leaving our encampment late in the day, we descended the river, which immediately opened out into a broad valley, furnishing good travelling ground. In a short distance we passed the village, a collection of straw huts; and a few miles below the guide pointed out the place where the whites had been encamped before they entered the mountain.

With our late start we made but ten miles, and encamped on the low river bottom, where there was no snow, but a great deal of ice; and we cut piles of long grass to lay under our blankets, and fires were made of large dry willows, groves of which wooded the stream. The river took here a northeasterly direction, and through a spur from the mountains on the left was the gap where we were to pass the next day.

January 31*st.*—We took our way over a gently rising ground, the dividing ridge being tolerably low; and travelling easily along a broad trail, in twelve or fourteen miles reached the upper part of the pass, when it began to snow heavily, with very cold weather. The Indians had only the usual scanty covering, and appeared to suffer greatly from the cold. All left us except our guide. Half-hidden by the storm, the mountains looked dreary; and, as night began to approach, the guide showed great reluctance to go forward. I placed him between two rifles, for the way began to be difficult. Travelling a little farther, we struck a ravine, which the Indian said would conduct us to the river; and as the poor fellow suffered greatly, shivering in the snow which fell upon his naked skin, I would not detain him any longer; and he ran off to the mountain, where, he said, there was a hut near by. He had kept the blue and scarlet cloth I had given him tightly rolled up, preferring rather to endure the cold than to get them wet.

In the course of the afternoon, one of the men had a foot frost-bitten; and about dark we had the satisfaction of reaching the bottoms of a stream timbered with large trees, among which we found a sheltered camp, with an abundance of such grass as the season afforded for the animals. We saw before us, in descending from the pass, a great continuous range, along which stretched the valley of the river; the lower parts steep, and dark with pines, while, above, it was hidden in clouds of snow. This we felt instantly satisfied was the central ridge of the Sierra Nevada, the great California Mountain, which only now intervened between us and the waters of the bay. We had made a forced march of twenty-six miles, and three mules had given out on the road. Up to this point, with the exception of two stolen by Indians, we had lost none of the horses which had been brought from the Columbia River, and a number of these were still strong and in tolerably good order. We had now sixty-seven animals in the band.

We had scarcely lighted our fires, when the camp was crowded with nearly naked Indians; some of them were furnished with long nets in addition to bows, and appeared to have been out on the sage hills to hunt rabbits.   These nets were, perhaps, thirty to forty feet long, kept upright in the ground by slight sticks at intervals, and were made from a kind of wild hemp, very much resembling, in manufacture, those common among the Indians of the Sacramento Valley.   They came among us without any fear, and scattered themselves about the fires, mainly occupied in gratifying their astonishment.   I was struck by the singular appearance of a row of about a dozen, who were sitting on their haunches perched on a log near one of the fires, with their quick sharp eyes following every motion.

We gathered together a few of the most intelligent of the Indians, and held this evening an interesting council.   I explained to them my intentions.   I told them that we had come from a very far country, having been travelling now nearly a year, and that we were desirous simply to go across the mountain into the country of the other whites.   There were two who appeared particularly intelligent—one, a somewhat old man.   He told me that, before the snows fell, it was six sleeps to the place where the whites lived, but that now it was impossible to cross the mountain on account of the deep snow; and showing us, as the others had done, that it was over our heads, he urged us strongly to follow the course of the river, which he said would conduct us to a lake in which there were many large fish. There, he said, were many people; there was no snow on the ground, and we might remain there until the spring.

From their descriptions we were enabled to judge that we had encamped on the upper water of the Salmon Trout River.   It is hardly necessary to say that our communication was only by signs, as we understood nothing of their language; but they spoke, notwithstanding, rapidly and vehemently, explaining what they considered the folly of our intentions, and urging us to go down to the lake.   *Táh-ve*, a word signifying snow, we very soon learned to know, from its frequent repetition.   I told him that the men and the horses were strong, and that we would break a road through the snow; and spreading before him our bales of scarlet cloth, and trinkets, showed him what we would give for a guide.   It was neces sary to obtain one, if possible; for I had determined here to attempt the passage of the mountain.

Pulling a bunch of grass from the ground, after a short discussion among themselves, the old man made us comprehend that if we could break through the snow, at the end of three days we would come down upon grass, which he showed us would be about six inches high, and where the ground was entirely free.   So far, he said, he had been in hunting for elk; but beyond that (and he closed his eyes) he had seen nothing; but there was one among them who had been to the whites, and, going out of the lodge, he returned with a young man of very intelligent appearance.   Here, said he, is a young man who has seen the whites with his own eyes; and he swore, first by the sky, and then by the ground, that what he said was true. With a large present of goods we prevailed upon this young man to be our guide, and he acquired among us the name Mélo—a word signifying friend, which they used very frequently. He was thinly clad, and nearly barefoot; his moccasins being about worn out. We gave him skins to make a new pair, and to enable him to perform his undertaking to us. The Indians remained in the camp during the night, and we kept the guide and two others to sleep in the lodge with us—Carson lying across the door, and having made them comprehend the use of our fire-arms.

The snow, which had intermitted in the evening, commenced falling again in the course of the night, and it snowed steadily all day. In the morning I acquainted the men with my decision, and explained to them that necessity required us to make a great effort to clear the mountains. I reminded them of the beautiful Valley of the Sacramento, with which they were familiar from the descriptions of Carson, who had been there some fifteen years ago, and who, in our late privations, had delighted us in speaking of its rich pastures and abounding game, and drew a vivid contrast between its summer climate, less than a hundred miles distant, and the falling snow around us. I informed them (and long experience had given them confidence in my observations and good instruments) that almost directly west, and only about seventy miles distant, was the great farming establishment of Captain Sutter—a gentleman who had formerly lived in Missouri, and, emigrating to this country, had become the possessor of a principality. I assured them that, from the heights of the mountain before us, we should doubtless see the Valley of the Sacramento River, and with one effort place ourselves again in the midst of plenty.

The people received this decision with the cheerful obedience which had always characterized them; and the day was immediately devoted to the preparations necessary to enable us to carry it into effect. Leggings, moccasins, clothing—all were put into the best state to resist the cold. Our guide was not neglected. Extremity of suffering might make him desert; we therefore did the best we could for him. Leggings, moccasins, some articles of clothing, and a large green blanket, in addition to the blue and scarlet cloth, were lavished upon him, and to his great and evident contentment. He arrayed himself in all his colors; and, clad in green, blue, and scarlet, he made a gay-looking Indian; and, with his various presents, was probably richer and better clothed than any of his tribe had ever been before.

I have already said that our provisions were very low; we had neither tallow nor grease of any kind remaining, and the want of salt became one of our greatest privations.   The poor dog which had been found in the Bear River Valley, and which had been a *compagnon de voyage* ever since, had now become fat, and the mess to which it belonged requested permission to kill it.   Leave was granted.   Spread out on the snow, the meat looked very good ; and it made a strengthening meal for the greater part of the camp.   Indians brought in two or three rabbits during the day, which were purchased from them.

The river was forty to seventy feet wide, and now entirely frozen over. It was wooded with large cotton-wood, willow, and *grains de bœuf*.   By observation, the latitude of this encampment was 38° 37′ 18″.

February 2d.—It had ceased snowing, and this morning the lower air was clear and frosty ; and six or seven thousand feet above, the peaks of the Sierra now and then appeared among the rolling clouds, which were rapidly dispersing before the sun.   Our Indian shook his head as he pointed to the icy pinnacles shooting high up into the sky, and seeming almost immediately above us.   Crossing the river on the ice, and leaving it immediately, we commenced the ascent of the mountain along the valley of a tributary stream.   The people were unusually silent ; for every man knew that our enterprise was hazardous, and the issue doubtful.

The snow deepened rapidly, and it soon became necessary to break a road.   For this service, a party of ten was formed, mounted on the strongest horses ; each man in succession opening the road on foot, or on horseback, until himself and his horse became fatigued, when he stepped aside ; and, the remaining number passing ahead, he took his station in the rear. Leaving this stream, and pursuing a very direct course, we passed over an intervening ridge to the river we had left.

On the way we passed two low huts entirely covered with snow, which might very easily have escaped observation.   A family was living in each ; and the only trail I saw in the neighborhood was from the door hole to a nut-pine tree near, which supplied them with food and fuel.   We found two similar huts on the creek where we next arrived ; and, travelling a little higher up, encamped on its banks in about four feet depth of snow. Carson found near, an open hill-side, where the wind and the sun had melted the snow, leaving exposed sufficient bunch-grass for the animals to-night.

The nut-pines were now giving way to heavy timber, and there were some immense pines on the bottom, around the roots of which the sun had melted away the snow ; and here we made our camps and built huge fires. To-day we had travelled sixteen miles, and our elevation above the sea was six thousand seven hundred and sixty feet.

February 3d.—Turning our faces directly toward the main chain, we ascended an open hollow along a small tributary to the river, which, according to the Indians, issues from a mountain to the south. The snow was so deep in the hollow, that we were obliged to travel along the steep hill-sides, and over spurs, where wind and sun had in places lessened the snow, and where the grass, which appeared to be in good quality along the sides of the mountains, was exposed.

We opened our road in the same way as yesterday, but made only seven miles ; and encamped by some springs at the foot of a high and steep hill, by which the hollow ascended to another basin in the mountain. The little stream below was entirely buried in snow. The springs were shaded by the boughs of a lofty cedar, which here made its first appearance ; the usual height was one hundred and twenty to one hundred and thirty feet, and one that was measured near by was six feet in diameter.

There being no grass exposed here, the horses were sent back to that which we had seen a few miles below. We occupied the remainder of the day in beating down a road to the foot of the hill, a mile or two distant ; the snow being beaten down when moist, in the warm part of the day, and then hard frozen at night, made a foundation that would bear the weight of the animals the next morning. During the day several Indians joined us on snow-shoes. These were made of a circular hoop, about a foot in diameter, the interior space being filled with an open network of bark.

February 4th.—I went ahead early with two or three men, each with a led horse, to break the road. We were obliged to abandon the hollow entirely, and work along the mountain-side, which was very steep, and the snow covered with an icy crust. We cut a footing as we advanced, and trampled a road through for the animals ; but occasionally one plunged outside the trail, and slided along the field to the bottom, a hundred yards below.

Late in the day we reached another bench in the hollow, where in summer the stream passed over a small precipice. Here was a short distance of dividing ground between the two ridges, and beyond an open basin, some ten miles across, whose bottom presented a field of snow. At the further or western side rose the middle crest of the mountain, a dark-looking ridge of volcanic rock.

The summit line presented a range of naked peaks, apparently destitute of snow and vegetation ; but below, the face of the whole country was covered with timber of extraordinary size. The view given of this ridge is from a camp on the western side of the basin.

Toward a pass which the guide indicated here, we attempted in the afternoon to force a road ; but after a laborious plunging through two or three hundred yards, our best horses gave out, entirely refusing to make any further effort ; and, for the time, we were brought to a stand. The guide informed us that we were entering the deep snow, and here began

the difficulties of the mountain ; and to him, and almost to all, our enterprise seemed hopeless.   I returned a short distance back, to the break in
the hollow, where I met Mr. Fitzpatrick.

The camp had been all the day occupied in endeavoring to ascend the
hill, but only the best horses had succeeded.   The animals, generally, not
having sufficient strength to bring themselves up without the packs ; and
all the line of road between this and the springs was strewed with camp
stores and equipage, and horses floundering in snow.

I therefore immediately encamped on the ground with my own mess,
which was in advance, and directed Mr. Fitzpatrick to encamp at the
springs, and send all the animals in charge of Tabeau, with a strong guard,
back to the place where they had been pastured the night before.   Here
was a small spot of level ground, protected on one side by the mountain,
and on the other sheltered by a little ridge of rock.   It was an open grove
of pines, which assimilated in size to the grandeur of the mountain, being
frequently six feet in diameter.

To-night we had no shelter, but we made a large fire around the trunk
of one of the huge pines ; and covering the snow with small boughs, on
which we spread our blankets, soon made ourselves comfortable.   The
night was very bright and clear, and though the thermometer was only
down to 10°, a strong wind which sprang up at sundown, made it intensely
cold ; and this was one of the bitterest nights during the journey.

Two Indians joined our party here ; and one of them, an old man, immediately began to harangue us, saying that ourselves and animals would
perish in the snow, and that if we would go back, he would show us another and a better way across the mountain.   He spoke in a very loud
voice, and there was a singular repetition of phrases and arrangement of
words which rendered his speech striking and not unmusical.

We had now begun to understand some words, and, with the aid of
signs, easily comprehended the old man's simple ideas.   " Rock upon
rock—rock upon rock—snow upon snow—snow upon snow," said he ;
" even if you get over the snow, you will not be able to get down from the
mountains."   He made us the sign of precipices, and showed us how the
feet of the horses would slip, and throw them off from the narrow trails
which led along their sides.

Our Chinook, who comprehended even more readily than ourselves,
and believed our situation hopeless, covered his head with his blanket,
and began to weep and lament.   " I wanted to see the whites," said he ;
" I came away from my own people to see the whites, and I wouldn't care
to die among them ; but here"—and he looked around into the cold night
and gloomy forest, and, drawing his blanket over his head, began again to
lament.

Seated around the tree, the fire illuminating the rocks and the tall bolls of the pines round about, and the old Indian haranguing, we presented a group of very serious faces.

February 5th.—The night had been too cold to sleep, and we were up very early. Our guide was standing by the fire with all his finery on; and seeing him shiver in the cold, I threw on his shoulders one of my blankets. We missed him a few minutes afterward, and never saw him again. He had deserted. His bad faith and treachery were in perfect keeping with the estimate of Indian character which a long intercourse with this people had gradually forced upon my mind.

While a portion of the camp were occupied in bringing up the baggage to this point, the remainder were busied in making sledges and snow-shoes. I had determined to explore the mountain ahead, and the sledges were to be used in transporting the baggage.

The mountains here consisted wholly of a white micaceous granite.

The day was perfectly clear, and while the sun was in the sky, warm and pleasant.

By observation, our latitude was 38° 42' 26"; and elevation, by the boiling-point, seven thousand four hundred feet.

February 6th.—Accompanied by Mr. Fitzpatrick, I set out to-day with a reconnoitring party, on snow-shoes. We marched all in single file, trampling the snow as heavily as we could. Crossing the open basin, in a march of about ten miles we reached the top of one of the peaks, to the left of the pass indicated by our guide.

Far below us, dimmed by the distance, was a large snowless valley, bounded on the western side, at the distance of about a hundred miles, by a low range of mountains, which Carson recognized with delight as the mountains bordering the coast. " There," said he, " is the little mountain —it is fifteen years ago since I saw it ; but I am just as sure as if I had seen it yesterday." Between us, then, and this low coast range, was the Valley of the Sacramento ; and no one who had not accompanied us through the incidents of our life for the last few months, could realize the delight with which at last we looked down upon it. At the distance of apparently thirty miles beyond us were distinguished spots of prairie ; and a dark line, which could be traced with the glass, was imagined to be the course of the river ; but we were evidently at a great height above the valley, and between us and the plains extended miles of snowy fields, and broken ridges of pine-covered mountains.

It was late in the day when we turned toward the camp ; and it grew rapidly cold as it drew toward night. One of the men, Fallon, became fatigued, and his feet began to freeze, and building a fire in the trunk of a dry old cedar, Mr. Fitzpatrick remained with him until his clothes could be dried, and he was in a condition to come on. After a day's march of twenty miles, we straggled into camp, one after another, at nightfall; the greater number excessively fatigued, only two of the party having ever travelled on snow-shoes before.

All our energies were now directed to getting our animals across the snow; and it was supposed that, after all the baggage had been drawn with the sleighs over the trail we had made, it would be sufficiently hard to bear our animals. At several places between this point and the ridge we had discovered some grassy spots, where the wind and sun had dispersed the snow from the sides of the hills, and these were to form resting-places to support the animals for a night in their passage across. On our way across we had set on fire several broken stumps, and dried trees, to melt holes in the snow for the camps. Its general depth was five feet; but we passed over places where it was twenty feet deep, as shown by the trees.

With one party drawing sleighs loaded with baggage, I advanced to-day about four miles along the trail, and encamped at the first grassy spot where we expected to bring our horses. Mr. Fitzpatrick, with another party, remained behind, to form an intermediate station between us and the animals.

February 8th.—The night had been extremely cold but perfectly still and beautifully clear. Before the sun appeared this morning the thermometer was 3° below zero; 1° higher, when his rays struck the lofty peaks; and 0° when they reached our camp.

Scenery and weather combined, must render these mountains beautiful in summer; the purity and deep-blue color of the sky are singularly beautiful; the days are sunny and bright, and even warm in the noon hours; and if we could be free from the many anxieties that oppress us, even now we would be delighted here; but our provisions are getting fearfully scant. Sleighs arrived with baggage about ten o'clock; and leaving a portion of it here, we continued on for a mile and a half, and encamped at the foot of a long hill on this side of the open bottom.

Bernier and Godey, who yesterday morning had been sent to ascend a higher peak, got in, hungry and fatigued. They confirmed what we had already seen. Two other sleighs arrived in the afternoon; and the men being fatigued, I gave them all tea and sugar. Snow-clouds began to rise in the south-southwest; and, apprehensive of a storm, which would destroy our road, I sent the people back to Mr. Fitzpatrick, with directions to send for the animals in the morning. With me remained Mr. Preuss, Mr. Talbot, and Carson, with Jacob.

Elevation of the camp, by the boiling-point, is seven thousand nine hundred and twenty feet.

February 9th.—During the night the weather changed, the wind rising to a gale, and commencing to snow before daylight; before morning the trail was covered. We remained quiet in camp all day, in the course of which the weather improved. Four sleighs arrived toward evening, with the bedding of the men. We suffer much from the want of salt; and all the men are becoming weak from insufficient food.

February 10th.—Taplin was sent back with a few men to assist Mr. Fitzpatrick; and continuing on with three sleighs carrying a part of the baggage, we had the satisfaction to encamp within two and a half miles of the head of the hollow, and at the foot of the last mountain ridge. Here two large trees had been set on fire, and in the holes, where the snow had been melted away, we found a comfortable camp.

The wind kept the air filled with snow during the day; the sky was very dark in the southwest, though elsewhere very clear. The forest here has a noble appearance: the tall cedar is abundant; its greatest height being one hundred and thirty feet, and circumference twenty, three or four feet above the ground; and here I see for the first time the white pine, of which there are some magnificent trees. Hemlock spruce is among the timber, occasionally as large as eight feet in diameter four feet above the ground; but, in ascending, it tapers rapidly to less than one foot at the height of eighty feet. I have not seen any higher than one hundred and thirty feet, and the slight upper part is frequently broken off by the wind. The white spruce is frequent; and the red pine (*Pinus colorado* of the Mexicans) which constitutes the beautiful forest along the flanks of the Sierra Nevada to the northward, is here the principal tree, not attaining a greater height than one hundred and forty feet, though with sometimes a diameter of ten. Most of these trees appeared to differ slightly from those of the same kind on the other side of the continent.

The elevation of the camp, by the boiling-point, is eight thousand and fifty feet. We are now one thousand feet above the level of the South Pass in the Rocky Mountains; and still we are not done ascending. The top of a flat ridge near was bare of snow, and very well sprinkled with bunch grass, sufficient to pasture the animals two or three days; and this was to be their main point of support. This ridge is composed of a compact trap, or basalt, of a columnar structure; over the surface are scattered large boulders of porous trap. The hills are in many places entirely covered with small fragments of volcanic rock.

Putting on our snow-shoes, we spent the afternoon in exploring a road ahead. The glare of the snow, combined with great fatigue, had rendered many of the people nearly blind; but we were fortunate in having some black silk handkerchiefs, which, worn as veils, very much relieved the eyes.

February 11*th.*—High wind continued, and our trail this morning was nearly invisible—here and there indicated by a little ridge of snow. Our situation became tiresome and dreary, requiring a strong exercise of patience and resolution.

In the evening I received a message from Mr. Fitzpatrick, acquainting me with the utter failure of his attempt to get our mules and horses over the snow—the half-hidden trail had proved entirely too slight to support them, and they had broken through, and were plunging about or lying half-buried in snow. He was occupied in endeavoring to get them back to his camp; and in the meantime sent to me for further instructions. I wrote to him to send the animals immediately back to their old pastures; and, after having made mauls and shovels, turn in all the strength of his party to open and beat a road through the snow, strengthening it with branches and boughs of the pines.

February 12*th.*—We made mauls, and worked hard at our end of the road all the day. The wind was high, but the sun bright, and the snow thawing. We worked down the face of the hill, to meet the people at the other end. Toward sundown it began to grow cold, and we shouldered our mauls, and trudged back to camp.

February 13*th.*—We continued to labor on the road; and in the course of the day had the satisfaction to see the people working down the face of the opposite hill, about three miles distant. During the morning we had the pleasure of a visit from Mr. Fitzpatrick, with the information that all was going on well. A party of Indians had passed on snow-shoes, who said they were going to the western side of the mountain after fish. This was an indication that the salmon were coming up the streams; and we could hardly restrain our impatience as we thought of them, and worked with increased vigor.

The meat train did not arrive this evening, and I gave Godey leave to kill our little dog (Tlamath) which he prepared in Indian fashion—scorching off the hair, and washing the skin with soap and snow, and then cutting it up into pieces, which were laid on the snow. Shortly afterward the sleigh arrived with a supply of horse meat; and we had to-night an extraordinary dinner—pea-soup, mule, and dog.

February 14*th.*—Opposite is given a view of the dividing ridge of the Sierra, taken from this encampment. With Mr. Preuss, I ascended to-day the highest peak to the right; from which we had a beautiful view of a mountain lake at our feet, about fifteen miles in length, and so entirely surrounded by mountains that we could not discover an outlet. We had taken with us a glass; but, though we enjoyed an extended view, the valley was half hidden in mist, as when we had seen it before. Snow could be distinguished on the higher parts of the coast mountains; eastward, as far as the eye could extend, it ranged over a terrible mass of broken snowy mountains, fading off blue in the distance.

The rock composing the summit consists of a very coarse dark volcanic conglomerate; the lower parts appeared to be of a slaty structure. The highest trees were a few scattering cedars and aspens. From the immediate foot of the peak, we were two hours in reaching the summit, and one hour and a quarter in descending. The day had been very bright, still, and clear, and spring seems to be advancing rapidly. While the sun is in the sky, the snow melts rapidly, and gushing springs cover the face of the mountain in all the exposed places; but their surface freezes instantly with the disappearance of the sun.

I obtained to-night some observations; and the result from these, and others made during our stay, gives for the latitude 38° 41' 57", longitude 120° 25' 57", and rate of the chronometer 25.82".

February 16th.—We had succeeded in getting our animals safely to the first grassy hill; and this morning I started with Jacob on a reconnoitring expedition beyond the mountain. We travelled along the crests of narrow ridges, extending down from the mountain in the direction of the valley, from which the snow was fast melting away. On the open spots was tolerably good grass; and I judged we should succeed in getting the camp down by way of these. Toward sundown we discovered some icy spots in a deep hollow; and, descending the mountain, we encamped on the head-water of a little creek, where at last the water found its way to the Pacific.

The night was clear and very long. We heard the cries of some wild animals, which had been attracted by our fire, and a flock of geese passed over during the night. Even these strange sounds had something pleasant to our senses in this region of silence and desolation.

We started again early in the morning. The creek acquired a regular breadth of about twenty feet, and we soon began to hear the rushing of the water below the icy surface, over which we travelled to avoid the snow; a few miles below we broke through, where the water was several feet deep, and halted to make a fire and dry our clothes. We continued a few miles farther, walking being very laborious without snow-shoes.

I was now perfectly satisfied that we had struck the stream on which Mr. Sutter lived; and, turning about, made a hard push and reached the camp at dark. Here we had the pleasure to find all the remaining animals, fifty-seven in number, safely arrived at the grassy hill near the camp; and here, also, we were agreeably surprised with the sight of an abundance of salt. Some of the horse-guard had gone to a neighboring hut for pine nuts, and discovered unexpectedly a large cake of very white, fine-grained salt, which the Indians told them they had brought from the other side of the mountain ; they used it to eat with their pine nuts, and readily sold it for goods.

On the 19th, the people were occupied in making a road and bringing up the baggage ; and, on the afternoon of the next day, *February* 20, 1844, we encamped with the animals and all the *materiel* of the camp, on the summit of the Pass in the dividing ridge, one thousand miles by our travelled road from the Dalles of the Columbia.

The people, who had not yet been to this point, climbed the neighboring peak to enjoy a look at the valley.

The temperature of boiling water gave for the elevation of the encampment nine thousand three hundred and thirty-eight feet above the sea.

This was two thousand feet higher than the South Pass in the Rocky Mountains, and several peaks in view rose several thousand feet still higher. Thus, at the extremity of the continent, and near the coast, the phenomenon was seen of a range of mountains still higher than the great Rocky Mountains themselves. This extraordinary fact accounts for the Great Basin, and shows that there must be a system of small lakes and rivers here scattered over a flat country, and which the extended and lofty range of the Sierra Nevada prevents from escaping to the Pacific Ocean. Latitude 38° 44′ ; longitude 120° 28′.

Thus this Pass in the Sierra Nevada, which so well deserves its name of Snowy Mountain, is eleven degrees west, and about four degrees south of the South Pass.

February 21*st.*—We now considered ourselves victorious over the mountain ; having only the descent before us, and the valley under our eyes, we felt strong hope that we should force our way down. But this was a case in which the descent was *not* facile. Still deep fields of snow lay between, and there was a large intervening space of rough-looking mountains, through which we had yet to wind our way.

Carson roused me this morning with an early fire, and we were all up long before day, in order to pass the snow-fields before the sun should render the crust soft. We enjoyed this morning a scene at sunrise, which even here was unusually glorious and beautiful.

Immediately above the eastern mountains was repeated a cloud-formed mass of purple ranges, bordered with bright yellow gold ; the peaks shot up into a narrow line of crimson cloud, above which the air was filled with a greenish orange ; and over all was the singular beauty of the blue sky.

Passing along a ridge which commanded the lake on our right, of which we began to discover an outlet through a chasm on the west, we passed over alternating open ground and hard-crusted snow-fields which supported the animals, and encamped on the ridge after a journey of six miles. The grass was better than we had yet seen, and we were encamped in a clump

PASS IN THE SIERRA NEVADA OF CALIFORNIA.

of trees twenty or thirty feet high, resembling white pine. With the exception of these small clumps, the ridges were bare; and, where the snow found the support of the trees, the wind had blown it up into banks ten or fifteen feet high. It required much care to hunt out a practicable way, as the most open places frequently led to impassable banks.

We had hard and doubtful labor yet before us, as the snow appeared to be heavier where the timber began farther down, with few open spots. Ascending a height, we traced out the best line we could discover for the next day's march, and had at least the consolation to see that the mountain descended rapidly. The day had been one of April; gusty, with a few occasional flakes of snow, which, in the afternoon, enveloped the upper mountain in clouds. We watched them anxiously, as now we dreaded a snow-storm.

Shortly afterward we heard the roll of thunder, and, looking toward the valley, found it all enveloped in a thunder-storm. ' For us, as connected with the idea of summer, it had a singular charm; and we watched its progress with excited feelings until nearly sunset, when the sky cleared off brightly, and we saw a shining line of water directing its course toward another, a broader and larger sheet. We knew that these could be no other than the Sacramento and the Bay of San Francisco; but, after our long wandering in rugged mountains, where so frequently we had met with disappointments, and where the crossing of every ridge displayed some unknown lake or river, we were yet almost afraid to believe that we were at last to escape into the genial country of which we had heard so many glowing descriptions, and dreaded again to find some vast interior lake, whose bitter waters would bring us disappointment. On the southern shore of what appeared to be the bay, could be traced the gleaming line where entered another large stream; and again the Buenaventura rose up in our minds.

Carson had entered the valley along the southern side of the bay, and remembered perfectly to have crossed the mouth of a very large stream, which they had been obliged to raft; but the country then was so entirely covered with water from snow and rain, that he had been able to form no correct impression of water-courses.

We had the satisfaction to know that at least there were people below. Fires were lit up in the valley just at night, appearing to be in answer to ours; and these signs of life renewed, in some measure, the gayety of the camp. They appeared so near, that we judged them to be among the timber of some of the neighboring ridges; but, having them constantly in view, day after day, and night after night, we afterward found them to be fires that had been kindled by the Indians among the *tulares*, on the shore of the bay, eighty miles distant.

Among the very few plants that appeared here, was the common blue flax. To-night a mule was killed for food.

February 22d.—Our breakfast was over long before day. We took advantage of the coolness of the early morning to get over the snow, which to-day occurred in very deep banks among the timber; but we searched out the coldest places, and the animals passed successfully with their loads the hard crust. Now and then the delay of making a road occasioned much labor and loss of time.

In the after part of the day we saw before us a handsome grassy ridge-point; and, making a desperate push over a snow-field ten to fifteen feet deep, we happily succeeded in getting the camp across; and encamped on the ridge, after a march of three miles. We had again the prospect of a thunder-storm below; and to-night we killed another mule—now our only resource from starvation.

We satisfied ourselves during the day that the lake had an outlet between two ranges on the right; and with this, the creek on which I had encamped, probably effected a junction below. Between these, we were descending.

We continued to enjoy the same delightful weather; the sky of the same beautiful blue, and such a sunset and sunrise as on our Atlantic coast we could scarcely imagine. And here among the mountains, nine thousand feet above the sea, we have the deep-blue sky and sunny climate of Smyrna and Palermo, which a little map before me shows are in the same latitude.

The elevation above the sea, by the boiling-point, is eight thousand five hundred and sixty-five feet.

February 23d.—This was our most difficult day: we were forced off the ridges by the quantity of snow among the timber, and obliged to take to the mountain-sides, where, occasionally, rocks and a southern exposure afforded us a chance to scramble along. But these were steep, and slippery with snow and ice; and the tough evergreens of the mountain impeded our way, tore our skins, and exhausted our patience. Some of us had the misfortune to wear moccasins with *parflèche* soles, so slippery that we could not keep our feet, and generally crawled across the snow-beds.

Axes and mauls were necessary to-day to make a road through the snow. Going ahead with Carson to reconnoitre the road, we reached in the afternoon the river which made the outlet of the lake. Carson sprang over, clear across a place where the stream was compressed among rocks, but the *parflèche* sole of my moccasin glanced from the icy rock, and precipitated me into the river. It was some few seconds before I could recover myself in the current, and Carson, thinking me hurt, jumped in after me, and we both had an icy bath. We tried to search awhile for my gun, which had been lost in the fall, but the cold drove us out ; and making a large fire on the bank, after we had partially dried ourselves we went back to meet the camp. We afterward found that the gun had been slung under the ice which lined the banks of the creek.

Using our old plan of breaking the road with alternate horses, we reached the creek in the evening, and encamped on a dry open place in the ravine.

Another branch, which we had followed, here comes in on the left ; and from this point the mountain-wall, on which we had travelled to-day, faces to the south along the right bank of the river, where the sun appears to have melted the snow ; but the opposite ridge is entirely covered. Here, among the pines, the hill-side produces but little grass—barely sufficient to keep life in the animals. We had the pleasure to be rained upon this afternoon ; and grass was now our greatest solicitude. Many of the men looked badly, and some this evening were giving out.

February 24th.—We rose at three in the morning, for an astronomical observation, and obtained for the place a latitude of 38° 46′ 58″ ; longitude 120° 34′ 20″. The sky was clear and pure, with a sharp wind from the northeast, and the thermometer 2° below the freezing-point.

We continued down the south face of the mountain : our road leading over dry ground, we were able to avoid the snow almost entirely. In the course of the morning we struck a footpath, which we were generally able to keep ; and the ground was soft to our animals' feet, being sandy or covered with mould. Green grass began to make its appearance, and occasionally we passed a hill scatteringly covered with it.

The character of the forest continued the same ; and among the trees, the pine with short leaves and very large cones was abundant, some of them being noble trees. We measured one that had ten feet diameter, though the height was not more than one hundred and thirty feet. All along the river was a roaring torrent, its fall very great ; and descending with a rapidity to which we had long been strangers ; to our great pleasure oak trees appeared on the ridge, and soon became very frequent ; on these I remarked unusually great quantities of mistletoe. Rushes began to make their appearance ; and at a small creek where they were abundant, one of the messes was left with the weakest horses, while we continued on.

The opposite mountain-side was very steep and continuous—unbroken by ravines, and covered with pines and snow ; while on the side we were travelling, innumerable rivulets poured down from the ridge. Continuing on, we halted a moment at one of these rivulets, to admire some beautiful evergreen trees, resembling live-oak, which shaded the little stream. They were forty to fifty feet high, and two in diameter, with a uniform tufted top ; and the summer green of their beautiful foliage, with the singing birds, and the sweet summer wind which was whirling about the dry oak leaves, nearly intoxicated us with delight; and we hurried on, filled with excitement, to escape entirely from the horrid region of inhospitable snow, to the perpetual spring of the Sacramento.

When we had travelled about ten miles the valley opened a little to an oak and pine bottom, through which ran rivulets closely bordered with rushes, on which our half-starved horses fell with avidity; and here we made our encampment. Here the roaring torrent has already become a river, and we had descended to an elevation of three thousand eight hundred and sixty-four feet.

Along our road to-day the rock was a white granite, which appears to constitute the upper part of the mountains on both the eastern and western slopes; while between, the central is a volcanic rock.

Another horse was killed to-night, for food.

February 25th.—Believing that the difficulties of the road were passed, and leaving Mr. Fitzpatrick to follow slowly, as the condition of the animals required, I started ahead this morning with a party of eight, consisting (with myself) of Mr. Preuss and Mr. Talbot, Carson, Derosier, Towns, Proue, and Jacob. We took with us some of the best animals, and my intention was to proceed as rapidly as possible to the house of Mr. Sutter, and return to meet the party with a supply of provisions and fresh animals.

Continuing down the river, which pursued a very direct westerly course through a narrow valley, with only a very slight and narrow bottom-land, we made twelve miles, and encamped at some old Indian huts, apparently a fishing-place on the river.

The bottom was covered with trees of deciduous foliage, and overgrown with vines and rushes. On a bench of the hill near by was a field of fresh green grass, six inches long in some of the tufts, which I had the curiosity to measure. The animals were driven here; and I spent part of the afternoon sitting on a large rock among them, enjoying the pauseless rapidity with which they luxuriated in the unaccustomed food.

The forest was imposing to-day in the magnificence of the trees; some of the pines, bearing large cones, were ten feet in diameter; cedars also abounded, and we measured one twenty-eight and one-half feet in circumference four feet from the ground. This noble tree seemed here to be in its proper soil and climate. We found it on both sides of the Sierra, but most abundant on the west.

February 26th.—We continued to follow the stream, the mountains on either hand increasing in height as we descended, and shutting up the river narrowly in precipices, along which we had great difficulty to get our horses.

It rained heavily during the afternoon, and we were forced off the river to the heights above ; whence we descended, at nightfall, the point of a spur between the river and a fork of nearly equal size, coming in from the right. Here we saw, on the lower hills, the first flowers in bloom, which occurred suddenly, and in considerable quantity ; one of them a species of *gilia*.

The current in both streams (rather torrents than rivers) was broken by large boulders. It was late, and the animals fatigued; and not succeeding to find a ford immediately, we encamped, although the hill-side afforded but a few stray bunches of grass, and the horses, standing about in the rain, looked very miserable.

February 27th.—We succeeded in fording the stream, and made a trail by which we crossed the point of the opposite hill, which, on the southern exposure, was prettily covered with green grass, and we halted a mile from our last encampment. The river was only about sixty feet wide, but rapid, and occasionally deep, foaming among boulders, and the water beautifully clear. We encamped on the hill-slope, as there was no bottom level, and the opposite ridge is continuous, affording no streams.

We had with us a large kettle ; and a mule being killed here, his head was boiled in it for several hours, and made a passable soup for famished people.

Below, precipices on the river forced us to the heights, which we ascended by a steep spur, two thousand feet high. My favorite horse, Proveau, had become very weak, and was scarcely able to bring himself to the top. Travelling here was good, except in crossing the ravines, which were narrow, steep, and frequent. We caught a glimpse of a deer, the first animal we had seen ; but did not succeed in approaching him. Proveau could not keep up, and I left Jacob to bring him on, being obliged to press forward with the party, as there was no grass in the forest. We grew very anxious as the day advanced and no grass appeared, for the lives of our animals depended on finding it to-night. They were in just such a condition that grass and repose for the night enabled them to get on the next day. Every hour we had been expecting to see open out before us the valley, which, from the mountain above, seemed almost at our feet.

A new and singular shrub, which had made its appearance since crossing the mountain, was very frequent to-day. It branched out near the ground, forming a clump eight to ten feet high, with pale-green leaves of an oval form ; and the body and branches had a naked appearance, as if stripped of the bark, which is very smooth and thin, of a chocolate color, contrasting well with the pale-green of the leaves. The day was nearly gone ; we had made a hard day's march and found no grass. Towns became light-headed, wandering off into the woods without knowing where he was going, and Jacob brought him back.

Near nightfall we descended into the steep ravine of a handsome creek thirty feet wide, and I was engaged in getting the horses up the opposite hill, when I heard a shout from Carson, who had gone ahead a few hundred yards—" Life yet," said he as he, came up, "life yet; I have found a hill-side sprinkled with grass enough for the night." We drove along our horses, and encamped at the place about dark, and there was just room enough to make a place for shelter on the edge of the stream. Three horses were lost to-day—Proveau; a fine young horse from the Columbia belonging to Charles Towns; and another Indian horse which carried our cooking utensils; the two former gave out, and the latter strayed off into the woods as we reached the camp.

February 29th.—We lay shut up in the narrow ravine, and gave the animals a necessary day; and men were sent back after the others. Derosier volunteered to bring up Proveau, to whom he knew I was greatly attached, as he had been my favorite horse on both expeditions. Carson and I climbed one of the nearest mountains; the forest land still extended ahead, and the valley appeared as far as ever. The pack-horse was found near the camp, but Derosier did not get in.

March 1st.—Derosier did not get in during the night, and leaving him to follow, as no grass remained here, we continued on over the uplands, crossing many small streams, and camped again on the river, having made six miles. Here we found the hill-side covered (although lightly) with fresh green grass; and from this time forward we found it always improving and abundant.

We made a pleasant camp on the river hill, where were some beautiful specimens of the chocolate-colored shrub, which were a foot in diameter near the ground, and fifteen to twenty feet high. The opposite ridge runs continuously along, unbroken by streams. We are rapidly descending into the spring, and we are leaving our snowy region far behind; everything is getting green; butterflies are swarming; numerous bugs are creeping out, wakened from their winter's sleep; and the forest flowers are coming into bloom. Among those which appeared most numerously to-day was *dodecatheon dentatum.*

We began to be uneasy at Derosier's absence, fearing he might have been bewildered in the woods. Charles Towns, who had not yet recovered his mind, went to swim in the river, as if it were summer and the stream placid, when it was a cold mountain-torrent foaming among rocks. We were happy to see Derosier appear in the evening. He came in, and, sitting down by the fire, began to tell us where he had been. He imagined he had been gone several days, and thought we were still at the camp where he had left us; and we were pained to see that his mind was deranged. It appeared that he had been lost in the mountain, and hunger and fatigue, joined to weakness of body and fear of perishing in the mountains, had crazed him. The times were severe when stout men lost their minds from extremity of suffering—when horses died—and when mules and horses, ready to die of starvation, were killed for food. Yet there was no murmuring or hesitation.

A short distance below our encampment the river mountains terminated in precipices, and, after a fatiguing march of only a few miles, we encamped on a bench, where there were springs and an abundance of the freshest grass. In the meantime, Mr. Preuss continued on down the river, and, unaware that we had encamped so early in the day, was lost. When night arrived, and he did not come in, we began to understand what had happened to him; but it was too late to make any search.

March 3d.—We followed Mr. Preuss' trail for a considerable distance along the river, until we reached a place where he had descended to the stream below and encamped. Here we shouted and fired guns, but received no answer; and we concluded that he had pushed on down the stream. I determined to keep out from the river, along which it was nearly impracticable to travel with animals, until it should form a valley.

At every step the country improved in beauty; the pines were rapidly disappearing, and oaks became the principal trees of the forest. Among these the prevailing tree was the evergreen oak (which, by way of distinction, we shall call the *live-oak*); and with these occurred frequently a new species of oak, bearing a long slender acorn from an inch to an inch and a half in length, which we now began to see formed the principal vegetable food of the inhabitants of this region.

In a short distance we crossed a little rivulet, where were two old huts, and near by were heaps of acorn hulls. The ground round about was very rich, covered with an exuberant sward of grass; and we sat down for a while in the shade of the oaks to let the animals feed. We repeated our shouts for Mr. Preuss, and this time we were gratified with an answer. The voice grew rapidly nearer, ascending from the river; but when we expected to see him emerge, it ceased entirely. We had called up some straggling Indian—the first we had met, although for two days back we had seen tracks—who, mistaking us for his fellows, had been only undeceived on getting close up. It would have been pleasant to witness his astonishment; he would not have been more frightened had some of the old mountain-spirits they are so much afraid of suddenly appeared in his path.

Ignorant of the character of these people, we had now an additional cause of uneasiness in regard to Mr. Preuss; he had no arms with him, and we began to think his chance doubtful. We followed on a trail, still keeping out from the river, and descended to a very large creek, dashing with great velocity over a pre-eminently rocky bed, and among large boulders. The bed has sudden breaks, formed by deep holes and ledges of rock running across. Even here it deserves the name of *Rock* Creek, which we gave to it. We succeeded in fording it, and toiled about three thousand feet up the opposite hill. The mountains now were getting sensibly lower; but still there is no valley on the river, which presents steep and rocky banks; but here, several miles from the river, the country is smooth and grassy; the forest has no undergrowth; and in the open valleys of rivulets, or around spring heads, the low groves of live-oak give the appearance of orchards in an old cultivated country.

Occasionally we met deer, but had not the necessary time for hunting. At one of these orchard grounds we encamped about noon to make an effort for Mr. Preuss. One man took his way along a spur leading in to the river, in hope to cross his trail; and another took our own back. Both were volunteers; and to the successful man was promised a pair of pistols—not as a reward, but as a token of gratitude for a service which would free us all from much anxiety.

We had among our few animals a horse which was so much reduced with travelling that even the good grass could not save him; and, having nothing to eat, he was killed this afternoon. He was a good animal, and had made the journey round from Fort Hall.

Dodecatheon dentatum continued the characteristic plant in flower; and the naked-looking shrub already mentioned continued characteristic, beginning to put forth a small, white blossom. At evening the men returned, having seen or heard nothing of Mr. Preuss; and I determined to make a hard push down the river the next morning, and get ahead of him.

March 4th.—We continued rapidly along on a broad, plainly beaten trail, the mere travelling and breathing the delightful air being a positive enjoyment. Our road led along a ridge inclining to the river, and the air and the open grounds were fragrant with flowering shrubs; and in the course of the morning we issued on an open spur, by which we descended directly to the stream.

Here the river issues suddenly from the mountains, which hitherto had hemmed it closely in; these now become softer, and change sensibly their character; and at this point commences the most beautiful valley in which we had ever travelled. We hurried to the river, on which we noticed a small sand beach, to which Mr. Preuss would naturally have gone. We found no trace of him, but, instead, were recent tracks of bare-footed Indians, and little piles of mussel-shells, and old fires where they had roasted the fish. We travelled on over the river grounds, which were undulating, and covered with grass to the river brink. We halted to noon a few miles beyond, always under the shade of the evergreen oaks, which formed open groves on the bottoms.

Continuing our road in the afternoon, we ascended to the uplands, where the river passes round a point of great beauty, and goes through very remarkable dalles, in character resembling those of the Columbia River. Beyond, we again descended to the bottoms, where we found an Indian village consisting of two or three huts; we had come upon them suddenly, and the people had evidently just run off. The huts were low and slight, made like beehives in a picture, five or six feet high, and near each was a crate formed of interlaced branches and grass, in size and shape like a very large hogshead. Each of these would hold from six to nine bushels. They were filled with the long acorns already mentioned, and in the huts were several neatly made baskets containing quantities of the acorns roasted. They were sweet and agreeably flavored, and we supplied ourselves with about half a bushel, leaving one of our shirts, a handkerchief, and some smaller articles in exchange.

The river again entered for a space among hills, and we followed a trail leading across a bend through a handsome hollow behind. Here, while engaged in trying to circumvent a deer, we discovered some Indians on a hill several hundred yards ahead, and gave them a shout, to which they responded by loud and rapid talking and vehement gesticulation, but made no stop, hurrying up the mountain as fast as their legs could carry them. We passed on, and again encamped in a grassy grove.

The absence of Mr. Preuss gave me great concern; and, for a large reward, Derosier volunteered to go back on the trail. I directed him to search along the river, travelling upward for the space of a day and a half, at which time I expected he would meet Mr. Fitzpatrick, whom I requested to aid in the search; at all events, he was to go no farther, but return to this camp, where a *cache* of provisions was made for him.

Continuing the next day down the river, we discovered three squaws in a little bottom, and surrounded them before they could make their escape. They had large conical baskets, which they were engaged in filling with a small leafy plant (*Erodium cicutarium*) just now beginning to bloom, and covering the ground like a sward of grass. These did not make any lamentations, but appeared very much impressed with our appearance, speaking to us only in a whisper, and offering us smaller baskets of the plant, which they signified to us was good to eat, making signs also that it was to be cooked by the fire. We drew out a little cold horse meat, and the squaws made signs to us that the men had gone out after deer, and that we could have some by waiting till they came in.

We observed that the horses ate with great avidity the herb which they had been gathering; and here, also, for the first time, we saw Indians eat the common grass—one of the squaws pulling several tufts, and eating it with apparent relish. Seeing our surprise, she pointed to the horses; but we could not well understand what she meant, except, perhaps, that what was good for the one was good for the other.

We encamped in the evening on the shore of the river, at a place where the associated beauties of scenery made so strong an impression on us that we have given it the name of the Beautiful Camp.   The undulating river shore was shaded with the live oaks, which formed a continuous grove over the country, and the same grassy sward extended to the edge of the water ; and we made our fires near some large granite masses which were lying among the trees.

We had seen several of the acorn *caches* during the day ; and here there were two which were very large, containing each, probably, ten bushels. Toward evening we heard a weak shout among the hills behind, and had the pleasure to see Mr. Preuss descending toward the camp.   Like ourselves, he had travelled to-day twenty-five miles, but had seen nothing of Derosier.   Knowing, on the day he was lost, that I was determined to keep the river as much as possible, he had not thought it necessary to follow the trail very closely, but walked on, right and left, certain to find it somewhere along the river, searching places to obtain good views of the country.   Toward sunset he climbed down toward the river to look for the camp ; but, finding no trail, concluded that we were behind, and walked back until night came on, when, being very much fatigued, he collected drift-wood and made a large fire among the rocks.   The next day it became more serious, and he encamped again alone, thinking that we must have taken some other course.   To go back, would have been madness in his weak and starved condition, and onward toward the valley was his only hope, always in expectation of reaching it soon.   His principal means of subsistence were a few roots, which the hunters call sweet onions, having very little taste, but a good deal of nutriment, growing generally in rocky ground, and requiring a good deal of labor to get, as he had only a pocket-knife.   Searching for these, he found a nest of big ants, which he let run on his hand, and stripped them off in his mouth ; these had an agreeable acid taste.   One of his greatest privations was the want of tobacco ; and a pleasant smoke at evening would have been a relief which only a voyageur could appreciate.   He tried the dried leaves of the live-oak, knowing that those of other oaks were sometimes used as a substitute ; but these were too thick, and would not do.   On the 4th he made seven or eight miles, walking slowly along the river, avoiding as much as possible to climb the hills.   In little pools he caught some of the smallest kind of frogs, which he swallowed, not so much in the gratification of hunger, as in the hope of obtaining some strength.   Scattered along the river were old fire-places, where the Indians had roasted mussels and acorns ; but though he searched diligently he did not there succeed in finding either.   He had collected firewood for the night, when he heard at some distance from the river the barking of what he thought were two dogs, and walked in that direction as quickly as he was able, hoping to find there some Indian hut, but met only two wolves; and, in his disappointment, the gloom of the forest was doubled.

Travelling the next day feebly down the river, he found five or six Indians at the huts of which we have spoken; some were painting themselves black, and others roasting acorns. Being only one man, they did not run off, but received him kindly, and gave him a welcome supply of roasted acorns. He gave them his pocket-knife in return, and stretched out his hand to one of the Indians, who did not appear to comprehend the motion, but jumped back, as if he thought he was about to lay hold of him. They seemed afraid of him, not certain as to what he was.

Travelling on, he came to the place where we had found the squaws. Here he found our fire still burning, and the tracks of the horses. The sight gave him sudden hope and courage, and, following as fast as he could, joined us at evening.

March 6th.—We continued on our road through the same surpassingly beautiful country, entirely unequalled for the pasturage of stock by anything we had ever seen. Our horses had now become so strong that they were able to carry us, and we travelled rapidly—over four miles an hour; four of us riding every alternate hour. Every few hundred yards we came upon a little band of deer; but we were too eager to reach the settlement, which we momentarily expected to discover, to halt for any other than a passing shot. In a few hours we reached a large fork, the northern branch of the river, and equal in size to that which we had descended. Together they formed a beautiful stream, sixty to one hundred yards wide, which at first, ignorant of the nature of the country through which that river ran, we took to be the Sacramento.

We continued down the right bank of the river, travelling for a while over a wooded upland, where we had the delight to discover tracks of cattle. To the southwest was visible a black column of smoke, which we had frequently noticed in descending, arising from the fires we had seen from the top of the Sierra.

From the upland we descended into broad groves on the river, consisting of the evergreen and a new species of white-oak with a large tufted top, and three to six feet in diameter. Among these was no brushwood; and the grassy surface gave to it the appearance of parks in an old-settled country. Following the tracks of the horses and cattle in search of people, we discovered a small village of Indians. Some of these had on shirts of civilized manufacture, but were otherwise naked, and we could understand nothing from them; they appeared entirely astonished at seeing us.

We made an acorn meal at noon, and hurried on ; the valley being gay with flowers, and some of the banks being absolutely golden with the California poppy (*Eschscholtzia crocea*). Here the grass was smooth and green, and the groves very open ; the large oaks throwing a broad shade among sunny spots.

Shortly afterward we gave a shout at the appearance on a little bluff of a neatly-built *adobe* house with glass windows. We rode up, but, to our disappointment, found only Indians. There was no appearance of cultivation, and we could see no cattle, and we supposed the place had been abandoned. We now pressed on more eagerly than ever; the river swept round in a large bend to the right ; the hills lowered down entirely ; and, gradually entering a broad valley, we came unexpectedly into a large Indian village, where the people looked clean, and wore cotton shirts and various other articles of dress. They immediately crowded around us, and we had the inexpressible delight to find one who spoke a little indifferent Spanish, but who at first confounded us by saying there were no whites in the country ; but just then a well-dressed Indian came up, and made his salutations in very well spoken Spanish. In answer to our inquiries he informed us that we were upon the *Rio de los Americanos* (the River of the Americans), and that it joined the Sacramento River about ten miles below. Never did a name sound more sweetly ! We felt ourselves among our countrymen ; for the name of *American*, in these distant parts, is applied to the citizens of the United States.

To our eager inquiries he answered, " I am a *vaquero* (cow-herd) in the service of Captain Sutter, and the people of this *rancheria* work for him." Our evident satisfaction made him communicative; and he went on to say that Captain Sutter was a very rich man, and always glad to see his country people. We asked for his house. He answered that it was just over the hill before us ; and offered, if we would wait a moment, to take his horse and conduct us to it. We readily accepted his civil offer. In a short distance we came in sight of the fort ; and, passing on the way the house of a settler on the opposite side (a Mr. Sinclair), we forded the river ; and in a few miles were met a short distance from the fort by Captain Sutter himself. He gave us a most frank and cordial reception—conducted us immediately to his residence—and under his hospitable roof we had a night of rest, enjoyment, and refreshment, which none but ourselves could appreciate. But the party left in the mountains with Mr. Fitzpatrick were to be attended to ; and the next morning, supplied with fresh horses and provisions, I hurried off to meet them. On the second day we met, a few miles below the forks of the Rio de los Americanos ; and a more forlorn and pitiable sight than they presented cannot well be imagined. They were all on foot—each man, weak and emaciated—leading a horse or mule

CAPTAIN SUTTER.

as weak and emaciated as themselves. They had experienced great difficulty in descending the mountains, made slippery by rains and melting snows, and many horses fell over precipices and were killed; and with some were lost the *packs* they carried. Among these was a mule with the plants which we had collected since leaving Fort Hall, along a line of two thousand miles travel. Out of sixty-seven horses and mules with which we commenced crossing the Sierra only thirty-three reached the Valley of the Sacramento, and they only in a condition to be led along. Mr. Fitzpatrick and his party, travelling more slowly, had been able to make some little exertion at hunting, and had killed a few deer. The scanty supply was a great relief to them; for several had been made sick by the strange and unwholesome food which the preservation of life compelled them to use. We stopped and encamped as soon as we met; and a repast of good beef, excellent bread, and delicious salmon, which I had brought along, were their first relief from the sufferings of the Sierra and their first introduction to the luxuries of the Sacramento. It required all our philosophy and forbearance to prevent plenty from becoming as hurtful to us now as scarcity had been before.

The next day, March 8th, we encamped at the junction of the two rivers, the Sacramento and Americanos; and thus found the whole party in the beautiful Valley of the Sacramento. It was a convenient place for the camp; and, among other things, was within reach of the wood necessary to make the pack-saddles which we should need on our long journey home, from which we were further distant now than we were four months before, when, from the Dalles of the Columbia, we so cheerfully took up the homeward line of march.

Captain Sutter emigrated to this country from the Western part of Missouri in 1838–39, and formed the first settlement in the valley on a large grant of land which he obtained from the Mexican Government. He had, at first, some trouble with the Indians; but, by the occasional exercise of well-timed authority, he has succeeded in converting them into a peaceable and industrious people.

The ditches around his extensive wheat-fields; the making of the sun-dried bricks, of which his fort is constructed; the ploughing, harrowing, and other agricultural operations, are entirely the work of these Indians, for which they receive a very moderate compensation—principally in shirts, blankets, and other articles of clothing. In the same manner, on application to the chief of a village, he readily obtains as many boys and girls as he has any use for. There were at this time a number of girls at the fort, in training for a future woollen factory; but they were now all busily engaged in constantly watering the gardens, which the unfavorable dryness of the season rendered necessary. The occasional dryness of some seasons I understood to be the only complaint of the settlers in this fertile valley, as it sometimes renders the crops uncertain. Mr. Sutter was about making arrangements to irrigate his lands by means of the Rio de los Americanos. He had this year sown, and altogether by Indian labor, three hundred *fanegas* of wheat.

A few years since the neighboring Russian establishment of Ross, being about to withdraw from the country, sold to him a large number of stock, with agricultural and other stores, with a number of pieces of artillery, and other munitions of war; for these a regular yearly payment is made in grain.

The fort is a quadrangular *adobe* structure, mounting twelve pieces of artillery (two of them brass), and capable of admitting a garrison of a thousand men; this, at present, consists of forty Indians, in uniform—one of whom was always found on duty at the gate. As might naturally be expected, the pieces are not in very good order.

The whites in the employment of Captain Sutter, American, French, and German, amount, perhaps, to thirty men. The inner wall is formed into buildings comprising the common quarters, with a blacksmith's and other work-shops; the dwelling-house, with a large distillery-house, and other buildings, occupying more the centre of the area.

It is built upon a pond-like stream, at times a running creek communicating with the Rio de los Americanos, which enters the Sacramento about two miles below. The latter is here a noble river, about three hundred yards broad, deep and tranquil, with several fathoms of water in the channel, and its banks continuously timbered. There were two vessels belonging to Captain Sutter at anchor near the landing—one a large two-masted lighter, and the other a schooner, which was shortly to proceed on a voyage to Fort Vancouver for a cargo of goods.

Since his arrival, several other persons, principally Americans, have established themselves in the valley. Mr. Sinclair, from whom I experienced much kindness during my stay, is settled a few miles distant, on the Rio de los Americanos.

Mr. Coudrois, a gentleman from Germany, has established himself on Feather River, and is associated with Captain Sutter in agricultural pursuits. Among other improvements, they are about to introduce the cultivation of rape-seed (*Brassica rapus*) which there is every reason to believe is admirably adapted to the climate and soil. The lowest average produce of wheat, as far as we can at present know, is thirty-five *fanegas* for one sown; but, as an instance of its fertility, it may be mentioned that Señor Vallejo obtained, on a piece of ground where sheep had been pastured, eight hundred *fanegas* for eight sown. The produce being different in various places, a very correct idea cannot be formed.

SUTTER'S FORT.

An impetus was given to the active little population by our arrival, as we were in want of everything. Mules, horses, and cattle were to be collected; the horse-mill was at work day and night, to make sufficient flour; the blacksmith's shop was put in requisition for horse-shoes and bridle-bits; and pack-saddles, ropes, and bridles, and all the other little equipments of the camp were again to be provided.

The delay thus occasioned was one of repose and enjoyment, which our situation required, and, anxious as we were to resume our homeward journey, was regretted by no one. In the meantime, I had the pleasure to meet with Mr. Childs, who was residing at a farm on the other side of the River Sacramento, while engaged in the selection of a place for a settlement, for which he had received the necessary grant of land from the Mexican Government.

It will be remembered that we had parted near the frontier of the States, and that he had subsequently descended the Valley of Lewis' Fork, with a party of ten or twelve men, with the intention of crossing the intermediate mountains to the waters of the Bay of San Francisco. In the execution of this design, and aided by subsequent information, he left the Columbia at the mouth of *Malheur* River; and, making his way to the head-waters of the Sacramento with a part of his company, travelled down that river to the settlements of Nueva Helvetia. The other party, to whom he had committed his wagons and mill-irons and saws, took a course farther to the south, and the wagons and their contents were lost.

On the 22d we made a preparatory move, and encamped near the settlement of Mr. Sinclair, on the left bank of the Rio de los Americanos. I had discharged five of the party: Neal, the blacksmith (an excellent workman, and an unmarried man, who had done his duty faithfully and had been of very great service to me) desired to remain, as strong inducements were offered here to mechanics. Although at considerable inconvenience to myself his good conduct induced me to comply with his request; and I obtained for him, from Captain Sutter, a present compensation of two dollars and a half per diem, with a promise that it should be increased to five if he proved as good a workman as had been represented. He was more particularly an agricultural blacksmith. The other men were discharged with their own consent.

While we remained at this place, Derosier, one of our best men, whose steady good conduct had won my regard, wandered off from the camp and never returned to it again; nor has he since been heard of.

March 24th.—We resumed our journey with an ample stock of provisions and a large cavalcade of animals, consisting of one hundred and thirty horses and mules, and about thirty head of cattle, five of which were milch cows. Mr. Sutter furnished us also with an Indian boy, who had been trained as a *vaquero* and who would be serviceable in managing our cavalcade, great part of which were nearly as wild as buffalo ; and who was, besides, very anxious to go along with us.

Our direct course home was east ; but the Sierra would force us south, above five hundred miles of travelling, to a pass at the head of the San Joaquin River. This pass, reported to be good, was discovered by Mr. Joseph Walker, of whom I have already spoken, and whose name it might, therefore, appropriately bear. To reach it, our course lay along the valley of the San Joaquin—the river on our right, and the lofty wall of the impassable Sierra on the left. From that pass we were to move southeastwardly, having the Sierra then on the right, and reach the "*Spanish trail*," deviously traced from one watering place to another, which constituted the route of the caravans from *Pueblo de los Angeles*, near the coast of the Pacific, to *Santa Fé* of New Mexico. From the pass to this trail was one hundred and fifty miles. Following that trail through a desert, relieved by some fertile plains indicated by the recurrence of the term *vegas*, until it turned to the right to cross the Colorado, our course would be northeast until we regained the latitude we had lost in arriving at the Utah Lake, and thence to the Rocky Mountains at the head of the Arkansas.

This course of travelling, forced upon us by the structure of the country, would occupy a computed distance of two thousand miles before we reached the head of the Arkansas ; not a settlement to be seen upon it ; and the names of places along it, all being Spanish or Indian, indicated that it had been but little trod by American feet.

Though long, and not free from hardships, this route presented some points of attraction, in tracing the Sierra Nevada—turning the Great Basin, perhaps crossing its rim on the south—completely solving the problem of any river, except the Colorado, from the Rocky Mountains on that part of our continent—and seeing the southern extremity of the Great Salt Lake, of which the northern part had been examined the year before.

Taking leave of Mr. Sutter, who, with several gentlemen, accompanied us a few miles on our way, we travelled about eighteen miles, and encamped on the *Rio de los Cosumnes*, a stream receiving its name from the Indians who live in its valley. Our road was through a level country, admirably suited to cultivation, and covered with groves of oak-trees, principally the evergreen oak, and a large oak already mentioned, in form like those of the white oak. The weather, which here at this season can easily be changed from the summer heat of the valley to the frosty mornings and bright days nearer the mountains, continued delightful for travellers, but unfavorable to the agriculturists, whose crops of wheat began to wear a yellow tinge from want of rain.

CHAPTER X.

March 25th.—We travelled for twenty-eight miles over the same delightful country as yesterday, and halted in a beautiful bottom at the ford of the *Rio de los Mokélumnes*, receiving its name from another Indian tribe living on the river. The bottoms on the stream are broad, rich, and extremely fertile; and the uplands are shaded with oak groves. A showy *lupinus* of extraordinary beauty, growing four to five feet in height, and covered with spikes in bloom, adorned the banks of the river and filled the air with a light and grateful perfume.

On the 26th we halted at the *Arroyo de las Calaveras* (Skull Creek), a tributary to the San Joaquin—the previous two streams entering the bay between the San Joaquin and Sacramento Rivers. This place is beautiful, with open groves of oak, and a grassy sward beneath, with many plants in bloom; some varieties of which seem to love the shade of the trees, and grow there in close, small fields.

Near the river, and replacing the grass, are great quantities of *amole* (soap plant), the leaves of which are used in California for making, among other things, mats for saddle-cloths. A vine with a small white flower (*melothria ?*), called here *la yerba buena*, and which, from its abundance, gives name to an island and town in the bay, was to-day very frequent on our road—sometimes running on the ground or climbing the trees.

March 27th.—To-day we travelled steadily and rapidly up the valley; for, with our wild animals, any other gait was impossible, and making about five miles an hour. During the earlier part of the day our ride had been over a very level prairie, or rather a succession of long stretches of prairie, separated by lines and groves of oak-timber, growing along dry gullies, which are filled with water in seasons of rain; and, perhaps, also by the melting snows. Over much of this extent the vegetation was sparse; the surface showing plainly the action of water, which, in the season of flood, the Joaquin spreads over the valley.

About one o'clock we came again among innumerable flowers; and a few miles farther, fields of the beautiful blue-flowering *lupine*, which seems to love the neighborhood of water, indicated that we were approaching a stream. We here found this beautiful shrub in thickets, some of them being twelve feet in height. Occasionally three or four plants were clustered together, forming a grand bouquet, about ninety feet in circumference and ten feet high; the whole summit covered with spikes of flowers, the perfume of which is very sweet and grateful. A lover of natural beauty can imagine with what pleasure we rode among these flowering groves, which filled the air with a light and delicate fragrance.

We continued our road for about half a mile, interspersed through an open grove of live oaks, which in form were the most symmetrical and beautiful we had yet seen in this country. The ends of their branches rested on the ground, forming somewhat more than a half-sphere of very full and regular figure, with leaves apparently smaller than usual.

The California poppy, of a rich orange color, was numerous to-day. Elk and several bands of antelope made their appearance.

Our road was now one continued enjoyment; and it was pleasant, riding among this assemblage of green pastures with varied flowers and scattered groves, and out of the warm green spring, to look at the rocky and snowy peaks where lately we had suffered so much. Emerging from the timber, we came suddenly upon the Stanislaus River, where we hoped to find a ford, but the stream was flowing by, dark and deep, swollen by the mountain snows; its general breadth was about fifty yards.

We travelled about five miles up the river, and encamped without being able to find a ford. Here we made a large *corral*, in order to be able to catch a sufficient number of our wild animals, to relieve those previously packed.

Under the shade of the oaks, along the river, I noticed *Erodium cicutarium* in bloom, eight or ten inches high. This is the plant which we had seen the squaws gathering on the Rio de los Americanos. By the inhabitants of the valley it is highly esteemed for fattening cattle, which appear to be very fond of it. Here, where the soil begins to be sandy, it supplies to a considerable extent the want of grass.

Desirous, as far as possible, without delay, to include in our examination the San Joaquin River, I returned this morning down the Stanislaus for seventeen miles, and again encamped without having found a fording place. After following it for eight miles farther the next morning, and finding ourselves in the vicinity of the San Joaquin, encamped in a handsome oak-grove, and, several cattle being killed, we ferried over our baggage in their skins. Here our Indian boy, who probably had not much idea of where he was going, and began to be alarmed at the many streams which we were rapidly putting between him and the village, deserted.

OLD BUILDING ADJOINING SUTER'S FORT.

Thirteen head of cattle took a sudden fright, while we were driving them across the river, and galloped off. I remained a day in the endeavor to recover them; but, finding they had taken the trail back to the fort, let them go without further effort. Here we had several days of warm and pleasant rain, which doubtless saved the crops below.

On April 1st we made ten miles across a prairie without timber, when we were stopped again by another large river, which is called the *Rio de la Merced* (River of our Lady of Mercy). Here the country had lost its character of extreme fertility, the soil having become more sandy and light; but, for several days past, its beauty had been increased by the additional animation of animal life; and now it is crowded with bands of elk and wild horses; and along the rivers are frequent fresh tracks of grizzly bears, which are unusually numerous in this country.

Our route had been along the timber of the San Joaquin, generally about eight miles distant, over a high prairie.

In one of the bands of elk seen to-day there were about two hundred: but the larger bands, both of these and wild horses, are generally found on the other side of the river, which, for that reason, I avoided crossing. I had been informed below that the droves of wild horses were almost invariably found on the western bank of the river; and the danger of losing our animals among them, together with the wish of adding to our reconnoissance the numerous streams which run down from the Sierra, decided me to travel up the eastern bank.

April 2d.—The day was occupied in building a boat, and ferrying our baggage across the river; and we encamped on the bank. A large fishing eagle, with white head and tail, was slowly sailing along, looking after salmon; and there were some pretty birds in the timber, with partridges, ducks, and geese innumerable, in the neighborhood. We were struck with the tameness of the latter bird at Helvetia, scattered about in flocks near the wheat-fields, and eating grass on the prairie; a horseman would ride by within thirty yards without disturbing them.

April 3d.—To-day we touched several times the San Joaquin River —here a fine-looking, tranquil stream, with a slight current, and apparently deep. It resembled the Missouri in color, with occasional points of white sand; and its banks, where steep, were a kind of sandy clay; its average width appeared to be about eighty yards. In the bottoms are frequent ponds, where our approach disturbed multitudes of wild fowl, principally geese. Skirting along the timber, we frequently started elk; and large bands were seen during the day, with antelope and wild horses.

The low country and the timber rendered it difficult to keep the main line of the river; and this evening we encamped on a tributary stream, about five miles from its mouth. On the prairie bordering the San Joaquin bottoms we found during the day but little grass, and in its place was a sparse and dwarf growth of plants; the soil being sandy, with small bare places and hillocks, reminded me much of the Platte bottoms; but, on approaching the timber, we found a more luxuriant vegetation; and at our camp was an abundance of grass and pea-vines.

The foliage of the oak is getting darker; and everything, except that the weather is a little cool, shows that spring is rapidly advancing; and to-day we had quite a summer rain.

April 4th.—Commenced to rain at daylight, but cleared off brightly at sunrise. We ferried the river without any difficulty, and continued up the San Joaquin. Elk were running in bands over the prairie and in the skirt of the timber. We reached the river again at the mouth of a large slough, which we were unable to ford, and made a circuit of several miles around. Here the country appears very flat; oak-trees have entirely disappeared, and are replaced by a large willow nearly equal in size. The river is about a hundred yards in breadth, branching into sloughs, and interspersed with islands. At this time it appears sufficiently deep for a small steamer, but its navigation would be broken by shallows at low water.

Bearing in toward the river, we were again forced off by another slough; and, passing around, steered toward a clump of trees on the river, and, finding there good grass, encamped. The prairies along the left bank are alive with immense droves of wild horses; and they had been seen during the day at every opening through the woods which afforded us a view across the river. Latitude, by observation, 37° 08′ 00″; longitude 120° 45′ 22″.

April 5th.—During the earlier part of the day's ride the country presented a lacustrine appearance; the river was deep, and nearly on a level with the surrounding country; its banks raised like a levee, and fringed with willows. Over the bordering plain were interspersed spots of prairie among fields of *tulé* (bulrushes), which in this country are called *tulares*, and little ponds. On the opposite side a line of timber was visible, which, according to information, points out the course of the slough, which, at times of high water, connects with the San Joaquin River—a large body of water in the upper part of the valley, called the Tulé Lakes.

The river and all its sloughs are very full, and it is probable that the lake is now discharging. Here elk were frequently started, and one was shot out of a band which ran around us.

On our left, the Sierra maintains its snowy height, and masses of snow appear to descend very low toward the plains; probably the late rains in the valley were snow on the mountains. We travelled thirty-seven miles, and encamped on the river. Longitude of the camp, 120° 28′ 34″, and latitude 36° 49′ 12″.

April 6th.—After having travelled fifteen miles along the river we made an early halt under the shade of sycamore-trees. Here we found the San Joaquin coming down from the Sierra with a westerly course, and checking our way, as all its tributaries had previously done. We had expected to raft the river; but found a good ford, and encamped on the opposite bank, where droves of wild horses were raising clouds of dust on the prairie.

Columns of smoke were visible in the direction of the Tulé Lakes to the southward—probably kindled in the *tulares* by the Indians, as signals that there were strangers in the valley.

We made, on the 7th, a hard march in a cold, chilly rain from morning until night—the weather so thick that we travelled by compass. This was a *traverse* from the San Joaquin to the waters of the Tulé Lakes, and our road was over a very level prairie country.

We saw wolves frequently during the day, prowling about after the young antelope, which cannot run very fast. These were numerous during the day, and two were caught by the people.

Late in the afternoon we discovered timber, which was found to be groves of oak-trees on a dry *arroyo.* The rain, which had fallen in frequent showers, poured down in a storm at sunset, with a strong wind, which swept off the clouds and left a clear sky. Riding on through the timber, about dark we found abundant water in small ponds, twenty to thirty yards in diameter, with clear, deep water and sandy beds, bordered with bog-rushes (*Juncus effusus*) and a tall rush (*Scirpus lacustris*) twelve feet high, and surrounded near the margin with willow-trees in bloom; among them one which resembled *Salix myricoides.* The oak of the groves was the same already mentioned, with small leaves, in form like those of the white oak, and forming, with the evergreen oak, the characteristic trees of the valley.

April 8th.—After a ride of two miles through brush and open groves we reached a large stream, called the River of the Lake, resembling in size the San Joaquin, and being about one hundred yards broad. This is the principal tributary to the Tulé Lakes, which collect all the waters in the upper part of the valley. While we were searching for a ford some Indians appeared on the opposite bank, and, having discovered that we were not Spanish soldiers, showed us the way to a good ford several miles above.

The Indians of the Sierra make frequent descents upon the settlements west of the Coast Range, which they keep constantly swept of horses; among them are many who are called Christian Indians, being refugees from Spanish missions. Several of these incursions occurred while we were at Helvetia. Occasionally parties of soldiers follow them across the Coast Range, but never enter the Sierra.

On the opposite side we found some forty or fifty Indians, who had come to meet us from the village below.   We made them some small presents and invited them to accompany us to our encampment, which, after about three miles through fine oak-groves, we made on the river.   We made a fort, principally on account of our animals.

The Indians brought otter-skins and several kinds of fish, and bread made of acorns, to trade.   Among them were several who had come to live among these Indians when the missions were broken up, and who spoke Spanish fluently.   They informed us that they were called by the Spaniards *mansitos* (tame), in distinction from the wilder tribes of the mountains : they, however, think themselves very insecure, not knowing at what unforeseen moment the sins of the latter may be visited on them.   They are dark-skinned, but handsome and intelligent Indians, and live principally on acorns and the roots of the tulé, of which also their huts are made.

By observation the latitude of the encampment is 36° 24′ 50″, and longitude 119° 41′ 40″.

April 9th.—For several miles we had very bad travelling over what is called rotten ground, in which the horses were frequently up to their knees. Making toward a line of timber we found a small fordable stream, beyond which the country improved and the grass became excellent ; and, crossing a number of dry and timbered *arroyos*, we travelled until late through open oak-groves, and encamped among a collection of streams.   These were running among rushes and willows ; and, as usual, flocks of blackbirds announced our approach to water.

We have here approached considerably nearer to the eastern Sierra, which shows very plainly, still covered with masses of snow, which yesterday and to-day has also appeared abundant on the Coast Range.

April 10th.—To-day we made another long journey of about forty miles, through a country uninteresting and flat, with very little grass and a sandy soil, in which several branches we crossed had lost their water. In the evening the face of the country became hilly ; and, turning a few miles up toward the mountains, we found a good encampment on a pretty stream hidden among the hills, and handsomely timbered, principally with large cotton-woods (*populus*, differing from any in Michaux's " Sylva "). The seed-vessels of this tree were now just about bursting.

Several Indians came down the river to see us in the evening : we gave them supper, and cautioned them against stealing our horses, which they promised not to attempt.

April 11th.—A broad trail along the river here takes out among the hills.   " Buen camino " (good road), said one of the Indians, of whom we had inquired about the pass ; and, following it accordingly, it conducted us beautifully though a very broken country, by an excellent way which, otherwise, we should have found extremely bad.   Taken separately, the hills present smooth and graceful outlines, but together, make bad travel-ling ground.

Instead of grass, the whole face of the country is closely covered with *Erodium cicutarium*, here only two or three inches high. Its height and beauty varied in a remarkable manner with the locality, being, in many low places which we passed during the day, around streams and springs, two and three feet in height. The country had now assumed a character of aridity; and the luxuriant green of these little streams, wooded with willow, oak, or sycamore, looked very refreshing among the sandy hills.

In the evening we encamped on a large creek with abundant water. I noticed here, for the first time since leaving the Arkansas waters, the *Mirabilis jalapa* in bloom.

April 12*th.*—Along our road to-day the country was altogether sandy, and vegetation meagre. *Ephedra occidentalis*, which we had first seen in the neighborhood of the Pyramid Lake, made its appearance here, and in the course of the day became very abundant, and in large bushes.

Toward the close of the afternoon we reached a tolerably large river, which empties into a small lake at the head of the valley: it is about thirty-five yards wide, with a stony and gravelly bed, and the swiftest stream we have crossed since leaving the bay. The bottoms produced no grass, though well timbered with willow and cotton-wood; and, after ascending it for several miles, we made a late encampment on a little bottom with scanty grass. In greater part, the vegetation along our road consisted now of rare and unusual plants, among which many were entirely new.

Along the bottoms were thickets consisting of several varieties of shrubs, which made here their first appearance; and among these was *Garrya elliptica* (Lindley), a small tree belonging to a very peculiar natural order, and, in its general appearance (growing in thickets), resembling willow. It now became common along the streams, frequently supplying the place of *Salix longifolia*.

April 13*th.*—The water was low, and a few miles above we forded the river at a rapid, and marched in a southeasterly direction over a less broken country. The mountains were now very near, occasionally looming out through fog. In a few hours we reached the bottom of a creek without water, over which the sandy beds were dispersed in many branches. Im-mediately where we struck it the timber terminated; and below, to the right, it was a broad bed of dry and bare sands. There were many tracks of Indians and horses imprinted in the sand, which, with other indications, informed us thus was the creek issuing from the pass, and which on the map we have called Pass Creek.

We ascended a trail for a few miles along the creek and suddenly found a stream of water, five feet wide, running with a lively current, but losing itself almost immediately.   This litttle stream showed plainly the manner in which the mountain waters lose themselves in sand at the eastern foot of the Sierra, leaving only a parched desert and arid plains beyond.   The stream enlarged rapidly, and the timber became abundant as we ascended.

A new species of pine made its appearance, with several kinds of oaks, and a variety of trees ; and the country changing its appearance suddenly and entirely, we found ourselves again travelling among the old orchard-like places.   Here we selected a delightful encampment in a handsome, green-oak hollow, where, among the open bolls of the trees, was an abundant sward of grass and pea-vines.

In the evening a Christian Indian rode into the camp, well dressed, with long spurs and a *sombrero*, and speaking Spanish fluently.   It was an unexpected apparition and a strange and pleasant sight in this desolate gorge of a mountain—an Indian face, Spanish costume, jingling spurs, and horse equipped after the Spanish manner.   He informed me that he belonged to one of the Spanish missions to the south, distant two or three days' ride, and that he had obtained from the priests leave to spend a few days with his relations in the Sierra.   Having seen us enter the *pass*, he had come down to visit us.   He appeared familiarly acquainted with the country, and gave me definite and clear information in regard to the desert region east of the mountains.   I had entered the pass with a strong disposition to vary my route, and to travel directly across toward the Great Salt Lake, in the view of obtaining some acquaintance with the interior of the Great Basin, while pursuing a direct course for the frontier ; but his representation, which described it as an arid and barren desert, that had repulsed by its sterility all the attempts of the Indians to penetrate it, determined me for the present to relinquish the plan ; and, agreeably to his advice, after crossing the Sierra, continue our intended route along its eastern base to the Spanish trail.   By this route a party of six Indians, who had come from a great river in the eastern part of the desert to trade with his people, had just started on their return.   He would himself return the next day to *San Fernando ;* and as our roads would be the same for two days, he offered his services to conduct us so far on our way.   His offer was gladly accepted.

The fog, which had somewhat interfered with views in the valley, had entirely passed off and left a clear sky.   That which had enveloped us in the neighborhood of the pass proceeded evidently from fires kindled among the tulares by Indians living near the lakes, and which were intended to warn those in the mountains that there were strangers in the valley.   Our position was in latitude 35° 17' 12", and longitude 118° 35' 03".

April 14th.—Our guide joined us this morning on the trail; and, arriving in a short distance at an open bottom where the creek forked, we continued up the right-hand branch, which was enriched by a profusion of flowers, and handsomely wooded with sycamore, oaks, cotton-wood, and willow, with other trees and some shrubby plants. In its long strings of balls this sycamore differs from that of the United States, and is the *Platanus occidentalis* of Hooker—a new species recently described among the plants collected in the voyage of the Sulphur. The cotton-wood varied its foliage with white tufts, and the feathery seeds were flying plentifully through the air. Gooseberries, nearly ripe, were very abundant on the mountain; and as we passed the dividing grounds, which were not very easy to ascertain, the air was filled with perfume, as if we were entering a highly-cultivated garden; and, instead of green, our pathway and the mountain sides were covered with fields of yellow flowers, which here was the prevailing color.

Our journey to-day was in the midst of an advanced spring, whose green and floral beauty offered a delightful contrast to the sandy valley we had just left. All the day snow was in sight on the butte of the mountain, which frowned down upon us on the right; but we beheld it now with feelings of pleasant security, as we rode along between green trees and on flowers, with humming-birds and other feathered friends of the traveller enlivening the serene spring air.

As we reached the summit of this beautiful pass, and obtained a view into the eastern country, we saw at once that here was the place to take leave of all such pleasant scenes as those around us. The distant mountains were now bald rocks again; and below, the land had any color but green. Taking into consideration the nature of the Sierra Nevada, we found this pass an excellent one for horses; and with a little labor, or perhaps with a more perfect examination of the localities, it might be made sufficiently practicable for wagons. Its latitude and longitude may be considered that of our last encampment, only a few miles distant. The elevation was not taken—our half-wild cavalcade making it too troublesome to halt before night, when once started.

We here left the waters of the Bay of San Francisco, and though forced upon them contrary to my intentions, I cannot regret the necessity which occasioned the deviation. It made me well acquainted with the great range of the Sierra Nevada of the Alta California, and showed that this broad and elevated snowy ridge was a continuation of the Cascade Range of Oregon, between which and the ocean there is still another and a lower range, parallel to the former and to the coast, and which may be called the Coast Range. It also made me well acquainted with the basin of the San Francisco Bay, and with the two fine rivers and their valleys (the Sacramento and San Joaquin) which are tributary to that bay ; and cleared up some points in geography on which error had long prevailed.

It had been constantly represented, as I have already stated, that the Bay of San Francisco opened far into the interior, by some river coming down from the base of the Rocky Mountains, and upon which supposed stream the name of Rio Buenaventura had been bestowed. Our observations of the Sierra Nevada, in the long distance from the head of the Sacramento to the head of the San Joaquin, and of the valley below it, which collects all the waters of the San Francisco Bay, show that this neither is nor can be the case. No river from the interior does, or can, cross the Sierra Nevada—itself more lofty than the Rocky Mountains ; and as to the Buenaventura, the mouth of which seen on the coast gave the idea and the name of the reputed great river, it is, in fact, a small stream of no consequence, not only below the Sierra Nevada, but actually below the Coast Range—taking its rise within half a degree of the ocean, running parallel to it for about two degrees, and then falling into the Pacific near Monterey. There is no opening from the Bay of San Francisco into the interior of the continent. The two rivers which flow into it are comparatively short, and not perpendicular to the coast, but lateral to it, and having their heads toward Oregon and Southern California. They open lines of communication north and south, and not eastwardly ; and thus this want of interior communication from the San Francisco Bay, now fully ascertained, gives great additional value to the Columbia, which stands alone as the only great river on the Pacific slope of our continent which leads from the ocean to the Rocky Mountains, and opens a line of communication from the sea to the Valley of the Mississippi.

Four *compañeros* joined our guide at the pass ; and two going back at noon, the others continued on in company. Descending from the hills, we reached a country of fine grass, where the *Erodium cicutarium* finally disappeared, giving place to an excellent quality of bunch grass. Passing by some springs where there was a rich sward of grass among groves of large black oak, we rode over a plain on which the guide pointed out a spot where a refugee Christian Indian had been killed by a party of soldiers which had unexpectedly penetrated into the mountains.

Crossing a low sierra, and descending a hollow where a spring gushed out, we were struck by the sudden appearance of *yucca* trees, which gave a strange and southern character to the country, and suited well with the dry and desert region we were approaching. Associated with the idea of barren sands, their stiff and ungraceful form makes them to the traveller the most repulsive tree in the vegetable kingdom. Following the hollow, we shortly came upon a creek wooded with large black oak, which yet had not put forth a leaf. There was a small rivulet of running water with good grass.

April 15*th.*—The Indians who had accompanied the guide returned this morning, and I purchased from them a Spanish saddle and long spurs, as reminiscences of the time ; and for a few yards of scarlet cloth they gave me a horse, which afterward became food for other Indians.

We continued a short distance down the creek, in which our guide informed us that the water very soon disappeared, and turned directly to the southward along the foot of the mountain ; the trail on which we rode appearing to describe the eastern limit of travel, where water and grass terminated.

Crossing a low spur, which bordered the creek, we descended to a kind of plain among the lower spurs ; the desert being in full view on our left, apparently illimitable. A hot mist lay over it to-day, through which it had a white and glistening appearance ; here and there a few dry-looking buttes and isolated black ridges rose suddenly upon it. " There," said our guide, stretching out his hand toward it, " there are the great *llanos* (plains) ; *no hay agua ; no hay zacate—nada* (there is neither water nor grass—nothing) ; every animal that goes out upon them dies." It was indeed dismal to look upon, and hard to conceive so great a change in so short a distance. One might travel the world over without finding a valley more fresh and verdant, more floral and sylvan, more alive with birds and animals, more bounteously watered, than we had left in the San Joaquin : here, within a few miles' ride, a vast desert plain spread before us, from which the boldest traveller turned away in despair.

Directly in front of us, at some distance to the southward, and running out in an easterly direction from the mountains, stretched a sierra, having at the eastern end (perhaps fifty miles distant) some snowy peaks, on which, by the information of our guide, snow rested all the year.

Our cavalcade made a strange and grotesque appearance, and it was impossible to avoid reflecting upon our position and composition in this remote solitude. Within two degrees of the Pacific Ocean ; already far south of the latitude of Monterey ; and still forced on south by a desert on one hand and a mountain range on the other ; guided by a civilized Indian, attended by two wild ones from the Sierra ; a Chinook from the Columbia ; and our own mixture of American, French, German—all armed ; four or five languages heard at once ; above a hundred horses and mules, half wild ; American, Spanish, and Indian dresses and equipments intermingled —such was our composition.

Our march was a sort of procession. Scouts ahead, and on the flanks ; a front and rear division ; the pack-animals, baggage, and horned cattle in the centre ; and the whole stretching a quarter of a mile along our dreary path. In this form we journeyed ; looking more as if we belonged to Asia than to the United States of America.

We continued in a southerly direction across the plain, to which, as well as to all the country so far as we could see, the *yucca* trees gave a strange and singular character. Several new plants appeared, among which was a zygophyllaceous shrub (*Zygophyllum Californicum* Torr. and Frem.) sometimes ten feet in height; in form, and in the pliancy of its branches, it is rather a graceful plant. Its leaves are small, covered with a resinous substance; and, particularly when bruised and crushed, exhale a singular, but very agreeable and refreshing odor. This shrub and the *yucca*, with many varieties of cactus, make the characteristic features in the vegetation for a long distance to the eastward.

Along the foot of the mountain, twenty miles to the southward, red stripes of flowers were visible during the morning, which we supposed to be variegated sandstones. We rode rapidly during the day, and in the afternoon emerged from the *yucca* forest at the foot of an outlier of the Sierra before us, and came among the fields of flowers we had seen in the morning, which consisted principally of the rich orange-colored Californian poppy, mingled with other flowers of brighter tints. Reaching the top of this spur, which was covered with fine bunch grass, and where the hills were very green, our guide pointed to a small hollow in the mountain before us, saying, " *En esta piedra hay agua.*" He appeared to know every nook in the country.

We continued our beautiful road, and reached a spring in the slope at the foot of the ridge, running in a green ravine, among granite boulders ; here nightshade, and borders of buckwheat, with their white blossoms among the granite rocks, attracted our notice as familiar plants. Several antelopes were seen among the hills, and some large hares. Men were sent back this evening in search of a wild mule with a valuable pack, which had managed (as they frequently do) to hide itself along the road.

By observation the latitude of the camp is 34° 41' 42", and longitude 118° 20' 00". The next day the men returned with the mule.

April 17*th.*—Crossing the ridge by a beautiful pass of hollows, where several deer broke out of the thickets, we emerged at a small salt lake in a *vallon* lying nearly east and west, where a trail from the mission of *San Buenaventura* comes in. The lake is about one thousand two hundred yards in diameter; surrounded on the margin by a white salty border, which, by the smell, reminded us slightly of Lake Abert. There are some cotton-woods, with willow and elder, around the lake; and the water is a little salt, although not entirely unfit for drinking.

Here we turned directly to the eastward along the trail, which, from being seldom used, is almost imperceptible ; and, after travelling a few miles, our guide halted, and, pointing to the hardly visible trail, " *Aqui es camino,*" said he, " *no se pierde—va siempre.*" He pointed out a black butte on the plain at the foot of the mountain, where we would find water to encamp at night ; and, giving him a present of knives and scarlet cloth, we shook hands and parted. He bore off south, and in a day's ride would arrive at San Fernando, one of several missions in this part of California, where the country is so beautiful that it is considered a paradise, and the name of its principal town (*Pueblo de los Angeles*) would make it angelic.

We continued on through a succession of valleys, and came into a most beautiful spot of flower fields ; instead of green, the hills were purple and orange, with unbroken beds, into which each color was separately gathered. A pale straw color, with a bright yellow, the rich red-orange of the poppy mingled with fields of purple, covered the spot with a floral beauty ; and, on the border of the sandy deserts, seemed to invite the traveller to go no farther. Riding along through the perfumed air we soon after entered a defile overgrown with the ominous *Artemisia tridentata*, which conducted us into a sandy plain covered more or less densely with forests of *yucca*.

Having now the snowy ridge on our right, we continued our way toward a dark butte belonging to a low sierra in the plain, and which our guide had pointed out for a landmark. Late in the day the familiar growth of cotton-wood, a line of which was visible ahead, indicated our approach to a creek, which we reached where the water spread out into sands, and a little below sank entirely. Here our guide had intended we should pass the night; but there was not a blade of grass, and, hoping to find nearer the mountain a little for the night, we turned up the stream. A hundred yards above we found the creek a fine stream, sixteen feet wide, with a swift current.

A dark night overtook us when we reached the hills at the foot of the ridge, and we were obliged to encamp without grass—tying up what animals we could secure in the darkness, the greater part of the wild ones having free range for the night. Here the stream was two feet deep, swift and clear, issuing from a neighboring snow-peak. A few miles before reaching this creek, we had crossed a broad, dry river bed, which, nearer the hills, the hunters had found a bold and handsome stream.

April 18*th*.—Some parties were engaged in hunting up the scattered horses, and others in searching for grass above ; both were successful, and late in the day we encamped among some spring heads of the river, in a hollow which was covered with only tolerably good grasses, the lower ground being entirely overgrown with large bunches of the coarse stiff grass (*Carex sitchensis*).

Our latitude, by observation, was 34° 27' 03" ; and longitude 117° 43' 21".

Travelling close along the mountain, we followed up, in the afternoon of the 19th, another stream, in hopes to find a grass patch like that of the previous day, but were deceived; except some scattered bunch grass, there was nothing but rock and sand; and even the fertility of the mountain seemed withered by the air of the desert. Among the few trees was the nut-pine (*Pinus monophyllus*).

Our road the next day was still in an easterly direction along the ridge, over very bad travelling ground, broken and confounded with crippled trees and shrubs; and, after a difficult march of eighteen miles, a general shout announced that we had struck the great object of our search—THE SPANISH TRAIL—which here was running directly north. The road itself and its course were equally happy discoveries to us. Since the middle of December we had continually been forced south by mountains and by deserts, and now would have to make six degrees of *northing* to regain the latitude on which we wished to cross the Rocky Mountains. The course of the road, therefore, was what we wanted; and, once more, we felt like going home-ward. A *road* to travel on and the *right* course to go were joyful conso-lations to us; and our animals enjoyed the beaten track like ourselves.

Relieved from the rocks and brush, our wild mules started off at a rapid rate, and in fifteen miles we reached a considerable river, timbered with cotton-wood and willow, where we found a bottom of tolerable grass. As the animals had suffered a great deal in the last few days, I remained here all next day to allow them the necessary repose; and it was now necessary, at every favorable place, to make a little halt. Between us and the Colo-rado River we were aware that the country was extremely poor in grass, and scarce for water, there being many *jornadas* (days' journey), or long stretches of forty to sixty miles, without water, where the road was marked by bones of animals.

Although in California we had met with people who had passed over this trail, we had been able to obtain no correct information about it; and the greater part of what we had heard was found to be only a tissue of falsehoods. The rivers that we found on it were never mentioned, and others, particularly described in name and locality, were subsequently seen in another part of the country. It was described as a tolerably good sandy road, with so little rock as scarcely to require the animals to be shod; and we found it the roughest and rockiest road we had ever seen in the country, and which nearly destroyed our band of fine mules and horses. Many ani-mals are destroyed on it every year by a disease called the foot-evil; and a traveller should never venture on it without having his animals well shod, and also carrying extra shoes.

Latitude 34° 34' 11", and longitude 117° 13' 00".

The morning of the 22d was clear and bright, and a snowy peak to the southward shone out high and sharply defined. As has been usual since we crossed the mountains and descended into the hot plains, we had a gale of wind. We travelled down the right bank of the stream, over sands which are somewhat loose and have no verdure, but are occupied by various shrubs.

A clear, bold stream, sixty feet wide and several feet deep, had a strange appearance, running between perfectly naked banks of sand. The eye, however, is somewhat relieved by willows, and the beautiful green of the sweet cotton-woods with which it is well wooded. As we followed along its course, the river, instead of growing constantly larger, gradually dwindled away, as it was absorbed by the sand.

We were now careful to take the old camping-places of the annual Santa Fé caravans, which, luckily for us, had not yet made their yearly passage. A drove of several thousand horses and mules would have entirely swept away the scanty grass at the watering places, and we should have been obliged to leave the road to obtain subsistence for our animals. After riding twenty miles in a northeasterly direction, we found an old encampment, where we halted.

By observation the elevation of this encampment is two thousand two hundred and fifty feet.

April 23d.—The trail followed still along the river, which, in the course of the morning, entirely disappeared. We continued along the dry bed, in which, after an interval of about sixteen miles, the water reappeared in some low places, well timbered with cotton-wood and willow, where was another of the customary camping-grounds.

Here a party of six Indians came into camp, poor and hungry, and quite in keeping with the character of the country. Their arms were bows of unusual length, and each had a large gourd, strengthened with meshes of cord, in which he carried water. They proved to be the Mohahve Indians mentioned by our recent guide ; and from one of them, who spoke Spanish fluently, I obtained some interesting information which I would be glad to introduce here.

An account of the people inhabiting this region would undoubtedly possess interest for the civilized world. Our journey homeward was fruitful in incident ; and the country through which we travelled, although a desert, offered much to excite the curiosity of the botanist ; but limited time and the rapidly advancing season for active operations oblige me to omit all extended descriptions, and hurry briefly to the conclusion of this report.

The Indian who spoke Spanish had been educated for a number of years at one of the Spanish missions, and, at the breaking up of those establishments, had returned to the mountains, where he had been found by a party of *Mohahve* (sometimes called *Amuchava*) Indians, among whom he had ever since resided.

He spoke of the leader of the present party as " *mi amo* " (my master). He said they lived upon a large river in the southeast, which the " soldiers called the Rio Colorado ; " but that, formerly, a portion of them lived upon this river and among the mountains which had bounded the river valley to the northward during the day, and that here along the river they had raised various kinds of melons.   They sometimes came over to trade with the Indians of the Sierra, bringing with them blankets and goods manufac- tured by the Moquis and other Colorado Indians.   They rarely carried home horses, on account of the difficulty of getting them across the desert and of guarding them afterward from the Pi-utah Indians, who inhabit the Sierra, at the head of the *Rio Virgen* (River of the Virgin).

He informed us that, a short distance below, this river finally disap- peared.   The two different portions in which water is found had received from the priests two different names ; and subsequently I heard it called by the Spaniards the *Rio de las Animas*, but on the map we have called it the *Mohahve* River.

April 24th.—We continued down the stream (or rather its bed) for about eight miles, where there was water still in several holes, and en- camped.   The caravans sometimes continue below to the end of the river, from which there is a very long *jornada* of perhaps sixty miles without water.

Here a singular and new species of acacia, with spiral pods or seed- vessels, made its first appearance ; becoming henceforward, for a consider- able distance, a characteristic tree.   It was here comparatively large, being about twenty feet in height, with a full and spreading top, the lower branches declining toward the ground.   It afterward occurred of smaller size, frequently in groves, and is very fragrant.   It has been called by Dr. Torrey *Spirolobium odoratum.*   The zygophyllaceous shrub had been con- stantly characteristic of the plains along the river ; and here, among many new plants, a new and very remarkable species of eriogonum (*Eriogonum inflatum* Torr. and Frem.) made its first appearance.

Our cattle had become so tired and poor by this fatiguing travelling that three of them were killed here, and the meat dried.   The Indians had now an occasion for a great feast, and were occupied the remainder of the day and all the night in cooking and eating.   There was no part of the animal for which they did not find some use, except the bones.

In the afternoon we were surprised by the sudden appearance in the camp of two Mexicans—a man and a boy.   The name of the man was Andres Fuentes ; and that of the boy (a handsome lad, eleven years old) Pablo Hernandez.   They belonged to a party consisting of six persons, the remaining four being the wife of Fuentes, the father and mother of Pablo, and Santiago Giacome, a resident of New Mexico.   With a cavalcade of about thirty horses they had come out from Pueblo de los Angeles, near the coast, under the guidance of Giacome, in advance of the great caravan, in order to travel more at leisure and obtain better grass. Having advanced as far into the desert as was considered consistent with their safety, they halted at the *Archilette*, one of the customary camping-grounds, about eighty miles from our encampment, where there is a spring of good water, with sufficient grass; and concluded to await there the arrival of the great caravan. Several Indians were soon discovered lurking about the camp, who, in a day or two after, came in, and, after behaving in a very friendly manner, took their leave without awakening any suspicions. Their deportment begat a security which proved fatal. In a few days afterward, suddenly a party of about one hundred Indians appeared in sight, advancing toward the camp. It was too late, or they seemed not to have presence of mind to take proper measures of safety; and the Indians charged down into their camp, shouting as they advanced and discharging flights of arrows. Pablo and Fuentes were on horse-guard at the time, and mounted, according to the custom of the country. One of the principal objects of the Indians was to get possession of the horses, and part of them immediately surrounded the band; but, in obedience to the shouts of Giacome, Fuentes drove the animals over and through the assailants, in spite of their arrows; and, abandoning the rest to their fate, carried them off at speed across the plain. Knowing that they would be pursued by the Indians, without making any halt except to shift their saddles to other horses, they drove them on for about sixty miles, and this morning left them at a watering place on the trail called Agua de Tomaso. Without giving themselves any time for rest they hurried on, hoping to meet the Spanish caravan, when they discovered my camp. I received them kindly, taking them into my own mess, and promised them such aid as circumstances might put it in my power to give.

April 25th.—We left the river abruptly and, turning to the north, regained in a few miles the main trail (which had left the river sooner than ourselves) and continued our way across a lower ridge of the mountain, through a miserable tract of sand and gravel. We crossed at intervals the broad beds of dry gullies, where in the season of rains and melting snows there would be brooks or rivulets; and at one of these, where there was no indication of water, were several freshly dug holes, in which there was water at the depth of two feet. These holes had been dug by the wolves, whose keen sense of smell had scented the water under the dry sand. They were nice little wells, narrow, and dug straight down, and we got pleasant water out of them.

The country had now assumed the character of an elevated and mountainous desert; its general features being black, rocky ridges, bald, and destitute of timber, with sandy basins between.   Where the sides of these ridges are washed by gullies, the plains below are strewed with beds of large pebbles or rolled stones, destructive to our soft-footed animals, accustomed to the grassy plains of the Sacramento Valley.   Through these sandy basins sometimes struggled a scanty stream, or occurred a hole of water, which furnished camping-grounds for travellers.   Frequently, in our journey across, snow was visible on the surrounding mountains ; but their waters rarely reached the sandy plain below, where we toiled along, oppressed with thirst and a burning sun.

But throughout this nakedness of sand and gravel were many beautiful plants and flowering shrubs, which occurred in many new species, and with greater variety than we had been accustomed to see in the most luxuriant prairie countries ; this was a peculiarity of this desert.   Even where no grass would take root, the naked sand would bloom with some rich and rare flower, which found its appropriate home in the arid and barren spot.

Scattered over the plain, and tolerably abundant, was a handsome leguminous shrub, three or four feet high, with fine bright-purple flowers.   It is a new *psoralea*, and occurred frequently henceforward along our road.

Beyond the first ridge our road bore a little to the east of north, toward a gap in a higher line of mountains ; and, after travelling about twenty-five miles, we arrived at the *Agua de Tomaso*—the spring where the horses had been left ; but, as we expected, they were gone.   A brief examination of the ground convinced us that they had been driven off by the Indians. Carson and Godey volunteered with the Mexican to pursue them ; and, well mounted, the three set off on the trail.   At this stopping-place there were a few bushes and very little grass.   Its water was a pool ; but near by was a spring, which had been dug out by Indians or travellers.   Its water was cool—a great refreshment to us under a burning sun.

In the evening Fuentes returned, his horse having failed ; but Carson and Godey had continued the pursuit.

I observed to-night an occultation of α^2 *Cancri*, at the dark limb of the moon, which gives for the longitude of the place 116° 23′ 28″ ; the latitude, by observation, is 35° 13′ 08″.   From Helvetia to this place the positions along the intervening line are laid down with the longitudes obtained from the chronometer, which appears to have retained its rate remarkably well ; but henceforward, to the end of the journey, the few longitudes given are absolute, depending upon a subsequent occultation and eclipses of the satellites.

In the afternoon of the next day a war-whoop was heard, such as Indians make when returning from a victorious enterprise ; and soon Carson and Godey appeared, driving before them a band of horses, recognized by

Fuentes to be part of those they had lost. Two bloody scalps, dangling from the end of Godey's gun, announced that they had overtaken the Indians as well as the horses.

They informed us that after Fuentes left them, from the failure of his horse, they continued the pursuit alone, and toward nightfall entered the mountains, into which the trail led. After sunset the moon gave light, and they followed the trail by moonshine until late in the night, when it entered a narrow defile and was difficult to follow. Afraid of losing it in the darkness of the defile, they tied up their horses, struck no fire, and lay down to sleep in silence and in darkness. Here they lay from midnight till morning. At daylight they resumed the pursuit, and about sunrise discovered the horses; and, immediately dismounting and tying up their own, they crept cautiously to a rising ground which intervened, from the crest of which they perceived the encampment of four lodges close by. They proceeded quietly, and had got within thirty or forty yards of their object, when a movement among the horses discovered them to the Indians: giving the war-shout, they instantly charged into the camp, regardless of the number which the *four* lodges would imply. The Indians received them with a flight of arrows shot from their long bows, one of which passed through Godey's shirt collar, barely missing the neck; our men fired their rifles upon a steady aim, and rushed in. Two Indians were stretched on the ground, fatally wounded; the rest fled, except a lad who was captured. The scalps of the fallen were instantly stripped off; but in the process one of them, who had two balls through his body, sprang to his feet, the blood streaming from his skinned head, and uttered a hideous howl. An old squaw, possibly his mother, stopped and looked back from the mountain side she was climbing, threatening and lamenting. The frightful spectacle appalled the stout hearts of our men; but they did what humanity required, and quickly terminated the agonies of the gory savage.

They were now masters of the camp, which was a pretty little recess in the mountain, with a fine spring, and apparently safe from all invasion. Great preparations had been made to feast a large party, for it was a very proper place for a rendezvous and for the celebration of such orgies as robbers of the desert would delight in. Several of the best horses had been killed, skinned, and cut up; for the Indians living in mountains, and only coming into the plains to rob and murder, make no other use of horses than to eat them. Large earthen vessels were on the fire, boiling and stewing the horse-beef; and several baskets, containing fifty or sixty pairs of moccasins, indicated the presence, or expectation, of a considerable party. They released the boy, who had given strong evidence of the stoicism, or something else, of the savage character, in commencing his breakfast upon a horse's head as soon as he found he was not to be killed, but only tied as a prisoner.

Their object accomplished, our men gathered up all the surviving horses, fifteen in number, returned upon their trail, and rejoined us at our camp in the afternoon of the same day. They had ridden about one hundred miles in the pursuit and return, and all in thirty hours. The time, place, object, and numbers considered, this expedition of Carson and Godey may be considered among the boldest and most disinterested which the annals of Western adventure, so full of daring deeds, can present. Two men, in a savage desert, pursue day and night an unknown body of Indians into the defiles of an unknown mountain—attack them on sight, without counting numbers —and defeat them in an instant—and for what? To punish the robbers of the desert, and to avenge the wrongs of Mexicans whom they did not know. I repeat: it was Carson and Godey who did this—the former an American, born in the Boonslick country of Missouri; the latter a Frenchman, born in St. Louis—and both trained to Western enterprise from early life.

By the information of Fuentes, we had now to make a long stretch of forty or fifty miles across a plain which lay between us and the next possible camp; and we resumed our journey late in the afternoon, with the intention of travelling through the night, and avoiding the excessive heat of the day, which was oppressive to our animals. For several hours we travelled across a high plain, passing, at the opposite side, through a cañon by the bed of a creek running *northwardly* into a small lake beyond, and both of them being dry.

We had a warm, moonshiny night; and, travelling directly toward the north star, we journeyed now across an open plain between mountain ridges; that on the left being broken, rocky, and bald, according to the information of Carson and Godey, who had entered here in pursuit of the horses. The plain appeared covered principally with the *Zygophyllum Californicum* already mentioned; and the line of our road was marked by the skeletons of horses, which were strewed to a considerable breadth over the plain. We were afterward always warned on entering one of these long stretches, by the bones of these animals, which had perished before they could reach the water. About midnight we reached a considerable stream-bed, now dry, the discharge of the waters of this basin (when it collected any) down which we descended in a *northwesterly* direction. The creek-bed was overgrown with shrubbery, and several hours before day it brought us to the entrance of a cañon where we found water and encamped. This word *cañon* is used by the Spaniards to signify a defile or gorge in a creek or river, where high rocks press in close, and make a narrow way, usually difficult, and often impossible to be passed.

In the morning we found that we had a very poor camping-ground: a

CARSON AND GODEY RETURNING FROM INDIAN FIGHT.

swampy, salty spot, with a little long, unwholesome grass ; and the water, which rose in springs, being useful only to wet the mouth, but entirely too salt to drink. All around were sand and rocks, and skeletons of horses which had not been able to find support for their lives. As we were about to start we found, at the distance of a few hundred yards, among the hills to the southward, a spring of tolerably good water, which was a relief to ourselves ; but the place was too poor to remain long, and therefore we continued on this morning. On the creek were thickets of *Spirolobium odoratum* (acacia) in bloom, and very fragrant.

Passing through the cañon, we entered another sandy basin, through which the dry stream-bed continued its northwesterly course, in which direction appeared a high snowy mountain.

We travelled through a barren district, where a heavy gale was blowing about the loose sand, and, after a ride of eight miles, reached a large creek of salt and bitter water, running in a westerly direction, to meet the stream-bed we had left. It is called by the Spaniards *Amargosa*—the bitter water of the desert. Where we struck it the stream bends ; and we continued in a northerly course up the ravine of its valley, passing on the way a fork from the right, near which occurred a bed of plants, consisting of a remarkable new genus of *cruciferæ*.

Gradually ascending, the ravine opened into a green valley, where, at the foot of the mountain, were springs of excellent water. We encamped among groves of the new *acacia*, and there was an abundance of good grass for the animals.

This was the best camping-ground we had seen since we struck the Spanish trail. The day's journey was about twelve miles.

April 29th.—To-day we had to reach the *Archilette*, distant seven miles, where the Mexican party had been attacked ; and, leaving our encampment early, we traversed a part of the desert, the most sterile and repulsive that we had yet seen. Its prominent features were dark *sierras*, naked and dry ; on the plains a few straggling shrubs—among them, cactus of several varieties. Fuentes pointed out one, called by the Spaniards *bisnada*, which has a juicy pulp, slightly acid, and is eaten by the traveller to allay thirst.

Our course was generally north ; and, after crossing an intervening ridge, we descended into a sandy plain or basin, in the middle of which was the grassy spot, with its springs and willow-bushes, which constitutes a camping-place in the desert, and is called the *Archilette*. The dead silence of the place was ominous ; and, galloping rapidly up, we found only the corpses of the two men : everything else was gone. They were naked, mutilated, and pierced with arrows. Hernandez had evidently fought, and with desperation. He lay in advance of the willow, half-faced tent, which sheltered his family, as if he had come out to meet danger, and to repulse it from that asylum. One of his hands and both his legs had been cut off. Giacome, who was a large and strong-looking man, was lying in one of the willow-shelters, pierced with arrows. Of the women no trace could be found, and it was evident they had been carried off captive. A little lap-dog, which had belonged to Pablo's mother, remained with the dead bodies, and was frantic with joy at seeing Pablo ; he, poor child, was frantic with grief, and filled the air with lamentations for his father and mother. *Mi padre !—mi madre !*—was his incessant cry. When we beheld this pitiable sight, and pictured to ourselves the fate of the two women, carried off by savages so brutal and so loathsome, all compunction for the scalped-alive Indian ceased ; and we rejoiced that Carson and Godey had been alive to give so useful a lesson to these American Arabs, who lie in wait to murder and plunder the innocent traveller.

We were all too much affected by the sad feelings which the place inspired to remain an unnecessary moment. The night we were obliged to pass there. Early in the morning we left it, having first written a brief account of what had happened, and put it in the cleft of a pole planted at the spring, that the approaching caravan might learn the fate of their friends. In commemoration of the event we called the place *Agua de Hernandez*—Hernandez' Spring. By observation its latitude was 35° 51′ 21″.

April 30th.—We continued our journey over a district similar to that of the day before. From the sandy basin in which was the spring we entered another basin of the same character, surrounded everywhere by mountains. Before us stretched a high range, rising still higher to the left, and terminating in a snowy mountain.

After a day's march of twenty-four miles we reached at evening the bed of a stream from which the water had disappeared ; a little only remained in holes, which we increased by digging ; and about a mile above, the stream, not yet entirely sunk, was spread out over the sands, affording a little water for the animals. The stream came out of the mountains on the left, very slightly wooded with cotton-wood, willow, and acacia, and a few dwarf oaks ; and grass was nearly as scarce as water. A plant with showy yellow flowers (*Stanleya integrifolia*) occurred abundantly at intervals for the last two days, and *Eriogonum inflatum* was among the characteristic plants.

May 1st.—The air is rough, and overcoats pleasant. The sky is blue, and the day bright. Our road was over a plain, toward the foot of the mountain ; *Zygophyllum Californicum*, now in bloom with a small yellow flower, is characteristic of the country ; and *cacti* were very abundant, and in rich fresh bloom, which wonderfully ornaments this poor country.

We encamped at a spring in the pass which had been the site of an old

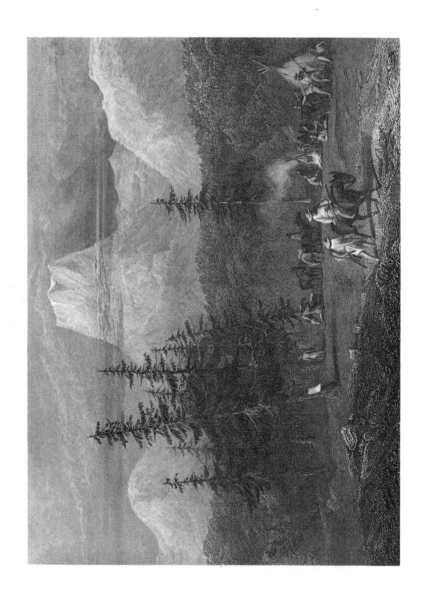

FOREST CAMP. SHASTL PEAK.

village; here we found excellent grass, but very little water.   We dug out the old spring, and watered some of our animals.   The mountain here was wooded very slightly with the nut-pine, cedars, and a dwarf species of oak; and among the shrubs were *Purshia tridentata*, *Artemisia*, and *Ephedra occidentalis*.   The numerous shrubs which constitute the vegetation of the plains are now in bloom, with flowers of white, yellow, red, and purple. The continual rocks, and want of water and grass, begin to be very hard on our mules and horses; but the principal loss is occasioned by their crippled feet, the greater part of those left being in excellent order, and scarcely a day passes without some loss ; and, one by one, Fuentes horses are constantly dropping behind.   Whenever they give out he dismounts, and cuts off their tails and manes to make saddle girths ; the last advantage one can gain from them.

The next day, in a short but rough ride of twelve miles, we crossed the mountain ; and, descending to a small valley-plain, encamped at the foot of the ridge, on the bed of a creek, where we found good grass in sufficient quantity, and abundance of water in holes.   The ridge is extremely rugged and broken, presenting on this side a continued precipice, and probably affords very few passes.   Many *Digger* tracks are seen around us, but no Indians were visible.

May 3d.—After a day's journey of eighteen miles, in a northeasterly direction, we encamped in the midst of another very large basin, at a camping-ground called *Las Vegas*—a term which the Spaniards use to signify fertile or marshy plains, in contradistinction to *llanos*, which they apply to dry and sterile plains.   Two narrow streams of clear water, four or five feet deep, gush suddenly, with a quick current, from two singularly large springs ; these, and other waters of the basin, pass out in a gap to the eastward.   The taste of the water is good, but rather too warm to be agreeable ; the temperature being 71° in the one and 73° in the other. They, however, afforded a delightful bathing-place.

May 4th.—We started this morning earlier than usual, travelling in a northeasterly direction across the plain.   The new acacia (*Spirolobium odoratum*) has now become the characteristic tree of the country ; it is in bloom, and its blossoms are very fragrant.   The day was still, and the heat, which soon became very oppressive, appeared to bring out strongly the refreshing scent of the zygophyllaceous shrubs and the sweet perfume of the acacia.   The snowy ridge we had just crossed looked out conspicuously in the northwest.   In about five hours' ride we crossed a gap in the surrounding ridge, and the appearance of skeletons of horses very soon warned us that we were engaged in another dry *jornada*, which proved the longest we had made in all our journey—between fifty and sixty miles without a drop of water.

Travellers through countries affording water and timber can have no conception of our intolerable thirst while journeying over the hot yellow sands of this elevated country, where the heated air seems to be entirely deprived of moisture. We ate occasionally the *bisnada,* and moistened our mouths with the acid of the sour dock (*Rumex venosus*). Hourly expecting to find water, we continued to press on until toward midnight, when, after a hard and uninterrupted march of sixteen hours, our wild mules began running ahead; and in a mile or two we came to a bold running stream— so keen is the sense of that animal, in these desert regions, in scenting at a distance this necessary of life.

According to the information we had received Sevier River was a tributary of the Colorado ; and this, accordingly, should have been one of its affluents. It proved to be the *Rio de los Angeles* (River of the Angels)— a branch of the *Rio Virgen* (River of the Virgin).

May 5th.—On account of our animals, it was necessary to remain to-day at this place. Indians crowded numerously around us in the morning ; and we were obliged to keep arms in hand all day, to keep them out of the camp. They began to surround the horses, which, for the convenience of grass, we were guarding a little above, on the river. These were immediately driven in, and kept close to the camp.

In the darkness of the night we had made a very bad encampment, our fires being commanded by a rocky bluff within fifty yards ; but, notwithstanding, we had the river and small thickets of willows on the other side. Several times during the day the camp was insulted by the Indians ; but peace being our object, I kept simply on the defensive. Some of the Indians were on the bottoms, and others haranguing us from the bluffs ; and they were scattered in every direction over the hills. Their language being probably a dialect of the *Utah,* with the aid of signs some of our people could comprehend them very well. They were the same people who had murdered the Mexicans ; and toward us their disposition was evidently hostile, nor were we well disposed toward them. They were barefooted and nearly naked ; their hair gathered up into a knot behind ; and with his bow each man carried a quiver with thirty or forty arrows, partially drawn out. Besides these, each held in his hand two or three arrows for instant service. Their arrows are barbed with a very clear translucent stone, a species of opal, nearly as hard as the diamond ; and, shot from their long bows, are almost as effective as a gunshot. In these Indians I was forcibly struck by an expression of countenance resembling that in a beast of prey ; and all their actions are those of wild animals. Joined to the restless motion of the eye there is a want of mind—an absence of thought—and an action wholly by impulse, strongly expressed, and which constantly recalls the similarity.

A man who appeared to be a chief, with two or three others, forced himself into camp, bringing with him his arms, in spite of my orders to the contrary.   When shown our weapons, he bored his ears with his fingers, and
said he could not hear.   " Why," said he, " there are none of you."
Counting the people around the camp, and including in the number a mule
which was being shod, he made out twenty-two.   " So many," said he,
showing the number, " and we—we are a great many ; " and he pointed
to the hills and mountains round about.   " If you have your arms," said he,
twanging his bow, " we have these."   I had some difficulty in restraining
the people, particularly Carson, who felt an insult of this kind as much as
if it had been given by a more responsible being.   " Don't say that, old
man," said he ; " don't you say that—your life's in danger"—speaking in
good English ; and probably the old man was nearer to his end than he
will be before he meets it.

Several animals had been necessarily left behind near the camp last
night ; and early in the morning, before the Indians made their appearance,
several men were sent to bring them in.   When I was beginning to be uneasy at their absence, they returned with information that the animals had
been driven off from the trail by Indians ; and, having followed the tracks
a short distance, they found them cut up and spread out upon bushes.

In the evening I gave a fatigued horse to some of the Indians for a
feast ; and the village which carried him off refused to share with the
others, who made loud complaints from the rocks of the partial distribution.
Many of these Indians had long sticks, hooked at the end, which they used
in hauling out lizards and other small animals from their holes.   During
the day they occasionally roasted and ate lizards at our fires.   These belong
to the people who are generally known under the name of *Diggers* ; and to
these I have more particularly had reference when occasionally speaking of
a people whose sole occupation is to procure food sufficient to support existence.

The formation here consists of fine yellow sandstone, alternating with a
coarse conglomerate, in which the stones are from the size of ordinary
gravel to six or eight inches in diameter.   This is the formation which renders the surface of the country so rocky, and gives us now a road alternately of loose, heavy sands, and rolled stones, which cripple the animals
in a most extraordinary manner.

On the following morning we left the *Rio de los Angeles*, and continued
our way through the same desolate and revolting country, where lizards
were the only animal, and the tracks of the lizard-eaters the principal sign
of human beings.   After twenty miles' march through a road of hills and
heavy sands we reached the most dreary river I have ever seen—a deep,
rapid stream, almost a torrent, passing swiftly by and roaring against ob-

structions.   The banks were wooded with willow, acacia, and a frequent plant of the country already mentioned (*Garrya elliptica*), growing in thickets, resembling willow, and bearing a small pink flower.

Crossing it, we encamped on the left bank, where we found a very little grass.   Our three remaining steers, being entirely given out, were killed here.   By the boiling point the elevation of the river here is four thousand and sixty feet; and latitude, by observation, 36° 41' 33".   The stream was running toward the southwest, and appeared to come from a snowy mountain in the north.   It proved to be the *Rio Virgen*—a tributary to the Colorado.

Indians appeared in bands on the hills, but did not come into camp. For several days we continued our journey up the river, the bottoms of which were thickly overgrown with various kinds of brush; and the sandy soil was absolutely covered with the tracks of *Diggers*, who followed us stealthily, like a band of wolves; and we had no opportunity to leave behind, even for a few hours, the tired animals, in order that they might be brought into camp after a little repose.   A horse or mule left behind was taken off in a moment.

On the evening of the 8th, having travelled twenty-eight miles up the river from our first encampment on it, we encamped at a little grass-plat where a spring of cool water issued from the bluff.   On the opposite side was a grove of cotton-woods at the mouth of a fork, which here enters the river.   On either side, the valley is bounded by ranges of mountains, everywhere high, rocky, and broken.   The caravan road was lost and scattered in the sandy country, and we had been following an Indian trail up the river.   The hunters the next day were sent out to reconnoitre, and in the meantime we moved about a mile farther up, where we found a good little patch of grass.   There being only sufficient grass for the night, the horses were sent with a strong guard in charge of Tabeau to a neighboring hollow, where they might pasture during the day; and to be ready in case the Indians should make any attempt on the animals, several of the best horses were picketed at the camp.   In a few hours the hunters returned, having found a convenient ford in the river and discovered the Spanish trail on the other side.

I had been engaged in arranging plants; and, fatigued with the heat of the day, I fell asleep in the afternoon and did not awake until sundown. Presently Carson came to me and reported that Tabeau, who early in the day had left his post, and, without my knowledge, rode back to the camp we had left in search of a lame mule, had not returned.   While we were speaking a smoke rose suddenly from the cotton-wood grove below, which plainly told us what had befallen him; it was raised to inform the surrounding Indians that a blow had been struck, and to tell them to be on their guard. Carson, with several men well mounted, was instantly sent down the river, but returned in the night without tidings of the missing man. They went to the camp we had left, but neither he nor the mule was there. Searching down the river, they found the tracks of the mule, evidently driven along by Indians, whose tracks were on each side of those made by the animal. After going several miles they came to the mule itself, standing in some bushes, mortally wounded in the side by an arrow, and left to die, that it might be afterwards butchered for food. They also found, in another place, as they were hunting about on the ground for Tabeau's tracks, something that looked like a little puddle of blood, but which the darkness prevented them from verifying. With these details they returned to our camp, and their report saddened all our hearts.

May 10*th.*—This morning, as soon as there was light enough to follow tracks, I set out myself with Mr. Fitzpatrick and several men in search of Tabeau. We went to the spot where the appearance of puddled blood had been seen ; and this, we saw at once, had been the place where he fell and died. Blood upon the leaves and beaten-down bushes showed that he had got his wound about twenty paces from where he fell, and that he had struggled for his life. He had probably been shot through the lungs with an arrow. From the place where he lay and bled, it could be seen that he had been dragged to the bank of the river, and thrown into it. No vestige of what had belonged to him could be found, except a fragment of his horse equipment. Horse, gun, clothes—all became the prey of these Arabs of the New World.

Tabeau had been one of our best men, and his unhappy death spread a gloom over our party. Men who have gone through such dangers and sufferings as we had seen become like brothers, and feel each other's loss. To defend and avenge each other is the deep feeling of all. We wished to avenge his death; but the condition of our horses, languishing for grass and repose, forbade an expedition into unknown mountains. We knew the tribe who had done the mischief—the same which had been insulting our camp. They knew what they deserved, and had the discretion to show themselves to us no more. The day before, they infested our camp; now, not one appeared ; nor did we ever afterward see but one who even belonged to the same tribe, and he at a distance.

Our camp was in a basin below a deep cañon—a gap of two thousand feet deep in the mountain—through which the *Rio Virgen* passes, and where no man or beast could follow it. The Spanish trail, which we had lost in the sands of the basin, was on the opposite side of the river. We crossed over to it, and followed it northwardly toward a gap which was visible in the mountain. We approached it by a defile, rendered difficult for our bare-footed animals by the rocks strewed along it ; and here the country changed its character.   From the time we entered the desert, the mountains had been bald and rocky ; here they began to be wooded with cedar and pine, and clusters of trees gave shelter to birds—a new and welcome sight—which could not have lived in the desert we had passed.

Descending a long hollow, toward the narrow valley of a stream, we saw before us a snowy mountain, far beyond which appeared another, more lofty still.   Good bunch grass began to appear on the hill-sides, and here we found a singular variety of interesting shrubs.   The changed appearance of the country infused among our people a more lively spirit, which was heightened by finding at evening a halting-place of very good grass on the clear waters of the *Santa Clara* Fork of the *Rio Virgen.*

CHAPTER XI.

May 11*th*.—The morning was cloudy and quite cool, with a shower of
rain—the first we have had since entering the desert, a period of twenty-
seven days ; and we seem to have entered a different climate, with the
usual weather of the Rocky Mountains. Our march to-day was very laborious, over very broken ground, along the Santa Clara River ; but then
the country is no longer so distressingly desolate.

The stream is prettily wooded with sweet cotton-wood trees—some of
them of large size ; and on the hills, where the nut-pine is often seen, a
good and wholesome grass occurs frequently. This cotton-wood, which is
now in fruit, is of a different species from any in Michaux's " Sylva." Heavy
dark clouds covered the sky in the evening, and a cold wind sprang up,
making fires and overcoats comfortable.

May 12*th*.—A little above our encampment the river forked ; and we
continued up the right-hand branch, gradually ascending toward the summit of the mountain. As we rose toward the head of the creek the snowy
mountain on our right showed out handsomely—high, and rugged with
precipices, and covered with snow for about two thousand feet from their
summits down.

Our animals were somewhat repaid for their hard marches by an excellent camping-ground on the summit of the ridge, which forms here the
dividing chain between the waters of the *Rio Virgen*, which goes south
to the Colorado, and those of Sevier River, flowing northwardly, and belonging to the Great Basin. We considered ourselves as crossing the
rim of the basin ; and, entering it at this point, we found here an extensive mountain meadow, rich in bunch grass, and fresh with numerous
springs of clear water, all refreshing and delightful to look upon. It was,
in fact, those *Las Vegas de Santa Clara*, which had been so long presented
to us as the terminating point of the desert, and where the annual caravan
from California to New Mexico halted and recruited for some weeks. It

was a very suitable place to recover from the fatigue and exhaustion of a month's suffering in the hot and sterile desert.   The meadow was about a mile wide and some ten miles long, bordered by grassy hills and mountains—some of the latter rising two thousand feet, and white with snow down to the level of the *vegas*.   Its elevation above the sea was five thousand two hundred and eighty feet; latitude, by observation, 37° 28' 28"; and its distance from where we first struck the Spanish trail about four hundred miles.

Counting from the time we reached the desert, and began to skirt, at our descent from Walker's Pass in the Sierra Nevada, we had travelled five hundred and fifty miles, occupying twenty-seven days, in that inhospitable region.   In passing before the great caravan we had the advantage of finding more grass, but the disadvantage of finding also the marauding savages who had gathered down upon the trail, waiting the approach of that prey.   This greatly increased our labors, besides costing us the life of an excellent man.   We had to move all day in a state of watch and prepared for combat—scouts and flankers out, a front and rear division of our men, and baggage animals in the centre.   At night, camp-duty was severe.   Those who had toiled all day had to guard, by turns, the camp and the horses all night.   Frequently one-third of the whole party were on guard at once ; and nothing but this vigilance saved us from attack.   We were constantly dogged by bands, and even whole tribes of the marauders; and although Tabeau was killed, and our camp infested and insulted by some, while swarms of them remained on the hills and mountain sides, there was manifestly a consultation and calculation going on to decide the question of attacking us.

Having reached the resting-place of the *Vegas de Santa Clara*, we had complete relief from the heat and privations of the desert, and some relaxation from the severity of camp-duty.   Some relaxation, and relaxation only —for camp-guards, horse-guards, and scouts are indispensable from the time of leaving the frontiers of Missouri until we return to them.

After we left the *Vegas* we had the gratification to be joined by the famous hunter and trapper, Mr. Joseph Walker, whom I have before mentioned, and who now became our guide.   He had left California with the great caravan ; and perceiving, from the signs along the trail, that there was a party of whites ahead, which he judged to be mine, he detached himself from the caravan with eight men (Americans), and ran the gauntlet of the desert robbers, killing two, and getting some of the horses wounded, and succeeded in overtaking us.   Nothing but his great knowledge of the country, great courage and presence of mind, and good rifles, could have brought him safe from such a perilous enterprise.

May 13*th.*—We remained one day at this noted place of rest and refreshment ; and, resuming our progress in a northeastwardly direction, we descended into a broad valley, the water of which is tributary to Sevier Lake. The next day we came in sight of the Wah-satch range of moun- tains on the right, white with snow, and here forming the southeast part of the Great Basin. Sevier Lake, upon the waters of which we now were, belonged to the system of lakes in the eastern part of the basin—of which the Great Salt Lake and its southern limb, the Utah Lake, were the prin- cipal—toward the region of which we were now approaching. We trav- elled for several days in this direction, within the rim of the Great Basin, crossing little streams which bore to the left for Sevier Lake ; and plainly seeing, by the changed aspect of the country, that we were entirely clear of the desert and approaching the regions which appertained to the system of the Rocky Mountains. We met, in this traverse, a few mounted Utah Indians, in advance of their main body, watching the approach of the great caravan.

May 16th.—We reached a small salt lake, about seven miles long and one broad, at the northern extremity of which we encamped for the night. This little lake, which well merits its characteristic name, lies immediately at the base of the Wah-satch range, and nearly opposite a gap in that chain of mountains through which the Spanish trail passes ; and which, again falling upon the waters of the Colorado, and crossing the river, proceeds over a mountainous country to Santa Fé.

May 17th.—After four hundred and forty miles of travelling on a trail which served for a road, we again found ourselves under the necessity of exploring a track through the wilderness. The Spanish trail had borne off to the southeast, crossing the Wah-satch range. Our course led to the northeast, along the foot of that range, and leaving it on the right. The mountain presented itself to us under the form of several ridges, rising one above the other, rocky, and wooded with pine and cedar ; the last ridge covered with snow. Sevier River, flowing northwardly to the lake of the same name, collects its principal waters from this section of the Wah-satch chain.

We had now entered a region of great pastoral promise, abounding with fine streams ; the rich bunch grass—soil that would produce wheat, and indigenous flax—growing as if it had been sown. Consistent with the general character of its bordering mountains, this fertility of soil and vege- tation does not extend far into the Great Basin. Mr. Joseph Walker, our guide, and who has more knowledge of these parts than any man I know, informed me that all the country to the left was unknown to him, and that even the *Digger* tribes, which frequented Lake Sevier, could tell him noth- ing about it.

May 20th.—We met a band of Utah Indians, headed by a chief who had obtained the American or English name of Walker, by which he is quoted and well known. They were all mounted, armed with rifles, and use their rifles well. The chief had a fusee, which he had carried slung, in addition to his rifle. They were journeying slowly toward the Spanish trail, to levy their usual tribute upon the great Californian caravan. They were robbers of a higher order than those of the desert. They conducted their depredations with form, and under the color of trade, and toll for passing through their country. Instead of attacking and killing, they affect to purchase—taking the horses they like, and giving something nominal in return. The chief was quite civil to me. He was personally acquainted with his namesake, our guide, who made my name known to him. He knew of my expedition of 1842 ; and, as tokens of friendship and proof that we had met, proposed an interchange of presents. We had no great store to choose out of; so he gave me a Mexican blanket, and I gave him a very fine one which I had obtained at Vancouver.

May 23*d.*—We reached Sevier River—the main tributary of the lake of the same name—which, deflecting from its northern course, here breaks from the mountains to enter the lake. It was really a fine river, from eight to twelve feet deep ; and, after searching in vain for a fordable place, we made little boats (or rather rafts) out of bulrushes, and ferried across. These rafts are readily made, and give a good conveyance across a river. The rushes are bound in bundles, and tied hard ; the bundles are tied down upon poles, as close as they can be pressed, and fashioned like a boat, in being broader in the middle and pointed at the ends. The rushes, being tubular and jointed, are light and strong. The raft swims well, and is shoved along by poles, or paddled, or pushed and pulled by swimmers, or drawn by ropes. On this occasion we used ropes—one at each end—and rapidly drew our little float backward and forward, from shore to shore. The horses swam.

At our place of crossing, which was the most northern point of its bend, the latitude was 39° 22′ 19″. The banks sustained the character of fertility and vegetation which we had seen for some days. The name of this river and lake was an indication of our approach to regions of which our people had been the explorers. It was probably named after some American trapper or hunter, and was the first American name we had met with since leaving the Columbia River. From the *Dalles* to the point where we turned across the Sierra Nevada, near one thousand miles, we heard Indian names, and the greater part of the distance none ; from Nueva Helvetia (Sacramento) to *Las Vegas de Santa Clara*, about one thousand more, all were Spanish ; from the Mississippi to the Pacific, French and American or English were intermixed ; and this prevalence of names indicates the national character of the first explorers.

THE DIGGER INDIAN.

We had here the misfortune to lose one of our people, François Badeau, who had been with me in both expeditions; during which he had always been one of my most faithful and efficient men. He was killed in drawing toward him a gun by the muzzle; the hammer, being caught, discharged the gun, driving the ball through his head. We buried him on the banks of the river.

Crossing the next day a slight ridge along the river, we entered a handsome mountain valley covered with fine grass, and directed our course toward a high snowy peak, at the foot of which lay the Utah Lake. On our right was a ridge of high mountains, their summits covered with snow, constituting the dividing ridge between the basin waters and those of the Colorado. At noon we fell in with a party of Utah Indians coming out of the mountain, and in the afternoon encamped on a tributary to the lake, which is separated from the waters of the Sevier by very slight dividing grounds.

Early the next day we came in sight of the lake; and, as we descended to the broad bottoms of the Spanish Fork, three horsemen were seen galloping toward us, who proved to be Utah Indians—scouts from a village which was encamped near the mouth of the river. They were armed with rifles and their horses were in good condition. We encamped near them, on the Spanish Fork, which is one of the principal tributaries to the lake. Finding the Indians troublesome, and desirous to remain here a day, we removed the next morning farther down the lake, and encamped on a fertile bottom near the foot of the same mountainous ridge which borders the Great Salt Lake, and along which we had journeyed the previous September.

Here the principal plants in bloom were two, which were remarkable as affording to the Snake Indians—the one an abundant supply of food, and the other the most useful among the applications which they use for wounds. These were the kooyah plant, growing in fields of extraordinary luxuriance, and *Convallaria stellata*, which, from the experience of Mr. Walker, is the best remedial plant known among those Indians. A few miles below us was another village of Indians, from which we obtained some fish—among them a few salmon-trout, which were very much inferior in size to those among the California mountains. The season for taking them had not yet arrived; but the Indians were daily expecting them to come up out of the lake.

We had now accomplished an object we had in view when leaving the Dalles of the Columbia in November last: we had reached the Utah Lake; but by a route very different from what we had intended, and without sufficient time remaining to make the examinations which were desired. It is a lake of note in this country, under the dominion of the Utahs, who resort to it for fish. Its greatest breadth is about fifteen miles, stretching far to the north, narrowing as it goes, and connecting with the Great Salt Lake. This is the report, and I believe it to be correct; but it is fresh water, while the other is not only salt, but a saturated solution of salt; and here is a problem which requires to be solved. It is almost entirely surrounded by mountains, walled on the north and east by a high and snowy range, which supplies to it a fan of tributary streams. Among these the principal river is the *Timpan-ogo*—signifying Rock River—a name which the rocky grandeur of its scenery, remarkable even in this country of rugged mountains, has obtained for it from the Indians. In the Utah language, *og-wáhbe*, the term for river, when coupled with other words in common conversation, is usually abbreviated to *ogo; timpan* signifying rock. It is probable that this river furnished the name which on the older maps has been generally applied to the Great Salt Lake; but for this I have preferred a name which will be regarded as highly characteristic, restricting to the river the descriptive term Timpan-ogo, and leaving for the lake into which it flows the name of the people who reside on its shores, and by which it is known throughout the country.

The volume of water afforded by the Timpan-ogo is probably equal to that of the Sevier River; and, at the time of our visit, there was only one place in the lake valley at which the Spanish Fork was fordable. In the range of mountains along its eastern shore the lake is bordered by a plain, where the soil is generally good, and in greater part fertile, watered by a delta of prettily timbered streams. This would be an excellent locality for stock farms; it is generally covered with good bunch grass, and would abundantly produce the ordinary grains.

In arriving at the Utah Lake we had completed an immense circuit, of twelve degrees diameter north and south and ten degrees east and west; and found ourselves in May, 1844, on the same sheet of water which we had left in September, 1843. The Utah is the southern limb of the Great Salt Lake; and thus we had seen that remarkable sheet of water both at its northern and southern extremity, and were able to fix its position at these two points.

The circuit which we had made, and which had cost us eight months of time and three thousand five hundred miles of travelling, had given us a view of Oregon and of North California from the Rocky Mountains to the Pacific Ocean, and of the two principal streams which form bays or harbors on the coast of that sea. Having completed this circuit, and being now about to turn the back upon the Pacific slope of our continent and to recross the Rocky Mountains, it is natural to look back upon our footsteps and take some brief view of the leading features and general structure of the country we had traversed.

These are peculiar and striking, and differ essentially from the Atlantic side of our country. The mountains are all higher, more numerous, and more distinctly defined in their ranges and directions; and, what is so contrary to the natural order of such formations, one of these ranges, which is near the coast (the Sierra Nevada and the Coast Range), presents higher elevations and peaks than any which are to be found in the Rocky Mountains themselves. In our eight months' circuit we were never out of sight of snow; and the Sierra Nevada, where we crossed it, was near two thousand feet higher than the South Pass in the Rocky Mountains. In height these mountains greatly exceed those of the Atlantic side, constantly presenting peaks which enter the region of eternal snow; and some of them volcanic and in a frequent state of activity. They are seen at great distances, and guide the traveller in his courses.

The course and elevation of these ranges give direction to the rivers and character to the coast. No great river does, or can, take its rise below the Cascade and Sierra Nevada range; the distance to the sea is too short to admit of it. The rivers of the San Francisco Bay, which are the largest after the Columbia, are local to that bay and lateral to the coast, having their sources about on a line with the Dalles of the Columbia, and running each in a valley of its own, between Coast Range and the Cascade and Sierra Nevada range. The Columbia is the only river which traverses the whole breadth of the country, breaking through all the ranges, and entering the sea. Drawing its waters from a section of ten degrees of latitude in the Rocky Mountains, which are collected into one stream by three main forks (Lewis', Clark's, and the North Fork) near the centre of the Oregon Valley, this great river thence proceeds by a single channel to the sea, while its three forks lead each to a pass in the mountains, which opens the way into the interior of the continent. This fact in relation to the rivers of this region gives an immense value to the Columbia. Its mouth is the only inlet and outlet to and from the sea; its three forks lead to the passes in the mountains; it is, therefore, the only line of communication between the Pacific and the interior of North America; and all operations of war or commerce, of national or social intercourse, must be conducted upon it. This gives it a value beyond estimation, and would involve irreparable injury if lost. In this unity and concentration of its waters the Pacific side of our continent differs entirely from the Atlantic side, where the waters of the Alleghany Mountains are dispersed into many rivers, having their different entrances into the sea, and opening many lines of communication with the interior.

The Pacific coast is equally different from that of the Atlantic. The coast of the Atlantic is low and open, indented with numerous bays, sounds, and river estuaries, accessible everywhere, and opening by many channels into the heart of the country. The Pacific coast, on the contrary, is high and compact, with few bays, and but one that opens into the heart of the country. The immediate coast is what seamen call *iron-bound*. A little within, it is skirted by two successive ranges of mountains, standing as ramparts between the sea and the interior country ; and to get through which there is but one gate, and that narrow and easily defended. This structure of the coast, backed by these two ranges of mountains, with its concentration and unity of waters, gives to the country an immense military strength and will probably render Oregon the most impregnable country in the world.

Differing so much from the Atlantic side of our continent, in coast, mountains, and rivers, the Pacific side differs from it in another most rare and singular feature—that of the great interior basin, of which I have so often spoken, and the whole form and character of which I was so anxious to ascertain. Its existence is vouched for by such of the American traders and hunters as have some knowledge of that region ; the structure of the Sierra Nevada range of mountains requires it to be there ; and my own observations confirm it.

Mr. Joseph Walker, who is so well acquainted in those parts, informed me that, from the Great Salt Lake west, there was a succession of lakes and rivers which have no outlet to the sea, nor any connection with the Columbia, or with the Colorado of the the Gulf of California. He described some of these lakes as being large, with numerous streams, and even considerable rivers, falling into them. In fact, all concur in the general report of these interior rivers and lakes ; and, for want of understanding the force and power of evaporation, which so soon establishes an equilibrium between the loss and supply of waters, the fable of whirlpools and subterraneous outlets has gained belief as the only imaginable way of carrying off the waters which have no visible discharge.

The structure of the country would require this formation of interior lakes ; for the waters which would collect between the Rocky Mountains and the Sierra Nevada, not being able to cross this formidable barrier, nor to get to the Columbia or the Colorado, must naturally collect into reservoirs, each of which would have its little system of streams and rivers to supply it. This would be the natural effect ; and what I saw went to confirm it. The Great Salt Lake is a formation of this kind, and quite a large one ; having many streams, and one considerable river, four or five hundred miles long, falling into it. This lake and river I saw and examined myself; and also saw the Wah-satch and Bear River Mountains, which enclose the waters of the lake on the east and constitute, in that quarter, the rim of the Great Basin.

Afterward, along the eastern base of the Sierra Nevada, where we travelled for forty-two days, I saw the line of lakes and rivers which lie at the foot of that Sierra ; and which Sierra is the western rim of the Basin. In going down Lewis' Fork and the main Columbia, I crossed only inferior streams coming in from the left, such as could draw their water from a short distance only ; and I often saw the mountains at their heads, white with snow ; which, all accounts said, divided the waters of the *desert* from those of the Columbia, and which could be no other than the range of mountains which form the rim of the basin on its northern side. And in returning from California along the Spanish trail, as far as the head of the Santa Clara Fork of the Rio Virgen, I crossed only small streams making their way south to the Colorado, or lost in sand—as the Mo-hah-ve ; while to the left, lofty mountains, their summits white with snow, were often visible, and which must have turned water to the north as well as to the south, and thus constituted on this part, the southern rim of the basin.

At the head of the Santa Clara Fork, and in the Vegas de Santa Clara, we crossed the ridge which parted the two systems of waters. We entered the basin at that point, and have travelled in it ever since, having its southeastern rim (the Wah-satch Mountain) on the right, and crossing the streams which flow down into it. The existence of the basin is, therefore, an established fact in my mind ; its extent and contents are yet to be better ascertained. It cannot be less than four or five hundred miles each way, and must lie principally in the Alta California ; the demarcation latitude of 42° probably cutting a segment from the north part of the rim. Of its interior but little is known. It is called a *desert*, and, from what I saw of it, sterility may be its prominent characteristic ; but where there is so much water there must be some *oases*. The great river and the great lake, reported, may not be equal to the report ; but where there is so much snow there must be streams ; and where there is no outlet there must be lakes to hold the accumulated waters, or sands to swallow them up. In this eastern part of the basin, containing Sevier, Utah, and the Great Salt Lakes, and the rivers and creeks falling into them, we know there is good soil and good grass adapted to civilized settlements. In the western part, on Salmon Trout River and some other streams, the same remark may be made.

The contents of this Great Basin are yet to be examined. That it is peopled we know, but miserably and sparsely. From all that I heard and saw, I should say that humanity here appeared in its lowest form and in its most elementary state. Dispersed in single families ; without fire-arms ; eating seeds and insects ; digging roots (and hence their name)—such is the condition of the greater part. Others are a degree higher, and live in communities upon some lake or river that supplies fish, and from which they repulse the miserable *Digger*. The rabbit is the largest animal known in this desert; its flesh affords a little meat; and their bag-like covering is made of its skins.   The wild sage is their only wood, and here it is of extraordinary size—sometimes a foot in diameter, and six or eight feet high. It serves for fuel, for building material, for shelter to the rabbits, and for some sort of covering for the feet and legs in cold weather.   Such are the accounts of the inhabitants and productions of the Great Basin; and which, though imperfect, must have some foundation, and excite our desire to know the whole.

The whole idea of such a desert, and such a people, is a novelty in our country, and excites Asiatic, not American ideas.   Interior basins, with their own systems of lakes and rivers, and often sterile, are common enough in Asia; people still in the elementary state of families, living in deserts, with no other occupation than the mere animal search for food, may still be seen in that ancient quarter of the globe; but in America such things are new and strange, unknown and unsuspected, and discredited when related.   But I flatter myself that what is discovered, though not enough to satisfy curiosity, is sufficient to excite it, and that subsequent explorations will complete what has been commenced.

This account of the Great Basin, it will be remembered, belongs to the Alta California, and has no application to Oregon, whose capabilities may justify a separate remark.   Referring to my journal for particular descriptions, and for sectional boundaries between good and bad districts, I can only say, in general and comparative terms, that, in the branch of agriculture which implies the cultivation of grains and staple crops, it would be inferior to the Atlantic States, though many parts are superior for wheat; while in the rearing of flocks and herds it would claim a high place.   Its grazing capabilities are great; and even in the indigenous grass now there, an element of individual and national wealth may be found.   In fact, the valuable grasses begin within one hundred and fifty miles of the Missouri frontier, and extend to the Pacific Ocean.   East of the Rocky Mountains it is the short curly grass on which the buffalo delight to feed, (whence its name of buffalo) and which is still good when dry and apparently dead.

West of those mountains it is a larger growth, in clusters, and hence called bunch grass, and which has a second or fall growth.   Plains and mountains both exhibit them; and I have seen good pasturage at an elevation of ten thousand feet.   In this spontaneous product, the trading or travelling caravans can find subsistence for their animals; and in military operations any number of cavalry may be moved and any number of cattle may be driven; and thus men and horses be supported on long expeditions, and even in winter in the sheltered situations.

Commercially, the value of the Oregon country must be great, washed as it is by the north Pacific Ocean—fronting Asia—producing many of the elements of commerce—mild and healthy in its climate—and becoming, as it naturally will, a thoroughfare for the East India and China trade.

Turning our faces once more eastward, on the morning of the 27th we left the Utah Lake, and continued for two days to ascend the Spanish Fork, which is dispersed in numerous branches among very rugged mountains, which afford few passes, and render a familiar acquaintance with them necessary to the traveller. The stream can scarcely be said to have a valley, the mountains rising often abruptly from the water's edge ; but a good trail facilitated our travelling, and there were frequent bottoms covered with excellent grass. The streams are prettily and variously wooded, and everywhere the mountain shows grass and timber.

At our encampment on the evening of the 28th, near the head of one of the branches we had ascended, strata of bituminous limestone were displayed in an escarpment on the river bluffs, in which were contained a variety of fossil shells of new species.

It will be remembered that in crossing this ridge about one hundred and twenty miles to the northward in August last, strata of fossiliferous rock were discovered, which have been referred to the oolitic period ; it is probable that these rocks also belong to the same formation.

A few miles from this encampment we reached the head of the stream ; and crossing, by an open and easy pass, the dividing ridge which separates the waters of the Great Basin from those of the Colorado, we reached the head branches of one of its larger tributaries, which, from the decided color of its waters, has received the name of White River. The snows of the mountains were now beginning to melt, and all the little rivulets were running by in rivers and rapidly becoming difficult to ford. Continuing a few miles up a branch of White River, we crossed a dividing ridge between its waters and those of the *Uintah.* The approach to the pass, which is the best known to Mr. Walker, was somewhat difficult for packs, and impracticable for wagons—all the streams being shut in by narrow ravines and the narrow trail along the steep hill-sides allowing the passage of only one animal at a time.

From the summit we had a fine view of the snowy Bear River range ; and there were still remaining beds of snow on the cold sides of the hills near the pass. We descended by a narrow ravine, in which was gathered a little branch of the Uintah, and halted at noon about one thousand five hundred feet below the pass, at an elevation, by the boiling point, of six thousand nine hundred feet above the sea.

The next day we descended along the river, and about noon reached a point where three forks come together. Fording one of these with some difficulty, we continued up the middle branch, which, from the color of its waters, is named the Red River. The few passes and extremely rugged nature of the country give to it great strength, and secure the Utahs from the intrusion of their enemies.

Crossing in the afternoon a somewhat broken highland, covered in places with fine grasses, and with cedar on the hill-sides, we encamped at evening on another tributary to the *Uintah*, called the *Duchesne* Fork. The water was very clear, the stream not being yet swollen by the melting snows; and we forded it without any difficulty. It is a considerable branch, being spread out by islands, the largest arm being about a hundred feet wide; and the name it bears is probably that of some old French trapper.

The next day we continued down the river, which we were twice obliged to cross; and, the water having risen during the night, it was almost everywhere too deep to be forded. After travelling about sixteen miles, we encamped again on the left bank.

I obtained here an occultation of δ *Scorpii* at the dark limb of the moon, which gives for the longitude of the place 112° 18′ 30″, and the latitude 40° 18′ 53″.

June 1st.—We left to-day the Duchesne Fork, and, after traversing a broken country for about sixteen miles, arrived at noon at another considerable branch, a river of great velocity, to which the trappers have improperly given the name of Lake Fork. The name applied to it by the Indians signifies great swiftness, and is the same which they use to express the speed of a race-horse. It is spread out in various channels over several hundred yards, and is everywhere too deep and swift to be forded.

At this season of the year there is an uninterrupted noise from the large rocks which are rolled along the bed. After infinite difficulty, and the delay of a day, we succeeded in getting the stream bridged, and got over with the loss of one of our animals. Continuing our route across a broken country, of which the higher parts were rocky and timbered with cedar, and the lower parts covered with good grass, we reached on the afternoon of the 3d the Uintah Fort, a trading post, belonging to Mr. A. Roubideau, on the principal fork of the Uintah River. We found the stream nearly as rapid and difficult as the Lake Fork, divided into several channels, which were too broad to be bridged. With the aid of guides from the fort, we succeeded, with very great difficulty, in fording it; and encamped near the fort, which is situated a short distance above the junction of the two branches that make the river.

By an immersion of the first satellite (agreeing well with the result of the occultation observed at the Duchesne Fork) the longitude of the post is 109° 56′ 42″, the latitude 40° 27′ 45″.

It has a motley garrison of Canadian and Spanish *engagés* and hunters, with the usual number of Indian women. We obtained a small supply of sugar and coffee, with some dried meat and a cow, which was a very acceptable change from the *pinole* on which we had subsisted for some weeks past. I strengthened my party at this place by the addition of Auguste Archambeau, an excellent voyageur and hunter, belonging to the class of Carson and Godey.

On the morning of the 5th we left the fort,* and the Uintah River, and continued our road over a broken country which afforded, however, a rich addition to our botanical collection ; and, after a march of twenty-five miles, were again checked by another stream, called Ashley's Fork, where we were detained until noon of the next day.

An immersion of the second satellite gave for this place a longitude of 109° 27' 07", the latitude by observation being 40° 28' 07".

In the afternoon of the next day we succeeded in finding a ford ; and, after travelling fifteen miles, encamped high up on the mountain side, where we found excellent and abundant grass, of a kind which we had not hitherto seen. A new species of *elymus*, which had a purgative and weakening effect upon the animals, had occurred abundantly since leaving the fort. From this point, by observation seven thousand three hundred feet above the sea, we had a view of the Colorado below, shut up among rugged mountains. It is the recipient of all the streams we had been crossing since we passed the rim of the Great Basin at the head of the Spanish Fork.

On the 7th we had a pleasant but long day's journey, through beautiful little valleys and a high mountain country, arriving about evening at the verge of a steep and rocky ravine, by which we descended to "*Brown's Hole.*" This is a place well known to trappers in the country, where the cañons through which the Colorado runs expand into a narrow but pretty valley, about sixteen miles in length. The river was several hundred yards in breadth, swollen to the top of its banks, near to which it was in many places fifteen to twenty feet deep. We repaired a skin boat which had been purchased at the fort, and, after a delay of a day, reached the opposite bank with much less delay than had been encountered on the Uintah waters.

According to information the lower end of the valley is the most eastern part of the Colorado ; and the latitude of our encampment, which was opposite to the remains of an old fort on the left bank of the river, was 40° 46' 27", and, by observation, the elevation above the sea five thousand one hundred and fifty feet. The bearing to the entrance of the cañon below was

---

* This fort was attacked and taken by a band of the Utah Indians since we passed it ; and the men of the garrison killed, the women carried off. Mr. Roubideau, a trader of St. Louis, was absent, and so escaped the fate of the rest.

south 20° east.   Here the river enters between lofty precipices of red rock, and the country below is said to assume a very rugged character ; the river and its affluents passing through cañons which forbid all access to the water.   This sheltered little valley was formerly a favorite wintering ground for the trappers, as it afforded them sufficient pasturage for their animals, and the surrounding mountains are well stocked with game.

We surprised a flock of mountain sheep as we descended to the river, and our hunters killed several.   The bottoms of a small stream called the Vermilion Creek, which enters the left bank of the river, a short distance below our encampment, were covered abundantly with *F. vermicularis*, and other chenopodiaceous shrubs.   From the lower end of Brown's Hole we issued by a remarkably dry cañon, fifty or sixty yards wide, and rising, as we advanced, to the height of six or eight hundred feet.   Issuing from this, and crossing a small green valley, we entered another rent of the same nature, still narrower than the other, the rocks on either side rising in nearly vertical precipices perhaps one thousand five hundred feet in height.

These places are mentioned, to give some idea of the country lower down on the Colorado, to which the trappers usually apply the name of a cañon-country.   The cañon opened upon a pond of water, where we halted at noon.   Several flocks of mountain sheep were here among the rocks, which rung with volleys of small arms.   In the afternoon we entered upon an ugly, barren, and broken country, corresponding well with that we had traversed a few degrees north, on the same side of the Colorado.   The Vermilion Creek afforded us brackish water and indifferent grass for the night.

A few scattered cedar-trees were the only improvement of the country on the following day ; and at a little spring of bad water, where we halted at noon, we had not even the shelter of these from the hot rays of the sun. At night we encamped in a fine grove of cotton-wood trees on the banks of the Elk Head River, the principal fork of the Yampah River, commonly called by the trappers Bear River.   We made here a very strong *corrál* and fort, and formed the camp into vigilant guards.   The country we were now entering is constantly infested by war parties of the Sioux and other Indians, and is considered among the most dangerous war-grounds in the Rocky Mountains ; parties of whites having been repeatedly defeated on this river.

On the 11th we continued up the river, which is a considerable stream fifty to a hundred yards in width, handsomely and continuously wooded with groves of the narrow-leaved cotton-wood (*Populus angustifolia*) ; with these were thickets of willow and *Grains de bœuf*.   The characteristic plant along the river is *F. vermicularis*, which generally covers the bottoms ; mingled with this, are saline shrubs and artemisia.   The new variety of grass which we had seen on leaving the Uintah Fort, had now disappeared.

The country on either side was sandy and poor, scantily wooded with cedars, but the river bottoms afforded good pasture. Three antelopes were killed in the afternoon, and we encamped a little below a branch of the river, called St. Vrain's Fork. A few miles above was the fort at which Frapp's party had been defeated two years since; and we passed during the day a place where Carson had been fired upon so close that one of the men had five bullets through his body. Leaving this river the next morning, we took our way across the hills, where every hollow had a spring of running water, with good grass.

Yesterday and to-day we have had before our eyes the high mountains which divide the Pacific from the Mississippi waters; and entering here among the lower spurs, or foot-hills of the range, the face of the country began to improve with a magical rapidity. Not only the river bottoms, but the hills, were covered with grass; and among the usual varied flora of the mountain region these were occasionally blue with the showy bloom of a *lupinus*.

In the course of the morning we had the first glad view of buffalo, and welcomed the appearance of two old bulls with as much joy as if they had been messengers from home; and, when we descended at noon on St. Vrain's Fork, an affluent of Green River, the hunters brought in mountain sheep and the meat of two fat bulls. Fresh entrails in the river showed us that there were Indians above; and, at evening, judging it unsafe to encamp in the bottoms, which were wooded only with willow-thickets, we ascended to the spurs above, and forted strongly in a small aspen-grove, near to which was a spring of cold water. The hunters killed two fine cows near the camp.

A band of elk broke out of a neighboring grove; antelopes were running over the hills; and on the opposite river plains herds of buffalo were raising clouds of dust. The country here appeared more variously stocked with game than any part of the Rocky Mountains we had visited; and its abundance is owing to the excellent pasturage and its dangerous character as a war-ground.

June 13th.—There was snow here near our mountain camp, and the morning was beautiful and cool. Leaving St. Vrain's Fork, we took our way directly toward the summit of the dividing ridge. The bottoms of the streams and level places were wooded with aspens; and as we neared the summit we entered again the piny region.

We had a delightful morning's ride, the ground affording us an excellent bridle-path, and reached the summit toward mid-day, at an elevation of eight thousand feet. With joy and exultation we saw ourselves once more on the top of the Rocky Mountains, and beheld a little stream taking its course toward the rising sun. It was an affluent of the Platte, called *Pullam's* Fork, and we descended at noon upon it. It is a pretty stream, twenty yards broad, and bears the name of a trapper who, some years since, was killed here by the *Gros Ventre* Indians.

Issuing from the pines, in the afternoon we saw spread out before us the Valley of the Platte, with the pass of the Medicine Butte beyond, and some of the Sweet Water Mountains; but a smoky haziness in the air entirely obscured the Wind River chain.

We were now about two degrees south of the South Pass, and our course home would have been eastwardly; but that would have taken us over ground already examined, and therefore without the interest which would excite curiosity.

Southwardly there were objects worthy to be explored, to wit: The approximation of the head-waters of three different rivers—the Platte, the Arkansas, and the Grand River Fork of the Rio Colorado of the Gulf of California; the passes at the heads of these rivers; and the three remarkable mountain coves, called parks, in which they took their rise. One of these parks was, of course, on the western side of the dividing ridge; and a visit to it would require us once more to cross the summit of the Rocky Mountains to the west, and then to recross to the east; making in all, with the transit we had just accomplished, three crossings of that mountain in this section of its course. But, no matter. The coves, the heads of the rivers, the approximation of their waters, the practicability of the mountain passes, and the locality of the THREE PARKS, were all objects of interest; and, although well known to hunters and trappers, were unknown to science and to history. We therefore changed our course, and turned up the Valley of the Platte, instead of going down it.

We crossed several small affluents, and again made a fortified camp in a grove. The country had now become very beautiful—rich in water, grass, and game; and to these were added the charm of scenery and pleasant weather.

June 14th.—Our route this morning lay along the foot of the mountain, over the long, low spurs which sloped gradually down to the river, forming the broad Valley of the Platte. The country is beautifully watered—in almost every hollow ran a clear, cool, mountain stream; and in the course of the morning we crossed seventeen, several of them being large creeks forty to fifty feet wide, with a swift current and tolerably deep. These were variously wooded with groves of aspen and cotton-wood, with willow, cherry, and other shrubby trees. Buffalo, antelope, and elk were frequent during the day; and, in their abundance, the latter sometimes reminded us slightly of the Sacramento Valley.

We halted at noon on Potter's Fork—a clear and swift stream forty yards wide, and in many places deep enough to swim our animals ; and in the evening encamped on a pretty stream, where there were several beaver-dams, and many trees recently cut down by the beaver. We gave to this the name of Beaver-dam Creek, as now they are becoming sufficiently rare to distinguish by their name the streams on which they are found. In this mountain they occurred more abundantly than elsewhere in all our journey, in which their vestiges had been scarcely seen.

The next day we continued our journey up the valley, the country presenting much the same appearance except that the grass was more scanty on the ridges, over which was spread a scrubby growth of sage ; but still the bottoms of the creeks were broad, and afforded good pasture-grounds. We had an animated chase after a grizzly bear this morning, which we tried to lasso. Fuentes threw the lasso upon his neck ; but it slipped off, and he escaped into the dense thickets of the creek, into which we did not like to venture. Our course in the afternoon brought us to the main Platte River, here a handsome stream with a uniform breadth of seventy yards, except where widened by frequent islands. It was apparently deep, with a moderate current, and wooded with groves of large willow.

The valley narrowed as we ascended, and presently degenerated into a gorge, through which the river passed as through a gate. We entered it, and found ourselves in the New Park—a beautiful circular valley of thirty miles diameter, walled in all round with snowy mountains, rich with water and with grass, fringed with pine on the mountain sides below the snow-line, and a paradise to all grazing animals. The Indian name for it signifies " *Cow Lodge*," of which our own may be considered a translation ; the enclosure, the grass, the water, and the herds of buffalo roaming over it, naturally presenting the idea of a park. We halted for the night just within the gate, and expected, as usual, to see herds of buffalo ; but an Arapahoe village had been before us, and not one was to be seen. Latitude of the encampment, 40° 52′ 44″. Elevation, by the boiling-point, seven thousand seven hundred and twenty feet.

It is from this elevated *cove*, and from the gorges of the surrounding mountains, and some lakes within their bosoms, that the Great Platte River collects its first waters and assumes its first form ; and certainly no river could ask a more beautiful origin.

June 16th.—In the morning we pursued our way through the park, following a principal branch of the Platte, and crossing, among many smaller ones, a bold stream, scarcely fordable, called Lodge Pole Fork, and which issues from a lake in the mountains on the right, ten miles long. In the evening we encamped on a small stream near the upper end of the park. Latitude of the camp, 40° 33′ 22″.

June 17*th*.—We continued our way among the waters of the park, over the foot-hills of the bordering mountains, where we found good pasturage, and surprised and killed some buffalo. We fell into a broad and excellent trail, made by buffalo, where a wagon would pass with ease; and in the course of the morning we crossed the summit of the Rocky Mountains, through a pass which was one of the most beautiful we had ever seen. The trail led among aspens, through open grounds richly covered with grass, and carried us over an elevation of about nine thousand feet above the level of the sea.

The country appeared to great advantage in the delightful summer weather of the mountains, which we still continued to enjoy. Descending from the pass we found ourselves again on the western waters, and halted at noon on the edge of another mountain valley, called the Old Park, in which is formed Grand River, one of the principal branches of the Colorado of California.

We were now moving with some caution, as, from the trail, we found the Arapahoe village had also passed this way. As we were coming out of their enemy's country, and this was a war-ground, we were desirous to avoid them. After a long afternoon's march we halted at night on a small creek, tributary to a main fork of Grand River, which ran through this portion of the valley. The appearance of the country in the Old Park is interesting, though of a different character from the New; instead of being a comparative plain, it is more or less broken into hills and surrounded by the high mountains, timbered on the lower parts with quaking asp and pines.

June 18*th*.—Our scouts, who were as usual ahead, made from a butte this morning the signal of Indians, and we rode up in time to meet a party of about thirty Arapahoes. They were men and women going into the hills—the men for game, the women for roots—and informed us that the village was encamped a few miles above, on the main fork of Grand River, which passes through the midst of the valley. I made them the usual presents; but they appeared disposed to be unfriendly, and galloped back at speed to the village. Knowing that we had trouble to expect, I descended immediately into the bottoms of Grand River, which were overflowed in places, the river being up, and made the best encampment the ground afforded. We had no time to build a fort, but found an open place among the willows which was defended by the river on one side and the overflowed bottoms on the other. We had scarcely made our few preparations when about two hundred of them appeared on the verge of the bottom, mounted, painted, and armed for war. We planted the American flag between us; and a short parley ended in a truce, with something more than the usual amount of presents. About twenty Sioux were with them

—one of them an old chief who had always been friendly to the whites. He informed me that, before coming down, a council had been held at the village, in which the greater part had declared for attacking us—we had come from their enemies, to whom we had doubtless been carrying assistance in arms and ammunition; but his own party, with some few of the Arapahoes who had seen us the previous year in the plains, opposed it.

It will be remembered that it is customary for this people to attack the trading parties which they meet in this region, considering all whom they meet on the western side of the mountains to be their enemies. They deceived me into the belief that I should find a ford at their village, and I could not avoid accompanying them; but put several sloughs between us and their village, and forted strongly on the banks of the river, which was everywhere rapid and deep, and over a hundred yards in breadth. The camp was generally crowded with Indians; and though the baggage was carefully watched and covered a number of things were stolen.

The next morning we descended the river for about eight miles, and halted a short distance above a cañon through which Grand River issued from the park. Here it was smooth and deep, one hundred and fifty yards in breadth, and its elevation at this point six thousand seven hundred feet. A frame for the boat being very soon made our baggage was ferried across; the horses, in the meantime, swimming over. A southern fork of Grand River here makes its junction, nearly opposite to the branch by which we had entered the valley, and up this we continued for about eight miles in the afternoon, and encamped in a bottom on the left bank, which afforded good grass. At our encampment it was seventy to ninety yards in breadth, sometimes widened by islands, and separated into several channels, with a very swift current and bed of rolled rocks.

On the 20th we travelled up the left bank, with the prospect of a bad road, the trail here taking the opposite side; but the stream was up, and nowhere fordable. A piny ridge of mountains, with bare, rocky peaks, was on our right all the day, and a snowy mountain appeared ahead. We crossed many foaming torrents with rocky beds, rushing down to the river; and in the evening made a strong fort in an aspen-grove. The valley had already become very narrow, shut up more closely in densely timbered mountains, the pines sweeping down to the verge of the bottoms. The *coq de prairie* (*Tetrao europhasianus*) was occasionally seen among the sage.

We saw to-day the returning trail of an Arapahoe party which had been sent from the village to look for Utahs in the Bayou Salade (South Park); and it being probable that they would visit our camp with the desire to return on horseback, we were more than usually on the alert.

Here the river diminished to thirty-five yards, and, notwithstanding the number of affluents we had crossed, was still a large stream, dashing swiftly by, with a great continuous fall, and not yet fordable.   We had a delightful ride along a good trail among the fragrant pines; and the appearance of buffalo in great numbers indicated that there were Indians in the Bayou Salade (South Park), by whom they were driven out.   We halted to noon under the shade of the pines, and the weather was most delightful.   The country was literally alive with buffalo; and the continued echoes of the hunters' rifles on the other side of the river for a moment made me uneasy, thinking perhaps they were engaged with Indians; but in a short time they came into camp with the meat of seven fat cows.

During the earlier part of the day's ride the river had been merely a narrow ravine between high piny mountains, backed on both sides, but particularly on the west, by a line of snowy ridges; but, after several hours' ride, the stream opened out into a valley with pleasant bottoms.   In the afternoon the river forked into three apparently equal streams; broad buffalo trails leading up the left-hand, and the middle branch indicating good passes over the mountains; but up on the right-hand branch, (which, in the object of descending from the mountain by the main head of the Arkansas, I was most desirous to follow) there was no sign of a buffalo trace.   Apprehending from this reason, and the character of the mountains, which are known to be extremely rugged, that the right-hand branch led to no pass, I proceeded up the middle branch, which formed a flat valley bottom between timbered ridges on the left, and snowy mountains on the right, terminating in large buttes of naked rock.   The trail was good, and the country interesting; and at nightfall we encamped in an open place among the pines, where we built a strong fort.   The mountains exhibit their usual varied growth of flowers, and at this place I noticed, among others, *Thermopsis montana*, whose bright-yellow color makes it a showy plant.   This has been a characteristic in many parts of the country since reaching the Uintah waters.   With fields of iris were *Aquilegia cœrulea*, violets, esparcette, and strawberries.

At dark we perceived a fire in the edge of the pines on the opposite side of the valley.   We had evidently not been discovered, and, at the report of a gun and the blaze of fresh fuel which was heaped on our fires, those of the strangers were instantly extinguished.   In the morning they were found to be a party of six trappers who had ventured out among the mountains after beaver.   They informed us that two of the number with which they started had been already killed by the Indians—one of them but a few days since—by the Arapahoes we had lately seen, who had found him alone at a camp on this river, and carried off his traps and animals. As they were desirous to join us the hunters returned with them to their encampment, and we continued up the valley, in which the stream rapidly diminished, breaking into small tributaries—every hollow affording water.

At our noon halt the hunters joined us with the trappers. While preparing to start from their encampment they found themselves suddenly surrounded by a party of Arapahoes, who informed them that their scouts had discovered a large Utah village in the Bayou Salade (South Park), and that a large war-party, consisting of almost every man in the village except those who were too old to go to war, were going over to attack them. The main body had ascended the left fork of the river, which afforded a better pass than the branch we were on; and this party had followed our trail, in order that we might add our force to theirs. Carson informed them that we were too far ahead to turn back, but would join them in the bayou; and the Indians went off apparently satisfied. By the temperature of boiling water our elevation here was ten thousand four hundred and thirty feet; and still the pine-forest continued, and grass was good.

In the afternoon we continued our road—occasionally through open pines, with a very gradual ascent. We surprised a herd of buffalo, enjoying the shade at a small lake among the pines; and they made the dry branches crack, as they broke through the woods. In a ride of about three-quarters of an hour, and having ascended perhaps eight hundred feet, we reached the SUMMIT OF THE DIVIDING RIDGE, which would thus have an estimated height of eleven thousand two hundred feet. Here the river spreads itself into small branches and springs, heading nearly in the summit of the ridge, which is very narrow. Immediately below us was a green valley, through which ran a stream; and a short distance opposite rose snowy mountains, whose summits were formed into peaks of naked rock.

We soon afterward satisfied ourselves that immediately beyond these mountains was the main branch of the Arkansas River—most probably heading directly with the little stream below us, which gathered its waters in the snowy mountains near by. Descriptions of the rugged character of the mountains around the head of the Arkansas, which their appearance amply justified, deterred me from making any attempt to reach it, which would have involved a greater length of time than now remained at my disposal.

In about a quarter of an hour we descended from the summit of the pass into the creek below, our road having been very much controlled and interrupted by the pines and springs on the mountain-side. Turning up the stream, we encamped on a bottom of good grass near its head, which gathers its waters in the dividing crest of the Rocky Mountains, and, according to the best information we could obtain, separated only by the rocky wall of the ridge from the head of the main Arkansas River.

By the observations of the evening, the latitude of our encampment was 39° 20' 24", and south of which, therefore, is the head of the Arkansas River. The stream on which we had encamped is the head of either the *Fontaine-qui-bouit*, a branch of the Arkansas, or the remotest head of the

South Fork of the Platte ; as which it is laid down on the map. But descending it only through a portion of its course, we have not been able to settle this point satisfactorily.

In the evening a band of buffalo furnished a little excitement, by charging through the camp.

On the following day we descended the stream by an excellent buffalo trail, along the open grassy bottom of the river.   On our right the bayou was bordered by a mountainous range, crested with rocky and naked peaks ; and below it had a beautiful park-like character of pretty level prairies, interspersed among low spurs, wooded openly with pine and quaking asp, contrasting well with the denser pines which swept around on the mountain sides.

Descending always the valley of the stream, toward noon we descried a mounted party descending the point of a spur, and, judging them to be Arapahoes—who, defeated or victorious, were equally dangerous to us, and with whom a fight would be inevitable—we hurried to post ourselves as strongly as possible on some willow-islands in the river.   We had scarcely halted when they arrived, proving to be a party of Utah women, who told us that on the other side of the ridge their village was fighting with the Arapahoes.   As soon as they had given us this information they filled the air with cries and lamentations, which made us understand that some of their chiefs had been killed.

Extending along the river, directly ahead of us, was a low piny ridge, leaving between it and the stream a small open bottom, on which the Utahs had very injudiciously placed their village, which, according to the women, numbered about three hundred warriors.   Advancing in the cover of the pines, the Arapahoes, about daylight, charged into the village, driving off a great number of their horses, and killing four men ; among them the principal chief of the village.   They drove the horses perhaps a mile beyond the village, to the end of a hollow, where they had previously forted at the edge of the pines.   Here the Utahs had instantly attacked them in turn, and, according to the report of the women, were getting rather the best of the day.   The women pressed us eagerly to join with their people, and would immediately have provided us with the best horses at the village ; but it was not for us to interfere in such a conflict.   Neither party were our friends, or under our protection ; and each was ready to prey upon us that could.   But we could not help feeling an unusual excitement at being within a few hundred yards of a fight in which five hundred men were closely engaged, and hearing the sharp cracks of their rifles.   We were in a bad position, and subject to be attacked in it.   Either party which we might meet, victorious or defeated, was certain to fall upon us ; and, gearing up immediately, we kept close along the pines of the ridge, having it between us and the village, and keeping the scouts on the summit, to give us notice of the approach of Indians. As we passed by the village, which was immediately below us, horsemen were galloping to and fro, and groups of people were gathered around those who were wounded and dead, and who were being brought in from the field. We continued to press on, and, crossing another fork, which came in from the right, after having made fifteen miles from the village, fortified ourselves strongly in the pines, a short distance from the river.

During the afternoon Pike's Peak had been plainly in view before us, and, from our encampment, bore north 87° east by compass. This was a familiar object, and it had for us the face of an old friend. At its foot were the springs, where we had spent a pleasant day in coming out. Near it were the habitations of civilized men ; and it overlooked the broad, smooth plains, which promised us an easy journey to our home.

The next day we left the river, which continued its course toward Pike's Peak ; and, taking a southeasterly direction, in about ten miles we crossed a gentle ridge, and, issuing from the South Park, found ourselves involved among the broken spurs of the mountains which border the great prairie plains. Although broken and extremely rugged, the country was very interesting, being well watered by numerous affluents to the Arkansas River, and covered with grass and a variety of trees. The streams which, in the upper part of their course, ran through grassy and open hollows, after a few miles all descended into deep and impracticable cañons, through which they found their way to the Arkansas Valley. Here the buffalo trails we had followed were dispersed among the hills, or crossed over into the more open valleys of other streams.

During the day our road was fatiguing and difficult, reminding us much, by its steep and rocky character, of our travelling the year before among the Wind River Mountains ; but always at night we found some grassy bottom, which afforded us a pleasant camp. In the deep seclusion of these little streams we found always an abundant pasturage and a wild luxuriance of plants and trees. Aspens and pines were the prevailing timber ; on the creeks oak was frequent ; but the narrow-leaved cotton-wood (*Populus angustifolia*), of unusually large size, and seven or eight feet in diameter, was the principal tree. With these were mingled a variety of shrubby trees, which aided to make the ravines almost impenetrable.

After several days' laborious travelling we succeeded in extricating ourselves from the mountains, and on the morning of the 28th encamped immediately at their foot, on a handsome tributary to the Arkansas River. In the afternoon we descended the stream, winding our way along the bottoms, which were densely wooded with oak, and in the evening encamped near the main river.

Continuing the next day our road along the Arkansas, and meeting on the way a war party of Arapahoe Indians (who had recently been committing some outrages at Bent's Fort, killing stock and driving off horses), we arrived before sunset at the *pueblo* near the mouth of the *Fontaine-qui-bouit* River, where we had the pleasure to find a number of our old acquaintances. The little settlement appeared in a thriving condition ; and in the interval of our absence another had been established on the river, some thirty miles above.

June 30th.—Our cavalcade moved rapidly down the Arkansas, along the broad road which follows the river, and on July 1st we arrived at Bent's Fort, about seventy miles below the mouth of the *Fontaine-qui-bouit.*

As we emerged into view from the groves on the river, we were saluted with a display of the national flag and repeated discharges from the guns of the fort, where we were received by Mr. George Bent with a cordial welcome and a friendly hospitality, in the enjoyment of which we spent several very agreeable days. We were now in the region where our mountaineers were accustomed to live ; and all the dangers and difficulties of the road being considered past, four of them, including Carson and Walker, remained at the fort.

On the 5th we resumed our journey down the Arkansas, travelling along a broad wagon road, and encamped about twenty miles below the fort. On the way we met a very large village of Sioux and Cheyenne Indians, who, with the Arapahoes, were returning from the crossing of the Arkansas, where they had been to meet the Kioway and Comanche Indians. A few days previous they had massacred a party of fifteen Delawares, whom they had discovered in a fort on the Smoky Hill River, losing in the affair several of their own people. They were desirous that we should bear a pacific message to the Delawares on the frontier, from whom they expected retaliation ; and we passed through them without any difficulty or delay. Dispersed over the plain, in scattered bodies of horsemen and family groups of women and children, with dog-trains carrying baggage, and long lines of pack-horses, their appearance was picturesque and imposing.

I left, at this encampment, the Arkansas River, taking a northeasterly direction across the elevated dividing grounds which separate that river from the waters of the Platte. On the 7th we crossed a large stream about forty yards wide, and one or two feet deep, flowing with a lively current on a sandy bed. The discolored and muddy appearance of the water indicated that it proceeded from recent rains ; and we are inclined to consider this a branch of the Smoky Hill River, although, possibly, it may be the Pawnee Fork of the Arkansas. Beyond this stream we travelled over high and level prairies, halting at small ponds and holes of

UPPER ARKANSAS RIVER, BELOW BENT'S FORT.

water, and using for our fires the *bois de vache*, the country being without timber. On the evening of the 8th we encamped in a cotton-wood grove on the banks of a sandy stream-bed, where there was water in holes sufficient for the camp. Here several hollows, or dry creeks with sandy beds, met together, forming the head of a stream which afterward proved to be the Smoky Hill Fork of the Kansas River.

The next morning, as we were leaving our encampment, a number of Arapahoe Indians were discovered. They belonged to a war party which had scattered over the prairie in returning from an expedition against the Pawnees.

As we travelled down the valley, water gathered rapidly in the sandy bed from many little tributaries ; and at evening it had become a handsome stream, fifty to eighty feet in width, with a lively current in small channels, the water being principally dispersed among quicksands.

Gradually enlarging, in a few days' march it became a river eighty yards in breadth, wooded with occasional groves of cotton-wood. Our road was generally over level uplands bordering the river, which were closely covered with a sward of buffalo grass.

On the 10th we entered again the buffalo range, where we had found these animals so abundant on our outward journey, and halted for a day among numerous herds, in order to make a provision of meat sufficient to carry us to the frontier.

A few days afterward we encamped, in a pleasant evening, on a high river prairie, the stream being less than a hundred yards broad. During the night we had a succession of thunder-storms, with heavy and continuous rain, and toward morning the water suddenly burst over the banks, flooding the bottoms, and becoming a large river five or six hundred yards in breadth. The darkness of the night and incessant rain had concealed from the guard the rise of the water ; and the river broke into the camp so suddenly, that the baggage was instantly covered, and all our perishable collections almost entirely ruined, and the hard labor of many months destroyed in a moment.

On the 17th we discovered a large village of Indians encamped at the mouth of a handsomely wooded stream on the right bank of the river. Readily inferring, from the nature of the encampment, that they were Pawnee Indians, and confidently expecting good treatment from a people who receive regularly an annuity from the Government, we proceeded directly to the village, where we found assembled nearly all the Pawnee tribe, who were now returning from the crossing of the Arkansas, where they had met the Kioway and Comanche Indians. We were received by them with the unfriendly rudeness and characteristic insolence which they never fail to display whenever they find an occasion for doing so with impunity.

The little that remained of our goods was distributed among them, but proved entirely insufficient to satisfy their greedy rapacity ; and, after some delay, and considerable difficulty, we succeeded in extricating ourselves from the village, and encamped on the river about fifteen miles below.*

The country through which we had been travelling since leaving the Arkansas River, for a distance of two hundred and sixty miles, presented to the eye only a succession of far-stretching green prairies covered with the unbroken verdure of the buffalo grass, and sparingly wooded along the streams with straggling trees and occasional groves of cotton-wood ; but here the country began perceptibly to change its character, becoming a more fertile, wooded, and beautiful region, covered with a profusion of grasses, and watered with innumerable little streams which were wooded with oak, large elms, and the usual varieties of timber common to the lower course of the Kansas River.

As we advanced, the country steadily improved ; gradually assimilating itself in appearance to the northwestern part of the State of Missouri. The beautiful sward of the buffalo grass, which is regarded as the best and most nutritious found on the prairies, appeared now only in patches, being replaced by a longer and coarser grass, which covered the face of the country luxuriantly. The difference in the character of the grasses became suddenly evident in the weakened condition of our animals, which began sensibly to fail as soon as we quitted the buffalo grass.

The river preserved a uniform breadth of eighty or a hundred yards, with broad bottoms continuously timbered with large cotton-wood trees, among which were interspersed a few other varieties.

While engaged in crossing one of the numerous creeks which frequently impeded and checked our way, sometimes obliging us to ascend them for several miles, one of the people (Alexis Ayot) was shot through the leg by the accidental discharge of a rifle—a mortifying and painful mischance, to be crippled for life by an accident, after having nearly accomplished in safety a long and eventful journey. He was a young man of remarkably good and cheerful temper, and had been among the useful and efficient men of the party.

After having travelled directly along its banks for two hundred and ninety miles, we left the river, where it bore suddenly off in a northwesterly direction, toward its junction with the Republican Fork of the Kansas, distant about sixty miles ; and, continuing our easterly course, in about twenty miles we entered the wagon-road from Santa Fé to Independence, and on

---

* In a report to the department, from Major Wharton, who visited the Pawnee villages with a military force some months afterward, it is stated that the Indians had intended to attack our party during the night we remained at this encampment, but were prevented by the interposition of the Pawnee Loups.

UPPER ARKANSAS.

the last day of July encamped again at the little town of Kansas, on the banks of the Missouri River.

During our protracted absence of fourteen months, in the course of which we had necessarily been exposed to great varieties of weather and of climate, no one case of sickness had ever occurred among us.

Here ended our land journey; and the day following our arrival we found ourselves on board a steamboat rapidly gliding down the broad Missouri.　Our travel-worn animals had not been sold and dispersed over the country to renewed labor, but were placed at good pasturage on the frontier, and were ready to do their part in the coming expedition.

On the 6th of August we arrived at St. Louis, where the party was finally disbanded; a greater number of the men having their homes in the neighborhood.

Andreas Fuentes also remained here, having readily found employment for the winter, and was one of the men engaged to accompany me the present year.

Pablo Hernandez remained in the family of Senator Benton, where he was well taken care of, and conciliated good-will by his docility, intelligence, and amiability.　General Almonte, the Mexican minister at Washington, to whom he was of course made known, kindly offered to take charge of him, and to carry him back to Mexico ; but the boy preferred to remain where he was until he got an education, for which he showed equal ardor and aptitude.

This was the promise of Pablo's childhood.　It might be supposed that the dreadful circumstances in which his father and mother met their death would have remained fixed in his memory, and that grief and compassion for them and gratitude to the strangers with whom he found safe refuge and who cared for him afterward as their own, would have taken possession of his mind and shaped his life.　We were all interested in him.　The disaster which had deprived him of parents and country seemed to make him our special charge, and it was settled that we would give him his start in life, confident that his winning manners and intelligence would carry him successfully on his way.　But the early promise was misleading. As he grew up toward manhood and his instincts developed, it was found that he would fit into nothing good.　The root of his character seemed strangely bad, and as it developed, led him into wrong courses and away from us.　He went to Mexico, where for a short time we heard of him disagreeably.

After some years the report came to us that he was the Joaquin who for some years was so well known as a robber chief in the San Joaquin Valley and the mountain country.　Whether or not this was so, it is the last that I heard of Pablo.

Our Chinook Indian had his wish to see the whites fully gratified.   He accompanied me to Washington, and, after remaining several months at the Columbia College, was sent by the Indian Department to Philadelphia, where, among other things, he learned to read and write well, and speak the English language with some fluency.

CHAPTER XII.

The eight months that I was to have been absent had extended to fourteen. Mrs. Frémont had been waiting in Saint Louis for me and suspense
had deepened into anxiety, for no word had been heard from me after I
had left the lower Columbia in November of '43. The Secretary of War,
Mr. Wilkins, had offered to send a party of dragoons to search for me,
but naturally it occurred to my friends to reply that if I could not find my
way out the dragoons could not do it for me. In those days there was
no communication possible to a party involved in the solitudes of the interior country beyond the mountains, and so it was that the first tidings
of our safety were brought by myself when I reached Saint Louis in August
of '44.

In Saint Louis, where the risks and uncertainties of the mountain country
were familiarly known, much sympathy had been felt for Mrs. Frémont
as the time wore on and no intelligence came. Many warm expressions
of welcome were given me, and we left for Washington animated and gratified by the hearty good wishes of strangers as well as friends.

I arranged for the two Indian boys, Juan and Gregorio, to winter on a
property belonging to Mr. Benton, near Lexington, Kentucky. They took
with them, to care for, a beautiful saddle-horse which I had brought from
California. He was to rest for the winter in the blue-grass region. Sacramento, as he was named, was gifted with two fine qualities—courage, and
a remarkable power for leaping—a specialty with him. He was beautifully
made, an iron-gray of the best California stock, about four years old, well
trained, a perfect saddle-horse.

Chinook I took with me to Washington. He parted with regret from
the other boys, but every feeling was soon absorbed in the delight of "seeing the whites" in their own homes and strange ways of travel.

I found the family well, but several lives had gone out from the circle
of our friends. Mr. Nicollet, Mr. Hassler, and Senator Linn had died soon
after my leaving in '43. The death of Mr. Nicollet in September, '43,

though expected was sudden.   From being restless he had become morbid and solitary, going off alone like a wounded animal trying to escape from its hurt.   He had come up to Washington and had gone to a hotel, where he was accidentally found by a friend of the Benton family, Dr. Martin. In his illness former scenes and his own language had taken possession of his mind, and it seems that he had not been able to make himself known to the people of the house.   The clerk at the office told Dr. Martin of the unknown French gentleman, and asked him to see who it was.   The doctor found him in this condition and arranged to notify his friends and have him removed at once to Baltimore.   When he came for him the next morning it was too late.   He had died in the night, alone.   It was the ending of a good, and useful, and pleasing life.   I deeply regretted him, and missed long his friendly and considerate presence.

After all it would have been a fitter end for him to have died under the open sky, and be buried, rolled up in a blanket, by the side of some stream in the mountains, than to have had life close in the night and alone at a hotel.

Mr. Hassler died in Philadelphia in the November of the same year. More fortunate than Mr. Nicollet, he was in the midst of his family.   This distinguished man was introduced here by his countryman, Albert Gallatin; and through him was sent as scientific ambassador to London and Paris with the outfit and salary of a foreign minister ; so far as I know the only occasion when science has been so honored by this country.

In October, Mr. Benton's friend and colleague, Senator Linn, had also died.   His death was a serious loss to the friends of Oregon.   Mr. Linn, though of a most pleasing and courteous manner, was unyielding and persistent.   This loss was felt, when in the following year a notice to England to terminate the joint occupation was introduced in the Senate.   The idea was created by the opposition that this was " a conspiracy to force war " and the Eastern commercial interest was roused to alarm, and brought to bear on the Senate—defeating the bill by 28 to 18.

On my arrival at Washington I reported my return to General Scott, and called upon the Secretary of War, Mr. Wilkins, of Pennsylvania, who in his frank quick manner unaffectedly expressed surprise at my apparent youth, but pleasantly qualified this by saying that in my case it was a good failing, as young men never saw the obstacles.

I had now returned to the satisfactions and enjoyment of family life. Living so long on the memory only of this it had become too unsubstantial. In the first weeks at Washington I had the great pleasure to see my mother again.   During recent years this had become rare.   To spare my time and be with me in the family surroundings she came to Washington and remained until the cold weather obliged me to take her back to the South.

With her presence the past time of careless boyhood was linked in a most satisfied and happy way to the serious labor of the maturer years which were advancing with their inevitable cares.

A responsible Quaker family of Philadelphia asked to have charge of Chinook for the winter, and he was accordingly placed in their care. While settling myself to work in preparing the results of the journey I found my time constantly broken in upon.

To Mr. Preuss had been assigned the congenial labor of making up the maps. He was now owner of a comfortable home of his own ; a good house near the Arsenal, which the locality brought within his means. The large front room he converted into his working-room, where he had space and good light, and there was a lookout over the river, and a long bit of grassed ground where Preuss made an arbor and where he smoked his pipe as he watched his child playing and the cow grazing.

The interesting character of the regions visited by this expedition, California chiefly, drew much attention and brought me many letters and personal inquiries. It became impossible to reconcile attention to visitors with work in hand ; and in order therefore to avoid this serious embarrassment I took for a workshop a small wooden two-story house not far from the residence of Mr. Benton. This was well apart from other buildings and had about it large enclosed grounds. I had here with me as assistant Mr. Joseph C. Hubbard, who, although no older than myself, was already a practical astronomer and a rapid and skilful computer, and with his aid the various calculations went fast. This was the occupation of the daylight. To keep ourselves in practice, both being fond of astronomical observations, we mounted a transit instrument, and the house being isolated, we were able to vary our work and have still an interesting point to it.

Wishing to prove the accuracy of a sextant by trying it against other observations, we went for several nights together quite late, when the streets were quiet and few passers to disturb the mercury, to a church near by where there was a large stone carriage-step near the curb on which to set the horizon. Waiting for the stars, which I wanted, to come into position I rested more agreeably on the ground half lying against the stone. A few days afterward a deacon of this church, who lived opposite, called upon Mr. Benton, regretting that he had disagreeable information to give, which still he thought it his duty to impart to him. He said that for several nights he had seen his son-in-law in a state of gross intoxication lying on the pavement in front of the church, and apparently unwilling to allow a more sober companion who was with him to take him to the house.

Mr. Benton did not receive this charitable information in the grateful spirit which the informer had expected. On the contrary the deacon was first frightened and then humiliated. Mr. Benton made him understand that he had converted an honorable fact into a damaging falsehood—in the way that slanders often originate—taking the color of the mind from which engenders them.

After the computations, came the writing of the Report. This had its great interest, but was still a task which required concentrated, systematic labor. Mrs. Frémont now worked with me daily at the little wooden house, but for her the work had its peculiar interest. Talking incidents over made her familiar with the minuter details of the journey, outside of those which we recorded, and gave her a realizing sense of the uncertainties and precarious chances that attend such travel, and which day and night lie in wait; and it gave her for every day an object unusual in the life of a woman.

To me, in drawing these results into visible form, there was now the impelling gratification of bringing into clear view the different face which our examination had given to the regions explored; their many points of general interest; their unexpectedly great resources and capacities for population and trade; thus vindicating the West in the importance which they attached to that Territory.

There was but brief time in which to do this writing. In the evenings the note-books were consulted, and the work thought out and prepared for the morning. Jacob kept up the camp habit and very early brought me coffee; and punctually at nine o'clock Mrs. Frémont joined me at the workshop. From that hour until one the writing went on, with seldom anything to break the thread; the dictation sometimes continuing for hours, interrupted only when an occasional point of exceptional interest brought out inquiry or discussion. After the four hours' stretch there was tea with a light luncheon and then a walk to the river; and after, work again until dusk.

Mrs. Benton was alarmed by this pull on her daughter, but Mr. Benton was delighted. He used sometimes to turn into our workroom to enjoy the pleasure he had in seeing the work grow. Another refreshing rest of the day came when we all met in the evening at dinner. Mr. Benton held to some observances in the family life which, though formal, were pleasant. He was fond of that degree of social decorum which respect for others' feelings should always exact and is grateful to every one. To him this was habitual. With the dressing for dinner were laid aside any subjects not suited to general harmony. Mr. Benton always relaxed to the enjoyment of the interesting and cheerful dinner-table—himself contributing his large share and example; except when, on rare occasions, he came down from the Senate preoccupied by some interesting debate. One day he was so much engrossed that he forgot his office of carver, on which he rather prided himself—but continued biting, as he thought, a piece of bread—until he was

George Bancroft

roused by the general laugh and "Father, that's the claret cork you are trying to eat." He laughed at himself but sent away the dish saying, " Child, don't ask me to carve anything until this Ashburton treaty is settled."

The completed Report of the journey was given in on March 1st, and 10,000 extra copies of the First and Second Report ordered by Congress.

An important event consequent upon the publication of these Reports was the settlement by the Mormons of the valley of the Great Salt Lake.

In this connection I give here the following letter from me published in New York in 1877:

GENERAL FRÉMONT AND THE GREAT SALT LAKE.

To the Editor of the New York Times:

Your paper of this morning contains a letter from Eli Perkins, giving an account of an interview between Governor Brigham Young and himself, in which there are several errors that I would like to correct.

Governor Young says that I made "a mistake." That I described the Great Salt Lake as one part salt and the other fresh, and that I had described the surrounding country as fertile, when he found the Salt Lake plain a desert. The passages I refer to in the letter are as follows :

" How came you to think of Utah?" I asked.

" Well, we had read an account of General Frémont's travels—how he found a large salt lake in the interior of our continent, in the middle of a great fertile plain. We read the account of his rowing to an island in the middle of the lake in an India-rubber boat, and how the south end of the lake was fresh and the north salt."

" But the south end of Salt Lake is not fresh, is it?" I asked.

" No; Frémont made a mistake. In going to the south of Salt Lake he struck Utah Lake—another lake —and thought it was a continuation of the same lake. Well, from Frémont's reports, we determined to get our wagons together, form a grand caravan and travel through the country to the Salt Lake, 1000 miles from any civilized settlement. We started out with 147 people and 73 wagons. This was in 1847. . . . On the 24th of July, 1847, we defiled down the Wasatch Mountains, and saw the plain of our New Jerusalem before us. . . . Salt Lake plain is a natural desert. When we struck this plain there was nothing on it but sage-bushes."

Governor Young was himself in error here. The report to which he refers contains no such statement, and I give the following extracts, which speak to the character of the lake and the country surrounding it. These, at this distance of time, Governor Young would only faintly remember:

SEPTEMBER 8, 1843.—The river here divided into several branches, filled with fluvials, and so very shallow that it was with difficulty we could get the boat along, being obliged to get out and wade. We encamped on a low point among rushes and young willows, where there was a quantity of drift-wood, which served for our fires. . . . Geese and ducks enough had been killed for an abundant supper at night and for breakfast the next morning.

SEPTEMBER 9.—. . . The channel in a short distance became so shallow that our navigation was at an end, being merely a sheet of soft mud, with a few inches of water, and sometimes none at all, forming the low-water shore of the lake. All this place was absolutely covered with flocks of screaming plover. We took off our clothes, and, getting overboard, commenced dragging the boat, making by this operation a very curious trail and a very disagreeable smell in stirring up the mud, as we sank above the knee at every step. The water here was still fresh, with only an insipid and disagreeable taste, probably derived from the fetid mud. After proceeding in this way about a mile we came to a small, black ridge on the bottom, beyond which the water became suddenly salt, beginning gradually to deepen, and the bottom was sandy and firm. It was a remarkable division separating the fresh waters of the rivers from the briny water of the lake, which was entirely saturated with common salt. Pushing our little vessel across the narrow boundary we sprang on board, and at length were afloat on the waters of the unknown sea.

．　．　．　．　．　．　．　．　．　．　．　．　．　．　．　．　．　．

SEPTEMBER 14.—Taking leave at this point of the waters of Bear River, and of the geographical basin which incloses the system of rivers and creeks which belong to the Great Salt Lake, and which so richly deserves a future detailed and ample exploration, I can say of it, in general terms, that the bottoms of this river (Bear), and of some of the creeks which I saw, form a natural resting and recruiting station for travellers now and all time to come. The bottoms are extensive, water excellent, timber sufficient, the soil good and well adapted to the grains and grasses suited to such an elevated region. A military post and a civilized settlement would be of great value here; and cattle and horses would do well where grass and salt so much abound. The lake will furnish exhaustless supplies of salt. All the mountain-sides here are covered with a valuable nutritious grass called bunch-grass, from the form in which it grows, which has a second growth in the fall. The beasts of Indians were fat upon it; our own found it a good subsistence; and its quantity will sustain any amount of cattle, and make this truly a bucolic region.

The character of fertility here attributed to the eastern shores of the lake and valleys of the tributary streams, which I visited at this time, would be abundantly borne out by a visit there to-day. The desert plain of the Great Salt Lake, which I did not then visit, lies west of it, and was not referred to in the report which guided the Mormon emigration.

The work was done as faithfully as was possible to us under restrictions of scanty means and time, but it has been a constant satisfaction to me to have had the approval which subsequent travellers and emigrants, and other authorities, have given to the correctness of the maps and reports belonging to these surveys.

In the recent adjustment of our Northwestern boundary with England (the San Juan case), I was informed by Commissioner Campbell that the determination of an important part of the line on the Pacific coast turned upon the maps of these surveys, and it was finally settled by my letter to him in explanation of it.

For the reasons above given I naturally desire to correct where it is susceptible of correction any accidental misstatement tending to lend character of looseness and inaccuracy to the work.

J. C. FRÉMONT.

NEW YORK, SATURDAY, JUNE 2, 1877.

This letter shows two things : it establishes the fact that it was upon my report of it that the Mormon community chose the Great Salt Lake for their place of settlement ; it also shows the ease with which recorded facts can be overlaid by loose or unfriendly statement.

In contrast to the facts set out by these Reports and to the rapid occupation by immigrants of the country examined, I insert the following extract from a book published in 1844 in London by an employé of the Hudson Bay Company, styled "History of the Oregon Territory and British North American Fur Trade ; by John Dunn." This goes to show the curious ignorance in regard to Oregon and the Rocky Mountain country which at this late date could find its way into print in England.

"Though several parties have penetrated into the Oregon territory from the United States through the gorges of the Rocky Mountains, yet it may be safely asserted, from the concurrent testimony of traders, trappers, and settlers, who have themselves passed these natural barriers, that the difficulties are so numerous and formidable, and the time necessary for the passage so long, that there is no secure, expeditious, or commodious track which can be ever used as a highway, so as to afford facilities for an influx of emigrants overland. Several routes have been tried of late ; and each differs only from the other in the privations which the passengers undergo. None but the wild and fearless free trappers can clamber over these precipices, and tread these deserts with security ; and even these are quitting them as haunts, and now using them only as unavoidable tracks. It is true, there have been published more favorable accounts within the last year or two by parties who have made the journey safely, and who encourage others to make a similar experiment. But these accounts are in such a spirit of *bravado*, and accompanied with expressions of thankfulness by the parties for their own success, that they are indirect proofs of the difficulty and danger of the undertaking, and of the utter hopelessness of such a route for general purposes. For hundreds of miles the several tracks present nothing but frightful barrenness underfoot, and overhead scorching heat, or piercing cold. The country, even west of the Rocky Mountains, is broken with towering cliffs, deep ravines, and sunken streams, from which the traveller cannot draw a drop to allay his burning thirst ; and the soil is either sandy, in which he sinks at every step, or of a black rugged stone which tears his feet. The travellers have been obliged to feed on the lean carcasses of their animals, which have died from hunger, thirst, or fatigue. Farnham says that his party were at last obliged to kill their universal favorite and pet—their dog—and economize his flesh. He further says that during eight days' journey—and he had proceeded with the expedition of one travelling for life—he had not met with a single acre of land capable of producing grain or vegetables."

Another American traveller—Townsend—says : " Our only food was dried, crumbling meat, which we carried and chewed like biscuits as we travelled. There are two reasons by which the extreme thirst which the wayfarer suffers in these regions may be accounted for ; first, the intense heat of the sun upon the open and exposed plains ; and secondly, the desiccation to which everything here is subject. The air feels like the breath of a sirocco ; the tongue becomes parched and horny, and the eyes, mouth, and nose are incessantly assailed by the fine pulverized lava, which rises from the ground with the least breath of air. Bullets, pebbles of chalcedony, and pieces of smooth obsidian were in great requisition ; almost every man was mumbling some of these substances in an endeavor to assuage his burning thirst. The lead bullets and the other substances which they chewed were for the purpose of producing spittle, which they would swallow to prevent inflammation and death. There are, however, certain declinations called *gaps* through which (though with great labor) a tedious and dreary passage can be effected. The most frequented of these is the most northern, between Mounts Brown and Hooker, through which the company's servants pass in their journey from Columbia to Hudson's Bay.   This is, comparatively, an easy passage.   There is another between the head-waters of the Flathead and Marias Rivers; another between Lewis and Clarke's River, in the Oregon, and the sources of the Missouri; and another, which is very important, lies between Long's Mountains and the Wind River cluster."

At the instance of General Scott I was given the double brevet of first lieutenant and captain.   He made my services the subject of a special report, which consisted of two parts: the first, an argument that a double brevet, under existing law, might be granted; the second, that in consideration of services rendered by me it ought to be granted.   The fact that General Scott was known to be tenacious of military observances increased the value of his recommendation.   Accordingly, I was appointed by President Tyler captain by brevet, "to rank as such from the 31st day of July, 1844 : for gallant and highly meritorious services in two expeditions commanded by himself; the first to the Rocky Mountains, which terminated October 17, 1842; and the second beyond those mountains, which terminated July 31, 1844."

This brevet has the greater value for me because it is the only recognition for "services rendered" that I have received from my own Government.

After the change of administration in March I accompanied Mr. Benton to visit the President, Mr. Polk.   In speaking to him of the interesting facts in the geography of the West I mentioned that I had shortly before, at the Library of Congress, drawn out from the map-stand one giving the United States and Territories, and found on it the Great Salt Lake represented as connected with the Pacific Ocean by three great rivers: one discharging into the Columbia River from the northwestern end; another from the southwestern end into the head of the Gulf of California; the third from the middle of the western side of the lake running westward, breaking through the Sierra Nevada and discharging into the Bay of San Francisco.   Bearing in mind the account given me at Vancouver of the Buenaventura River, the known fact of the Great Colorado, and the existence of large streams flowing into the lake, it is easy to see how the reports of trappers scattered over that region, who had seen it only in widely separated parts, might be connected together in the compilation of maps so as to give the lake these outlets.

The President seemed for the moment sceptical about the exactness of my information and disposed to be conservative.   He evidently "respected that ancient chaos" of the western geography as it existed on the old maps.   Like the Secretary, he found me "young," and said something of the "impulsiveness of young men," and was not at all satisfied in his own mind that those three rivers were not running there as laid down.

It may be remembered that Alexis Ayot was severely wounded at the frontier, just when reaching the end of the journey. As an evidence of the interest felt in the expeditions, I anticipate here to say in what way he was not lost sight of. He was a French Canadian, young, and with simple faith in "government." He believed, that, as he had been crippled in its service, he only needed to show himself in Washington to be provided for. To his surprise and distress he was told that as he was not an enlisted soldier the pension laws could not apply to him. "*Je vais mourir de faim,*" he said to Mrs. Frémont; "*je ne suis pas clerc, je n'avais que mes jambes.*" That evening Mrs. Frémont was telling of this disappointment to herself as well as to the poor voyageur to Mrs. Dix, a charming, sympathetic woman with whom as with her husband the family intimacy was great. A large, rather bashful gentleman waiting to see Mr. Dix sat apart taking no share in the talk of the two ladies; but after he had made his visit to the Senator, Mr. Dix came in from his library to say that this was the chairman of the Committee on Pensions; that he had been so interested for the crippled man that he had asked him to say that if Mrs. Frémont would write out briefly—just as she told it—the man's case, he thought he could help him. This was Preston King, of New York.

He made good his offer. A special act was introduced by Mr. King for his relief, and within a few days it had gone through both houses, received the signature of President Polk, and Ayot found himself with not only his pension, but back pay from the date of his wound. Swaying on his crutches he tried to thank Mrs. Frémont, and with tears running down his dark face said, "I cannot kneel to thank you—*je n'ai plus de jambes*—but you are my *Sainte Madonne et je vous fais ma prière.*" To draw his pension he had to become an American resident. He was thorough; becoming also a citizen and marrying an American girl. And as a shoemaker in Montpelier, Vermont, I learned of his friendly arguments, and his voting for me there, many years after.

I had returned inspired with California. Its delightful climate and uncommon beauty of surface; the great strength of its vegetation and its grand commercial position; took possession of my mind. My wish when I first saw it settled into intention, and I determined to make there a home.

With all these advantages it was unused. Its great forests and fertile lands, the fish that crowded its waters, the noble harbor and great commerce that waited for it, were all unused; lying waste like an Indian country, as in greater part it was. Its fertile sea-board was one great stock-farm and its whole population only a few thousands ; so far distant from the Central Government that it was ready at any moment to break off. It had now come to share the great interest which the men in control of affairs at Washington had felt for the more northern coast of the Pacific. Mr. Webster invited me to dine with him "to talk about California." I found that his mind was specially fixed upon the Bay of San Francisco and the commanding advantage it would give us for war and commerce. He drew his line, however, at the coast. Coming as he did from a part of our coun- try where grass contends with rocks for possession of the fields, it was diffi- cult to make him realize the wonderful fertility of the unobstructed soil of California, where wild oats make unbroken fields from valley to mountain- top. For him the Rocky Mountains extended the influence of their name to the sea-beaches and mingled their rocks with the sands; making in his mind the picture which he afterward gave of California: "a strip of sandy land along the Pacific Ocean with here and there an oasis of fertile soil; offering no inducements for us except the fine harbors indented upon its coast."

What Mr. Webster thought of these harbors he says in a letter written to his son March 11, 1845, quoted by Mr. George Ticknor Curtis in his well-studied and admirable life of Buchanan. In this letter Mr. Webster is speaking of the improbability that England would go to war with us to prevent the annexation of Texas. "But," he says, "she will now take care that Mexico shall not cede California, or any part thereof, to us. You know my opinion to have been, and now is, that the port of San Francisco would be twenty times as valuable to us as all Texas."

I communicated my inspiration to others. For this Mr. Benton's mind was open. Many clients from among old Spanish families in Florida and Lou- isiana ; his practice in defending their interests ; the knowledge acquired of the usage as well as the laws under which their old land grants had been held ; his knowledge of the language which led to friendships with his clients ; all gave him unusual interest now in Mexico. Out of this had come his sympathy for them as a people. He had always held that toward Mex- ico our relation should be that of the Great Republic aiding a neighboring state in its early struggles ; and he belonged with those who preferred the acquiring of Texas by treaty and purchase, not by war. This he opposed and denounced. He came now to hold the same views concerning California.

President Polk entered on his office with a fixed determination to acquire California, if he could acquire it in an honorable and just manner.

The President and Mr. Bancroft held it impossible for Mexico, situated as things then were, to retain possession of California ; and therefore it was right to negotiate with Mexico for the acquisition of that which to her could be of no use. This it was hoped to accomplish by peaceful negotiation ;

but if Mexico in resenting our acceptance of the offer of Texas to join us, should begin a war with us, then, by taking possession of the province.

To acquire California by all honorable means had been the desire of Mr. Bancroft much before this time, but the relations with Mexico growing out of the Texas situation soon became critical and threatened war ; leaving no room for further negotiation.

The Secretary of State, Mr. Buchanan, and Senator Dix, of New York, came frequently to confer with Senator Benton. As chairman of the Committee on Military Affairs he was the centre of information and conference. Mr. Buchanan had discovered a leak in his Department, and not knowing the Spanish language himself brought his confidential letters and documents from Mexico to be read to him by Mr. Dix and Mr. Benton, who knew the language well. Mr. Dix was a near neighbor for the whole of his senatorial term, a member of the Military Committee and also personally intimate with Mr. Benton from similarity of tastes. In the security of Mr. Benton's library these despatches were read and discussed and many translations made for Mr. Buchanan's use by Mrs. Frémont and her elder sister. Baron Gerolt, the Prussian Minister, who had been for twenty years Minister to Mexico and who had now his continued confidential relations with chief men in that country, was also our valued friend ; with a friendship uninterrupted while he lived. From his outset in life Humboldt had been his friend and watched over his career. He had been chosen by him for the mission to Mexico, and during his long absence abroad their friendly correspondence had been maintained.

The following letter to Mr. Buchanan from Mr. Bancroft gives the state of affairs from authentic information and shows the friendly interest of Baron Gerolt:

WASHINGTON, August 7, 1845.

MY DEAR MR. BUCHANAN :

You remember what I told you, before you left, that Baron Gerolt predicted war on the part of Mexico. Yesterday morning, at the President's request, I went to see him, and found him very ready to communicate all his intelligence, concealing only the name of his informant, and desiring that his own name may not be used.

His letters came by way of Havana, and Charleston, S. C., and are from Mexico City, of the date of June 28th. He vouches for the entire authenticity and good opportunity of information on the part of his correspondent.

General Arista, with three thousand men, chiefly cavalry, himself the best cavalry officer in Mexico, had been directed to move forward towards the Del Norte ; but whether he had orders to cross the Del Norte was not said.

At San Louis Potosi, General Paredes, the commander-in-chief, had his general quarters, with an army of seven thousand men. These also were directed to move forward, in small divisions, towards the Del Norte.

From Mexico City, General Felisola, the old woman who was with Santa Anna in Texas, was soon to leave with three thousand men to join the army of Paredes.

Thus far positive information. It was stated by the Baron as his *opinion* that Mexico would certainly consider the armistice with Texas broken by the action of the Texas convention ; that she would shun battles and carry on an annoying guerilla warfare ; that she would protract the war into a very expensive length ; that she would agree to no settlement of boundary with us, but under the guarantee of European powers.

On these opinions I make no comment. The seemingly authentic news of hostile intentions has led Governor Marcy, under proper sanctions, to increase his little army in Texas, and Mr. Mason has written all the necessary letters. I do not see but that the sun rises this morning much as usual. The President, too, is in excellent spirits, and will grow fat in your absence, he sleeps so well *now*, and sees nothing before him but the plain, though steep and arduous path of duty.

So wishing you well,

Your faithful friend,

GEORGE BANCROFT.

Of his solicitude for my personal welfare Baron Gerolt gave a marked proof during my absence on the third expedition, by coming to Mr. Benton to warn him that I would be in danger from an unexpected quarter in California ; for he had received positive information from the City of Mexico that orders had been sent by the Mexican Government to the commanding general of that Department directing him to drive me from any part of the territory in which I might appear.

Concurrently with the Report upon the second expedition the plans and scope of a third one had been matured. It was decided that it should be directed to that section of the Rocky Mountains which gives rise to the Arkansas River, the Rio Grande del Norte of the Gulf of Mexico, and the Rio Colorado of the Gulf of California ; to complete the examination of the Great Salt Lake and its interesting region ; and to extend the survey west and southwest to the examination of the great ranges of the Cascade Mountains and the Sierra Nevada, so as to ascertain the lines of communication through the mountains to the ocean in that latitude. And in arranging this expedition, the eventualities of war were taken into consideration.

The geographical examinations proposed to be made were in greater part in Mexican territory. This was the situation : Texas was gone and

UPPER SACRAMENTO VALLEY.

California was breaking off by reason of distance ; the now increasing American emigration was sure to seek its better climate. Oregon was still in dispute ; nothing was settled except the fact of a disputed boundary ; and the chance of a rupture with Great Britain lent also its contingencies.

Mexico, at war with the United States, would inevitably favor English protection for California. English citizens were claiming payment for loans and indemnity for losses. Our relations with England were already clouded, and in the event of war with Mexico, if not anticipated by us, an English fleet would certainly take possession of the Bay of San Francisco.

For use in such a contingency the only available force was our squadron in the North Pacific, and the measures for carrying out the design of the President fell to the Navy Department. During the year such precautionary measures as were practicable were taken, especially by the vigilant Secretary of the Navy, Mr. Bancroft, whose orders continuously evince comprehending foresight and insistance. Imbued with the philosophy of history, his mind was alive to the bearing of the actual conditions, and he knew how sometimes skill and sometimes bold action determine the advantages of a political situation ; and in this his great desire was to secure for the United States the important one that hung in the balance. In the government at Washington he was the active principle, having the activity of brain and keen perception that the occasion demanded. With him Mr. Benton had friendly personal relations of long standing.

As affairs resolved themselves, California stood out as the chief subject in the impending war ; and with Mr. Benton and other governing men at Washington it became a firm resolve to hold it for the United States. To them it seemed reasonably sure that California would eventually fall to England or to the United States and that the eventuality was near. This was talked over fully during the time of preparation for the third expedition, and the contingencies anticipated and weighed. The relations between the three countries made a chief subject of interest about which our thoughts settled as the probability of war grew into certainty. For me, no distinct course or definite instruction could be laid down, but the probabilities were made known to me as well as what to do when they became facts. The distance was too great for timely communication; but failing this I was given discretion to act. The instructions early sent, and repeatedly insisted upon, to the officer commanding our Pacific squadron, gave specific orders to be strictly followed in the event of war. But these frequent discussions among the men who controlled the action of the Government, gave to me the advantage of knowing more thoroughly what were its present wishes, and its intentions in the event of war. And so it came that as soon as war was sure between Mexico and ourselves, Lieutenant Gillespie was despatched with instructions ; and with letters which, if intercepted when crossing Mexico, would convey no meaning to others while to me they would be clear. Plans and expressions relating to the future home in California were known by me to be intended as relating to its occupation by the United States.

Mrs. Frémont was to have accompanied me to the frontier, but the dangerous illness of Mrs. Benton kept her at home. I went off with only Jacob and Chinook, who had been recalled from Philadelphia, and was glad to go back to his people.

The Quaker family had been interested in him and careful to give him such rudiments of practical knowledge as he might be able to put to good use. But he was about twenty years old when he left the Columbia with me; intelligent, with set character formed among the habits of Indian life, as ineradicable from Indian manhood as his love of free range from a wild horse. How far his brief education was likely to influence his life was made strikingly clear to us when on the evening he reached Washington he exhibited the parting gifts which he had received from his friends. Among these was a large Bible which had been made attractive in his eyes by its ornamentation. " Chinook been a Quaker all winter," he said; and opening this at the blank leaves for " Family Record "—" Here," he added, with the short Indian laugh of pleasure, " Chinook put here name all wife, and all horse."

The knowledge which his eyes had taken in would be useful among his people. He was the son of a chief, and the stories he could tell of his life among the whites would add to his importance; and the kind treatment he had received would dispose himself and them to be friendly to the Americans.

The Indian boys who had spent a happy winter in Kentucky met me at Saint Louis, bringing with them Sacramento, aggressively well.

On the frontier I formed a camp where my party was quickly organized. For this expedition ampler means had been provided, and in view of uncertain conditions the force suitably increased. In addition to the usual outfit of arms I had procured about a dozen rifles, the best that could be found; with the object of setting them up as prizes for the best marksmen, to be shot for during the journey. Many of my old men joined me. And I had again Godey.

The animals I had left on pasture were in fine condition; hardened by the previous journey and thoroughly rested they were well fitted to endure a campaign. From the Delaware nation twelve men had been chosen to go with me. These were known to be good hunters and brave men and two of them were chiefs, Swanok and Sagundai. Mr. Preuss was not with me this time; but was now in assured employment and preferred in his comfortable home to rest from the hardships of the last journey. In his place Mr. Edward M. Kern, of Philadelphia, went with me as topographer. He was besides an accomplished artist; his skill in sketching from nature and in accurately drawing and coloring birds and plants made him a valuable accession to the expedition. Lieutenants Abert and Peck had been attached to my command, and also with me were Mr. James McDowell, a nephew of Mrs. Benton, and Mr. Theodore Talbot, whose health had been restored by the previous journey.

It was getting late in the year. The principal objects of the expedition lay in and beyond the Rocky Mountains, and for these reasons no time could be given to examinations of the prairie region. The line of travel was directed chiefly to pass over such country as would afford good camping-grounds; where water and grass, and wood and abundant game would best contribute to maintain the health of the men and the strength of the animals. Along the route we met the usual prairie incidents of Indians and large game, which furnished always wholesome excitement. In those days these broke pleasantly in upon the silence and uniformity of the prairie and made a good school for the men. On the high plains we encountered a Cheyenne village which was out on a hunt. The men came to meet us on the plain, riding abreast and their drums sounding. They were in all their bravery, and the formidable line was imposing, and looked threatening to those of our people who were without experience in an Indian country. Men, tried and fearless in accustomed dangers, are often at the first encounter nervous in those that are unfamiliar. But the Cheyennes were friendly, and we on our side were too strong for any exhibition of hostility or rudeness; and so we gave the usual present in exchange for friendly conduct and good wishes.

We had lost an animal which in the night had strayed off from the band, and early on the march next morning Basil, with a companion, had been sent out to look for it. He did not get in at night nor in the morning. I therefore remained encamped and with a small party went in turn to look for him. After a search of an hour or two we discovered them halted, and apparently scanning the horizon around, in some uncertainty where to look for us. We were down in a swale in the ground about three hundred yards away, and so out of sight that we had not been seen. We thought to try them, and quickly throwing off the greater part of our clothes we raised an Indian yell and charged. But there was no hesitation with them. They were off their horses in an instant and their levelled pieces brought us to an abrupt halt and a hearty laugh which we all enjoyed in having found them safe and well.

Returning to camp our first experiment suggested another. The camp lay in a sort of broad gully below the level of the prairie. It was midday and the people were careless and more occupied by getting the dinner than with Indians. Riding quietly down to the hollow which gave an easy approach we charged them with the usual yell. Our charge gave them a good lesson, though it lasted but a moment. It was like charging into a beehive; there were so many men in the camp ready with their rifles that it was very unsafe to keep up our Indian character beyond the moment of the charge. Still, like all excitements, it stirred the blood pleasantly for the moment.

On the second of August we reached Bent's Fort, on the Arkansas River. This was our real point of departure. It was desirable to make a survey of the prairie region to the southward, embracing the Canadian and other rivers. I accordingly formed a detached party, in charge of which I placed Lieutenants Abert and Peck, Lieutenant Abert being in chief command. Including these officers, the command consisted of thirty-three men, and I had the good fortune to secure my friend Mr. Fitzpatrick for their guide. I had endeavored to obtain the services of an Indian who knew well the country, and was a man of great influence, especially among the Camanches, but no offer that I could make him would induce him to go. It happened that the Fort was well provisioned, and from its supplies we were able to furnish the party with a good outfit. This consisted principally of coffee and sugar for two months, several boxes of macaroni, and a quantity of rice, together with four fanegas of Mexican flour. In addition they took with them eight steers brought up on the prairie and therefore easy to drive. They were furnished with four large circular tents, and as the face of the country which was covered by the projected survey was not much broken, four wagons were added for their outfit and camp equipage. This outfit may appear luxurious for the prairie, but provisions go fast where thirty healthy men taking just the right quantity of exercise are to be fed three times a day.

Mr. Hatcher, who was a good hunter, was to accompany them as far as Bent's Post on the Canadian.

On the 12th Mr. Fitzpatrick took leave of me and joined the party. On the same day Lieutenant Abert changed his encampment preparatory to making his start, and on the 14th the two officers came to take leave of me.

It is well to say here that on the journey to Bent's Fort I had been much prepossessed in their favor. They had shown themselves well qualified for such an expedition which as of course was entirely new to them. In this journey they had given evidence of the prudence and good judgment which enabled them to carry through successfully the expedition entrusted to their care.

The next day I sent Lieutenant Abert his instructions, which were to survey the Canadian from its source to its junction with the Arkansas, taking in his way the Purgatory River, and the heads of the Washita; and on the 16th he commenced his journey down the Arkansas.

With Lieutenant Abert also went Mr. James McDowell, who decided to avail himself of this survey to return for the reason that his work would not be carried into the winter, while my journey to the Pacific was expected to be of long duration.

From the Fort I sent an express to Carson at a rancho, or stock farm, which with his friend Richard Owens he had established on the Cimarron, a tributary to the Arkansas River. But he had promised that in the event I should need him, he would join me. And I knew that he would not fail to come. My messenger found him busy starting the congenial work of making up a stock ranch. There was no time to be lost, and he did not hesitate. He sold everything at a sacrifice, farm and cattle ; and not only came himself but brought his friend Owens to join the party. This was like Carson, prompt, self-sacrificing, and true. I received them both with great satisfaction.

That Owens was a good man it is enough to say that he and Carson were friends. Cool, brave, and of good judgment ; a good hunter and good shot ; experienced in mountain life ; he was an acquisition, and proved valuable throughout the campaign.

Godey had proved himself during the preceding journey, which had brought out his distinguishing qualities of resolute and aggressive courage. Quick in deciding and prompt in acting he had also the French *élan* and their gayety of courage.

" Gai, gai, avançons nous."

I mention him here because the three men come fitly together, and because of the peculiar qualities which gave them in the highest degree efficiency for the service in which they were engaged.

The three, under Napoleon, might have become Marshals, chosen as he chose men. Carson, of great courage; quick and complete perception, taking in at a glance the advantages as well as the chances for defeat; Godey, insensible to danger, of perfect coolness and stubborn resolution; Owens, equal in courage to the others, and in coolness equal to Godey, had the *coup-d'œil* of a chess-player, covering the whole field with a glance that sees the best move. His dark-hazel eye was the marked feature of his face, large and flat and far-sighted.

Godey was a Creole Frenchman of Saint Louis, of medium height with black eyes and silky curling black hair which was his pride. In all situations he had that care of his person which good looks encourage. Once when with us in Washington, he was at a concert; immediately behind him sat the wife of the French Minister, Madame Pageot, who, with the lady by her, was admiring his hair, which was really beautiful, " but," she said, " *C'est une perruque.*" They were speaking unguardedly in French.

Godey had no idea of having his hair disparaged and with the prompt coolness with which he would have repelled any other indignity turned instantly to say, "*Pardon, Madame, c'est bien a moi.*" The ladies were silenced as suddenly as the touch on a tree trunk silences a katydid.

On the 16th of August I left Bent's Fort with a well-appointed compact party of sixty; mostly experienced and self-reliant men, equal to any emergency likely to occur and willing to meet it.

On the 20th of August we encamped on the Arkansas at the mouth of the *Fontaine qui Bouit* River. I had with me good instruments for astronomical observations, among them a portable transit instrument. This I set up, and established here one of the four principal positions on which depend the longitudes of the region embraced in the expeditions. The longitude was determined by moon culminations and the latitude by sextant observations of Polaris and stars in the south.

The resulting longitude at this position is 104° 42′ 41″. The latitude 38° 15′ 18″.

On the 26th we encamped at the mouth of the Great Canyon, and next morning leaving the river passed in our way over a bench of the mountain which the trappers believed to be the place where Pike was taken prisoner by the Mexicans. But this side of the river was within our territory. He supposed himself to be on the Arkansas when he was taken prisoner on the Rio del Norte, where he had built a stockade.

Crossing various forks of the river we finally, on September 2d, reached and continued up the main branch, having on our right the naked rock ridge of the mountain, and encamped at night on the head-waters of the Arkansas in Mexican territory; in latitude 39° 20′ 38″, longitude 106° 27′ 15″.

This was pleasant travelling. The weather now was delightful and the country beautiful. Fresh and green, aspen groves and pine woods and clear rushing water, cool streams sparkling over rocky beds.

In a pine grove at the head of the river we came to our delighted surprise upon a small herd of buffalo, which were enjoying themselves in the shade and fresh grass and water. It was now very rare that these animals were found so far west, and this made for us a most pleasant and welcome incident, as it was long now since we had parted from the buffalo. This must have been a stray herd which had found its way into the upper mountains and they had remained for a long time undisturbed. Sometimes in severe winters deer find their way into the highest parts of the wooded mountains, and remain there, keeping fat and sheltered in the aspen groves which furnish them food. Probably this little herd of buffalo had done the same. The Utah Pass was several days' journey to the southeast, and this part of the mountain was out of the way of ordinary travel.

Here along in these mountains was one of the pleasantest grounds in the journey. Game was plenty; deer and elk. We were some days after on the mountain slopes, where a lovely view extended across a broad valley to the opposite ridges. It was so fine a view that Kern sketched it. In looking over the country I had ridden off a mile or two from the party, keeping along the heights to enjoy the air and views, when I came upon a small band of buffalo, doubtless part of the herd which we had found in the pines at the top of the mountain. The ground was rough, but we had a fine race. I had closed up and was about to fire when the pistol which I held raised went off, and the ball passed so close to my head that I reined up in surprise. My holster pistols were a hair-trigger pair, and old companions which I liked for that, and because they were true as a rifle. "*Sacré bon coup*," Basil said of them once when he saw the head of a quail cut off at long range. This time it was my own head. It is in this way that men have been sometimes lost in the mountains and never found. They lie like the trunk of a fallen tree worn by the snow and rain until the tall, rank grass covers and hides them. My trail would not have been taken in time and it would have been by the merest chance that any hunter would have passed the spot.

One of the Delawares had killed a fat buffalo cow. This singular meeting with the buffalo was our last; and they were probably the last stragglers that ever reached the western slope of the mountains. This was the general opinion of our people, whose experience would be likely to make it correct. The places where I have described them made then the broadest range of the buffalo from east to west, and make a fair exhibit of the abounding animal life of the country.

Passing the night of the 4th on Piny River, an affluent of Grand River, of the Colorado of the Gulf of California, we encamped the next day on the same river at "Williams Fishery," in longitude 106° 44′ 21″, latitude 39° 39′ 12″. We caught here a singular fish, which was called buffalo-fish from a hump on the back, rising straight up immediately behind the head.

Between fishermen and hunters the camp was abundantly supplied in all this part of our journey. These wood-clothed ranges, with their abundant game and healthful air, we have seen described as "impenetrable deserts whose rugged inaccessibility barred all passage, amid whose parched sterility unfortunate travellers were exposed to death from thirst and hunger."

The character of the mountain country has been so fully given in the previous journeys, that it does not need to be longer dwelt upon here. On the 2d of October I encamped on a branch of the Timpanogos River, and on the 10th reached the shore of the lake, and its outlet at the mouth of Hugh's Creek, on the 12th. The geographical features of the country were carefully sketched; and astronomical observations, for which the continued fine weather favored us, were made on the different affluents to the Grand

and Green River forks of the Great Colorado.   The next day we encamped at a creek on the shore of the Great Salt Lake, where I made the second principal station for longitude.   These observations resulted in longitude 112° 06′ 08″, and latitude 40° 45′ 53″.

It will be remarked that our journey from the head of the Arkansas River had been continuously in Mexican territory, as was all of the Salt Lake valley.   Two weeks were spent in this valley and on its tributary streams, during which we were occupied in fixing the positions of various points, and extending our examination into and around the lake.

The rocky shores of its islands were whitened by the spray which leaves salt on everything it touches, and a covering like ice forms over the water which the waves throw among the rocks.   This seems to be the dry season when the waters recede ; and the shores of the lake, especially on the south side, are whitened with incrustations of fine white salt.   The shallow arms of the lake, under a slight covering of briny water, present beds of salt extending for miles.   Plants and bushes blown by the winds upon these fields are entirely incrusted with crystallized salt.   The stem of a small twig, less than the size of a goose-quill, from the southeastern shore, showed a formation of more than an inch thick of crystallized salt.   The fresh water received by the lake is great in quantity, from the many fresh-water streams flowing into it, but they seem to have no perceptible effect.   We could find in it no fish, or animal life of any kind, the larvæ which were accumulated in beds on the shore being found to belong to winged insects.   On the contrary, the upper lake—the Timpanogos—which discharges into this by a stream about thirty-five miles long, is fresh water, and affords large trout and other fish in great numbers.   These constitute the food of the Indians during the fishing season.

The mineral or rock salt is found in beds of great thickness at the heads of a stream in the mountains to the eastward behind the lakes.   These strata probably underlie the bed of the Great Lake, and constitute the deposit from which it obtains its salt.   It was found by us in the place marked by Humboldt on his map of New Spain as derived from the journal of the missionary Father Escalante, who towards the close of the last century attempted to penetrate the unknown country from Santa Fé of New Mexico to Monterey of California.   But he does not seem to have got further in his adventurous journey—and this at that time was far—than the south end of the Timpanogos.   Southeast of this lake is the chain of the Wahsatch Mountains, which make in that part the rim of the Great Basin.   In this mountain, at the place where Humboldt has written " *Montagnes de sel Gemme* " (Rock Salt Mountain), the strata of salt are found in thick beds of red clay, at the heads of a small stream tributary to the Utah or Timpanogos Lake on its southeasterly side.

THE CLAIMANT.

There is at the southern end of the lake a large peninsular island, which the Indians informed me could at this low stage of the water be reached on horseback. Accordingly on the 18th I took with me Carson and a few men and rode from our encampment near the southeastern shore across the shallows to the island—almost peninsular at this low stage of the waters— on the way the water nowhere reaching above the saddle-girths. The floor of the lake was a sheet of salt resembling softening ice, into which the horses' feet sunk to the fetlocks. On the island we found grass and water and several bands of antelope. Some of these were killed, and, in memory of the grateful supply of food they furnished, I gave their name to the island. An observation of the meridian altitude of the sun, taken on the summit of the peak of the island, gave for its latitude 40° 58′ 48″.

Returning to the shore we found at the camp an old Utah Indian. See- ing what game we had brought in he promptly informed us that the ante- lope which we had been killing were his—that *all* the antelope on that island belonged to him—that they were all he had to live upon, and that we must pay him for the meat which we had brought away. He was very serious with us and gravely reproached me for the wrong which we had done him. Pleased with his readiness, I had a bale unpacked and gave him a present— some red cloth, a knife, and tobacco, with which he declared himself abun- dantly satisfied for this trespass on his game preserve. With each article laid down, his nods and gutturals expressed the satisfaction he felt at the success of his imaginary claim. We could see, as far as an Indian's face lets expression be seen, that he was thinking, " I went to the White Chief who killed my antelope, and made him pay for it." There is nothing new under the sun.

The climate of this lake country does not present the rigorous winter due to its elevation and mountainous structure. Observations made during our stay here show that around the southern shore of the lake, latitude 40° 30′ to 41°, for two weeks in the month of October, from the 13th to the 27th, the mean temperature was 40° at sunrise, 70° at noon, and 54° at sunset; ranging at sunrise from 28° to 57°; at noon, from 62° to 76°; at four in the afternoon, from 58° to 69°; and at sunset, from 47° to 57°.

Until the middle of the month the weather remained fair and very pleas- ant. On the 15th it began to rain in occasional showers which whitened with snow the tops of the mountains on the southeast side of the lake valley. Flowers were in bloom during all the month. About the 18th, when we visited the large island in the south of the lake, *helianthus,* sev- eral species of *aster, erodium cicutarium,* and several other plants were in fresh and full bloom; the grass of the second growth was coming up finely, and vegetation generally betokened the lengthened summer of the climate.

The 16th, 17th, and 18th were stormy with rain; heavy at night; the peaks of the Bear River range and tops of mountains covered with snow. On the 18th the sky cleared with weather like that of late spring, and continued mild and clear until the end of the month, when the fine weather was again interrupted by a day or two of rain. No snow showed within 2000 feet above the level of the valley.

On the 23d I encamped at a spring in a valley opening on the southern shore of the lake. On the way, near the shore, we came to a small run flowing into the lake, where an Indian was down on his hands and knees, drinking. Going there also to drink, we were surprised to find it salt. The water was clear, and its coolness indicated that it came from not far below the surface.

On the 25th we moved camp to a valley near the southwestern shore about fifty miles from the station creek, and in longitude 113° 05' 09", latitude 40° 38' 17".

At this point we were to leave the lake. From any neighboring mountain height looking westward, the view extended over ranges which occupied apparently the whole visible surface—nothing but mountains, and in winter-time a forbidding prospect. Afterwards, as we advanced, we found the lengthening horizon continued the same prospect until it stretched over the waters of the Pacific. Looking across over the crests of these ridges, which nearly all run north and south, was like looking lengthwise along the teeth of a saw.

Some days here were occupied in deciding upon the direction to be taken for the onward journey. The route I wished to take lay over a flat plain covered with sage-brush. The country looked dry and of my own men none knew anything of it; neither Walker nor Carson. The Indians declared to us that no one had ever been known to cross the plain, which was desert; so far as any of them had ventured no water had been found. It was probably for this reason Father Escalante had turned back. Men who have travelled over this country in later years are familiar with the stony, black, unfertile mountains, that so often discouraged and brought them disappointment. Nearly upon the line of our intended travel, and at the farther edge of the desert, apparently fifty to sixty miles away, was a peak-shaped mountain. This looked to me to be fertile, and it seemed safe to make an attempt to reach it. By some persuasion and the offer of a tempting reward, I had induced one of the local Indians to go as guide on the way to the mountain; willing to profit by any side knowledge of the ground, or water-hole that the rains might have left, and about which the Indians always know in their hunts through the sage after small game.

I arranged that Carson, Archambeau, and Maxwell should set out at night, taking with them a man having charge of a pack-mule with water and provisions, and make for the mountain. I to follow with the party the next day and make one camp out into the desert. They to make a signal by smoke in case water should be found.

The next afternoon, when the sun was yet two hours high, with the animals rested and well watered, I started out on the plain. As we advanced this was found destitute of any vegetation except sage-bushes, and absolutely bare and smooth as if water had been standing upon it. The animals being fresh I stretched far out into the plain. Travelling along in the night, after a few hours' march, my Indian lost his courage and grew so much alarmed that his knees really gave way under him and he wabbled about like a drunken man. He was not a true Utah, but rather of the Pi-utes, a Digger of the upper class, and he was becoming demoralized at being taken so far from his *gîte*. Seeing that he could be of no possible use I gave him his promised reward and let him go. He was so happy in his release that he bounded off like a hare through the sage-brush, fearful that I might still keep him.

Sometime before morning I made camp in the sage-brush, lighting fires to signal Carson's party. Before daybreak Archambeau rode in ; the jingling of his spurs a welcome sound indicating as it did that he brought good tidings. They had found at the peak water and grass, and wood abundant. The gearing up was quickly done and in the afternoon we reached the foot of the mountain, where a cheerful little stream broke out and lost itself in the valley. The animals were quickly turned loose, there being no risk of their straying from the grass and water. To the friendly mountain I gave the name of Pilot Peak. From my observation this oasis is in the latitude 41° 00' 28'' longitude 114° 11' 09''. Some time afterward, when our crossing of the desert became known, an emigrant caravan was taken by this route, which then became known as *The Hastings Cut-off*.

We gave the animals a day's rest here. The crossing of the desert had been a little strain upon them ; many of them being grain-fed horses, unused to travelling on grass. These cannot stand being over-fatigued, soon reaching the stage which is called in the language of the country *resté ;* from which they cannot recover without time, and must be left on the trail. With a mule it is very different. He may be *resté* at night, but give him plenty of good grass and water and he is ready for service in the morning.

On the 1st of November we resumed our journey. The ridges which occupied the basin and which lay across our route are short, being the links which form the ranges ; and between their overlapping points were easy passes by which the valleys connect. This is their regular structure.

Through these passes we wound our way and in the evening encamped at a spring in the head of a ravine which my observations put in longitude 114° 26' 22'', latitude 40° 43' 29'', and the next day I made camp at a spring to which I gave the name of Whitton, one of my men who discovered it.

In advancing, the country was always carefully examined, so far as the eye could form any judgment upon it; and from the early morning start the men were spread over it to search for a camping-place which with water should give the best grass.

The winter was now approaching and I had good reason to know what the snow would be in the Great Sierra. It was imprudent to linger long in the examination of the Great Basin. In order therefore to use to the best advantage the interval of good weather I decided to divide my party and run two separate lines across the Basin.

On the evening of the 8th I encamped on a small stream which I called Crane's Branch after one of my Delaware hunters. Crane was a good judge of country with a quick eye exercised in hunting. He was one of the men I liked to have near me. He was usually serious and dignified even for an Indian, who are naturally grave men. The objects which furnish ideas to the mind of an Indian are very few and mostly what he sees within a limited range. Within this, the game and other natural objects which come before his eyes; and outside of it, the enemies whom he goes to fight and scalp, if he can. These make his two sets of ideas. Nearer to the whites, other subjects force their way in confused shape through the barriers of an unknown language, but these are quite outside of the usual Indian under-standing. The subjects belonging to their manner of life they hesitate to talk about with the whites; this and the difference of language make them reserved to us. With me the Delawares were now making the grand tour.

Crane's Branch led into a larger stream that was one of two forks form-ing a river to which I gave the name of Humboldt. I am given by himself the honor of being the first to place his great name on the map of the continent.

Both the river and mountain to which I gave his name are conspicuous objects; the river stretching across the Basin to the foot of the Sierra Nevada, and the mountain standing out in greater bulk and length than its neighbors, and being one of those which I have named fertile mountains, having on it abundant water and grass, and woods.

Years after in travelling through that country I was glad to find that river and mountain held his name, not only on the maps, but in usage by the people.

I now divided the party, giving to Mr. Kern the charge of the main body with instructions to follow down and survey the Humboldt River and its valley to their termination in what was called " the Sink." This is a broad level bottom of fertile land ; probably once the bed of the lake when over all this region, at a time not very remote, the waters were higher. When I passed there two years later it was covered with grass and several varieties of clover. Thence to continue on along the eastern foot of the Sierra to a lake to which I have given the name of Walker, who was to be his guide on this survey. I had engaged Mr. Walker for guide in this part of the region to be explored, with which, and the southern part of the " California Mountain " he was well acquainted. The place of meeting for the two par-ties was to be the lake.

This party would have a secure line of travel in following the river, which would furnish grass and water for the entire journey and so keep the greater number of the animals in as good condition as the season admitted.

To accompany myself I selected ten men, among whom were some of the Delawares. I took leave of the main party and set out on a line westward directly across the Basin, the look of the country inducing me to turn somewhat to the south.

We lost no time in pressing forward ; but the tortuous course rendered unavoidable by the necessity of using just such passes as the mountains gave, and in searching for grass and water, greatly lengthened our road. Still it gave me knowledge of the country. The early morning began the day's work by the usual careful study of the ground ahead for indications to the best line of travel, and so soon as they were ready the hunters started out to the right and left, scouring the country as we advanced. When anything worthy of note was discovered a shot was fired, or the horseman would make a few short turns backward and forward as a signal that something requiring attention had been found.

We succeeded in finding always good camping-grounds, usually avail-ing ourselves of the Indian trails which skirted the foot of the ridges. When well marked showing use, these never failed to lead to water and the larger the trail the more abundant the water. This we always found at the edge of the mountain, generally in some ravine, and quickly sinking into the ground ; never reaching the valley except in seasons of rain. Doubtless artesian wells would find it and make fertile these valleys, which now are dry and barren.

Travelling along the foot of a mountain on one of these trails we dis-covered a light smoke rising from a ravine, and riding quietly up, found a single Indian standing before a little sage-brush fire over which was hanging a small earthen pot, filled with sage-bush squirrels. Another bunch of squirrels lay near it and close by were his bow and arrows. He was deep in a brown study, thinking perhaps of some game-trail which he had seen and intended to follow that afternoon, and did not see or hear us until we were directly upon him, his absorbed thoughts and the sides of the ravine cutting off sounds. Escape for him was not possible and he tried to seem pleased, but his convulsive start and wild look around showed that he thought his end had come. And so it would—abruptly— had the Delawares been alone. With a deprecating smile he offered us part of his *pot-au-feu* and his bunch of squirrels. I reassured him with a friendly shake of the hand and a trifling gift. He was a good-looking young man, well made, as these Indians usually are, and naked as a worm.

The Delawares lingered as we turned away, but I would not let them remain. Anyhow they regarded our journey as a kind of war-path, and no matter what kind of path he is upon a Delaware is always ready to take a scalp when he is in a country where there are strange Indians. We had gone but a short distance when I found they had brought away his bow and arrows, but I had them taken immediately back. These were well made ; the bow strong, and made still stronger with sinews, and the arrows were all headed with obsidian worked in the usual spear shape by patient labor, and nearly as sharp as steel. The Delawares took them back willingly when I reminded them that they had exposed the poor fellow to almost certain starvation by depriving him at the beginning of winter of his only means to procure food.

At one of our camps on the foot-slopes of a ridge we found again springs of boiling water; but a little way distant from the spring of cold water which supplied us.

A day or two after we saw mountain sheep for the first time in crossing the Basin. None were killed, but that afternoon Carson killed an antelope. That day we travelled late, making for the point of a wooded mountain where we had expected to find water, but on reaching it found only the dry bed of a creek where there was sometimes running water. It was too late to go farther and I turned up the creek bed, taking the chance to find it above as the mountain looked promising. Well up, towards the top of the mountain, nearly two thousand feet above the plain, we came upon a spring where the little basin afforded enough for careful use. A bench of the mountain near by made a good camping-ground, for the November nights were cool and newly-fallen snow already marked out the higher ridges of the mountains. With grass abundant, and pine wood and cedars to keep up the night fires, we were well provided for.

Sagundai who had first found the spring saw fresh tracks made in the sand by a woman's naked foot, and the spring had been recently cleaned out. But he saw no other indications of human life. We had made our supper on the antelope and were lying around the fire, and the men taking their great comfort in smoking. A good supper and a pipe make for them a comfortable ending no matter how hard the day has been. Carson who was lying on his back with his pipe in his mouth, his hands under his head and his feet to the fire, suddenly exclaimed, half rising and pointing to the other side of the fire, " Good God! look there!" In the blaze of the fire, peering over her skinny, crooked hands, which shaded her eyes from the glare, was standing an old woman apparently eighty years of age, nearly

OLD DIGGER WOMAN ABANDONED BY HER PEOPLE.

naked, her grizzly hair hanging down over her face and shoulders. She had thought it a camp of her people and had already begun to talk and gesticulate, when her open mouth was paralyzed with fright, as she saw the faces of the whites. She turned to escape, but the men had gathered about her and brought her around to the fire. Hunger and cold soon dispelled fear and she made us understand that she had been left by her people at the spring to die, because she was very old and could gather no more seeds and was no longer good for anything. She told us she had nothing to eat and was very hungry. We gave her immediately about a quarter of the antelope, thinking she would roast it by our fire, but no sooner did she get it in her hand than she darted off into the darkness. Some one ran after her with a brand of fire, but calling after her brought no answer. In the morning, her fresh tracks at the spring showed that she had been there for water during the night. Starvation had driven her to us, but her natural fear drove her away as quickly, so soon as she had secured something to eat. Before we started we left for her at the spring a little supply from what food we had. This, with what she could gather from the nut-pine trees on the mountain, together with our fire which she could easily keep up, would probably prolong her life even after the snows came. The nut-pines and cedars extend their branches out to the ground and in one of their thickets, as I have often proved, these make a comfortable shelter against the most violent snow-storms.

This was Sangundai's Spring. The names of my camps here along become the record of the rivalry of the men in finding good camps. It became the recurring interest of each day to prove their judgment of country as well as their skill as hunters.

The region here along had a special interest for me and our progress was slow for the two following days. We had now reached a low valley line that extends along the eastern foot of the ridges which constitute the Sierra Nevada. Into this low ground the rivers from the Sierra as well as from the Basin gather into a series of lakes extending south towards the head of the Gulf of California. I had a reason for carefully examining this part of the Basin, but the time needed for it would interfere with other objects and the winter was at hand.

The place appointed for meeting the main party was on the eastward shore of Walker's Lake near the point where the river to which I had given the same name empties into it. Making our way along the foot of the mountain towards our rendezvous we had reached one of the lakes where at this season the scattered Indians of the neighborhood were gathering to fish. Turning a point on the lake shore the party of Indians some twelve or fourteen in number came abruptly into view. They were advancing along in Indian file, one following the other, their heads bent forward and eyes fixed on the ground. As our party met them the Indians did not turn their heads nor raise their eyes from the ground. Their conduct indicated unfriendliness, but, habituated to the uncertainties of savage life, we too fell readily into their humor, and passed on our way without word or halt. Even to us it was a strange meeting.

It was the solitary occasion where I met with such an instance of sullen and defiant hostility among Indians and where they neither sought nor avoided conflict. I judged that they either regarded us as intruders, or that they had received some recent injury from the whites who were now beginning to enter California, and which they wished but feared to avenge.

In this region the condition of the Indian is nearly akin to that of the lower animals. Here they are really *wild men.* In his wild state the Indian lives to get food. This is his business. The superfluous part of his life, that portion which can be otherwise employed, is devoted to some kind of warfare. From this lowest condition, where he is found as the simplest element of existence, up to the highest in which he is found on this continent, it is the same thing. In the Great Basin, where nearly naked he travelled on foot and lived in the sage-brush, I found him in the most elementary form; the men living alone, the women living alone, but all after food. Sometimes one man cooking by his solitary fire in the sage-brush which was his home, his bow and arrows and bunch of squirrels by his side; sometimes on the shore of a lake or river where food was more abundant a little band of men might be found occupied in fishing; miles away a few women would be met gathering seeds and insects, or huddled up in a shelter of sage-brush to keep off the snow. And the same on the mountains or prairies where the wild Indians were found in their highest condition, where they had horses and lived in lodges. The labor of their lives was to get something to eat. The occupation of the women was in gleaning from the earth everything of vegetable or insect life; the occupation of the men was to kill every animal they could for food and every man of every other tribe for pleasure. And, in every attempt to civilize, these are the two lines upon which he is to be met.

On the 24th we encamped at our rendezvous on the lake where beds of rushes made good pasturage for our animals. Three days afterward the main party arrived. They were all in good health, and had met with no serious accident. But the scarcity of game had made itself felt, and we were now all nearly out of provisions. It was now almost midwinter, and the open weather could not be expected to last.

In this journey across the Basin, between latitudes 41° and 38,° during the month of November from the 5th to the 25th, the mean temperature was 29° at sunrise and 40° at sunset, ranging at noon between 41° and 60°. There was a snow-storm between the 4th and 7th, snow falling principally at night, and the sun occasionally breaking out in the day. The lower hills and valleys were covered only a few inches deep with snow, which the sun carried off in a few hours after the storm was over. The weather continued uninterruptedly clear and beautiful until the close of the month. But though the skies were clear it was colder now that we had come within the influence of the main Sierra.

I was in the neighborhood of the passage which I had forced across it a year before, and I had it on my mind. Heavy snows might be daily expected to block up the passes, and I considered that in this event it would be hopeless to attempt a crossing with the material of the whole party.

I therefore decided again to divide it, sending the main body under Kern to continue southward along the lake line and pass around the Point of the California Mountain into the head of the San Joaquin valley. There, as already described, the great Sierra comes down nearly to the plain, making a Point, as in the smaller links, and making open and easy passes where there is never or rarely snow. As before, Walker, who was familiar with the southern part of Upper California, was made the guide of the party; and, after considering the advantages of different places, it was agreed that the place of meeting for the two parties should be at a little lake in the valley of a river called the Lake Fork of the Tularé Lake.

With a selected party of fifteen, among whom were some of my best men, including several Delawares, I was to attempt the crossing of the mountain in order to get through to Sutter's Fort before the snow began to fall. At the fort I could obtain the necessary supplies for the relief of the main party.

Leaving them in good order, and cheerful at the prospect of escaping from the winter into the beautiful " California Valley," as it was then called, we separated, and I took up my route for the river which flows into Pyramid Lake, and which on my last journey I had named Salmon-Trout River.

I now entered a region which hardship had made familiar to me, and I was not compelled to feel my way, but used every hour of the day to press forward towards the Pass at the head of this river.

On the 1st of December I struck it above the lower cañon, and on the evening of the 4th camped at its head on the east side of the pass in the Sierra Nevada. Our effort had been to reach the pass before a heavy fall of snow, and we had succeeded. All night we watched the sky, ready to attempt the passage with the first indication of falling snow; but the sky continued clear. On our way up, the fine weather which we had left at the foot of the mountain continued to favor us, and when we reached the pass the only snow showing was on the peaks of the mountains.

At three in the afternoon the temperature was 46°; at sunset, 34°. The observations of the night gave for the longitude of the pass, 120° 15′ 20″, and for latitude, 39° 17′ 12″. Early the next morning we climbed the rocky ridge which faces the eastern side, and at sunrise were on the crest of the divide, 7200 feet above the sea; the sky perfectly clear, and the temperature 22°. There was no snow in the pass, but already it showed apparently deep on higher ridges and mountain-tops. The emigrant road now passed here following down a fork of Bear River, which leads from the pass into the Sacramento valley. Finding this a rugged way, I turned to the south and encamped in a mountain-meadow where the grass was fresh and green. We had made good our passage of the mountain and entered now among the grand vegetation of the California valley. Even if the snow should now begin to fall, we could outstrip it into the valley, where the winter king already shrunk from the warm breath of spring.

The route the next day led over good travelling ground; gaining a broad leading ridge we travelled along through the silence of a noble pine forest where many of the trees were of great height and uncommon size. The tall red columns standing closely on the clear ground, the filtered, flickering sunshine from their summits far overhead, gave the dim religious light of cathedral aisles, opening out on every side, one after the other, as we advanced. Later, in early spring, these forest grounds are covered with a blue carpet of forget-me-nots.

The pines of the European forests would hide their diminished heads amidst these great columns of the Sierra. A species of cedar (*Thuya gigantea*) occurred often of extraordinary bulk and height. *Pinus Lambertiani* was one of the most frequent trees, distinguished among cone-bearing tribes by the length of its cones, which are sometimes sixteen or eighteen inches long. The Indians eat the inner part of the burr, and I noticed large heaps of them where they had been collected.

Leaving the higher ridges we gained the smoother spurs and descended about 4000 feet, the face of the country rapidly changing as we went down. The country became low and rolling; pines began to disappear, and varieties of oak, principally an evergreen resembling live oak, became the predominating forest growth. The oaks bear great quantities of acorns, which are the principal food of all the wild Indians; it is their bread-fruit tree. At a village of a few huts which we came upon there was a large supply of these acorns: eight or ten cribs of wicker-work containing about twenty bushels each. The sweetest and best acorns, somewhat resembling Italian chestnuts in taste, are obtained from a large tree belonging to the division of white oaks, distinguished by the length of its acorn, which is commonly an inch and a half and sometimes two inches. This long acorn characterizes the tree, which is a new species and is accordingly specified by Dr. Torrey as *Quercus longiglanda* (Torr. and Frem.)—long-acorn oak. This tree is

TLAMATH LAKE

very abundant and generally forms the groves on the bottom-lands of the streams; standing apart with a green undergrowth of grass which gives the appearance of cultivated parks. It is a noble forest tree, sixty to eighty feet high with a summit of wide-spreading branches, and frequently attains a diameter of six feet; the largest that we measured reached eleven feet. The evergreen oaks generally have a low growth with long branches and spreading tops.

At our encampment on the evening of the 8th, on a stream which I named Hamilton's Creek, we had come down to an elevation of 500 feet above the sea. The temperature at sunset was 48°, the sky clear, the weather calm and delightful, and the vegetation that of early spring. We were still upon the foot-hills of the mountains, where the soil is sheltered by woods and where rain falls much more frequently than in the open Sacramento Valley near the edge of which we then were. I have been in copious continuous rains of eighteen or twenty hours' duration, in the oak region of the mountain, when none fell in the valley below. Innumerable small streams have their rise through these foot-hills, which often fail to reach the river of the valley, but are absorbed in its light soil; the large streams coming from the upper part of the mountain make valleys of their own of fertile soil, covered with luxuriant grass and interspersed with groves.

The oak belt of the mountain is the favorite range of the Indians. I found many small villages scattered through it. They select places near the streams where there are large boulders of granite rock, that show everywhere holes which they had used for mortars in which to pound the acorns. These are always pretty spots. The clean, smooth granite rocks standing out from the green of the fresh grass over which the great oaks throw their shade, and the clear running water are pleasant to eye and ear.

After the rough passage and scanty food of the Basin these lovely spots with the delightful spring weather, fresh grass and flowers, and running water, together with the abundant game, tempted us to make early camps; so that we were about four days in coming down to the valley.

Travelling in this way slowly along, taking the usual astronomical observations and notes of the country, we reached on the 9th of December the Grimes Rancho on what was then still known as *Rio de los Americanos*— the American Fork, near Sutter's Fort.

Captain Sutter received me with the same friendly hospitality which had been so delightful to us the year before. I found that our previous visit had created some excitement among the Mexican authorities. But to their inquiries he had explained that I had been engaged in a geographical survey of the interior and had been driven to force my way through the snow of the mountains simply to obtain a refuge and food where I knew it could be had at his place, which was by common report known to me.

Being ourselves already recruited by the easy descent into the valley I did not need to delay long here. A few days sufficed to purchase some animals and a small drove of cattle, with other needed supplies.

Leaving the upper settlements of *New Helvetia*, as the Sutter settlement was called, on the 14th of December, I started to find my party which I had left in charge of Talbot when we had separated in the Basin on Walker Lake. Passing through the groves of oak which border the American Fork, we directed our route in a southeasterly course towards the Cosumné River.

The Cosumné Indians, who have left their name on this river, and which I had preserved on my map of the country, have been driven away from it within a few years and dispersed among other tribes; and several farms of some leagues in extent had already been commenced on the lower part of the stream. At one of these we encamped about eight miles above the junction of the Cosumné with the Mokelumné River, which a few miles below enters a deep slough in the tide-water of the San Joaquin delta.

Our way now lay over the well-remembered plains of the San Joaquin valley, the direction of our route inclining towards the mountains. We crossed wooded sloughs, with ponds of deep water, which nearer the foot-hills are running streams with large bottoms of fertile land ; the greater part of our way being through evergreen, and other oaks. The rainy season, which commonly begins with November, had not yet commenced, and the streams were at the low stage usual to the dry season and easily forded. The Mokelumné where we crossed it is about sixty yards wide ; the broad alluvial bottoms were here about five hundred yards wide. Leaving this river on the morning of the 16th, we travelled about twenty miles through open woods of white oak, crossing in the way several stream-beds, among them the Calaveras Creek. These have abundant water with good land nearer the hills; and the Calaveras makes some remarkably handsome bottoms.

Issuing from the woods we rode about sixteen miles over open prairie partly covered with bunch-grass, the timber reappearing on the rolling hills of the river Stanislaus in the usual belt of evergreen oaks. The level valley was about forty feet below the upland, and the stream seventy yards broad, with the usual fertile bottom-land which was covered with green grass among large oaks. We encamped in one of these bottoms, in a grove of the large white oaks previously mentioned.

The many varieties of deciduous and evergreen oaks which predominate throughout the valleys and lower hills of the mountains afford large quantities of acorns. Their great abundance in the midst of fine pasture-land must make them an important element in the farming economy of the country.

The day had been very warm. At sunset the temperature was 55° and the weather clear and calm.

MEDICINE MAN.

At sunrise next morning the thermometer was at 22° with a light wind from the Sierra N. 75° E. and a clear pure sky, against which the blue line of the mountains showed clearly marked. The way for about three miles was through woods of evergreen and other oaks with some shrubbery intermingled. Among this was a lupine of extraordinary size, not yet in bloom. Emerging from the woods we travelled in a southeasterly direction, over a prairie of rolling land, the ground becoming more broken as we approached the Tuolumné River, one of the finest tributaries to the San Joaquin.

The hills were generally covered with a species of geranium (*erodium cicutarium*), in the language of the country *alfalferia*, a valuable plant for stock and considered very nutritious. With this was frequently interspersed good and green bunch-grass, and a plant commonly called *bur-clover*. This plant, which in some places is very abundant, bears a spirally twisted pod, filled with seeds that remain on the ground during the dry season, well preserved. This affords good food for the cattle until with the spring rains new grass comes up.

We started a band of wild horses on approaching the river and the Indians ran off from a village on the bank; the men lurking round to observe us.

The trail led sidling down the steep face of the hill to the river-bottom. The horse I was riding, one of those gotten at Sutter's, had been reclaimed from the wild herds, and seeing this wild herd scouring off he remembered his own free days and in mid-trail set himself to bucking, in the way a California horse—wild or tame—knows how to do exceptionally. A wild horse broken to the saddle never forgets, and takes advantage of every chance he has to rid himself of his rider. If a girth breaks or a saddle turns he knows it. A rifle across the saddle and Indians to be watched and a bucking horse on a steep hill-side make a complicated situation, but we got to the bottom without parting company and my horse seemed only pleased by the excitement.

I give place to a recollection of another bucking horse which illustrates well the capacity in that way of the Californian horse of the civilized breed and the capacity of the Californian to sit him. After the capitulation of Couënga I was riding into Los Angeles at the head of the battalion and was met by Don Francisco de la Guerra and other officers of the Californian force, who brought with them for me two fine horses, one a gray, the other a *palomino* or tan-colored cream; both uncommonly large for Californian horses and just the size for a saddle-horse. Before changing my saddle I took a look at the two, and not liking the eyes of the gray I had Jacob put the saddle on the *palomino*. My friend Don Pedro Carillo, a Californian, educated at Harvard—and who had taken sides with me and was one of my aides—took the gray. Of course, like all Californians, Don Pedro was a splendid horseman. He sprang lightly into the saddle, which was that of the country, with the usual *mochila* or large, stiff, leather covering to the saddle. But his right foot had not reached the stirrup when the gray commenced. He bucked from the start, going around in a circle about thirty yards across, bucking right along and with so much force that he jerked Don Pedro's sword from its scabbard, the pistols from the holsters and the *mochilas* from between him and the saddle. Everybody applauded his horsemanship. Francisco de la Guerra cried out " *Todavia es Californio!* " ("He is a Californian still.")

Californians generally were handsome, but even among them Don Pedro was a fine-looking man. He is yet living at Los Angeles, and we remain friends.

We encamped on the Tuolumné on bottom-land, open-wooded with large white oaks of the new species; and excellent grass furnished good food for the animals. The usual order of the camp was enlivened by the Indians, who were soon reconciled to our presence. About their huts were the usual *acorn cribs*, containing each some twenty or thirty bushels. The sunset temperature was pleasant, at 54°, and a clear atmosphere. Multitudes of geese and other wild fowl made the night noisy.

In the morning the sky was clear, with an air from the southeast and a hoar frost covering the ground like a light fall of snow. At sunrise the thermometer was at 24°, a difference from the preceding sunset of thirty degrees. Our course now inclined more towards the foot of the mountain and led over a broken country. In about seventeen miles we reached the Auxumné River—called by the Mexicans *Merced*—another large affluent of the San Joaquin, and continued about six miles up the stream, intending gradually to reach the heart of the mountains at the head of the *Lake Fork* of the Tularé.

We encamped on the southern side of the river, where broken hills made a steep bluff, with a narrow bottom. On the northern side was a low, undulating wood and prairie land, over which a band of about three hundred elk was slowly coming to water, feeding as they approached.

The next day was December the 19th; the weather continuing clear and pleasant, very unlike the winter days to which we were accustomed. We continued our journey in a southeasterly direction, over a broken and hilly country without timber, and showing only scattered clumps of trees from which we occasionally started deer.

In a few hours we reached a beautiful country of undulating upland, openly wooded with oaks, principally evergreen, and watered with small streams which together make the MARIPOSAS River. Continuing along we

A FLOCK OF WILD GEESE.

came upon broad and deeply-worn trails which had been freshly travelled by large bands of horses, apparently coming from the San Joaquin valley. But we had heard enough to know that they came from the settlements on the coast. These and indications from horse-bones dragged about by wild animals, wolves or bears, warned us that we were approaching villages of Horse-thief Indians, a party of whom had just returned from a successful raid. Immediately upon striking their trail I sent forward four of my best men, Dick Owens and Maxwell and two Delawares. I followed after with the rest of the party, but soon the Indian signs became so thick, trail after trail coming into that on which we were travelling, that I saw we were getting into a stronghold of the Horse-thieves, and we rode rapidly forward. After a few miles of sharp riding, a small stream running over a slaty bed, with clumps of oaks around, tempted me into making an early halt. Good grass was abundant, and this spot not long since had been the camping-ground of a village, and was evidently one of their favorite places, as the ground was whitened with the bones of many horses. We had barely thrown off our saddles and not yet turned the horses loose, when the intermittent report of rifles, in the way one does not mistake, and the barking of many dogs and sounds of shouting faintly reaching us, made us quickly saddle up again and ride to the sounds at speed.

Four men were left to guard the camp. In a short half mile we found ourselves suddenly in front of a large Indian village not two hundred yards away. More than a hundred Indians were advancing on each side of a small hill, on the top of which were our men where a clump of oaks and rocks amidst bushes made a good defence. My men had been discovered by the Indians and suddenly found themselves in the midst of them, but jumped from their horses and took to the rocks, which happened to be a strong place to fight from. The Indians were shouting at them in Spanish, and the women and children at the village howling at their best. Our men were only endeavoring to stand them off until we should get up, as they knew we would not be far behind. The Indians had nearly surrounded the knoll and were about getting possession of the horses when we came into view. Our shout as we charged up the hill was answered by the yell of the Delawares as they dashed down the hill to recover their animals, and the report of Owens' and Maxwell's rifles. Owens had singled out the foremost Indian, who did not go any farther up the hill, and the others drew a little back towards the village. Anxious for the safety of the men left behind, I profited by the surprise to withdraw towards our camp; checking the Indians by an occasional rifle shot, with the range of which they seemed to think they were acquainted. They followed us to the camp and scattered around among the rocks and trees, whence they harangued us, bestowing on us liberally all the epithets they could use, telling us what they would do with us.   Many of them had been Mission Indians and spoke Spanish well.   " Wait," they said.   " *Esperate Carrajos*—wait until morning.   There are two big villages up in the mountains close by; we have sent for the Chief ; he'll be down before morning with all the people, and you will all die.   None of you shall go back ; we will have all your horses."

I divided the camp into two watches, putting myself into the last one. As soon as it was fully dark each man of the guard crept to his post.   We heard the women and children retreating towards the mountains.   Before midnight the Indians had generally withdrawn, only now and then a shout to show us that they were on hand and attending to us.   Otherwise nothing occurred to break the stillness of the night, but a shot from one of the Delawares fired at a wolf as it jumped over a log.   In our experienced camp no one moved, but Delaware Charley crept up to me to let me know what had caused the shot of the Delaware who, with hostile Indians around, instinctively fired at a moving thing that might have been an Indian crawling towards our horses.

The Horse-thief tribes have been " Christian Indians " of the Missions, and when these were broken up by Mexico the Indians took to the mountains.   Knowing well the coast country, and the exact situation of the Missions where they had lived and the ranchos and the range which their horses were accustomed to, they found it easy to drive off the animals into the mountains, partly to use as saddle-horses, but principally to eat.

In time they became a scourge to the settlements.   The great ranges which belonged with the ranchos not only supported many thousands of cattle, but also many hundreds of horses which were divided into bands, " *manadas.*"   The Indians were the vaqueros or herdsmen who attended to both; herding the cattle, and breaking in the colts.   The Californians had great pleasure in their horses.   On some ranchos there would be several hundred saddle-horses, in bands of eighty or a hundred of different colors; *Alazan* (sorrel) always the favorite color.   Deprived of their regular food, the Indians took to the mountains and began to drive off horses.   Cattle would not drive fast enough to avoid the first pursuit.   In their early condition they had learned to eat wild horse-meat and liked it.   Familiarity with the whites and the success of their predatory excursions made the Horse-thief Indians far more daring and braver than those who remained in fixed villages, whether in the mountains or on the valley streams which carried the name of the different tribes—the Cosumné, Mokelumné, Towalumné, and Auxumné Rivers.   Probably all the streams if their Indian names could have been known, received their names from the small tribes who lived upon them.

The Indians of this country finding their food where they lived were

SCENE OF FREMONT CAMP, 1845.

not nomadic. They were not disposed to range, and seemed unaccustomed to intrude upon the grounds which usage probably made the possession of other tribes. Their huts were easily built and permanent ; the climate was fine, they lived mostly in the open air, and when they died they were not put in the ground but up in the branches of the trees. The climate is such that a dead animal left on the ground simply dries up and only the eye gives knowledge of its presence.

The springs and streams hereabout were waters of the Chauchiles and Mariposas Rivers and the Indians of this village belonged to the Chauchiles tribe.

On some of the higher ridges were fields of a poppy which, fluttering and tremulous on its long thin stalk, suggests the idea of a butterfly settling on a flower, and gives to this flower its name of *Mariposas*—butterflies— and the flower extends its name to the stream.

The encounter I had here with the Indians was a premonitory symptom of the contests I afterward had with the State and Federal governments when the place became my property.

We were only sixteen men. Keeping in the oak belt on the course I was pursuing would bring us farther among these villages, and I would surely have lost the cattle and perhaps some men and horses in attacks from these Indians. In the morning therefore I turned down one of the streams and quickly gained the open country of the lower hills. We had gained but a little distance on this course when an Indian was discovered riding at speed towards the plain, where the upper San Joaquin reaches the valley. Maxwell was ahead and not far from the Indian when he came into sight, and knowing at once that his object was to bring Indians from the river to intercept us, rode for him. The Indian was well mounted but Maxwell better. With Godey and two of the Delawares I followed. It was open ground over rolling hills and we were all in sight of each other, but before we could reach them a duel was taking place between Maxwell and the Indian— both on foot, Maxwell with pistols, the Indian with arrows. They were only ten or twelve paces apart. I saw the Indian fall as we rode up. I would have taken him prisoner and saved his life, but was too late. The Delawares captured his horse.

Riding along the open ground towards the valley after a mile or two we discovered ten Indians ahead going in the same direction. They saw us as well, but took no notice and did not quicken their gait. When we were about overtaking them they quietly turned into a close thicket which covered about eight acres. We gave the thicket a wide berth; for ten Indians in such a place were more dangerous than so many gray bear.

Turning now to the southward we continued on our way, keeping a few men towards the mountain to give early notice of the approach of any Indians. At evening we encamped in a spring hollow leading to the upper San Joaquin where it makes its way among the hills towards the open valley. We were at an elevation of 1000 feet above the sea; in latitude by observation 37° 07' 47''. The day had been mild with a faint sun and cloudy weather; and at sunset there were some light clouds in the sky and a northeasterly wind, and a sunset temperature of 45°; probably rendered lower than usual by the air from the mountains, as the foot-hills have generally a warmer temperature than the lower valley.

During the day elk were numerous along our route, making at one time a broken band several miles in length.   On the 21st the thermometer was at sunrise 33°; the sky slightly clouded, and in the course of the morning clouds gathered heavy in the southwest.   Our route lay in a southeasterly direction, still toward the upper Joaquin, crossing among rolling hills, a large stream, and several sandy beds and affluents to the main river.   On the trees along these streams as well as on the hills I noticed *mosses*.   In the afternoon we reached the upper San Joaquin River, which was here about seventy yards wide and much too deep to be forded; a little way below we succeeded in crossing at a rapid made by a bed of rock below which, for several miles, the stream appeared deep and not fordable.   We followed down it for six or eight miles and encamped on its banks on the verge of the valley plain.

At evening rain began to fall, and with this the spring properly commenced.   In November there had been a little rain, but not sufficient to revive vegetation.

December 22d.   Temperature at sunrise was 39°.   During the night there had been heavy rain, with high wind, and there was a thick fog this morning, but it began to go off at 8 o'clock when the sun broke through.   We crossed an open plain still in a southeasterly direction, reaching in about twenty miles the *Tuláre Lake* River.   This is the Lake Fork; one of the largest and handsomest streams in the valley, being about one hundred yards broad and having perhaps a larger body of fertile lands than any one of the others.   It is called by the Mexicans the *Rio de los Reyes*.   The broad alluvial bottoms were well wooded with several species of oaks.   This is the principal affluent of the Tuláre Lake, a strip of water which receives all the rivers in the upper or southern end of the valley.   In time of high water it discharges into the San Joaquin River, making a continuous water-line through the whole extent of the valley.   The lake itself is surrounded by lowlands and its immediate shores are rankly overgrown with bulrushes.

According to the appointment made when I left my party under Talbot, it was a valley upon the Lake Fork to which the guide Walker was to conduct him. Here I expected to find him. The men, as well as the cattle and horses, needed rest; a strict guard had been necessary, as in the morning Indian sign was always found around our camp. The position was good in the open ground among the oaks, there being no brush for cover to the Indians, and grass and water were abundant. Accordingly we remained here a day and on the 24th entered the mountain, keeping as nearly as possible the valley ground of the river. While in the oak belt the travelling was easy and pleasant, but necessarily slow in the search for our people, especially here in this delightful part of the mountain where they should be found. Several days were spent here. At the elevation of 3500 feet the ridges were covered with oaks and pines intermixed, and the bottom-lands with oaks, cottonwoods, and sycamores. Continuing upward I found the general character of the mountain similar to what it was in the more northern part, but rougher, and the timber perhaps less heavy and more open, but some trees extremely large. I began to be surprised at not finding my party, but continued on, thinking that perhaps in some spread of the river branches I was to find a beautiful mountain valley. Small varieties of evergreen oaks were found at the observed height of 9840 feet above the sea, at which elevation *pinus Lambertiani* and other varieties of pine, fir, and cypress were large and lofty trees. The distinctive oak belt was left at about 5000 feet above the sea.

Indians were still around the camp at night and the necessity of keeping the animals closely guarded prevented them from getting food enough and, joined with the rough and difficult country, weakened them. For this, I usually made the day's journey short. I found the mountain extremely rocky in the upper parts, the streams breaking through cañons, but wooded up to the granite ridges which compose its rocky eminences. We forced our way up among the head springs of the river and finally stood upon the flat ridge of naked granite which made the division of the waters and was 11,000 feet above the sea. The day was sunny and the air warm enough to be not only very agreeable, but with exercise exhilarating, even at that height. Lying immediately below, perhaps 1000 feet, at the foot of a precipitous descent was a small lake, which I judged to be one of the sources of the main San Joaquin. I had grown, by occasional privation, to look upon water as a jewel beyond price, and this was rendered even more beautiful by its rough setting. The great value to us of the first necessaries of life made a reason why we so seldom found gold or silver or other minerals. Ores of iron and copper, and gold and silver, and other minerals we found, but did not look for. A clear cold spring of running water or a good camp, big game, or fossils imbedded in rock, were among the prized objects of our daily life. Owens, after the discovery of the gold in California, reminded me that he had once on the American Fork noticed some little shining grains which he could see from his horse and which afterward we decided was gold, but we were not interested enough at the time to give it attention; and Breckenridge too reminded me that he brought me in his hand some large grains which I carelessly told him were sulphurets of iron. These too were probably gold. As I said, this bed of summit granite was naked. Here and there a pine or two, stunted and twisted, and worried out of shape by the winds, and clamping itself to the rock. But immediately below we encamped in the sheltering pine woods which now were needed, for towards evening the weather threatened change. The sky clouded over and by nightfall was a uniform dull gray, and early in the night the roar of the wind through the pines had at times the sound of a torrent. And the camp was gloomy. We had ridden hard, and toiled hard, and we were all disappointed and perplexed, wondering what had become of our people. During the night the Indians succeeded in killing one of our best mules. He had fed quietly into one of the little ravines, wooded with brush pines, just out of sight of the guard near by, and an Indian had driven an arrow nearly through his body. Apparently he had died without sound or struggle, just as he was about to drink from the little stream.

The next day, December 31st, I made a short camp, the cattle being tender-footed and scarcely able to travel. To descend the mountain we chose a different way from that by which we had come up, but it was rocky and rough everywhere. The old year went out and the new year came in, rough as the country. Towards nightfall the snow began to come down thickly, and by morning all lay under a heavy fall. The chasms through which the rivers roared were dark against the snow, and the fir branches were all weighed down under their load. This was the end of the few remaining cattle. It was impossible to drive them over the treacherous ground. The snow continued falling, changing the appearance of the ground and hiding slippery breaks and little rocky hollows, where horse and man would get bad falls. Left to themselves cattle could easily work their way to the lower grounds of the mountain if not killed by Indians. We had great trouble in getting out from the snow region. The mountain winter had now set in, and we had some misgivings as we rode through the forest, silent now without a sound except where we came within hearing of water roaring among rocks or muffled under snow. There were three ridges to surmount, but we succeeded in crossing them, and by sunset when the storm ceased we made a safe camp between 9000 and 10,000 feet above the sea. The temperature at sunset when the sky had cleared was between eight and nine degrees.

The next day we reached the oak region, where spring weather, rain and sunshine, were found again. At an elevation of 4500 feet the temperature at the night encampment of the 3d of January was 38° at sunset and the same at sunrise; the grass green and growing freshly under the oaks. The snow line at this time reached down to about 6000 feet above the sea. On the 7th of January we encamped again on the Lake Fork in the San Joaquin valley. Our camp was in a grove of oaks at an Indian village, not far from the lake. These people recognized the horse of the Indian who had been killed among the hills the day after our encounter with the Horse-thief village, and which had been captured by the Delawares. It appeared that this Indian had belonged to their village and they showed unfriendly signs. But nothing took place during the day and at night I had a large oak at the camp felled. We were unencumbered and its spreading summit as it fell made a sufficient barricade in event of any sudden *alerte*.

We found the temperature much the same as in December. Fogs, which rose from the lake in the morning, were dense, cold, and penetrating; but after a few hours these gave place to a fine day. The face of the country had already much improved by the rains which had fallen while we were travelling in the mountains. Several humble plants, among them the golden-flowered violet (*viola chrysantha*) and *erodium cicutarium*, the first valley flowers of the spring, and which courted a sunny exposure and warm sandy soil, were already in bloom on the southwestern hill slopes. In the foot-hills of the mountains the bloom of the flowers was earlier. Descending the valley we travelled among multitudinous herds of elk, antelope, and wild horses. Several of the latter which we killed for food were found to be very fat. By the middle of January, when we had reached the lower San Joaquin, the new grass had covered the ground with green among the open timber upon the rich river bottoms, and the spring vegetation had taken a vigorous start.

We had now searched the San Joaquin valley, up to the head-waters of the Tuláre Lake Fork, and failed to find my party. They were too strong to have met with any serious accident and my conclusion was that they had travelled slowly in order to give me time to make my round and procure supplies; the moderate travel serving meanwhile to keep their animals in good order, and from the moment they would have turned the point of the California Mountain the whole valley which they entered was alive with game—antelope and elk and bear and wild horses. Accounting in this way for their failure to meet me I continued on to Sutter's Fort, at which place I arrived on the 15th of the month, and remaining there four days I sailed on Sutter's launch for San Francisco, taking with me eight of my party. From Captain Sutter, who was a Mexican magistrate, I had obtained a passport to Monterey for myself and my men. At Yerba Buena, as it was then called, I spent a few days, which Leidesdorff, our vice-consul, and Captain Hinckley made very agreeable to me. With Captain Hinckley I went to visit the quicksilver mine at New Almaden, going by water to please the captain.   We were becalmed on the bay and made slow progress, failing in the night to find the entrance to the Alviso *embarcadero* and spending in consequence a chilled and dismal night in the open boat tied up to the rushes.   When the light came we found without difficulty the *embarcadero*, and the discomforts of the night were quickly forgotten in a fortifying breakfast.   As may be supposed, the mineral being so rare, this visit to the quicksilver mine was very interesting.   The owner, a Mexican of Mexico, who was also, I think, the discoverer, received us very agreeably and showed us over the mine and gave us all the specimens we were able to carry away from some heaps of the vermilion-colored ore which was being taken out.   At the time of our visit it could have been purchased for $30,000.   While at Yerba Buena I wrote to Mrs. Frémont the following letter, which sums up briefly the incidents of our journey so far, and gives something of the plans I had in my mind for the future:

"YERBA BUENA, January 24, 1846.

"I crossed the Rocky Mountains on the main Arkansas, passing out at its very head-water; explored the southern shore of the Great Salt Lake, and visited one of its islands.   You know that on every extant map, manuscript or printed, the whole of the Great Basin is represented as a sandy plain, barren, without water, and without grass.   Tell your father that, with a volunteer party of fifteen men, I crossed it between the parallels of 38° and 39°.   Instead of a plain, I found it, throughout its whole extent, traversed by parallel ranges of lofty mountains, their summits white with snow (October); while below, the valleys had none.   Instead of a barren country, the mountains were covered with grasses of the best quality, wooded with several varieties of trees, and containing more deer and mountain sheep than we had seen in any previous part of our voyage.   So utterly at variance with every description, from authentic sources, or from rumor or report, it is fair to consider this country as hitherto wholly unexplored, and never before visited by a white man.   I met my party at the rendezvous, a lake southeast of the Pyramid Lake; and again separated, sending them along the eastern side of the Great Sierra, three or four hundred miles in a southerly direction, where they were to cross into the valley of the San Joaquin, near its head.   During all the time that I was not with them, Mr. Joseph Walker was their guide, Mr. Talbot in charge, and Mr. Kern the topographer.   The eleventh day after leaving them I reached Captain Sutter's, crossing the Sierra on the 4th December, before the snow had fallen there.   Now, the Sierra is absolutely impassable, and the place of our passage two years ago is luminous with snow.   By the route I have explored I can ride in thirty-five days from the *Fontaine qui Bouit* River to Captain Sutter's; and, for wagons, the road is decidedly better.

"I shall make a short journey up the eastern branch of the Sacramento, and go from the Tlamath Lake into the Wahlahmath valley, through a pass alluded to in my report; in this way making the road into Oregon far shorter, and a *good* road in place of the present very bad one down the Columbia. When I shall have made this short exploration, I shall have explored from beginning to end *this road to Oregon*.

"I have just returned with my party of sixteen from an exploring journey in the *Sierra Nevada*, from the neighborhood of Sutter's to the heads of the Lake Fork. We got among heavy snows on the mountain summits; they were more rugged than I had elsewhere met them; suffered again as in our first passage; got among the 'Horse-thieves' (Indians who lay waste the California frontier), fought several, and fought our way down into the plain again and back to Sutter's. Tell your father that I have something handsome to tell him of some exploits of Carson and Dick Owens, and others.

"I am now going on business to see some gentlemen on the coast, and will then join my people, and complete our survey in this part of the world as rapidly as possible. The season is now just arriving when vegetation is coming out in all the beauty I have often described to you; and in that part of my labors I shall gratify all my hopes. I find the theory of our Great Basin fully confirmed in having for its southern boundary ranges of lofty mountains. The Sierra, too, is broader where this chain leaves it than in any other part that I have seen. So soon as the proper season comes, and my animals are rested, we turn our faces homeward, and be sure that grass will not grow under our feet.

"All our people are well, and we have had no sickness of any kind among us; so that I hope to be able to bring back with me all that I carried out. Many months of hardships, close trials, and anxieties have tried me severely, and my hair is turning gray before its time. But all this passes, *et le bon temps viendra*."

After finishing my letter I set out towards evening for Monterey with Mr. Leidesdorff, who was kind enough to give me the advantage of his company. His house was one of the best among the few in Yerba Buena—a low bungalow sort of adobe house with a long piazza facing the bay for the sunny mornings, and a cheerful fire within against the fog and chill of the afternoons. His wife, a handsome, girl-like woman, Russian from Sitka, gave the element of home which had been long missing to my experience. He was a cheerful-natured man, and his garden and his wife spoke pleasantly for him.

We had started rather late and on the plain beyond the Mission Dolores in the darkness and the fog we lost our way, but wandering around we were at last rejoiced by hearing the barking of dogs. This soon brought us to the rancho of Don Francisco Sanchez, for which we were looking, and where we were received with the cordial hospitality which in those days assured a good bed and a savory supper to every traveller, and if his horse happened to be tired or hurt by any accident a good one to replace it for the journey.

The next day we rode along the bay shore, the wooded and fertile character of which needs no describing, and stopped for the night with Don Antonio Sunol. This was my first ride down the valley of San José, and I enjoyed even the passing under the oak groves with the branches cut off to a uniform height by the browsing herds of cattle, listening the while to Leidesdorff's account of the fertility of the country's vegetation. His descriptions of this part of the country were especially interesting to me. He was a lover of nature and his garden at San Francisco was, at that time, considered a triumph.

After a half day's riding from the Gomez rancho, across the Salinas plains, we reached Monterey and went directly to the house of our consul, Mr. Larkin. I had come to Monterey with the object of obtaining leave to bring my party into the settlements in order to refit and obtain the supplies that had now become necessary. All the camp equipment, the clothes of the men and their saddles and horse gear, were either used up or badly in want of repair.

The next morning I made my official visits. I found the governor, Don Pio Pico, absent at Los Angeles. With Mr. Larkin I called upon the commanding general, Don José Castro, the prefect, alcalde, and ex-Governor Alvarado. I informed the general and the other officers that I was engaged in surveying the nearest route from the United States to the Pacific Ocean. I informed them farther that the object of the survey was geographical, being under the direction of the Bureau of Topographical Engineers, to which corps I belonged; and that it was made in the interests of science and of commerce, and that the men composing the party were citizens and not soldiers.

The permission asked for was readily granted, and during the two days I stayed I was treated with every courtesy by the general and other officers.

This permission obtained I immediately set about arranging for supplies of various kinds and for sending fresh horses to meet our people; with such supplies of lesser luxuries as I knew would be grateful to them; and by the middle of February we were all reunited in the valley of San José, about thirteen miles south of the village of that name on the main road leading to Monterey, which was about sixty miles distant.

When we separated at the lake which bears his name there was a singular mistake between Walker and myself. The understanding was that we were to meet on the Tuláre Lake Fork.   This is the large tributary to the lake, which had been known to myself and party in the campaign of the preceding year as the Lake River.   Mr. Walker apparently did not know this river, but took it for granted that a much smaller one coming from the end of the range and discharging where there are two small lakes amidst bulrushes at the head of the valley, was the river which was intended for the place of meeting.   These lakes are eighty or ninety miles south of the Tuláre Lake.   At the end of the mountain there were lower passes which were used by trappers and others coming from the basin into the country about Los Angeles, and the rivers there were known to Mr. Walker, while probably he had never seen the Tuláre Lake Fork.

Mr. Talbot, with the detached party, had crossed the California Mountain towards the "Point" and nearly opposite the southern end of the Tuláre Lakes, and remained encamped in a valley or cove, near the summit of the Sierra, at the head of the river, from December 27th to January 17th.   The cove was well wooded with evergreen oaks, some varieties of pine, firs, and cedars, maintaining the usual majestic growth which characterizes the cone-bearing trees of the Sierra.   Until the 12th of January the weather was almost that of summer, when the rains commenced, almost three weeks later than in latitude 37°, where I was.   On the 17th there was a fall of snow, washed off by a cold fall of rain in the afternoon, the high ranges remaining covered a foot deep.   After that, snow and rain alternated with sunshine, snow remaining on the ridges; and winter set in fairly on all the upper half of the mountain.   To this river I gave the name of my topographer, Kern.

Finding that I did not arrive, Mr. Talbot, counseling with Walker, judged it expedient to descend into the valley; and on the morning of the 19th resumed his journey down the San Joaquin to the Cósumne River, where they made an encampment to wait until hearing from me.   Meantime Mr. Walker, in his turn, set out on a search for me which was happily terminated by meeting Carson and Owens, who were looking for him.

The people were all in good health, having been well supplied with game, and the animals were in improving condition.   The route of the party had been an easy one along the base of the Sierra and the pass at the head of the river was low, broad, and open, without any impediment.   To one of the lakes along their route on the east side of the range I gave Owens' name.

During the stay of the party on the Cósumne a grizzly bear showed the value of a sudden onset.   One of these animals ranging the river bottom after acorns had accidentally discovered the camp, which was at breakfast, and charged into it, scattering the men, driving some into trees, and holding possession until some of the men got hold of their guns.   The bear treed even the Delawares. He had four inches thickness of fat on his back and on his belly, and was estimated to weigh a thousand pounds. This shows the fine quality of the range.

The place which I had selected for rest and refitting was a vacant rancho called the *Laguna*, belonging to Mr. Fisher. I remained here until February, in the delightful spring season of a most delightful climate. The time was occupied in purchasing horses, obtaining supplies, and thoroughly refitting the party.

I established the rate of the chronometer and made this encampment a new point of departure. Observations put it in longitude 121° 39′ 08″, latitude 37° 13′ 32″. This point is but a few miles distant from what is now the Lick Observatory.

Many Californians visited the camp, and very friendly relations grew up with us. One day amusements were going on as usual, the Californians showing our men their admirable horsemanship. One of the large vultures which are often seen floating about overhead had been brought down with a broken wing by one of our rifles. This was the point on which we excelled, as the others in perfect horsemanship. The vulture was sitting on the frame of a cart to which he had been tied; he had gotten over his hurt and would have been treated as a pet, but his savage nature would not permit of any approach. By accident a Californian had gotten a fall and the whole camp was shouting and laughing, and Owens, his mouth wide open, was backing towards the cart to rest his arm on the wheel, forgetful of the vulture. The vulture with his long, red neck stretched out was seizing the opportunity—we all saw it and Owens saw our amusement, but not quite in time to escape the grip of the vulture.

It was quite a picture. The vulture lying in wait, and Owens' unconsciousness, and the hearty laugh which cheered the bird's exploit. Owens got off with a sharp pinch and a torn sleeve.

The fertile valley of San José is a narrow plain of rich soil lying between equally fertile ranges from two thousand to three thousand feet high, covered on one side with wild oats, and wooded on the range toward the sea. The valley is openly wooded with groves of oak free from underbrush, and after the spring rains covered with grass. On the west it is protected from the chilling influence of the northwest winds by the *Cuesta de los Gatos*— Wild-Cat Ridge—which separates it from the coast.

Resuming the work of the expedition, on the 22d March we encamped on the Wild-Cat Ridge on the road to Santa Cruz, and again on the 23d near the summit. The varied character of the woods and shrubbery on this mountain, which lay between my camp and the Santa Cruz shore, was very interesting to me, and I wished to spend some days there, as now the spring season was renewing vegetation, and the accounts of the great trees in the forest on the west slope of the mountain had roused my curiosity. Always, too, I had before my mind the home I wished to make in this country, and first one place and then another charmed me. But none seemed perfect where the sea was wanting, and so far I had not stood by the open waves of the Pacific. The soft climate of the San José valley was very enticing, and in the interior I had seen lovely spots in the midst of the great pines where the mountains looked down, but the sea was lacking. The piny fragrance was grateful, but it was not the invigorating salt breeze which brings with it renewed strength. This I wanted for my mother. For me, the shore of "the sounding sea" was a pleasure of which I never wearied, and I knew that along this coast the sea broke deep against bold rocks or shining sands. All this I had reason to believe I would find somewhere on the Santa Cruz shore. We remained on the upper portion of the mountain several days. The place of our encampment was two thousand feet above the sea, and was covered with a luxuriant growth of grass a foot high in many places.

At sunrise the temperature was 40°; at noon, 60°; at four in the afternoon, 65°, and 63° at sunset, with very pleasant weather. The mountains were wooded with many varieties of trees, and in some parts with heavy forests. These forests are characterized by a cypress (*taxodium*) of extraordinary dimensions, which I have already mentioned among the trees in the Sierra Nevada as distinguished among the forest trees of America by its superior size and height. Among many we measured in this part of the mountain a diameter of nine or ten feet was frequent, sometimes eleven; but going beyond eleven only in a single tree, which reached fourteen feet in diameter. Above two hundred feet was a frequent height. In this locality the bark was very deeply furrowed and unusually thick, being fully sixteen inches on some of the trees. It was now in bloom, flowering near the summit, and the flowers consequently difficult to procure.

This is the staple timber-tree of the country, being cut into both boards and shingles, and is the principal timber sawed at the mills. It is soft and easily worked, wearing away too quickly to be used for floors; but it seems to have all the durability which anciently gave the cypress so much celebrity. Posts which had been exposed to the weather three-quarters of a century, since the foundation of the Missions, showed no marks of decay in the wood and are now converted into beams and posts for private dwellings. In California this tree is called the *Palo Colorado*, Redwood.

Among the oaks in this mountain is a handsome, lofty evergreen tree, specifically different from those of the lower grounds, and in its general appearance much resembling hickory. The bark is smooth, of a white color, and the wood hard and close-grained. It seems to prefer the north hill-sides, where some were nearly four feet in diameter and a hundred feet high.

Another remarkable tree of these woods is called in the language of the country *Madrona*. It is a beautiful evergreen with large, thick, and glossy digitated leaves; the trunk and branches reddish colored and having a smooth and singularly naked appearance, as if the bark had been stripped off. In its green state the wood is brittle, very heavy, hard, and close-grained; it is said to assume a red color when dry, sometimes variegated, and susceptible of a high polish. This tree was found by us only in the mountains. Some measured nearly four feet in diameter and were about sixty feet high.

A few scattered flowers were now showing throughout the forests, and on the open ridges shrubs were flowering; but the bloom was not yet general.

On the 25th of February we descended to the coast near the north-western point of Monterey Bay, losing our fine weather, which in the evening changed to a cold southeasterly storm that continued with heavy and constant rains for several days.

The rain-storm closed with February, and the weather becoming fine, on the 1st of March we resumed our progress along the coast. Over the face of the country between Santa Cruz and Monterey, and around the plains of San Juan, the grass, which had been eaten down by the large herds of cattle, was now everywhere springing up and flowers began to show their bloom. In the valleys of the mountains bordering the Salinas plains wild oats were three feet high and well headed. The Salinas River runs through these plains, which are some fifty miles in length.

Pursuing our course to the southward I encamped on the afternoon of March 3d at the Hartnell rancho, which is on a small creek-bed well out on the plain. We were now passing Monterey, which was about twenty-five miles distant.

The Salinas valley lay outside of the more occupied parts of the country; and I was on my way to a pass, opening into the San Joaquin valley, at the head of a western branch of the Salinas River.

CHAPTER XIII.

In the afternoon the quiet of the camp was disturbed by the sudden appearance of a cavalry officer with two men. The officer proved to be Lieutenant Chavez, with a communication from the commanding general. He seemed disposed to be somewhat rude and abrupt as I have remarked that subalterns usually are when they represent unfriendly masters. This one brought to me peremptory letters from the general and prefect, ordering me forthwith out of the department, and threatening force in the event that I should not instantly comply with the order.

Surprised both at the message and the terms in which it was worded, I expressed to the envoy my astonishment at General Castro's breach of good faith, and the rudeness with which he committed it; both of which, I remarked to him, were unworthy of an officer in his position. And I desired him to say in reply to General Castro that I peremptorily refused compliance to an order insulting to my government and myself.

And with this message the envoy went off to his general.

Like myself my men were roused by the offence of the message, and were more than ready to support me in any course I saw fit to adopt.

Early in the morning I moved camp a few miles to the foot of the ridge, which separates the Salinas from the San Joaquin, at the house of Don Joaquin Gomez. A stream here issues from the mountain which is called the Gavilan Peak. The road from Monterey passes by this place, entering the neighboring San Juan valley by way of a short pass called the Gomez Pass.

From the Gomez rancho there is a wood-road leading up to the top of the ridge; following this in the morning I moved up the mountain and encamped on a small wooded flat at the summit of the Sierra. This was a convenient position. It afforded wood, water, and grass; and commanded a view of the surrounding country, including the valley of San Juan and the Salinas plain. In case of exigency it opened a retreat to the San Joaquin.

Arriving at the summit, I proceeded immediately to build a rough but strong fort of solid logs, for which we found good trees abundant on the ridge. While this was being built a tall sapling was prepared, and on it, when all was ready, the American flag was raised amidst the cheers of the men. The raising of this flag proved to be a premonitory symptom.

Meantime I opened communication with a rancho in the valley and a steer was brought up to me by two Californian vaqueros. The wild steer never could have been driven up by the vaqueros, but they had made him fast by a riata to a work-ox which tugged it up to the camp; they butchered it immediately, and the smell and sight of the blood so excited the "tame" ox, that he became wild and commenced hostilities by charging into and scattering the camp.

I remained in position, our flag flying, for three days; during which I received information from Mr. Larkin and from Californians of what was going on below. From the fort by aid of the glass we could see below, at the Mission of San Juan, Castro's troops gathering, and by the vaqueros we were informed that Indians (*Mansos*) were being brought into their camp and kept excited by drink.

Late in the afternoon of the second day we discovered a body of cavalry coming up the wood-road which led from the Monterey road to our camp. With about forty men I went quickly down the wood-road to where a thicket along the creek made a good ambush, and waited for them. They came up to within a few hundred yards, when they halted; but after some consultation they turned back. Had they come on they would have had to pass within a few paces of us.

Late in the afternoon of the third day the pole bearing our flag fell to the ground. Thinking I had remained as long as the occasion required, I took advantage of the accident to say to the men that this was an indication for us to move camp, and accordingly I gave the order to prepare to move. The protecting favor which the usage of all civilized governments and peoples accords to scientific expeditions imposed on me, even here, a corresponding obligation; and I now felt myself bound to go on my way, having given General Castro sufficient time to execute his threat. Besides I kept always in mind the object of the Government to obtain possession of California and would not let a proceeding which was mostly personal put obstacles in the way. In a letter written shortly afterwards to Mrs. Fremont I make the allusion which she would fully comprehend:

"SACRAMENTO RIVER (latitude 40°), April 1, 1846.

". . . The Spaniards were somewhat rude and inhospitable below, and ordered us out of the country, after having given me permission to winter there. My sense of duty did not permit me to fight them, but we retired slowly and growlingly before a force of three or four hundred men, and three pieces of artillery. Without a shadow of a cause, the governor suddenly raised the whole country against us, issuing a false and scandalous proclamation. Of course I did not dare to compromise the United States, against which appearances would have been strong; but, although it was in my power to increase my party by many Americans, I refrained from committing a solitary act of hostility or impropriety."

On the morning of the 11th, after I had left my camp on the hill, Mr. John Gilroy, an Englishman resident in California, came to my camp with a message from General Castro, offering to make an arrangement with me. Mr. Gilroy found our fires burning. I was afterwards informed that the proposition was that I should unite my force with his and jointly march against the Governor Don Pio Pico. This agreed so well with the Mexican revolutionary habit, and subsequent confirmatory facts, that I fully believe it.

In his letters Mr. Larkin says that the Californian who had brought them to my camp reported to him that 2000 of his countrymen would not be sufficient to compel me to leave the country, although my party was small. The letters of Mr. Larkin to the Secretary of State, Mr. Parrott the American Consul at Mazatlan, and myself, give a clear view of the extraordinary circumstances through which I had just passed, and accordingly I insert them here.

The change in the action of the Californian authorities towards me seemed inexplicable until when afterwards I learned that within three weeks after granting me permission to refresh my party in California, General Castro had received by the *Hannah* from the home government at Mexico positive orders to drive me from the territory. Later I learned from Washington of this action taken against me by the Mexican Government.

The following letters cover fully the actual situation:

CONSULATE OF THE UNITED STATES,
MONTEREY, CALIFORNIA, March 4, 1846.

SIR: The undersigned has the honor to inform the Honorable Secretary that Captain J. C. Frémont arrived within this department in January last, with his party of fifty men, and was at the home of the undersigned a few days during the last month, for the purpose of getting funds for refitting and clothing his party, which he received as far as could be procured. He is now in this vicinity surveying, and will be again at this consular house during this month. He then proceeds for the Oregon, returns here in May, and expects to be in Washington about September. To this gentleman is due, from the Government, unqualified praise for the patience, industry, and indefatigable perseverance in attaining the object he is engaged in.

Captain Frémont passed three degrees south of Fort Hall, having taken a route supposed to be a desert, which made his distance to California eight or nine hundred miles less.   He considers the distance from Independence to Monterey about one thousand nine hundred miles.   He describes the new route he followed far preferable, not only on account of the less distance, but it is less mountainous, with good pasturage, and well watered.   The second day of his arrival in Monterey, he visited the commandante general, prefecto, and alcalde, and by verbal request of the general, informed him officially of his object in visiting California.   The undersigned forwards, with this, the two annexed letters respecting Captain Frémont's arrival.

I am, sir, with the highest respect and consideration, your most obedient servant,   (Signed)   THOMAS O. LARKIN.

To the Hon. Secretary of State, City of Washington.

CONSULATE OF THE UNITED STATES,
MONTEREY, March 9, 1846.

SIR : Enclosed you have a copy of my answer to the general and pre-fecto of this place, one to Captain Frémont, and the second letter from the prefect.   Captain Frémont is eight or nine leagues from this place encamped, intending to move as soon as the state of his horses will permit.   There will be two to three hundred people collected together to-morrow, with the intention of attacking the camp.   Captain Frémont has about fifty men— all men of confidence, and remarkably well armed.   Neither himself nor men have any fears respecting the result of the present state of affairs; yet, be the result for or against him, it may prove of a disadvantage to the resident Americans in California.   I have at some (risk) despatched out two couriers to the camp, with duplicate letters, and this letter I send to Santa Barbara, in expectation of finding a vessel bound to Mazatlan.   Having had over one-half of my hospital expenses of 1844 cut off, and know not why, and even my bill for a flag, I do not feel disposed to hazard much for government, though the life of Captain Frémont and party may need it.   I hardly know how to act.   I have only received one letter (of June) from the department for the year 1845.   In the month of February, Captain Frémont, in my company, visited the general, prefecto, and alcalde of this place, and informed them of his business; and there was no objection made. Within twenty days the general says he had received direct and specific orders from Mexico not to allow Captain Frémont to enter California; which, *perhaps*, accounts for the change of feelings with the people.

I am, sir, with the highest respect and consideration, your obedient servant,   (Signed)   THOMAS O. LARKIN.

To the Hon. Secretary of State, City of Washington.

It will be noticed that Mr. Larkin says in this letter to the Secretary that he had " only received one letter (of June) from the department for the year 1845." From this it does not appear that the State Department was watchful. The Navy Department was.

NOTE IN PENCIL FROM CAPTAIN FRÉMONT TO THE CONSUL LARKIN FROM HIS ENTRENCHED CAMP ON THE PIC DEL GABELANO, THIRTY MILES FROM MONTEREY, MARCH 9, 1846.

MY DEAR SIR : I this moment received your letters, and, without waiting to read them, acknowledge the receipt which the courier requires immediately. I am making myself as strong as possible, in the intention that if we are unjustly attacked we will fight to extremity and refuse quarter, trusting to our country to avenge us. No one has reached our camp, and from the heights we are able to see with the glass troops mustering at San Juan and preparing cannon.

I thank you for your kindness and good wishes, and would write more at length as to my intentions did I not fear that my letter would be intercepted. We have in nowise done wrong to the people or the authorities of the country, and if we are hemmed in and assaulted here we will die every man of us under the flag of our country.

Very truly yours,

J. C. FRÉMONT.

P.S.—I am encamped on the top of the Sierra at the head-waters of a stream which strikes the road to Monterey at the house of Don Joaquin Gomez. J. C. F.

Thomas O. Larkin, Esq., Consul for the United States, Monterey.

LETTER FROM CONSUL O. LARKIN TO THE U. S. CONSUL AT MAZATLAN, ASKING NAVAL ASSISTANCE FOR CAPTAIN FRÉMONT.

CONSULATE OF THE UNITED STATES,
MONTEREY, CALIFORNIA, March 9, 1846.

SIR : Enclosed with this, you will receive several copies of correspondence in this town, for the present week ; also an official letter for the captain of any of our ships of war you may have in your port on your receiving this letter. It is impossible to say whether Señor Castro, the prefecto, and the general will attack Captain Frémont ; we expect such will be the case. I am just informed by Señor Arcé, the general's secretary, who has just come in from the general's camp (St. John's), that the whole country will be raised to force Captain Frémont, if they require so many. Señor Arcé further says, the camp of the Americans is near Mr. Hartnell's rancho, on a high hill, with his flag flying ; of the latter I am not certain.   As you are acquainted with this country, and its people, you will advise with our naval captains on the subject of sailing immediately for this port.   If the vessel is not actually obliged to go elsewhere, it is my earnest desire she sails for Monterey on the receipt of this, although everything may end peaceably amongst us.

Believe me to be, yours, sincerely,

(Signed)   THOMAS O. LARKIN.

To John Parrott, Esq., United States Consul, Mazatlan.

[*Copy.*]

CONSULATE OF THE UNITED STATES,

MONTEREY, CALIFORNIA, March 9, 1846.

SIR : Captain J. C. Freemont with a party of fifty men has been within the limits of California about two months, within a few days encamped about eight leagues from this Town, resting his men & animals, he has two letters from the General and Prefecto, wherein he is ordered to leave this Country, or they will take immediate measures to compel him, they sent me copies of the same, which I have sent in English to Captain Freemont.   I have not heard from the camp since, this morning I wrote to Captain Free-mont in duplicate, one by a Native, the other by a Foreigner, by to-morrow there will be collected togather nearly three hundred men, with the intention to drive out the strangers, and if required, there will be by the next week, a much larger body collected ; should this force be used against Captain Freemont, much blood will be shed, his party though of only fifty in number, have from three to six guns, rifles, and pistols each,—and very determined, both Commander & men, having every confidence in each other.   It was the intention of Captain Freemont, to leave this week, if his animals were in good condition, perhaps he may not now be willing, as the people wish to force him ; he was at my house alone in February, and in company with me, visited the General, Prefecto & Alcalde, informed them of his orders to survey the nearest route to the Pacific, and had come into California to purchase provisions, clothes & other necessaries, including horses ; no objection was made at the time, since then, the General states, that he has received by the " Hannah," positive orders from Mexico, to drive Captain Freemont from the country.   I shall send this letter open to Consul Parrott of Mazatlan, with copies of this weeks correspondence.   If there is a fight between these people & Captain Freemont, be the result for or against him ; the American residents are under some apprehensions of their safety hereafter.   I would therefore request you, if in your power, to despatch a Sloop of War, to this Port, from Mazatlan, on the receipt of this.

I understand there were in December, five of our Ships of War then in that Port, should this be the case, I hope it will not be inconvenient to comply with this request. I have looked for the Portsmouth over two months; Captain Montgomery informed me he was to return.

I remain, Sirs', your respectfull servant,

(Signed)   THOMAS O. LARKIN.

To the Commander of any American Ship of War,
    in San Blas, or Mazatlan.
Monterey, May 29, 1846.

The above is a copy of the original—drawn off at the request of Captain Montgomery—Captain Freemont was not attacked—the Californians did not come within three leagues of his camp—he is now on his way to Origon.

(Signed)   THOMAS O. LARKIN.

COPY SENT CAPTAIN FRÉMONT BY CONSUL LARKIN.

CONSULSHIP OF THE UNITED STATES,
MONTEREY, March 10, 1846.

MY DEAR SIR : I am ignorant if it would meet with the approbation of Captain Frémont, that I should permit, that of the note which he wrote with so much precipitation, the translation should be made which you so-licit. But since it pleases you to allow that my courier should pass to the encampment of said officer, and trusting that the contents of the said note will contribute to calm the minds, and preserve harmony, I consent that the translation which you wish may be made.

Perhaps the authorities have conceived suspicions in relation to my person, considering the difficulty of the circumstance, being Consul of the United States, but I cannot remedy it. Nevertheless, you may know that verbally I have offered my services, always when I have judged them in any manner useful, the same as now I am lending them by writing. Captain Frémont has his particular instructions, which it is not one of the attributes of this consulship to alter, nevertheless I will do as much as may be reconcilable with my functions to avoid any conflict whatever.

It only remains for me to ask you respectfully, that when you write to-day to the General, that you make known to him on my part, that I take the liberty to propose to him that before proceeding to extremities, he will please to address a communication to Captain Frémont, in which he shall ask of him an hour's interview. I am in the firm belief that there will be a copious effusion of blood, if the officer in question is attacked, and there would result from a step of such a nature, not only, that many lives would be lost on both sides, but it would be the origin of great expenses, considerable damages, and perhaps a greater flow of blood in the future, between the citizens of our respective nations. Finally, intimately convinced I am, that forcible measures will not produce a single good, but evils of great magnitude now and in the time to come.

I have powerful motives for believing that Captain Frémont yet remains where he is, with the sole end of affording his horses some rest (since he has already bought his provisions), and immediately afterwards, he will go out of the Department of California. But he cannot verify this, inasmuch as he sees himself surrounded by people in whom he observes decided intentions of hostility.

I beg you to send a copy of this note to the Commandant General D. José Castro, and I have the honor to subscribe myself with the greatest respect,

(Signed)   THOMAS O. LARKIN.

To Don Manuel Diaz, Alcalde of Monterey.

CAPTAIN FREMONT : I direct this with the correspondence of the Alcalde to the General, I know not, if it will arrive or not in your possession. By the Blacksmith Joseph who formerly belonged to that Company under your command, I remit the original of the letter that I received.

LETTER FROM THE CONSUL, THOMAS O. LARKIN, TO CAPTAIN FRÉMONT.

CONSULATE OF THE UNITED STATES,
MONTEREY, CALIFORNIA, March 10, 1846.

SIR : Your letter of yesterday I received last night at eight o'clock ; I thank you for the same ; it took from me a weight of uneasiness concerning your situation. The alcalde of Monterey has requested of me a copy in Spanish of your letter. Not knowing what you might approve of in the case, I had some objection; on second thoughts I considered that the alcalde, having given the courier a passport (without which he would not go) for carrying of the letters both ways, were made public, and people might put a wrong construction on our correspondence, I gave it to him with the following additions. I also considered the letter contained nothing of importance to keep secret, and now annex my letter of this morning to the alcalde. As you may not have a copy of your letter, I send one. My native courier said he was well treated by you—*that two thousand men could not drive you.* In all cases of couriers, order your men to have no words or hints with them, as it is magnified. This one said a man pointed to a tree and said, "There's your life;" he expected to be led to you blind-folded; says you have sixty-two men, well armed, etc., etc., etc.

You will, without thought of expense or trouble, call on me, or send to me, in every case of need, not only as your consul, but as your friend and countryman.   I am yours, truly,
        (Signed)   THOMAS O. LARKIN.

To Captain J. C. Frémont, United States Army.

EXTRACTS FROM LETTERS OF CONSUL LARKIN TO THE SECRETARY
OF STATE.

CONSULATE OF THE U. S. OF AMERICA,
MONTEREY, March 27, 1846.

SIR: Captain J. C. Frémont, of the United States Army, arrived at this United States consular house in Monterey, on the 27th of January, 1846. Being very anxious to join his party of fifty men at the second place of rendezvous, without the settlement, they having missed the first place by mistake, he remained but two days; in which time, with myself, he visited the commandant general, prefecto, alcalde, and Colonel Alvarado, informing them that he was surveying the nearest route from the United States to the Pacific Ocean. This information, and that his men were not United States soldiers, was also, by myself, officially given to the prefecto. Having obtained funds and supplies from myself, he returned to his camp; it being well known in Monterey that he was to return, when he collected his men. Some fifteen or twenty days after this, Captain Frémont, with his party, encamped at a vacant rancho belonging to Captain Fisher (about ninety miles from here), to recruit his men and animals. From there he proceeded towards Santa Cruz, making short journeys. On the 3d of March he encamped on the rancho of Mr. E. P. Hartnell, where he received letters from the general and prefecto, ordering him out of the country, and to obey the order without any pretext whatever, or immediate measures would be taken to compel him to do so. This, not corresponding with assurances received at Monterey, it was not answered, and he gave orders to hoist the United States flag the next morning, as the only protection his men were to look to. From the 7th to the 10th of March, they fortified their camp with a breastwork of logs. Encamped on a high hill, which commanded a view of the surrounding country, they could see (with the use of spy-glasses) the general and his troops, numbering about two hundred men, at their camp, in the Mission of St. John's, preparing their cannon. On the 9th inst., I sent duplicate letters; one by an American, who lost his papers, and the other by a Californian, to Captain Frémont, informing him of the movements of the Californians. The California courier returned to the consulate in about nine or ten hours, bringing a letter from Captain Frémont having travelled in that time sixty miles. He reported being well treated by Captain Frémont and his men ; *and that two thousand of his countrymen would not be sufficient to compel him to leave the country, although his party was so small.* At the earnest request of the alcalde for a translation of Captain Frémont's letter, it was given, and immediately despatched to the general at St. John's ; and one also to the governor of the Puebla of Los Angeles. The general informed the alcalde on the night of the 10th instant, that Captain Frémont had left his encampment, and that he (the general) would pursue and attack him the first opportunity, and chastise him for hoisting a foreign flag in California. In the postscript of the same letter, the general stated that Captain Frémont had crossed a small river, and was then about three miles distant from them; but the general made no preparation to follow him. On the morning of the 11th, General Castro sent John Gilroy, an Englishman, long resident in this country, to make offers of arrangement to Captain Frémont. On his arrival at the camp-ground, he found Captain Frémont had left that morning with his party; the camp-fires were still burning. He found in the camp the staff used for the flag, tent-poles (cut on the spot), some old clothes, and two old and useless pack-saddles which the Californians have magnified into munitions of war. General Castro informed his party that he had received various messages from the camp of Captain Frémont, threatening to exterminate the Californians, etc. (but will hardly name his messengers, nor did they put any confidence in it themselves). From the 11th to the 13th, the natives had returned to their respective homes, to resume their customary occupation. A few people that were ordered to march from San Francisco to join the general at his camp, returned to their homes. On the 12th, a proclamation was put up by the general in the billiard-room (not the usual place), informing the inhabitants that a band of highwaymen ("*bandoleros*") under Captain Frémont, of the United States Army, had come within the towns of this department; and that he, with two hundred patriots, had driven them out, and sent them into the back country. Some of the officers of the two hundred patriots (and more were expected to join them) arrived in Monterey, and reported that the cowards had run, and that they had driven them to the Sacramento River; some added that they drove them into the bullrushes, on the plains of the Sacramento; and that, in their haste, they had left some of their best horses behind. The horses proved to be those belonging to the Californians themselves, and had strayed into Captain Frémont's band (being an every-day occurrence in California), and on raising camp, they were turned out and left behind. Instead of the Americans being driven out of the country, they travelled less distance, for three or four days, than the natives did in returning to Monterey; moving from four to six miles per day, in order to recruit.

CONSULATE OF THE U. S. OF AMERICA,
MONTEREY, April 2, 1846.

SIR: In giving my first information to the department respecting Captain Frémont's arrival in California, I did not anticipate such an extensive correspondence as it has now reached. Captain Frémont was well received in this place, and to the last day we heard of him, by the natives individually, who sold him provisions, and liked his presence. During his encampment, thirty or forty miles from here, despatches were received by the commandant, General José Castro (a native of Monterey), from Mexico, ordering him to drive Captain Frémont out of this department; which order, with one hundred and seventy or two hundred men present, and over one hundred more daily expected, he pretended to execute. Captain Frémont left his camp a few hours after he received the undersigned's letter of the 9th of March (not from fright of General Castro), as he had been preparing the week before to travel. It is supposed he has gone to Santa Barbara, where an American was sent by the undersigned in February, with funds and provisions for his use. From there he proceeds on his journey, according to his instructions from his department in Washington. Although from the correspondence it may appear that in the centre of a strange country, among a whole people with real or apparent hostile intentions towards him, that Captain Frémont was in much danger, it can be believed that he was only annoyed. Whether he will visit Monterey after this unexpected affair or not, is uncertain.

The undersigned has not supposed, during the whole affair, that General Castro wished to go after Captain Frémont, and was very confident that with all California he would not have attacked him, even had he been sure of destroying the whole party, as five times their number could have taken their place before the expected battle. Captain Frémont received verbal applications from English and Americans to join his party, and could have mustered as many men as the natives. He was careful not to do so. Although he discharged five or six of his men, he took no others in their place. On the return of General Castro, he published a flaming proclamation to the citizens, informing them that a band of *bandoleros* (highwaymen or freebooters), under Captain Frémont of the United States Army, had come into this district; but with the company of two hundred patriots he had driven them away, and exhorted his companions and countrymen to be always ready to repel others of the same class. This proclamation was missing, from the place it was put up, on the third day.

From the foregoing series of letters it appears that under date of March 9th Mr. Larkin addressed a letter to the commander of any American ship of war in San Blas or Mazatlan; setting out the existing circumstances at that date, and asking that a sloop of war be despatched to Monterey from Mazatlan on the receipt of his letter, which was sent open to Mr. Parrott, our Consul at Mazatlan.

In it he mentions my arrival in California, and my visit with himself to the commanding general and other authorities at Monterey with the object of obtaining permission to recruit my party and purchase supplies in the settlements—that the permission applied for was granted, but that afterward General Castro had received from Mexico, by the "Hannah," positive orders to drive Captain Frémont from the country—that at the time of his writing I was encamped about eight leagues from Monterey, resting my animals—that three hundred men would be ready on the day following to drive me out of the department, and should this intention be carried out there would be much bloodshed, as my party consisted of well-armed and determined men, having every confidence in themselves and in their commander. And further, that I had intended to leave during the week, but might not now be willing, as the people wish to force me, and that if there should be a fight between the Californians and myself, the American residents were under apprehensions for their safety afterward.

Subsequently to these proceedings I learned through the Prussian Minister at Washington, Baron Gerolt, of this intended hostile action against me by the Mexican Government.

Descending the southeastern side of the ridge we halted for the night on a stream about three miles from the camp of General Castro, a few miles from our fort. The next day we resumed our route, and emerging into the valley of the San Joaquin on the 11th we found almost a summer temperature and the country clothed in the floral beauty of spring. Travelling by short stages we reached the Towalumne River on the evening of the 14th. By observation, in latitude 37° 25' 53", and longitude 120° 35' 55".

On the 21st we entered the Sacramento valley, and on the 22d encamped at a favorite spot opposite the house of Mr. Grimes. As already mentioned, his house was not far from Sutter's Fort. We remained several days here on the American River, to recruit our animals on the abundant range between the Sacramento and the hills.

On the 24th we broke up camp with the intention of making an examination of the lower Sacramento valley, of which I had seen but little above Sutter's Fort. I left the American River ten miles above its mouth; travelling a little east of north in the direction of the Bear River settlements. The road led among oak timber, over ground slightly undulating, covered with grass intermingled with flowers.

At sunrise on the 25th the temperature was a few degrees above the freezing point with an easterly wind and a clear sky.

In about thirty miles' travel to the north, we reached the Keyser rancho, on Bear River; an affluent to *Feather* River, the largest tributary of the Sacramento. The route lay over an undulating country—more so as our course brought us nearer the mountains—wooded with oaks and shrubbery in blossom, with small prairies intervening. Many plants were in flower, and among them the California poppy, unusually magnificent. It is the characteristic bloom of *California* at this season, and the Bear River bottoms, near the hills, were covered with it. The blue fields of the nemophyla and this golden poppy represent fairly the skies and gold of California.

I was riding quietly along with Godey through the oak groves, the party being several miles off nigher to the hills, when we discovered two Indian women busily occupied among the trees on the top of a hill, gathering plants or clover-grass into their conical baskets. Taking advantage of the trees we had nearly reached the top of the hill, thinking to surprise these quick-eyed beings. Reaching the top we found nothing there except the baskets —apparently suddenly dropped and the grass spilled out. There were several bushes of a long-stemmed, grass-like shrub, and searching around to see what had become of them, we discovered two pairs of naked feet sticking out just above the top of the bushes.

At the shout we raised two girls to whom the feet belonged rolled out of the bushes into which they had only time to dive as we neared the top of the hill, thinking perhaps that we had not seen them. They were but little alarmed and joined in the laugh we had at their ostrich-like idea of hiding. It appeared that they belonged to a village not far away towards the hills. Ranging around in that beautiful climate, gathering where they had not the trouble to sow, these people had at that time their life of thorough enjoyment. The oaks and pines and grasses gave them abundant vegetable food, and game was not shy.

We crossed several small streams, and found the ground miry from the recent rains. The temperature at four in the afternoon was 70°, and at sunset 58°, with an easterly wind, and the night bright and clear.

The morning of the 26th was clear, and warmer than usual ; the wind southeasterly, and the temperature 40°. We travelled across the valley plain, and in about sixteen miles reached Feather River at twenty miles from its junction with the Sacramento, near the mouth of the *Yuba*, so called from a village of Indians who live on it. The river has high banks —twenty or thirty feet—and was here one hundred and fifty yards wide, a deep, navigable stream. The Indians aided us across the river with canoes and small rafts. Extending along the bank in front of the village was a range of wicker cribs, about twelve feet high, partly filled with what is there the Indians' staff of life—acorns. A collection of huts, shaped like bee-hives, with naked Indians sunning themselves on the tops, and these acorn cribs, are the prominent objects in an Indian village.

There is a fine farm, or rancho, on the Yuba, stocked with about three thousand head of cattle, and cultivated principally in wheat, with some other grains and vegetables, which are caried by means of the river to a market at San Francisco. Mr. Cordua, a native of Germany, who is proprietor of the place, informed me that his average harvest of wheat was twenty-five bushels to the acre, which he supposed would be about the product of the wheat lands in the Sacramento valley. The labor on this and other farms in the valley is performed by Indians.

The temperature here was 74° at two in the afternoon, 71° at four, and 69° at sunset, with a northeasterly wind and a clear sky.

At sunrise of the 27th the temperature was 42°, clear, with a northeasterly wind. We travelled northwardly, up the right bank of the river, which was wooded with large white and evergreen oaks, interspersed with thickets of shrubbery in full bloom. This was a pleasant journey of twenty-seven miles, and we encamped at the bend of the river, where it turns from the course across the valley to run southerly to its junction with the Sacramento. The thermometer at sunset was 67°, sky partially clouded, with southerly wind.

The thermometer at sunrise on the 28th was at 45° 5′, with a northeasterly wind. The road was over an open plain, with a few small sloughs or creeks that do not reach the river. After travelling about fifteen miles, we encamped on *Butte* Creek, a beautiful stream of clear water about fifty yards wide, with a bold current running all the year. It has large, fertile bottoms, wooded with open groves, and having a luxuriant growth of pea vine among the grass. The oaks here were getting into general bloom. Fine ranchos have been selected on both sides of the stream, and stocked with cattle, some of which were now very fat. A rancho here is owned by Neal, who formerly belonged to my exploring party. It may be remembered that in my last expedition I had acceded to his request to be left at Sutter's, where he was offered high wages, with a certain prospect of betterment, where good mechanics were in great request. He was a skilful blacksmith, and had been and was very useful to me, as our horses' feet were one of the first cares. But his uniform good conduct rendered him worthy of any favor I could grant, and he was accordingly left at Sutter's when we resumed our march homeward. In the brief time which had elapsed he had succeeded in becoming a prospering stockman, with a good rancho. There is a *rancheria* (Indian village) near by, and some of the Indians gladly ran races for the head and offals of a fat cow which had been presented to us. They were *entirely* naked. The thermometer at two in the afternoon was at 70°, two hours later at 74°, and 65° at sunset; the wind east, and the sky clear only in the west.

The temperature at sunrise the next day was 50°, with cumuli in the south and west, which left a clear sky at nine, with a northwest wind, and temperature of 64°.   We travelled twenty miles, and encamped on Pine Creek, another fine stream, with bottoms of fertile land, wooded with groves of large and handsome oaks, some attaining to six feet in diameter, and forty to seventy feet in height.   At four in the afternoon the thermometer showed 74° and 64° at sunset; and the sky clear, except in the horizon.

MARCH 30.—The sun rose in masses of clouds over the eastern mountains.   A pleasant morning, with a sunrise temperature of 46° 5′, and some *mosquitoes*—never seen, it is said, in the coast country; but at seasons of high water abundant and venomous in the bottoms of the Joaquin and Sacramento.   On the tributaries nearer the mountains but few are seen, and those go with the sun.   Continuing up the valley, we crossed in a short distance a large wooded creek, having now about thirty-five feet breadth of water.   Our road was over an upland prairie of the Sacramento, having a yellowish, gravelly soil, generally two or three miles from the river, and twelve or fifteen from the foot of the eastern mountains.   On the west it was twenty-five or thirty miles to the foot of the mountains, which here make a bed of high and broken ranges.   In the afternoon, about half a mile above its mouth, we encamped on Deer Creek, another of these beautiful tributaries to the Sacramento.   It has the usual broad and fertile bottom-lands common to these streams, wooded with groves of oak and a large sycamore (*platanus occidentalis*), distinguished by bearing its balls in strings of three to five, and peculiar to California.   Mr. Lassen, a native of Germany, has established a rancho here, which he has stocked, and is gradually bringing into cultivation.   Wheat, as generally throughout the north country, gives large returns ; cotton, planted in the way of experiment, was not injured by frost, and succeeded well ; and he has lately planted a vineyard, for which the Sacramento valley is considered to be singularly well adapted.   The seasons are not yet sufficiently understood, and too little has been done in agriculture, to afford certain knowledge of the capacities of the country.   This farm is in the 40th degree of latitude ; our position on the river being in 39° 57′ 00′′, and longitude 121° 56′ 44′′ west from Greenwich, and elevation above the sea five hundred and sixty feet.   About three miles above the mouth of this stream are the first rapids —the present head of navigation—in the Sacramento River, which, from the rapids to its mouth in the bay, is more than two hundred miles long, and increasing in breadth from one hundred and fifty yards to six hundred yards in the lower part of its course.

During six days that we remained here, from the 30th March to the 5th April, the mean temperature was 40° at sunrise, 52°.5 at nine in the morning, 57°.2 at noon, 59°.4 at two in the afternoon, 58°.8 at four, and 52° at sunset ;

at the corresponding times the dew point was at 37°.0, 41°.0, 38°.1, 39°.6, 44°. 9, 40°. 5; and the moisture in a cubic foot of air 2.838 grs., 3.179 grs., 2.935 grs., 3.034 grs., 3.766 grs., 3.150 grs. respectively. Much cloudy weather and some showers of rain, during this interval, considerably reduced the temperature, which rose with fine weather on the 5th. Salmon was now abundant in the Sacramento. Those which we obtained were generally between three and four feet in length, and appeared to be of two distinct kinds. It is said that as many as four different kinds ascend the river at different periods. The great abundance in which this fish is found gives it an important place among the resources of the country. The salmon crowd in immense numbers up the Umpqua, Tlamath, and Trinity Rivers, and into every little river and creek on the coast north of the Bay of San Francisco ; and up the San Joaquin River, into the Stanislaus, beyond which the Indians say they do not go. Entering all the rivers of the coast far to the north, and finding their way up into the smaller branches which penetrate the forests of the interior country, climbing up cataracts and lesser falls, this fish had a large share in supporting the Indians—who raised nothing, but lived on what Nature gave. "A Salmon-Water," as they named it, was a valuable possession to a tribe or village, and jealously preserved as an inheritance. I found the "Salmon-waters" in the forests along the eastern flank of the Cascade range below the Columbia River.

In the evening of the 5th we resumed our journey northward, and encamped on a little creek near the Sacramento, where an emigrant from "the States" was establishing himself, and had already built a house. It is a handsome place, wooded with groves of oak, and along the creek are sycamore, ash, cottonwood, and willow. The day was fine, with a northwest wind.

The temperature at sunrise the next day (April 6th) was 42°, with a northeasterly wind. We continued up the Sacramento, which we crossed in canoes at a farm on the right bank of the river. The Sacramento was here about one hundred and forty yards wide, and with the actual stage of water, which I was informed continued several months, navigable for a steamboat. We encamped a few miles above, on a creek wooded principally with large oaks. Grass was good and abundant, with wild oats and pea vine in the bottoms. The day was fine, with a cool northwesterly breeze, which had in it the air of the high mountains. The wild oats here were not yet headed.

The snowy peak of Shastl bore directly north, showing out high above the other mountains. Temperature at sunset 57°, with a west wind and sky partly clouded.

APRIL 7.—The temperature at sunrise was 37°, with a moist air ; and a faintly clouded sky indicated that the wind was southerly along the coast.

We travelled toward the Shastl peak, the mountain ranges on both sides of the valleys being high and rugged, and snow-covered. Some remarkable peaks in the Sierra, to the eastward, are called *the Sisters*, and, nearly opposite, the Coast Range shows a prominent peak, to which in remembrance of my friend Senator Linn, I gave the name MOUNT LINN, as an enduring monument to recall the prolonged services rendered by him in securing to the country our Oregon coast. I trust this reason will protect it from change. These giant monuments, rising above the country and seen from afar, keep alive and present with the people the memory of patriotic men, and so continue their good services after death. Mount Linn and Mount Shastl keep open to the passing glance each an interesting page of the country's history—the one recording a successful struggle for the ocean boundary which it overlooks, the other the story of a strange people passed away. And so, too, these natural towers call attention from the detail of daily occupation to the larger duties which should influence the lives of men.

Leaving the Sacramento, at a stream called Red Bank Creek, we entered on a high and somewhat broken upland, timbered with at least four varieties of oaks, with *mansanita* (*arbutus Menziesii*) and other shrubbery interspersed. The *mansanita* is the strange shrub which I met in March of '44 in coming down from the Sierra Nevada to Sutter's Fort, and which in my journal of that time I described as follows : " A new and singular shrub, which had made its appearance since crossing the mountain, was very frequent to-day. It branched out near the ground, forming a clump eight to ten feet high, with pale green leaves of an oval form, and the body and branches had a naked appearance as if stripped of the bark, which is very smooth and thin, of a chocolate color, contrasting well with the pale green of the leaves." Out of its red berries the Indians make a cider which, put to cool in the running streams, makes a pleasant, refreshing drink. A remarkable species of pine, having leaves in threes (sometimes six to nine inches long), with bluish foliage, and a spreading, oak-shaped top, was scattered through the timber. I have remarked that this tree grows lower down the mountains than the other pines, being found familiarly associated with oaks, the first met after leaving the open valleys, and seeming to like a warm climate. It seems that even among inanimate things association levels differences. This tree, growing among oaks, forgets its narrow piny form and color, and takes the spreaded shape of the oaks, their broad summits, and lesser heights. Flowers were as usual abundant. The splendid California poppy characterized all the route along the valley. A species of clover was in bloom, and the berries of the *mansanita* were beginning to redden on some trees, while others were still in bloom We encamped, at an elevation of about one thousand feet above the sea, on a large stream called Cottonwood Creek, wooded on the bottoms with oaks, and with cotton-woods along the bed, which is sandy and gravelly. The water was at this time about twenty yards wide, but is frequently fifty. The face of the country traversed during the day was gravelly, and the bottoms of the creek where we encamped have a sandy soil.

There are six or seven rancherias of Indians on the Sacramento River between the farm where we had crossed the Sacramento and the mouth of this creek, and many others in the mountains about the heads of these streams.

The next morning was cloudy, threatening rain, but the sky grew brighter as the sun rose, and a southerly wind changed to northwest, which brought, as it never fails to bring, clear weather.

We continued sixteen miles up the valley, and encamped on the Sacramento River. In the afternoon (April 8th) the weather again grew thick, and in the evening rain began to fall in the valley and snow on the mountains. We were now near the head of the lower valley, and the face of the country and the weather began sensibly to show the influence of the rugged mountains which surround and terminate it.

The valley of the Sacramento is divided into upper and lower—the lower two hundred miles long, the upper known to the trappers as Pitt river, about one hundred and fifty ; and the latter not merely entitled to the distinction of upper, as being higher up the river, but also as having a superior elevation of some thousands of feet above it. The division is strongly and geographically marked. The Shastl peak stands at the head of the lower valley, rising from a base of about one thousand feet out of a forest of heavy timber. It ascends like an immense column upwards of fourteen thousand feet (nearly the height of Mont Blanc), the summit glistening with snow, and visible, from favorable points of view, at a distance of one hundred and forty miles down the valley. The river here, in descending from the upper valley, plunges down through a cañon, falling two thousand feet in twenty miles. This upper valley is one hundred and fifty miles long, heavily timbered, the climate and productions modified by its altitude, its more northern position, and the proximity and elevation of the neighboring mountains covered with snow. It contains valleys of arable land, and is deemed capable of settlement. Added to the lower valley, it makes the whole valley of the Sacramento three hundred and fifty miles long,

APRIL 9.—At ten o'clock the rain which commenced the previous evening had ceased, and the clouds clearing away, we boated the river, and continued our journey eastward toward the foot of the Sierra. The Sacramento bottoms here are broad and prettily wooded, with soil of a sandy character. Our way led through very handsome, open woods, principally of oaks, mingled with a considerable quantity of the oak-shaped pine. Interspersed among these were bosquets or thickets of *mansanita*, and an abundant white-flowering shrub, now entirely covered with small blossoms. The head of the valley here (lower valley) is watered by many small streams, having fertile bottom-lands, with a good range of grass and acorns. In about six miles we crossed a creek twenty or twenty-five feet wide, and several miles farther descended into the broad bottoms of a swift stream about twenty yards wide, called Cow Creek, so named as being the range of a small band of cattle, which ran off here from a party on their way to Oregon. They are entirely wild, and are hunted like other game. A large band of antelope was seen in the timber, and five or six deer came darting through the woods. An antelope and several deer were killed. There appear to be two species of these deer—both of the kind generally called black-tailed; one, a larger species frequenting the prairies and lower grounds ; the other, much smaller, and found in the mountains only. The mountains in the northeast were black with clouds when we reached the creek, and very soon a fierce hailstorm burst down on us, scattering our animals and covering the ground an inch in depth with hailstones about the size of wild cherries. The face of the country appeared as whitened by a fall of snow, and the weather became unpleasantly cold. The evening closed in with rain, and thunder rolling around the hills. Our elevation here was between one thousand and eleven hundred feet. At sunrise the next morning the thermometer was at 33°. The surrounding mountains showed a continuous line of snow, and the high peaks looked wintry. Turning to the southward, we retraced our steps down the valley, and reached Lassen's, on Deer River, on the evening of the 11th. The Sacramento bottoms between Antelope and Deer River were covered with oats, which had attained their full height, growing as in sown fields. The country here exhibited the maturity of spring. The California poppy was everywhere forming seed-pods, and many plants were in flower and seed together. Some varieties of clover were just beginning to bloom. By the middle of the month the seed-vessels of the California poppy which, from its characteristic abundance, is a prominent feature in the vegetation, had attained their full size ; but the seeds of this and many other plants, although fully formed, were still green-colored, and not entirely ripe. At this time I obtained from the San Joaquin valley seeds of the poppy, and other plants, black and fully ripe, while they still remained green in this part of the Sacramento—the effect of a warmer climate in the valley of the San Joaquin. The mean temperature for fourteen days, from the 10th to the 24th of April, was 43° at sunrise, 58° at nine in the morning, 64° at noon, 66° at two in the afternoon, 69° at four, and 58° at sunset (latitude 40°). The thermometer ranged at sunrise from 38° to 51°, at four (which is the hottest of those hours of the day when the temperature was noted) from 53° to 88°, and at sunset from 49° to

65°. The dew point was 40°.3 at sunrise, 47°.3 at 9 in the morning, 46°.1 at noon, 49°.2 at 2 in the afternoon, 49°.2 at 4, and 46°.6 at sunset ; and the quantity of moisture in a cubic foot of air at corresponding times was 3.104 grs., 3.882 grs., 3.807 grs., 4.213 grs., 4.217 grs., 3.884 grs., respectively. The winds fluctuated between northwest and southeast, the temperature depending more upon the state of the sky than the direction of the winds—a clouded sky always lowering the thermometer fifteen or twenty degrees in a short time. For the greater number of the days above given the sky was covered and the atmosphere frequently thick with rain at intervals from the 19th to the 23d.

Here at Lassen's I set up the transit and during the nights of the 14th and 16th (April) obtained good observations of moon culminations which established the longitude of the place in 120° 56′ 44″, latitude obtained 39° 57′ 04″. This was the third of my main stations and the place of observation was upon Deer River half a mile above its mouth in the Sacramento and opposite Lassen's house.

On the 24th I left Lassen's, intending to penetrate the country, along the Cascade ranges north into Oregon, and connect there with the line of my journey of '43, which lay up the Fall River of the Columbia and south to the great savannah, or grassy meadow-lake through which flows from among the ridges of the Cascade Mountains the principal tributary, or rather the main stream of the waters which make the Tlamath Lake and River. It is a timbered country, clothed with heavy pine forests that nourish many streams.

Travelling up the Sacramento over ground already described, we reached the head of the lower valley in the evening of the second day, and in the morning of the 26th left the Sacramento, going up one of the many pretty little streams that flow into the main river around the head of the lower valley. On either side low, steep ridges were covered along their summits with pines, and oaks occupied the somewhat broad bottom of the creek. Snowy peaks which made the horizon on the right gave a cool tone to the landscape, and the thermometer showed a temperature of 71°, but there was no breeze and the air was still and hot. There were many runs and small streams, with much bottom-land, and the abundant grass and acorns, both of excellent quality, made it a favorite resort for game. The frequent appearance of game furnished excitement, and together with the fine weather, which made mere breathing an enjoyment, kept the party in exhilarated spirits. At our encampment among oak groves in the evening, we found ourselves apparently in a bear garden, where the rough denizens resented our intrusion and made a lively time for the hunters, who succeeded in killing four of them after we had encamped. During our skirmishing among the bear this afternoon we had overtaken and slightly wounded one, just enough to irritate him. At this moment Delaware Charley's horse fell near by the bear. To save Charley we had all to close in on the bear, who was fortunately killed before he could get the Delaware. In his fall the hammer of his gun struck Charley on the bridge of his nose and broke it in the middle. We had no surgeon, but I managed to get it into good shape and it healed without trace of injury. I was always proud of this surgical operation, and the Delaware was especially pleased. He was a fine-looking young man, and naïvely vain of his handsome face, which now had a nose unusual among his people; the aquiline arch had been broken to knit into a clear straight line, of which he became very vain.

At sunset the weather was pleasant, with a temperature of 56°. I had only an observation for latitude, which put the camp in 40° 38' 58", and the elevation above the sea was one thousand and eighty feet. The day following we found a good way along a flat ridge; there was a pretty stream in a mountain valley on the right, and the face of the country was already beginning to assume a mountainous character, wooded with mingled oak and long-leaved pine, and having a surface of scattered rocks, with grass or flowers, among them the three-leaved poppy, its parti-colored blossoms waving on the long stem above the grass, and gaining for itself the name *mariposas*, already mentioned because of its resembling living butterflies. I speak often of the grass and the flowers, but I have learned to value the one and the other lends a beauty to the scenery which I do not like to omit, and the reader can always imagine for himself the brightness they give when once he has had described the glorious flowers of this country, where the most lovely hues are spread in fields over both hill and plain. At noon, when we were crossing a high ridge, the temperature was down to 61°, and where we encamped at an elevation of two thousand four hundred and sixty feet, on a creek that went roaring into the valley, the sunset temperature was 52°.

The next day I continued up the stream on which we had slept, and with it the mountain slope rose rapidly, clothed with heavy timber. On crossing one of the high ridges, snow and the great pine *Lambertiani* appeared together, and an hour before noon we reached a pass in the main ridge of the Sierra Nevada, in an open pine forest at an elevation of only four thousand six hundred feet, where the snow was in patches and the deciduous oaks were mingled with the pines. The thermometer was at 50°, and we were not above the upper limit of the oak region. This pass is in about the fortieth degree of latitude, and is in the terminating point of the northern link of the Sierra Nevada chain, which the Cascade range takes up with the link of the Shastl peak. Between the points of these links the upper Sacramento River breaks down on its way to the Bay of San Francisco and the Tlamath River to the sea.

Going through this pass and descending the mountain, we entered into what may be called a basin or mountain valley, lying north and south along the ranges of the Cascade Mountains. Here we found a region very different from the valley of California. We had left behind the soft, delightful climate of the coast, from which we were cut off by the high, snowy mountains, and had ascended into one resembling that of the Great Basin, and under the influence of the same elevation above the sea; but more fertile and having much forest land, and well watered. The face of the country was different from that of the valley which we had just left, being open and more spread into plain, in which there were frequent lakes as well as rivers. The soil itself is different; sometimes bare. At times we travelled over stretches in the forest where the soil was a gray or yellowish-white pumice-stone, like that which I have seen along the Cascade range in travelling south from the Columbia River, where the soil was covered with splendid pine forests, but where there was hardly a blade of grass to be found. Very different from this the compact growth of grass and flowers which belong to the California valley, where the rich soil had accumulated the wash of ages from the mountains, and where the well-watered land and moisture of the air combine to cover the country with its uncommon and profuse vegetation. The country where we now were was not known to any of the men with me, and I was not able to communicate with any of the Indians, who in this region were unfriendly—from these I might have learned the names by which the natural features were known to them. Except in some of its leading features I regarded this district as not within the limits of fixed geography, and therefore I thought it well to give names to these; to some at the time, and to others afterward, when I came to making up a map of the country. And this was also necessary, as otherwise I could not conveniently refer to them.

On the 29th of April I encamped on the upper Sacramento, above Fall River, which is tributary to it. I obtained observations here, which gave for longitude 121° 07′ 59″, and for latitude 40° 58′ 43″; and the next day again encamped on it at the upper end of a valley, to which, from its marked form, I gave the name *Round Valley.* By observation the longitude here is 121° 01′ 23″, latitude 41° 17′ 17″. On the first of May I encamped on the southeastern end of a lake, which afterwards I named Lake Rhett in friendly remembrance of Mr. Barnwell Rhett, of South Carolina, who is connected with one of the events of my life which brought with it an abiding satisfaction. I obtained observations here which placed this end of the lake in longitude 121° 15′ 24″, and latitude 41° 48′ 49″.

This camp was some twenty-five or thirty miles from the lava beds, near which Major-General Canby was killed by the Modocs, twenty-seven years later; and when there was some of the hardest fighting known in Indian history between them and our troops.

This Indian fighting is always close, incurring more certain risk of life and far more sanguinary, than in the ordinary contests between civilized troops. Every Indian fights with intention, and for all that is in him; he waits for no orders, but has every effort concentrated on his intention to kill. And, singularly, this Indian fighting, which calls for the utmost skill and courage on the part of men, is not appreciated by the Government, or held worthy of the notice given to the milder civilized warfare.

When we left Round Valley in the morning Archambeau, who was an inveterate hunter, had gone off among the hills and towards the mountain in search of game.

We had now entered more into the open country, though still a valley or high upland along the foot of the main ridge, and were travelling north; but the route of the day is often diverted from its general course by accidents of country and for convenient camping grounds. Archambeau did not come in at night, and when the morning came and did not bring him I did not move camp, but sent out men to look for him. Since leaving the California Mountains we had seen no Indians, though frequently we came upon their tracks and other sign. All through this country there were traces of them. Doubtless our camp-fires had discovered us to them, but they hovered around out of our way and out of sight. The second day passed and still no trace of Archambeau had been found, and the greater part of the third was passed in scouring the country. There would have been little difficulty in a prairie region, but in a broken or hilly country much ground cannot be covered and the search is restricted to a small area. We had now been in camp three days and I began to be seriously disturbed by his absence. Game had been found scarce in the immediate neighborhood. He had nothing with him but a little dried meat when he turned off from the party, expecting to rejoin us before night, and the Indians in the region through which we were travelling were known to be hostile and treacherous, with a fixed character for daring. Parties from as far north as the Hudson Bay Company's post who had penetrated here had met with some rough experiences, and the story of trapper adventure hereabout was full of disaster. On one occasion a large party of trappers from the north were encamped on one of the streams of the Cascade range, and having been led into carelessness by the apparent friendly conduct of the Indians, were every man killed. It was easy to waylay a single man, especially if he were intent on game. I had always been careful of my men, and in all my journeyings lost but few, and with rare exceptions those were by accident or imprudence. Naturally disposed that way, I had always endeavored to provide for their safety so far as the nature of our exposed life permitted, for in case of accident, as we had no surgeon, I was myself the only resource. A man lost from camp was likely also to lose his life. In such circumstances every hour increases the danger of his situation. And so about sunset we were greatly relieved when a shout from the men on guard roused the camp and we saw Archambeau creeping slowly in, man and horse equally worn out. Searching for game, he had been led off and entangled among the hills until the coming night roused him and the darkness cut off all chance of reaching camp. His search was as fruitless on the following days. He did not meet game, and his horse being kept close at hand at night had no chance to feed, and was nearly as tired as himself. And he had probably owed his life to his good eyes. These were unusually fine, with an instant quickness to catch a moving object or any slight difference in color or form of what lay before him. I was riding with him on the prairie one day, off from the party, when he suddenly halted. "Stop," he said, "I see an antelope's horns." About fifty steps away an antelope was lying in the tall grass, and the tip of its horn was barely visible above it, but he not only saw it but shot and killed it. And this time his eyes had served him well again. They were ranging around taking in all before him when he caught sight of a party of Indians. They were travelling directly across his line of way, making towards the coast mountains, probably going to some river in which there were salmon. If they had been coming towards him they would have seen him, or if they had crossed his trail behind him his life would have been lost. He saw them as they were coming up out of a broad ravine and in the instant got his horse out of sight down the slope of a hill. "My heart was in my mouth for a moment," he said. The danger of his situation had already brought on the hurry and excitement which often deprives a man of all prudence. In such mishaps a man quickly loses his head, but at this stage, happily, he struck our trail.

The arrival of Archambeau relieved and spread pleasure through the camp, where he was a general favorite. He was Canadian, tall, fine-looking, very cheerful, and with all the gayety of the *voyageur* before hard work and a rough life had driven it out. He had that light, elastic French temperament that makes a cheerful companion in travelling; which in my experience brings out all there is of good or bad in a man. I loved to have my camp cheerful and took care always for the health and comfort which carry good temper with them. Usually, on leaving the frontier, I provided the men with tents or lodges, but by the time we had been a month or two on the road, they would come to me to say that it was hard on them to have to put up their lodge at night when they were tired, and that they made a delay in the morning when starting. So usually their shelters were gladly left behind and they took the weather as it came.

Meantime the days while we had been waiting here were not lost. Our animals had been resting on good grass, and when in the morning the welcome order was given to move camp, they made the lively scene which Mr. Kern gives in the picture. This was an order which the animals were always prone to resist promptly, and their three days' rest made them do it now with unusual vigor. But the men, too, refreshed by rest and cheered by the recovery of their companion, entered with equal spirit into the fray, and soon we were again on the trail, the animals settled down to their orderly work.

Archambeau was himself again in the morning after a night's rest, and good meals among companions, but his horse was let to run loose for some days, in order to recover its useful strength. With the animals refreshed we made a long stretch and encamped on a stream flowing into Lake Rhett, which I called McCrady. This was the name of one of my boyhood's friends, living in Charleston, who came this evening into my mind, and I left his memory on the stream. In such work as I was engaged in there is always much time for thinking, or ruminating, as it may better be called; not upon the road, but often at night, waiting for the hour when the work belonging to it may begin.

In the forenoon of the sixth we reached the Tlamath Lake at its outlet, which is by a fine, broad stream, not fordable. This is a great fishing station for the Indians, and we met here the first we had seen since leaving the lower valley. They have fixed habitations around the shores of the lake, particularly at the outlet and inlet, and along the inlet up to the swamp meadow, where I met the Tlamaths in the winter of '43–'44, and where we narrowly escaped disaster.

Our arrival took them by surprise, and though they received us with apparent friendship, there was no warmth in it, but a shyness which came naturally from their habit of hostility.

At the outlet here were some of their permanent huts. From the lake to the sea I judged the river to be about two hundred miles long; it breaks its way south of the huge bulk of Shastl Peak between the points of the Cascade and Nevada ranges to the sea. Up this river the salmon crowd in great numbers to the lake, which is more than four thousand feet above the sea. It was a bright spring morning, and the lake and its surrounding scenery looked charming. It was inviting, and I would have been glad to range over it in one of the Indian canoes. The silent shores and unknown mountains had the attraction which mystery gives always. It was all wild and unexplored, and the uninvaded silence roused curiosity and invited research. Indigenous, the Indians like the rocks and trees seemed part of the soil, growing in a state of rude nature like the vegetation, and like it nourished and fed by nature. And so it had been back to a time of which nothing was known. All here was in the true aboriginal condition, but I had no time now for idling days, and I had to lose the pleasure to which the view before me invited. Mr. Kern made the picture of it while we were trading with the Indians for dried fish and salmon, and ferrying the camp equipage across the outlet in their canoes.

The Indians made me understand that there was another large river which came from the north and flowed into the lake at the northern end, and that the principal village was at its mouth, where also they caught many fish.

Resuming our journey, we worked our way along between the lake and the mountain, and late in the day made camp at a run, near where it issued from the woods into the lake and where our animals had good feed. For something which happened afterward, I gave this run the name of Denny's Branch. Animals and men all fared well here.

May 7.—The weather continued refreshingly cool. Our way led always between the lake and the foot of the mountains, frequently rough and blocked by decaying logs and fallen trees, where patches of snow still remained in the shade, over ground rarely trodden even by an Indian foot. In the timber the snow was heavy and naturally much heavier towards the summits and in the passes of the mountains, where the winter still held sway. This year it had continued late and rough. In the late afternoon we reached a piece of open ground through which a stream ran towards the lake. Here the mountain receded a little, leaving a flat where the woods, which still occupied the ground, left us a convenient open space by the water, and where there was grass abundant. On the way along from the outlet no Indians had been seen and no other sign of life, but now and then when the lake was visible a canoe might be seen glancing along. But in the morning, as we were about to leave camp, a number of them came in. I could not clearly find where they had come from, though they pointed up the lake. Perhaps from some valley in the mountain on this stream, or perhaps they had followed our trail. This was most likely, but if so they were not willing to tell. They would not have done so with any good intent, and they knew well enough that we were aware of it. They said that they were hungry, and I had some mules unpacked and gave them part of our remaining scanty supply of dried meat and the usual present which an Indian, wild or tame, always instinctively expects.

We continued our route over the same kind of ground, rendered difficult by the obstructions which the wash of the rain and snow, and the fallen timber, the undisturbed accumulations of the many years, had placed in these forests. Crossing spurs of mountains and working around the bays or coves between the ridges or winding among the hills, it is surprising how a long day's march dwindles away to a few miles when it comes to be laid down between the rigorous astronomical stations. We had travelled in this direction many such days when we encamped in the afternoon of the 8th of May. A glance at the mountains, which are shown in the view of the lake, gives some idea of the character of this unexplored region. By unexplored, I wish to be understood to say that it had never been explored or mapped, or in any way brought to common knowledge, or rarely visited except by strong parties of trappers, and by those at remote intervals, doubtless never by trappers singly. It was a true wilderness. There was the great range of mountains behind the coast, and behind it the lakes and rivers known to the trappers, and that was all, and the interest attached to it was chiefly from the disasters which had befallen them. And from their reports, rude and exaggerated outlines, and Turtle Lakes and Buenaventura Rivers, had been marked down at the stations of the Fur Company. All this gave the country a charm for me. It would have been dull work if it had been to plod over a safe country and here and there to correct some old error.

And I had my work all planned. The friendly reader—and I hope that no unfriendly eyes will travel along with me over these lines; the friends may be few and the many are the neutral minds who read without reference to the writer, solely for the interest they find. To these I write freely, letting the hues of my mind color the paper, feeling myself on pleasant terms with them, giving to them in a manner a life confession in which I hope they find interest, and expecting to find them considerate and weighing fairly, and sometimes condoning the events as we pass them in review. My reading friend, then, who has travelled with me thus far will remember that some seventeen months before this time, in the December of '43, in coming south from the Columbia, I encamped on a large savannah, or meadow-lake, which made the southern limit of my journey. I met there a Tlamath chief and his wife, who had come out to meet me and share his fate, whether good or bad, and the chief had afterward accompanied me and piloted me on my way through the forest and the snow. Where I had encamped this night I was only some twenty miles in an air-line from their village and I was promising myself some pleasure in seeing them again. According to what the Indians at the south end of the lake had told me, I had only to travel eastward a short march and I would find a large village at the inlet of the river, which I knew must be that on which my friendly chief lived, some twenty miles above. And his Indians, too, like all the others along these mountains, had the character of normal hostility to the whites.

My plans when I started on my journey into this region were to connect my present survey of the intervening country with my camp on the savannah, where I had met the Tlamaths in that December ; and I wished to penetrate among the mountains of the Cascade ranges. As I have said, except for the few trappers who had searched the streams leading to the ocean, for beaver, I felt sure that these mountains were absolutely unknown. No one had penetrated their recesses to know what they contained, and no one had climbed to their summits; and there remained the great attraction of mystery in going into unknown places —the unknown lands of which I had dreamed when I began this life of frontier travel. And possibly, I thought, when I should descend their western flanks some safe harbor might yet be found by careful search along that coast, where harbors were so few; and perhaps good passages from the interior through these mountains to the sea. I thought that until the snow should go off the lower part of the mountains I might occupy what remained of the spring by a survey of the Tlamath River to its heads, and make a good map of the country along the base of the mountains. And if we should not find game enough to live upon, we could employ the Indians to get supplies of salmon and other fish. But I felt sure that there was game in the woods of these mountains as well as in those more to the south. Travelling along the northern part of this range in December of '43, I had seen elk tracks in the snow, and at an old Cayuse village in the pine forest at the foot of the mountains, only about sixty miles farther north, there were many deer horns lying around. This showed that we should probably find both elk and deer, and bear, in the mountains, and certainly on the slope towards the sea, where every variety of climate would be found, and every variety of mast-bearing trees, as in the oak region of the Sierra Nevada. And I had not forgotten how fascinated I had been with the winter beauty of the snowy range farther north, when at sunrise and at sunset their rose-colored peaks stood up out of the dark pine forests into the clear light of the sky. And my thoughts took the same color when I remembered that Mr. Kern, who had his colors with him, could hold these lovely views in all their delicate coloring.

How fate pursues a man! Thinking and ruminating over these things, I was standing alone by my camp-fire, enjoying its warmth, for the night air of early spring is chill under the shadows of the high mountains. Suddenly my ear caught the faint sound of horses' feet, and while I was watching and listening as the sounds, so strange hereabout, came nearer, there emerged from the darkness—into the circle of the firelight—two horsemen, riding slowly as though horse and man were fatigued by long travelling. In the foremost I recognized the familiar face of Neal, with a companion whom I also knew. They had ridden nearly a hundred miles in the last two days, having been sent forward by a United States officer who was on my trail with despatches for me; but Neal doubted if he would get through. After their horses had been turned into the band and they were seated by my fire, refreshing themselves with good coffee while more solid food was being prepared, Neal told me his story. The officer who was trying to overtake me was named Gillespie. He had been sent to California by the Government and had letters for delivery to me. Neal knew the great danger from Indians in this country, and his party becoming alarmed and my trail being fresh, Mr. Gillespie had sent forward Neal and Sigler upon their best horses to overtake me and inform me of his situation. They had left him on the morning of the day before, and in the two days had ridden nearly a hundred miles, and this last day had severely tried the strength of their horses. When they parted from him they had not reached the lake, and for greater safety had not kept my trail quite to the outlet, but crossed to the right bank of the river, striking my trail again on the lake shore. They had discovered Indians on my trail after they had left Gillespie, and on the upper part of the lake the Indians had tried to cut them off, and they had escaped only by the speed and strength of their horses, which Neal had brought from his own rancho. He said that in his opinion I could not reach Gillespie in time to save him, as he had with him only three men and was travelling slow.

A quick eye and a good horse mean life to a man in an Indian coun-try. Neal had both. He was a lover of horses and knew a good one; and those he had with him were the best on his rancho. He had been sent forward by the messenger to let me know that he was in danger of being cut off by the Indians.

The trail back along the shore at the foot of the mountains was so nearly impassable at night that nothing could be gained by attempting it, but everything was made ready for an early start in the morning. For the relief party, in view of contingencies, I selected ten of the best men, including Carson, Stepp, Dick Owens, Godey, Basil, and Lajeunesse, with four of the Delawares.

When the excitement of the evening was over I lay down, speculating far into the night on what could be the urgency of the message which had brought an officer of the Government to search so far after me into these mountains. At early dawn we took the backward trail. Snow and fallen timber made the ride hard and long to where I thought to meet the messenger. On the way no Indians were seen and no tracks later than those where they had struck Neal's trail. In the afternoon, having made about forty-five miles, we reached the spot where the forest made an opening to the lake, and where I intended to wait. This was a glade, or natural meadow, shut in by the forest, with a small stream and good grass, where I had already encamped. I knew that this was the first water to which my trail would bring the messenger, and that I was sure to meet him here if no harm befell him on the way. The sun was about going down when he was seen issuing from the wood, accompanied by three men.

He proved to be an officer of the navy, Lieutenant Archibald Gillespie of the Marine Corps. We greeted him warmly. All were glad to see him, whites and Indians. It was long since any news had reached us, and every one was as pleased to see him as if he had come freighted with letters from home, for all. It was now eleven months since any tidings had reached me.

Mr. Gillespie informed me that he had left Washington under orders from the President and the Secretary of the Navy, and was directed to reach California by the shortest route through Mexico to Mazatlan.

He was directed to find me wherever I might be, and was informed that I would probably be found on the Sacramento River. In pursuance of his instructions he had accordingly started from Monterey to look for me on the Sacramento. Learning upon his arrival at Sutter's Fort that I had gone up the valley, he made up a small party at Neal's rancho, and, guided by him, followed my trail and had travelled six hundred miles to overtake me; the latter part of the way through great dangers.

The mission on which I had been originally sent to the West was a peaceful one, and Mr. Bancroft had sent Mr. Gillespie to give me warning of the new state of affairs and the designs of the President. Mr. Gillespie had been given charge of despatches from the Secretary of the Navy to Commodore Sloat, and had been purposely made acquainted with their import. Known to Mr. Bancroft as an able and thoroughly trustworthy officer, he had been well instructed in the designs of the Department and with the purposes of the Administration, so far as they related to California.

Through him I now became acquainted with the actual state of affairs and the purposes of the Government. The information through Gillespie had absolved me from my duty as an explorer, and I was left to my duty as an officer of the American Army with the further authoritative knowledge that the Government intended to take California. I was warned by my Government of the new danger against which I was bound to defend myself; and it had been made known to me now on the authority of the Secretary of the Navy that to obtain possession of California was the chief object of the President.

He brought me also a letter of introduction from the Secretary of State, Mr. Buchanan, and letters and papers from Senator Benton and family. The letter from the Secretary was directed to me in my private or citizen capacity, and though importing nothing beyond the introduction, it accredited the bearer to me as coming from the Secretary of State, and in connection with the circumstances and place of delivery it indicated a purpose in sending it. From the letter itself I learned nothing, but it was intelligibly explained to me by the accompanying letter from Senator Benton and by communications from Lieutenant Gillespie.

This officer informed me that he had been directed by the Secretary of State to acquaint me with his instructions, which had for their principal objects to ascertain the disposition of the California people, to conciliate their feelings in favor of the United States; and to find out, with a view to counteracting, the designs of the British Government upon that country.

The letter from Senator Benton, while apparently of friendship and family details, contained passages and suggestions which, read by the light of many conversations and discussions with himself and others at Washington, clearly indicated to me that I was required by the Government to find out any foreign schemes in relation to California and, so far as might be in my power, to counteract them.

Neal had much to talk over with his old companions and pleasurable excitement kept us up late; but before eleven o'clock all were wrapped in their blankets and soundly asleep except myself. I sat by the fire in fancied security, going over again the home letters. These threw their own light upon the communication from Mr. Gillespie, and made the expected signal. In substance, their effect was: The time has come. England must not get a foothold. We must be first. Act; discreetly, but positively.

Looking back over the contingencies which had been foreseen in the discussions at Washington, I saw that the important one which carried with it the hopes of Senator Benton and the wishes of the Government was in the act of occurring, and it was with thorough satisfaction I now found myself required to do what I could to promote this object of the President. Viewed by the light of these deliberations in Washington, I was prepared to comprehend fully the communications brought to me by Mr. Gillespie.

Now it was officially made known to me that my country was at war, and it was so made known expressly to guide my conduct. I had learned with certainty from the Secretary of the Navy that the President's plan of war included the taking possession of California, and under his confidential instructions I had my warrant. Mr. Gillespie was directed to act in concert with me. Great vigilance and activity were expected of us both, for it was desired that possession should be had of California before the presence in her ports of any foreign vessel of war might make it inconvenient.

I had about thought out the situation when I was startled by a sudden movement among the animals. Lieutenant Gillespie had told me that there were no Indians on his trail, and I knew there were none on mine. This night was one of two when I failed to put men on guard in an Indian country—this night and one spent on an island in the Great Salt Lake. The animals were near the shore of the lake, barely a hundred yards away. Drawing a revolver I went down among them. A mule is a good sentinel, and when he quits eating and stands with his ears stuck straight out taking notice, it is best to see what is the matter. The mules knew that Indians were around, but nothing seemed stirring, and my presence quieting the animals I returned to the fire and my letters.

I saw the way opening clear before me. War with Mexico was inevitable; and a grand opportunity now presented itself to realize in their fullest extent the far-sighted views of Senator Benton, and make the Pacific Ocean the western boundary of the United States. I resolved to move forward on the opportunity and return forthwith to the Sacramento valley in order to bring to bear all the influences I could command.

Except myself, then and for nine months afterward, there was no other officer of the army in California. The citizen party under my command was made up of picked men, and although small in number, constituted a formidable nucleus for frontier warfare, and many of its members commanded the confidence of the emigration.

This decision was the first step in the conquest of California.

My mind having settled into this conclusion, I went to my blankets under a cedar. The camp was divided into three fires, and near each one, but well out of the light, were sleeping the men belonging to it. Close up along the margin of the wood which shut us in on three sides were some low cedars, the ends of their boughs reaching nearly to the ground. Under these we made our beds.

One always likes to have his head sheltered, and a rifle with a ramrod or a branch or bush with a blanket thrown over it answers very well where there is nothing better. I had barely fallen to sleep when I was awakened by the sound of Carson's voice, calling to Basil to know " what the matter was over there ? " No reply came, and immediately the camp was roused by the cry from Kit and Owens, who were lying together— "Indians." Basil and the half-breed, Denny, had been killed. It was the sound of the axe being driven into Basil's head that had awakened

SAGUNDAI.

Carson. The half-breed had been killed with arrows, and his groans had replied to Carson's call, and told him what the matter was. No man, with an Indian experience, jumps squarely to his feet in a night attack, but in an instant every man was at himself. The Delawares who lay near their fire on that side sprung to cover, rifle in hand, at the sound of the axe. We ran to their aid, Carson and I, Godey, Stepp, and Owens, just as the Tlamaths charged into the open ground. The fires were smouldering, but gave light enough to show Delaware Crane jumping like a brave as he was from side to side in Indian fashion, and defending himself with the butt of his gun. By some mischance his rifle was not loaded when he lay down. All this was quick work. The moment's silence which followed Carson's shout was broken by our rifles. The Tlamath chief, who was at the head of his men, fell in front of Crane, who was just down with five arrows in his body—three in his breast. The Tlamaths, checked in their onset and disconcerted by the fall of their chief, jumped back into the shadow of the wood. We threw a blanket over Crane and hung blankets to the cedar boughs and bushes near by, behind my camp-fire, for a defence against the arrows. The Indians did not dare to put themselves again in the open, but continued to pour in their arrows. They made no attempt on our animals, which had been driven up by Owens to be under fire of the camp, but made frequent attempts to get the body of their chief. We were determined they should not have it, and every movement on their part brought a rifle-shot; a dozen rifles in such hands at short range made the undertaking too hazardous for them to persist in it. While both sides were watching each other from under cover, and every movement was followed by a rifle-shot or arrow, I heard Carson cry out: " *Look at the fool. Look at him, will you?* " This was to Godey, who had stepped out to the light of my fire to look at some little thing which had gone wrong with his gun; it was still bright enough to show him distinctly, standing there—a fair mark to the arrows—turning resentfully to Carson for the epithet bestowed on him, but in no wise hurrying himself. He was the most thoroughly insensible to danger of all the brave men I have known.

All night we lay behind our blanket defences, with our rifles cocked in our hands, expecting momentarily another attack, until the morning light enabled us to see that the Indians had disappeared. By their tracks we found that fifteen or twenty Tlamaths had attacked us. It was a sorrowful sight that met our eyes in the gray of the morning. Three of our men had been killed: Basil, Crane, and the half-breed Denny, and another Delaware had been wounded ; one-fourth of our number. The chief who had been killed was recognized to be the same Indian who had given Lieutenant Gillespie a salmon at the outlet of the lake. Hung to his wrist was an English half-axe. Carson seized this and knocked his head to pieces with it, and one of the Delawares, Sagundai, scalped him. He was left where he fell. In his quiver were forty arrows ; as Carson said, " the most beautiful and warlike arrows he had ever seen." We saw more of them afterward. These arrows were all headed with a lancet-like piece of iron or steel—probably obtained from the Hudson Bay Company's traders on the Umpqua—and were poisoned for about six inches. They could be driven that depth into a pine tree.

This event cast an angry gloom over the little camp. For the moment I threw all other considerations aside and determined to square accounts with these people before I left them. It was only a few days back that some of these same Indians had come into our camp, and I divided with them what meat I had, and unpacked a mule to give them tobacco and knives.

On leaving the main party I had directed it to gear up as soon as the men had breakfasted and follow my trail to a place where we had encamped some days back. This would put them now about twenty-five miles from us. Packing our dead men on the mules, we started to rejoin the main camp, following the trail by which we had come. Before we had been two hours on the way many canoes appeared on the lake, coming from different directions and apparently making for a point where the trail came down to the shore. As we approached this point the prolonged cry of a loon told us that their scout was giving the Indians warning of our approach. Knowing that if we came to a fight the care of our dead men would prove a great hindrance and probably cost more lives, I turned sharply off into the mountain, and buried, or *cached* them in a close laurel thicket.

With our knives we dug a shallow grave, and wrapping their blankets round them, left them among the laurels. There are men above whom the laurels bloom who did not better deserve them than my brave Delaware and Basil. I left Denny's name on the creek where he died.

The Indians, thrown out by our sudden movement, failed in their intended ambush, and in the afternoon we found our people on the stream where we had encamped three days before. All were deeply grieved by the loss of our companions. The Delawares were filled with grief and rage by the death of Crane and went into mourning, blackening their faces. They were soothed somewhat when I told them that they should have an opportunity to get rid of their mourning and carry home scalps enough to satisfy the friends of Crane and the Delaware nation. With blackened faces, set and angry, they sat around brooding and waiting for revenge.

The camp was very quiet this evening, the men looking to their arms, rubbing and coaxing them. Towards evening I went over to the Delaware fire and sat down among them. They were sitting around their fire, smoking and silent. It did not need to speak ; our faces told what we were all thinking about. After a pause I said, " Swonok, bad luck come this time. Crane was a brave. Good man, too. I am very sorry." " Very sick here," he said, striking his hand against his breast ; " these Delaware all sick." " There are Indians around the camp, Swonok," I replied. " Yes, I see him. Me and Sagundai and Charley gone out and see him in woods." " How many ? " " Maybe ten, maybe twenty, maybe more." " Where did they go ? " " Up mountain. He not long way." " Listen, Swonok, we kill some. These same men kill Crane. How best kill him ? " The chief's eyes glittered and his face relaxed, and all the Delawares raised their heads. " You go in morning ? Which way ? " " Only three, four mile, to creek which you know over there," said I pointing up the lake; " next day, big Indian village." Swonok turned to Sagundai and the two chiefs spoke earnestly together for a few mo-ments, the others deeply interested, but gravely listening without speak-ing. " Captain," said Sagundai, "in the morning you go little way, stop. These Delaware stay here. Indian come in camp, Delaware kill him."

In the morning, when we were ready to start, the Delawares rode out some moments ahead, halting after a few hundred yards until we came up; then, leaving their horses with us, they returned on foot and got into a thicket among some young pines near the camp ground. We contin-ued our way and halted, no one dismounting, at a little run about a quarter of a mile distant. It was not long before the stillness was broken by a scattered volley, and after that, nothing. Shortly Swonok came up " Better now," he said; " very sick before, better now." They had taken two scalps. The Tlamaths, as expected, had rushed into the camp ground, so soon as they thought it safe, and met the rifles of the Dela-wares. Two were killed and others wounded, but these were able to get away. Fortunately for them, the cracking of a dry branch startled the Tlamaths and the Delawares were too eager to shoot as well as usual. I moved on about three miles to a stream where the grass was good and en-camped. Choosing an open spot among the pines we built a solid corral of pine logs and branches. It was six feet high and large enough to contain all our animals. At nightfall they were driven into it, and we took up our quarters outside, against the corral; the fires being at a little distance farther out and lighting up, while they lasted, the woods beyond. I obtained obser-vations which put this camp in longitude 121° 58′ 45″ and latitude 42° 36′ 45″.

Continuing our route along the lake we passed around the extreme northwestern bay and after a hard day's march encamped in the midst of woods, where we built again a corral for the night. In the morning there were many canoes on the lake, and Indians had been about during the night, but the lesson they had learned served to keep them warily aloof in daylight. We were not very far from the principal village at the inlet which the Indians whom I had met when I first reached the lake had described to me; and the arms being all carefully examined and packs made secure, we started for it. When within a few miles I sent Carson and Owens ahead with ten men, directing them to reconnoitre the position of the Indians, but if possible to avoid engaging them until we could come up. But, as we neared the mouth of the river, the firing began. The party was discovered and had no choice but to open the fight, driving the Indians who were on this side to the other side of the river. As I rode up I saw a dead Indian sitting in the stern of a canoe, which the current had driven against the bank. His hand was still grasping the paddle. On his feet were shoes which I thought Basil wore when he was killed. The stream was about sixty yards wide and a rapid just above the mouth made it fordable. Without drawing rein we plunged in and crossed to the farther side and joined our men, who were pressed by a large body of Indians. They had abandoned their village and were scattered through a field of sage-brush, in front of the woods. But this time the night was not on their side and the attack was with us. Their arrows were good at close quarters, but the range of the rifle was better. The firing was too severe for them to stand it in open ground and they were driven back into the pine woods with a loss of fourteen killed. They had intended to make a hard fight. Behind the sage-bushes where they had taken their stand every Indian had spread his arrows on the ground in fan-like shape, so that they would be ready to his hand. But when our close fire drove them from the brush they were compelled to move so quickly that many did not have time to gather up their arrows and they lay on the ground, the bright, menacing points turned toward us. Quantities of fish were drying, spread on scaffolds, or hung up on frames. The huts, which were made of tall rushes and willow, like those on the savannah above, were set on fire, and the fish and scaffolds were all destroyed.

About a mile from the village I made my camp on a *clairière* in the midst of woods, where were oaks intermingled with pines, and built a strong corral. Meantime I kept out scouts on every side and horses were kept ready saddled. In the afternoon Indians were reported advancing through the timber; and taking with me Carson, Sagundai, Swonok, Stepp, and Archambeau, I rode out to see what they were intending. Sacramento knew how to jump and liked it. Going through the wood at a hand-gallop we came upon an oak tree which had been blown down; its summit covered quite a space, and being crowded by the others so that I was brought squarely in front of it, I let Sacramento go and he cleared the whole green mass in a beautiful leap. Looking back, Carson called out, " Captain, that horse will break your neck some day." It never happened to Sacramento to hurt his rider, but afterward, on the Salinas plain, he brought out from fight and back to his camp his rider who had been shot dead in the saddle.

In the heart of the wood we came suddenly upon an Indian scout. He was drawing his arrow to the head as we came upon him, and Carson attempted to fire, but his rifle snapped, and as he swerved away the Indian was about to let his arrow go into him ; I fired, and in my haste to save Carson, failed to kill the Indian, but Sacramento, as I have said, was not afraid of anything, and I jumped him directly upon the Indian and threw him to the ground. His arrow went wild. Sagundai was right behind me, and as I passed over the Indian he threw himself from his horse and killed him with a blow on the head from his war-club. It was the work of a moment, but it was a narrow chance for Carson. The poisoned arrow would have gone through his body.

Giving Sacramento into the care of Jacob, I went into the lodge and laid down on my blankets to rest from the excitement of which the day had been so full. I had now kept the promise I made to myself and had punished these people well for their treachery ; and now I turned my thoughts to the work which they had delayed. I was lost in conjectures over this new field when Gillespie came in, all roused into emotion. " By Heaven, this is rough work," he exclaimed. " I'll take care to let them know in Washington about it." " Heaven don't come in for much about here, just now," I said ; " and as for Washington, it will be long enough before we see it again ; time enough to forget about this."

He had been introduced into an unfamiliar life in joining me and had been surprised into continued excitements by the strange scenes which were going on around him. My surroundings were very much unlike the narrow space and placid uniformity of a man-of-war's deck, and to him the country seemed alive with unexpected occurrences. Though himself was not, his ideas were, very much at sea. He was full of admiration for my men and their singular fitness for the life they were leading. He shared my lodge, but this night his excitement would not let him sleep, and we remained long awake ; talking over the incidents of the day and speculating over what was to come in the events that seemed near at hand. Nor was there much sleeping in the camp that night, but nothing disturbed its quiet. No attack was made.

The night was clear and I obtained observations here which gave what may be assumed for the longitude of the outlet 121° 52′ 08″, and for its latitude 42° 41′ 30″. To this river I gave the name of my friend, Professor Torrey, who, with all the enthusiasm that goes with a true love of science, had aided me in determining the botany of the country.

The next day we moved late out of camp and travelled to the southward along the lake. I kept the ground well covered with scouts, know-ing the daring character of the Tlamaths. We made a short day's march and encamped in woods and built a corral. On the following day we con-tinued the march, still in the neighborhood of the lake, and in the evening made camp at its southeastern end, on a creek to which I gave the name of one of the Delaware, We-to-wah. Indians were seen frequently during the day. Observations placed the mouth of this creek in longitude 121° 41′ 23″, latitude 42° 21′ 43″. As had become usual we made a corral to secure the safety of the animals. This was our last camp on the lake. Here I turned away from our comrades whom I had left among the pines. But they were not neglected. When the Tlamaths tell the story of the night attack where they were killed, there will be no boasting. They will have to tell also of the death of their chief and of our swift retaliation; and how the people at the fishery had to mourn for the loss of their men and the destruction of their village. It will be a story for them to hand down while there are any Tlamaths on their lake.

The pines in these forests were mostly full-grown trees, and for many a year our log forts around the lake will endure, and other travellers may find refuge in them, or wonder, in the present quiet, what had once broken the silence of the forest. Making open spots in the woods where the sun-shine can rest longest, the trees that encircle them will be fuller-headed, and grass and flowers will be more luxuriant in the protection of their enclosure, so that they may long remain marked places.

The next day brought no unusual incident. On the day following I was travelling along a well-worn trail when I came upon a fresh scalp on an arrow which had been stuck up in the path. Maxwell and Archambeau were ahead, and in the evening they reported that riding along the trail they met an Indian who, on seeing them, laid down a bunch of young crows which he had in his hand, and forthwith and without parley let fly an arrow at Maxwell, who was foremost. He threw himself from his horse just in time to escape the arrow, which passed over the seat of his saddle, and, after a brief interchange of rifle-balls and arrows, the Indian was killed and his scalp put up in the trail to tell the story. We were getting rough-ened into Indian customs.

Our route was now among the hills over ground where we had already just travelled in going north and bordering the valley of the upper Sacra-mento, which, as I have said, was known to trappers under the name of Pitt River. The spring now gave its attraction and freshness to the whole region. The rolling surface of the hills was green up to the timbered ridges of the Cascade range which we were skirting along; but, above, the unconquerable peaks still were clothed with snow, and glittered cool in their solitary heights.

TLAMATH RIVER. ATTACK BY TLAMATHS.

CHAPTER XIV.

On one of these days, being hurried forward by rifle-shots ahead, we found Owens, with Stepp and Jacob, engaged with a party of Indians who had attacked them with as little ceremony as the Indian who had taken Maxwell for a mark. One of them was left behind when the others took to the thicker timber. These Indians deserve their reputation for daring, but their bravery is imprudent and uncalculating. Like tigers, their first spring is the dangerous one.

We were skirting still the wooded foot-hills of the great mountains, and, journeying along, had reached the head of a rocky, wooded ravine, down which a trail that we had been following led into a cañon. I was passing along its edge when a strong party of Indians suddenly issued from among the rocks and timber, and commenced an attack. They were promptly driven into cover of the wood and down the ravine into the brush, with a number wounded. One brave refused to be dislodged from behind a rock in the brush on the side of the ravine, from which he kept up a dangerous flight of arrows. He had spread his arrows on the ground and held some in his mouth, and drove back the men out of range for some moments, until Carson crept around to where he could get a good view of him and shot him through the heart. Carson gave the bow and arrows to Mr. Gillespie. The Indians had seemed bent on speeding their parting guest, but this was the last encounter we had with them.

Their ambush had been well laid. They had thought we would certainly follow the trail into the cañon, where, between their arrows and the rocks which they would have hurled down upon us, we would have had a *mauvais quart d'heure* and lost men as well as animals. But in a bad country I usually kept clear of such places, and in all this journey, except on the night at Denny's Creek, committed but one imprudence, which was in passing along the shore of the lake where a high, naked ridge, its face so literally strewed over with jagged fragments of rock as to be absolutely inaccessible from below, skirted the water for a number of miles. The Indians could have rained arrows and rock down upon us, and we could neither have got at them without great loss, nor got our animals out of the way. I breathed more freely when I was at the end of this pass, and felt mortified that I needed a lesson.

We were now approaching the rougher country into which breaks the point of the last link of the Sierra Nevada, and at nightfall encamped on its waters. We crossed the mountain upon a different line, nearer to the head of the lower Sacramento valley, and, descending, entered into a truly magnificent forest. It was composed mainly of a cypress and a lofty white cedar (*Thuya gigantea*) one hundred and twenty to one hundred and forty feet high, common in the mountains of California. All were massive trees, but the cypress was distinguished by its uniformly great bulk. None were seen so large as are to be found in the coast mountains near Santa Cruz, but there was a greater number of large trees—seven feet being a common diameter—carrying the bulk eighty or a hundred feet without a limb.

At an elevation of four thousand six hundred feet the temperature at sunset was 48° and at sunrise 37°. Oaks already appeared among the pines, but did not show a leaf. In the meadow-marshes of the forest grass was green, but not yet abundant, and the deer were poor. Descending the flanks of the mountain, which fell gradually toward the plain, the way was through the same deep forest. At the elevation of about three thousand feet the timber had become more open, the hills rolling, and many streams made pretty bottoms of rich grass ; the black oaks in full and beautiful leaf were thickly studded among the open pines, which had become much smaller and fewer in variety, and when we halted near midday, at an elevation of two thousand two hundred feet, we were in one of the most pleasant days of early spring, cool and sunny, with a pleasant breeze, amidst a profusion of flowers; many trees in dark summer foliage, and some still in bloom. Among these the white spikes of the horse-chestnut, common through all the oak regions, were conspicuous. We had again reached summer weather, and the temperature at noon was 70°. The plants we had left in bloom were now generally in seed, and many, including the characteristic plants, perfectly ripe.

In the afternoon we descended to the open valley of the Sacramento, one thousand feet lower, where the thermometer was 68° at sunset and 54° at sunrise. This was the best timbered region that I had seen, and was the more valuable from its position near the head of the valley of the lower Sacramento, and accessible from its waters.

On the 24th of May we reached again Lassen's, and in the evening I wrote to Senator Benton; a guarded letter, chiefly to call the attention of

Mr. Buchanan to the Indians among whom I had been travelling, especially to the fact that they were unfriendly to us but friendly to the English, by whom they were supplied with arms from a Hudson Bay's post on the Umpqua conveniently near to the coast. In the vague condition of affairs until the arrival of Commodore Sloat, my own movements depended upon circumstances and of them I could say but little.

SACRAMENTO RIVER (latitude 40°), May 24, 1846.

MY DEAR SIR : Most unexpectedly, and in a remote region of the Northern Mountains, I had the great pleasure to receive your letters. An express from Mr. Gillespie overtook me, the man being Neal, whom you will remember as having been left by me here in the last expedition. No other man here would have had the courage and resolution to follow us. I had the good fortune to save the lives of Mr. Gillespie and party from the Indians. In a charge at night by the Tlamath Indians I lost three men killed and had one dangerously wounded, being then with a detached party of fourteen men. You will regret to hear that among the killed was my old companion, Basil Lajeunesse. We afterwards fought the nation from one extremity to the other, and have ever since been fighting, until our entrance into the Lower Sacramento valley. I have but a faint hope that this note will reach you before I do; but the object for which I write is a pressing one, and therefore I make the experiment. The Tlamath Lake on our last map I find to be only an expansion of the river above, which passes by an outlet through a small range of mountains into a large body of water to the southward. This is the true Tlamath Lake, and the heart of the Tlamath nation. It is on the east side of a range of mountains (the Cascade). Directly west, and comparatively near at hand, is the Umpqua River. *Here the British have a post.* Why do they keep it there ? The fur trade will not justify it. If there is to be any war with England, it is of great importance that they should instantly be driven from this and similar posts before they furnish the Indians with firearms, and engage them in their service. These Indians are considered by the Willamette missionaries (who have been able to have only a slight knowledge of those on the north) as the most savage and warlike Indians on the continent. So said Mr. Lee. This post maintains an intercourse with the Tlamaths and other mountain Indians, and furnishes them with the tomahawks and iron arrow-heads with which they fought us. They are the bravest Indians we have ever seen ; our people (my camp, Carson, etc.) consider them far beyond the Blackfeet, who are by no means so daring. You know that the Indians along the line of the Columbia are well supplied with firearms, ammunition, and horses—hardly a man having less than forty or fifty of the latter—that they are brave, friendly to the British, and unfriendly to us. These things may be worthy of Mr. Buchanan's attention. Your letter led me to expect some communication from him, but I *received nothing*. I shall now proceed directly homewards, by the Colorado, but cannot arrive at the frontier until late in September. I saw a notice of your illness in the papers, and your letter relieved me of much anxiety. I trust that I will be able to force my way through this rough voyage, and find all well on the frontier. We certainly commenced our voyage when some malicious and inauspicious star was in the ascendant, for we find enemies and difficulty everywhere. I detain Mr. Gillespie's courier to write only to yourself ; believing, too, that when this reaches you I shall be near at hand. The letters from home have taken off half the length of the journey, and I have courage now for the rest.

> Very truly and respectfully,
> J. C. FRÉMONT.

The interest and conjecture following Lieutenant Gillespie's arrival at Sutter's, and his obtaining the services of Neal to aid him in overtaking me had spread over the valley, and I found the people anxiously waiting the result of his journey; and expecting so see me return with him. In the dearth of information and rumors of war, his coming was a significant event. I found myself welcomed.

Here in the lower valley of the Sacramento among the settlements I began to hear of the great change in the affairs of the country during my absence. Rumors of hostile proceedings on the part of the commanding general were current ; and the warning of Baron Gerolt made me now understand that the action of Castro against me was not merely a precautionary and isolated movement, but that it was Mexico against the United States.

From official records now in my possession I subjoin here the following resolutions adopted at a council of war held at Monterey on the 11th of April, consequent on the instructions which General Castro had received from the Home Government by the *Hannah :*

PREAMBLE AND RESOLUTIONS.

In the port of Monterey on the 11th day of April, one thousand eight hundred and forty-six, there met in the hall of the General Commandancia the officers of this garrison and other points of the Department, in unity with the Prefect of the District, for the purpose of proposing measures for security against the dangers which threaten the country. The Commanding General having shown the imminent risk of an invasion founded on the extravagant design of an American Captain of the United States Army, " Mr. N. (*sic*)

Frémont," which individual, although he has retired to the interior of the Department toward the North, we have, according to notices received, sufficient foundation to fear that his object is to strengthen and provide himself with a superior force, capable of making resistance and carrying forward his views—which he has not thought proper to disclose, either at the time he found himself sufficiently prepared on the mountain of the Gavilan, or since. From the latter place he sent a letter to the American Consul, in which he did not wish to explain himself for fear of a discovery. All this gives good foundation for suspicion which obliges this General Commandancia to keep in view the interest of the northern frontiers.

I likewise inform you that by the means of the Commissioner, Don Andres Castillero, application has been made to the Supreme Government for prompt assistance, but notwithstanding whatever confidence we may have in the energy and efficaciousness of the Supreme Government, or in the zeal and activity of the Commissioner, I believe it indispensable in the meantime to take such provisional steps as may be necessary so far as to defend the northern frontiers from the imminent dangers which threaten them, and by this means save the National integrity. I likewise submit an invitation I received from his Excellency, the Governor of the Department, in which his Excellency invites an interview in Santa Barbara. I conclude by expressing my wish that each and every person in this junta will express his opinion, and hope that through his patriotic deliberations, his prudence, and his judgment which he owes to his country in this dangerous crisis, and that we shall have the advantage of his advice in taking the following timely foresighted indications, such as that of guarding the Northern points, establishing general quarters in Santa Clara, the same being the resolution indicated to the Supreme Government.

Each person having in succession pledged himself the junta after a long discussion determined on the following:

ARTICLE 1st.—That, with the distressing situation of the Department in view, and until the danger of the invasion which threatens is past, the presence of the Commanding General is indispensably necessary in the Northern points; these being the points most threatened by the enemy, and the only ones where the danger is positive, consequently they must have the preference of being first attended, fortified, and covered.

2. That this shall be laid before his Excellency, the Governor, inviting him to come to this Port, that by his presence and co-operation the necessary assistance may be more efficaciously resorted to for the salvation of the Department, and the integrity of the Nation.

3. That if, against all probability, his Excellency should not find it convenient to comply with this invitation, the Commanding General may proceed with the most just and best regulated measures, establishing general quar-

ters in Santa Clara; this being the most convenient point for military operations, as being the nearest in contact with the Northern points. The
General, being in good understanding with the Superior authorities of the
District and their subalterns, on whose well-disposed and patriotic sentiments
he may rely, will find sufficient force for the present defence of the territory.

4. The propositions made and determined on in the foregoing article will
stand good, until we obtain from the Supreme Government its resolutions
and assistance by the aforesaid Captain Andres Castillero, and solicited by
the principal authorities of these ports.

5. There shall be made an act of these presents signed by the Commanding General and all the individuals of the junta by him accepted; there shall
be one copy remitted to the Supreme Government; another to his Excellency, the Governor of the Department, and the original shall remain in
the archives of the Commandancia General.

(Signed)   COL. M. G. VALLEJO.
LIEUT-COL. V. PRUDON.
COMD'G GEN'L JOSÉ CASTRO.
COL. JUAN B. ALVARADO.
JOSÉ ANTONIO CARILLO, *Comdte de Esquadra.*
CAPT. MANUEL CASTRO, *Prefect.*

Remaining two days at Lassen's, I moved on to Neal's rancho. During
my stay here neighboring settlers came to my camp bringing me information that the Indians of the valley were leaving their *rancherias* and taking
to the mountains; a movement which indicated preparations for active hostility. Shortly after my arrival a courier arrived from Captain Sutter bringing me from him a message to warn me that two Californians had been sent
by General Castro amongst the different Indian tribes to raise them against
the settlers, and that it was with this intention that they had taken to the
mountains.

Other reports received here confirmed this information; the Indians of
the valley near by having taken to the mountains and on their way killed an
Indian boy employed on the rancho who had refused to follow them. The
settlers who had now learned of my arrival in the valley, men with their
families, came in appealing to me to give them protection. Looking upon
these people and knowing the hardships and dangers of the long road they
had travelled to reach this country, I remembered the barbarities of Indians,
some of which I had seen, and towards women so cruel that I could not
put them upon paper. An Indian let loose is of all animals the most savage.
He has an imagination for devilment that seems peculiar to him, and a
singular delight in inflicting suffering. I had once come upon a scene
where a band of savages had had their own way—no relief could come,

as they thought—the men had been killed and mutilated—the women, pinned to the ground by stakes driven through their bodies, while yet alive.

Bearing these in mind I resolved that there should be no such scenes here—no more men skinned alive—no more women impaled—and I told the men to take their families home and have them rest in quiet; I would take charge of the Indians and they might surely rely on me not to leave the valley while there was any danger. Thenceforward I kept careful watch over the Indians and their instigators.

The following *Banda* or proclamation issued on the 30th of April had increased the alarm created by the movements of the Indians:

" Being informed that a multitude of foreigners abusing our local circumstances without having come with the requisites provided by law, are residing in the district, and that many of them who should not be admitted into this country, have made themselves owners of real property, this being a right belonging only to citizens;

" I have concluded to instruct all the Judges having towns under their (respective) charge, that they cannot, without incurring great responsibility, permit or authorize any sale or cession whatever of land, or of said class of property, outside of established regulations and in favor of Mexican citizens; advising those foreigners that are not naturalized and legally introduced that whatever purchase or acquisition they may make will be null and void; and that they will be subject, unless they retire voluntarily from the country, to be expelled from it whenever the Government may find it convenient.

" GOD AND LIBERTY.

" MONTEREY, April 30, 1846."

" The foregoing order was forwarded by Don Manuel Castro, Prefect of Monterey, to his Sub-Prefect in San Francisco, and transmitted by the latter to the U. S. Vice-Consul at that port, Leidesdorf, to be by him made known to the American settlers."

The condition of affairs was getting serious. The California authorities were evidently reaching out into the Sacramento valley. There was enough to satisfy us that we would soon be called upon to meet their measures, and meantime it was prudent to prepare. Rumor indicated that they intended to make use of the Indians ; who were, as we have told, numerous throughout the valleys of the Sacramento and San Joaquin.

After consulting together it was therefore decided that Mr. Gillespie should go down to the Bay of San Francisco with a requisition upon Commander Montgomery, who was then lying at the anchorage of Yerba Buena, with the sloop of war *Portsmouth;* and that, obtaining our needed supplies from the ship's stores, he should acquaint him, so far as he felt authorized, with our instructions and probable movements.

The following was the requisition made upon him for the few things absolutely essential to the health and comfort of the camp.

By this time the usual camp supplies of provisions had been exhausted. Beef we could get, but we had long been without bread and there was not salt for the meat.

REQUISITION.

LASSEN'S RANCHO, SACRAMENTO RIVER, May 25, 1846.

SIR : There is required for the support of the exploring party under my command, at present almost entirely destitute, the following amount of supplies with which I respectfully request that I may be furnished from the public stores.

The unfriendly disposition of this Government in the present doubtful position of affairs, has made it very difficult for me to obtain provisions, in any case only to be had at very exorbitant prices; and to obtain them from our Squadron would materially aid the surveys with which I am charged and very much expedite my return to the States.

Lead (American rifle)	300 lbs.
Powder	1 keg.
Percussion Caps	8000
Russia Duck	25 yds.
Flour	5 bbls.
Sugar	600 lbs.
Coffee, Tea	
Pork	1 bbl.
Medicines (common cases, emetics, purges, fevers and agues, etc.)	
Soap	1 box.
Salt	1 sack.
Tobacco	300 lbs.
Half-inch rope for tent	30 Faths.
Iron for Horseshoes	

Very respectfully, sir, your obedient servant,

(Signed)   J. C. FRÉMONT,

Bt. Capt. U. S. Topl. Engineers.

LIEUTENANT ARCHIBALD GILLESPIE,

U. S. Marine Corps, Sacramento River.

LIEUTENANT GILLESPIE'S LETTER WITH REQUISITION.

YERBA BUENA, June 9, 1846.

SIR: Herewith I have the honor to enclose a Requisition for supplies, made upon me by Capt. Frémont, of United States Topographical Engi-

UPPER SACRAMENTO HILLS.

neers, who is in command of a party of some fifty men, engaged upon an important Scientific Expedition.

You will perceive that Capt. Frémont states " his party to be nearly destitute, and under the unfriendly feeling of the Government of this country, in the existing position of affairs, he is unable to obtain supplies; and, in any case, only at very exorbitant prices." From the above-mentioned circumstances, I am induced to enclose this requisition, and respectfully request you to supply the same or such parts of it as you may be able to spare; being fully assured it will afford you great pleasure to render assistance to a different arm of the Service, engaged upon a laborious and dangerous expedition, exposed to every kind of danger and the greatest hardships men can endure; oftentimes living upon horseflesh, and at times without any provisions whatever.

Capt. Frémont is also in want of funds for the purchase of animals, as, upon leaving for the United States, it will be necessary for him to purchase more horses, his present supply being travel-worn and almost unfit for the saddle.

The exorbitant rate at which the Government Bills are exchanged induce me to beg you to supply Capt. Frémont with fifteen hundred dollars ($1500), if the same can be furnished without injury to your own particular service; for which he will give the necessary receipts or bills upon the Department. For these supplies and any others he may receive, Capt. Frémont will make due settlement upon his arrival at Headquarters, Washton City.

Capt. Frémont is now encamped on the Sacramento, at the mouth of the Feather River, where he awaits my return with such provisions as I may be able to obtain.

Hoping you will be able to make the supply, I will only add that, in the event of the party receiving from you the assistance requested, you may be assured the same will not only be highly appreciated by the President and Departments, confer an obligation upon Capt. Frémont and myself, but will receive the heartfelt thanks of a party of some of the bravest and most determined men, who are happy in suffering privations while serving their country with a zeal and fidelity unsurpassed by any other.

I am, sir, very respectfully, your obedient servant,

(Signed)   ARCHIE H. GILLESPIE,
1st Lieut. U. S. M. Corps, and Special and Confidential Agent for California.

To JNO. B. MONTGOMERY, ESQ., *Commanding U. S. Ship Portsmouth, Sausalito, Bay of San Francisco.*

Lieut. Gillespie left my party on the 28th of May and on the following day left Cordua's rancho for Sutter's Fort, going down the Sacramento by canoe.

Neal, who had been on a visit to the coast settlements, returned in company with Mr. Samuel Hensley, of Missouri, who was now one of the leading American Settlers. From him I learned that recently, at Yerba Buena, he had met with General Guadalupe Vallejo, who was in command of the northern district of the Department, and one of the most influential men of upper California. The General had informed him that recently he had attended a convention composed of General Castro, himself, and five others, delegates from the different districts in California, at which the proposition to separate from Mexico and establish an independent government under the protection of a foreign power had been debated; but that the majority in the convention was not in favor of placing the country under the protection of the United States.

Mr. Hensley had returned to Sutter's Fort in a few days after the conversation with General Vallejo. He had there learned from Captain Sutter that there was great excitement among the Indians in the neighborhood and that he had just sent for the Cosumné chief, who had recently returned from the California settlements on the coast. Mr. Hensley waited for the chief, who, on his coming, was examined by Captain Sutter, as the Alcaldé and Magistrate of the District. The chief stated that he had seen General Castro during his visit to the settlements, and that he had received from Castro promise of great reward on condition that he would excite the Indians to burn the wheat crops of the American settlers whom Castro was preparing to drive out of the country.

Learning of my return into the valley, Hensley had come immediately to me with this and other information which he had gathered concerning the designs of the leading men among the Californians. His conviction was that the American residents would have to leave the country or fight for the homes which they had made.

Neal made a similar report about the condition of the country. The growing hostility of the Californian authorities towards Americans and the insecurity in which these found themselves placed is shown by the following letter. This letter sets out that arbitrary and flagrant abuses of authority, and denial of just attention to their representations, and to their proofs of ill treatment by Mexicans, had brought affairs to such a condition that they petition for the presence of an American man-of-war in the harbor of Yerba Buena ; they declare " that the situation of all foreign residents at this place is extremely insecure and precarious ; and that the immediate presence of an American vessel of war is absolutely needed." The signatures comprise all the best names of business men, of ship-captains, and of both the English and American vice-consuls, Forbes and Leidesdorf.

This was October 15, 1845 ; nearly half a year before I was made a pretext by Castro. The enmity and injuries to foreigners were already existing facts, and in keeping with the special orders of the Home Government against me by the *Hannah*.

MEMORIAL OF AMERICAN RESIDENTS.

To the Commander of the United States ship *Levant* or any other United States vessel of war, this memorial of the masters and supercargoes of the American vessels, citizens of the United States, and other foreign residents at the port of San Francisco, Upper California, respectfully showeth:

That on the night of the 11th of October, 1845, Captain Elliot Libbey, of the American barque *Tasso*, now lying at anchor in this port, was assaulted on the public street of the town of Yerba Buena by a party of armed natives of this country, and after being grievously wounded by sundry stabs in his body, a dreadful gash upon his head and divers other bruises about his face and body, was left on the street weltering in his blood.

That the perpetrators of this outrage were recognized and complaint made in form to the local authority by Henry Mellus, Esq., supercargo of the barque *Tasso ;* who received an official answer that judicial proceedings had been instituted against those individuals ; which of course implied that those offenders had been placed separately in confinement to await their trial, even according to the laws of this country.

That it is a notorious fact that all the individuals who co-operated in the assault upon Captain Libbey have been entirely at liberty, and still continue so, walking about the streets of this town and pursuing their customary avocations at their residences on the neighboring farms and Mission.

That the repeated arbitrary and flagrant abuses of the power vested in the Sub-Prefect of the Second District of this Department and the indifference with which the Departmental Executive has viewed these abuses, particularly with respect to foreigners, have led to the barbarous treatment of Captain Libbey. For the perpetrators thereof declared before witnesses on the spot, that they only acted in conformity to orders they had received from the Sub-Prefect. And he having arrogated to himself the right to authorize the appearance of an armed mob under the pretext of their being a patrol, violated the very laws that he has sworn to enforce and respect. And in consequence he should be held responsible for such violation.

That the proper authority in whom resides the power to establish patrols or any armed person whatever, and to designate their duty, is the Military Commandant, who solemnly denies ever having received any communication relative to ordering out any patrol on the night Captain Libbey was assaulted or of having been aware of that outrage, until the fact was made known to him by an eyewitness.

That Mr. Nathan Spear, a citizen of the United States of America, and for a number of years a resident of this country, was also assaulted by the same party that wounded Captain Libbey, and received from them several severe contusions upon the head and shoulders, causing him grievous injury, having only escaped being murdered by a precipitate flight.

That your memorialists are aware that in cases of this kind they should have recourse to the local authorities. This has been already done in another cause of complaint some two months since, but without effect. And now these authorities sanction by a tacit consent the infamous proceedings of these lawless people and thereby become accessories. The persons who attempted to assassinate Messrs. Libbey and Spear are not even arrested, but on the contrary are applauded by their companions for their valor. And their next act may be to murder some supercargo or seize some of the American vessels lying here, under the plea that they are enemies. Your memorialists do not hesitate to declare, that the situation of all foreign residents at this place is extremely insecure and precarious ; and that the immediate presence of an American vessel of war in this port is absolutely necessary to inspire a salutary terror into the authorities ; and to compel them to render justice according to their own laws, for the barbarous treatment received by Messrs. Libbey and Spear.

Your memorialists, therefore, respectfully request that you will be pleased to take their case under your serious consideration.

And your memorialists will ever pray, etc.

Yerba Buena, San Francisco Upper California, 15th October, 1845.

(Signed)   HENRY MELLUS.   NATHAN SPEAR.
            T. C. EVERETT.   WILLIAM S. HINCKLEY.
            JOSEPH P. THOMPSON.   ELIAB GRIMES.
            JOHN WILSON.   JAMES ALEX. FORBES.
            JAMES ORBELL.   WM. A. LEIDESDORFF.
            G. H. NYE.   MIGUEL DE PEDRORENA.
            A. B. THOMPSON.   ROBERT S. RIDLE.
            WILLIAM FISHER.

My geographical work in the valley had been finished, and having nothing more to do than observe the changes made in the face of the country by the progress of the seasons, I had abundant time to think over the political situation and to settle upon the course to pursue. I clearly saw that my proper course was to observe quietly the progress of affairs and take advantage of any contingency which I could turn in favor of the United States, and, where uncertainties arose, to give my own country the benefit of any doubts by taking decided action.

Leaving Lassen's and travelling south into a more open and wider part

THE BUTTES. SACRAMENTO VALLEY.

SIERRA NEVADA IN THE DISTANCE

of the valley, where the bordering mountains are low and showed less snow, the temperature increased rapidly.

Hensley and Neal left the rancho at the same time with my party; their object being to notify the American settlers in the valley to meet and take measures for the common safety.

My camp, wherever it might be, was appointed the place of meeting. I commissioned Hensley to visit Dr. Marsh, an American living on the southern side of the bay. He was a man of marked intelligence and sagacity; favorable to American interests and likely to be well informed of any intended movement by the Californian authorities.

On the 29th we encamped on Bear River. Among the settlers was a man named Ezekiel Merritt. He was tall and spare, what I understand by "rawboned;" a rugged man, fearless and simple; taking delight in incurring risks, but tractable and not given to asking questions when there was something he was required to do. Merritt was my Field-Lieutenant among the settlers.

Information was brought in that a band of horses had been gathered for Castro in Sonoma, and were then on their way to his camp. These were intercepted by Merritt, the guard and vaqueros dispersed, and the horses brought to my camp.

Looking over the field I saw that prompt precautionary measures were necessary in order to avail myself of such advantages as my position offered. Acting upon this necessity I sent Merritt into Sonoma instructed to surprise the garrison at that place.

On the 30th we encamped at the " Buttes of Sacramento." This is an isolated mountain ridge about six miles long, and at the summit about 2690 feet above the sea. At our encampment on a small run at the southeastern base we were about eight hundred feet above the sea. The mornings here were pleasantly cool for a few hours, but before ten the heat of the sun became very great, usually tempered by a refreshing breeze. Our camp was in one of the warmest situations of the Sacramento Valley. The summer winds being steadily from the northwest, this block of mountains entirely intercepted them. We felt the heat here more sensibly than at any other place to which our journeying brought us in California. The hunters always left the camp before daylight, and were in by nine o'clock, after which the sun grew hot. Game was very fat and abundant; upwards of eighty deer, elk, and bear were killed in one morning. This country was a perpetual delight to the Delawares. Its wonderful abundance of game, always in fine condition, and its comfortable climate, with everywhere water and wood and grass, giving the hunter a good camp wherever night might overtake him, kept them constantly happy. If they could have been suddenly transported into it they might have thought that they had

OLD CUSTOM HOUSE, MONTEREY, CAL.

died and awakened in the happy hunting grounds.   It was a lovely camp for the animals; the range consisted of excellent grasses, wild oats in fields, red and other varieties of clover, some of which were now in mature seed and others beginning to flower.   Oats were already drying in level places where exposed to the full influence of the sun, remaining green in moister places and on the hill-slopes.

At this point I established the last main point for longitude, making observations of moon culminations on the 4th and 5th of June.   These gave for the longitude 121° 38' 04".   The latitude was 39° 12' 03".

During our stay at the Buttes, camp was moved to a small run or spring at the northeastern base in longitude 121° 33' 36", latitude 39° 14' 41".   I give the position of both these points because they were the last astronomical observations made during this journey.

Here terminated the geographical work of the expedition.   We remained at the Buttes until the 8th of June, during which time the mean temperature was 64° at sunrise, 79° at 9 in the morning, 86° at noon, 90° at 2 P.M., 91° at 4, and 80° at sunset; ranging from 50° to 79° at sunrise, from 85° to 98° at 4 P.M., and from 73° to 89° at sunset.

The longitudes established on the line of this journey are based on a series of astronomical observations resting on the four positions, determined by lunar culminations.   The position established here was the last of the four.   This line of astronomical observations, thus carried across the continent, reaches the Pacific Ocean on the northern shore of the Bay of Monterey.

The first of these main positions is at the mouth of the *Fontaine qui Bouit* River, on the upper Arkansas; the second is on the eastern shore of the Great Salt Lake ; and two in the valley of the Sacramento.   Later, on my return to Washington when these observations were calculated, it was found that they carried the coast valleys of the Sacramento and San Joaquin about twenty miles east, and the line of the coast about fourteen miles west of their positions on the maps and charts in general use ; giving an increase of more than thirty miles in the breadth of the country below the Sierra Nevada.   Upon examination it was found that my positions agreed, nearly, with the observations of Captain Beechey at Monterey.   The corrections required by the new positions were then accordingly made; the basin of the Sacramento and the San Joaquin valleys was moved to the eastward, and the line of the coast was placed farther west, conformable to my observations, retaining the configurations given to it by the surveys of Vancouver.

When the United States sloop of war *Portsmouth*, Commander Montgomery, reached Boston in February of 1848, on her return from the Pacific Ocean, she brought the information that an American whale-ship had been recently lost on the coast of California in consequence of errors in the charts then in general use, locating the coast and islands, from Monterey south, too far east.*

The observations made by me across the continent in this expedition were calculated by Prof. Hubbard, then of the National Observatory in Washington City, during the winter of 1847–48; and a note from him on the subject of these observations will be added in the concluding chapter of this volume.

While interested in examining into the true position of the coast of California I found it worthy of notice that the position given to it on the charts of the old Spanish navigators agrees nearly with that which would be assigned to it by the observations of the most eminent naval surveyors of our time. The position which I have adopted for Monterey and the adjacent coast agrees nearly with that in which it had been placed by Malespina, in 1791.

Of this skilful, intrepid, and unfortunate navigator, Humboldt in his essay on " New Spain " says: " The peculiar merit of his expedition consists not only in the number of astronomical observations, but principally in the judicious method which was employed to arrive at certain results. The latitude and longitude of four points on the coast, Cape San Lucas, Monterey, Nootka, and Fort Mulgrave, were fixed in an absolute manner."

In closing up the geographical work which was proposed by this exploration I think it well to give a condensed view of the leading features of California as I saw it at the time of which I am writing; and for the reason that an examination of the face of the country and the connection of the interior with the coast country through the barriers of its mountains was one of the chief objects of the expedition.

BAY OF SAN FRANCISCO AND DEPENDENT COUNTRY.

The Bay of San Francisco has been celebrated, from the time of its first discovery, as one of the finest in the world, and is justly entitled to that character even under the seamen's view of a mere harbor. But when all the accessory advantages which belong to it—fertile and picturesque dependent country; mildness and salubrity of climate; connection with the great interior valley of the Sacramento and San Joaquin; its vast resources for ship timber, grain and cattle—when these advantages are taken into the account,

---

* " NAVAL.—The United States sloop of war *Portsmouth*, Commander John B. Montgomery, arrived at Boston on Friday, from the Pacific Ocean, last from Valparaiso, February 23d. Commander Montgomery states that the British frigate *Herald*, and the brig *Pandora*, are engaged in making a new survey of the gulf and coast of California.

" The whale-ship *Hope*, of Providence, was recently lost on the coast, in consequence of an error in the charts now in general use, which locate the coast and islands from Monterey to Cape St. Lucas from fifteen to forty miles too far to the eastward."—*National Intelligencer.*

with its geographical position on the line with Asia, it rises into an importance far above that of a mere harbor, and deserves a particular notice in any account of maritime California. Its latitudinal position is that of Lisbon; its climate is that of southern Italy; settlements upon it for more than half a century attest its healthfulness; bold shores and mountains give it grandeur; the extent and fertility of its dependent country give it great resources for agriculture, commerce, and population.

The Bay of San Francisco is separated by the sea by low mountain ranges. Looking from the peaks of the Sierra Nevada, the coast mountains present an apparently continuous line, with only a single gap, resembling a mountain pass. This is the entrance to the great bay, and is the only water communication from the coast to the interior country. Approaching from the sea, the coast presents a bold outline. On the south, the bordering mountains come down in a narrow ridge of broken hills, terminating in a precipitous point, against which the sea breaks heavily. On the northern side, the mountain presents a bold promontory, rising in a few miles to a height of two or three thousand feet. Between these points is the strait —about one mile broad in the narrowest part, and five miles long from the sea to the bay. To this Gate I gave the name of *Chrysopylæ*, or GOLDEN GATE; for the same reasons that the harbor of Byzantium (Constantinople afterwards), was called *Chrysoceras*, or GOLDEN HORN.* Passing through this gate, the bay opens to the right and left, extending in each direction about thirty-five miles, having a total length of more than seventy, and a coast of about two hundred and seventy-five miles. It is divided, by straits and projecting points, into three separate bays, of which the northern two are called San Pablo and Suisoon Bays. Within, the view presented is of a mountainous country, the bay resembling an interior lake of deep water, lying between parallel ranges of mountains. Islands, which have the bold character of the shores—some mere masses of rock, and others grass-covered, rising to the height of three and eight hundred feet—break its surface, and add to its picturesque appearance. Directly fronting the entrance, mountains a few miles from the shore rise about two thousand feet above the water, crowned by a forest of lofty cypress, which is visible from the sea, and makes a conspicuous landmark for vessels entering the bay. Behind, the rugged peak of Mount Diavolo, nearly four thousand feet high (three thousand seven hundred and seventy), overlooks the sur-

---

* NOTE.—The form of the harbor and its advantages for commerce, and that before it became an entrepot of Eastern commerce, suggested the name to the Greek founders of Byzantium. The form of the entrance into the Bay of San Francisco and its advantages for commerce, Asiatic inclusive, suggested to me the name which I gave to this entrance and which I put upon the map that accompanied a geographical Memoir addressed to the Senate of the United States in June, 1848.

rounding country of the bay and San Joaquin. The immediate shore of the bay derives, from its proximate and opposite relation to the sea, the name of *Contra-costa* (counter-coast, or opposite coast). It presents a varied character of rugged and broken hills, rolling and undulating land, and rich alluvial shores backed by fertile and wooded ranges, suitable for towns, villages, and farms, with which it is beginning to be dotted. A low alluvial-bottom land, several miles in breadth, with occasional open woods of oak, borders the foot of the mountains around the southern arm of the bay, terminating on a breadth of twenty miles in the fertile valley of San José, a narrow plain of rich soil, lying between ranges from two to three thousand feet high. The valley is openly wooded with groves of oak, free from underbrush, and after the spring rains covered with grass. Taken in connection with the valley of San Juan, with which it forms a continuous plain, it is fifty-five miles long and one to twenty broad, opening into smaller valleys among the hills. At the head of the bay it is twenty miles broad; and about the same at the southern end, where the soil is beautifully fertile, covered in summer with four or five varieties of wild clover, several feet high. In many places it is overgrown with wild mustard, growing ten or twelve feet high, in almost impenetrable fields, through which roads are made like lanes. On both sides the mountains are fertile, wooded, or covered with grasses and scattered trees. On the west it is protected from the chilling influence of the northwest winds by the *Cuesta de los Gatos* (wild-cat ridge) which separates it from the coast. This is a grassy and timbered mountain, watered with small streams, and wooded on both sides with many varieties of trees and shrubbery, the heaviest forests of pine and cypress occupying the western slope. Timber and shingles are now obtained from this mountain; and one of the recently discovered quicksilver mines is on the eastern side of the mountain, near the Pueblo of San José. This range terminates on the south in the *Anno Nuevo* point of Monterey Bay, and on the north declines into a ridge of broken hills about five miles wide, between the bay and the sea, and having the town of San Francisco on the bay shore, near its northern extremity.

Sheltered from the cold winds and fogs of the sea, and having a soil of remarkable fertility, the valley of San José is capable of producing in great perfection many fruits and grains which do not thrive on the coast in its immediate vicinity. Without taking into consideration the extraordinary yields which have sometimes occurred, the fair average product of wheat is estimated at fifty fold, or fifty for one sown. The mission establishments of Santa Clara and San José, in the north end of the valley, were formerly, in the prosperous days of the missions, distinguished for the superiority of their wheat crops.

The slope of alluvial land continues entirely around the eastern shore of the bay, intersected by small streams, and offering some points which good landing and deep water, with advantageous positions between the sea and interior country, indicate for future settlement.

The strait of *Carquines*, about one mile wide and eight or ten fathoms deep, connects the San Pablo and Suisoon Bays.   Around these bays smaller valleys open into the bordering country, and some of the streams have a short launch navigation, which serves to convey produce to the bay.   Missions and large farms were established at the head of navigation on these streams, which are favorable sites for towns or villages.   The country around the Suisoon Bay presents smooth, low ridges and rounded hills, clothed with wild oats, and more or less openly wooded on their summits.   Approaching its northern shores from *Sonoma* it assumes, though in a state of nature, a cultivated appearance.   Wild oats cover it in continuous fields, and herds of cattle and bands of horses are scattered over low hills and partly isolated ridges, where blue mists and openings among the abruptly terminating hills indicate the neighborhood of the bay.

The Suisoon is connected with an expansion of the river formed by the junction of the Sacramento and the San Joaquin, which enter San Francisco Bay in the same latitude, nearly, as the mouth of the Tagus at Lisbon. A delta of twenty-five miles in length, divided into islands by deep channels, connects the bay with the valley of the San Joaquin and Sacramento, into the mouths of which the tide flows, and which enter the bay together as one river.

Such is the bay, and the proximate country and shores of the bay of San Francisco.   It is not a mere indentation of the coast, but a little sea to itself, connected with the ocean by a defensible gate, opening out between seventy and eighty miles to the right and left, upon a breadth of ten to fifteen, deep enough for the largest ships, with bold shores suitable for towns and settlements, and fertile adjacent country for cultivation.   The head of the bay is about forty miles from the sea, and there commences its connection with the noble valleys of San Joaquin and Sacramento.

WESTERN SLOPE OF THE SIERRA NEVADA.

The western flank of this Sierra belongs to the maritime region of California, and is capable of adding greatly to its value.   It is a long, wide slope, timbered and grassy, with intervals of arable land, copiously watered with numerous and bold streams, and without the cold which its name and altitude might imply.   In length it is the whole extent of the long valley at its base, five hundred miles.   In breadth, if is from forty to seventy miles from the summit of the mountain to the termination of the foot-hills in the edge of the valleys below, and almost the whole of it available for some useful purpose—timber, pasturage, some arable land, mills, quarries—and so situated as to be convenient for use, the wide slope of the mountain being of easy descent. Timber holds the first place in the advantages of this slope, the whole being heavily wooded, first with oaks, which predominate to about half the elevation of the mountain; and then with pines, cypress, and cedars, the pines predominating; and hence, called the pine region, as that below is called the oak region, though mixed with other trees. The highest summits of the Sierra are naked, massive granite rock, covered with snow, in sheltered places, all the year round. The oaks are several varieties of white and black oak, and evergreens, some of them resembling live oak. Of the white oak there are some new species, attaining a handsome eleva- tion, upon a stem six feet in diameter. Acorns of uncommon size, and not bad taste, used regularly for food by the Indians, abound on these trees, and will be of great value for stock. The cypress, pine, and cedar are betweeu one hundred and two hundred and fifty feet high, and five to twelve feet in diameter, with clean solid stems. Grass abounds on almost all parts of the slope; except towards the highest summits, and is fresh and green all the year round, being neither killed by cold in the winter, nor dried by want of rain in the summer. The foot-hills of the slope are sufficiently fertile and gentle to admit of good settlements; while coves, benches, and mead- ows of arable land are found throughout. Many of the mountain streams, some of them amounting to considerable rivers, which flow down the mountain-side, make handsome, fertile valleys. All these streams furnish good water-power. The climate in the lower part of the slope is that of constant spring, while above, the cold is not in proportion to the elevation. Such is the general view of the western slope of the great Sierra.

COAST COUNTRY NORTH OF THE BAY OF SAN FRANCISCO.

Between the Sacramento valley and the coast, north of the bay of San Francisco, the country is broken into mountain ridges and rolling hills, with many very fertile valleys, made by lakes and small streams. In the interior it is wooded, generally with oak, and immediately along the coast presents open prairie lands, among heavily-timbered forests, having a greater variety of trees, and occasionally a larger growth than the timbered region of the Sierra Nevada. In some parts it is entirely covered, in areas of many miles, with a close growth of wild oats, to the exclusion of almost every other plant. In the latter part of June and beginning of July, we found here a cli- mate sensibly different from that of the Sacramento valley, a few miles east, being much cooler and moister. In clear weather, the mornings were like those of the Rocky Mountains in August, pleasant and cool, following cold, clear nights. In that part lying nearer the coast, we found the mornings sometimes cold, accompanied with chilling winds; and fogs frequently came rolling up over the ridges from the sea. These sometimes rose at evening, and continued until noon of the next day. They are not dry, but wet mists, leaving the face of the country covered as by a drizzling rain. This sometimes causes rust in wheat grown within its influence, but vegetables flourish and attain extraordinary size.

I learned from Captain Smith, a resident at Bodega, that the winter months make a delightful season—rainy days (generally of warm showers) alternating with mild and calm, pleasant weather, and pure, bright skies— much preferable to the summer, when the fogs and strong northwest winds, which prevail during the greater part of the year, make the morning part of the day disagreeably cold.

Owing probably to the fogs, spring is earlier along the coast than in the interior, where, during the interval between the rains, the ground becomes very dry. Flowers bloom in December, and by the beginning of February grass acquires a strong and luxuriant growth, and fruit trees, peach, pear, apple, etc., are covered with blossoms. In situations immediately open to the sea the fruit ripens late, generally at the end of August, being retarded by the chilling influence of the northwest winds; a short distance inland, where intervening ridges obstruct these winds and shelter the face of the country, there is a different climate and a remarkable difference in the time of ripening fruits; the heat of the sun has full influence on the soil, and vegetation goes rapidly to perfection.

The country in July began to present the dry appearance common to all California as the summer advances, except along the northern coast within the influence of the fogs, or where the land is sheltered by forests, and in the moist valleys of streams and coves of the hills. In some of these was an uncommonly luxuriant growth of oats, still partially green, while elsewhere they were dried up; the face of the country presenting generally a mellowed and ripened appearance, and the small streams beginning to lose their volume, and draw up into the hills.

This northern part of the coast country is heavily timbered, more so as it goes north to the Oregon boundary (42°), with many bold streams falling directly into the sea.

My camp at the Buttes became a rendezvous for the settlers, and a centre of information for me and of confidence for them. It was evident from movements of the Indians that the rumored attack on the settlers was certainly intended, and all signs indicated that the time for it was at hand. The wheat throughout the valley was now dry and ready for the harvest or the torch.

Keeping in mind my promise to the settlers, and being now about to move towards Sutter's Fort, where I intended to occupy a more central position, I thought that the time for me too had come. I resolved to anticipate the Indians and strike them a blow which would make them recognize that Castro was far and that I was near. And I judged it expedient to take such precautionary measures as in my forward movement would leave no enemy behind to destroy the strength of my position by cutting off my supply in cattle and break communication with the incoming emigrants.

Accordingly, early in the morning I moved quietly out of camp with the greater number of men, taking the right or western bank of the Sacramento.

In describing the lower division of this river I have already mentioned the many *rancherias* towards the head of its valley. Some of the largest were scattered along the right bank of the river, where fish and the abundant acorn-bearing trees made a preferred ground. These numbered more men than the smaller *rancherias* which lay farther out in the valley and among the hills.

My movement was unexpected, and riding rapidly up the river we reached without discovery the first rancheria among the hostiles. The scouts who had been sent forward reported the Indians with feathers on their heads, and faces painted black, their war color; and in the midst of their war ceremonies.

Intending to surprise and scatter them we rode directly upon them, and at this place several Indians were killed in the dispersion. In the panic made by our sudden charge the Indians jumped into and swam the river, a few escaping into shelter on our side of the river.

With scarcely a halt we rode on towards the other *rancherias*, but the news of our attack apparently reached these as soon as ourselves, for the Indians were escaping from their villages as we rode in among them. Before the close of the day nearly all the *rancherias* had been visited and the Indians dispersed; as we rode down the hill which commanded a view of the river-plain, on which stood the farthest village that we reached, we could see the Indians in commotion, some running off from the river and others jumping into it. When we reached the rancheria the water was dotted with the heads of the Indians swimming across. We had surprised them assembled in the height of their war ceremonies.

This put an end to the intended attack upon the whites. The Indians of the California Valley had their fixed places of habitation where they lived. The tribes on one river were rarely friendly to those on another. They knew that I came from the mountains, so that they could not take refuge there. That if I should drive them into the upper valley they would encounter hostile tribes, who would destroy them. So that with the return to their villages the dread of another visitation would keep them on their good behavior.

This was a rude but necessary measure to prevent injury to the whites. And it had the effect which I intended.

While encamped at the Buttes I received by the hand of Neal the following letter from Captain Montgomery:

U. S. Ship Portsmouth,
Bay of San Francisco, June 3, 1846.

Sir : On the 31st ulto., the day previous to my sailing from Monterey, a courier from Lieut. Gillespie to the U. S. Consul arrived bringing the only definite intelligence of your movements and position since my arrival at that port on the 22d of April last.   The instructions under which I am now serving and which may detain me until late in the fall, or longer, upon this coast, have relation specifically to the objects of affording protection to the persons and property of citizens of the United States, and of maintaining a watchful care over the general interests of our country.   Without reference in any manner to the enterprise in which you are so actively engaged, the nature and subject of which, except so far as I may have been rightly informed by paragraph casually met with in public prints, I am totally ignorant.

I beg leave, however (availing myself of the return of the messenger), to assure you, sir, of the interest I feel in the successful prosecution and issue of the public interests committed to your direction, and without desiring information further than you may deem necessary to enable me to aid and facilitate your operations, to express my sincere desire and readiness to serve you in any manner consistent with other duties.

Permit me to say, sir, that if you should find it convenient to visit the U. S. Ship *Portsmouth* during her stay in this port, that I, with the officers of the ship, will be most happy to see you.

I shall remain here probably three weeks unless unforeseen circumstances require an earlier movement, and my present intention is to return to Monterey.

I am, sir, very respectfully,
Your obedient servant,
(Signed)   Jno. B. Montgomery,
Commander U. S. N.

To Capt. J. C. Frémont, Upper California.

On the 8th of June I broke up camp at the Buttes and moved down the valley to my old encampment on the American Fork, which I reached on the 12th.   The range here was broad, extending towards the hills; the feed for the animals excellent and abundant; and the position was near the Fort, which naturally became the base of operations.

On the 13th I went with a small party to " Sutter's Landing," which was the place appointed to meet Lieut. Gillespie. He had reached the place at midnight, in the *Portsmouth's* launch, which was in charge of Lieut. B. F. Hunter, bringing the stores for which I had made requisition. Mr. Hunter was accompanied by Purser Watmough and Asst. Surgeon Duvall; the latter having volunteered to visit my camp in order to arrange my medicine chest and render any other assistance in his power.

Lieut. Hunter brought me from Commander Montgomery the following letter, dated June 10th, 1846:

SECOND LETTER TO CAPT. FRÉMONT BY LIEUT. HUNTER.

U. S. SHIP PORTSMOUTH,
BAY OF SAN FRANCISCO, June 10, 1846.

SIR: Since writing you by Neal on the 3d inst., I have been by Lieut. Gillespie informed of your present position and circumstances, and made acquainted with your design to proceed south with your party as far as Santa Barbara before striking across the country for the United States. I am also informed by Lieut. G. of your having expressed to him a desire for the presence of a vessel of war at Santa Barbara, during the period of your temporary sojourn in the vicinity of that port.

Now, sir, I am happy to say that I feel myself at liberty to visit any or all ports upon this coast should the public interest require it, and if, on the receipt of this, you shall still think that the presence of a ship of war at Santa Barbara may prove serviceable to you in carrying out the views of our Government, and will do me the favor by the return boat to communicate your wishes with information as to the time you will probably reach that part of the coast, I shall not fail (Providence permitting) to meet you there with the *Portsmouth*.

I feel gratified, sir, in having it in my power to forward you by Lieut. Hunter the amount of funds asked for in your name by Lieut. Gillespie, with most of the articles of store, etc., required to meet the demand of your urgent necessity, regretting only my inability to furnish the whole. You will oblige me by signing the Requisitions and Receipts annexed to the several invoices transmitted by Lieut. Hunter, and with a view to the settlement of Purser James H. Watmough's accounts at the Navy Department, be pleased to give an order or bill (in duplicate) on the proper Department of Government, payable to Purser Watmough's order to the Fourth Auditor of the Treasury for the aggregate amount of money and purser's stores supplied. Articles having no prices affixed need only be receipted for.

Lieut. Gillespie informs me that you may find it convenient to visit the *Portsmouth* at Santa Barbara should we have occasion to go there; with this prospect in view I beg leave again to assure you that we shall all on board be most happy to see you.

Very respectfully,

I am your obedient servant,

(Signed) JNO. B. MONTGOMERY,

Commander U. S. N.

To Capt. J. C. Frémont,

Bt. Capt.U. S. Topol. Engineers, N. California.

Not finding me at the rendezvous, Mr. Gillespie had taken the launch up into the American Fork to await my arrival and found there my main party. For a few days I remained at the Landing.

During these days Merritt came in with a small party, bringing with him as prisoners General Vallejo, Col. Salvador Vallejo, Col. Prudon, and Mr. Jacob Leese. A party of about forty settlers having surprised and taken Sonoma, which was the first military post in that part of the country, General Vallejo had asked to be brought to me, but I declined to receive the prisoners, there being in my camp no suitable accommodation, and they were taken to Sutter's Fort.

Affairs had now assumed a critical aspect and I presently saw that the time had come when it was unsafe to leave events to mature under unfriendly, or mistaken, direction. I decided that it was for me rather to govern events than to be governed by them.

I knew the facts of the situation. These I could not make known, but felt warranted in assuming the responsibility and acting on my own knowledge.

Against the Mexican Government, with which I knew we were contending, the individual action of the settlers could have only a temporary success, to result in inevitable disaster so soon as the government troops were brought to bear upon them.

But I represented the Army and the Flag of the United States. And the Navy was apparently co-operating with me. This gave to my movements the national character which must of necessity be respected by Mexico, and by any foreign power to which she might ally herself; and would also hold offensive operations in check until actual war between the governments should make an open situation. And, in order to place it in the power of my government to disavow my action should it become expedient to do so, I drew up my resignation from the Army to be sent by the first opportunity to Senator Benton for transmission to the War Department, in the event of such a contingency. Captain Sutter was an officer under the Mexican Government, and I thought it best to place in charge of the Fort

Mr. Edward Kern, who is already known as the topographer and artist of my exploring expedition.

I think I have said enough in journeying along to have it understood that the men of my party were exceptionally good; in fact, through all circumstances upon the surveys, and here in a compromising situation, they went with me as one man. I hold myself excused to the reader if I dwell upon them when the occasion naturally offers. I like to do so as upon things pleasant to remember. Among them were two upon whom my eyes always rested with satisfaction on account of the fine specimens they were of vigorous manhood. The calm resolution expressed in their faces reminded me of Cromwellian faces I had seen in pictures. The two were relatives, Hughes and Moore. They were of Illinois; full six feet high, and perfectly well-built, fair specimens of Western men.

Risdon Moore was a reasoning man and to my surprise undertook to question the expediency of the course upon which I was moving, and to foresee bad consequences probable from it. He expressed dissent, verging on disobedience. Under the circumstances such an example was impossible. There was at one of the angles of the Fort a rather dungeon-like room which had the ground for its floor; unoccupied except by those active insects which I believe always accompany cattle ranges, and which in California at this time commanded respect by their multitude and indiscriminate ferocity. This " dungeon " was a hot-bed of them and an intruder was as promptly repulsed as if he had entered an abandoned Pawnee hut.

Moore, as I have said, was of the kind of men who are reasoning beings; he was open to conviction and not obstinate, and a night of solitary reflection —not calm—satisfied him that good reason was on my side and he rehabilitated himself forthwith and resumed his place. Nor did he bear malice, of which in truth he was not capable, for he remained with me during the California campaign through to Washington where he stood by me as solidly as he had done in the field. This I mention as the confirmatory example in my command.

Shortly after my arrival on the American Fork, Mr. William Loker, of Ohio, who was then staying at the Fort, came to me at the camp. He gave me much detailed information concerning what had been going on in the neighborhood and in the coast settlements. He informed me that the authorities at Monterey had published a *Banda* or Proclamation, ordering all foreigners to leave the country at any date fixed by the government or they would otherwise be driven out by force. The *Banda* had been translated and sent up the valley and one of them was put up by Mr. Loker at Sutter's Fort.*

* This was the proclamation of April 30th, already forwarded officially to Leidesdorf, U. S. Vice Consul, for notice to the American settlers.

Among the stories spread abroad to excite the Indians was one to the effect that all their land would be taken from them by the Americans. Some of General Castro's officers too took down to Monterey with them an Indian of the Mokelumné tribe named Eusebio, who was by trade a weaver. He had been one of the Mission Indians and spoke Spanish understandingly. Presents and promises had been made him and he had been engaged to burn the wheat of the settlers in the Sacramento valley. Upon his return Eusebio went about among the Indians of the neighboring rancherias fomenting discontent among the Indians and inciting them to join in the work of destruction for which he had been engaged. But forewarned of danger, the settlers were watchful and Eusebio and his Indian confederates lost their lives.

On the 20th of this month Mr. Pearson B. Reading and Mr. Hensley came to my camp. They brought positive information that General Castro was organizing a force of Californians and Indians, with the declared purpose of attacking my camp. Through Dr. Marsh and other friendly foreign settlers, Mr. Hensley had been able to inform himself thoroughly as to the condition of affairs and the views of the Californians. At the same time a courier arrived from the small garrison at Sonoma asking for assistance against a threatened attack by a large force. The courier informed me that Lieut. Missroom, of the sloop of war *Portsmouth*, had been sent to Sonoma by Commander Montgomery to inquire concerning the rumors of outrages said to have been committed against the people of the country by the settlers. He brought also information that one of the settlers named Ide had issued a proclamation declaring California independent of Mexico and that he had hoisted a flag bearing a grizzly bear upon a white field.

It breaks a little the course of the narrative, to give here the following letters, but they serve to make the situation at this time more clearly comprehended:

(COPY OF MR. WM. B. IDE'S LETTER.)

SONOMA, June 15, 1846.

OUR PRESENT HEADQUARTERS.

DEAR SIR: I beg leave to inform you by express, of a change in the political affairs of Sonoma, and the Sacramento valley; which has taken place within the last week. With the circumstances which led to this change you are doubtless acquainted, viz.: the hostility of the Spaniards to the American emigrants. About forty days since a proclamation was issued by the Spaniards, ordering all foreigners to leave the country, and forbidding them to take any of their property with them, at the same time threatening them with extermination should they presume to remain in the country. The immigration to the States was gone; the company for Oregon had left us. There was now no alternative but to die silently, and singly by the hands of our enemies or fly to meet the foe. Information had reached the upper end of Sacramento valley (where I resided) that two hundred Spaniards were on their way up the valley for the purpose of destroying our wheat, burning our houses, and driving off our cattle. Aroused by appearances so shocking, a very few of us resolved to meet our enemy (being encouraged by the known presence of Captain Frémont's command in the valley) and dispose of our difficulties in the best possible manner. The two hundred Spaniards proved to be a band of horses (about two hundred) guarded by a Spanish officer and fifteen men, being driven up the valley as far as Captain Sutter's, thence across the river for the lower settlements, for the declared and express purpose of being mounted by soldiers and sent back to enforce said proclamation. In self-defence, those few men (viz., twelve) seized the moment and pursued those horses, captured their guard and drove the horses to the neighborhood of Captain Frémont's camp. Still writhing under the dreadful necessity above alluded to, we pursued our way night and day, adding to our number a few true hearts to the number of thirty-four men, until the dawn of the morning of the 14th inst., when we charged upon the Fortress of General Guadaloupe Vallejo, and captured eighteen prisoners (among whom were three of the highest officers in the Californian Government and all the military officers who reside in Sonoma) eight field-pieces, two hundred stand of arms, a great quantity of cannon, canister, and grape-shot, and a little less than one hundred pounds of powder (quite too little to sustain us against an attack by the use of cannon). By the articles of capitulation it was contemplated we were to be provisioned by the generosity of our captured general, while we can keep possession or while opposition renders possession necessary. By another arrangement of cannon and field-pieces, we have strengthened our position and continue to hold it, under the authority of twenty-four well-armed men and (as we have good right to believe) the will of the people. The Alcaldé we discharged under a new appointment, the soldiers were set at liberty, and the said officers were escorted by ten armed men to an asylum under the generous protection of Captain Frémont. This day we proclaim California a Republic, and our pledge of honor that private property shall be protected. With this, as we hear from various parts of the country, the Spaniards are not only satisfied, but pleased. We are situated three or four miles north of the north end of the bay, and are liable to be attacked by an enemy from beyond the bay but would repel any that should be made by the use of small arms. We have not powder to work our cannon, and therefore, with our small force, could not long resist the operations of cannon against us

Destined as we are to certain destruction should we prove unsuccessful, we have the honor to be your *Fellow Countrymen*, and whether we conquer or perish we are resolved to approve ourselves not unworthy the kindly regards of those who "build to the honor and glory of the American flag."

It is our object and earnest desire to embrace the first opportunity to unite our adopted and rescued country, to the country of our early home.

With every consideration and by the will of the people, I have the honor to be, etc.

Wm. B. Ide,
Commander-in-Chief at the Fortress of Sonoma.
To Commodore Stockton, of the U. S. Navy.

ANSWER TO MR. IDE.

U. S. Ship Portsmouth,
Sausalito, Bay of San Francisco, June 16, 1846.

Sir: On the point of despatching an officer to Sonoma to confer with you respecting the state of alarm and apprehension into which your sudden movement seems to have thrown the helpless people of Sonoma and the country around, your messenger, Mr. Todd, arrived and handed me your communication of yesterday, addressed to Commodore Stockton, but designed, as Mr. Todd said, for me. The circumstances therein stated, which has led to the hasty organization of the foreign population of this part of California in opposition to the constituted authorities, had in part previously reached me through irregular channels not entirely to be relied on; and in respect to which I would only observe as a general rule without direct application or reference to the position in which you stand, that I hold it to be the privilege of all men everywhere, by such proper means as they possess, to counteract the sinister designs of treachery, and resist oppression in whatever form or manner they may be assailed by them, and that a right motive and a just cause will be always characterized by a miid, tender, and humane regard for the security of the happiness, proper interests, and privileges of others.

I am most happy, sir, to understand from Mr. Todd, that these (by proclamation) have been guaranteed to your prisoners and the defenceless people within your reach, and I sincerely hope that whatever may be the future course of the popular movement in which you are engaged that this policy may distinguish the conduct of your party as well as that of your opposers.

Permit me, sir, in response to your call for powder for the use of your party, to say that I am here as a representative of a government at peace (as far as I know) with Mexico and her province of California, having in charge the interests and the security of the commerce and citizens of the United States lawfully engaged in their pursuits, and have no right or authority to furnish munitions of war, or in any manner to take sides with any political party, or even indirectly to identify myself, or official name, with any popular movement (whether of foreign or native residents) of the country, and thus, sir, must decline giving the required aid.

Lieutenant Missroom, the executive officer of the U. S. Ship *Portsmouth*, under my command, who will hand you this, will explain more fully than the few moments allowed me to answer your letter will permit me to do.

I am, sir, your obedient servant,

(Signed) JNO. B. MONTGOMERY,

Commander.

To Wm. B. Ide, Esq.,
Commanding the Fortress of Sonoma, Upper California.

In answer now to the urgent appeals made by the settlers for assistance, I started for Sonoma, where I arrived with my party on the afternoon of the 25th. Here I learned that the settlers had defeated a party of Californians seventy strong, killing one and wounding four and rescuing two prisoners who were being taken to the headquarters of General Castro.

I was informed that a few days previous a party of Californians had captured two Americans on their road to Sonoma from Bodega; that they had tied them to trees and butchered them with knives.

A force under the command of De la Torre, a captain of Mexican cavalry, was on this side of the bay near the Mission San Rafael, and a report being brought to me that this officer was being reinforced by troops crossing at San Pablo under General Castro, I pushed forward to the Mission. Arriving there in the forenoon of the 26th, I found no force, but learned that it was upon the Point of San Pablo waiting an opportunity to cross. During the afternoon of the same day letters were intercepted which required De la Torre to send horses to the Point the next morning to meet troops from the other side; but the enemy did not cross the straits. On the contrary De la Torre retreated with his command to Sausalito, where he availed himself of a launch belonging to Mr. Richardson, a resident there, to escape across the bay.

Both the settlers and the men of my command were excited against the Californians by the recent murder of the two Americans, and not by the murder only, but by the brutal circumstances attending it. My scouts, mainly Delawares, influenced by these feelings, made sharp retaliation and killed Bereyasa and de Haro, who were the bearers of the intercepted letters.

I found here at Sausalito the master of the American vessel *Moscow*, Captain William D. Phelps, of Worcester, Massachusetts. His was a trading vessel visiting the coast of California with a mixed cargo for the purpose of exchanging goods with the Californians for hides and tallow, which made his return cargo. With him I arranged for the use of one of his boats, with which he met me at the landing before daylight in the morning. I took with me twelve of my men singled out as the best shots;—Captain Phelps and his boat's crew excited and pleased to aid in the work on hand. The captain happened to have on board his ship a quantity of rat-tail files, with some of which we supplied ourselves. I had learned that little or no guard was maintained at the fort, which was at the point on the southern side of the gate which makes the entrance to the bay and which I named *Golden Gate*. Pulling across the strait or avenue of water which leads in from the Gate we reached the Fort Point in the gray dawn of the morning and scrambled up the steep bank just in time to see several horsemen escaping at full speed towards *Yerba Buena*. We promptly spiked the guns—fourteen—nearly all long brass Spanish pieces. The work of spiking was effectually done by Stepp, who was a gunsmith, and knew as well how to make a rifle as to use one.

The measures which I had taken, ending with the retreat of De la Torre, had freed from all Mexican authority the territory north of the Bay of San Francisco, from the sea to Sutter's Fort.

Leaving a force to protect San Rafael, I returned to Sonoma upon the 4th of July, when the day was celebrated by salutes and a ball in the evening.

During that and the following day the settlers were organized into a battalion consisting of four companies numbering two hundred and twenty-four men. The force with which I had recently been acting was one hundred and sixty men.

It had now become necessary to concentrate the elements of this movement, in order to give it the utmost efficiency of which it was capable. As was reasonably to be expected under the circumstances, the people desired me to take charge of it. Its existence was due to my presence in the valley, and at any time upon my withdrawal it would have collapsed with absolute ruin to the settlers.

Accordingly, the settlers having met together, I addressed them briefly, accepting the position. In doing so I dwelt on the responsibility which I had assumed as an officer of the United States Army, trusting to them to do nothing which would discredit themselves or our country.

I sent out parties for horses to mount the battalion and to bring in cattle for their support. The horses were taken principally from the estate of General Vallejo, and the cattle from the government stock-farm at Suscol.*

* The value of these and all other supplies taken during my operations in California was afterward estimated by a Board of Officers at Washington appointed by the Government, and the estimated value was appropriated by Congress and paid to the respective owners. Sutter also was paid for the use of his fort.   J. C. F.

U. S. Ship Portsmouth,
Sausalito, June 23, 1846.

Sir : By Lieutenant Hunter, who reached the ship on Saturday evening from your camp, I had the pleasure to receive your letter of the 16th inst., announcing the seasonable reception of the stores forwarded by him.   The last few days have teemed with important events ; pointing, in my view, to results momentous to the interests of California and our own country.   I have determined to remain where I am at present, looking after the interests of our country and countrymen requiring to be watched at this crisis, and readily comply with your suggestion to keep open the communication with your camp, by means of my boats ; in pursuance of which it is intended to send a boat in the morning (to-morrow) in charge of Lieutenant Revere (who will hand you this) and another on Saturday next, by the return of which you will be pleased to inform me whether a third boat will be likely to reach you at your present camp or not.   The surgeon of the *Portsmouth*, Dr. Henderson, goes in the boat with the orders to remain with you until the return of the next boat, or longer should you desire it.   Although aware that the public mind in California was prepared for a change of government, I little expected the movement to take place at this time or in the manner it has.   The capture of the horses and the surprise of Sonoma were master-strokes, but should have been followed up by a rush upon Santa Clara, where Castro, with the residue of ordnance and munitions of the country, might have been taken by thirty men at any time previous to Saturday evening.   Castro must feel sensibly the loss of the two Vallejos and Pruden, as well as that of the arms and munitions taken at Sonoma.   I have exchanged communications with the commanders on both sides, and others, preserving a strict neutrality and avowing my purpose of scrupulously adhering to this principle ; while I confess my sympathies are wholly with the gallant little band in arms for mutual defence.

Individuals and small parties from this section have been joining the insurgents at Sonoma daily, I am informed, and Lieutenant Hunter brings intelligence of Sutter's union with them. An irregular force of one hundred and fifty are said to have joined Castro at Santa Clara on Saturday, brought from the vicinity of Monterey by Manuel Castro, the sub-prefect of that place, and I am just informed that they are expected to cross the straits and take horses at Point San Pedro, where a number have been collected for their use, this evening, and move directly upon Sonoma.   If this is the case we shall soon know the result.   I yesterday heard of the arrival of the United States ship *Cyane* at Monterey, where the *Congress* is also daily looked for from the Islands, where she arrived on the 13th of May.   Not a word of news have I yet received by the *Cyane*, but I think she must bring from Mazatlan something respecting our Mexican concerns.

I received a letter from Castro a few days since, a copy of which, as it related solely to your imagined operations, I have thought it well to send you with my reply.   Also two proclamations this moment received.   Should anything of consequence reach me from the *Cyane* before sending the next boat I will not fail to communicate it to you.

In the meantime permit me to subscribe myself

Your obedient servant,
(Signed)   Jno. B. Montgomery,
Commander U. S. N.

To Captain J. C. Frémont, U. S. Topl. Engineers, Sacramento, U. California.

N.B.—Since writing the above I have heard there is no probability of Castro s movement upon Sonoma for several days ; they are using great efforts to purchase arms, etc.

Respectfully,
(Signed)   Jno. B. Montgomery.

U. S. Ship Portsmouth,
Yerba Buena, June 26, 1846.

Sir : Since writing to you by Lieutenant Revere a force of seventy Californians, moving from Santa Clara towards Sonoma, after passing the narrows of this bay twelve miles to the Northerd of my anchorage, were met by a party of fifteen of the revolutionists, and checked or, as reported, compelled to fall back with the loss of two killed and two wounded, two of the fifteen also falling by the fire of their opponents. This first success, though seemingly a small affair, cannot fail I think to give a favorable impulse to the operations of the insurgents and attract at once numbers of the foreign residents to their aid. Although neutral in my position, I cannot be so in feeling and am anxiously looking for farther intelligence, believing that inactivity in the circumstances can form no part of the policy of the Sonoma party.

Castro has written to me, saying that "he had received advice from various sources, that the boats of the American ship *Portsmouth* go about the Bay of San Francisco armed for the purpose of examining its trade, etc." This, of course, I have very honestly denied, but informed him that I had sent two boats since the 10th inst. to your camp, and deemed it proper in the circumstances to notify him of my intention to despatch another for the purpose of communicating with you at the close of this week, since which I have heard nothing from him. He is at Santa Clara with about seventy men, it is said.

I have directed Lieutenant Bartlett to bring Surgeon Henderson with him when he returns, unless your detention beyond the period named for your final departure for the United States should render his further continuance important, of which you will please be the judge. Lieutenant Bartlett will hand you, sir, a package for the Honorable Secretary of the Navy, which (if perfectly convenient, not otherwise), I will thank you to take charge of, and forward from any point of communication most convenient to yourself.

Wishing you, sir, a safe and pleasant journey to your country and home, I have the honor to subscribe myself,

Very respectfully, your obedient servant,
(Signed)   JNO. B. MONTGOMERY,
Commander U. S. N.

To Captain J. C. Frémont,
U. S. Topl. Engineers, Upper California.

TRANSLATION OF GENERAL CASTRO'S LETTER.

OFFICE OF THE COMMANDANT-GENERAL OF UPPER CALIFORNIA,
HEADQUARTERS, SANTA CLARA, June 23, 1846.

The undersigned, Commander-in-Chief of the Department, has had advice from various sources, that the boats of the American ship of war *Portsmouth*, now anchored in San Francisco, go about the bay armed for the purpose of examining its trade, and as in the opinion of the undersigned, the aforesaid ship cannot practise such acts in a port which belongs to the Mexican nation, he addresses himself to the commander of the aforesaid ship, to the end that he will please inform him, in reply, with what object he takes those measures; that, in consequence, he may act in conformity with his orders from his Government.

The undersigned has the honor to repeat to the commander of the aforesaid ship assurances of his most respectful consideration.

God and Liberty.

(Signed)   JOSÉ CASTRO.
To the Commander of the American Sloop of War Portsmouth,
anchored in the Bay of San Francisco.

SAUSALITO, July 1, 1846.

SIR: Captain Frémont has requested me to address you upon the subject of a surgeon being ordered to his command. The daily application of sick alone induces him to urge the necessity of his having a medical officer; and he hopes you will feel that he would not make the request, without being satisfied of your concurrence with the application solely with reference to the return of Dr. Henderson to the ship.

Captain Frémont would address you himself, were he not so much occupied, and being away from his writing utensils, which are left at San Rafael.

We move to San Rafael to-morrow morning. In the meantime we hope to learn your favorable decision as to the foregoing application.

I have the honor to be, very respectfully,

Your obedient servant,

(Signed)   ARCHI. H. GILLESPIE,

Lieut. U. S. Marine Corps, etc., etc.

To Captain J. B. Montgomery,

Commanding U. S. Ship Portsmouth, Yerba Buena.

P.S.—I write this in haste on board the Barque *Moscow.*

Respectfully,

(Signed)   ARCHI. H. GILLESPIE.

U. S. SHIP PORTSMOUTH,

YERBA BUENA, July 1, 1846.

SIR: I have just received your note by Captain Hall, requesting, in the name of Captain Frémont, that one of the medical officers of the *Portsmouth* might be ordered to his command. However happy, sir, I should feel in complying with the wishes of Captain Frémont in this respect, there are reasons why, in my view, it would be improper to detach one of them for an indefinite period of time from the ship; but be pleased with my respectful regards to Captain Frémont to assure him of my readiness to send one of my medical officers to his camp, wherever that may be, at any time he may require his services, and also, that I will receive such of my sick or wounded countrymen, or others under his command, as shall stand in need of accommodation and medical attendance on board the *Portsmouth.*

I am, sir, very respectfully,

Your obedient servant,

(Signed)   JNO. B. MONTGOMERY,

Commanding U. S. Ship Portsmouth.

To Lieutenant A. H. Gillespie, Sausalito.

SONOMA, July 5, 1846.

SIR: I have the pleasure to acknowledge the receipt at this place of your two communications, dated June 23d and 26th, the latter highly interesting, in connection with the present crisis. I trust that by the time you receive this note, the arrival of Commodore Sloat will have put an end to your neutral position.

Besides owing you my acknowledgments for the professional aid of Dr. Henderson, I am much indebted to you for the pleasure of his acquaintance, as our pursuits appear to have been somewhat similar. I found him with Lieutenant Bartlett here on my arrival, two days since.

A military organization of the force under arms was yesterday made at this place, and farther than this I have nothing of present interest to communicate to you. I shall to-day continue my road towards Sutter's Fort, on the Sacramento. Foreigners from below are daily arriving at this post, and we have information that upwards of a hundred good men are now in the upper part of the Sacramento valley, on their road from Oregon. The intelligence was brought by a party of seven men who were in advance. Of these, five were wounded, one very dangerously, in an attack by the Indians. This man was shot through the body and is lying at one of the upper settlements.

I forward this by Lieutenant Bartlett, who is about starting, and to my great regret, Dr. Henderson accompanies him.

I trust that in case anything of moment should occur, you will not find it inconsistent with your convenience and the strict neutrality of your position to give me some information. Thanking you in the meantime for your recent kindness,

I am, sir, very respectfully,

Your obedient servant,

(Signed)   J. C. FRÉMONT,

Bt. Capt. U. S. Topl. Engineers.

Captain Jno. B. Montgomery,

U. S. Ship Portsmouth, Bay of San Francisco.

Leaving one company of fifty men under Captain John Grigsby in command at Sonoma, on the 6th I set out on my return; taking with me some small brass field-pieces from the fort, and reached my encampment on the American Fork on the 9th. Before we arrived at that place, General Castro had evacuated Santa Clara, and with a force reported to be about four hundred men and two pieces of artillery, commenced his retreat upon San Juan, a former mission near Monterey, now occupied as a post and fortified with eight pieces of artillery.

On the evening of the 10th we were roused into enthusiasm by the arrival of an express from Captain Montgomery, to inform me that Commodore Sloat had raised the flag at Monterey—that he had hoisted the flag at Yerba Buena, and sent one to Sonoma to be hoisted at that place. He also sent one with a request to have it hoisted at Sutter's Fort; and accordingly with great satisfaction I had this done at sunrise the next morning, under a salute of twenty-one guns amid the general rejoicing of the people. This event paralyzed all opposition.

The raising of the flag at Monterey was communicated by Commodore Sloat to Commander Montgomery, who made known to me the contents of the letter as requested. The following is a copy:

FLAG-SHIP SAVANNAH, MONTEREY, July 6, 1846.

SIR : Since I wrote you last evening, I have determined to hoist the flag of the United States at this place to-morrow, as I would prefer being sacrificed for doing too much than too little.　.　.　.　.　.　.　.　.　.　.　.　.　.

If you consider that you have sufficient force, or if *Frémont* will join you, you will hoist the flag of the United States at Yerba Buena, or at any other proper place, and take possession, in the name of the United States, of the fort, and that portion of the country.

.　.　.　.　.　.　.　.　.　.　.　.　.　.

I am very anxious to know if *Captain Frémont* will co-operate with us. Mr. Larkin is writing to him by the launch, and you will please put him in possession of this letter as soon as possible. I have no time to write more at present.

Very respectfully, your obedient servant,
(Signed)　　　　JOHN D. SLOAT,
Commander-in-Chief, etc.

Commander J. B. Montgomery,
　　U. S. Ship Portsmouth, San Francisco..

On the 12th I received an express from Commodore Sloat, transmitting to me his proclamation, and with a request to proceed with the force under my orders to Monterey.

FLAG-SHIP SAVANNAH, BAY OF MONTEREY, July 9, 1846.

SIR : You will, no doubt, have received the information before this that I have hoisted the flag of the United States at this place, on the 7th instant ; as yet all is quiet and no resistance of any kind has been made.

I immediately sent to General Castro a copy of my proclamation to the inhabitants of California, and a summons to surrender forthwith to the American arms the forts, military posts, and stations, under his command, together with all troops, arms, munitions of war, and public property of every description under his control and jurisdiction, with an invitation for him to meet me immediately at this place to enter into articles of capitulation, that himself, officers, soldiers, and the inhabitants of California, may receive assurances of perfect safety to themselves and property.

I have this moment learned, by an Englishman just arrived from General Castro, at the Pueblo, that General Castro was probably at St. John's last evening, and that you would probably be at the Pueblo at the same time.

I have not as yet received any communication from General Castro.

It is thought he will be in to-morrow, or send some communication. This Englishman says that when the general read my proclamation to his troops, he expressed his approbation of it; if he is wise, he will make no resistance.

I have here the frigate *Savannah*, of fifty-four guns, the sloops of war *Cyane* and *Levant*, of twenty-four guns each, armed with 32-pounder long guns, 68-pounder shell guns, and 42-pounder carronades, with a large complement of men, and am every moment in expectation of the arrival of the frigate *Congress*, with sixty 32-pounder long guns, at this place, and the sloop *Erie* with long 18's at San Francisco. I am extremely anxious to see you at your earliest convenience; and should General Castro consent to enter into a capitulation, it is of the utmost importance that you should be present. I hope, therefore, that you will push on with all possible despatch, or, at any rate, let me hear from you immediately.

Captain Montgomery sent his launch down, which I despatched on the 6th, informing him that I should take possession of this place on the next day in the name of the United States, and sent him a copy of my summons and proclamation, and also orders to take possession of Yerba Buena and the Bay of San Francisco immediately, requesting him to inform you of these facts without delay. I have also sent him three couriers with the same orders (in cipher), which I have no doubt have reached him, and am confident that the flag of the United States is now flying there.

Although I am in expectation of seeing General Castro, to enter into satisfactory terms with him, there may be a necessity of one hundred men, well mounted, who are accustomed to riding, to form a force to prevent any further robbing of the farmers' houses, etc., by the Indians. I request you to bring in as many men up to that number with you, or send them on under charge of a trusty person, in case you may be delayed for a day or two. Should you find any Government horses on the road, please bring them in.

Very respectfully, your obedient servant,

JOHN D. SLOAT,
Commander-in-Chief of the U. S. Naval Forces in the Pacific Ocean, etc.

Captain J. C. Frémont.

A few days had been occupied in mounting guns, preparing ammunition, and making other preparations for a campaign, and in arranging for the tranquillity of the Sacramento valley during my absence. Before I set out on this third expedition the emigration from the Western States had received a strong impulse from the accounts spread abroad of the singular beauty and fertility of the California valley; and I considered it safe to count upon the incoming emigrants for a steady increase of our strength. Of their hearty support I had no doubt.

Shortly after the receipt of the message from Commodore Sloat, I set out upon the march to Monterey, going by the way of the San Joaquin valley and crossing the mountains to San Juan. General Castro had made here but brief halt, and with the force which he had collected was withdrawing towards Los Angeles; realizing that war had begun in earnest, and that he was unable to contend with the land and naval forces suddenly combined in the north. I took possession of San Juan, putting only a few men in charge, for the reason that no further opposition was to be apprehended in the north. A few hours after my arrival Lieutenant McLane and Mr. Fauntleroy came in with a reconnoitring party.

On the 19th we continued our road through the Gomez Pass towards Monterey, giving on the way a marching salute to the Cavilan Peak, where in March, four months before, we had hoisted the flag.

It was a day of excitement when we entered Monterey. I was glad again to meet the ocean breeze and surf. Many of my men had never seen the ocean, or the English flag. Four of our men-of-war were lying in the harbor, and also the *Collingwood*, eighty guns, flag-ship of Admiral Seymour. The men looked upon the *Collingwood* with the feeling of the racer who has just passed the winning post.

On the 16th a sail hove in sight which was made out to be an English line-of-battle ship, and the vessels of the American squadron were signalled to prepare for action. I learned from Midshipman Beale, who was on shore at the time with a party of men engaged in building a block-house on the hill, that the signal was also made recalling to their ships all officers and men from shore; and when he reached the *Congress* he found the men at quarters. The stranger vessel proved to be the eighty-gun ship *Collingwood*, bearing the flag of Rear-Admiral Sir George Seymour.

The uncertainty which existed in the American squadron concerning the action which might be taken by the English admiral is shown in the following extract from a letter of the 11th of July from Commander Montgomery to Commodore Sloat:

" This afternoon the *Juno* arrived and anchored at Sausalito. I sent a boat with offer of service, and, at the same time, notified Captain Blake of the existing state of things in California, and that the flag of the United States was now flying at Yerba Buena, which he appeared satisfied with on receiving information of the commencement of hostilities between the armies f the United States and Mexico. On the appearance of that ship, the necessary preparation was made to defend our position in the event of English opposition to our claims. In such a contingency being twenty odd men short, it would become absolutely necessary to withdraw the marines from the shore to the ship; and to show the spirit of our ' Volunteer Guards of Yerba Buena,' I will add, that to-day they were assembled and informed by Mr. Watson that the flag of the United States would, by our necessity, have to be committed to their care, and that we trusted to their spirit and honor to keep it flying; when they unanimously gave the strongest assurances that it should wave while a single man of the " Guards " lived to defend it."

ENGLISH LINE OF BATTLE SHIP.   AMERICAN MEN-OF-WAR.

ENGLAND AND THE UNITED STATES AT MONTEREY.

The rough and travel-worn appearance of our men was in strong contrast with the fresh looks of the uniformed officers and men in their clean sailor dress. But our men were in fine condition and looked serviceable as well as service-worn. The town now presented a different face from that which it wore when I visited it in January under a Mexican passport to ask permission to recruit my party on the San Joaquin. Three nations now were represented in those quiet streets, and our men made a strong impression as they rode through the crowd on the way to their encampment.

Lieutenant Minor, of the frigate *Savannah*, was on shore when we entered Monterey. In giving his testimony before the Committee of Military Affairs of the Senate when the California war claims were being examined, he took occasion to say " that the appearance of this body of men and the well-known character of its commander not only made a strong impression upon the British admiral and officers, but an equally impressive and more happy one upon those of the American Navy then in Monterey." For himself, he said, " that, after he had seen Captain Frémont's command, all his doubts regarding the conquest of California were removed."

The following extract is from " FOUR YEARS IN THE PACIFIC in Her Majesty's ship *Collingwood*, from 1844 to 1848, by Lieutenant the Hon. Fred. Walpole, R.N."

" During our stay in Monterey," says Lieutenant Walpole, " Captain Frémont and his party arrived. They naturally excited curiosity. Here were true trappers, the class that produced the heroes of Fenimore Cooper's best works. The men had passed years in the wilds, living upon their own resources; they were a curious set. A vast cloud of dust appeared first, and thence in long file emerged this wildest wild party. Frémont rode ahead, a spare, active-looking man." . . . " He was dressed in a blouse and leggings, and wore a felt hat. After him came five Delaware Indians, who were his body-guard, and have been with him through all his wanderings; they had charge of two baggage-horses. The rest, many of them blacker than the Indians, rode two and two, the rifle held by one hand across the pommel of the saddle. His original men are principally backwoodsmen, from the State of Tennessee and the banks of the upper waters of the Missouri. He has one or two with him who enjoy a high reputation in the prairies. Kit Carson is as well known there as the duke is in Europe. The dress of these men was principally a long loose coat of deerskin, tied with thongs in front; trowsers of the same, of their own manufacture. They are allowed no liquor, tea and sugar only; this, no doubt, has much to do with their good conduct; and the discipline, too, is very strict. They were marched up to an open space on the hills near the town, under some long firs, and there took up their quarters, in messes of six or seven, in the open air. The Indians lay beside their leader. In justice to the Americans I must say, they seemed to treat the natives well, and their authority extended every protection to them. The butts of the trappers' rifles resemble a Turkish musket, therefore fit light to the shoulder; they are very long and very heavy, carry ball about thirty-eight to the pound."

I went into camp beyond the town, near the sea, on a flat among firs and pines towards the top of the ridge fronting the bay. This was a delightful spot. Before us, to the right, was the town of Monterey with its red-tiled roofs and large gardens enclosed by high adobe walls, capped with red tiles; to the left the view was over the ships in the bay and on over the ocean, where the July sun made the sea-breeze and the shade of the pine trees grateful.

The camp was frequently visited by the officers and men of both the *Collingwood* and the American squadron, to whom our men and their rough camp life were objects of curiosity. All, especially the English officers, were interested in the shooting of the Delawares and the men of the exploring party. Consequently there was much shooting at marks put up against pine trees.

Immediately after my arrival I went on board the frigate *Savannah* and waited upon Commodore Sloat. I was accompanied by Lieutenant Gillespie. Commodore Sloat was glad to see me. He seemed excited over the gravity of the situation in which he was the chief figure; and now, wholly responsible for its consequences. After a few words to introduce the subject he informed me that he had applied to Lieutenant Gillespie, whom he knew to be an agent of the Government, for his authority. But he had declined to give it. He then asked to know under what instructions I had acted in taking up arms against the Mexican authorities. " I do not know by what authority you are acting. I can do nothing. Mr. Gillespie has told me nothing; he came to Mazatlan, and I sent him to Monterey, but I know nothing. I want to know by what authority you are acting."

I informed him that I had acted solely on my own responsibility, and without any expressed authority from the Government to justify hostilities.

He appeared much disturbed by this information, and gave me distinctly to understand, that in raising the flag at Monterey he had acted upon the faith of our operations in the north.

Commodore Sloat was so discouraged that the interview terminated abruptly and was without sequence. He did not ask me for another interview. He had expected to find that I had been acting under such *written* authority as would support his action in raising the flag. Disappointed in this expectation his mind closed against anything short of the written paper; the full information that I might have given should, in my judgment, have been sufficient to satisfy him that the taking possession of California, as had been done, would exactly meet the wishes of the Government. I should have been glad to do so. But for this he made no occasion, and, as a much younger officer, it did not become me to urge upon one of his rank and

POINT OF PINES.

present command, to change his course of action; especially as I felt there was an atmosphere of resistance that I could not penetrate.

Naturally I was surprised by the result of the interview. Aware of what would be the general nature of the instructions to our officers on the Pacific coast, I could not have supposed that the officer commanding the squadron was relying upon me to justify his actions. And the situation now had something in it so grand that hesitation was incomprehensible.

I had returned into the California valley two months before with my mind full of one purpose. I was so inspired with watchful excitement that the nights were almost as wakeful as the day. I saw the lovely country which had charmed my senses with admiration for its beauty dangerously near to becoming the appanage of a foreign power. I knew that the men who understood the future of our country, and who at this time ruled its destinies and were the government, regarded the California coast as the boundary fixed by nature to round off our national domain. From Mexico it was naturally separated, and events were pointing to its sure and near political separation from that power.

I had left Washington with full knowledge of their wishes, and also of their purposes so far as these could be settled in the existing circumstances; and I was relied upon to do what should be in my power in the event of opportunity to further their designs. And now that the opportunity came I had entered among the surrounding circumstances with great joy and a resolution to give to my own country the benefit of every chance as these circumstances changed. And, as I have just said, with great joy, for to what their sagacity of statesmen had brought them, I brought the enthusiasm which the wonderful value and beauty of California had created in me.

Now two months had wrought the change, and my work, too, was done. With the sight of our flag floating over the town when I entered it all my excitement subsided, and care and responsibility fell together from me.

Returning to the shore from my visit to the *Savannah*, I walked out towards the Point of Pines, which juts into the sea. No matter how untoward this interview had been I felt that the die was cast, and as trifles float into a mind at ease I pleased myself with thinking it a good augury that as Savannah was my birthplace, the birth of this new child of our country should have been presided over by this *Savannah* of the seas.

Sitting here by the sea and resting and gathering about me these dreams which had become realities, I thought over the long way from Washington to this spot and what little repose of body or mind I had found, less of the last. But now I was having an ideal rest.

Looking out over the bay, the dark hulls of the war-vessels and the slumbering cannon still looked ominous and threatening. But the Cross of St. George hung idly down from the peak of the great ship, the breeze occasionally spreading out against the sky the small red patch which repre-sented centuries of glory. There lay the pieces on the great chess-board before me with which the game for an empire had been played. At its close we had, to be sure, four pieces to one, but that one was a Queen. I was but a pawn, and like a pawn I had been pushed forward to the front at the open-ing of the game.

The actual situation is best explained by a knowledge of Commodore Sloat's condition of mind when he left Mazatlan on the 8th of June for Mon-terey. On the 6th he had written to the Secretary of the Navy that he had resolved that he would not take possession of any part of California or undertake any hostile measure against Mexico until either Mexico or the United States had declared war; notwithstanding the fact that our consul, Mr. Parrott, by an express, had informed him that the battles of Palo Alto and Resaca de la Palma had been fought. This resolution he had com-municated to the Secretary of the Navy by his letter of June 6th, in which he expresses his deep regret that the orders given him should have been of such a nature as to compel him to this humiliating decision while it appeared to the world that we were actually at war on the other coast.

The reply of the Secretary taking a widely different view of the situation did not reach him until he had returned to the East.

It was in this frame of mind that Commodore Sloat reached Monterey on the 2d of July.

To make the situation distinct I give here the two letters:

No. 51.

FLAG-SHIP SAVANNAH, June 6, 1846.

SIR: Since my No. 50, of the 31st May, I have, upon more mature reflection, come to the conclusion that your instructions of the 24th June last, and every subsequent order, will not justify my taking possession of any part of California, or any hostile measure against Mexico (notwithstanding their attack upon our troops), as neither *party have declared war.* I shall, therefore, in conformity with those instructions, be careful to avoid any act of aggression until I [am] certain one or the other party have done so, or until I find that our squadron in the Gulf have commenced *offensive* operations, presuming that, as they are in daily communication with the Department, their proceedings are authorized.

The want of communication with, and information from, the Department and our consul, render my situation anything but pleasant; indeed it is humiliating and mortifying in the extreme, as by my orders I cannot act, while it appears to the world that we are actually at war on the other coast.

Three of the sloops are on the coast of California, where I shall proceed, leaving the *Warren* here to bring intelligence. The *Shark* is at Columbia River.

Most respectfully, I am your obedient servant,

J. D. SLOAT, *Commodore.*

To the Honorable Secretary of the Navy, Washington.

NAVY DEPARTMENT, January 11, 1848.

The foregoing is a translation of a letter received at this Department in cipher.

J. Y. MASON.

(Duplicate.)

U. S. NAVY DEPARTMENT,
WASHINGTON, August 13, 1846.

COMMODORE: The Department has received your letter No. 51, of June 6th, from which it appears that while you were aware of the existence of "actual war" between the United States and Mexico, you remained in a state of inactivity and did not carry out the instructions of June 24, 1845, framed to be executed even in the event of the mere declaration of war, much more in the event of actual hostilities. Those instructions you were ordered to carry out "at once."

In my letter of August 5, 1845, the receipt of which you acknowledged on the 28th January, 1846, referring to them, I said, "In the event of war, you will obey the instructions recently addressed to you via Panama."

In my letter of October 17, 1845, of which you acknowledge the receipt on the 17th of March, 1846, referring to these instructions once more, I said further, "In the event of actual hostilities between the Mexican Government and our own, you will so dispose of your whole force as to carry out most effectually the objects specified in the instructions forwarded to you from the Department in view of such a contingency." And surely there is no ambiguity in this language.

And in my letter of 23d February last, sent through Mexico, I remarked, "This letter is sent to you overland, enclosed as you suggest, to Messrs. Mott, Talbot & Co., Mazatlan, and you will readily understand the reserve with which it is written."

The Department on August 5, 1845, had also told you that "your force should not be weakened, while hostilities are threatened by Mexico." Your course was particularly approved in detaining the frigate *Constitution*. The Department will hope that a more urgent necessity than as yet appears existed for the otherwise premature return of that vessel.

The Department ~~does not charge you with disobedience of orders. It~~* willingly believes in the purity of your intentions. But your anxiety not to do wrong has led you into a most unfortunate and unwarranted inactivity.   Very respectfully yours,

(Signed)   GEORGE BANCROFT.

*Commodore John D. Sloat, Commanding U. S. Naval Forces
in the Pacific Ocean.*

When Commodore Sloat on the 2d of July entered the port of Monterey he sent an officer on shore with a tender of the usual civilities, by an offer to salute the Mexican flag; but the offer was declined on the pretext that there was no powder with which to return it.

"It was a matter of great surprise on the part of many officers of the squadron that the Commodore should have tendered these civilities, knowing as we all did that the Mexican Government had already commenced offensive operations against our army on the Rio Grande, and that the squadron of the United States was blockading the coast of Mexico on the Gulf."†

Rumors of hostilities which had reached us many days previously through Indian sources were confirmed on the arrival of Commodore Sloat. In sparsely settled and grazing countries, especially where there are Indians, news travels with great rapidity from village to village and from rancho to rancho. In the country between Monterey and the Rio Grande horses are abundant and the Indians and ranchmen spend a good part of their lives in the saddle. The friendly custom was to change horses at every rancho, so

* This, is the original letter received by Commodore Sloat.
† Sworn testimony of Midshipman Wilson.

that news really went by courier and posting; and now with extraordinary swiftness in this situation, when events on the Rio Grande were anxiously watched by all the Mexican people.

That battles had taken place all knew. But as will be seen by this interview Commodore Sloat did not intend to move farther and had gone back to the position taken in his letter to the Secretary of the 6th of June.

In his letter of the 6th to Commander Montgomery he directs that officer to hoist the flag if he has sufficient force, " or if Frémont will join you," and expresses his great anxiety that I should join him.

In the following letter to me of July the 9th, informing me of his operations and of his force in the harbor of Monterey, he tells me that he is extremely anxious to see me at my earliest convenience and that it is of the utmost importance that I be present in the event that General Castro should consent to a capitulation. And in the event of my being delayed for a day or two, he requests me to send in a mounted force of 100 men and to bring in any Mexican government horses that I may find on the road.

FLAG-SHIP SAVANNAH, BAY OF MONTEREY, July 12, 1846.

SIR: I have one hundred marines and two hundred men on shore, well armed, and also two 18-pounder carronades, mounted for field-pieces, and can land the remainder of my force in a few minutes, if necessary. By the best information I can obtain, Frémont was at the Pueblo (of St. Joseph) the day before yesterday, and probably at St. Johns yesterday. I sent a letter to him two days since, by express, and yesterday a message by an American who was on his way to Yerba Buena, who promised to see him; he has also a message for you; therefore I am in momentary expectation of hearing from him. Castro buried two field-pieces, with their shot, at St. Johns, and is flying before Frémont.

.   .   .   .   ,   , ...

I have information from the Pueblo (of St. Joseph) that yesterday forty foreigners in that town wanted to hoist our flag, but had no bunting. I shall send them some the first opportunity, and shall direct them to organize themselves into a company of cavalry, choose their own officers, for the protection of their own property against marauders and the Indians, and then report to me. When organized and reported they will be mustered into service and receive instructions from me. . . . .

Very respectfully, your obedient servant,

JOHN D. SLOAT,

Commander-in-Chief, etc.

Commandant J. B. Montgomery, U. S. Ship Portsmouth,
Bay of San Francisco.

Before Commodore Sloat knew that I was not acting under written orders he was, as will be seen by his letters, " extremely anxious " that I should co-operate with him. Now his activity seemed paralyzed, and what he said at our interview seemed true, " that he could do nothing." And he did nothing.

The story of the night preceding the raising of the flag is best told in the words of Ex-Governor Rodman Price of New Jersey, who was at that time an officer in the squadron under Commodore Sloat, and who had a deciding

GOV. RODMAN M. PRICE, OF NEW JERSEY.

part in that event.   This statement was written for me by Governor Price:

In July, 1845, the United States sloop of war *Cyane*, Captain William Mervine, sailed from Norfolk under orders to join the Pacific Squadron. (Mr. Price was purser of the *Cyane*.) Just before he left he saw President Polk, who, in the then disturbed relations between the United States and Mexico, expressed great anxiety in regard to the possible contingency of hostilities occurring between the two countries, and said, "that should it happen, California should be seized by the naval forces in the Pacific and held as indemnification for the expenses of carrying on such a war," and Mr. Price was fully impressed with the policy of the President.*

The *Cyane* joined the Pacific squadron in January, 1846, finding Commodore Sloat then commanding the squadron in the flag-ship frigate *Savannah*, at Mazatlan, on the west coast of Mexico, where a large naval force was concentrated of American and English ships—Sir George Seymour, the English admiral, having his flag on the *Collingwood*, a hundred-gun ship.

At the time of the *Cyane's* arrival, much excitement existed in both squadrons and on shore in regard to the anticipated rupture between the United States and Mexico. It was understood and believed that the English Government meant to seize or throw protection over California in case of war, as indemnity for the debt owing by Mexico to England. Therefore there was great anxiety for news, and much importance placed as to which squadron would first receive intelligence of war, as the fate of California depended upon it.

Soon after the *Cyane's* arrival, Lieutenant Archibald Gillespie, United States Marine Corps, came to Mazatlan, having crossed Mexico with despatches to Commodore Sloat and Captain Frémont. The latter was then supposed to be in California or Oregon, and Captain Mervine was ordered to land him (Gillespie) at some port where he could best communicate with Frémont, and about February 1st the *Cyane* sailed for the Sandwich Islands to deceive the English admiral as to her ultimate destination, and the offer to carry the English mail to the islands was made and accepted. The *Cyane* sailed direct for Honolulu, and thence to Monterey, Cal., arriving about March 1st, when we learned through our consul, Thomas O. Larkin, that Frémont had been at San Juan (some forty miles from Monterey) a short time previous to our arrival, and had sent a messenger to Mr. Larkin requesting supplies for his party, and that the Mexican authorities had forbidden any supplies being sent to him, and that General Castro, the Military Governor of California, had ordered Frémont to leave Mexican territory. As no attention was paid to this, Castro sent a very insolent note threatening to drive him out by military force. This threat Frémont treated with silent contempt, but he could get no supplies, which his command greatly needed.

General Castro then marched a strong military force against him. Frémont fortified himself and waited to receive him. Castro's force lay in sight some time without attacking, but made every effort to cut off his supply of water, and by siege compel him to surrender.

Frémont was starved out and left his position, and offered battle, which Castro declined, and Frémont went north.

Gillespie was left at Monterey, and pursued and overtook Frémont, who returned with him to Sutter's Fort. The *Cyane* returned to Mazatlan in April, and reported these facts to the commodore. The excitement had greatly intensified by the rumor that General Santa Anna had crossed the Rio Grande with a large force, and that General Taylor was in command of the American forces in Texas, and a battle anticipated.

Soon the sloop of war *Portsmouth*, Captain Montgomery, was despatched to San Francisco, Cal., and the *Levant*, Captain Page, to Monterey, Cal.; the *Warren*, Captain Hull, having been previously sent there. The destination of these vessels was not made known to the English admiral, who had sent the English frigate *Juno* to sea, without the usual formality of informing Commodore Sloat of her destination. But an English priest, Father McNamara, who had come across Mexico, had mysteriously taken passage in her. About June 1st the *Cyane* was again ordered to Monterey, Cal.—the belief then existing, from rumors, that a fight had occurred be-

---

* Mr. Price had recently been a guest at the White House, on a visit there to Knox Walker, secretary and nephew of the President.

tween the American and Mexican forces, and this belief was largely entertained by our consul, Mr. Parrott, who, about that time, set out for the City of Mexico—Commodore Sloat and the English admiral having all this time remained at Mazatlan.

After the *Cyane* sailed, the commodore received a despatch from Guadalajara, from Mr. Parrott, informing him of the battles of Palo Alto and Resaca de la Palma, which occurred in May.

The *Cyane* arrived at Monterey the last of June, and found the *Levant* and *Warren* at anchor, and heard that the *Portsmouth* was at (Yerba Buena) San Francisco, and what is curious, rumors were afloat that a battle had occurred on the Rio Grande, and the result detailed with some minuteness, which had come through Indian sources, which afterwards proved to be very accurate.

It was also learned that the English frigate *Juno* was at Santa Barbara, and that Father McNamara was negotiating with the Civil Governor and authorities for a grant of land in California, intended for European colonization, which was a part of the English design to acquire California, and so understood at the time.

Some days after our arrival, about July 1st, Commodore Sloat arrived, and it was confidently believed by the officers of the squadron that he would land at once, hoist our flag, and take possession of California, and all felt that the Fourth day of July was an appropriate day to do it.

The positive news of the battles through Mr. Parrott, and the feeling to chastise General Castro for his insult to our flag, and the wanton outrage upon Frémont, fully justified and demanded such a course: but to the disappointment and chagrin of all, the commodore sent his flag-lieutenant, Joseph Adams, ashore, and, as if a friendly port, desired to know when salutes would be exchanged.

In the meantime a very strong feeling had arisen with the native Californians against us, induced by English and French agents and the anticipated war with us. The friendly influences which had been cultivated by American residents, and our consul, Mr. Larkin, who had been many years in California, had made many friends among the Californians, and our trading-ships on the coast, which supplied all their wants and had taken all their exports (hides and tallow) and dealt honestly with the people, had contributed to American influence; but all this had been greatly changed, and the English sentiment had arisen, and a preference expressed for England's protection: a majority of the people greatly preferred that California should fall to England rather than to the United States. The French people, also, in California were against us and in favor of English plans.

The French consul, after we occupied Monterey, was detected in communicating with the Californians, and giving them information as to our military movements. So flagrant was his conduct that Commodore Stockton confined him to his house until he left the country.

Several days after Commodore Sloat's arrival, and on Sunday afternoon, July 5th, a sail was reported coming into the Bay of Monterey. All glasses were turned upon it, and it was watched with great interest. It proved to be the launch of the sloop of war *Portsmouth*, with Past-Midshipman Napoleon Harrison and sixteen men, sent by Captain Montgomery—he having heard of the *Cyane's* arrival at Monterey (Captain Mervine being his senior officer). The presence of the commodore was not known when the launch left. Harrison went to the flag-ship and delivered despatches.

Captain Montgomery had been requested by Frémont to send him supplies and munitions of war, and Major Gillespie had come from Sutter's fort to receive them, Frémont stating that American settlers in the Sacramento and San Joaquin valleys were much alarmed by the Californians' threatening movements, and had asked his protection, and that he needed the supplies to defend his own party and protect the lives and property of the Americans, and Montgomery wanted to know whether he should comply with Frémont's request.

Sloat immediately replied, instructing Montgomery *not to give Frémont any aid whatever*, but to obey strictly our treaty stipulations with Mexico. He also ordered his answer to be handed to Lieutenant Harrison, directing him to shove off, and return to his ship at once. It was then growing dark, and a high westerly wind prevailing. The men had been in the launch fifty-six hours. The order seemed so harsh to send Harrison off at night-fall in such tempestuous weather to the executive officer of the *Savannah* (Livingston), that he appealed to the commodore to allow Harrison to remain until daylight the next morning, and to allow his men to come on board and sleep, and be refreshed—they were wet and their limbs had been cramped. This request was granted.

These circumstances and facts had been learned by Mr. Price immediately from Captain Mervine, who was on board the flag-ship when the despatches were received from Montgomery, and Sloat had told him the character of his reply and instructions, at which he was greatly disappointed, and thought it a grave mistake of the commodore's.

Mr. Price made the facts known to the ward-room officers, who discussed them, and all felt that it was a fatal error, that the commodore was not carrying out the policy or wishes of the Government—jeopardizing its interests and sacrificing its honor.

Mr. Price considered the moment so critical that, as if by inspiration, he said, that if it were possible to get a boat, it then being quite late at night and after the crew had turned in, he felt he would be only doing a duty to go and see the commodore and urge him to reconsider his action. Upon reflection he decided to ask Captain Mervine for a boat, and stated his object for desiring it. Mervine said there was no use of going to see the commodore, that he himself had said everything against his order to Montgomery, but wished him to give all the aid and supplies that Frémont required, but added, "*you* shall have it if *you* desire it." The request was repeated, Mr. Price saying that he would like to present to the commodore the views of President Polk, as given to him a few days before the *Cyane* sailed from Norfolk.

First-Lieutenant Rowan, executive officer of the *Cyane*, was ordered to have the captain's gig called away for Mr. Price to go on board the flag-ship. Mr. Price was received on board the flag-ship by First-Lieutenant Livingston, who said the commodore had turned in, his cabin lights were out, and it was doubtful whether he would receive him, but would send in an orderly and see; and an answer was returned that he would. The cabin was lighted and the commodore came out of his state-room in his night-dress.

Mr. Price apologized for disturbing him, and stated that his visit was induced at that unusual hour by information he had received from Captain Mervine, who had informed him of the character of the communication from Captain Montgomery, and the reply to it—that he must pardon the intrusion and venture of coming to him, under the circumstances, to urge the reconsideration of his letters of instruction to Captain Montgomery denying Frémont the supplies he wanted to defend himself and protect American citizens and their property.

Feeling as Mr. Price did, that upon the decision of the commodore rested the loss or gain of California to the United States, he urged upon him every view and reason possible to recall the letter and show the evils which would result to himself as well as to his country, if Frémont was not sustained and our flag immediately raised on shore and a military occupation declared.

The evidence of hostilities existing between us and Mexico was dwelt upon—his delay would certainly give California to England. The English policy and intention was clear—the English frigate *Juno* was at Santa Barbara; that Admiral Seymour was following him with the intention of landing and occupying California. Under the circumstances, there was only one course to pursue to meet the expectations of his country. The first and only reply Sloat made was, that he did not want to fall into the same mistake that Commodore Jones made two years before. The great difference of circumstances which existed at that time and the present were pointed out, and that delay would undoubtedly bring about a serious complication with the English, if not a fight; that he could not witness the raising of the English flag over California without remonstrance, active and forcible. After silent reflection, Sloat yielded to the entreaty of Mr. Price, and decided to recall the letter to Captain Montgomery, and not only ordered him to furnish all the supplies and all the aid to Fremont he required, but also, on the receipt of the order, to raise the flag immediately at San Francisco, informing him the flag would be raised by him the next morning, being July 7, 1846, at Monterey. That he would receive therewith a copy of the proclamation under which California would be occupied by us. The proclamation was written that night before Mr. Price had left the *Savannah ;* and he returned to his ship, receiving the congratulations of his captain and mess-mates as having performed a signal service. He bore orders to Captain Mervine, the senior officer of the fleet, to go ashore at daylight in the morning and notify the Mexican military and civil authorities that the commodore would land a force at ten o'clock that day to take possession of California in the name of the United States Government.

Captain Mervine performed this service, taking with him Lieutenant Edward Higgins, and Purser Price as his aides. Arrangements were accordingly made, and a force of sailors and marines numbering about two hundred and fifty, taken from the different vessels, were landed, and the flag, in charge of Lieutenant Higgins, was raised on the flag-staff of the Custom-House, and the Proclamation of Occupation was read by Purser Price, in Spanish and in English, before our own force and the assembled citizens of the place, from the porch of the Custom-House. Our sailors and marines then occupied the Mexican barracks, which the troops of General Castro had just vacated, and every military precaution was taken to resist attack.

The English admiral arrived a few days afterward, and the first thing he said on receiving the commodore was, "Sloat, if your flag was not flying on shore I should have hoisted mine there."

Purser Price was appointed prefect and alcalde, and has the distinction of having first administered American law in California, under the "Proclamation of Occupation."

Frémont organized a military battalion, and afforded protection to Americans at Sutter's Fort, and marched south to punish General Castro for the warfare they had waged against him. This military organization of Frémont's is historically known as the renowned California Battalion, and became the active power of subduing California. And in a revolt of the Californians to our authority after their submission, Frémont's command again brought them to submission. About two weeks after the flag was raised, Frémont came with his command to Monterey and volunteered their services to Commodore Stockton, who had succeeded Sloat, and was anxious to carry an active war against the Californians in arms against us.

The English admiral was still at Monterey when Frémont came, and looked on with his officers with much interest. It was, indeed, a novel and interesting sight—the command, numbering two or three hundred men, marching in a square, within which was the cattle which they were driving for their subsistence. They were mostly clothed in buckskin, and armed with Hawkins rifles. The individuality of each man was very remarkable. When they dismounted, their first care was their rifle. Frémont, by his explorations and the geographical and scientific knowledge he had given to the world, was the conspicuous figure. The hunters and guides of his exploring party were the next objects sought for. Kit Carson and the Indians accompanying him were the objects of much attention.

The command carried terror and dismay to the Californians; the unerring and deadly rifle in the hands of the frontiersmen was equally dreaded by the Indian.

The prompt, decisive action taken by Frémont before Sloat raised the flag forced Sloat to do so, and was the great cause which conspired to the acquisition of California.

CHAPTER XV.

Reviewing now, long afterward, the events of that time I come to the belief that the pause which Commodore Sloat made at Monterey in executing the orders of his chief, the Secretary of the Navy, was occasioned by the conflicting despatch of the Secretary of State to his consul; which was pressed upon Commodore Sloat, by the consul, Mr. Larkin, but which had been already rendered wholly inapplicable to the existing condition of affairs before it was delivered to him by Gillespie.

Days of indecision followed, during which the only indication of future action came from Commodore Stockton.

In company with Lieutenant Gillespie I went on board the *Congress* to talk over the situation with Commodore Stockton. I informed him fully of the interview with Commodore Sloat, and its result in being told " that he could do nothing."

The commodore said to us in reply that he was only second in command, and could not with propriety express any opinion upon the conduct of Commodore Sloat. I remarked to him, that in the course of the night I would decide whether I should return to the United States, or remain in the territory. Commodore Stockton then informed me that within a few days he would be in command of the forces on shore and afloat, and that on assuming the command he would immediately communicate to me his intentions as to future operations. Meantime, he requested me to remain.

The next day he addressed the following letter to Commodore Sloat:

U. S. FRIGATE CONGRESS, July 23, 1846.

MY DEAR COMMODORE: It is very important to take General Castro or to drive him out of the country. Until one or the other is done, I see no hope of restoring peace and good order to this territory.

I wish to send the *Cyane* with Captain Frémont's men to the southward, to head him off, and drive him back here.

Had you not better send me an order to take command at once, and make my own arrangements?

It will facilitate operations, and relieve you from a great deal of trouble.

Faithfully your obedient servant,

(Signed)   R. F. STOCKTON.

To Commodore J. D. Sloat, etc., etc., Flag-Ship Savannah.

In reply to the urgent request of Commodore Stockton he was then told by Commodore Sloat that on account of his ill health he would return to the United States as soon as possible, but was not yet disposed to give him the command of the squadron.   Commodore Stockton says: " I then stated that it was very important that these Mexican officers should be driven out of the country or taken prisoners, and requested him to place under my command the United States ship of war *Cyane*, then lying in the harbor; he did so.   Having then the command of all the forces on shore, and the *Congress* and the *Cyane*, I immediately sent word to Captain Frémont of what had occurred, and to let him know, that if he and Lieutenant Gillespie, with the men who were with them, would volunteer to serve under my command as long as I was in possession of the territory and desired their services, that I would form a battalion and appoint Captain Frémont the major and Lieut. Gillespie a captain, and all the other necessary officers."

This was all done in the course of the day and the next morning; and they were ordered to embark on board the United States ship *Cyane*, to be landed at San Diego.   In this way was the Navy Battalion of mounted riflemen formed, and brought into the service of the United States.

To accept the proposal of Commodore Stockton was to abandon the strong and independent position in which I had left Washington and under which I had continuously acted, and in which I knew I would have the support of the Government.

My plan had been, with the willing co-operation of Commander Montgomery, who had agreed to meet me with the *Portsmouth* at Santa Barbara, and the enthusiastic support of the settlers and immigrants, to continue the movement south until it terminated in the complete conquest of the department.

But the proposal of Commodore Stockton was not what Commodore Sloat had in mind when he wrote to ask my co-operation.   His withdrawal gave a new face to affairs.   There was for me no longer any initiative.   If Commodore Stockton could bring himself to make this request I had no other course than to acquiesce, and accept the new situation into which circumstances forced me.

Knowing that the men under my command would go with me, I accepted Commodore Stockton's proposal to take service under him and remain with him as long as he required my services.   And I adhered to this engagement at the cost of my commission in the army.

CARMEL MISSION CHURCH.

The temporary indecision over, and a line of action adopted, I wrote from the old mission of Carmel to Senator Benton; giving him a summary of events up to the date of writing.

MISSION OF CARMEL,* July 25, 1846.

MY DEAR SIR: When Mr. Gillespie overtook me in the middle of May, we were encamped on the northern shore of the greater Tlamath Lake. Snow was falling steadily and heavily in the mountains, which entirely surround and dominate the elevated valley region into which we had penetrated; in the east, and north, and west, barriers absolutely impassable barred our road; we had no provisions; our animals were already feeble, and while any other way was open, I could not bring myself to attempt such a doubtful enterprise as a passage of these unknown mountains in the dead of winter. Every day the snow was falling; and in the face of the depressing influence exercised on the people by the loss of our men, and the unpromising appearance of things, I judged it inexpedient to pursue our journey further in this direction, and determined to retrace my steps, and carry out the views of the Government by reaching the frontier on the line of the Colorado River. I had scarcely reached the Lower Sacramento, when General Castro, then in the north (at Sonoma, in the Department of Sonoma, north of the bay of San Francisco, commanded by General Vallejo), declared his determination immediately to proceed against the foreigners settled in the country, for whose expulsion an order had just been issued by the governor of the Californias. For these purposes Castro immediately assembled a force at the Mission of Santa Clara, a strong place, on the northern shore of the Francisco Bay. You will remember how grossly outraged and insulted we had already been by this officer; many in my own camp, and throughout the country, thought that I should not have retreated in March last. I felt humiliated and humbled; one of the main objects proposed by this expedition had been entirely defeated, and it was the opinion of the officers of the squadron (so I was informed by Mr. Gillespie) that I could not again retreat consistently with any military reputation. Unable to procure supplies elsewhere, I had sent by Mr. Gillespie to Captain Montgomery, commanding the United States ship of war *Portsmouth*, then lying at Monterey, a small requisition for such supplies as were indispensably necessary to leave the valley; and my animals were now in such a state that I could not get out of the valley, without reaching the country which lies on the east side of them in an entirely destitute condition. Having carefully examined my position, and foreseeing, I think, clearly, ALL the consequences which may eventuate to me from such a step, I determined to take such active and anticipatory measures as should seem to me most expedient to protect my party and justify my own character. I was well aware of the grave responsibility which I assumed, but I also determined that, having once decided to do so, I would assume it and its consequences fully and entirely, and go through with the business completely to the end. I regret that, by a sudden emergency, I have only an hour for writing to all friends, and that therefore from the absence of detail, what I say to you will not be clearly understood. Castro's first measure was an attempt to incite the Indian population of the Joaquin and Sacramento valleys, and the neighboring mountains, to burn the crops of the foreigners and otherwise proceed immediately against them. These Indians are extremely numerous, and the success of his measure would have been very destructive; but he failed entirely. On the 6th of June I decided on the course which I would pursue, and immediately concerted my operations with the foreigners inhabiting the Sacramento valley. A few days afterwards, one of Castro's officers, with a party of fourteen men, attempted to pass a drove of two hundred horses from Sonoma to Santa Clara, via New Helvetia, with the avowed purpose of bringing troops into the country. On the 11th they were surprised at daylight on the Consumné River by a party of twelve from my camp. The horses were taken, but they were (the men) dismissed without injury. At daybreak on the 15th, the military fort of Sonoma was taken by surprise, with 9 brass pieces of artillery, 250 stands of muskets, some other arms, and a quantity of ammunition. General Vallejo, his brother (Captain Vallejo), Colonel Prudon, and some others were taken prisoners, and placed at New Helvetia, a fortified post under my command. In the meantime a launch had reached New Helvetia with stores from the ship *Portsmouth*, now lying at Yerba Buena, on

---

* The Mission of Carmel is three miles south of Monterey.

Francisco Bay. News of General Castro's proceedings against me in *March* had reached Commodore Sloat at Mazatlan at the end of that month, and he had immediately despatched the ship *Portsmouth* to Monterey, with general instructions to protect American interests in California.

These enterprises accomplished I proceeded to the American settlements on the Sacramento, and the Rio de los Americanos, to obtain reinforcements of men and rifles.

The information brought by Mr. Gillespie to Captain Montgomery, in relation to my position, induced that officer immediately to proceed to Yerba Buena, whence he despatched his launch to me. I immediately wrote to him, by return of the boat, describing to him fully my position and intentions, in order that he might not, by supposing me to be acting under orders from our Government, unwittingly commit himself in affording me other than such assistance as his instructions would authorize him naturally to offer an officer charged with an important public duty ; or, in fine, to any citizen of the United States.

Information having reached me from the commanding officer at Sonoma, that his post was threatened with an attack by a force under General Castro, I raised camp on the American Fork on the afternoon of the 23d, and, accompanied by Mr. Gillespie, at two in the morning of the 25th, reached Sonoma, with ninety mounted riflemen, having marched eighty miles. Our people still held the place, only one division of Castro's force, a squadron of cavalry, numbering seventy men, and commanded by Joaquin de la Torre (one of his best officers), having succeeded in crossing the straits (Francisco Bay). This force had attacked an advanced party of twenty Americans, and (was) defeated with the loss of two killed and two or three wounded. The Americans lost none. This was an unexpected check to the Californians, who had announced their intentions to defeat our people without firing a gun ; to beat out their brains with their "tapaderos," and destroy them "con cuchillos puros." They were led to use this expression from the circumstance that a few days previous they had captured two of our men (an express), and after wounding, had bound them to trees, and cut them to pieces while alive, with an exaggeration of cruelty which only Indians would be capable of. In a few days de la Torre was driven from the country, having barely succeeded in effecting his escape across the straits, the guns (six large and handsome pieces) spiked at the fort on the *south* side of the entrance to Francisco Bay, and the communication with the opposite side entirely broken off, the boats and launches being either destroyed or in our possession. Three of Castro's party having landed on the Sonoma side in advance, were killed on the beach ; and beyond this there was no loss on either side. In all these proceedings, Mr. Gillespie has acted with me. We reached Sonoma again on the evening of July 4th, and in the morning I called the people together, and spoke to them in relation to the position of the country, advising a course of operations which was unanimously adopted. California was declared independent, the country put under martial law, the force organized and officers elected. A pledge, binding themselves to support these measures, and to obey their officers, was signed by those present. The whole was placed under my direction. Several officers from the *Portsmouth* were present at this meeting. Leaving Captain Grigsby with fifty men in command of Sonoma, I left that place on the 6th, and reached my encampment on the American Fork in three days. Before we arrived at that place, General Castro had evacuated Santa Clara, which he had been engaged in fortifying, and with a force of about four hundred men, and two pieces of artillery, commenced his retreat upon St. John's, a fortified post, having eight pieces of artillery, principally brass. On the evening of the 10th we were electrified by the arrival of an express from Captain Montgomery, with the information that Commodore Sloat had hoisted the flag of the United States at Monterey, and taken possession of the country. Captain Montgomery had hoisted the flag at Yerba Buena, and sent one to Sonoma, to be hoisted at that place. One also was sent to the officer commanding at New Helvetia, requesting that it might be hoisted at his post.

Independence and the flag of the United States are synonymous terms to the foreigners here (the northern, which is the stronger part, particularly), and accordingly I directed the flag to be hoisted with a salute the next morning. The event produced great rejoicing among our people. The next day I received an express from Commodore Sloat, transmitting to me his proclamation, and directing me to proceed with the force under my orders to Monterey. The registered force, actually in arms, under my orders, numbered two hundred and twenty riflemen, with one piece of field artillery, and ten men, in addition to the artillery of the garrison.

INTERIOR OF CARMEL MISSION IN ITS MOST RUINOUS CONDITION.

We were on the eve of marching on Castro when this intelligence arrived; accordingly, I directed my march upon Monterey, where I arrived on the evening of the 19th, with a command of one hundred and sixty mounted riflemen, and one piece of artillery. I found also there Commodore Stockton in command of the *Congress*, and Admiral Seymour, in command of her Britannic majesty's ship *Collingwood*, of eighty guns. I have been badly interrupted, and shall scarcely be able to put you in full possession of occurrences.

To come briefly to a conclusion, Commodore Sloat has transferred the squadron, with California and its appurtenances, into the hands of Commodore Stockton, who has resolved to make good the possession of California. This officer approves entirely of the course pursued by myself and Mr. Gillespie, who, I repeat, has been hand-in-hand with me in this business. I received this morning from Commodore Stockton a commission of major in the United States army, retaining command of my battalion, to which a force of eighty marines will be attached. We are under orders to embark to-morrow morning on board the *Cyane* sloop of war, and disembark at San Diego, immediately in the rear of Castro. He is now at the Puebla de los Angeles, an interior city, with a force of about five hundred men, supposed to be increasing. The design is to attack him with my force at that place. He has there seven or eight pieces of artillery.

Commodore Sloat, who goes home by way of Panama, promises to hand or send you this immediately on his arrival at Washington, to which he goes direct. It is my intention to leave this country, if it is within the bounds of possibility, at the end of August. I could then succeed in crossing without fear on account of the snow; and by that time a territorial government will be in operation here.

Yours very truly,

J. C. FRÉMONT.

Hon. Thomas H. Benton, United States Senate, Washington City, D. C.

For the reason that will be naturally conceded to me, that I feel special interest in having this part of California history understood, I introduce here some extracts from a discussion in the Senate of the United States immediately upon the close of the war. In this I anticipate somewhat, but I do so in order to complete the record by showing how these events were viewed at the time they took place by men in the Government who were in the best position to have correct information and to understand them.

In a speech in the Senate by Senator Dix to which fuller reference will be made when I reach a later subject, he gives clearly the attitude of England towards us at the time immediately preceding the declaration of war against Mexico; and, from a discussion in the House of Lords in 1845, the Earl of Aberdeen defending the Ministry, shows the power England gives her admirals on foreign stations and the use she makes of the results in cases similar to that of California. Her usage was to leave to them unlimited discretion in great contingencies; reserving it to herself to support or disavow their acts, but always demanding action. Senator Dix makes it forcibly clear that, if the work on land had not been done on which Commodore Sloat based his raising of the American flag, Admiral Seymour would have raised that of England, and California would have been lost to us; for with her vastly superior navy the chances of war were largely against us.

It will be borne in mind that this speech was not made by an incautious or inadequately informed person. General Dix was a member of the Military Committee of the Senate and Senator from New York; his military service and high social position gave him habits of restraint and respect for the courtesies of his position; and he would not have made these assertions in the presence of the English Minister unless facts and the occasion called for and justified them.

"The objects accomplished by Colonel Frémont, as subsequent events have shown, were far more important than those I have referred to. There is no doubt that his rapid and decisive movements kept California out of the hands of British subjects and perhaps out of the hands of the British Government; and it is in this point of view that I desire to present the subject to the Senate." . . . "The grant to MacNamara is so connected with the movements of the public vessels and public agents of Great Britain as to raise a strong presumption that he was secretly countenanced by the British Government." . . . "I have referred to the connection of MacNamara's movements with the public vessels of Great Britain as presumptive evidence of the connection of the British Government with them. I do not inquire whether Admiral Seymour had special instructions or not. From the declaration of Admiral Purvis, in the intervention of La Plata, it is highly probable that British naval officers cruising in distant seas have general instructions *to protect British interests at all hazards.*" . . . "From all the circumstances connected with the transactions in California, we are constrained to believe that the British naval commander was fully apprised of MacNamara's objects, as well as the design to place that country under the protection of Great Britain, and that he was there co-operating in the one, and ready to co-operate in the other." . . . "It is impossible that the success of these movements should not have brought us into direct collision with Great Britain. We could not have failed to regard them, considered in connection with her proceedings in Oregon, and more recently in Central America, as part of a deliberate design to environ us with her colonies, and especially to shut us out from the Pacific and its extending commerce. From all the facts, we can hardly doubt either that she would have taken possession of the country in her own name, or, what is perhaps more probable, that she would in the first instance have taken it under her protection." . . . "It is in this point of view that these transactions possess the greatest interest and importance, and that the sagacity, promptitude, and decision of our youthful commander in California, at the time the disturbance broke out, have given him the strongest claims on his countrymen. Any faltering on his part—any hesitancy in acting promptly—might have lost us millions of dollars and thousands of lives; and it might also have cost us a contest of which the end is not readily foreseen."

Senator Atchison, of Missouri, from the different stand-point of specially Western interests, said "that he felt it his duty to say something on this

FALSE BAY, NEAR CARMEL.

Bill ('California Claims') because some of the claimants were citizens of Missouri, and personal friends with whom he had been long acquainted. He gave it as his opinion not only that the conquest of California was effected by Colonel Frémont, but that the United States had derived the advantage of this conquest at comparatively little cost. He justified Colonel Frémont in all that he had done." He made some references to the course which Colonel Frémont pursued—" a course in some instances rendered indispensable for his own preservation, and always characterized by skill and promptitude. War had existed before Colonel Frémont struck a blow; so that the United States Government is properly liable for the claims which are provided for by this Bill. The emigrants left their families in the mountains and joined the battalion for the defence of Colonel Frémont and had received not a cent of pay during nine months in which they served."

Senator Cass, of Michigan:
" One point, however, has been touched upon which I think it would be proper to mention. These operations took place at a great distance off, and under peculiar circumstances. A great responsibility devolved upon the officer at the head of the expedition; and I think he is entitled to great credit for the course which he pursued in getting possession of the country."

Senator Clarke, of Rhode Island, said " that Colonel Frémont in turning back from his scientific investigations to mingle in the revolutionary scenes in California was influenced by the letter of the President of the United States, and the letter of Mr. Buchanan, conveyed to Colonel Frémont by Lieutenant Gillespie, and therefore that the claims are entitled to recognition, because they arose out of instructions sent out by Government. All services which Colonel Frémont performed after the receipt of these letters were strictly legal, and authorized by the Executive; and the Government was as much bound to pay for them as for any other services."

Senator Crittenden, of Kentucky, said :
. . . " There is but one other question, and upon that I need say nothing—it is, whether Congress is disposed to pay these claims or not. I think we are bound to pay them. They have originated in a manner that is not regular, I admit. They have grown up under peculiar circumstances. These services have been valuable to the country. They are such as we would have directed if we had been acquainted with the circumstances, and it is but just and proper that we should legalize them. Upon every principle of equity we are bound to pay the claims. The parties claiming compensation are entitled, upon every consideration, patriotism, hardihood,

courage, and the sacrifices incurred in rendering these services, and by every other consideration that can entitle men to remuneration. The courage and conduct of Colonel Frémont have signalized his name. His services were peculiar, attended with great responsibility to himself—characterized by great firmness and humanity, as well as devotion to his country."

Senator Allen, of Ohio, said :

"This is all that I intended to say on the subject ; but if I were to indulge myself in commenting on the events out of which this claim grew, I should be inclined to occupy some of the time of the Senate in giving my opinion in regard to the conduct of Lieutenant-Colonel Frémont, and the gallant men under his command." . . . "Nor is this my opinion of him just now or recently formed ; for at the opening of the war with Mexico, I took occasion to suggest his name in connection with a command in the war which would have enabled him to exert that military genius and energy which I knew him to possess, and by which he would have conferred yet greater services on his country."

Senator Badger, of North Carolina, said :

. . . "We next find him in Oregon, where he is overtaken by a messenger, an officer of the Government, who bore to him a letter, and—there is no use in concealing it, sir—although it purported to be a mere letter of introduction, it was, in reality, an official document, accrediting the bearer of it to Colonel Frémont, with a view to the union of the two, in devising some means to counteract the designs of the British emissaries. Captain Gillespie, the officer to whom I allude, in his evidence before the Committee on Military Affairs, states, that he was directed to convey the order of the Government to Colonel Frémont, to watch the interests of the United States in California. This, sir, was the purport of Captain Gillespie's mission ; and so soon as the communication was made to him, Colonel Frémont returned to California, under the order of his Government, and by its express authority." . . .

The Very Rev. Father MacNamara was an apostolic missionary who had projected a far-reaching plan to colonize California with emigrants from Ireland. Evidently, in the exercise of his special functions, he had selected California as the field for his labors. Looking back to the work of the early missionaries, it was surely a great field, and a noble ambition to revive on a higher plane the power of the Church as it had existed in the old missions. In this he was strongly supported by the Archbishop of Mexico who earnestly recommended his plan to the authorities. During his stay in the city of Mexico, he lived either in the family of the English consul or the Chargé d'Affaires. Early in January he laid before the President of Mexico his plan " to colonize California with Irish Catholics." In his application to the President he says that no people of the old continent are better fitted for colonization and better adapted to the religion, character, and temperament of the inhabitants of Mexico ; " that the Irish people are devout Catholics, moral, industrious, sober, and brave. He says, that in making this proposition he has in view three objects : first to advance the cause of Catholicism ; secondly, to contribute to the happiness of his countrymen ; and in the third place, he wishes to place an impediment to further usurpations on the part of an irreligious and anti-Catholic nation. And for these objects he proposes that an extensive territory upon the sea-coast of Upper California be granted to him. The first colonists were to be established on the Bay of San Francisco ; to begin, one thousand families would be brought, and afterward a second colony to be established about Monterey, and a third about Santa Barbara. In this way the whole coast, at least that part of it where there was danger to be apprehended, would remain completely assured against the invasions and robberies of foreigners. One square league was to be given to each family, free of all cost ; and to those children of the colonists who should marry, half a league each, as a gift of the nation. An exemption from all taxation was to be granted for a certain number of years ; and the colonists were to be considered under the protection of the Government and in the enjoyment of all their rights, upon taking possession of their lands.

In a reply under date of the 19th of January from the Minister of Foreign Relations, Father MacNamara is informed that the project of colonization in California which he had presented to the supreme Government had been considered by the Cabinet, which had decided that, in view of the necessity of adopting some vigorous measures upon that subject and other concessions which were properly functions of Congress, an account of the whole matter would be referred to that body, and that this would be done at a fitting time.

It appears that there was some hesitation on the part of the Government ; but the principal and only objection to taking immediate steps for founding the colony was the difficulty of obtaining the necessary means for transporting the colonists to their destination. To this objection Father MacNamara replies in another communication to the President. In this he sets out the means by which he proposes to obtain the necessary funds ; one, by the sale of the small properties of the colonists, another, by hypothecation of a grant of lands which could be given him ; and finally, the use of the import duties at the port of San Francisco, which he asks from the Government. And he urges upon the Mexican President the expediency of

losing no time in this important affair, " if success is to be looked for."
" Your Excellency," he says, " knows too well that we are surrounded by a
vile and skilful enemy who loses no means, however low they may be, to
possess himself of the best lands of that country, and who hates to the death
your race and your religion." " If," he continues, " the means I propose to
you are not promptly adopted, your Excellency may rest assured that before
a year the Californias will form part of the American Union." . . . " I
have no personal interest in this affair, save the progress of the Holy Religion of God, and the happiness of my countrymen ; as for the loyalty and
fidelity of these to the Mexican Government, I answer with my life. And
as there can be brought a sufficient number of colonists, at least ten thousand,
I am of opinion and can affirm with certainty that this number would be
sufficient to repel both the secret intrigues and the open attacks of the
American usurpers."

It is in evidence that his project secured the approbation of the Mexican
Government ; and that he went to California to perfect his plans under the
auspices of the English Government. On the 20th of June he arrived at
Santa Barbara, California, in the frigate *Juno* which had brought him up
from Mazatlan.

It appears that, immediately upon his arrival, MacNamara submitted his
plans to the Governor Don Pio Pico, who urged them favorably upon the
Departmental Assembly in his official note of the 24th June. On the 1st of
July he addressed to the Governor a petition, in the usual form, setting out
the fact that he had arrived in California with the object of establishing a
colony of his countrymen ; that he had received the benign co-operation of
the venerable and illustrious Archbishop of Mexico and the cordial recognition of the supreme Government, which had recommended him to come in
person to the department to select the land adapted to his purpose ; to set
out to the governor his project of colonization ; and to go through the customary formalities.

He offers to contract with the Government to introduce into the department, in the shortest possible time, two thousand families of Irish people,
and he solicits the governor to cause to be adjudicated to him in ownership
the lands situated between the river San Joaquin, from its source to its
mouth, and the Sierra Nevada ; the northern boundary to be the Consumné
River, and the southern the extremity of the Tuláres in the vicinity of San
Gabriel. This application was dated Santa Barbara, July 1st. Before the
arrival of Commodore Sloat, tidings of the battles of the Rio Grande had
already reached California through New Mexico and Arizona overland ;
and the authorities, who were all favorably disposed to the MacNamara
project, hurried forward the issue of this and a number of other land grants.
The governor immediately referred the application of Father MacNamara

to the Departmental Assembly, with a request that it should give its opinion upon the subject and return it to him for final action.

On the 4th of July the governor issued a grant conformably to the application, reciting that the Departmental Assembly had agreed to grant, for colonization by Irish families, the lands solicited by the Father Eugenio MacNamara, subject to the approval of the Supreme National Government and under the usual conditions which accompanied grants of land in California. The boundaries were the same as I have already stated, and the number of families to constitute the colony was fixed at three thousand, to each of whom a square league of land was to be assigned, making in all thirteen and a half millions of acres.

Upon the 7th of July at Los Angeles the Departmental Assembly transmitted to the governor the report of a special committee, approved by the Assembly in extra session of that date, upon the colonization project which he had " referred to them with the expression of his great desire that it be given immediate effect."

But it was too late. On the morning of the day that the Departmental Assembly communicated to the governor their formal approval of the Mac-Namara grant the flag of the United States was hoisted at Monterey, and the Mexican authority ended in California.

The Mexican archives comprehending the titles to land in California were taken possession of by me, and among them the grant to MacNamara. This, with the documents relating to it, I delivered to the Government in Washington. All other titles to land I delivered afterward to General Kearny.

We cannot fail to sympathize with the grief of a mind which had conceived a project so far-reaching and which had experienced the shock of overthrow in the moment of its complete success. The time, the thought, the labor of solicitation, the patient endurance with slower or inferior minds—all, had resulted in the blank of absolute failure.

In the interest of his Church it was a nobly conceived plan ; one among the great ideas which affect nations. Doubtless, in looking abroad for a field of missionary labor, he had chosen this, as out of all others that one which combined singular advantages and promised the most glorious results for the Church of which he was a devoted servant ; laboring with no selfish aim other than the satisfaction which he promised himself in the advancement of his religion and the happiness of his countrymen. Under his direction the three thousand families would have spread over the whole beautiful valley of the San Joaquin. Farms would have occupied the river lands, and the plains between would have served as cattle ranges in that climate of wonderful animal growth ; and among the innumerable springs and streams of the foot-hills, and up to the snow of the Sierra would have been happy and prosperous homesteads. Under the guidance of an intelligent and stable authority the groves of grand old oaks, and the magnificent pine forests would not have been swept away. With its advantages of climate and soil and abundant streams the whole valley would have presented a picture of agricultural beauty unsurpassed on earth.

The mountain Indians would have been reclaimed and made useful herdsmen and laborers, and the abandoned missions along the coast would have been restored on a higher level and made centres of productive labor. The Indians would have been held under the steady influence of a firm government and educated to the advantages of civilization and not left only to the degrading contact with its vices. This is not merely an opinion asserted. It had been a reality proved by the successful work of the missions when the country was very remote and the resources were only from within themselves.

I realized fully at the time what I have been here writing, for it happened that just in those days when the colonization project failed, I wrote from the quiet of the beautiful ruin of the old Carmel Mission to Senator Benton, of the events which had brought me to that date and place. The date of the letter, "Carmel Mission, July 24, 1846," carried with it, for me, a marked significance; it ended my mission as well as that of Mac-Namara. After the wreck of his hopes, Father MacNamara left California in Admiral Seymour's flag-ship, the *Collingwood.*

From early in '45, through to the commencement of hostilities, war with Mexico, though not begun, was accepted as imminently certain. The hostile forces faced each other on the banks of the Rio Grande. On the Pacific coast we were facing England. Her fleet there, commanded by Rear Admiral Sir George Seymour, was the largest she had ever sent to those waters. Mexico had no fleet, and her coast on the Pacific was comparatively defenceless. The chief anxiety of our Government was to be the first to seize California, and with or without war, and in no event, and under no disguise, to let England take possession of that country. The English fleet watched closely the movements of the American commodore. Being aware of this fact Commodore Sloat, upon hearing of the first battle on the Rio Grande, got under way in the frigate *Savannah*, then at anchor off Mazatlan, for the ostensible purpose of proceeding to California ; an English vessel of war weighed soon after the *Savannah*, and stood in the direction of San Blas, where it was known the English admiral was; after cruising in the Gulf two days, the commodore returned to his anchorage off Mazatlan, when another English ship got under way and stood in the direction of San Blas. It is believed that this manœuvre of Commodore Sloat was intended to mislead the English admiral. On the 8th June the *Savannah* again made sail and after a passage of twenty-three days, during which a press of canvas was carried, she arrived on the 2d of July at the port of Monterey, in Upper California. The *Collingwood* of eighty guns, flag-ship of Admiral Seymour, entered the harbor on the 16th of July.

Concurrent events make it clear that it was Admiral Seymour's intention to hoist the English flag at Monterey, but the movements of Commodore Sloat misled him and he came into the harbor too late. Still he did not admit that California was lost to England. This will be recognized in the letter by which he instructed English consuls at the different ports in the attitude they were to maintain. These instructions show that he looked upon the question as only adjourned, and that the raising of the flag of the United States operated simply as a stay of proceedings.

The cool and defiant tone of the note, with which he communicated a copy of these instructions to commodore Sloat, shows that it was in this light he wished that officer to know that he regarded the situation.

H. B. M. SHIP COLLINGWOOD.
MONTEREY, July 22, 1846.

SIR: As I think it desirable that you should be in possession of my view of the present occupation of this province by the force under your command, and the duties and conduct which I have recommended to Her Britannic Majesty's vice-consul under the circumstances, I beg to enclose, for your information, a copy of a letter I have this day addressed to Mr. Forbes; and, with every consideration, have the honor to remain

Your most obedient servant,
(Signed)   G. F. SEYMOUR,
Rear Admiral and Commander-in-Chief of H. B. M.'s Squadron in the Pacific.

To Commodore Sloat, Commander-in-Chief of the United States Squadron, Pacific.

[*Copy.*]
H. M. SHIP COLLINGWOOD,
MONTEREY, 22d July, 1846.

SIR: On quitting the coast of Upper California, it may be useful to you that I should shortly state my views of your situation as Her Majesty's vice-consul in that Province, under present circumstances.

The squadron of the United States having taken forcible possession of the principal ports, in consequence of hostilities having occurred on the Rio Grande between the armies of the United States and Mexico, the value of the services of the consuls of the different powers is enhanced, in order that they may assist in affording or obtaining protection for their fellow-subjects, whose interests may be compromised in the distracted state of affairs which exists, or may be expected to prevail; I am, therefore, glad to have been informed by the commodore commanding the United States squadron that there is no intention to disturb the foreign consuls in the exercise of their functions.

I observe in the proclamation issued on the 7th of July, that he acquaints the inhabitants that California will henceforward be a portion of the United States.

Whatever may be the expectations of that officer, I apprehend he would not be warranted by the practice or law of nations, nor, I believe, by the Constitution of the United States, to declare that California has been annexed to that Republic; and that the tenure under which the forces of the United States at present hold this province should, therefore, be regarded as a provisional occupation pending future decisions, or the issue of the contest between the United States and Mexico; and in that light alone it should be regarded by you, until you receive instructions from the department under which you act, for your conduct.

I recommend to you to preserve the strictest neutrality between contending parties, and to conduct yourself with the prudence and circumspection which are so essential to make your services as Her Majesty's vice-consul beneficial in the present state of Upper California.

I have the honor to be, sir, your obedient servant,

(Signed)   G. F. SEYMOUR,

Rear Admiral and Commander-in-Chief.

To James Alexander Forbes, Esq.,

Her Majesty's Vice-Consul in California.

The nation seems now in the humor to read its titles to its lands and its honors. In this interval of renewed prosperity, and rest from great agitations which were made personal to all, they look back, and read with comprehending interest of the men concerned in shaping affairs, judging for themselves what influence their personal character had upon national events. In reading history the time which nurses great events seems long, but the culminating moments which bring triumph or disaster, and in which men display their real character, are swift in passing and demand action equally swift.

Up to the time of the Louisiana purchase our western coast line had been the bank of the Mississippi. That great transfer of territory extended our limits to the Pacific and the settlement of the Oregon question now confirmed our title to a coast line on that ocean. With this question of Oregon the country had been made familiar by the efforts of the statesmen who had successfully defended and finally enforced our title. The great value of California in itself, and by its position commercially so advantageous, and geographically appurtenant to the United States, were until recently so little known as not to have attracted public attention in this country. Its acquisition by us was a new idea; and entertained only by the few men with whom an increase of territory, which should secure for the Republic enduring existence and with it unlimited prosperity, was a fixed idea. The history of the time shows that these men were few. Fewer still are living now to witness the marvellous result of their forethought. As its value to us became gradually recognized the idea of its acquisition by purchase from Mexico, as an ontlier useless to her, took definite shape. War had interfered to prevent acquiring a title to this valuable territory by purchase alone; but the course of events had ended in possession by force, finally confirmed to us both by treaty and purchase. Now in the possession of California the country had rounded off its grand domain, and could say with Senator Benton, " We own the country from sea to sea—from the Atlantic to the Pacific—and upon a breadth equal to the length of the Mississippi and embracing ths whole temperate zone."

The President had proposed to himself the acquisition of California as one of the chief measures of his administration. In his Cabinet he was energetically supported by his Secretary of the Navy, Mr. Bancroft, who had long before had this in view as a cherished political measure; for reasons which time has singularly justified.

Outside of his Cabinet he had the powerful aid of Senator Benton, who was Chairman of the Committee on Military Affairs and the head of the Democratic party; and who, as is known, was imbued with the subject as belonging with his plan of western expansion.

The remoteness of California rendered it practically impossible to operate there by land force instantly upon the breaking out of the war, and Mr. Marcy made no preparation for such an exigency there, but occupied himself with Texas and Mexico on the Rio Grande.

To reach California by a force overland needed months of time, and required that first possession should be had of the intervening province of New Mexico which lay across the road. This was also in the nature of a midway station which could furnish supplies to an invading army, and through it and by way of the Spanish trail was the only road known at that time.

The Secretary of State, Mr. Buchanan, was a man by nature habitually courteous and conciliatory ; of a temperament averse to disturbed conditions. While agreeing with Mr. Polk in this administrative measure, he naturally wished that California, if acquired, should come to us through the Department of State and by his diplomacy. But in the progress of affairs it soon became evident that the outcome would be war. The duty of taking possession of California as a war measure fell to the willing hands of Mr. Bancroft. He had ample means to know, and reason to believe, that Mexico intended to make war upon us, and every possible measure of precautionary readiness was put in motion by him. In less than four months after the inauguration, on the 24th day of June, 1845, he sent orders to the commanding officer of the naval forces on the Pacific that, if he should ascertain that Mexico had declared war against the United States, he should at once possess himself of the port of San Francisco and such other ports as his force would permit. The Secretary of the Navy repeated these orders in August and in October of 1845, and in February and March of 1846. To get these orders through Mexico was a service of danger, requiring judgment ; and the naval officers carrying them were selected accordingly. These were Lieutenant Gillis, Midshipmen McRae and Beale ; and, as the plan of the President became more definite and the need for action more pressing, Lieutenant Gillespie, who was well instructed in the designs of the Department and with the purposes of the Administration so far as they related to California.

Mr. George Ticknor Curtis, in his memoir of Mr. Buchanan, gives, in Chapters 21 and 22, Volume 1, a compact and clear view of English policy towards the United States at this time. He says : " In the meantime,

Mr. Buchanan had not only to manage the relations between the United States and Mexico, under circumstances of great delicacy, with firmness as well as conciliation, but also to keep a watchful eye upon the course of England and France in reference to this measure.   It must be remembered that Mr. Buchanan had succeeded, as Secretary of State, to the management of the Oregon question with England, as well as to the completion of the arrangements for annexing Texas to the United States.   He was informed, both privately and officially, by the Ministers of the United States at London and Paris, of the danger of an intervention by England and France in the affairs of Mexico.   .   .   .

THE PRESIDENT TO MR. BUCHANAN.

WASHINGTON CITY, August 7, 1845.

MY DEAR SIR : I enclose you a letter from Mr. Bancroft, and will add, to what he has said, that the information from Mexico comes in so authentic a shape as to entitle it to entire credit.   .   .   .

You may consider me impatient on this subject.   I do not consider that I am so, but still I have a great desire that what is contemplated should be done as soon as it may suit your convenience.   I have felt great reluctance in saying this much, because I desired not to interfere with your arrangements during the short recreation which you have taken from your arduous labors.

I am, very faithfully and truly, your friend,   JAMES K. POLK.

P.S.—If you determine to anticipate the period of your return to Washington, you will see the propriety of leaving Bedford in a way to produce no public sensation as to the cause of your departure.   That it may not be known that you leave on receiving a letter from me, I will not place my frank on this letter.

Yours, etc.,   J. K. P.

The letter of Mr. Bancroft, enclosed by the President to Mr. Buchanan, and in which he asks his immediate return to Washington, has been already given.   From exceptional sources of information in the City of Mexico Baron Gerolt gave the same warning concerning the danger of intervention by European powers of which Mr. Buchanan was informed, both " privately and officially," by our Ministers at London and Paris.

" In 1845, when the war between the United States and Mexico was impending, there was reason to believe that England was aiming to obtain a footing in the then Mexican province of California, by an extensive system of colonization.   Acting under Mr. Buchanan's advice, President Polk, in his first annual message of December 2, 1845, not only reasserted the Monroe doctrine in general terms, but distinctly declared that no future European colony or dominion shall, with the consent of the United States, be planted or established on any part of the American continent.   This declaration was confined to North America, in order to make it emphatically applicable to California.

July 5, 1846.

What are you going to do with the Mexican War? I hope there will be no treaty without the acquisition of California. The loss of California to Mexico will be nothing, as it will aid in consolidating her Government, and finally strengthen it, while its acquisition will be immense to us. . . .

If we had California, with its vast harbors, in the next fifty years we could control the commerce of the Pacific and the wealth of China and India, and the future destiny of our glorious Republic would be to accumulate as vast wealth and power on the Pacific as we have on the Atlantic. Some people seem to have very tender consciences of late as to conquests. I should like to know if half the earth is not now owned by the rights of conquests?

F. W. PICKENS,*

Edgewood, S. C.

What Governor Pickens says here is in the philosophy of history. From the brother of Esau down to Bismarck the story is the same of the acquisition of lands. It is an inherent desire ; and, whether by arts of diplomacy or by the strong hand, makes a continuous chain in the world's story.

Upon current knowledge it was believed by the men concerned in watching over the interests of the country that England, having failed in Oregon, was intending to gain a foothold in California. A year later, after the experience of California, Mr. Buchanan, in the instructions prepared for the Chargé to Guatemala, Mr. Hise, speaking of England's "encroachments," says: "Her object in this acquisition is evident from the policy which she has uniformly pursued throughout her past history—of seizing upon every valuable point throughout the world, wherever circumstances have placed this in her power." †

But upon Mr. Bancroft's distinctly military plans Mr. Buchanan now intervened. His desire to avert war led him to send the Slidell mission with its offer to purchase California. In the angry condition of the political atmosphere this mission resulted only in the affront from Mexico of refusing to receive our Minister. In the same clinging to peace when events showed that the time for peace was past, the State Department ordered its Consul in California to make a tentative effort to induce California to offer herself to us. The object proposed to be accomplished by this eleventh-hour effort was, to conciliate the people of California in favor of the United States, so as to induce them to ask its protection against Mexico. But the rapid progress of affairs had already rendered this inapplicable; there was no time for such an experiment—no time now left for a gradual acquisition of California. It only remained to carry out the ultimate purpose of the Government.

Had there lived in California such a man as Magoffin was in Santa Fé, with his will and intelligence, his wealth, and long close relations with leading men, the successful experiment made by him soon after in New Mexico might have been equally successful in California.

* Afterwards Governor of South Carolina under the first period of Secession.
† Curtis' Memoir of Mr. Buchanan.

California was already semi-independent, setting aside the authority of the home Government when it suited its chiefs to do so. Among its lead-ing men—leaders, because of large property and strong personal force—were some who had also within themselves ideas and influences resulting from their foreign education, and which made them feel disapprobation and resentment against the capricious and inadequate policy pursued toward California by the home Government. Had these leading men decided upon a separation from Mexico, with the aid of the immigrants already in the country, a strength might readily have been drawn together sufficient to render abortive any attempt from Mexico to reclaim it when the time came to declare independence. The certain immigration that would have taken place would have made a background of constantly increasing strength.

When Commodore Sloat arrived at Monterey, affairs had reached a culminating point. England had then just failed in Oregon. California remained open to her. Mexico, resolved on war, had determined that for-eign powers also should settle the terms of its close. In this intervention England would have had the first voice.

California could be made an English colony and the debts of Mexico paid through that outlying province. The intended colonization is proved. So much of the history of the day as can be gleaned from London, Paris, and Mexico, and California, goes to show the intention of England to occupy that territory.

At the critical moment, when the squadrons of the two nations were watching each other, when the moment had arrived which would force Cal-ifornia into the arms of the boldest, Mr. Buchanan sends to his consul at Monterey the despatch which had no place in the occurring events, but which influenced the American Commander to pause in the execution of his strict orders, making a delay that left the field broadly open to Eng-land ; and brought upon himself a severe reprimand, and which might have cost him his commission. Had those two, the Commodore and the Consul, been the only two men acting for the United States a page in our history would have been left open for a story to be written upon it very different from that which we read there to-day.

A few words may here well be used to show how sometimes the turn given to great events is narrowed down at the decisive moments.

At this time, as the shifting uncertainties settled into the realities of war, it chanced that four men had been drawn into such positions that the result for California was centred in them. All power to this end on land and sea was in the will of Mr. Bancroft. His executive officer was Commodore Sloat, and upon him the Secretary mainly depended for the carrying out of his plans. There being no land force available, Mr. Bancroft sent Mr. Gillespie to me. He reached me after a land journey from Monterey of more than six hundred miles, the greater part of which was through the country of the Modocs and Tlamaths, the most daring and savage Indians of the continent. Had he been killed on that journey—as it nearly chanced —the communications which he bore for me from the President, the Secretary of the Navy, and Senator Benton would not have reached me.

And on the night when I found him on the lake shore and the Tlamaths attacked us, the chance was even that I might have been killed— or both of us—instead of Basil and the Delaware. There would then have been no act of mine in northern California to furnish Commodore Sloat his reason for raising the flag at Monterey.

I write here only of such scenes and incidents as had connection with the current of my own life, and which were chiefly directed by me ; which occupied my mind at the time and so stand out prominent in my memory now ; holding so far as possible to my own path among the events of the time, and dwelling only upon those which had for myself some personal interest.

Renouncing my independent position by taking service under Commodore Stockton, I was no longer burdened with responsibilities ; but also I had no longer that initiative in which there is always the necessity for the thought and resource that in difficult situations gives the highest pleasure and rouses the mind into the highest excitement, while it calls for the exercise of its best powers.

The plan of campaign on which I had been acting was very different from that which Commodore Stockton had conceived. Under the plan of operations which I had proposed to myself I had intended to travel down the coast road through that part of the country which was occupied by towns and ranchos ; drawing into my force, or into my support, the foreigners already settled in the country and the incoming emigrants from Oregon and our West ; meantime getting into communication with the Californians on their ranchos, paying, or arranging to pay, for what supplies we needed from them ; and " conciliating " the rancheros in favor of the new order of things, not by promises but by acts which would give assurance of friendly intentions. In this way I was satisfied I could keep open my communication with the Sacramento valley, through a country that would be not ill-disposed, but of necessity friendly. It had been arranged with Captain Montgomery that he would meet me at Santa Barbara with the *Portsmouth.* Looking back over events, it is clear they would have justified this plan by complete success, had Commodore Sloat not arrived. The news of the battles on the Rio Grande would have authorized us to raise the flag at Santa Barbara. Now with Commodore Stockton the same plan of campaign would have brought me to Los Angeles at the head of a strong and efficient, and constantly increasing force, well mounted and supplied, with a pacified country behind me and the coast towns garrisoned by the fleet.   And again this was proved by subsequent events.

Landing on the coast in the country of an enemy who could easily sweep out of reach horses and cattle was not the way to intercept a leader at the head of a well-mounted body of cavalry, operating among his own friends and people, and familiar with every pass and trail.

We were ready to embark.   My camp was always in a state of readiness, and it needed but a few hours to prepare.   The emigrants, who composed the greater part of my force, were accustomed to the use of arms, strong men seasoned to hardship, roughened to field life by the exposure of their overland journey, and full of the courage and energy which brought them to make it, and which were now roused into a generous excitement by the call made upon them to serve their country.

The men of my exploring party had been trained every man to his horse and his rifle, until the use of both had become an instinct, will and hand and eye going together.   As my reader by this time knows, if he has had the patience to go with me in the preceding journeys, many of them had had experience of uncommon bodily hardship and times of danger, all of which they had gone through with cheerful obedience and splendid resolution.   In the sudden emergencies which sometimes came, every one of them knew what to do and every one might be relied on to do it.   Living an uncontrolled life, ranging prairies and mountains subject to no will but their own, it was a great sacrifice for these border chiefs to lay aside their habits of independence and subordinate their knowledge and experience to the contrarieties of discipline.   But once undertaken they did it thoroughly.

Coming back one day from the State Department, where the urgent business on which he had been sent had been met by fresh delay, Carson said : " They are princes here in their big houses, but out on the plains *we* are the princes.   What would their lives be worth without *us* there? "   And when the battalion was being organized and they were told by me that Commodore Stockton " felt authorized to pay them ten dollars a month," they simply laughed at the value set upon their services, but said they would give them, all the same, and leave it to the Government to pay what it could afford.

We were now about to change from the nature of the work in which we had been engaged together.   And in parting from that I gratify myself and do some justice to them by recording the fidelity and courage with which they had done their part.

The appearance of the men when we entered Monterey merited the encomiums given them by the American and the English officers, Lieutenants Minor and Walpole.   The only trace of uniform worn by them were sailor shirts of blue or white, with low falling collars of the contrasting color, bearing a star in the broad points. These, through the kindness of Captain Montgomery, I had obtained for some of the men from the *Portsmouth's* stores to supply the damage from the wear and tear of travel. Except the tall man in buckskins of whom Mr. Walpole speaks, few or none wore such clothes. He was probably a new-comer and not a Western-frontier man. Many years before, when solitary trappers spent their hardy lives in remote mountain districts where all the necessaries, or if it is better to call them so, the luxuries, of life were difficult to procure, they wore buckskin clothes made from the skins which they dressed themselves or traded from the Indians. But that was long ago. In later years, when trading posts were established within easier reach, cloth, which was warmer for the winter, and lighter stuffs for the summer, were always worn by hunters and trappers. "Bill Williams" even, whom I had with me as guide for a time and who had spent the greater part of his life and until he had become an old man trapping alone among the mountains, never wore buckskin; and he was the most careless and slovenly of all the mountain men. Of course, as these men are exposed to all weathers, their clothes are frequently wet, and buckskin shrinks and dries very hard. A buckskin dress in these days, so far as my knowledge goes, is worn only by amateurs or in order to produce some scenic effect; a pair of leggings, perhaps, but nothing more in the country where the real work is done or the real hunter lives.

On the 25th of July we embarked on the *Cyane*. My men were all greatly pleased at the novelty of a voyage in a man-of-war, which they anticipated would be very pleasant now when the regular northwest wind belonging to the season was blowing, and there was no prospect of storms. But like many prospective enjoyments this one proved to be all in the anticipation. By the time we had been a few hours at sea we were all very low in our minds; and there was none of the expected enjoyment in the sparkling waves and the refreshing breeze, and the sail along the mountainous shore as the ship rolled her way down the coast. Carson was among those who were badly worsted by this enemy to landsmen, and many were the vows made to the winds that never again would they put trust in the fair-weather promises of the ocean. But all was forgotten when at the end of three days the ship entered the land-locked bay of San Diego, where the still waters reflected the quiet of the town. Here no enemy was found. On the contrary, we were received on the footing of friends by Don Juan Bandini, the chief citizen of the place, and by Don Santiago Arguello, the Captain of the Port.

Señor Bandini was a native of Spain; of slight and thin person, sarcastic and cynical of speech, often the shape in which a keen intelligence, morbid because without outlet, expresses itself.   He realized for himself and his interesting family the isolation to which the slumber of this remote place condemned them.   He knew that from our regular force no acts of violence would take place, and that we owed it to ourselves to prevent disturbances and maintain good order.   And he was glad of the relief from the monotony of the place, and so, immediately, a friendly intercourse was established, which was aidful to us.   One of Don Juan's daughters was married to Don Abel Stearns, whose residence was at Los Angeles, the seat of the Governors-General of California, and distant about a hundred and forty miles from San Diego.   In sounding the chief men of the South concerning the mooted change in the sovereignty of the Department, Don Abel would naturally have conferred with him as the most influential personage, in whom also he could have the fullest confidence.   From himself and his family I received the social attentions and kindly aid which, in our condition, was not only very agreeable but extremely valuable.   We were entirely ignorant of the surrounding country, and consequently, where best and most quickly to obtain horses to mount my command, and beef cattle for its subsistence. These were the first necessity, but very difficult to procure.   The large ranchos in this part of Southern California were few and distant; there were not enough horses at hand to mount a party to send after animals to distant places through an enemy's country.   In the midst of these difficulties, the aid which Bandini and Arguello were willing to give was most fortunate.

Exploring for horses, we became well acquainted with the general character of this district.   Every farm or rancho had its own spring or running stream sufficient for the supply of stock, which hitherto had made the chief object of industry in California.   In this neighborhood there are places of extraordinary fertility.   Cultivation has always been by irrigation, and the soil seems to require only water to produce vigorously.   Among the arid, brush-covered hills south of San Diego we found little valleys converted by a single spring into crowded gardens, where pears, peaches, quinces, pomegranates, grapes, olives, and other fruits grew luxuriantly together, the little stream acting upon them like a principle of life.   This southern frontier of Upper California seems eminently adapted to the cultivation of the vine and the olive.   A single vine has been known to yield a barrel of wine, and the olive trees are burdened with the weight of fruit.

While we remained between San Diego and Los Angeles during this month, the days were bright and hot, the sky pure and entirely cloudless, and the nights cool and beautifully serene.   In this month fruits generally ripen—melons, pears, peaches, prickly-fig (*cactus-tuña*), and others of like kind—and large bunches of ripe grapes are scattered numerously through the vineyards, but do not reach maturity until in September.   After the vintage, grapes are hung up in the houses and so kept for use during the winter. On one of these excursions we came upon a pretty spot where the noon-day heat enticed us into making a halt. It was in garden grounds, not far from the house of the rancho, where the water from a little stream was collected in a basin about fifteen feet across, around which ran a low, cement-covered wall. Fruit trees, among them pomegranates, hung over the basin, making a cool, pleasant place with the water and shade. With a portion of lamb, which we got at the house and cooked ourselves, we had a hearty luncheon after our own fashion, with appetites the better for their late interruption by the sea.

The forced delay at an end, after little more than a week occupied in this way with the aid of Don Juan, the sufficient number of animals were obtained to enable me to move, and on the eighth of the month we moved out on the road to Los Angeles. The marines and about fifty of my men were left in garrison under Lieutenant Minor at the port.

If little gifts nourish friendship a timely one lays a good foundation for it, because it shows a really kind intent behind. Just before leaving the town an uncommonly beautiful sorrel horse, thoroughly trained, was brought me from Señor Bandini. It had been brought up to hand in the family, was accustomed to take a sup of coffee and eat sugar and other horse delicacies; and when brought to me its tail and mane were plaited and tied with green ribbons. It was a gift from the family.

From this time forward I felt safe in relying upon the influence of Don Juan and Don Santiago to support us in the endeavor to obtain quiet possession of the territory, while disturbing the people as little as possible in their customary pursuits, and giving them no unnecessary alarm by our presence. And in this reliance upon his co-operation to this end I authorized Bandini to extend this assurance as far as practicable among the Californians. Coming from him and Arguello these assurances would go far to allay the natural excitement created by our invasion. In this way I acted upon the instructions sent me to " conciliate the people."

The march to Los Angeles was a pleasant one. Necessary food was always to be had, the fine beef of the country being equal to game; good water was frequent, and the animals we rode were accustomed to the grasses of the country, their usual feed, good throughout the year; and they knew how to provide for themselves. This was the dry season when there was no rain, but the face of this country is always beautiful. Its great fertility forces itself on the attention, and at the ranchos there were the grain fields and the green of the vineyards with the cluster of ripening grapes. With the aid of my friends at San Diego I had felt the country well up towards Los Angeles, and had ascertained that General Castro was encamped at the mesa near the city with a force of about five hundred men and ten pieces of artillery. Commodore Stockton had informed me of his landing at San Pedro with a force of three hundred and sixty men and several pieces of artillery, and that he would move about the 10th on Los Angeles, expecting me to join him upon his march, which was about twenty-eight miles. On my own road I was in constant expectation of an attack from General Castro. Having but one hundred and twenty men I naturally supposed that he would endeavor to intercept my march before I could effect a junction with Stockton. But with the exception of scattered horsemen occasionally seen, and disappearing as quickly, there was no demonstration of any kind, and on the 13th I joined Commodore Stockton outside of the city.

In the afternoon the combined force entered Los Angleles without opposition, our entry having more the effect of a parade of home guards than of an enemy taking possession of a conquered town.

General Castro in the meantime had broken up his camp on the mesa, buried part of his guns, and his force had dispersed over the country; himself, as reported, finding temporary refuge in the mountain which overlooks the San Gabriel plain. Detachments from my command were sent out to scour the country and to capture and bring into Los Angeles any of his officers who might be still within reach, together with any of the leading citizens who under the alarm of unfounded rumors had fled from their homes. A number were made prisoners and others surrendered; all of whom were either released on parole or set at liberty after being notified that they would be required to comply with the necessary police regulations, and expected to aid in the preservation of order. Before our occupation of the city, the governor, Don Pio Pico, had retired to one of his estates, lying near the coast about forty miles to the southward of Los Angeles.

I wrote to him, assuring him of protection to his person and property, and inviting him to return to the city. I knew afterwards that he thoroughly appreciated my sincere desire to save himself from annoyance and his affairs from derangement, and to publicly show my respect for him and his official position ; and although he did not then decide to return, my action led to the most friendly relations with his brother, Don Andres Pico.

On the 17th Commodore Stockton issued a proclamation for the information and government of the people. There seemed to him no apparent reason why the conquest thus easily made should not become permanent, as the acquiescent condition of the people seemed to indicate that it would. So considering it, and treating California as already a territorial possession of the United States, he occupied himself immediately in organizing a civil government and formulating such regulations as, in his opinion, would best tend to preserve order and guard against any attempt at surprises from the Californians.

His reason for speedy action was his desire to go at once himself to the southern coast of Mexico. In his arrangements for the more convenient government of the Territory, he divided it into three districts, and on the 24th of August, in anticipation of his speedy return to the sea, he completed them by appointing me Military Governor of the Territory and Gillespie Commandant of the Southern District, with headquarters at Los Angeles, and a garrison from the battalion of fifty men. Notwithstanding the existence of martial law, the civil officers of the country were permitted to proceed with the usual exercise of their functions, and were not to be interfered with, except in cases where the peace and safety of the district required aid or interference from the military authority.

In his letter to me he says : " I propose, before I leave the Territory, to appoint you to be governor, and Captain Gillespie to be secretary; and to appoint also the Council of State, and all the necessary officers. You will, therefore, proceed to do all you can to further my views and intentions thus frankly manifested. Supposing that by the 25th of October you will have accomplished your part of these preparations, I will meet you at San Francisco on that day, and place you as Governor of California."

A copy of this letter with a copy of all the rest of the acts of Commodore Stockton up to the 28th of August, as governor and commander-in-chief in California, were sent now to Mr. Bancroft. To insure the safety and speedy delivery of these important papers, and as a reward for brave and valuable service on many occasions, we decided to make Carson the bearer of these despatches, which announced to the Government that its orders concerning California had been successfully carried out. And I was pleased to procure for Carson any occasion where he would meet with the personal recognition which he had earned by good service. He was to go direct to Senator Benton at Washington, who would personally introduce him to the President and Secretary of the Navy, and to whom he could give in fulness the incidental detail always so much more interesting than the restricted official report.

On the way he would see his family at Taos, New Mexico, through which lay his shortest road to the frontier. It was a service of high trust and honor, but of great danger also. The shortest way led through Mexican territory and through the dangerous Indians we have already described along the Spanish trail. He went off, charged with personal messages and personal feelings, and I looked to his arrival at home and the deep interest and pleasure he would bring to them there, almost with the pleasure I should feel in getting there myself—it was touching home. Going off at the head of his own party with *carte blanche* for expenses and the prospect of novel pleasure and honor at the end was a culminating point in Carson's life.

He had been so part of all my life for eighteen months that my letters were chiefly indications of points which he would tell them at home in fulness.

The despatches reached Washington safely; but by another hand.

The chief points they contained concerning California affairs were embodied in the message of the President and the reports of the Secretaries of War and of the Navy. When the courier reached Washington, Mr. Bancroft was no longer in the Cabinet, but was already at sea on his way to England, having been appointed Minister from the United States.

EXTRACT FROM THE PRESIDENT'S ANNUAL MESSAGE, DECEMBER, 1846.

Our squadron in the Pacific, with the co-operation of a gallant officer of the army, and a small force hastily collected in that distant country, have acquired bloodless possession of the Californias, and the American flag has been raised at every important point in that province. I congratulate you on the success which has thus attended our military and naval operations. In less than seven months after Mexico commenced hostilities, at a time selected by herself, we have taken possession of many of her principal ports, driven back and pursued her invading army, and acquired military possession of the Mexican provinces of New Mexico, New Leon, Coahuila, Tamaulipas, and the Californias, a territory larger in extent than that embraced in the original thirteen States of the Union, inhabited by a considerable population, and much of it more than a thousand miles from the points at which we had to collect our forces and commence our movements. By the blockade, the import and the export trade of the enemy have been cut off. By the law of nations a conquered territory is subject to be governed by the conqueror during his military possession, and until there is either a treaty of peace, or he shall voluntarily withdraw from it. The old civil government being necessarily superseded, it is the right and duty of the conqueror to secure his conquest, and to provide for the maintenance of civil order and the rights of the inhabitants. This right has been exercised and this duty performed by our military and naval commanders, by the establishment of temporary governments in some of the conquered provinces in Mexico, assimilating them, as far as practicable, to the free institutions of our own country. In the provinces of New Mexico and of the Californias little, if any, further resistance is apprehended from the inhabitants to the temporary governments which have thus, from the necessity of the case and according to the laws of war, been established.

It may be proper to provide for the security of these important conquests, by making an adequate appropriation for the purpose of erecting fortifications and defraying the expenses necessarily incident to the maintenance of our possession and authority over them.

EXTRACT FROM THE REPORT OF THE SECRETARY OF WAR, DECEMBER, 1846.

Commodore Stockton took possession of the whole country as a conquest of the United States, and appointed Colonel Frémont governor, under the law of nations, to assume the functions of that office when he should return to the squadron.

EXTRACT FROM THE REPORT OF THE SECRETARY OF THE NAVY, DECEMBER, 1846.

On the 25th of July, the *Cyane*—Captain Mervine—sailed from Monterey, with Lieutenant-Colonel Frémont and a small volunteer force on board, for San Diego, to intercept the retreat of the Mexican General Castro. A few days after, Commodore Stockton sailed in the *Congress*, frigate, for San Pedro, and, with a detachment from his squadron of three hundred and sixty men, marched to the enemy's camp. It was found that the camp was broken up, and that the Mexicans, under Governor Pico and General Castro, had retreated so precipitately that Lieutenant-Colonel Frémont was disappointed in intercepting him. On the 13th, the commodore was joined by this gallant officer, and marched a distance of thirty miles from the sea, and entered without opposition the Cindad de los Angeles, the capital of the Californias; and, on the

THE HUERFANO BUTTE.

22d of August, the flag of the United States was flying at every commanding position, and California was in the undisputed military possession of the United States. The conduct of the officers and men of the squadron in these important operations has been characterized by activity, courage, and steady discipline, and entitles them to the thanks of the department. Efficient aid was rendered by Lieutenant-Colonel Frémont and the volunteers under his command. In his hands, Commodore Stockton informs the department, he will leave the military government when he shall leave California, in the further execution of his orders.

In anticipating to insert these extracts I have made a long detour of some two thousand miles or more from the actual scenes and places of which I am writing, but though the distance is long the connection is close, and to borrow a favorite quotation of Mrs. Frémont's, from Montaigne, " *Je divague fort, mais j'y retourne.*"

His plans having been all formulated and put in movement, Commodore Stockton was ready to leave by the end of the month on his voyage north to Santa Barbara and San Francisco to prepare for his expedition to the southern coast of Mexico. In furtherance of his plans he had directed me, so soon as certain work about Los Angeles was completed, to go to the Sacramento valley, with the purpose of increasing the force of the battalion to three hundred men, and of ascertaining how many men I could influence to embark with him in an expedition against Mazatlan or Acapulco, " where, if possible, he intended to land and fight his way as far on to the city of Mexico as he could." The number required was one thousand.

It must be conceded to Commodore Stockton that if he was bold in the conception of his plans, he was equally prompt in the endeavor to execute them. In this one his expectation was at least to distract the attention of Mexico, and, in the presumable event that her forces would be fully occupied by ours, on the eastern side, he might find an open way to " shake hands with General Taylor at the gates of Mexico."

All arrangements being completed, he re-embarked his men and sailed for San Francisco on the 5th of September, touching at Santa Barbara to take on board the garrison which had been left there. The civil government, as he had formed it, was in quiet operation there, the American flag flying peaceably; and the prefect and alcalde, appointed by himself, in the undisturbed execution of their duties.

I did not remain at Los Angeles many days after his departure. During this time I made occasional excursions into the neighborhood, and in ranging over the country and visiting different ranchos made friendly acquaintance with the rancheros which, in making us known to each other, proved afterwards useful; some of them were Californians and others Englishmen or Americans who had for many years been citizens of California. These were all owners of tracts of land, large enough to be called domains, under grants from the Mexican Government. Among the places which I had pleasure in visiting was the Mission of San Fernando, which my Spanish-speaking Indian guide, who had shown me the way over the desert two years before, and parted from me within a day's ride of this mission, had described to me as most beautiful and the surrounding country most lovely. It is at the foot of the pass of its own name, and after occurrences made it a marked point in my memory, The large buildings gave it to me an imposing appearance, as I approached. A tall palm tree which extended its branches over the high garden wall gave it at once a southern, character. I spent some pleasant hours in going over the buildings and the church, and in the vineyards then just ready for the vintage. The *ceps* or vines here were forty years old. At Los Angeles the September mornings were cool and generally delightful, at times almost cold enough to freeze; the midday hours bright and sometimes hot enough to keep the native bitumen, with which many of the roofs are covered, dripping from the eaves like raindrops. But a breeze usually made the shade pleasant. The evenings were calm and the nights cool and clear when they were unobscured by fogs, and the dews were occasionally heavy. The first clouds I saw appeared on the 6th of September, at sunset, gradually spreading over the sky, and the morning following was cloudy, but clear again before noon. Lightning at this time was visible in the direction of Sonora, where the rainy season had already this commenced, and the cloudy weather was perhaps indicative of its approach to California.

In the early part of September I left Los Angeles for the Sacramento valley with about thirty-five men. Travelling along at sunrise the morning was cool enough to make the barrel of my rifle disagreeably cold to my hand, but the day soon became pleasantly warm; it was just the weather for days on horseback when there is no special care to interfere with the enjoyment of fine weather and exercise. Journeying along the coast towards Santa Barbara fogs occasionally obscured the sunset over the ocean, and rose next morning with the sun. There is a fertile wooded plain stretching along the foot of the San Gabriel Mountain, and frequently on the way, and in the neighborhood of Santa Barbara, I noticed that some of the trees were partly covered with moss, indicating in this locality a moist climate. The great variety of soil and climate which valleys and plains, the hills and mountains afford, will give a great variety and difference in quality to the products of California. When I first came to the country it was supposed that nothing could be produced without irrigation, not even the ordinary vegetables used in the household economy. Where only a little patch of these was cultivated because there was but little water, I soon afterwards saw a ten-thousand-acre field of barley, and a hundred miles of wire-fencing enclosing the cultivated fields, nearly all potatoes, belonging to one man. And all without any other moisture than the regular season and the soil afforded. Near the sea in this journey I came across some very attractive spots.

The garden of Dr. Den, near Santa Barbara, was one of these. It extended to the verge of a low sea-bluff on the level lowland between the mountains and the sea; and in the midst of the many fruits which were clustered together in a luxuriance almost wild, and the home comforts around, the sheltered security was made felt by the sullen waves as they were thrown back, disappointed, from the shore. It was pleasant to look out over the sea from the stillness of such lovely surroundings and picture its blind rages and deceptive calms.

We were travelling one morning down the Salinas valley, three or four of us some distance ahead of the party. The river was spread over several hundred yards in little streams and water-holes and threads of water, and densely covered over the whole space of the bed with matted thickets of tall willow. Where we were riding on the prairie bottom, between the willows and the river hills, some clumps of shrubbery hid for the moment an open ground on which were several of the long-acorn oaks. Suddenly we saw among the upper boughs a number of young grizzly bears, busily occupied in breaking off the smaller branches which carried the acorns, and throwing them to the ground. Seeing us as soon as we discovered them, they started to climb down but, were apparently checked and driven back, running backward and forward in great alarm. Dismounting quickly and running into the open we found the ground about the trees occupied by full-grown bears, which had not seen us, and were driving the young ones back until the jingle of our spurs attracted their attention. In their momentary pause the young ones clambered down and scampered into the brush, as did some of the larger ones. Others stood their ground for fight, some charging on us, and for awhile the skirmish was close and dangerous. The party behind came up at full speed, thinking we were engaged with the Californians. We drove the bears into the willows, on to the sand-bars, and into the water holes, among which our men were dispersed in parties of three or four. When the *mêlée* was over twelve bears, old and young, were found killed. During the fight at a moment when the bears made the firing rapid, I saved the life of Davis, who, looking to his own bear, stepped in front of King just as he fired upon another. I jerked him aside and saved him by an instant's breadth. Our noon-day halt was made on the field. In the afternoon we came upon a stretch of the river where it had collected into a stream about eighty yards wide and on the opposite side a fine-looking grizzly, with shining coat so dark as to be almost black, came out of the willows to the water's edge and stood looking at us. We fired upon him, but he retreated immediately into the thicket. It was a question for a moment whether we should follow, but finally Dick Owens, Knight, and I waded across the river and went in after him. We were moving slowly abreast, among the willow clumps, when Knight, who was one of the outside men at my side, found the bear right behind him, hidden for the moment by the clump which he had just passed. His favorite weapon was a double-barrelled gun, and he had just time to turn and fire both barrels into the bear as it sprang upon him. It was close quarters; a few feet distance, with a big grizzly—fortunately he was killed. The skin was very large, with thick and glossy fur. Writing in this desultory way, which in fact only followed my life, for that was desultory, I have not before spoken of William Knight. How long he had been in the country I do not know. He was one of the settlers and one of the best;—afterwards well known by his ferry and rancho on the Stanislaus. I had engaged him as scout, for which he proved excellently well qualified. His specialty was hunting, and this made him know the country intimately; and in both capacities of scout and hunter he will appear again.

In the latter part of September I reached the Sacramento valley. The three months which had elapsed since I came down from the Tlamath Lake had worked a change. There were no rumors now of burning grain fields, or of driving emigrants beyond the mountains. From north and east they were fast finding their way into the valley, looking about undisturbed for farming land, buying cattle, and laying the foundation for homes.

I dispersed a number of my men over the country, with the object of ascertaining by inquiry among the immigrants the probability of any sufficient number being found willing to engage in the expedition of Commodore Stockton against southern Mexico. With the same object I went myself to the ranchos of several men whose prudence and means of information would enable me to form some idea of probable success in my mission. I found the prospect not encouraging. There was no difficulty in obtaining the aid of the immigrants to hold the country we had taken. They had come to California to live there and make homes for their families, and were eagerly ready to defend what I felt authorized to assure them would be permanently ours. The greater number had left their women and children behind until they should have built a home and prepared means for them to live in it. They were mostly intelligent men, with a purpose, and the men who had crossed the continent with a purpose had will and energy behind it—usually men of the best kind in their particular business. Generally, now, I found them indisposed to break up their plans, which in the favorable change in the condition of the country they saw would be successful, to go off on a doubtful enterprise, that, in any event, would surely bring to them, individually, no corresponding advantage. And I met with a serious difficulty in the fact that when appealed to by them for my own opinion, I did not have enough confidence in the enterprise to advise them to embark in it. So that when I received the following note I was unable to give Commodore Stockton any reasonable encouragement:

U. S. Frigate Congress,
Harbor of San Francisco, September 28, 1846.

(*Private.*)

Sir: I am here, anxious to know what prospect there is of your being able to recruit my thousand men for a visit to Mexico.

Let me know as soon as possible. Many serious arrangements will have to be made, all requiring more or less time, which, you know, in war is more precious than "rubies."

Your faithful friend and obedient servant,

(Signed) R. F. Stockton,

Governor, etc.

To Major Frémont,
Military Commander of the Territory of California.

But meantime events were occurring which compelled an abrupt change in his plans. A few days after this note reached me I received an order from Commodore Stockton to come forthwith to San Francisco with as many men and saddles as I could obtain for immediate service in southern California. An insurrection had broken out in the south under José Maria Flores, a captain in the Mexican Army, and the Mexican officers generally had broken their parole and joined him. Gillespie was besieged in the Government House at Los Angeles.

The territory had been placed by Commodore Stockton under martial law and in his arrangements at Los Angeles for their government he had acted with little or no knowledge of the Californians, who, without pretence or declarations, had been in fact and in practice essentially a free people, and governed themselves. Their tie to the mother government was simply one of feeling and race as to a country which was hereditary; but they were capricious and refractory children, fond of having their own way. A large part of their time they were accustomed to spend on horseback without let or hindrance. There were no restrictions of ground—no fences or barred up roads—the country was everywhere open to horse and rider. They led wholesome and careless lives. The little care their cattle required was only healthy exercise. On the great ranges these were like game, and supplied them with abundant food. The hides and tallow which made their chief value brought trading vessels to the coast and procured for them all the ordinary necessaries of life; and the rich soil gave them abundant vegetables and fruit. They were a happy people, living without restraint or vexatious authority, one large family, with kinships ramified throughout the whole. Mostly, in the towns, the evenings were spent in social gatherings, with only the light refreshments of the wines of the country. Healthy and good-tempered, they had their pleasure in the friendly meeting and the dancing, for other amusements there were none. And each one had the old Spanish pride in his personality, for every ranchero was a grandee of the country. Such a people, free to range at pleasure by night as by day, would hardly endure any restraints upon that personal liberty, where any oppression is most quickly felt.   Among the police regulations laid down by Commodore Stockton were two which jarred against all the instincts of this people.   These two were, first, that any one who wished to be out of his house before sunrise must have a pass from Captain Gillespie, the commandant of the district.   And, second, that any persons who wished to carry arms for protection to themselves and servants must have a written pass from the same authority.

As a naturally to be expected consequence from these and other exactions, we had hardly left the south before the people rose against the new order of things, which had been decreed but not established, because they could not take root.   This was the natural result of those ill-adapted regulations which interfered directly with the personal convenience and habits of the Californians.   In the same spirit, afterward, were the arbitrary exactions, amounting to confiscation, rigorously enforced against them by the government in regard to the lands which were absolutely their sole means of existence.   All this regardless of the usages and tenure of a century.   The promises of our Government, while the object was to " conciliate " and disarm any hostile feelings of the people, were full of good-will and consideration; but their acts, when they had acquired the power to act, were not only ill-judged and ill-adapted to the interests of these people, but arbitrary and oppressive; and while apparently only in the exercise of rights which they had purchased, singularly inequitable and false in the highest degree to their promises and treaty obligations.

To bring my command to San Francisco Commodore Stockton had sent a fleet of boats in charge of Midshipman Edward Beale, whom I had met in Monterey in July.   At our meeting now commenced intervals of agreeable companionship on interesting occasions that resulted in a family friendship which has continued for forty years.

General Beale, at the date to which I refer, was a real midshipman of the old type; happy and spilling over with uncontrolled good spirits, as mostly midshipmen are used to be when away from the restraints of the ship.   Many miles of a delta, broad and long, have been made by the San Joaquin and Sacramento Rivers, covered with *tule* and intersected by a network of sloughs.   The bay and its sloughs at that time were not familiar to seagoing men, or indeed to men of any kind.   Of his navigation through the *tuláres* in search of me I will let Beale speak for himself.

I remember the lovely spring-like morning (I think it was autumn, but it ought to have been spring because I was so happy) when I was ordered to command a squadron of boats (what is the Presidency to that at nineteen or twenty?) and go to find Frémont—Sir Galahad going to search for the Holy Grail.   Wide and beautiful before us was the splendid and lovely bay.   So far as we were concerned, " we were the first that ever burst into that lonely sea."

We looked curiously at Red Rock, passed *La ysle de las yeguas* and met the furious tide of Garquinez Straits.   My remembrance is *it* steered us, and we camped for the night.   The next day we looked over the vast ocean of Tules which make at Suisun and towards where the Sacramento and San Joaquin come together in the great middle mere of that wonderful delta. There was everything curious to us that sunset. Monte Diavolo, with double peaks—a long white line, very distant, which told of the Sierra Nevada, and the bewitching contour of the nearer coast range and quiet and lovely valleys lying close aboard—I believe there were mosquitoes in those Tules, but I never saw one until after I became fifty and died to all there is worth living for in life. Anyhow, we were more interested in raccoons, which the sailors, who always know, said were *mungooses;* and the coyotes, which they knew to be *painters*, because one of them had read Cooper's "Leather-Stocking;" all of which I firmly believed until a venerable captain of the fore-top told me he had read "Horace Pottle" and knew them to be the American lion—he got the lie on me that time and I lost faith in him to a great extent. Well, we pulled in and tied up to the Tules that night, and next day I took the disciple of "Horace Pottle" with me, and wading a long time, we at last reached dry land and cast about for something to shoot. Not far off were some animals which the captain of the top told me were cows. He said he knew they were cows, because all cows had horns excepting buffaloes. Nevertheless, as we were out of meat and in a foreign country with which we proposed a little war, I fired and killed one of them, and after some discussion, in which the boats' crews took part as jurors, we decided it could not be a cow. Next day—the philosopher still with me—we discovered a man on horseback, whereupon we prepared to give him a broadside, as we were at some distance from camp, and were already owners (in fancy) of a horse and saddle, when, to our intense disgust, he spoke to us in English and proved to be Jake Snyder, of Frémont's Battalion. Then I had found my Holy Grail and went with him to Sonoma, or some such place. We went like the knightly Hospitalers, two on one horse, I holding on to the taffrail when at a gallop.

The town was all ablaze. Old Ide—I wonder if he was descended of that Alexander Iden who slew Jack Cade—was there, and Cosgrove and Snyder and Hensley and Bidwell and Gibson and a lot of others—perhaps I have named some who were not, as the names all come by a hazy sort of mist to my memory. Very soon, mayhap it was the next day, we all went to the boats and soon set sail for the bay again. Major Frémont being naturally in the fastest boat with me, we outsailed the fleet and at nightfall hauled up on an island. Here I went to work to signal by a fire where we were. I pulled all sorts of bushes and among these a lot of poison-oak. When the boats had all come safely to us we had supper, at which our cow played the part of first lady. After supper to bed. With my usual providence I had brought no blankets, and Mr. Frémont offered me part of his bed, which was a monstrous grizzly bear-skin. I soon began to itch so much I told him there must be fleas in his bear-skin, at which he laughed. Very soon I seemed to be on fire and got up and went to where the water was lapping on the crag, but there was no balm in Gilead for me that night nor for many after. I could do nothing but swell and swear and swear and swell. Soon my head was as big as a flour-barrel and Job had no harder time than I. Howsomever, we got under way, and by the time we reached the old frigate *Congress*, I had no need to pray, "Oh, for an hour of blind old Dandolo!" for I was blind as ever he was. I remember the old surgeon, who must have got his diploma in a Sioux lodge, poured arnica over me, for which I promised him if I ever caught him ashore to pay him off with a vitriol bath. And all this happened in the fall of forty-six, and a few unimportant matters have happened since, but hardly worth recording.

P.S.—I forgot to say that Jake Snyder said our cow was an *elk*, an assertion which the philosopher received and disputed with contempt.

While engaged in operations at the south I had the great regret to learn that in just such a boat-voyage through the Straits of Carquinez, Commander Montgomery had the shock of losing his eldest two sons. He had been appointed Military Commandant of the Northern District, which included the Sutter Fort. There was need to send some supplies to the fort by boat, in charge of which were these sons, accompanied by Midshipman Huganin. A violent gale overtook them in the straits, where the wind against the swift current (which forced Beale to encamp for the night) raises heavy seas. In these it is believed the boat was swamped, and all on board were lost.

It happened that, although we had worked cordially together, I had never met Commander Montgomery, but the generous promptness with which his mind rose to the spirit of the occasion, and the willing activity with which he had entered into my plans in the Sacramento valley, had given me a feeling of comradeship with him that made his loss almost personal to me. The aid which he gave had encouraged the settlers, added strength to my movements, and embarrassed the Mexican authorities. He was a man of quick and generous impulses, and with that kind of loyal patriotism which sets country above self and does not stop to calculate the cost when the occasion offers to serve it. He did not fail to comprehend that there was purpose in my movements, and, from his interview with Gillespie, he learned enough to satisfy himself that I had authority for what I was doing. From that moment I had his willing aid and cordial sympathy. He could not go beyond a certain limit, but he chafed with the restraint of his position, and was eager for open action. The year for which the name of a "*missing*" officer is still carried on the rolls was about to expire, and brought the official inquiry which is answered in the following official reports to the Navy Department. They show that all search had been in vain, and that no trace of the missing boat could be found. Such an accident, surrounded by land and so near, seemed harder than if it had occurred on the open sea.

(*No.* 43.—*Copy.*)
U. S. SHIP INDEPENDENCE, MONTEREY, September 30, 1847.

SIR: I enclose a report, from Commander J. B. Hull, of all that is known in relation to the loss of the launch of the *Warren* and Midshipmen Montgomery and Huganin.

The boat is supposed to have foundered in the Straits of Carquinez, through which the ebb-tide sets with great velocity against a strong wind and caused, of course, a dangerous sea.

The shores in the neighborhood and wherever it was supposed the wreck might have drifted, have been carefully and frequently examined, but nothing that was in the boat has been found, and I regret to say that there is not a shadow of doubt that all on board perished.

I am respectfully your obedient servant,
W. BRANFORD SHUBRICK,
Commanding Pacific Squadron.

Hon. *John Y. Mason,*
Secretary of the Navy, Washington. D. C.

(*Copy.*)
U. S. SHIP WARREN, MONTEREY BAY, September 30, 1847.

SIR: In reply to your letter of this date. directing me to make to you a detailed report of the loss of the launch in which Midshipman Montgomery perished, I have the honor to submit the following statement of that melancholy occurrence. On the 13th of November last, the launch of this ship left San Francisco to go up the Sacramento to Sutter's Fort, on public service, under the order of Commander Montgomery, then in command of the Northern Department of California. She was in charge of Acting Master William H. Montgomery, and had on board a brother of W. Montgomery and Midshipman D. C. Huganin, of the *Portsmouth*, and the following men belonging to the ship, viz.: Geo. Redmore, C. A. G.; Milton Ladd, seaman; Anthony Sylvester, seaman; John Dowd, seaman; Alexr. McDonald, O. S.: Philip L. Lee, seaman; Saml. Lane, O. S.; Gilman Hilton, O. S.; Saml. Turner, landsman. And a quantity of arms and ammunition sufficient for her defence. There was also on board the sum of about nine hundred dollars sent to pay bills due at the fort on account of the service.

After she had been absent longer than was thought necessary to perform the trip, great anxiety was felt for her safety, and on the 30th of the month a hired boat with some men from this ship was sent, by my direction, in search of her: on the 18th of December the boat returned, after having searched the river and inlets as far as Fort Sacramento, without hearing anything of the missing launch. A day or two after the launch left the ship there was a violent gale, in which it was afterwards thought she must have been lost, and no definite intelligence has since been heard of her.

Very respectfully, your obedient servant,
J. B. HULL,
Commander.

Commodore W. B. Shubrick,
   Commanding U. S. Squadron, Pacific Ocean.

The next morning I reported to the commodore my arrival with one hundred and seventy good men, well armed and with their horse equipments ready for service when horses could be had to mount them. The day following we were embarked on the ship *Stirling*, under orders to proceed to Santa Barbara and endeavor to surprise the enemy at that place. The commodore meanwhile had ordered Captain Mervine, then lying at Monterey in the frigate *Savannah* under sailing orders for the coast of Mexico, to go direct to San Pedro and give all possible support to the little garrison at Los Angeles.

The *Stirling* got underway at the same time with the *Congress*, but the commodore having crossed the bar and got to sea before us, hove to until we were also fairly at sea, and both vessels headed their way with a fair wind down the coast. In the afternoon of the day of sailing we separated, in a fog, from the *Congress*.

The events which were involved in the movements of the commodore influenced the course of my own life, and for this reason I will leave the *Stirling* out of sight in the fog and follow him. Between San Francisco and Monterey the commodore spoke the merchant ship *Barnstable*, with despatches to himself from Captain Maddox at Monterey, informing him that an attack on the town was expected and asking immediate aid. Running the *Congress* into the bay of Monterey, he reinforced the garrison with two officers and fifty men and some artillery; and continuing down the coast, he touched at Santa Barbara to ascertain if I, with my sailing vessel, had succeeded in " surprising " that town. Not finding me there, he continued on to San Pedro, where he found the *Savannah*.

Upon his capitulation at Los Angeles, Captain Gillespie had retreated with his garrison to San Pedro and the merchant ship *Vandalia*, then lying there. Shortly after, Captain Mervine entered with the frigate *Savannah,* under orders from Commodore Stockton, to afford all the aid within the compass of the *Savannah's* resources to the little garrison at Los Angeles. Acting in the spirit of his instructions, Mervine landed part of his crew of sailors and marines with Gillespie's men, but without artillery, and attempted to force his way across the plain to Los Angeles.   Early on the march he was met by a body of Californians with a single piece of artillery, which they used so effectually to harass him that he was compelled to abandon his attempt to reach the town and retreat to his ship, with a loss of four killed and several wounded.   Wherever horses could be brought into play the Californians were at home, and being naturally brave, could be used to the utmost advantage that man and horse, acting together, were capable of. Men growing up on foot will be equally brave but not equally bold as men growing up on horseback.   Here in California we had the spectacle of ranchmen, without discipline and fresh from their ranchos, attacking and defeating a regular force having the prestige which regular forces always have in their favor against irregular troops.   In this skirmish their simple tactics were to run down upon Mervine's troops within fair range of their single gun and open fire upon them; continuing it until the Americans got near enough to make their fire in turn effectual, when the vaqueros would lasso their gun and gallop off with it at full speed to another convenient distance; keeping up this manœuvre until Captain Mervine found that he could not reach Los Angeles without great loss, if in fact he should find himself able to reach it before being surrounded and cut off by the accumulating force of the Californian cavalry, which in the meantime was suffering no loss.   Mervine repeatedly attempted to charge the Californians, his men bravely seconding him and making every effort to reach them, but it was literally impossible; he being on foot and they being on horseback.

The commodore was displeased with this incident and with its natural result in the encouragement it would give to the Californians, and proceeded at once to remove this impression. " Elated by this transient success which the enemy, with his usual want of veracity, magnified into a great victory, they collected in large bodies on all the adjacent hills, and would not permit a hoof except their own horses to be within fifty miles of San Pedro."   I have a reason for letting Commodore Stockton speak here-along for himself.

In the instructions given to me I had been informed that he would land here to co-operate with me on my approach from Santa Barbara.   Orders were accordingly given to prepare for the landing of the troops in the morning, and a party of volunteers were ordered to land before daylight, " to cover the general landing which was to be made up a very steep bank and in the face of the enemy. The volunteers failing to land in time, in consequence of a fancied force of the enemy; not so with the sailors and marines, who were ready in the boats alongside the two ships, and who, as soon as I discovered that the volunteers had not succeeded, I ordered to land. The boats of the *Savannah* were under the immediate command of Captain Mervine; those of the *Congress* under the immediate command of Lieutenant Commander Livingston, and performed the service in a most gallant manner, being myself present."

" On our approach to the shore, the enemy fired a few muskets without harm and fled; we took possession and once more hoisted our flag at San Pedro."

The commander-in-chief commended " the determined courage with which the officers, sailors, and marines landed (in despite of the false alarm as to the enemy's force), and again hoisted the American standard at San Pedro."

" The troops remained encamped at that place for several days before the insurgents, who covered the adjacent hills, and until both officers and men had become almost worn out by chasing and skirmishing with and watching them, and until I had given up all hope of the co-operation of Major Frémont. Besides, the enemy had driven off every animal, man and beast, from that section of the country, and it was not possible, by any means in our power, to carry provisions for our march to the city."

" I resolved, therefore, to embark the troops, and waste no more time there, but to go down south and, if possible, to get animals somewhere along the coast before the enemy could know or prevent it, and to mount my own men and march to the city by the southern route."

Sometimes, however, infantry has been known to carry rations enough for support during a march of thirty miles. Tired of waiting on me, the commodore left the *Savannah* to look out for me, and sailed to San Diego, where Lieutenant Minor was in command. Arriving off the harbor he attempted to cross the bar, but the ship got ashore, and he was obliged to return to the outside anchorage.

Lieutenant Minor reporting the town besieged by the Californians and that more men and provisions were required for the garrison, Captain Gillespie was sent on shore with supplies and that part of my battalion which had formed the garrison at Los Angeles.

At Lieutenant Minor's request Captain Gibson of the battalion was sent with a party to a locality of ranchos near the coast, to the southward, indicated by Señor Bandini, where some horses and cattle might be obtained.

Two days after his arrival at San Diego, the *Malek Adhel* came in from Monterey with despatches from me, in which I wrote to Commodore Stockton: " We met the *Vandalia* with information of the occurrences below.

Mr. Howard represented that the enemy had driven off all the horses and cattle, so that it would be impossible to obtain either for transportation or supplies. Under the circumstances, and using the discretionary authority you have given me, I judged it of paramount necessity to haul up immediately for this port, with the intention to send for all the men who could be raised in the north, and for the band of horses which I had left on the Consumné. In the meantime we should be able to check the insurrection here, and procure horses and supplies, so as to be in readiness to march to the southward immediately on the arrival of our reinforcements." I have sometimes wondered, since reading the commodore's letters to the Secretary of the Navy, in which he kept him informed of my failure to connect, if it never occurred to Stockton that the same difficulties which blocked his march upon Los Angeles were also in the way of my command, which was expected to operate as a mounted force in the interior.

Upon the receipt of my letter the commodore went back with his ship to San Pedro and sent the *Savannah* to Monterey to aid me in preparing for the march on Los Angeles. Returning to San Diego he buoyed the bar and succeeded in getting the *Congress* into the harbor, where she could lie undisturbed by the southeast storms. Meantime Gibson had succeeded in bringing into San Diego some horses and cattle, but the horses were in such poor condition that it would require weeks of rest to fit them for service. On the afternoon of the commodore's arrival the Californians made an attack on the town, but were driven back with the loss of two men killed and four wounded. Such skirmishes were of almost daily occurrence, resulting mostly from the attempts of the garrison to reach the ranchos for supplies.

During the time that he remained at San Diego the unreflecting impatience which belonged to the temperament of Commodore Stockton experienced some useful schooling. Inside the bulwarks of a ship of war patience in the commander was an unknown quantity. He could hold coast towns under the fire of his guns; but when it came to equipping a force on the coast of an enemy's country for a march into the interior he saw with surprise that such things as obstacles to his will could exist. Finding that his alert enemy had driven every animal off from the coast in the neighborhood of San Diego, and refused to let him have any horses or cattle or fresh provisions of any kind, he bethought himself of the sea which he knew about, and decided to deceive the Californians by sending a vessel down the coast several hundred miles away to a part of Lower California, where the tidings of war had probably not yet reached the scattered ranchos, or where, if they had, one of the usual trading vessels would arouse no suspicion. Accordingly about the end of November Captain Hensley, with Company B of the battalion, was embarked in the merchant

" MIDSHIPMAN BEALE."

ship *Stonington*, directed to go down the coast of California to try there for horses and mules, saddles and saddle gearing, cattle and working bullocks for the guns; all of which were essential for the march on Los Angeles. The saddle tree and horse-hair girth and saddle gear generally of the Californians are made for hard service and very strong, especially the tree and girth; and usually were made on the ranchos. While efforts were made to procure these from the outside, the men inside the town were kept at work to contribute to the necessary equipment.

About this time two men came into San Diego from the enemy's camp at San Bernardo, reporting it to consist of only about fifty men. Thereupon Captain Gillespie was ordered, with as many men as horses could be found to mount, and one field-piece, to make an attempt to " surprise " them. During his day of preparation for this service an English resident of California, Mr. Stokes, came into San Diego, bearing the following letter to Commodore Stockton from Brigadier-General Kearny, of the United States Army, who had just reached by overland journey the frontier of inhabited California:

HEADQUARTERS, ARMY OF THE WEST,
CAMP AT WARNER'S, December 2, 1846.

SIR: I (this afternoon) reached here, escorted by a party of the First Regiment Dragoons. I came by orders from the President of the United States. We left Santa Fé on the 25th of September, having taken possession of New Mexico, annexed it to the United States, established a civil government in that territory, and secured order, peace, and quietness there.

If you can send a party to open a communication with us, on the route to this place, I wish you would do so, and as quickly as possible.

The fear of this letter falling into Mexican hands prevents me from writing more.

Your express by Mr. Carson was met on the Del Norte, and your mail must have reached Washington at least ten days since.

Very respectfully, your obedient servant,
S. W. KEARNY,
Brigadier-General, U. S. A.

It will be remarked that in this letter no mention is made of Carson, other than the reference to him as bearer of an " express."

A good pass called by the name of Warner led directly from the desert through the lower mountain onto Warner's rancho. Stockton replied as follows:

HEADQUARTERS, SAN DIEGO,
December 3, 1846, half-past 6 o'clock P.M.

SIR: I have this moment received your note of yesterday, by Mr. Stokes, and have ordered Captain Gillespie, with a detachment of mounted riflemen and a field-piece, to your camp without delay.

Captain Gillespie is well informed in relation to the present state of things in California, and will give you all needful information. I need not, therefore, detain him by saying anything on the subject. I will merely say that I have this evening received information, by two deserters from the rebel camp, of the arrival of an additional force in this neighborhood of one hundred men, which in addition to the force previously here, makes their number about one hundred and fifty.

I send with Captain Gillespie, as a guide, one of the deserters, that you may make inquiries of him, and, if you see fit, endeavor to surprise them.

Faithfully, your obedient servant,

R. F. STOCKTON,

Commander-in-Chief and Governor of the Territory of California.

By Kearny's letter it appeared that he had not only taken possession of New Mexico, but had " annexed " it to the United States. Giving my story here along as briefly as I can, to do so clearly, I still thought it well to insert some letters in order to give at their source statements of facts or events, which have special bearing on my narrative, and I have not given much space to minor occurrences of the time, but occupied myself with the men who were chief actors in the more important events, and who made them. And in order to isolate them from their surroundings and give them the greater prominence, I have let them tell their own story, and disclose their thoughts in their letters; so, giving a truer idea of their characters than I should have done if I had transfused their thoughts through my own mind and language. Gillespie's command being immediately available, he was ordered to proceed forthwith to General Kearny's camp. His party consisted of twenty-six men from the battalion under Captain Gibson; with a detachment of ten carbineers and a brass four-pounder field-piece from the *Congress,* under Acting-Lieutenant Beale and Midshipman Duncan.

Among the men from the battalion was Godey, who had been made by Stockton a first lieutenant. His knowledge of the country and experience in it made him at this juncture a valuable man. Captain Gillespie left San Diego with his command about seven o'clock in the evening of the 3d, in all but forty men, every horse fit for service having been taken for the use of the party. With every effort made, the few animals brought in by Captain Gibson were all that could be gleaned from the country. Mr. Stokes accompanied the party, and with it went also one of the Californians who had come in from their camp at San Bernardo. He was sent to guide General Kearny in the event that he should wish to attack it.

On the day but one following his departure from San Diego, Gillespie met General Kearny about one o'clock in the afternoon, in the mountains between Santa Maria and Santa Ysabel, and put himself at his orders. Small as it was, his party proved a seasonable addition to the force which the general had with him. Informed by Gillespie of the proximity of the small force of the Californians, the general decided to attack, and, if possible, to " surprise " them. In the evening of the same day he encamped near San Pasqual.

A few days after Gillespie had left San Diego Mr. Stokes returned, bringing information that General Kearny had attempted to "surprise" the Californians at San Bernardo, and that sharp fighting had followed the attack, in which the general had lost many killed and wounded, and one of his guns; and had been worsted. What was the final result he did not know, as he had left before the action was over, without communicating with any one on the field of battle. It suggests itself naturally here that Gillespie would have fared badly had he, as was intended, attempted the same performance with his forty men. Mr. Stokes, in his excitement, had seen a great many men on the field, and he reported General Kearny's force as three hundred and fifty.

The day after the arrival of Stokes, Lieutenant Godey, on the 7th, with two men, came in, having been hurried forward from San Pasqual with the following letter:

HEADQUARTERS, CAMP NEAR SAN PASQUAL, December 6, 1846.

SIR: I have the honor to report to you that at early dawn this morning General Kearny, with a detachment of the United States dragoons and Captain Gillespie's company of mounted riflemen, had an engagement with a very considerable Mexican force near this camp.

We have about eighteen killed and fourteen or fifteen wounded; several so severely that it may be impracticable to move them for several days. I have to suggest to you the propriety of despatching, without delay, a considerable force to meet us on the route to San Diego, via the Soledad and San Bernardo, or to find us at this place; also, that you will send up carts or some other means of transporting our wounded to San Diego. We are without provisions, and in our present situation find it impracticable to obtain cattle from the ranches in the vicinity.

General Kearny is among the wounded, but it is hoped not dangerously; Captains Monroe and Johnson, First Dragoons, killed; Lieutenant Hammond, First Dragoons, dangerously wounded. I am, sir, very respectfully,
Your obedient servant,
H. S. TURNER,
Captain U. S. A., comdg.

Commodore R. F. Stockton, U. S. Navy, San Diego.

Godey was unable to give any certain account of the force engaged on either side, and the result of the action, together with Stokes' report, induced Stockton to believe that the Californian strength was much greater than he had been led to suppose. He therefore prepared to set out himself to Kearny's relief with his whole force.

Preparations were at once made for his advance, with two pieces of artillery, to move forward at seven o'clock of the same evening to the Mission of San Diego, about nine miles from the town; the commodore intending to join it with the remainder of his force the next day.

Meantime, great was his surprise to learn from Godey that Carson was in General Kearny's camp, and he lost himself in conjectures as to how he came there.

Preparations for the intended march were being pushed at all points when in the evening of the 9th an Indian who had been with Beale as a servant came into San Diego. He reported that Beale and Carson, with himself, had been sent for relief and had succeeded in getting through the lines of the Californians who were surrounding the American camp. On approaching San Diego the three had separated, taking different routes, in the hope that at least one of them would reach the town. Living at San Diego, he was familiar with the ground and was the first to get in. About ten o'clock Beale came in, and, following him, Carson. They stated that the force under General Kearny's command had attempted to surprise the insurgents on the morning of the 6th at San Pasqual; that in the fight which ensued General Kearny had been defeated, with the loss of eighteen or nineteen killed and thirteen or fourteen wounded; that General Kearny and his whole force were besieged on a small hill of rocks, and so surrounded by the enemy that it was impossible for them to escape unless immediate assistance was sent to them; that all their cattle had been taken away from them and that they were obliged to eat their mules; that they were burning and destroying a quantity of public property—tents, saddles and bridles, and camp equipage of every description, as well as private stores and clothing. On the side of the Californians Don Andres Pico, the brother of the governor, was in command.

These tidings showed that the urgency of General Kearny's situation admitted of no delay and the advance at San Diego Mission was detained and increased to the number of two hundred and fifteen men and one field-piece, it being found impracticable to get ready the artillery which Commodore Stockton had intended to take with him. The relief force was put under the command of Lieutenant Andrew Gray, of the *Congress*, and hurried off. He was directed to march until near daylight, when he was to make some convenient camp where his men might lie concealed during the day; resuming his march at nightfall, and to avoid engaging the enemy before effecting a junction with General Kearny.

Quickly as possible, after his arrival with the letter from Captain Turner, Lieutenant Godey had been sent off to the American camp with tidings of the coming relief. By habit, mindful of the trifles that make comfort in camp, he carried with him some supplies to Captain Gillespie, who had been wounded. Afterward, I regretted to learn that Captain Gibson had been lanced through the body. Among other incidents of the fight, which I heard when we met at Los Angeles, there was one which long remained fresh in my memory. One of the Californians in the *mêlée* ran his sword through the body of a Christian or Mexican Indian who was fighting on the American side. When he felt the sword go through him the Indian knew that he was killed and called out " *Basta*." " *Otra vez*," said the soldier-murderer, and ran him through the second time. " *Ahi*

VIEW OF MONTEREY AND REMAINS OF OLD FORT.

esta," said he. " *Si Señor,"* said the dying man, with the submission of an Indian to his fate.*

Stockton was angered when he learned from Carson how it was that he came to be in General Kearny's camp. A few days out from Santa Fé he had met the general, who, after hearing from him what had taken place in California, had turned him back to act as his guide and given the despatches of which he was the bearer to Fitzpatrick, to be carried to Washington.

Cuvier said that give him a bone and he would construct the animal. It has been remarked a little way back that, in the letter announcing to Commodore Stockton his arrival, General Kearny mentioned Carson's name only incidentally as having met him as the bearer of Stockton's despatches. He said nothing of having stopped him on his road and turned back the trusted man whom Commodore Stockton and myself had chosen to be the bearer of important despatches, and equally important verbal communications, to the Government and friends in Washington, nor of having taken away from him the despatches and sent them forward through a man of his own selection. Merely, he " *had met him."* That misleading letter was the bone out of which to make the man. The concealment of an act which was wrong in itself and which it so much interested Commodore Stockton to know, showed with the clearness of light the quality which was the root of his character—a falseness which contaminated every other quality.

EXTRACT FROM SPEECH OF SENATOR BENTON IN U. S. SENATE.

" Mr. Carson has since arrived in Washington and given me the following statement in relation to the turning back, the truth of which, as of everything else that he says, I underwrite :

" ' STATEMENT OF MR. C. CARSON.

" ' I met General Kearny, with his troops, on the 6th of October, about — miles below Santa Fé. I had heard before of their coming ; and when I met them, the first thing I told them was that they were " too late "—that California was conquered, and the United States flag raised in all parts of the country. But General Kearny said he would go on ; and said something about going to establish a civil government. I told him a civil government was already established, and Colonel Frémont appointed governor, to commence as soon as he returned from the north, some time in that very month (October). General Kearny said that was no difference ; that he was a friend of Colonel Frémont, and he would make him governor himself. He began from the first to insist on my turning back to guide him into California. I told him I could not turn back—that I had pledged myself to Commodore Stockton and Colonel Frémont to take their despatches through to Washington City, and to return with them as far as New Mexico, where my family lived, and to carry them all the way back if I did not find some one at Santa Fé that I could trust as well as I could myself ; that I had promised them I would reach Washington in sixty days, and that they should have return despatches from the Government in one hundred and twenty days. I had performed so much of the journey in the appointed time, and, in doing so, had already worn out and killed thirty-four mules ; that Stockton and Frémont had given

---

* The Indian knew that he was killed, and called out " *Enough."* " *Another time,"* said the soldier-murderer, and ran him through the body a second time. " *There it is,"* said he. " *Yes, Señor,"* said the dying man, with the submission of an Indian to his fate.

me letters of credit to persons on the way to furnish me with all the animals I needed, and all supplies to make the trip to Washington and back in the one hundred and twenty days; and that I was pledged to them, and could not disappoint them; and, besides that I was under more obligations to Colonel Frémont than to any other man alive. General Kearny would not hear any such thing as my going on. He told me he was a friend to Colonel Frémont and Colonel Benton, and all the family, and would send on the despatches by Mr. Fitzpatrick, who had been with Colonel Fremont in his exploring party, and was a good friend to him, and would take the despatches through and bring them back as quick as I could. When he could not persuade me to turn back, he then told me that he had a right to make me go with him, and insisted on his right; and I did not consent to turn back till he had made me believe that he had a right to order me; and, then, as Mr. Fitzpatrick was going on with the despatches, and General Kearny seemed to be such a good friend of the colonel's, I let him take me back; and I guided him through, but with great hesitation, and had prepared everything to escape in the night before they started, and made known my intention to Maxwell, who urged me not to do so.

" ' More than twenty times on the road, General Kearny told me about his being a friend of Colonel Benton and Colonel Frémont and all their family, and that he intended to make Colonel Frémont the governor of California, and all this of his own accord, as we were travelling along or in camp, and without my asking him a word about it.

" ' This statement I make at the request of Senator Benton, but had much rather be examined in a court of justice, face to face with General Kearny, and there tell at once all that I know about General Kearny's battles and conduct in California.' "

Later, the mischievous results brought upon us by the turning back of our messenger to Washington will fully appear.

The estimate which I had made of the frank and brave character of the Californians is well sustained by the conduct of Don Andres Pico, as told in the same speech of Senator Benton:

The four days' siege of the hill was the period of interesting events, which it was the duty of the general to have told, and which he suppressed to keep up his assumed character of victor. First, there was the capture of the generous and daring Godey, with his two companions in full view of Kearny's camp, after his adventurous run to San Diego, forty miles, to get aid for Kearny; and rapid return with the tidings that it was coming—tidings which he could not deliver because he was captured in view of Kearny by his besiegers. This fact had to be suppressed, or the illusive cry of victory was at an end. It was suppressed—doubly suppressed—not noticed in the official report, and not confessed on interrogation before the court-martial. Then there was the chivalry of Don Andres Pico, worthy of Castilian blood, in his conduct to his enemies. He treated the captured men with the utmost kindness—Godey as a brother, because he knew his renown, and honored heroism in his person. He inquired for the killed, and especially for Gillespie, whom he personally knew, and whom he had reported among the dead. Godey told him that he was not dead, but badly lanced, and that his servant in San Diego had made up some supplies for him, which he had brought—sugar, coffee, tea, fresh linen. Pico put the supplies under a flag, and sent them to Gillespie, with an invitation to come to his camp and receive better treatment than he could get on the dry rocks of San Bernardo; which he did, and was treated like a brother, returning when he pleased. The same flag carried a proposition to exchange prisoners. Kearny was alarmed at it, and saw nothing in it, or in the noble conduct to Gillespie, but a trick and a lure to perfidy. He was afraid to meet the flag. None of those for whom he reserved the honors of his report to the Government would venture to go. There was a lad present—one of those sent out by Stockton, a midshipman, the son of a widow in sight of this Capitol, the grandson of Truxton, and no degenerate scion of that illustrious stock; his name, Beale. This lad volunteered to go and hear the propositions of exchange. Great was the alarm at his departure, and *American* was one of the precautions for his safety. A six-barrelled revolver, in addition to the sword, perfectly charged and capped, was stowed under his coat. Thus equipped, and well mounted, he set out, protected by a flag, and followed by anxious eyes.

The little river San Bernardo was crossed at a plunging gallop, without a drink, though rabid for water both the horse and his rider, the rider having a policy which the horse could not comprehend. Approaching a picket guard, a young *alfarez* (ensign) came out to inquire "for what purpose?" The mission was made known, for Beale spoke Spanish; and while a sergeant was sent to the general's tent to inform him of the flag, a soldier was despatched to the river for water. "Hand it up to the gentleman," was the Castilian command. Beale put the cup to his lips, wet them, in token of acknowledging a civility, and passed it back; as much as to say we have water enough on the hill. The *alfarez* smiled; and, while waiting the arrival of Don Andres, a courteous dialogue went on. "How do you like the country?" inquired the *alfarez*. "Delighted with it," responded Beale. "You occupy a good position to take a wide view." "Very good: can see all round." "I don't think your horses find the grass refreshing on the hill." Not very refreshing, but strong." There was, in fact, no grass on the hill, nor any shrub but the one called wire-wood, from the close approximation of its twigs to that attenuated preparation of iron which is used for making knitting-needles, card-teeth, fishing-hooks, and such small notions! and upon which wood, down to its roots, the famished horses gleaned until compassionate humanity cut the halters, and permitted them to dash to the river and grassy banks, and become the steeds of the foe. By this time three horsemen were seen riding up, as all Californians ride. Arriving within a certain distance, they halted, as only Californians and Mamelukes can halt; the horse, at a pull of the bridle and lever bit, thrown back upon his haunches, fixed in his tracks, and motionless as the equestrian statue of Peter the Great. One of the three advanced on foot, unbuckling his sword and flinging it twenty feet to the right. The *alfarez* had departed. Seeing the action of the gentlemen, Beale did the same—unbuckled his sword and flung it twenty feet to the right. The swords were then forty feet apart. But the revolver: there it stuck under the coat—unmistakable symptom of distrust or perfidy—sign of intended or apprehended assassination, and outlawed by every code of honor from the field of parley. Confusion filled his bosom; and for a moment honor and shame contended for the mastery. To try and hide it, or pull it out, expose it, and fling it away, was the question; but with the grandson of Truxton it was a brief question. High honor prevailed. The clean thing was done. Abstracted from its close concealment, the odious tool was bared to the light, and vehemently dashed far away—the generous Californian affecting not to have seen it. Then the boy breathed "easier and deeper."

The business of the parley was soon arranged. Pico had three Americans, and Kearny had but one Californian, sole fruit of the "*victory*" of San Pasqual. Pico offered to exchange man for man. Beale was anxious to redeem Godey, yet would not name him, only described him. Pico smiled. "That is Godey," said he. "You can't have him; but he will be treated well. Describe another." Beale, supposing he was to be refused again, and so reduced to the one which he least wanted, described Burgess, a brave man, but the least intelligent of the three. "You shall have him," was the ready reply. "Send our man, and he shall redeem Burgess." It was done, and the exchange effected.

True to his instincts (to give dangers to others and honors to his own *sequitors*), Kearny sent out Captain Emory to consummate the exchange; and he, improving upon the act of his general, falsified his story, in his journal, by omitting all mention of Beale, and taking to himself the sole credit of the parley. He thus relates the transaction in his journal, p. 110: "December 8th.—In the morning a flag of truce was sent into our camp, informing us that Andres Pico, the commander of the Mexican forces, had just captured *four* Americans, and wished to exchange them for a like number of Californians. We had but one to exchange, and with this *fellow* I was sent to meet Andres Pico, whom I found to be a gentlemanly looking and rather handsome man. The conversation was short; for *I saw the man he wished to exchange was Burgess*, one of those sent on the morning of the 6th to San Diego; and we were very anxious to know the result of his mission. Taking rather a contemptuous leave of his late captors, he informed us of the safe arrival of himself and Godey at San Diego. He also stated, that when captured, his party, consisting of himself and two others, on their return from San Diego, had previously *cached* their letters under a tree, which he pointed out to me; but, on subsequent examination, we found the letters had been extracted."

So far the journal; and so far as honor is concerned, Brevet Lieutenant-Colonel Emory may wear what he has won by his own account of himself in the transaction. I let him alone. I perform a cherished duty to a heroic boy by placing the truth where history will find it—in the parliamentary history of the country ; where the future veracious historian will look for his materials. As for Brevet Lieutenant-Colonel Emory, if he feels the credit of his journal and the honor of an officer impugned, he has only to take the requisite steps for an investigation. The proofs are present. Major Gillespie, also brevetted, was there, and is here ; others also.

Of course, General Kearny, in his official report to the Government, makes no mention of this honorable conduct on the part of Beale and Pico.

The results of the astuteness of Pico, in giving up the least intelligent of his prisoners, was soon visible, and lamentably so, in the American camp. Burgess could tell nothing about the mission to Stockton—nothing about his response in answer to Godey's mission—nothing about help ; for he was only one of the escort for the personal safety of Godey, in his dangerous mission, traversing eighty miles (going and coming) of insurgent country, filled with a hostile population, and rode over by fleet cavalry, flushed with victory. The secret of the mission asking for aid was confined to Godey—not to be committed to others, for fear of multiplying the chances of its getting to the knowledge of the enemy. Burgess could tell nothing. Then it was that black despair fell upon the American camp. Without provisions, without power to move, besieged by conquerors, without the hope of relief—a surrender at discretion, or death in a vain effort to escape, were the only alternatives. In this mournful dilemma, American spirit rose to the level of the occasion. Men and officers, one and all, the unhappy wounded with the rest, demanded to be led forth. All the baggage was burnt—everything that would encumber the march. The helpless wounded were put on ambulances. At one o'clock the devoted column began to move—Pico, on the watch, observing the movement. In a moment his lancers were in the saddle, mounted on their fleet, docile, daring, and " *educated* " horses, such as the Mameluke never rode. He was then in front, in the open and beautiful valley through which the road lay down the river to San Diego. Suddenly the lancers defiled to the right—came round into the rear of the hill—halted, and formed at six hundred yards' distance : as much as to say, " We open the road to you. Take it." Then Kearny halted his column, and consulted his officers, *and others*, Carson knows who. The question was, to go or not ? The solution seemed to depend upon the possibility of getting relief from Stockton : if there was a chance for that relief, wait for it ; if not, go forward. Stockton was thirty-five miles distant, and nothing heard from him ; for Burgess, as I have said, could tell nothing. To send another express to Stockton seemed hopeless, the distance and dangers were so great. Besides, who would venture to go, seeing the fate of Godey, and knowing the state of the country ? It was a moment to find a hero ; and one presented himself. It was the lad Beale. It was then one o'clock ; the column fell back into camp ; early dark was fixed for the departure of the daring messenger ; and he was asked who he would have for his companion. " Carson and my Indian servant," was the reply, The general answered that he could not spare Carson—*that general* who swore before the court-martial that he had never seen the *man* before or since who brought him Frémont's letter of the 17th of January—*that man* being Carson ! He could not spare him. He wanted a counsellor as well as a guide and a hero. " Then," said Beale, " no other can help me ; I will go with the Indian servant." General Kearny then said Carson might go. Carson has since told me that Beale volunteered first.

The brief preparations for the forlorn hope were soon made ; and brief they were. A rifle each, a revolver, a sharp knife, and no food ; there was none in the camp. General Kearny invited Beale to come and sup with him. It was not the supper of Antony and Cleopatra ; for when the camp starves, no general has a larder. It was meagre enough. The general asked Beale what provision he had to travel on ; the answer was nothing. The general called his servant to inquire what his tent afforded ; a handful of flour was the answer. The general ordered it to be baked into a loaf and be given to Beale. When the loaf was brought the servant said that was the last, not of bread only, but of everything ; that he had nothing left for the general's breakfast. Beale directed the servant to carry back the loaf, saying that he would provide for himself. He did provide for himself ; and how ? By going to the smouldering fire where the baggage had been burnt in the morning, and scraping from the ashes and embers the half-burnt peas and grains of corn which the conflagration had spared, filling his pockets with the unwonted food. Carson and the faithful Indian provided for themselves some mule-beef.

The darkness of night fell upon the camp, and the moment arrived for descending from

DISTANT VIEW OF CARMEL MISSION: CARMEL BAY AND POINT LABOR IN THE DISTANCE.

the hill and clearing the open valley, two miles to the nearest cover. It was a perilous descent, for at the approach of night it was the custom of Pico to draw a double chain of sentinels around the hill, and to patrol the valley with mounted lancers—precautions more vigilantly enforced since he learned from the captured men that Carson was on the hill. " Be on the, alert," he said to his men—" Carson is there ; " and applying to Kearny's command one of the figurative expressions so common in the Spanish language—*se escapara el lobo ;* the wolf will escape the hunters if you do not watch him close. The descent was perilous and painful, all done by crawling ; for the upright figure of a man could not be exhibited where the horizon was watched for all that appeared above it. Shoes were pulled off to avoid cracking a stick or making a sound which the ear of the listener pressed upon the ground could catch, and the naked feet exposed to the prickly pear. They passed between sentinels, waiting and watching their time to move an inch. They heard them whisper and smelled the smoke of the cigarito. At one time Beale thought it was all over with them. Pressing Carson's thigh to get his attention, and putting his mouth upon his ear, he whispered into it : " We are gone ; let us jump and fight it out." Carson said : " No ; I have been in worse places before, and Providence saved me." His religious reliance encouraged the sinking hopes of Beale. The hill cleared, two miles of prairie in the open valley, all covered with prickly pears, remained to be crawled over, for no one could stand upright without detection where the mounted vedette and the horizontal view of the recumbent sentinel observed every object that rose above the level plain. Clear of the valley, and gaining the first woods, they travelled all night without shoes, having lost them in the dark. Rocks, stones, pebbles, prickly pears, there of exuberant growth, were their carpet. At daylight they took a gorge of a mountain, and laid by, for movement by day was impossible to them ; the whole country was on the alert, animated to the highest by the success over Kearny, and all on the search for fugitives. At nightfall the expedition was resumed and within twelve miles of San Diego the three adventurers separated, each to take his chance of getting in, and thus multiply chances for getting relief to Kearny ; for San Diego also was surrounded and invested, and Stockton had not a horse (having sent all to Kearny) to scour the country a furlong in front of his infantry pickets. The Indian got in first, Beale next, Carson third, all in a state of utter exhaustion ; and Beale only getting into town by the help of the men (picket guard) who carried him, and with injuries from which he has not yet recovered. They found Stockton's relief in the act of setting out.

On the 12th day of December Lieutenant Gray, with General Kearny and what remained of his party, were reported in sight from the fort on the hill at San Diego. It is illustrative of a sailor's habitual disuse of his legs that in his report of Kearny's arrival Commodore Stockton makes pointed notice of the fact that there was no horse for him to ride, because he had sent them all with Captain Gillespie to General Kearny, but that he walked out to meet them. General Kearny and his officers were received with all the kindness and attention that their situation demanded, and given the best quarters that the town afforded. After General Kearny had been made welcome and comfortable in his quarters, Commodore Stockton offered to make him commander-in-chief over his entire force and go with him as his aide-de-camp. He said no. That the force was Stockton's, and that he would go as his aide-de-camp, or accompany him. This offer was a few days afterward formally repeated in presence of all the officers that could be spared from duty, and again declined. Commodore Stockton wished Kearny to understand that he was willing to waive all question of the right to the chief command, in the circumstances, and give all power into his hands. Subsequently, and whilst still at San Diego, General Kearny intimated to Stockton that he thought he ought to be the governor of the territory, under his instructions. Surprised at this demand, the commodore reminded Kearny that he had more than once offered to place him at the head of affairs in California, but that he had as often refused. The subject was argued between them upon the point of right, General Kearny relying upon his instructions. To this Commodore Stockton replied that the language of the instructions was, "Should you conquer the country, you will establish a civil government;" but that he had conquered the country; that he had established a civil government therein, which government was in successful operation at the moment throughout the territory, except at Santa Barbara and Los Angeles, where it had been interrupted, temporarily, by the insurgents; that all that the Government had ordered to be done had already been accomplished; that nothing remained to be done; that he had informed the Government of these things; and that he had stated to the Government that he intended to appoint Major Frémont governor of the territory and Captain Gillespie the secretary. The argument ended without, apparently, disturbing the amicable relations of the two officers, but the refusal to recognize his claim to be governor rankled in Kearny's mind and guided his conduct.

About the 22d of December Captain Hensley arrived, by land, with a convoy of horses and cattle, which he succeeded in driving into San Diego through the insurgent parties that were still engaged in cutting off communication from the town with the interior. After some ineffectual attempts to land, he had disembarked at San Domingo, about two hundred and forty miles down the coast of Lower California. In landing, two boats were swamped, with the loss of seven or eight rifles, several pistols, blankets, and clothing of the men. They succeeded in getting about one hundred and forty head of horses and mules, some saddles, and three hundred head of cattle, which belonged to Señor Bandini, to whose instructions Hensley was indebted for any success at all.

These supplies met the absolute necessities of the hour, and Commodore Stockton set vigorously to work in his preparations for the march towards Los Angeles. In the disposition of the horses Captain Turner was offered his choice for the dragoons, but after looking them over he replied as follows:

SAN DIEGO, December 23, 1846.

COMMODORE: In compliance with your verbal instructions to examine and report upon the condition of the public horses turned over to me, for the use of C Company, First Dragoons, I have the honor to state that, in my opinion, not one of the horses referred to is fit for dragoon service, being too poor and weak for any such purpose; also, that the company of dragoons under my command can do much better service on foot than mounted on those horses.

I am, sir, with high respect, your obedient servant,

H. S. TURNER,

Captain First Dragoons, Commanding Company C.

Meanwhile Commodore Stockton continued his preparations for the march towards Los Angeles. About this time he received the following letter :

SAN DIEGO, December 22, 1846.

DEAR COMMODORE : If you can take from here a sufficient force to oppose the Californians now supposed to be near the Pueblo and waiting for the approach of Lieutenant-Colonel Frémont, I advise you to do so, and that you march with that force as early as possible in the direction of the Pueblo, by which you will either be able to form a junction with Lieutenant-Colonel Frémont or make a diversion very much in his favor.

I do not think that Lieutenant-Colonel Frémont should be left unsupported to fight a battle upon which the fate of California may, for a long time, depend, if there are troops here to act in concert with him. Your force, as it advances, might surprise the enemy at the Saint Louis Mission, and make prisoners of them.

I shall be happy, in such an expedition, to accompany you, and to give you any aid, either of head or hand, of which I may be capable.

Yours truly,

S. W. KEARNY, *Brigadier-General.*

To Commodore Stockton,
Commanding United States Forces, San Diego.

To which Commodore Stockton replied as follows :

HEADQUARTERS, SAN DIEGO, December 23, 1846.

DEAR GENERAL : Your note of yesterday was handed to me last night by Captain Turner, of the dragoons.

In reply to that note, permit me to refer you to the conversation held with you yesterday morning at your quarters. I stated to you distinctly that I intended to march upon St. Louis Rey as soon as possible with a part of the force under my command, and that I was very desirous to march on to the Pueblo to co-operate with Lieutenant-Colonel Frémont ; but my movements after, to St. Louis Rey, would depend entirely upon the information that I might receive as to the movements of Colonel Frémont and the enemy. It might be necessary for me to stop the pass of San Felipe, or march back to San Diego.

Now, my dear General, if the object of your note is to advise me to do anything which would enable a large force of the enemy to get into my rear and cut off my communication with San Diego, and hazard the safety of the garrison and the ships in the harbor, you will excuse me for saying I cannot follow such advice.

My purpose still is to march for St. Louis Rey as soon as I can get the dragoons and riflemen mounted, which I hope to do in two days.

Faithfully, your obedient servant,

R. F. STOCKTON,

Commander-in-Chief and Governor
of the Territory of California.

To Brigadier-General S. W. Kearny,
United States Army.

This letter brought the following :

SAN DIEGO, December 23, 1846.

DEAR COMMODORE : I have received yours of this date, repeating, as you say, what you stated to me yesterday, and in reply I have only to remark that, if I had so understood you, I certainly would not have written my letter to you of last evening.

You certainly could not for a moment suppose that I would advise or suggest to you any movement which might endanger the safety of the garrison and the ships in the harbor.

My letter of yesterday's date stated that " if you can take from here," etc., of which you were the judge, and of which I knew nothing.

Yours truly,

S. W. KEARNY, *Brigadier-General.*

Commodore R. F. Stockton,
Commanding United States Navy, etc., San Diego.

The troops were about starting for San Luis Rey and Commodore Stockton, as he himself described the occasion, was about mounting his horse when General Kearny came to him and inquired who was to command the troops. In reply the commodore told him that Lieutenant Rowan, first lieutenant of the *Cyane,* commanded them. General Kearny gave him then to understand that he would like to command the troops himself; and after some further conversation Commodore Stockton agreed to give him the command which he asked for. Lieutenant Rowan was sent for, and the officers near at hand assembled and informed that the commodore had appointed General Kearny to command the troops, but that he himself retained his own position as commander-in-chief. Accordingly, under this arrangement the troops moved out of the town and took up the line of march for San Luis Rey, about forty miles distant from San Diego.

Leaving them on their march, I return to myself and my ship, which I left shut out of sight in the fog, boggling her uncertain way along the rocky coast.

This happened to be one of the severe winters on the western coast. The snow fell deep in the mountains, and in the low country travelling in large bodies of men was made hard and difficult by prolonged easterly storms, during which cold rains flooded the country. This was the winter of the Donner disaster; snows had already barred the passes of the Sierra Nevada, when that party reached the pass at the head of the Salmon Trout River.

I had left a large band of horses and some artillery in the Sacramento valley. These I sent for, and I commissioned Mr. William H. Russell, who had arrived in August from Missouri with a party of emigrants, and was a man of standing in that State, to return into the valley with the purpose of enlisting men for the battalion. Originally from Kentucky, he had served in its Legislature, and was an active friend of Henry Clay. Having been United States Marshal in Missouri and several times in its Legislature, he had a large acquaintance with its people. He had served in the Florida war, and had been on a board of visitors to West Point, appointed by President Van Buren, and was in many ways well qualified to be successful among the emigrants, to most of whom he was personally known. Meantime, the resources of Monterey and the neighborhood were exhausted in procuring material for the equipment of the battalion.

Among the residents of Monterey, to whom I was indebted for much useful aid, was Mr. William Swasey. He was a young American of education and handsome presence; at this time consular secretary to Mr. Larkin, and from the knowledge his position gave him he was able to be of unusual service. He had become familiar with the personal history of many Californians and with the resources of the locality where he lived, which came to me now in direct aid; and when he was on my staff as assistant commissary of subsistence his activity and steady good temper smoothed out many a difficulty. He rendered to the country in that time the willing service which young men give to the cause which excites their enthusiasm, and to me he has always been a loyal friend.

Since the outbreak at Los Angeles the northern country had remained quiet. Don Manuel Castro, the former Prefect of Monterey, had broken his parole, and had been appointed by Flores commander-in-chief in the north, with Don Francisco Rico and Don Jesus Pico as his lieutenants. Flores' plan of campaign was to confine our naval forces strictly to the seaports which they held under the guns of their men-of-war; the Californians meanwhile to hold possession of their whole interior country, leaving the fate of California, as an integral part of the Mexican territory, to be decided by negotiation between the two governments at the close of the war. This was the mode of settlement referred to by Admiral Sir George Seymour in his instructions to the English consuls, and of which he gave notice to Commodore Sloat. The plan which Flores adopted was well considered and naturally suggested by the circumstances of the country where the business was stock-raising and all the men herdsmen and horsemen. His intention was, to make it impossible for the Americans to move from their ships, by driving all the stock into the interior; and to secure this end he adopted stringent measures, which otherwise were easily carried into effect in the midst of a friendly population, themselves most deeply concerned in having it done.

Against the naval force only, his plan would have been easily successful, but it became impossible when in addition he had against him the active force of my command, which cut his plan at the root and turned it against himself. I had at my back the constantly increasing emigrant force, and the mountains, which I knew better than himself.

At Monterey Governor Alvarado and some other officers had stood to their parole. Don Pablo Noriega, who was among the most influential and far the most able of the Northern Californians, had been unreasonably imprisoned in order to paralyze his influence. He had been educated in the United States and had too much intelligence to engage in an attempt which he knew to be fruitless of good consequences, in any possible issue of the war. Don Manuel Castro had been drawing together any force possible under the circumstances, with the object, probably, of getting in a stroke in some unguarded spot, but beyond uncertain and contradictory rumors, I had heard nothing of him. In the night of the 16th Tom Hill and another Delaware from the Columbia River arrived at Monterey, with news from the San Juan valley. Charles Burroughs, in command of some thirty-five men, enlisted for the battalion and having in charge the fine band of horses, for which I had sent, had reached the San Juan Mission the day before, followed shortly after by another party of about equal strength. Their arrival with the horses was quickly reported to Castro, who was moving from Soledad. On the night of the 15th his scouts had found Mr. Larkin at the house of Don Joaquin Gomez, at the foot of the Gavilan peak. That day the consul had left Monterey for San Francisco, and had halted for the night at the house of Gomez, where he was captured by this party during the night and taken to Castro, who was encamped on the Monterey River. Through the capture of Larkin, Captain Burroughs learned of the neighborhood of the Californian troop, and in the morning of the 16th sent a squad of men over into the Salinas valley to ascertain its strength and position. This reconnoitring party was of ten men, two of them emigrants, George Foster and James Hayes; of the eight, six were Wallawallah Indians and the remaining two Delawares, Tom Hill and James Salmon—all from the Columbia River. I give the names as far as I know them, for their signal bravery against heavy odds deserves it.

Meanwhile, Castro was cautiously advancing, having his scouts well spread out in order to be instantly advised of any movement by Burroughs from San Juan, or by me from Monterey. In the afternoon they came upon Burroughs' scouts, some eight of whom retreated to cover in the Encinal— a low ground covered with oaks—the other two riding back to let Burroughs know of the Californians' approach. These eight brave men for a full hour held their ground in the Encinal against the whole Californian force, numbering about one hundred and thirty men. Mr. Larkin, who had been brought along and was present during this unequal encounter, writes of it that he " was several times requested, then commanded to go among the oaks and bring out his countrymen, and offer them their lives on giving up their rifles and persons. He at last offered to go and call them out, on condition that they should return to San Juan, or go to Monterey with their arms; this being refused, he told the commanding officer to go himself." At this, an officer crept on his hands and knees in the grass to get a fair view, but instead received a ball in his body and was carried off on a horse by a companion. At the end of an hour Burroughs, with his available force of about fifty men, came in sight and with his appearance relieved the brave men who were beleaguered in the Encinal. Burroughs' men were new to discipline and not properly subordinate, so that he lost the benefit of their rifles and gave the advantage to the Californians by a disorderly charge.

My gray horse, Sacramento, was with the band I had sent back for, and Captain Burroughs was mounted on him when the charge was made, and was shot through the body at the outset, but the horse wheeled from an attempt to seize him and carried his rider back among his own men. The fight lasted less than half an hour, the Californians dropping out of it in small parties, until the Americans only remained on the field. They had lost Captain Burroughs, and two others killed, and several wounded. Captain Foster was killed in the Encinal. The Californians lost three killed and seven wounded. Their small loss shows how heedlessly the action was fought on our side.

In the morning after Hill's arrival I marched out of Monterey across the Salinas plain to San Juan, where I made my camp, to wait for the reinforcements from the valley and get otherwise ready for the march to Los Angeles. I scoured the country in search of any remaining parties of Castro's force, but they had all taken flight and settled down again on ranchos around about, or in the mountains.

I have dwelt a little on this action in the Salinas plain, partly because it is due to the men who fought it and to those who fell, and partly to show what good fighting material the emigrants made. The men who took to the cover of the oaks in the Encinal were mountaineers and woodsmen. Fearless, and accustomed to rely on their good rifles, knowing how to fight and to take advantage of ground, they stood off, for more than an hour, the whole Californian force of one hundred and thirty men.

I defer, for the present, giving the roll of my battalion, but I pause to say that only in the emergencies which call out the best men could any four hundred be collected together among whom would be found an equal number of good, self-respecting men as were in the ranks and among the officers of the companies and of the staff of this corps.

Many of the men in my command were splendid fighters, and, handling them as I knew how to fight them and giving them the advantage of ground as I had learned how to do it, the reader can judge how much reason there was in Kearny's fear that I too would be defeated, or how much I needed a sailor's advice how to manage my woodsmen. There was no point on the line which I chose for my march from San Juan to San Fernando—no camp by night—where I could have been taken at disadvantage. The advantage of ground was always on my side. I had always the timber, or the brush, or the broken ground of the hills; and in an encounter the defeat of the Californians was easily certain, and at great loss to them. A good commander spares his men. He fights to win, and to do this his head is the best weapon at his command. The plan of Flores was to convert all California into a guerilla war field; of all kinds of warfare the most harassing. A French writer, speaking of General Hoche and the war in the Vendée, says: " Soldiers great in their profession never enter but with repugnance upon the field of irregular warfare; as practised swordsmen do not like to cross steel with a resolute novice whose unregulated violence disconcerts all the combinations of art."

The skill which wins without fighting is never appreciated as is the battle, with what Wellington called " the butcher's bill," and which precaution might have averted.

Lieutenant Louis McLane,* of the navy, who had volunteered for the battalion, was sent with the artillery to Gilroy's, where he was engaged in mounting it.

On my way up the coast from Los Angeles in September I left ten men at Santa Barbara. This was done at the request of the citizens of the town, who thought they would feel safer with even a small guard of Americans in the event of some disorder. Theodore Talbot was one of the party and in charge of it.† The men with him were Thomas Breckenridge, Eugene Russell (son of Mr. William H. Russell), Charles Scriver, William Chinook, an Indian lad from the Columbia River, John Stevens, two French creoles, Durand and Moulton, Francis Briggs, and a New Mexican named Manuel. Except Moulton, Durand, and Manuel, they were all about twenty years of age. Shortly after I had left, news of the insurrection reached Santa Barbara, and the little garrison were assured they would be attacked. I tell the story of their escape in their own words.

The ladies of Santa Barbara gave them the first intimation of danger and urged them to escape, and, when they refused, offered to conceal them. In a few days a mounted force of about a hundred and fifty appeared, with a written summons from Flores to surrender, with promise to spare their lives and let them go on parole; and two hours were allowed for them to decide. It was then near dusk. The American residents in Santa Barbara came in and recommended them to surrender, saying it was impossible to escape. One of them, named Sparks, of St. Louis, said that at the fire of the first gun they might count him one; he afterwards joined me.

They determined not to surrender, but to make their way to the mountains, a spur from which came down to the town. In about half an hour

---

* His father was at that time Minister to England ; himself at present Minister to France.

† It will be remembered that I left Mr. Talbot in charge when, on two occasions, I separated from my party in the Great Basin. He had been with me on two occasions, and, though young, had a sense of responsibility. His father was a United States Senator from Kentucky, and his mother an English lady, and, now a widow, was among our friends in Washington. In 1847 he was made a lieutenant of artillery in the United States Army, and was with Major Anderson at Sumter, and the last officer permitted to leave the fort with despatches, in April, 1861.

they started—the moon shining—and soon approached a small picket-guard. This gave way and let them pass. They then gained the mountains and relied on their rifles to keep off both men and cavalry. On the mountain they stayed eight days, in sight of Santa Barbara, watching for some American vessel to approach the coast. They suffered greatly for want of food, and attempted to take cattle or sheep in the night, but for want of a lasso could only get a lean old white mare, which was led up on the mountain and killed, and all eaten up. Despairing of relief by sea, and certain that they could not reach me in the north by going through the settled country, they undertook to cross the mountains nearly east into the San Joaquin valley, and through the Tuláre Indians. Before they left their camp in the mountains the Californians attempted to burn them out by starting fires on the mountain around them, and once sent a foreigner to urge them to surrender. The enemy did not often venture near enough to be fired upon, but would circle round on the heights and abuse them. When they had any chance of hitting they fired, and once saw a horse fall. It took them three days to cross the first ridge of the mountains, during which time they had nothing but rosebuds to eat. The ascent was so steep, rocky, and bushy, that at one time it took them half the night to gain some three hundred yards; after crossing the first mountain they fell in with an old Spanish soldier at a rancho, who gave them two horses and some dried beef and became their guide over the intervening mountains, about eighty miles wide, to the San Joaquin valley. They followed that valley down towards the Monterey settlements, where they joined me; being about thirty-four days from Santa Barbara and having travelled about five hundred miles. When the battalion passed through Santa Barbara their old acquaintances there were glad to see them. They had been thought all dead; the bones of the old mare found at their camp being taken to be theirs and all that remained of them after the fires had burned them out. The people of Santa Barbara generally, and the compassionate ladies especially, showed real joy at seeing them alive and treated them hospitably while the battalion halted at the town.

Working and waiting for the reinforcements from the valley, the weeks passed on until the end of November, when we moved out from San Juan, and, halting a few days for our supply of beef cattle, took up the line of march for Los Angeles. Our route lay up the San Benito River, and thence over the hills into the Salinas valley. The march was made under difficult circumstances. Winter weather and cold rain-storms for days together ; the roads and trails muddy ; the animals weak for want of food ; the strength of the old grass washed out by the rains, and the watery new grass without sustenance. Many of the horses, too weak for use, fell out by the way and were left behind, and part of the battalion were soon on foot.

Attached to the battalion was a company of Indians ; some Wallawallahs and a few Delawares from the Columbia River, the rest Indians from the Sacramento. These were to act as scouts under the command of Captain Richard Jacob,* of Louisville, Kentucky. Regularly during the march a part of this company encamped, without fires, one to three miles in advance of the battalion ; the other part about the same distance in the rear ; so that no traveller on the road escaped falling into our hands.

The battalion numbered about four hundred and thirty men. Their only provision was the beef which was driven along, but this was good, and the men were in fine health. Cold weather and the exposed marches gave wholesome appetites. Perfect order was maintained on the march and in the camp, and private property was respected absolutely. No man left the camp without a pass, and the column passed over the country without giving reasonable cause for complaint to any Californian.

In such a march, it may be supposed, there was no superfluity of baggage, and the men rode or walked in the rain and slept wet at night, but there was surprisingly little complaint and no disorder. As always, there were in the command some men who were useless and some who were worse, but these were kept under watchful eyes, and gave little trouble. In the forepart of the day of the 14th December I encamped on the mountain near San Luis Obispo. In the afternoon I went with William Knight to a point on the hills which overlooked the mission, and watched for awhile, but in the distance we could discover nothing to indicate whether or not there was a force at the place. The night was rainy. Saddling up after nightfall, about nine o'clock we surrounded the mission buildings and captured the few people found there. Some took to the roofs of the mission, but none got away. To avoid turning the people out of their houses in the stormy weather, I quartered the battalion in the mission church, putting a regular guard over the altar and church property. We found in the town some *frijoles* and other vegetables, and crushed wheat, which were bought and distributed among the men by way of luxuries.

Upon information, I sent men around the neighborhood, and in all some thirty men fell into our hands, among them an officer who had been wounded at the Encinal, and Don Jesus Pico, who was at the head of the insurrection in that quarter. Don Jesus had broken his parole, and was put before a court-martial and sentenced to be shot.

Among the papers seized here was an original despateh from General Flores, by which we learned of the action at San Pasqual, but it made no mention of the officer commanding on the American side.

The hour for the execution of Don Jesus Pico had arrived and the bat-

* Afterwards Lieutenant-Governor of Kentucky and son-in-law of Senator Benton.

talion was drawn up in the plaza in front of my windows. The rough travelling had put the men in bad humor and they wanted to vent it upon something. They looked upon Pico as in part cause of their hardships and
wanted to see him die. Don Jesus was about to be led out. The door of
my room was abruptly opened by Captain Owens, who showed in a lady in
black, followed by a group of children. They were the wife and children
of Pico. She had prevailed upon Owens, who was kind as well as brave, to
bring her to me. On entering, the lady threw herself on her knees, she im-
ploring the life of her husband, the children crying and frightened. " He did
not know," she said, " that he was committing such a crime. He went with
the *hijos del pais* to defend the country because he was ashamed to stay
behind when the others went to fight. He did not know it was so wrong."
I raised her from her knees and told her to go home and remain quiet, and
I would presently let her know.

I sent Owens to bring me Don Jesus. He came in with the gray face
of a man expecting death, but calm and brave, while feeling it so near. He
was a handsome man, within a few years of forty , with black eyes and
black hair. I pointed through the window to the troops paraded in the
square. He knew why they were there. " You were about to die," I
said, " but your wife has saved you. Go thank her."

He fell on his knees, made on his fingers the sign of the cross, and said:
"I was to die—I had lost the life God gave me—you have given me
another life. I devote the new life to you." And he did it, faithfully.

Don Jesus was a cousin of Don Andres Pico who commanded at San
Pasqual, and was married to a lady of the Carrillo family. When the
march was resumed he accompanied me and remained with me until I left
California, always an agreeable companion and often rendering me valuable
service—perhaps sometimes quite unknown to myself.

Contracting space requires me here to pass lightly over incidents of
the march, beyond the Mission. On Christmas eve we encamped on the
ridge of Santa Ines behind Santa Barbara. The morning of Christmas
broke in the darkness of a southeasterly storm with torrents of cold rain,
which swept the rocky face of the precipitous mountain down which we
descended to the plain. All traces of trails were washed away by the
deluge of water, and pack-animals slid over the rocks and fell down the
precipices, blinded by the driving rain. In the descent over a hundred
horses were lost. At night we halted in the timber at the foot of the
mountain, the artillery and baggage strewed along our track, as on the
trail of a defeated army. The stormy day was followed by a bright morning, with a welcome sun, and gathering ourselves into an appearance of
order we made our way into the town. There was nothing to oppose us,
and nothing to indicate hostility; the Californian troops having been drawn

together in a main body near Los Angeles. I remained here some days to refresh the battalion and repair damages. The gun crews wanted sights to their guns, and to please them I had the guns tried and sighted.

Pending this delay Don Jesus brought me word that a lady wished to confer with me. He informed me that she was a woman of some age, highly respected and having a strong connection, over which she had the influence sometimes accorded to women of high character and strong individuality.*

In the interview I found that her object was to use her influence to put an end to the war, and to do so upon such just and friendly terms of compromise as would make the peace acceptable and enduring. And she wished me to take into my mind this plan of settlement, to which she would influence her people; meantime, she urged me, to hold my hand, so far as possible. Naturally, her character and sound reasoning had its influence with me, and I had no reserves when I assured her that I would bear her wishes in my mind to act when the occasion came, and that she might with all confidence speak on this basis with her friends. Here began the Capitulation of Couenga.

With damage from hard marching and stormy weather repaired, and the men restored by their rest in comfortable quarters to good condition and good humor, the march was resumed on the 17th. On our way across the plain below Santa Barbara a corps of observation of the enemy's cavalry, some fifty to one hundred men, hovered about us, without doing or receiving any harm. It did not come within my policy to have any of them killed, and a few shots from our guns that went uncomfortably near dispersed them.

There is a maritime defile called the *Rincon*, about fifteen miles south of Santa Barbara and fifteen miles long. A mountain ridge here skirts the sea, leaving a narrow beach floored with a hard, parti-colored bitumen. The defile was passed without opposition. Here-along we were flanked by a gunboat, under the command of Lieutenant Selden, of the navy, which Commodore Stockton had sent, to be of aid to me in some possible emergency. He was watchful over the whole situation and prompt to aid wherever he saw an opening. On the morning of the 9th Captain Hamlyn, master of the *Stonington*, which had so useful a part at San Diego, came into my camp at " The Willows," below the Rincon.

---

* I had retained only the Christian name of this lady, but in reply to a letter I have received the following telegram :

SAN LUIS OBISPO, CALIFORNIA, November 10, 1886.

To GENERAL J. C. FRÉMONT, 1310 *Nineteenth Street, Washington, D. C.*

Received your letter. The lady who urged you for peace with the Californians at Santa Barbara is Bernarda Ruiz. She died eight years ago.

J. DE JESUS PICO.

Captain Hamlyn was the bearer of a despatch to me from Commodore Stockton, whom he had left at San Luis Rey, and passing through San Diego had embarked on the brig *Malek Adhel* and landed at San Buena-ventura, which is at the southern entrance of the Rincon Pass. He was ac-companied by my friend, Don Pedro Carillo, by whose aid he had found an Indian who guided them past the camp of the horsemen who had been ob-serving us, and brought them to me at " The Willows."

This is the letter which he brought me from the commodore:

CAMP AT SAN LUIS REY, January 3, 1847.

MY DEAR COLONEL: We arrived here last night from San Diego, and leave to-day on our march for the City of the Angels, where I hope to be in five or six days. I learn this morning that you are at Santa Barbara, and send this despatch by the way of San Diego, in the hope that it may reach you in time. If there is one single chance against you, you had better not fight the rebels until I get up to aid you, or you can join me on the road to Pueblo.

These fellows are well prepared, and Mervine's and Kearny's defeat have given them a deal more confidence and courage. If you do fight before I see you, keep your forces in close order; do not allow them to be separated, or even unnecessarily extended. They will probably try to deceive you by a sudden retreat, or pretended runaway, and then unexpectedly return to the charge after your men get in disorder in the chase. My advice to you is, to allow them to do all the charging and running, and let your rifles do the rest.

In the art of horsemanship, of dodging, and running, it is in vain to attempt to compete with them.

In haste, very truly, your friend and obedient servant,

R. F. STOCKTON.

To Lieutenant-Colonel Fremont, etc., etc., etc.

I understand that it is probable they will try to avoid me and fight you separately.

We entered the Pass of San Bernardo on the morning of the 12th, ex-pecting to find the enemy there in force, but the Californians had fallen back before our advance and the Pass was undisputed. In the afternoon we en-camped at the mission of San Fernando, the residence of Don Andres Pico, who was at present in chief command of the Californian troops. Their en-campment was within two miles of the mission, and in the evening, Don Jesus, with a message from me, made a visit to Don Andres. The next morning, accompanied only by Don Jesus, I rode over to the camp of the Californians, and, in a conference with Don Andres, the important features of a treaty of capitulation were agreed upon.

A truce was ordered; commissioners on each side appointed; and the same day a capitulation agreed upon. This was approved by myself as Military Commandant representing the United States, and Don Andres Pico, Commander-in-Chief of the Californians. With this treaty of Couenga hostilities ended, and California left peaceably in our possession ; to be finally secured to us by the treaty of Guadalupe Hidalgo in 1848.

Writing from Los Angeles on the 15th of January to the Secretary of the Navy concerning the capitulation, Commodore Stockton says :

It seemed that, not being able to negotiate with me, and having lost the battles of the 8th and 9th, they met Colonel Frémont on the 12th instant on his way here, who, not knowing what had occurred, entered into the capitulation with them, which I now send to you ; and, although I refused to do it myself, still I have thought it best to approve it. I am glad to say that, by the capitulation, we have recovered the gun taken by the insurgents at the sad defeat of General Kearny at San Pasqual.

And in a letter of the 22d of January he informs the Secretary that " the civil government of this Territory is in successful operation, that Colonel Frémont is acting as governor, and Colonel Russell as secretary, and that I am on board of the *Congress* preparing her for the coast of Mexico."

With this event I close the volume which contains that part of my life which was of my own choosing, which was occupied in one kind of work, and had one chief aim. I lived its earlier part with the true Greek joy in existence—in the gladness of living. An unreflecting life, among chosen companions ; all with the same object, to enjoy the day as it came, without thought for the morrow that brought with it no reminders, but was all fresh with its own promise of enjoyment. Quickly as the years rolled on and life grew serious, the light pleasures took wing and the idling days became full of purpose ; and, as always, obstacles rose up in the way of the fixed objects at which I had come to aim. But it had happened to me that the obstacles which I had to encounter were natural ones, and I could calculate unerringly upon the amount of resistance and injury I should have to meet in surmounting them. Their very opposition roused strength to overcome them. The grand mountains stood out fairly in their armor of ice and snow ; the sterile face of the desert warned the traveller off ; and if he ventured there it was with full knowledge of his danger. No treachery lurked behind the majesty of the mountain or lay hidden in the hot glare of the inhospitable plain. And though sometimes the struggle was hard, it was an honest one and simple ; and I had my own free will how to combat it. There was always the excitement which is never without pleasure, and it left no griefs behind.

So that all this part of my narrative has been the story of an unrestrained life in open air, and the faces which I had to look upon were those of nature's own, unchanging and true. Now this was to end. I was to begin anew, and what I have to say would be from a different frame of mind. I close the page because my path of life led out from among the grand and lovely features of nature, and its pure and wholesome air, into the poisoned atmosphere and jarring circumstances of conflict among men, made subtle and malignant by clashing interests.

CHAPTER OF RESULTS.

Reasons for this Chapter—Humboldt : Extracts from Cosmos on Value of Surveys, and Volcanic Disturbances in Oregon, etc.—Aid rendered by Professors Torrey and Hall in Analysis of Collections, Botanical and Geological—Notes on Astronomical Observations by Professor Hubbard—Capitulation of Couenga—Completing Government Policy to Conquer and Conciliate.

WHEN I laid down for myself the plan on which this memoir should be written, I thought that I would not introduce anything relating to the scientific work of the several expeditions in which I had been engaged, but that I would give only the events and incidents that make up daily life; whether mine was for the time over uninhabited countries, where there was nature only to be described, or among men where nature and natural things were effaced, and only the acts of men toward each other in society, and their effects upon the common welfare were concerned. And I stated this in the scope of the work as the purpose with which I set out to travel again over the road of my life. But I had not advanced far, when I found that in this way I would leave unrecorded the efforts of many laborious days and nights, and that the great fields of the prairies would lose their true coloring and variety of attraction when I failed to individualize the flowers, so many of which have legends; and the rocks of the mountains would lose their interest and be trodden over with me as ordinary ground, without any particular interest to arrest attention. What they were, and what their uses were, and what their relations to other rocks in distant regions, would remain untold; and they would occur in the narrative as simply rocks, if they occurred at all. And in going over waste regions which were but little known, or not at all, to other parts where people get their knowledge by reading only, I found that it would be necessary to give the relative position to those other parts, and to say also what means I used to fix these positions. Then, the flower and the rock, with the fixed locality, would together tell their own useful story about soil and climate, and give valuable indications to men who travel for scientific knowledge, or to emigrants searching for new homes. And so these would, in travelling over the pages of the book, find a guide to show them the way to the objects they had in mind. A man reading to find something of interest in his particular science would find, and perhaps have lively pleasure in finding, that in the central ridges of the Sierra Nevada is the same gray rock of which his house is built on the shore of the Atlantic. And, sitting in some English home, reading along simply for the pleasure of an imagined travel through distant scenes, another would be delighted to find on the plains of the San Joaquín the little golden violet—his Shakespeare's " Love-in-idleness "—or, on the foot-hills of the Sierra, in the shade of the evergreen oaks, little fields of the true English crimson-tipped daisy ; and straightway home associations would cluster round the page. It is true that in the lapse of time the face of these regions has changed, but the change is only in degree.

And as in drawing together the materials for these volumes, I recalled to my mind the men who had been with me in the long journeys, I remembered also the men who had aided me in giving value to them ; who had given me the benefit which came from years of study and laborious thought ; and I found that I could not be satisfied to omit from the record the results, however small might be their contribution to knowledge. Though they were, in fact, only nurselings which, under the culture of other hands, have taken their full growth, still I am not willing to let pass out of sight and memory the results of years of labor under difficult circumstances, and which afterward had been made useful by the perfected knowledge of such men as Torrey and Hall, whose only reward was in the delight they found in extending the confines of knowledge, and in their feeling of satisfaction at the reciprocated pleasure this contribution would give to their *confrères* in other parts of the world. For the men of science are the true cosmopolitans.

So I may be pardoned if instead of some incidents, which indeed are only the ripple on the stream of events, I retract the promise I made at the outset, and give the closing pages of this volume to the useful results of the time, the record of which precedes and fills it.

And I do not like to call by the name of appendix that which is not an appendage, but the result of foregoing thought and effort, flowing from these and part of them as consequences, not appended to them. And that may certainly be called " a chapter of results," which contains as consequences the approbation of Humboldt ; the Capitulation of Couenga, which completed the policy of the Government to " conquer and conciliate ; " and the fruits of many days of labor and exposure which had well-nigh worn out, heart and body, the men who were striving to reach them.

Note at page 248 refers to this Extract.

[I had, later, much satisfaction in learning that my description of past volcanic action displayed over this region between the Rocky Mountains and Pacific Ocean, had attracted the interested attention of Humboldt. Because of this, and because of the interest to be found in the general view which, in that connection, he gives of the western part of the continent, I subjoin here from the " Cosmos" the extract in which he makes these references, and in which also he anticipates the use which already has been made of the " great Columbia River" as a channel for commerce.

J. C. F.]

EXTRACT FROM HUMBOLDT'S COSMOS.

" Thus, though, previous to the commencement of the nineteenth century, not a single altitude had been barometrically taken in the whole of New Spain, the hypsometrical and, in most cases also astronomical observations for thirty-two places in the direction from north to south, in a zone of nearly sixteen and one-half degrees of latitude, between the town of Santa Fé and the capital of Mexico, have been accomplished. We thus see that the surface of the wide elevated plain of Mexico assumes an undulating form varying in the centre from 5,850 to 7,500 feet in height. The lowest portion of the road from Parras to Albuquerque is even one thousand and sixty-six feet higher than the highest point of Vesuvius.

" The great, though gentle, swelling of the soil, whose highest portion we have just surveyed, and which from south to north, from the tropical part to the parallels of 42° and 44°, so increases in extent from east to west that the Great Basin, westward of the great Salt Lake of the Mormons, has a diameter of upward of three hundred and forty geographical miles, with a mean elevation of nearly five thousand eight hundred feet, differs very considerably from the rampart-like mountain chains by which it is surmounted. Our knowledge of this configuration is one of the chief points of Frémont's great hypsometrical investigations in the years 1842 and 1844. This swelling of the soil belongs to a different epoch from that late upheaval which we call mountain chains and systems of varied direction. At the point where, about 32° latitude, the mountain mass of Chihuahua, according to the present settlement of the boundaries, enters the western territory of the United States (in the provinces taken from Mexico), it begins to bear the not very definite title of the Sierra Madre. A decided bifurcation, however, occurs in the neighborhood of Albuquerque, and at this bifurcation the western chain still maintains the general title of the Sierra Madre, while the eastern branch has received, from latitude 36° 10' forward (a little to the north of Santa Fé), from American and English travellers, the equally ill-chosen, but now universally accepted, title of the Rocky Mountains. The two chains form a lengthened valley, in which Albuquerque, Santa Fé, and Taos lie, and through which the Rio Grande del Norte flows. In latitude $38\frac{1}{2}°$, this valley is closed by a chain running east and west for the space of eighty-eight geographical miles, while the Rocky Mountains extend undivided in a meridional direction as far as latitude 41°. In this intermediate space rise somewhat to the east the Spanish Peaks, Pike's Peak (5,800 feet), which has been beautifully delin-

eated by Frémont, James' Peak (11,434 feet), and the three Park Mountains, all of which enclose three deep valleys, the lateral walls of which
rise up, along with the eastern Long's Peak, or Big Horn, to a height of
9,060 and 11,191 feet.   On the eastern boundary, between Middle and
North Park, the mountain chain all at once changes its direction and runs,
from latitude 40¼° to 44°, for a distance of about two hundred and sixty geographical miles, from southeast to northwest.   In this intermediate space
lie the South Pass (7,490 feet), and the famous Wind River Mountains, so
singularly pointed, together with Frémont's Peak (latitude 43° 8'), which
reaches the height of 13,567 feet.   In the parallel of 44°, in the neighborhood of the Three Tetons, where the northwesterly direction ceases,
the meridian direction of the Rocky Mountains begins again, and continues
as far as Lewis and Clarke's Pass, which lies in latitude 47° 2' and longitude 112° 9' 30''.   Even at this point, the chain of the Rocky Mountains
maintains a considerable height (5,977 feet), but from the many deep river-
beds in the direction of Flathead River (Clarke's Fork), it soon decreases
to a more regular level.   Clarke's Fork and Lewis or Snake River, unite in
forming the great Columbia River, which will one day prove an important
channel for commerce.

" As in Bolivia, the eastern chain of the Andes furthest removed from
the sea, that of Sorata (21,287 feet) and Illimani (21,148 feet), furnish no
volcano now in a state of ignition, so also in the western part of the United
States, the volcanic action on the coast chain of California and Oregon is
at present very limited.   The long chain of the Rocky Mountains, at a
distance from the shores of the South Sea varying from four hundred
and eighty to eight hundred geographical miles, without any trace of still
existing volcanic action, nevertheless shows, like the eastern chain of
Bolivia in the vale of Yucay, on both of its slopes, volcanic rock, extinct
craters, and even lavas enclosing obsidian, and beds of scoriæ.   In the
chain of the Rocky Mountains which we have here geographically described in accordance with the admirable observations of Frémont, Emory,
Abbot, Wislizenus, Dana, and Jules Marcou, the latter, a distinguished
geologist, reckons three groups of old volcanic rock on the two slopes.
For the earliest notices of the vulcanicity of this district we are also indebted to the investigations made by Frémont since the years 1842 and
1843." *

In the departments of geological and botanical science I submitted on
my return from the expeditions all my specimens to Dr. John Torrey of
New Jersey, and Dr. James Hall of New York, who kindly classified and
arranged all that I had been able to preserve through the difficult transportation and accidents of travel.   Both furnished me with full statements

* Humboldt's Cosmos, vol. v., pp. 410–415.

of the results of their examinations.   To the aid given by the skill of Dr. Hall I am indebted for the discovery of an oolitic formation in the region west of the Rocky Mountains, which further examination may prove to assimilate the geology of the New to that of the Old World in a rare particular which had not before been discovered in either of the two Americas.

It will be noticed in the descriptions of the geological formations given by Dr. Hall that he considers the discovery of the coal and fossil ferns which I found in the ridge connecting the Utah or Bear River Mountains with the Wind River chain, to be of great economical importance, as indicating the wide extent of this modern coal period.*

SKETCH OF THE VEGETABLE AND GEOLOGICAL CHARACTER OF THE REGION
COVERED BY THE FIRST REPORT.

The collection of plants submitted to me for examination, though made under unfavorable circumstances, is a very interesting contribution to North American botany.   From the mouth of the Kansas River to the " Red Buttes," on the North Fork of the Platte, the transportation was effected in carts ; but from that place to and from the mountains, the explorations were made on horseback, and by such rapid movements (which were necessary, in order to accomplish the objects of the expedition), that but little opportunity was afforded for collecting and drying botanical specimens. Besides, the party was in a savage and inhospitable country, sometimes annoyed by Indians, and frequently in great distress from want of provisions ; from which circumstances, and the many pressing duties that constantly engaged the attention of the commander, he was not able to make so large a collection as he desired.   To give some general idea of the country explored by Lieutenant Frémont, I recapitulate, from his report, a brief sketch of his route.   The expedition left the mouth of the Kansas on June 10, 1842, and, proceeding up that river about one hundred miles, then continued its course generally along the " bottoms " of the Kansas tributaries, but sometimes passing over the upper prairies.   The soil of the river bottoms is always rich, and generally well timbered ; though the whole region is what is called a prairie country.   The upper prairies are an immense deposit of sand and gravel, covered with a good, and, very generally, a rich soil.   Along the road, on reaching the little stream called Sandy Creek (a tributary of the Kansas), the soil became more sandy. The rock-formations of this region are limestone and sandstone.   The *Amorpha canescens* was the characteristic plant, it being in many places as abundant as the grass.

---

* [It will be remembered that I am writing of conditions as they were known to me more than forty years ago.]

Crossing over from the waters of the Kansas, Lieutenant Frémont arrived at the Great Platte, two hundred and ten miles from its juncture with the Missouri. The valley of this river, from its mouth to the great forks, is about four miles broad, and three hundred and fifteen miles long. It is rich, well timbered, and covered with luxuriant grasses. The purple *Liatris scariosa* and several *asters* were here conspicuous features of the vegetation. I was pleased to recognize among the specimens collected near the forks the fine large-flowered asclepias, that I described many years ago in my account of James' " Rocky Mountain Plants," under the name of *A. speciosa*, and which Mr. Geyer also found in Nicollet's expedition. It seems to be the plant subsequently described and figured by Sir W. Hooker, under the name of *A. Douglasii.* On the Lower Platte, and all the way to the Sweet Water, the showy *Cleome integrifolia* occurred in abundance. From the Forks to Laramie River, a distance of about two hundred miles, the country may be called a sandy one. The valley of the North Fork is without timber; but the grasses are fine, and the herbaceous plants abundant. On the return of the expedition in September, Lieutenant Frémont says the whole country resembled a vast garden; but the prevailing plants were two or three species of *helianthus* (sun-flower). Between the main forks of the Platte, from the junction, as high up as Laramie's Fork, the formation consisted of marl, a soft earthy limestone, and a granite sandstone. At the latter place that singular leguminous plant, the *Kentrophyta montana* of Nuttall was first seen, and then occurred at intervals to the Sweet Water River. Following up the North Fork, Lieutenant Frémont arrived at the mouth of the Sweet Water River, one of the head-waters of the Platte. Above Laramie's Fork to this place the soil is generally sandy. The rocks consist of limestone, with a variety of sandstones (yellow, gray, and red argillaceous), with compact gypsum of alabaster, and fine conglomerates.

The route along the North Fork of the Platte afforded some of the best plants in the collection. The *Senecio rapifolia,* Nutt., occurred in many places, quite to the Sweet Water; *Lippia* (*zapania*) *cuneifolia* (Torr. in James' " Plants," only known before from Dr. James' collection); *Cercocarpus parvifolius,* Nutt.; *Eriogonum parvifolium,* and *cæspitosum,* Nutt.; *Shepherdia argentea,* Nutt., and *Geranium Fremontii,* a new species (near the Red Buttes), were found in this part of the journey. In saline soils, on the Upper Platte, near the mouth of the Sweet Water, were collected several interesting CHENOPODIACEÆ. One of which was first discovered by Dr. James in Long's expedition; and although it was considered as a new genus, I did not describe it owing to the want of the ripe fruit. It is the plant doubtfully referred by Hooker, in his " Flora Boreali Americana," to Batis. He had seen the male flowers only. As it is certainly a new genus, I have dedicated it to the excellent commander of the expedition, as a well-merited compliment for the services he has rendered North American botany.

The Sweet Water Valley is a sandy plain, about one hundred and twenty miles long, and generally about five miles broad ; bounded by ranges of granitic mountains, between which the valley formation consists, near the Devil's Gate, of a grayish micaceous sandstone, with marl and white clay. At the encampment of August 5th to 6th, there occurred a fine white argillaceous sandstone, a coarse sandstone or pudding-stone, and a white calcareous sandstone. A few miles to the west of that position, Lieutenant Frémont reached a point where the sandstone rested immediately upon the granite, which thenceforward, along his line of route, alternated with a compact mica slate.

Along the Sweet Water, many interesting plants were collected, as may be seen by an examination of the catalogue ; I would, however, mention the curious *Œnothera Nuttallii*, Torr. and Gr. ; *Eurotia lanata*, Mocq. (Diotis lanata, *Pursh.*), which seems to be distinct from *E. ceratoides ; Thermopsis montana*, Nutt. ; *Gilia pulchella*, Dougl. ; *Senecio spartioides*, Torr. and Gr. ; a new species, and four or five species of wild currants (*Ribes irriguum*, Dougl., etc.). Near the mouth of the Sweet Water was found the *Plantago eriophora*, Torr., a species first described in my Dr. James' "Rocky Mountain Plants." On the upper part, and near the dividing ridge, were collected several species of *castilleja ; Pentstemon micrantha*, Nutt. ; several *gentians ;* the pretty little *Androsace occidentalis*, Nutt. ; *Solidago incana*, Torr. and Gr., and two species of *eriogonum*, one of which was new.

On August 8th, the exploring party crossed the dividing ridge or pass, and found the soil of the plains at the foot of the mountains, on the western side, to be sandy. From Laramie's Fork to this point, different species of Artemisia were the prevailing and characteristic plants; occupying the place of the grasses, and filling the air with the odor of camphor and turpentine. Along Little Sandy, a tributary of the Colorado of the West, were collected a new species of *phaca* (*P. digitata*) and *Parnassia fimbriata.*

On the morning of August 10th they entered the defiles of the Wind River Mountains, a spur of the Rocky Mountains, or Northern Andes, and among which they spent about eight days. On the borders of a lake, embosomed in one of the defiles, were collected *Sedum rhodiola*, DC. (which had been found before, south of Kotzebue's Sound, only by Dr. James) ; *Senecio hydrophilus*, Nutt. ; *Vaccinium uliginosum ; Betula glandulosa*, and *B. occidentalis*, Hook. ; *Eleagnus argentea*, and *Shepherdia Canadensis.* Some of the higher peaks of the Wind River Mountains rise one thousand feet above the limits of perpetual snow.   Lieutenant Frémont, attended by four of his men, ascended one of the loftiest peaks on August 15th.   On this he found the snow-line twelve thousand five hundred feet above the level of the sea.   The vegetation of the mountains is truly Alpine, embracing a considerable number of species common to both hemispheres, as well as some that are peculiar to North America.   Of the former, Lieutenant Frémont collected *Phleum alpinum ; Oxyria reniformis ; Veronica alpina ;* several species of *salix ; Carex atrata ; C. panicea ;* and, immediately below the line of perpetual congelation, *Silene acaulis* and *Polemonium cæruleum β,* Hook.   Among the Alpine plants peculiar to the Western Hemisphere, there were found *Oreophila myrtifolia* Nutt. ; *Aquilegia cærulea,* Torr. ; *Pedicularis surrecta,* Benth. ; *Pulmonaria ciliata,* James ; *Silene Drummondii,* Hook. ; *Menziesia empetriformis, Potentilla gracilis,* Dougl. ; several species of *pinus ; Frasera speciosa,* Hook. ; *Dodecatheon dentatum,* Hook. ; *Phlox muscoides,* Nutt. ; *Senecio Fremontii,* n.sp., Torr. and Gr. ; four or five *asters,* and *Vaccinium myrtilloides,* Mx. ; the last seven or eight very near the snow-line.   Lower down the mountain were found *Arnica angustifolia,* Vahl. ; *Senecio triangularis,* Hook. ; *S. subnudus,* DC. ; *Macrorhynchus troximoides,* Torr. and Gr. ; *Helianthella uniflora,* Torr. and Gr. ; and *Linosyris viscidiflora,* Hook.

The expedition left the Wind River Mountains about August 18th, returning by the same route as that by which it ascended, except that it continued its course through the whole length of the Lower Platte, arriving at its junction with the Missouri on October 1st.

As the plants of Lieutenant Frémont were under examination while the last part of the "Flora of North America" was in the press, nearly all the new matter relating to the Compositæ was inserted in that work.   Descriptions of a few of the new species were necessarily omitted, owing to the report of the expedition having been called for by Congress before I could finish the necessary analyses and comparisons.   These, however, will be inserted in the successive numbers of the work to which I have just alluded.

JOHN TORREY.

NEW YORK, *March,* 1843.

A—GEOLOGICAL FORMATIONS.

Nature of the geological formations occupying the portion of Oregon and North California included in a geographical survey under the direction of Captain Frémont: by James Hall, palæontologist to the State of New York.

The main geographical features of every country, as well as its soils and vegetable productions, depend upon the nature of its geological formations. So universally true is this, that a suite of the rocks prevailing in any country, with their mineral and fossil contents, will convey more absolute information regarding the agricultural and other capabilities of that country than could be given by a volume written without reference to these subjects. Indeed, no survey of any unknown region should be made without at the same time preserving collections of the prevailing rocks, minerals, and fossils. The attention given to this subject in the foregoing report renders the information of the highest value, and perfectly reliable in reference to opinions or calculations regarding the resources of the country.

The specimens examined present a great variety of aspect and composition; but calcareous rocks prevail over a large portion of the country traversed between longitude 98° and the mouth of the Columbia River, or 122° west from Greenwich. That portion of the route embraced in this notice varies in latitude through seven degrees, viz., 38° to 45° north; and specimens are presented in nearly every half-degree of latitude. Such a collection enables us to form a very satisfactory conclusion regarding this portion of the country, seven degrees in width and twenty-four degrees in length; having an extent east and west equal to the distance between the Atlantic coast of New York and the Mississippi River, and lying in the temperate latitudes which extend from Washington City to the northern limit of the State of New York.

Although we are far from being able to fix the minute or detailed geology, this collection presents us with sufficient materials to form some probable conclusions regarding the whole region from this side of the Rocky Mountains westward to the mouth of the Columbia River. But it is not within my province to dwell upon the advantages opened to us in the vast field which the researches of Captain Frémont have made known. I therefore proceed to a description of the specimens as they occur, taking them in the order from east to west. This, in connection with the section of altitudes on which the rocks are marked, will show the comparative extent of different formations.

Longitude 96¼°, latitude 38¾°; *Otter Creek.*—The single specimen from this locality is a yellowish, impure limestone, apparently containing organic remains, whose structure is obliterated by crystallization. From its position relatively to the formations farther east, I am inclined to refer it to the cretaceous formation.

Longitude 98°, latitude 39°; *Smoky Hill River.*—The specimens from this locality are numbered 26, 29, 31, 33, and 88. They all bear a similar character, and the fossils are alike in each. The rock is an impure limestone, pretty compact, varying in color from dull yellowish to ashy brown, and abounding in shells of a species of *Inoceramus.* (See description.)

This rock probably belongs to the cretaceous formation; the lower part of which has been indicated by Dr. Morton as extending into Louisiana, Arkansas, and Missouri.

Although the specimens from this locality bear a more close resemblance to the upper part of the formation, I do not feel justified in referring them to any other period. This formation evidently underlies large tracts of country, and extends far toward the base of the Rocky Mountains.

Longitude 105°, latitude 39°.—The specimens from this locality are a somewhat porous, light-colored limestone, tough and fine-grained. One or two fragments of fossils from this locality still indicate the cretaceous period; but the absence of any perfect specimens must deter a positive opinion upon the precise age of the formation. One specimen, however, from its form, markings, and fibrous structure, I have referred to the genus *Inoceramus.*

It is evident, from the facts presented, that little of important geological change is observed in travelling over this distance of seven degrees of longitude. But at what depths beneath the surface the country is underlaid by this formation I have no data for deciding. Its importance, however, must not be overlooked. A calcareous formation of this extent is of the greatest advantage to a country; and the economical facilities hence afforded, in agriculture and the uses of civilized life, cannot be overstated.

The whole formation of this region is probably, with some variations, an extension of that which prevails through Louisiana, Arkansas, and Missouri.

The strata at the locality last mentioned are represented as being vertical, standing against the eastern slope of the Rocky Mountains immediately below Pike's Peak.

Longitude 106°, latitude 41°.—At this point, although only one degree west of the last-named specimens, we find a total change in the geology of the region. The specimens are of a red feldspathic granite, showing a tendency to decomposition; and, from the information accompanying the same, this rock overlies a mass of similar granite in more advanced stages of decomposition. The specimens present nothing peculiar in their appearance; and the only apparent difference between these and the ordinary red feldspathic granites of more eastern localities is their finer grain and dingy color.

Longitude 107°, latitude 41½°.—The specimens from this locality are of crystalline feldspathic granite, of a flesh-red color, apparently not acted on by the weather, and presenting the common appearance of this kind of granite in other localities.

No. 95, "above the third bed of coal, in the lower hill, North Fork of Platte River," is a siliceous clay slate, having a saline taste.

Longitude 110°, latitude 41¼°; Nos. 99 and 104.—No. 99 is a fine-grained, soft, argillaceous limestone, of a light ash-color, evidently a modern formation; but, from the absence of fossils, it would be unsatisfactory to assign it any place in the scale of formations. The other specimen, No. 104, is a compact serpentine, having the aspect of a greenstone trap; and, from the account given, is probably interstratified with the limestone. The limestone is more friable and chalky than any specimen previously noticed.

Longitude 110¼°, latitude 41½°.—The specimens from this locality are very peculiar and remarkable. The first is a friable or pulverulent green calcareous sand, unctuous to the touch, but remaining unaltered on exposure to the atmosphere. Its character is very similar to the green sands of New Jersey; but it is of a brighter color and less charged with iron. The second specimen is of similar composition, but quite solid—being, in fact, a green limestone. The singularity of the specimen, and that which first attracted my attention, was the efflorescence of a salt upon its surface, which appears to be, in part, chloride of sodium. Supposing this to be accidental, I broke a specimen, and after a day or two a similar efflorescence appeared from the fresh fracture; leaving no doubt but the salts arise from decomposition of substances within the stone itself.

Longitude 111°, latitude 41½°; *Muddy River.*—These specimens are of a yellowish-gray oolitic limestone, containing turbo, cerithium, etc. The rock is a perfect oolite; and, both in color and texture, can scarcely be distinguished from specimens of the Bath oolite. One of these specimens is quite crystalline, and the oolitic structure somewhat obscure. In this instance the few fossils observed seem hardly sufficient to draw a decisive conclusion regarding the age of the formation; but when taken in connection with the oolitic structure of the mass, its correspondence with the English oolites, and the modern aspect of the whole, there remains less doubt of the propriety of referring it to the oolitic period. A further collection from this interesting locality would doubtless develop a series of fossils which would forever settle the question of the relative age of the formation.

A few miles up this stream Captain Frémont has collected a beautiful series of specimens of fossil ferns. The rock is an indurated clay, wholly destitute of carbonate of lime, and would be termed a " fire clay." These are probably, geologically as well as geographically, higher than the oolite specimens, as the rocks at this place were observed to dip in the direction of north 65° west at an angle of twenty degrees. This would show, conclusively, that the vegetable remains occupy a higher position than the oolite. Associated with these vegetable remains were found several beds of coal, differing in thickness. The section of strata at this place is as follows:

	ft.	in.
Sandstone	1	0
Coal	1	3
Coal	1	3
Indurated clay, with vegetable remains	20	0
Clay	5	0
Coal	0	0
Clay	5	0
Coal	0	0
Clay	5	0
Coal	0	0

The stratum containing the fossil ferns is about twenty feet thick; and above it are two beds of coal, each about fifteen inches. These are succeeded by a bed of sandstone. Below the bed containing the ferns there are three distinct beds of coal, each separated by about five feet of clay. Before examining the oolitic specimens just mentioned, I compared these fossil ferns with a large collection from the coal measures of Pennsylvania and Ohio, and it was quite evident that this formation could not be of the same age. There are several specimens which I can only refer to the *Glossopteris Phillipsii* (see description), an oolitic fossil; and this alone, with the general character of the other species, and the absence of the large stems so common in the coal period, had led me to refer them to the oolitic period. I conceive, however, that we have scarcely sufficient evidence to justify this reference; and though among the fossil shells there are none decidedly typical of the oolite, yet neither are they so of any other formation, and the lithological character of the mass is not reliable evidence. Still, viewed in whatever light we please, these fossil ferns must, I conceive, be regarded as mostly of new species, and in this respect form a very important addition to the flora of the more modern geological periods.

In passing from this locality westward to the Bear River, Captain Frémont crossed a high mountain chain, which is the dividing ridge between the waters of Muddy River, flowing eastward, and those of Muddy Creek, flowing into Bear River on the west. The gap where the ridge was crossed is stated to be eight thousand two hundred feet above the level of the sea. In this ridge, one hundred and fifteen miles to the southward of the locality of the fossils last mentioned, were collected the specimens next to be named. These were obtained near the summit of the ridge, and probably higher than the point where Captain Frémont's party crossed.

The collection from this locality (longitude 111°, latitude 40°) consists of several specimens of an argillaceous, highly bituminous, and somewhat slaty limestone, loaded with fossils. It is very brittle, and easily shivered into small fragments by a blow of the hammer. Its natural color is a light sepia, but it bleaches on exposure to the atmosphere. In structure it is not unlike some of the limestones of the lias or oolite formations. The fossils are chiefly one species of cerithium and one of mya; and besides these, another species of cerithium and a nucula can be identified. So far as I am able to ascertain, these fossils are undescribed, and will therefore be regarded as new species.

It may be considered premature to decide upon the geological position of this mass. It may belong to the same period, though far higher in the series than those in the same longitude which have just been described. In the locality of the fossil plants the strata dip west by north; but, from the structure of the country, it is evident that there is a change in the direction of the dip before reaching the high ridge from which the specimens under consideration were taken. Further examination, I have no doubt, will set this question at rest.

I may here notice the interesting fact of the wide extent of these formations, showing the existence in this longitude of these calcareous beds, of a nature precisely like those of the modern formations of Western Europe.

A few miles south of the locality of these fossils Captain Frémont describes the occurrence of an immense stratum of fossil salt; and the same ridge is represented as bounding the Great Salt Lake. There would therefore seem no doubt that the salt in question is associated with the strata of this period, and probably coeval with the same.

I may remark, in the same connection, that the surfaces of the specimens containing the fossil ferns also effloresce a salt, which is apparently chloride of sodium. This fact seems to indicate the presence of fossil salt at this distance north of the known locality, and is a circumstance which we naturally appropriate as part of the evidence of identity in the age of the formations.

This region is unquestionably one of the highest interest, both as regards its economical resources and equally so in the contributions which it will yield to geological science.   In the specimens from the vegetable locality I have been able to indicate seven or eight species of fossil ferns, most of which are new.   Further researches will doubtless greatly multiply this number.   Besides these, as new species probably peculiar to our continent, they have a higher interest, inasmuch as they show to us the wide extent and the nature of the vegetation of this modern coal period.   In the broad fields of the West we shall have an opportunity of tracing it over large and unbroken areas, and many highly interesting results may follow its comparison with the vegetation of the true carboniferous period.

Again : since these deposits have evidently been made over large tracts of country, it is not unreasonable to suppose that the quantity of materials accumulated will be very great, and that we may expect to find profitable coal-beds in the rocks of this age.   This subject, besides being of high interest to science, is of some prospective economical importance, though perhaps too remote to dwell upon while the country remains so little explored as at present.

Longitude 112°, latitude 42°.—The specimen No. 72 is a grayish-blue limestone, efflorescing a salt upon the surface, " from the Hot Salt Springs of September 13, 1843."   No. 108 is a siliceous limestone of a brownish-gray color ; where exposed the surface becomes porous, from the solution and removal of the lime, while the siliceous particles remain.   From the general lithological characters of the specimen it is probably a modern rock, but its precise age cannot be decided.

Longitude 112°, latitude 41½°.—The single specimen from this locality is, in its present state, " granular quartz."   It is, however, very evidently an altered sedimentary rock, with the lines of deposition quite distinctly preserved.   This rock probably comes out from under the siliceous limestone last described, both having been altered by modern igneous action.   The character of the specimens from the next locality—three-quarters of a degree farther west—may perhaps throw some light upon the present condition of those last named.

Longitude 112¾°, latitude 42¾° ; *at the American Falls of Snake River.*—The collection from this point presents the following, in a descending order.   These specimens are numbered 94, 96, 97, 101, 102, 106, and 107 :

1. A botryoidal or concretionary lava, No. 94.
2. Obsidian, No. 102.
3. Vitrified sandstone, No. 106.
4. A whitish ash-colored chalk or limestone, No. 107.
5. A light ashy volcanic sand, No. 97.
6. Brown sand, volcanic (?).

These are all apparently volcanic products, with, probably, the exception of Nos. 106 and 107, which may be sedimentary products, the first altered by heat. The two lower deposits are evidently volcanic sand or "ashes;" the upper of these, or No. 5, has all the characters of pulverized pumice-stone, and is doubtless of similar origin.

No. 107 is an impure limestone, but little harder than common chalk; and, but for its associations, would be regarded as of similar origin.*

No. 106 is apparently a vitrified sandstone, the grains all rounded and the surfaces of the mass highly polished.

No. 102 is a beautiful black obsidian.

No. 94 is a mammillary or botryoidal lava; the concretions having a radiated structure, the mass is easily frangible, and readily separates into small angular fragments.

The whole of this series, with the exception of No. 107, may be regarded as of volcanic origin; for the apparently vitrified sandstone may be, in its composition, not very distinct from trap or basalt, though it is more vitreous and its fracture fresher and brighter.

Longitude $114\frac{1}{2}°$, *latitude* $42\frac{1}{2}°$.—The specimens marked No. 3 are of light-colored tufaceous limestone and siliceous limestone. The specimens appear as if from some regular formation, broken up and thinly coated by calcareous matter from springs. From the fact observed by Captain Frémont, that these fragments enter largely into the composition of the soil, we may presume that the same is highly calcareous.

The specimen No. 12, from the same locality, consists mainly of small fragments of the crust, claws, etc., of some crustacean—probably of fresh-water origin. There are also some vertebræ and ribs of fishes. The whole is so unchanged, and of such recent appearance, as to induce a belief that the deposit is of fresh-water origin, and due to the desiccation of some lake or stream. Should such a deposit be extensive, its prospective value to an agricultural community will be an important consideration. But, as before remarked, there is evidently a preponderance of calcareous matter throughout the whole extent of country traversed.

Longitude $115,°$ *latitude* $43°$.—The specimens from this locality are numbered 16, 21, and 39. Nos. 16 and 21 are angular fragments of impure

---

* Since this was written a specimen of No. 107 has been submitted to the examination of Professor Bailey, who finds it highly charged with "calcareous polythalamia" in excellent preservation. He remarks that "the forms are, many of them, such as are common in chalk and cretaceous marls; but as these forms are still living in our present oceans, their presence does not afford conclusive evidence as to the age of the deposit in which they occur. I have, however, invariably found that in our tertiary deposits the chalk polythalamia are accompanied by large species of genera *peculiar* to the tertiary. Now, as these are entirely wanting in the specimen from Captain Frémont, the evidence, *as far as it goes*, is in favor of the view that the specimen came from a cretaceous formation."

limestone of some recent geological period, and No. 39 consists of an aggregation of pebbles and gravel. The pebbles are of black siliceous slate, which are represented as forming a conglomerate with the limestone fragments just mentioned. The limestone specimens are probably broken fragments from some stratum *in situ* in the same vicinity, and the conglomerate is one of very recent formation. The slate pebbles are from a rock of much older date, and worn very round and smooth, while the limestone bears little evidence of attrition.

The gray siliceous limestone specimens contain a species of turritella, and a small bivalve shell. (See descriptions and figures.)

Longitude 115½°, latitude 43½°.—The two specimens from this locality are of volcanic origin. No. 46 is a reddish compact trap or lava, with small nodules or cavities filled with analcime and stilbite. No. 52 is a coarse and porous trap, or ancient lava.

Longitude 116°, latitude 43½°.—The single specimen from this place is a white feldspathic granite, with a small proportion of quartz, and black mica in small scales. The specimen contains a single garnet. The structure is somewhat slaty, and from appearances it is rapidly destructible from atmospheric agency.

Longitude 117°, latitude 44½°.—These specimens, from Brulé River, are numbered 4, 19, 41, and 48.

No. 4 is a slaty limestone, partially altered, probably from the proximity of igneous rocks.

No. 41 is of similar character, very thinly laminated, and of a dark color.

No. 19 is of similar character, but more altered, and partially crystalline. The lines of deposition are, however, preserved.

No. 48 has the appearance of a compact, gray feldspathic lava ; but there are some apparent lines of deposition still visible, which incline me to the opinion that it is an altered sedimentary rock.

Longitude 117½°, latitude 45°.—The specimen is a compact, dark-colored basalt, showing a tendency to desquamate upon the exposed surfaces. This rock forms the mountains of Brulé River.

Longitude 117½°, latitude 45½°.—The specimen No. 110 is a fine-grained basalt or trap, with a few small cells filled with analcime. This is of the rock forming the Blue Mountain.

Longitude 118°, latitude 45°.—The single specimen (No. 43) from this locality is apparently an altered siliceous slate. It is marked by what appear to be lines of deposition, the thin laminæ being separated by layers of mica.

Longitude 119°, latitude 38½°.—The specimens Nos. 14, 23, 45, and 51, are all from this locality.

No. 14 appears to be a decomposed feldspar, having a slightly porous structure; it is very light, and adheres strongly to the tongue.

No. 23. A friable, argillaceous sandstone, somewhat porous upon the exposed surfaces.

No. 45. A compact lava of a sienitic structure, containing obsidian. This specimen appears much like some of the porous portions of trap dikes which cut through the sienitic rocks of New England.

No. 51. Feldspar, with a little black mica. The specimen is probably from a granite rock, though its structure is that of compact feldspar.

Longitude 120°, latitude 45½°.—The single specimen (No. 20) from this locality is a compact, fine-grained trap, or basalt, with a few round cavities of the size of peas.

Longitude 120½°, latitude 38½°.—The specimens are numbered 91, 109, and 117.

No. 91 has the appearance of a porous trap, or basalt, though possibly the production of a modern volcano. It is thickly spotted with crystals of analcime, some apparently segregated from the mass, and others filling vesicular cavities.

No. 117 is a compact basalt, the specimen exhibiting the character of the basalt of the Hudson and Connecticut River valleys.

No. 109 is a fine-grained granite, consisting of white quartz and feldspar, with black mica. Captain Frémont remarks that this rock forms the eastern part of the main California Mountain. From its granular and rather loose structure, it is to be inferred that it would undergo rapid decomposition in a climate like ours.

Longitude 121°, latitude 44½°.—The specimens from this locality are numbered 53, 54, 55, 56, 57, 58, 59, 60, and 61. These are characteristic specimens of the strata composing a bluff seven hundred feet high, and are numbered in the descending order.

The specimens 59, 60, and 61, are three specimens of what appears to be very fine clay, perfectly free from carbonate of lime, and nearly as white as ordinary chalk. These three specimens, which are understood to be from three distinct strata, vary but slightly in their characters—No. 61 being of the lightest color.

No. 58 is a specimen of grayish volcanic breccia, the larger portion consisting of volcanic sand or ashes.

Nos. 55, 56, and 57, are of the same character, being, however, nearly free from fragments or pebbles, and composed of light volcanic sand, or scoria, with an apparently large admixture of clay from the strata below. The whole is not acted on by acids, and, so far as can be judged, is of volcanic origin.

No. 58 is of similar character to the preceding three specimens, but contains more fragments, and has a generally coarser aspect.*

Longitude 121°, latitude 45°.—These specimens are numbered 7, 35, 40, 47, and 49.

No. 7 is a siliceous sinter, coated externally with hydrate of iron.

No. 35. A reddish, rather compact lava. The color is owing to the presence of iron, which hastens its decomposition on exposure.

No. 40. A reddish brecciated feldspathic lava, embracing fragments of light-colored siliceous sandstone or lava.

No. 47. Compact trap, or basalt, with a few rounded cavities. This specimen is precisely like No. 20, longitude 120°; and, from the description given, appears to be a prevailing rock along the valley of the Columbia River.

* The specimens Nos. 59, 60, and 61, which are from three different but contiguous strata, have since been examined by Professor J. W. Bailey, of West Point, who finds them charged with fluviatile infusoria of remarkable forms.

Below are descriptions (accompanied by a plate) of some of the most interesting forms, which were sketched by him with a camera-lucida attached to his microscope. It has not been considered necessary to distinguish, particularly, to which of the strata the individuals figured belong, as no species occur in one, which are not present in the others. They are evidently deposits of the same epoch, and differ very slightly in their characters.

Figs. 3, 2, and 4. Side views of *Eunotia librile* of Ehrenberg. The species is figured and described by Ehrenberg, who received it from Real del Monte, Mexico. It resembles *Eunotia Westermanni* (Ehr.), but differs in its granulations. The three figures are from individuals of different age.

Figs. 8 and 9. *Eunotia gibba* (Ehr.).—Identical with a common fresh-water species now living at West Point.

Fig. 10. *Pinnularia pachyptera ?* (Ehr.).—Ehrenberg's figure of P. pachyptera from Labrador is very similar to the Oregon species here represented.

Figs. 12, 15, and 17. *Cocconema cymbiforme ?* (Ehr.).—These are probably merely varieties of the same species. Fig. 8 is rather larger than C. cymbiforme usually grows at West Point.

Fig. 19. *Gomphonema clavatum ?* (Ehr.).—Front view.

Fig. 20. *Gomphonema clavatum ?* (Ehr.).—Side view.

Fig. 25. *Gomphonema minutissimum* (Ehr.).—A cosmopolite species.

Fig. 1. *Gallionella (new species, a).*—This is evidently identical with a large species which I have described and figured as occurring at Dana's locality. (See Silliman's Journal for April, 1845.)

Figs. 5 and 7. *Gallionella, new species ?* δ (a—edge view ; b—side view).—This species presents remarkably compressed frustules, which are marked on their circular bases with radiant lines. It is particularly abundant in Nos. 59 and 61.

Fig. 11. *Gallionella distans ?*—This very minute species constitutes the chief mass of No. 60, but also abounds in Nos. 59 and 61.

Figs. 14 and 13. *Cocconeis prætexta* (Ehr.).—Appears to agree with a species from Mexico figured by Ehrenberg.

Fig. 16. *Fragillaria ——.*

Fig. 18. *Surirella ——.*—A fragment only. I have seen several fragments of beautiful Surirellæ, but have not yet found a perfect specimen to figure.

Fig. 23. *Fragillaria rhabdosoma ?*—Fragment.

Figs. 6 and 21. *Spiculæ of fresh-water sponges.*—Spongilla.

Fig. 24. Four-sided crystal of—— ?

Fig. 22. Scale=10-100ths of millimetre magnified equally with the drawings.

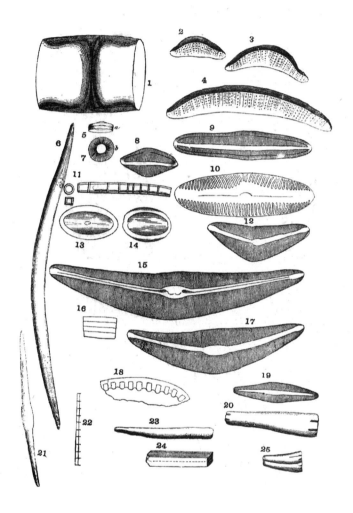

FOSSIL FRESH WATER INFUSORIA FROM OREGON.

No. 49. An imperfect striped agate, with the centre of siliceous sinter. This, with Nos. 7 and 40, is doubtless associated with the basalt, No. 47, which is the prevailing rock.

Longitude 122°, latitude 45½° ; *Cascades of the Columbia River.*—From this place are the specimens numbered 9, 10, 13, 17, 18, 22, 24, 25, 27, 30, 36, 37, 38, and 44.

Of these specimens, Nos. 13 and 24 are indurated clay, with impressions of leaves of dicotyledonous plants.

No. 17 is a fine argillaceous sandstone, with stems and leaves, which still retain their fibrous structure.

No. 30 is a specimen of dicotyledonous wood, partially replaced by stony matter, and a portion still retaining the fibrous structure and consistency of partially carbonized wood.

Nos. 10, 25, 27, and 38 are specimens of coal from the same locality. (For further information of these, see analysis of specimens appended.)

No. 22. Carbonaceous earth, with pebbles, evidently a part of the formation to which the previous specimens are referred.

No. 18 is a compact trap, apparently having a stratified structure.

No. 36. A porous basaltic lava, with crystals of analcime, etc.

No. 37. Two specimens—one a porous or rather scoriaceous lava of a reddish color ; and the other a compact gray lava, with a few small cavities.

No. 44. A brown scoriaceous lava.

No. 44*a*. A small specimen of compact lava.

Miscellaneous Specimens.

No. 62. A coral in soft limestone ; the structure too much obliterated to decide its character. (From the dividing ridge between Bear Creek and Bear River, at a point 8,200 feet above tide-water.)

No. 71. Calcareous tufa, containing the remains of grasses, twigs, moss, etc.

No. 81. Calcareous tufa stained with iron.

No. 98. Ferruginous calcareous tufa, containing remains of twigs, etc.

These three last-named specimens are evidently the calcareous deposits from springs holding carbonate of lime in solution.

B—ORGANIC REMAINS.

Descriptions of organic remains collected by Captain J. C. Frémont, in the geographical survey of Oregon and North California : by James Hall, palæontologist to the State of New York.

PLATES I. AND II.

Fossil Ferns, etc.

The specimens here described are all from one locality, in longitude 111°, latitude 41½°. They occur in a light-gray indurated clay, which is entirely free from calcareous matter, very brittle, and having a very imperfect slaty structure. Nearly all the species differ from any described in Brongniart's "*Hist. Veg. Foss.*," in Goppert's "*Systema Filicum Fossilium,*" or in Phillips' "*Geology of Yorkshire.*"

1. SPHENOPTERIS FREMONTII. Pl. 2, figs. 3, 3*a*. (No. 118 of collection.) Compare *sphenopteris crenulata;* Brong. Hist. Veg. Foss., i., p. 187, t. 56, f. 3.

Description.—Frond bipinnate (or tripinnate?); rachis moderately strong, striated; pinnæ oblique to the rachis, rigid, moderately approximate, alternate; pinnules subovate, somewhat decurrent at the base, about three-or four-lobed; fructification very distinct in round dots (capsules) of carbonaceous matter upon the margins of the pinnules; *3a*, a portion twice magnified.

I have named this beautiful and unique species in honor of Captain Frémont, and as a testimony of the benefits that science has derived from his valuable explorations on the west of the Rocky Mountains.

2. SPHENOPTERIS TRILOBA. Pl. 1, fig. 10. (Nos. 65, 79, and 80 of collection.)

Description.—Frond bipinnate, or tripinnate; rachis slender, flexuous; pinnæ long, flexuous, distant, opposite, perpendicular to the rachis; pinnules oblong, subtrilobate, opposite or alternate, narrow at base, distant, perpendicular.

The distant, long, and flexuous pinnæ, with the small trilobate pinnules, distinguish this species. In general features it approaches somewhat the *sphenopteris rigida* (Brong.), but differs essentially in the smaller pinnules, which are usually nearly opposite, and in never being more than sub-trilobate, while in *S. rigida* they are often deeply five-lobed.

3. SPHENOPTERIS (?) PAUCIFOLIA. Pl. 2, figs. 1, 1*a*, 1*b*, 1*c*, 1*d*. (No. 118 of collection.)

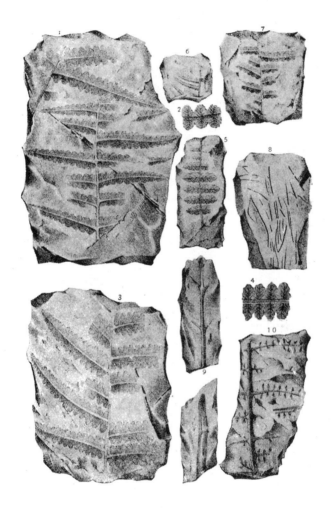

FOSSIL FERNS.

Description.—Frond tripinnate ; rachis rather slender, with long, lateral, straight branches, which are slightly oblique ; pinnæ slender, nearly at right angles, alternate and opposite ; pinnules minute, oval-ovate, somewhat distant, opposite or alternate, expanded or attenuate at base, sometimes deeply bilobed or digitate ; midrib not apparent.

This species was evidently a beautiful fern of large size, with slender, sparse foliage, giving it a peculiarly delicate appearance. In some of its varieties (as fig. 1*b*) it resembles *Sphenopteris digitata ;* Phillips' Geol. Yorkshire, p. 147, pl. 8, figs. 6 and 7 ; *Sphen. Williamsonii*, Brong., Hist. Veg. Foss., i., p. 177, t. 49, figs. 6, 7, 8. The fossil under consideration, however, is quite a different species. In the fig. 1*a*, the branches and pinnules are more lax ; fig. 1*d* is a magnified portion.

In its general aspect this fossil resembles the genus *Pachypteris*, to which I had been inclined to refer it, but for the digitate character of the pinnules manifested by some specimens.

4. SPHENOPTERIS (?) TRIFOLIATA. Pl. 2, figs. 2, 2*a*. (No. 86 of collection.)

Description.—Frond bipinnate ; pinnæ trifoliate ; pinnules elliptic, narrowing at the base ; rachis slender, flexuous ; fructification terminal, raceme-like, from the pinnules gradually becoming single and fructiferous.

Fig. 2*a*. Part of the fructiferous portion enlarged, showing the capsules, apparently immersed in a thickened pinnule. This is a most beautiful and graceful species, approaching in some respects to the *S. paucifolia* just described.

5. GLOSSOPTERIS PHILLIPSII (?). Pl. 2, figs. 5, 5*a*, 5*b*, 5*c*. (Nos. 69, 82, and 86 of the collection.) Compare *Glossopteris Phillipsii*, Brong., Hist. Veg. Foss., p. 225, t. 61 bis, fig. 2 ; *Pecopteris paucifolia*, Phillips' Geol. Yorkshire, p. 119, pl. viii., fig. 8.

Description.—"Leaves linear lanceolate, narrow, narrowing toward the base and apex ; nervules oblique, dichotomous, lax, scarcely distinct, subimmersed in the thick parenchyma." Brong., *ut sup.*, p. 225.

The specimen fig. 5 corresponds precisely with the figure of Brongniart, pl. 61 bis, fig. 5, both in form of the leaf and arrangement of the nervules, so as to leave little doubt of their identity. Fig. 5 is a nearly perfect leaf of this species ; fig. 5*a* is the base of another specimen, having a long foot-stalk ; fig. 5*b* is the base of another leaf with fructification (?) ; fig. 5*c*, the same magnified. This structure is so partial, that it can only with doubt be referred to the fructification of the plant ; and it is not improbable that the same may be some parasitic body, or the eggs of an insect which have been deposited upon the leaf. Whatever this may have been, it does not appear to have been calcareous ; and the total absence of calca-reous matter in the rock is an objection to referring the same to *flustra*, or any of the parasitic corals.　The ferns are abundant in the rock at this point, and many of them unbroken, and evidently not far or long trans-ported—which, had they been, would have given support to the supposition of this body being coral.

I have referred this species to the *Glossopteris Phillipsii*, as being the only description and figure accessible to me to which this fossil bears any near resemblance.　The geological position of that fossil is so well ascer-tained to be the schists of the upper part of the oolitic period that, relying upon the evidence offered by a single species, we might regard it as a strong argument for referring all the other specimens to the same geolog-?ical period.

The two following species, or varieties of the same species, have been referred with doubt to the genus *pecopteris ;* but a close examination shows the midrib only partially distinct, and in some cases scarcely visible, while the nervules radiate from the base.　In other cases the midrib appears well marked at the base, but disappears in numerous ramifications before reaching the apex.　The character, therefore, given by Brongniart, of "*nervo medio valde notato, nec apice evanescente*," is inapplicable to these species ; but the same feature may be observed in some figured by Bron-gniart himself.

6. PECOPTERIS UNDULATA.　Pl. 1, figs. 1 and 2.　(Nos. 83 and 118 of col-lection.)

Description.—Frond bipinnate; rachis slender ; pinnæ long, slightly oblique to the rachis, opposite and alternate ; pinnules oblique, oval-ovate, broad at the base, and the lower ones sometimes lobed, gradually becom-ing coadunate toward the extremity of the pinnæ.

The pinnules have often an apparently continuous smooth outline ; but, on closer examination, they appear undulated, or indented upon the mar-gin, and many of them are obviously so.

7. PECOPTERIS UNDULATA ; *var.*　Pl. 1, figs. 3, 4, 5.　(No. 78 of col-lection.)

Description.—Frond bipinnate ; rachis slender ; pinnæ numerous, long, and gradually tapering, oblique to the rachis ; pinnules oval-ovate, broad at base ; midrib evanescent ; nervules strong, bifurcating toward the apex ; margins lobed or indented, particularly in those near the base of the pinnæ.

This species may be regarded as a variety of the last, though the pin-nules are longer and less broad proportionally ; but the general aspect is similar, and the habit of the plant precisely the same.

The specimen fig. 5 can only be regarded as an extreme variety of the same species, which is approached in some of the enlarged pinnules, as fig. 4.

8. PECOPTERIS (?) ODONTOPTEROIDES. Pl. 1, figs. 6 and 7. (Nos. 78 and 118 of collection.)

Description.—Frond bipinnate (?) ; pinnæ long and slender ; secondary pinnæ subdistant, gradually tapering, nearly perpendicular ; pinnules subrotund, obtuse, small, approximate, oblique, alternate, and coadunate at base ; nervules strong, diverging from base ; no distinct midrib.

Fig. 7. A few of the pinnæ near the termination of a frond.

The arrangement of the pinnules and nerves in this species strongly reminds one of the *Odontopteris Schlotheimii*, Brong., Hist. Veg. Foss., p. 256, t. 78, fig. 5—a fossil fern of the Pennsylvania coal measures ; but this is essentially different.

The aspect of the three last-named plants is more like that of the true coal-measure ferns than any of the others ; but the whole association, and their fossil condition, demand that they should be referred to a very modern period.

New Genus—TRICHOPTERIS.

Character.—Frond slender, flexuous, in tufts or single, branching or pinnate ; branches long, very slender.

9. TRICHOPTERIS FILAMENTOSA. Pl. 2, fig. 6. (No. 78 of collection.) Compare *Fucoides æqualis*, Brong., Hist. Veg. Foss., p. 58, t. 5, figs. 3 and 4.

Description.—Frond pinnate or bipinnate ; rachis long, and almost equally slender throughout ; branches numerous, regular, alternate, simple, elongated, very slender, and flexuous.

The branches are frequently folded back upon themselves, and undulated, lying like the finest thread upon the surface of the stone. This species is very delicate and graceful, and can scarcely be examined without the aid of a magnifier. This fossil is very similar to the *Fucoides æqualis* of Brong. (from the lower chalk), except that the branches are longer and undivided.

10. TRICHOPTERIS GRACILIS. Pl. 1, fig. 8. (No. 84 of collection.)

Description.—Slender, stems numerous, flexuous, in a tuft, branched ; branches numerous, slender, oblique, stronger than in the last species.

This species is more robust than the first described, but evidently belongs to the same genus. I had first supposed that this might be a collection of fern stems, stripped of their foliage; but their slender structure, long branches, and peculiar arrangement, with the appropriate proportion of all the parts, forbid its reference to anything of this kind; it is therefore placed in a new genus.

11. STEMS OF FERNS. Pl. 1, fig. 9.

The stems of ferns, denuded of leaves, and portions only of the branches remaining. Great numbers of these stems occur, mingled with fragments of leaves and other portions of ferns still perfect.

12. LEAF OF A DICOTYLEDONOUS PLANT (?). Pl. 2, fig. 4. (Fr. Aug. 17, and No. 201 of collection.)

Description.—Leaf ovate-lanceolate, lobed; lobes acute, mucronate; midrib straight, distinct, dichotomous; principal divisions going to the mucronate points.

This leaf has the aspect of the leaf of a dicotyledonous plant, and approaches remotely only to the character of species of the genus *Phlebopteris* of Brongniart, which are regarded as such by Phillips, and by Lindley and Hutton. The specimen was not observed soon enough to make a satisfactory comparison.

Locality, in the neighborhood of the specimens containing the preceding fossils, and regarded by Captain Frémont as belonging to the same formation. The rock containing them is a soft or very partially indurated clay, very unlike the hard and brittle mass containing the other species.

PLATE III.

Fossil Shells, etc.

Figs. 4, 6, 5, 7, 9, and 12 are from longitude 111°, latitude 40°.
Figs. 18, 19, and 20 are from longitude 111 latitude 41$\frac{1}{2}$°.
Figs. 13, 15, and 16 are from longitude 115°, latitude 43°.
Figs. 22 and 23, leaves, from longitude 122°, latitude 45$\frac{1}{4}$°.

13. MYA TELLINOIDES.* Pl. 3, figs. 4 and 6. Compare *unio peregrinus;* Phillips' Geol. Yorkshire, pl. 7, fig. 12. (Nos. 8, 28, and 32 of collection.)

Description.—Ovate, posterior side extended, slope gentle, rounded at the extremity; anterior side regularly rounded; surface nearly smooth, or marked only by lines of growth; beaks slightly wrinkled; moderately prominent.

The specimen fig. 4 is an entire shell; fig. 6 is a cast of the two valves of a smaller specimen, retaining a small portion of the shell. Another

* The species, where no authority is given, are regarded as new, and will be so understood.

PLATE 3.

PLATE 4.

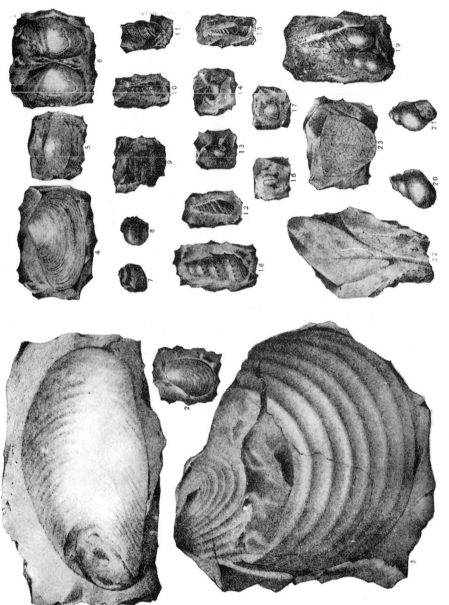

FOSSIL SHELLS.

specimen, larger than either of these, presents the inside of both valves, with the hinge broken.

Locality, in longitude 111°, latitude 40°, in slaty bituminous limestone.

14. NUCULA IMPRESSA (?) G. Pl. 3, fig. 5. (No. 32 of collection.)

Description.—Subelliptical ; posterior extremity somewhat expanded ; surface smooth. A few of the teeth are still visible on the anterior hinge margin, but the greater part of the hinge line is obscured.

Locality, in longitude 111°, latitude 40°, in slaty bituminous limestone.

15. CYTHEREA PARVULA. Pl. 3, figs. 16 and 17. (No. 21 of collection.) Compare *Isocardia angulata* (?), Phillips' Geol. Yorkshire, pl. 9, fig. 9.

Description.—Ovate trigonal ; umbones elevated ; beaks incurved ; surface marked by regular concentric lines of growth ; umbones and beaks with a few stronger wrinkles. The umbones of this shell are scarcely diverging or involute enough to place it in the genus *Isocardia*, where it would otherwise very naturally belong.

Locality, in longitude 115°, latitude 43°, in gray argillaceous limestone. Two other specimens of the same shell were noticed.

16. PLEUROTOMARIA UNIANGULATA. Pl. 3, figs. 7 and 9. (Nos. 8 and 32 of collection.)

Description.—Turbinate ; whorls, about six, gradually enlarging ; convex below, and angular above ; suture plain ; surface marked by fine lines of growth ; aperture round-oval ; shell thin, fragile.

The specimens are all imperfect, and more or less crushed ; the figures, however, are good representations of the fossil. It is readily distinguished by its fine lines of growth, resembling a species of helix, and by the angular character of the upper part of each whorl.

Locality, in longitude 111°, latitude 40°, in a dark slaty bituminous limestone.

17. CERITHIUM TENERUM. Pl. 3, figs. 10, 11. (Nos. 8, 32, and 34 of collection.)

Description.—Elongated, subulate ; whorls, about ten, marked with strong ridges, which are again crossed by finer lines in the direction of the whorls. The strong vertical ridges are often obsolete on the last whorl, as in fig. 11, and the spiral lines much stronger.

This shell is very strongly marked, and its external aspect is sufficient to distinguish it ; it is easily fractured, and, from the nature of the matrix, it has been impossible to obtain a specimen exhibiting the mouth perfectly.

Locality, same as the preceding.

18. Cerithium Fremontii.   Pl. 3, fig. 12.   (No. 28 of collection.)

Description.—Shell terete, ovate, acute ; whorls, about nine, convex ; summit of each one coronated ; surface marked by regular rows of pustular knobs, often with smaller ones between ; beak small, sharp ; mouth not visible in the specimen.

This is a very beautifully marked shell, with the summit of each whorl crowned with a row of short spines.

Locality, same as the preceding.

19. Natica (?) occidentalis. Pl. 3, figs. 13 and 14. (Nos. 16 and 21 of collection.)

Description.—Depressed, conical, or subglobose ; spire short, consisting of about five whorls, the last one comprising the greater part of the shell ; aperture semioval, rounded at both extremities ; umbilicus small ; surface marked by lines of growth.

There is a single perfect specimen and several casts of this delicate little shell.   The mouth is not entire, but enough remains to show that the lip was a little expanded ; but whether the columella covered a part of the umbilicus is uncertain.

Locality, in longitude 115°, latitude 43°, in a gray siliceous limestone.

20. Turritella bilineata.   Pl. 3, fig. 15.   (No. 21 of collection.)

Description.—Elongated, subulate, spire rapidly ascending ; whorls marked by a double, elevated, spiral line, which is notched in the lower whorls.

The specimen figured is imperfect, only the upper part of the shell remaining.   Several casts of the same species occur in the specimens.

Locality, same as the preceding.

21. Cerithium nodulosum.   Pl. 3, figs. 18 and 19.   (Nos. 64, 68, and 74 of collection.)

Description.—Elongated, subulate ; spire rapidly ascending ; whorls about seven ; the sutures marked by a spiral band ; surface of whorls marked by curved striæ, or elevated lines, in the direction of the lines of growth ; whorls carinated, with a row of protuberances along the centre.

The arched lines of growth are more distinct upon the last whorl, and it is marked beneath by a few spiral lines.

Fig. 18 is a perfect specimen.   Fig. 19. The left-hand figure is a cast of the same species ; the right-hand figure retains the shell upon the upper part, while it is removed from the lower part.

Locality, in longitude 111°, latitude 41½°, in yellowish-gray oolitic limestone.

22. TURBO PALUDINÆFORMIS. Pl. 3, fig. 20. (No. 64 of collection.)

Description.—Whorls, about four, rapidly enlarging, convex, smooth; mouth round-oval; columella slightly reflected; volutions marked by fine arched striæ in the direction of the lines of growth.

A small portion only of the shell remains upon the specimen figured, but it is retained in the matrix. This fossil occurs in gray or yellowish oolite, associated with *Cerithium nodulosum*, and other shells. It resembles *Paludina* in form.

Locality, same as the preceding.

23. LEAVES OF DICOTYLEDONOUS PLANTS. Pl. 3, figs. 22 and 23.

The specimens have not been satisfactorily identified, but doubtless belong to a very modern tertiary deposit.

Locality, Cascades of the Columbia River.

PLATE IV.

24. INOCERAMUS————? Pl. 4, figs. 1 and 2. (Nos. 26, 29, 21, 33, and 38 of collection.) Compare *Inoceramus mytiloides*, Sow. Min. Con., tab. 442.

Description.—Inequavalved, depressed, and elongated; surface marked by numerous waved lines and ridges; convex toward the beaks; beaks short and obtuse, somewhat obsolete in old specimens; hinge line oblique.

In the old specimens, the shell appears much flattened, except toward the beaks; while in the younger specimens it is more convex, and particularly so toward the beaks. The youngest specimens are finely lined, and the whole surface of one valve quite convex.

This fossil apparently exists in great numbers, as in the specimens examined there were individuals in all stages of growth, though mostly broken or separated valves. The same species was collected by the late Mr. Nicollet, near the Great Bend of the Missouri.

Locality, Smoky Hill River, longitude 98°, latitude 38°, in yellowish and gray limestone of the cretaceous formation.

25. INOCERAMUS————? Pl. 4, fig. 3. (No. 42 of collection.) Compare *Inoceramus involutus*, Sow. Min. Con., tab. 583.

Description.—Semicircular; surface flat, with the margin deflected; marked by strong, regular concentric ridges, which become attenuated on either side, and are nearly obsolete toward the beak; beak of one valve small, not elevated; hinge line nearly rectangular.

The strong concentric ridges distinguish this fossil from any other species. The specimen figured is probably the flat valve, as a fragment of a large and much more convex valve accompanies this one, from the same locality. The shell, particularly toward the margin, is very thick and fibrous.

Locality, near the eastern slope of the Rocky Mountains, in longitude 105°, latitude 39°, in light yellowish-gray limestone, probably of the cretaceous formation.

Note.—The specimens figured on Plate III., Nos. 4, 6, 5, 7, and 10, have the appearance of fluviatile shells, and would have been so regarded but for the occurrence of fig. 5, which appears to be a Nucula, and fig. 12, in the same association, the sculpturing of which is unlike any of the Melania known to me. It is not improbable, however, that this may prove a fresh-water deposit of vast interest, as it appears to be of great extent, and occurs at a great elevation. The researches of Captain Frémont, in his future explorations, will doubtless set this question at rest, by a larger collection of fossils from the same region.

C. Note Concerning the Plants Collected in the Second Expedition of Captain Frémont.

When Captain Frémont set out on his second expedition, he was well provided with paper and other means for making extensive botanical collections ; and it was understood that, on his return, we should, conjointly, prepare a full account of his plants, to be appended to his report. About fourteen hundred species were collected, many of them in regions not before explored by any botanist. In consequence, however, of the great length of the journey, and the numerous accidents to which the party were exposed, but especially owing to the dreadful flood of the Kansas, which deluged the borders of the Missouri and Mississippi Rivers, more than half of his specimens were ruined before he reached the borders of civilization. Even the portion saved was greatly damaged ; so that, in many instances, it has been extremely difficult to determine the plants. As there was not sufficient time, before the publication of Captain Frémont's report, for the proper study of the remains of his collection, it has been deemed advisable to reserve the greater part of them to incorporate with the plants which we expect he will bring with him on returning from his third expedition, upon which he has just set out.

The loss sustained by Captain Frémont, and, I may say, by the botanical world, will, we trust, be partly made up the present and next seasons, as much of the same country will be passed over again, and some new regions explored. Arrangements have also been made by which the botanical collections will be preserved, at least from the destructive effects of water ; and a person accompanies the expedition, who is to make drawings of all the most interesting plants. Particular attention will be given to the forest trees and the vegetable productions that are useful in the arts, or that are employed for food or medicine.—JOHN TORREY.]

Descriptions of some new genera and species of plants, collected in Captain J. C. Frémont's exploring expedition to Oregon and North California, in the year 1843–44. By John Torrey and J. C. Frémont.

CLEOMELLA (?) OBTUSIFOLIA. *Torr. and Frém.*

Branching from the base, and diffuse; leaflets cuneate-obovate, obtuse; style filiform.

Annual, stem smooth, the branches spreading, about a span long, hairy in the axils. Leaves, or petioles, an inch or more in length; the lamina of the leaflets four to six lines long, apiculate with a deciduous bristle, nearly smooth above, sparsely strigose underneath. Pedicles solitary and axillary in the upper part of the branches, longer than the petioles. Calyx much shorter than the corolla; the sepals lacerately three to five-toothed. Petals yellow, oblong-lanceolate, obtuse, about three lines in length. Stamens six, unequal, a little exserted; anthers linear-oblong, recurved when old. Torus hemispherical. Ovary on a long slender stipe, obovate; style longer than the ovary.

On the American Fork of the Sacramento River; March. The specimens are not in fruit, so that we cannot be certain as to the genus; but it seems to be a Cleomella.

MECONELLA CALIFORNICA. *Torr. and Frém.*

Leaves obovate-spatulate; stamens 11 to 12.

On the American Fork of the Sacramento River.

This species is intermediate between Meconella and Platystigma. It is a slender annual, three to four inches high, with the radical leaves in rosulate clusters, and more dilated at the extremity than in *M. Oregana*. The flowers also are much larger. The torus, which is like that of Eschscholtzia, is very distinct.

ARCTOMECON. *Torr. and Frém.—n. gen.*

Calyx of three smooth imbricated caducous sepals. Petals four, obovate, regular. Stamens numerous; anthers oblong-linear, the cells opening longitudinally. Ovary obovoid, composed of six carpels, with as many narrow intervalvular placentæ; styles none; stigmas coalescing into a small hemispherical, six-angled, sessile head, the angles of which are opposite the placentæ, not forming a projecting disk. Capsule (immature) ovoid, the placentæ almost filiform, opening at the summit by six valves, which separate from the persistent placentæ. Seeds oblong, smooth, strophiolate. A perennial herb, with a thick woody root. Leaves numerous, mostly crowded about the root, flabelliform-cuneate, densely clothed with long gray, upwardly barbellate hairs, three to five lobed at the summit ; the lobes with two to three teeth, which are tipped with a rigid pungent, upwardly scabrous bristle. Stems cape-like, about a foot high, furnished about the middle with one or two small bract-like leaves, smooth above, rough toward the base. Flowers in a loose, somewhat umbellate, simple or somewhat compound panicle ; the peduncles elongated, erect. Petals about an inch long, yellow.

ARCTOMECON CALIFORNICUM. *Torr. and Frém.*

This remarkable plant was found in only a single station in the Californian Mountains, on the banks of a creek ; flowering early in May. The soil was sterile and gravelly. Although very near Papaver, it differs so much in habit and in the strophiolate seeds, as well as in other characters, that it must be a distinct genus.

KRAMERIA.

A shrubby species of this genus was found on the *Virgen* River, in California. It seems to be *K. parvifolia* of Bentham, described in the voyage of the Sulphur. His plant, however, was only in fruit, while our specimens are only in flower. Ours grows in thick bunches one to two feet high, of a gray aspect, with numerous very straggling and somewhat spinescent branches. Leaves scarcely one-third of an inch long, obovate-spatulate. The flowers are scarcely more than half as large as in *K. lanceolata.* Sepals five, unequal ; claws of the three upper petals united into a column below ; lamina more or less ovate ; the two lower petals short and truncate. Stamens shorter than the upper petals ; the filaments united at the base with the column of the petals ; anthers one-celled, with a membranaceous summit, the orifice of which is somewhat dilated, and finally lacerated. Ovary hairy and spinulose; style rigid, declined.

OXYSTYLIS. *Torr. and Frém.—n. gen.*

Sepals linear ; petals ovate, somewhat unguiculate ; ovary two-celled ; the cells subglobose, each with two ovules ; style pyramidal, much larger than the ovary. Silicle didymous ; the carpels obovoid-globose, one-seeded (or rarely two-seeded), indehiscent, separating from the base of the persistent subulate spinescent style; pericarp crustaceo-coriaceous. Seed ovate, somewhat compressed; testa membranaceous, the lining much thickened and fleshy. Cotyledons incumbent, linear-oblong; radicle opposite the placentæ. A smooth annual herb. Leaves ternately parted, on long petioles; the leaflets ovate or oblong, entire petiolulate. Flowers in numerous axillary, crowded, short capitate racemes, small and yellow.

OXYSTYLIS LUTEA. *Torr. and Frém.*

On the Amargosa River, at the foot of a sandy hill; only seen in one place, but abundant there. The specimens were collected on April 28th, and were in both flower and fruit.

A rather stout plant; the stem erect, a foot or fifteen inches high, simple or a little branching below, leafy. Leaflets one to one and a half inch long, obtuse. Heads of flowers about half an inch in diameter, not elongating in fruit. Calyx shorter than the corolla; the sepals acute, yellowish, tipped with orange. Petals about two lines long. Fruit consisting of two roundish indehiscent carpels, which at maturity separate by a small base, leaving the indurated pointed style. The epicarp is thin, membranaceous, and slightly corrugated.

This remarkable plant seems to connect Cruciferæ with Capparidaceæ. The clusters of old flower stalks, with their numerous crowded spinescent styles, present a singular appearance.

THAMNOSMA. *Torr. and Frém.—n. gen.*

Flowers hermaphrodite (or polygamous)? Calyx four-cleft. Corolla four-petalled, much longer than the calyx; the æstivation valvate. Stamens eight, in a double series, all fertile. Ovaries two, sessile and connate at the summit of a stipe, each with five or six ovules in two series; styles united into one; stigma capitate. Capsules two, sessile at the summit of stipe, subglobose, united below (one of them sometimes abortive), coriaceous, one- to three-seeded. Seeds curved, with a short beak, black and minutely wrinkled; the radicle inferior. Embryo curved; cotyledons broadly linear, incumbent.

THAMNOSMA MONTANA. *Torr. and Frém.*

A shrub of the height of one or two feet, branching from the base, with simple, very small linear wedge-shaped leaves. The flowers are apparently dark purple, in loose terminal clusters. The whole plant has a strong aromatic odor, and every part of it is covered with little glandular dots.

Although nearly allied to Xanthoxylum, we regard it as a peculiar genus. It grows in the passes of the mountains, and on the Virgen River in Northern California. The greater part of it was already in fruit in the month of May.

Prosopis odorata. *Torr. and Frém.*

Branches and leaves smooth ; spines stout, mostly in pairs, straight ; pinnæ a single pair ; leaflets six to eight pairs, oblong-linear, slightly falcate, somewhat coriaceous, rather obtuse ; spikes elongated, on short peduncles ; corolla three times as long as the calyx ; stamens exserted ; legume spirally twisted into a compact cylinder.

A tree about twenty feet high, with a very broad full head, and the lower branches declining to the ground ; the thorns sometimes more than an inch long. Leaves smooth ; the common petiole one to two inches long, and terminated by a spinescent point ; leaflets from half an inch to an inch long, and one to two lines broad, somewhat coriaceous, sparingly but prominently veined underneath. Spikes two to four inches long, and about one-third of an inch in diameter. Flowers yellow, very fragrant, nearly sessile on the rachis. Calyx campanulate, somewhat equally five-toothed, smooth. Petals ovate-oblong, hairy inside. Stamens ten, one-third longer than the corolla. Anthers tipped with a slightly stipitate gland. Ovary linear-oblong, villous ; style smooth ; stigma capitate, concave at the extremity. Legumes clustered, spirally twisted into a very close rigid cylinder, which is from an inch to an inch and a half long, and about two lines in diameter, forming from ten to thirteen turns, many seeded. Sarcocarp pulpy ; the two opposite sides of the firm endocarp are compressed together between the seeds, forming a longitudinal kind of septum, which divides the pulp into two parts. Seeds ovate, kidney-form, compressed, very smooth and hard. Embryo yellowish, surrounded with a thin albumen.

A characteristic tree in the mountainous part of Northern California, particularly along the Mohahve and Virgen Rivers, flowering the latter part of April.

This species belongs to the section *strombocarpa* of Mr. Bentham,[*] which includes the *Acacia strombulifera* of Wildenow. In the structure of the pod it is so remarkable that we at one time regarded it as a distinct genus, to which we gave the name of Spirolobium.

There are numerous other Leguminosæ in the collection, including, as might be expected, many species of Lupinus, Astragalus, Oxytropis, and Phaca, some of which are new ; also, Thermopsis rhombifolia and montana,

---

[*] In Hooker's Journal of Botany, iv., p. 351.

and a beautiful shrubby Psoralea (or some allied genus) covered with bright violet flowers.

COWANIA PLICATA. *D. Don.* (?)

Specimens of this plant, without a ticket, were in the collection ; doubt-less obtained in California.   It may prove to be a distinct species from the Mexican plant, for the leaves are more divided than they are described by Don, and the flowers are smaller.   The genus Cowania is very nearly al-lied to Cercocarpus and Purshia, notwithstanding its numerous ovaries. The lobes of the calyx are imbricated, as in those genera, and not valvate, as in *Eudryadeæ*, to which section it is referred by Endlicher.

Purshia tridentata formed a conspicuous object in several parts of the route, not only east of the mountains, but in Oregon and California.   It is covered with a profusion of yellow flowers, and is quite ornamental. Sometimes it attains the height of twelve feet.

Spiræa ariæfolia, var. *discolor*, was found on the upper waters of the Platte, holding its characters so well that it should perhaps be regarded as a distinct species.

ŒNOTHERA CLAVÆFORMIS. *Torr. and Frém.*

Leaves ovate or oblong, denticulate or toothed, pinnatified at the base, with a long naked petiole ; scape with several small leaves, eight- to twelve-flowered ; segments of the calyx longer than the tube ; capsules clavate-cylindrical, nearly twice as long as the pedicel.   Flowers about as large as in *Œ. pumila.*   Grows with the preceding.

This new species belongs to the section *Chylismia* of Nutt.   (*Torr. and Gr. Fl. N. Am.* i, p. 506.)

ŒNOTHERA DELTOIDES. *Torr. and Frém.*

Annual ; canescently strigose ; stem low and stout ; leaves rhombico-vate, repandly denticulate, acute ; flowers (large) clustered at the summit of the short stem ; tube of the calyx nearly twice the length of the seg-ments ; petals entire, one-third longer than the slightly declined stamens ; anthers very long, fixed by the middle ; style exserted ; capsules prismatic-cylindrical.

Allied to *Œ. Jamesii, Torr. and Gr.*, and belongs, like that species, to the section EUŒNOTHERA and sub-section *Onagra.*

ŒNOTHERA CANESCENS.   *Torr. and Frém.*

Strigosely canescent; leaves narrowly lanceolate, rather obtuse, remotely denticulate; flowers in a leafy raceme; tube of the calyx rather slender, three times as long as the ovary, and one-third longer than the segments; petals broadly ovate, entire.

This species was collected (we believe) on the upper waters of the Platte. It belongs to the section Euœnothera, and to a sub-section which may be called GAUROPSIS, and characterized as follows: Perennial diffuse herbs; tube of the calyx linear; capsule obovate, sessile, with four-winged angles and no intermediate ribs, tardily opening; seeds numerous, horizontal; the testa membranaceous; leaves opaque.

Besides these new species, many other Œnothera were collected; among which may be mentioned *Œ. albicaulis, alyssoides, montana,* and *Missouriensis.* Also, *Gayophytum diffusum* (from the Snake country, growing about two feet high) *Stenosiphon virgatum,* and *Gaura coccinea.*

COMPOSITÆ.

The plants of this family were placed in the hands of Dr. Gray for examination; and he has described some of them (including four new genera) in the *Boston Journal of Natural History* for January, 1845. He has since ascertained another new genus among the specimens; and we fully concur with him in the propriety of dedicating it to the late distinguished I. N. Nicollet, Esq., who spent several years in exploring the country watered by the Mississippi and Missouri Rivers, and who was employed by the United States Government in a survey of the region lying between the sources of those rivers. This gentleman exerted himself to make known the botany of the country which he explored, and brought home with him an interesting collection of plants, made under his direction, by Mr. Charles Geyer, of which an account is given in the report of Mr. N. The following is the description of this genus by Dr. Gray:

NICOLLETIA.   *Gray.*

" Heads heterogamous, with few rays, many flowered. Involucre campanulate, consisting of about eight oval membranaceous scales in a single series; the base calyculate, with one or two smaller scales. Receptacle convex, alveolate. Corolla of the disk flowers equally five-toothed. Branches of the style terminated by a subulate hisped appendage. Achenia elongated, slender, canescently pubescent. Pappus double, scarcely shorter than the corolla ; the exterior of numerous scabrous, unequal bristles ; the inner of five linear-lanceolate chaffy scales, which are entire, or two-toothed at the summit, and furnished with a strong central nerve, which is produced into a short scabrous awn.—A humble, branching (and apparently annual) herb. Leaves alternate, pinnatified, and somewhat fleshy (destitute of glands?) ; the lobes and rachis linear. Heads terminal, solitary, nearly sessile, large (about an inch long), with one or two involucrate leaves at the base. Corolla yellow."

Nicolletia occidentalis. *Gray.*

On the banks of the Mohahve River, growing in naked sands ; flowering in April. The plant has a powerful and rather agreeable odor. This interesting genus (which is described from imperfect materials) belongs to the tribe Senecionideæ, and the sub-tribe Tagitineæ. It has the habit of Dissodia, and exhibits both the chaffy pappus of the division *Tageteæ,* and the *pappus pilosus* of *Porophyllum.*—Gray.*

Franseria dumosa. *Gray.*

Shrubby, much branched ; leaves pinnatified, canescent on both sides, as are the branchlets ; the divisions three to seven, oval, entire, and somewhat lobed ; heads rather loosely spiked ; involucre of the sterile flowers five- to seven-cleft, strigosely canescent; of the fertile, ovoid, two-celled, two-flowered.

A shrub, one to two feet high, with divaricate rigid branches. Leaves scarcely an inch long. Fertile (immature) involucre clothed with straight soft lanceolate-subulate prickles, which are short and scale-like.

On the sandy uplands of the Mohahve River, and very common in all that region of North California. Flowering in April.

Amsonia tomentosa. *Torr. and Frém.*

Suffrutescent ; clothed with a dense whitish pubescence ; leaves lanceolate and ovate-lanceolate, acute at each end ; segments of the calyx lanceolate-subulate ; corolla slightly hairy externally.

Stems numerous, erect, twelve to eighteen inches high, woody, below simple or branching. Leaves alternate ; the lowest small and spatulate,

---

* It should be stated here, that the notice of this genus by Dr. Gray was drawn up in Latin; but we have given it in English, that it may be uniform with our own description.

or reduced to scales; the others about two inches long, and varying from four to eight lines in breadth; entire, acuminate at the base. Flowers in rather dense, somewhat fastigiate terminal clusters, nearly three-fourths of an inch long. Calyx about one-third the length of the corolla, five-parted to the base; the segments narrow and hairy. Corolla with the tube ventricose above; the segments ovate-oblong. Stamens included; filaments short; anthers ovate-sagittate. Ovaries oblong, united below, distinct above, smooth; style slender; stigma capitate, with a membranaceous collar at the base.

The specimens of this plant were without tickets; but they were probably collected west of the Rocky Mountains. They were without fruit.

ASCLEPIAS SPECIOSA. *Torr. in Ann. Lyc. New York*, ii., *p.* 218.

This (as was stated in the first report) is *A. Douglasii* of Hooker, well figured in his "Flora Boreali Americana," 2, t. 142. It has a wide range, being found on both sides of the Rocky Mountains, and from the sources of the St. Peter's to those of the Kansas and Canadian. The fruit was collected from specimens on the banks of the Snake River. It is almost exactly like that of *A. Cornuti*, being inflated, woolly, and covered with soft spines.

ACERATES LATIFOLIA. *Torr. and Frém.*

Stem simple, erect, smooth; leaves roundish-ovate, nearly sessile, obtuse, with a small mucro, smooth on both sides; umbel solitary, on a terminal peduncle, few-flowered; pedicels slender; segments of the corolla ovate-lanceolate; lobes of the crown semilunar-ovate, as long as the column, rather obtuse, cucullate.

On Green River, a tributary of the Colorado of the West; June. About a span high. Leaves about an inch and a half long, and more than an inch wide. Flowers few, very large, apparently yellowish. Fruit not seen.

ERIOGONUM INFLATUM. *Torr. and Frém.*

Smooth, bi-trichotomous; the lower part, and sometimes the two primary divisions of the stem, much inflated and clavate; peduncles divaricately branched, the ultimate divisions filiform and solitary; involucre few-flowered, smooth; the teeth equal, erect.

The specimens of this plant are imperfect, being destitute of leaves, which are probably wholly radical. It is a foot or more high. The first joint of the stem, or rather scape, is remarkably dilated and fistular upward. This divides into three or more branches, the two primary ones of which are sometimes inflated like the first; the subdivisions are dichotomous, with a pedicellate involucre in each fork. The involucres are about a line in diameter, smooth, five- to six-flowered; and, in all the specimens that I examined, only five-toothed. The plant was found on barren hills in the lower part of North California.

ERIOGONUM RENIFORME. *Torr. and Frém.*

Annual; leaves radical, on long petioles, reniform, clothed with a dense hoary tomentum; stem scape-like, naked, three-forked from the base-glaucous, and nearly smooth; the divisions divaricately two- to three-forked; involucres two to four together, on slender peduncles, smooth, campanulate, five-toothed, the teeth nearly equal, obtuse; perigonium smooth.

On the Sacramento River; March. Allied to *E. vimineum* of Bentham. A small species, with very minute flowers.

ERIOGONUM CORDALUM. *Torr. and Frém.*

Annual; leaves all radical, on long petioles, roundish-ovate, cordate, very obtuse, slightly pubescent above, hairy underneath; scape naked, slender, smooth and glaneous divaricately branched, the divisions slender; involucres solitary, on filiform peduncles, campanulate, smooth, five-toothed, the teeth nearly equal, rather obtuse; perigonium hairy.

With the preceding, from which it is easily distinguished by the form of its leaves and color of the pubescence, many other species of this genus were collected in California and the Snake country, some of which are probably new, and will be described in the next report.

FREMONTIA VERMICULARIS. *Torr. in Frém., 1st report.*

This curious plant is always found in saline soils, or where the atmosphere is saline. Its greatest height is eight feet. It is a characteristic feature of the vegetation throughout a great part of Oregon and North California. About Brown's Hole, on Green River, it occupies almost exclusively the *bottoms* of the neighboring streams. It is abundant also on the shores of a salt lake in latitude 38° and longitude 113°; and constantly occurs in the desert region south of the Columbia, and between the Cascade range and the Rocky Mountains, as far south as latitude 34°. The branches, when old, become spiny, as in many other plants of this family.

Since the description of this genus was published in the first report (March, 1843) Nees has given it the name of SARCOBATUS; and Dr. Seubert has published an account of it, with a figure, in the *Botanische Zeitung* for 1844. This we have not yet seen; but, from the remarks of Dr. Lindley, who has given a note on the genus in Hooker's *Journal of Botany* for January, 1845, it would seem that some doubt existed among European botanists as to its affinities, as they had not seen the ripe seeds. These we have long possessed, and unhesitatingly referred it to Chenopodiaciæ. We regret that our sketches of the staminate flowers were mislaid when the artist was engraving the figure.

OBIONE CONFERTIFOLIA.   *Torr. and Frém.*

Stem pubescent, much branched, erect; leaves alternate, ovate, rather obtuse, petiolate, much crowded, entire, somewhat coriaceous, white with a mealy crust; bracts broadly ovate, obtuse, entire, and the sides without appendages or tubercles.

A small shrub, with rigid crooked and somewhat spinescent branches, and of a whitish aspect. Leaves varying from one-third to half an inch in length, abruptly narrowed at the base into a petiole, thickly clothed with a white mealy substance.

Flowers apparently diœcious. Sterile not seen. Bracts of the fruit three to four lines long, united about half way up, distinct above, indurated at the base. Styles distinct. Pericarp very thin. Seed roundish-ovate, rostellate upward; the testa coriaceous. Embryo two-thirds of a circle.

On the borders of the Great Salt Lake. From the description of *O. coriacea*, Moq., our plant seems to be a near ally of that species.

PTEROCHITON.   *Torr. and Frém.—n. gen.*

Flowers diœcious. STAMINATE . . . PISTILLATE. Perigonium ovoid-tubular, four-winged, two-toothed at the summit. Ovary roundish; style short; stigmas two, linear. Ovule solitary, ascending from the base of the ovary, campulitropous. Fructiferous perianth indurated, broadly four-winged, closed, minutely two-toothed at the summit; the wings veined and irregularly toothed. Utricle very thin and membranaceous, free. Seed ovate, somewhat compressed; the podosperm lateral and very distinct, rostrate upward. Integument double, the exterior somewhat coriaceous, brownish, the inner one thin. Embryo nearly a circle, surrounding copious mealy albumen.

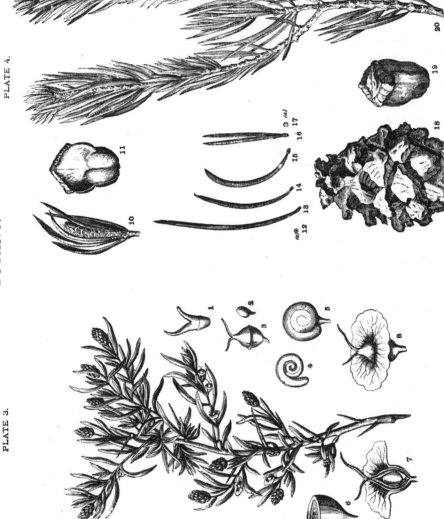

BOTANY.

PLATE 3.

PLATE 4.

FREMONTIA VERMICULARIS.

PIMES MONOPHYLLUS—THE NUT PINE.

PTEROCHITON OCCIDENTALE. *Torr. and Frém.*

An unarmed shrub, one to two feet high, with numerous slender branches, which are clothed with a grayish nearly smooth bark. Leaves alternate or fasciculate, linear oblanceolate, narrowed at the base, flat, entire, covered with a whitish mealy crust. Flowers somewhat racemose, on short pedicels. Fructiferous calyx, with the wings two to three lines wide, semi-orbicular, coriaceo-membranaceous, mealy like the leaves, strongly veined; the margin more or less toothed. Utricle free from the indurated cavity of the perianth, extremely thin and transparent. Seed conformed to the utricle, the conspicuous podosperm passing along its side; the beak pointing obliquely upward.

This is one of the numerous shrubby plants of the Chenopodiaceous family that constitute a large part of the vegetation in the saline soils of the west. The precise locality of this plant we cannot indicate, as the label was illegible; but it was probably from the borders of the Great Salt Lake. It is allied to Grayia of Hooker and Arnott, a shrub of the same family, which was found in several places on both sides of the Rocky Mountains, often in great abundance.

PINUS MONOPHYLLUS. *Torr. and Frém.* (*The nut pine.*)

Leaves solitary, or very rarely in pairs, with scarcely any sheaths, stout and rigid, somewhat pungent; cones ovoid, the scales with a thick obtusely pyramidal and protuberant summit, unarmed; seeds large, without a wing.

A tree with verticillate branches and cylindrical-clavate buds, which are about three-fourths of an inch in length. The leaves are from an inch to two and a half inches long: often more or less curved, scattered, very stout, terete (except in the very rare case of their being in pairs, when they are semi-cylindrical) ending in a spiny tip. Cones about two and a half inches long, and an inch and three-fourths broad in the widest part. The scales are of a light-brown color, thick; the summit obtusely pyramidal and somewhat recurved, but without any point. The seeds are oblong, about half an inch long, without a wing; or rather the wing is indissolubly adherent to the scale. The kernel is of a very pleasant flavor, resembling that of *Pinus Pembra.*

This tree, which is remarkable among the true pines for its solitary leaves, is extensively diffused over the mountains of Northern California, from longitude 111° to 120°, and through a considerable range of latitude. It is alluded to repeatedly, in the course of the narrative, as the *nut pine.*

The Coniferæ of the collection were numerous, and suffered less than most of the other plants. Some of them do not appear to have been hitherto described. There was also an Ephedra, which does not differ essentially from *E. occidentalis,* found in great plenty on the sandy uplands of the Mohahve River.

Description of the Plates.

Plate 1. ARCTMOECON CALIFORNICUM. *Fig.* 8, a stamen, *magnified; fig.* 11, an ovule, *magnified; fig.* 12, capsule, *natural size; fig.* 5, (*a*) stigma, *magnified; fig.* 6, the same cut horizontally, showing the sutures ; *fig.* 13, a seed, *magnified; fig.* 14, portion of a hair from the leaf, *magnified; fig.* 7, bristle from the extremity of a leaf lobe, *magnified; figs.* 9 and 10, leaves, *natural size.*

Plate 2. PROSOPIS ODORATA. *Fig.* 1, a flower, *magnified; fig.* 2, pistil, *magnified; fig.* 3, cluster of ripe legumes, *natural size.*

Plate 3. FREMONTIA VERMICULARIS. *Fig.* 1, a very young fertile flower, *magnified; fig.* 2, an ovule, *magnified; fig.* 3, a fertile flower more advanced, *magnified; fig.* 8, a fertile flower at maturity, showing the broadwinged border of the calyx, *magnified; fig.* 7, the same cut vertically ; *fig.* 6, the same cut horizontally ; *fig.* 5, a seed, *magnified; fig.* 4, embryo, *magnified.*

Plate 4. PINUS MONOPHYLLUS. *Fig.* 10, a bud, *natural size; figs.* 13, 14, 15, and 16, leaves, *natural size; fig.* 12, section of a single leaf; *fig.* 17, section of a pair of leaves ; *fig.* 18, a cone, *natural size; fig.* 19, a scale, as seen from the outside; *fig.* 11, inside view of the same.

I. Note from Professor Hubbard (of the National Observatory, Washington City), describing the instruments used by J. C. Frémont in making the astronomical observations in his third or last expedition, and the methods followed by Professor Hubbard in reducing them.

II. A table of astronomical observations made by J. C. Frémont at the four principal stations determined in this third expedition, namely : 1, The mouth of Fontaine Qui Bouit, on the Upper Arkansas. 2, Southeastern shore of the Great Salt Lake. 3, Lassen's Farm, Deer Creek, in the Valley of the Sacramento. 4, The Three Buttes, Valley of the Sacramento.

III. A table of latitudes and longitudes, deduced from the foregoing astronomical observations, calculated by Professor Hubbard.

I. NOTE FROM PROFESSOR HUBBARD.

The instruments employed in the determination of astronomical positions were :

A portable transit instrument, by Young, of Philadelphia.

A sextant, by Troughton.

A sextant, by Gambey.

Two pocket chronometers (Nos. 438 and 443), by Appleton.

The transit instrument was made by Mr. William J. Young, of Philadelphia. The length of the telescope was 26 inches, the diameter of the

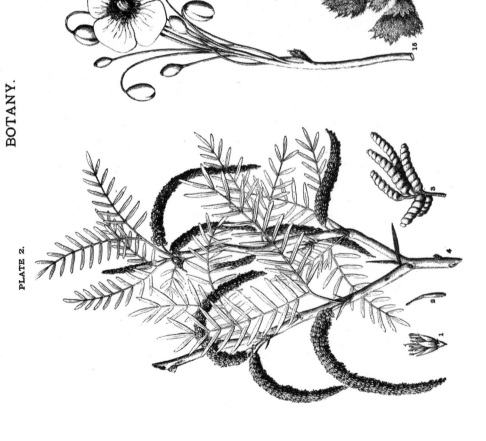

BOTANY.

PLATE 1.

PLATE 2.

ARCTOMECON CALIFORNICUM.

PROSOPIS ADORATA.

object glass 2½ inches, and the axis 16 inches between the shoulders. A circle was attached to the instrument, having a diameter of 11 inches, graduated to read to 10 seconds, and furnished with 3 verniers. The stand was of iron, and four feet in height.

Of the sextants, the one by Gambey, a new instrument, was most frequently used. The other, by Troughton, is the same that was carried in the previous exploration, and was now only used in observing at night, its divided arc being more readily illuminated than that of the other. The index errors of both were carefully and often determined, in order that any possible change of adjustment might be readily detected.

The sextant observations consist of single altitudes of a star or the sun for time, and of Polaris or a star in the south, for latitude. They have been reduced in the usual manner, the formulæ being too well known to need quoting. All the latitudes, and the several links of the chain of longitudes connecting the primary stations, depend upon the data thus furnished. In deducing the differences of longitude, in order to obviate, so far as possible, all error arising from eccentricity of the sextant or any like cause, comparison has been made, when practicable, with observations in the same quarter of the heavens.

The rates of the chronometers depend entirely upon sextant observations. The comparison of these rates, determined at different times and under different circumstances of climate and usage, has shown that but one of the chronometers (No. 438) was entitled to confidence. All differences of longitude from the principal stations have therefore been determined by this one, and the results thus obtained are, as will hereafter be seen, highly satisfactory. The following are the observed rates, deduced, with but a single exception, from altitudes of the sun ; the sign + indicates a gaining rate :

Locality.	Dates of Observation.	Rate of 443.	Rate of 438.
		S.	S.
Bent's Fort	August 3 to August 15, 1845	+ 2.020	+ 3.386
Camp at Salt Lake	October 14 to October 20, 1845	+ 0.883	3.317
Laguna Farm	February 11 to February 19, 1846 ..	-- 1.754	2.146
	March 30 to April 14, 1846	....	2.193
	April 14 to May 22, 1846	....	+ 2.980

The whole route has been divided into three distinct lines. The first, commencing at Bent's Fort, extends to the camp of January 4, 1846. The chronometers were then for a time subjected to a rapid travel over a rough road, and their rates were thereby changed. The second line commences with the Laguna Farm, between which and the camp of January 4th no observations were made, and extends to the camp of March 30th to April 14th, where the chronometers stopped, and another change of rate took place. The last line extends from this camp to that of June 7th, after which date no more longitudes were determined.

By combining the above rates for the same line, giving to each a weight equivalent to the number of days elapsed between the observations on which it depends, we get the following:

Rates of chronometer No. 438.

                                                                      s.
August 21, 1845, to January 4, 1846.................................... + 3.363
February 18, 1846, to March 30, 1846 .... + 2.175
April 14, 1846, to June 7, 1846....................................... + 2.980

The transit instrument has given, by moon culminations, the longitudes of four camps with an accuracy much more than sufficient for ordinary geographical purposes. These camps being connected, as we have already seen, by chronometric differences, an excellent check of the whole work is thus afforded. When we remember that an error of one second of time in the observed transit of the moon induces an average error in the resulting longitude of the place of nearly seven minutes of arc, the agreement of these independent determinations, thus referred to the same point, is unexpectedly great. The following is the method by which the transit observations have been reduced:

An estimated longitude for each of the camps in question gave the means of computing, with sufficient accuracy, the "tabular mean time of transit" of the stars observed; their places in the heavens being taken from the catalogue of the British Association. The "observed mean time of transit" was next to be obtained. Where the passage of the star over all the wires had been observed, the mean, reduced to the middle wire, gave at once the time sought. For the purpose of correcting imperfect transits, a determination of the equatorial intervals of the transit wires was necessary. These wires were originally seven in number; their intervals are given below (I.). They were broken out after October 21, 1845, and were replaced by a set of five (II.), which in their turn were broken, and the last set (III.) inserted. Of these last the second wire was broken before the commencement of observations, and the reduction of the mean to the middle wire of course includes the correction for the deficiency. The following, then, are the adopted intervals of the several wires and the mean of the whole from the middle wire:

No.	Dates.	A.	B.	C.	Mean.	E.	F.	G.
		s.	s.	s.	s.	s.	s.	s.
I.	Aug. 12 to Oct. 21, 1845 .	+ 55.49	+ 36.78	+ 18.52	+ 00.69	− 18.12	− 34.63	− 53.18
II.	April 14 to April 23, 1846.	....	36.59	17.99	00.00	18.14	36.45	....
III.	June 4 to June 6, 1846 ...	+ 54.96	....	+ 18.84	− 05.17	− 17.41	− 35.19	− 51.95

From this table the corrections to the mean of wires for imperfect transits have been deduced by dividing the sum of the intervals for the wires observed by the product of the number of wires into the cosine of the star's declination. In the single case of an imperfect transit of the moon, allowance has been made for the moon's motion during the interval of time indicated by the correction.

In deducing the instrumental and chronometer errors by comparison of the observed and computed times of transit, the formula of M. Hansen has been employed.

Denoting by L the latitude of the place.
 " " D the declination of the star.
 " " Z the zenith distance of the star.
 " " i the correction of instrument for error of level.
 " " n the correction of instrument for deviation at the pole.
 " " c the correction of instrument for error of collimation.

Then the reduction of the observed transit to the meridian has the form

$$i \sec L - n \sin Z \sec L \sec D + c \sec D.$$

The value of one division of the level tube accompanying the instrument was unknown; and the instrument itself being in California, this value could not be determined; but, knowing from the observing-books that the axis was always kept as nearly horizontal as possible, we may neglect the constant term i sec L, or rather may include it in the chronometer correction, and this without affecting the observed right ascensions.

Denote also by A the computed mean time of star's transit.
 " " " T the observed mean time of star's transit.
 " " " ΔT the correction of the chronometer.

Then every observation will give an equation of the following form:

$$O = T + \Delta T - A - \sin Z \sec L \sec D \, n + \sec D \, c.$$

Or for brevity:

$$O = T + \Delta T - A - a \, n + b \, c.$$

putting a and b for the co-efficients of n and c. By help of this formula approximate values were obtained for n and c from two or more observations. These were generally taken on different days, and the equations furnished by them were only limited by the condition that the value of c should remain constant for these days, allowance being afterward made for the error of this assumption. The values of n and c thus obtained were substituted in the equation furnished by each observation. The mean of the chronometer corrections thus determined being compared with the individual results, a new set of equations of condition was arranged, of the following form :

$$O = d\Delta T - a.\ dn + b.\ dc.$$

where $d\Delta T$ is the residual quantity obtained by the above comparison. The solution of these differential equations by the method of least squares gave the corrections of n and c, which, applied to the assumed, gave the most probable values. The assumed and adopted n and c are given below. The application of these final values to the original equations gave now the most probable chronometer correction, and this, applied to the corrected transit of the moon's limb, gave the mean time of transit, and finally the right ascension.

Table of Assumed and Adopted Values of n and c.

DATE.	ASSUMED.		ADOPTED.	
	n	c	n	c
	S.	S.	S.	S.
August 21, 22, 1845	+ 3.702	− 3.237	+ 3.702	− 3.237
October 20, 1845	+ 1.633	− 3.237	+ 1.343	− 3.062
April 14, 1846	+ 1.02	+ 0.183	+ 1.648	+ 0.890
April 16, 1846	+ 52.07	+ 0.183	+ 52.265	− 0.084
June 4, 1846	+ 0.574	− 0.145	+ 0.574	− 0.145
June 5, 1846			+ 0.689	− 0.183

The following longitudes were assumed as the basis of the comparison of the observed with the tabulated moon culminations :

	h.	*m.*	*s.*
I. August 22, 1845...	6	58	30
II. October 20, 1845...	7	29	31
III. April 14, 1846..	8	08	20
IV. June 4, 1846	8	01	52

By help of these the moon's Æ and hourly motion at transit were computed from the moon-culminating list of the Nautical Almanac, using fourth differences. A comparison of the computed Æ with that observed gave the numerator—the hourly motion being the denominator—of the fraction expressing the correction of the assumed longitudes. Those corrections, and the resulting longitudes, are as follows :

	m.	*s.*	*h.*	*m.*	*s.*
I.	+ 0	15.52	6	58	45.52
II.	− 1	15.65	7	28	15.35
III.	− 0	37.54	8	07	42.46
IV.	+ 4	36.70	8	06	28.70

Camps I. and II., as well as III. and IV., being connected by chronometric differences, it becomes important to test the results above given by a comparison of the two differences.   We have then

	m.	*s.*	*m.*	*s.*
By lunars	29	29.83	1	13.76
By chro...	29	33.83	1	10.67
L–C..		− 4.00		+ 3.09

The chronometric difference is adopted as the most exact—apportioning the errors of the other among the longitudes by lunars, remembering that Camp II. is determined by a single culmination, while at each of the others two were observed, we should now have, were the lunar tables correct, the best system of longitudes.   Mr. S. C. Walker states that a correction of the present residual errors of the lunar tables would increase all the longitudes depending upon moon culminations by about six seconds of time.   Adding, therefore, six seconds to the above corrected longitudes, we get finally, as the basis of the whole work, the following adopted longitudes.

	h.	*m.*	*s.*	°	′	″
I. Mouth of the Fontaine-qui-bouit, August 22, 1845.....	6	58	50.72 =	104	42	41
II. Camp at Salt Lake, October 14th, 20th	7	28	24.55 =	112	06	08
III. Lassen's Farm, Deer Creek, April 14, 1846	8	07	46.92 =	121	56	44
IV. Buttes, Sacramento Valley, June 4, 1846	8	06	36.24 =	121	39	04

Upon these and the sextant observations is based the accompanying table of latitudes and longitudes.

J. S. HUBBARD.

II.—Observations made by J. C. Frémont, with the Transit Instrument, determining the Four Principal Positions mentioned in his Memoir, reduced by Professor Hubbard.

Camp at the Mouth of the Fontaine-qui-Bouit.

Ref. No.	Date 1845.	Object.	Declination. (° ′)	Transits Observed. (s.)							Mean of observed wires. (H. M. S.)	Reductions to		Observed transit. (H. M. S.)	Computed transit. (H. M. S.)	Chronometer fast. (H. M. S.)
				I.	II.	III.	IV.	V.	VI.	VII.		Middle wire. (M. S.)	Meridian. (M. S.)			
1	Aug. 21.	η Piscium	+ 14 33	24.5	04.0	22.4	42.5	00.5	18.0	36.5	15 44 41.20	+ 0 00.72	− 0 05.29	15 44 36.63	15 20 57.04	0 23 39.59
2		Moon's II. L.	+ 13 51	59.4	18.5	38.4	58.0	16.4	35.0	54.4	16 21 57.16	+ 0 00.72	− 0 05.29	16 21 52.59		
3	Aug. 22.	θ¹ Arietis	+ 19 11	54.4	14.5	33.4	52.5	12.0	30.4	50.0	16 30 52.47	+ 0 00.73	− 0 05.09	16 30 48.11	16 07 08.36	0 23 39.75
4		α Aquilæ	+ 18 50	48.0	06.7	02.0	44.4	02.0	19.0	37.0	10 01 43.11	+ 0 00.71	− 0 05.64	10 01 38.18	9 37 58.02	0 23 40.16
5		β Ceti		36.0	52.0	11.0	31.0	50.0	08.0	28.0	14 53 30.29	+ 0 00.73	− 0 07.61	14 53 23.41	14 29 45.08	0 23 38.33
6		Polaris	+ 88 29	53.5	38.5	12.0	57.4	11.5	45.5	17.0	15 21 25.06	+ 0 26.32	+ 0 14.54	15 22 05.92	14 58 25.22	0 23 40.70
7		ι Draconis, S. P.	+ 114 31	36.0	51.5	05.5	22.0	....	55.0	....	16 05 28.75	− 1 06.78	− 0 03.23	16 04 18.74	15 40 34.95	0 23 43.79
8		ψ Arietis	+ 19 31	....	19.4	39.0	59.0	17.4	35.0	55.0	16 26 57.83	+ 0 00.73	− 0 05.06	16 26 53.50	16 03 12.48	0 23 41.02
9		ψ Arietis	+ 17 01	46.0	06.0	25.0	45.0	03.5	20.5	40.0	16 39 43.71	+ 0 00.73	− 0 05.18	16 39 39.26	16 05 58.46	0 23 40.80
10		Moon's II. L.	+ 15 30	47.0	07.4	26.5	46.5	05.5	23.4	43.4	17 10 45.67	+ 0 00.73	− 0 05.25	17 10 41.15	......	......

Camp on the Salt Lake.

Ref. No.	Date 1845.	Object.	Declination. (° ′)	Transits Observed. (s.)							Mean of observed wires. (H. M. S.)	Reductions to		Observed transit. (H. M. S.)	Computed transit. (H. M. S.)	Chronometer fast. (H. M. S.)
				I.	II.	III.	IV.	V.	VI.	VII.		Middle wire. (M. S.)	Meridian. (M. S.)			
11†	Oct. 20.	Polaris	+ 88 29	....	04.0	....	....	27.0	00.2	46.8	12 25 24.67	− 22 22.51	− 1 13.08	12 01 49.08	11 06 38.20	0 55 10.88
12†		β Ursæ Min., S. P.	+ 105 13	14.8	46.5	51.2	49.0	32.5	39.5	21.0	13 47 46.14	− 0 02.64	+ 0 06.63	13 47 50.13	12 52 34.16	0 55 15.97
13		γ¹ Eridani	− 21 57	27.3	53.5	12.0	24.0	43.5	01.0	19.0	14 47 23.90	+ 0 00.72	− 0 03.82	14 47 20.86	13 52 08.92	0 55 11.88
14		β Orionis	− 8 23	33.5	35.0	54.7	29.2	49.0	05.2	23.2	16 03 29.37	+ 0 00.70	− 0 03.68	16 03 26.39	15 08 13.81	0 55 12.58
15		α Leporis	− 17 56	16.0	54.3	13.5	13.0	33.2	50.8	09.7	16 22 13.20	+ 0 00.73	− 0 03.95	16 22 09.98	15 26 58.70	0 55 11.28
16		χ¹ Orionis	+ 20 14	34.3	23.0	42.5	33.5	53.5	09.8	30.2	16 41 32.73	+ 0 00.74	− 0 03.39	16 41 30.08	15 46 14.99	0 55 15.09
17		χ² Orionis	+ 20 08	03.8	05.8	26.0	02.5	22.5	39.5	59.0	16 51 01.83	+ 0 00.74	− 0 03.39	16 50 59.18	15 55 44.04	0 55 15.14
18		Moon's II. L.	+ 19 41	45.5	24.0	....	45.5	05.4	22.5	43.0	17 30 44.81	+ 0 00.74	− 0 03.39	17 30 42.16		....
19		δ Geminorum	+ 20 47	05.0	....	44.0	03.4	23.0	40.0	....	17 51 02.77	+ 0 00.74	− 0 03.38	17 51 00.13	16 55 45.67	0 55 14.46

1846.

Lassen's Farm, Deer Creek, Sacramento Valley.

Date	No.	Star	±								±		±				
April 14.	20	α Virginis	−	10 20	57.2	16.0	34.3	53.0	11.2	15 51 34.34	.....	.....	−	0 00.76	15 51 33.58	11 44 45.72	4 06 47.86
	21	β¹ Scorpii	−	19 21	54.6	14.3	33.2	52.5	11.0	18 30 33.12	.....	.....	−	0 01.02	18 30 32.10	14 23 43.86	4 06 48.30
	22	Moon's II. L.	−	19 05	11.0	31.5	51.3	10.5	31.0	19 14 51.66	.....	.....	−	0 01.02	19 14 50.04	.....	.....
	23	35 Draconis	+	76 59	36.5	56.5	15.5	35.2	54.5	20 38 36.90	.....	.....	+	0 09.70	20 38 07.38	16 23 19.30	4 06 48.08
	24	μ¹ Sagittarii	−	21 05	.....	39.2	59.3	14.5	48.2	20 38 15.64	+ 1 20.78		−	1 01.66	20 38 14.58	16 31 26.13	4 06 48.45
April 16.	25	ρ Cassiopeæ, S. P.	+	123 22	09.5	34.0	08.5	25.2	51.0	14 15 57.80	0 16.56		−	2 03.19	14 13 38.05	10 06 43.24	4 06 54.81
	26	β Cassiopeæ, S. P.	+	121 42	35.0	55.0	14.5	33.0	51.0	14 29 59.80	.....	.....	−	2 08.41	14 27 51.39	10 49 58.16	4 06 53.23
	27	β Corvi	−	22 33	40.2	07.5	35.4	04.0	32.0	14 54 14.30	.....	.....	+	1 05.42	14 53 08.88	10 53 08.88	4 06 53.29
	28	α Cassiopeæ, S. P.	+	124 19	30.0	33.0	02.0	45.2	04.0	15 00 35.82	.....	.....	+	2 00.06	14 58 35.76	10 51 41.74	4 06 54.02
	29†	Polaris, S. P.	+	91 30	38.0	58.2	18.0	37.0	56.3	16 03 58.84	.....	.....	+	33 48.98	15 30 09.86	11 23 18.86	4 06 51.00
	30	58 Ophiuchi	−	21 36	53.5	13.5	33.2	52.5	11.7	20 01 17.50	.....	.....	+	1 04.38	20 00 13.12	15 53 17.58	4 06 55.54
	31	μ¹ Sagittarii	−	21 05	17.5	37.6	58.0	18.0	37.0	20 31 32.88	.....	.....	+	1 03.85	20 30 29.03	16 23 34.37	4 06 54.66
	32	β Moon's II. L.	−	18 29	.....	.....	.....	.....	.....	21 09 57.46	.....	.....	−	1 03.00	21 08 54.46	.....	.....

Three Buttes, Sacramento Valley.

Date	No.	Star	±								±		±				
June 4.	33	γ Virginis	−	0 36	54.7	13.0	30.2	48.7	05.0	11 49 30.32	− 0 17.14		−	0 00.62	11 49 12.56	7 41 07.60	4 08 04.96
	34	Moon's I. L.	−	8 24	48.2	07.0	25.2	43.8	01.2	12 16 12.57	− 0 05.30		−	0 00.72	12 16 06.55	.....	.....
	35	Polaris, S. P.	+	91 31	01.7	.....	.....	13.5	23.0	12 12 40.57	+ 6 46.18		+	0 16.69	12 19 10.66	8 11 05.46	4 08 04.66
	36	ω Virginis	−	10 22	42.0	19.0	37.7	55.8	12.7	12 32 14.30	+ 0 24.59		−	0 00.72	12 32 18.99	8 24 14.59	4 08 04.40
	37†	φ Centauri	−	41 21	25.2	06.5	30.5	54.8	17.0	13 04 14.30	− 0 05.90		−	0 01.17	13 04 07.23	8 56 01.28	4 08 05.95
	38	φ Centauri	+	35 37	40.7	41.8	09.7	31.6	52.3	13 12 54.53	− 0 06.36		−	0 01.05	13 12 47.12	9 04 41.92	4 08 05.20
	39	ι Lupi	+	45 21	24.7	54.2	07.7	33.0	86.5	13 24 49.88	− 0 07.35		−	0 01.21	13 24 41.32	9 16 36.71	4 08 04.61
	40	β Ursæ Minoris	+	76 23	.....	41.8	16.8	38.2	02.3	13 44 09.19	− 1 12.84		+	0 01.28	13 42 57.63	9 34 52.72	4 08 04.91
	41	δ Ursæ Minoris	+	74 47	.....	54.2	40.2	20.5	29.0	14 07 15.50	− 0 05.32		−	0 01.09	14 07 11.27	9 58 07.06	4 08 04.21
	42*	Virginis	−	4 43	.....	58.0	.....	23.7	16.0	14 13 58.10	− 0 37.03		−	0 00.43	14 13 20.64	10 05 14.71	4 08 05.93
June 5.	43†	Polaris, S. P.	+	91 31	51.0	50.0	50.0	.....	34.2	12 15 47.42	+ 5 04.71		+	0 33.56	12 15 09.15	10 07 10.32	4 07 58.83
	44	a³ Virginis	−	10 22	32.2	24.3	42.7	.....	20.2	12 28 19.45	+ 0 35.26		−	0 00.50	12 28 24.21	10 20 18.69	4 08 05.52
	45	ε Cassiopeæ, S. P.	+	112 45	34.5	50.0	.....	59.2	.....	12 43 59.23	+ 1 35.14		+	0 02.67	12 42 17.42	10 34 11.41	4 08 05.52
	46	φ Centauri	+	117 06	55.3	40.2	57.5	38.2	38.2	12 54 29.54	+ 0 30.14		−	0 02.31	12 54 36.54	10 40 30.48	4 08 06.06
	47	φ Centauri	−	41 21	25.0	10.0	36.2	.....	.....	12 59 48.38	− 0 22.83		−	0 00.93	13 00 10.28	8 52 05.37	4 08 04.91
	48	Moon's I. L.	−	12 11	39.2	15.0	35.2	00.2	13.0	13 08 10.07	.....	.....	−	0 00.53	13 04 14.94	.....	.....
	49	θ Centauri	+	35 37	48.5	52.0	15.2	46.2	00.2	13 08 46.02	− 0 06.36		−	0 00.83	13 08 51.55	9 00 46.01	4 08 05.54
	50	χ Virginis	−	9 33	17.5	52.5	12.0	49.2	.....	13 15 47.82	− 0 05.24		−	0 00.51	13 15 52.55	9 07 47.30	4 08 05.25
	51	λ Virginis	−	12 39	22.5	57.2	17.2	54.5	.....	13 21 52.82	− 0 05.30		−	0 00.53	13 21 57.59	9 13 52.18	4 08 05.41
	52	5 Ursæ Minoris	+	76 23	28.8	26.6	19.0	36.5	51.6	13 53 22.83	− 0 21.97		+	0 01.58	13 39 01.58	9 30 56.77	4 08 04.81
	53	a² Libræ	−	15 24	52.3	10.2	48.2	25.2	25.2	13 53 22.83	+ 0 05.36		+	0 00.56	13 53 27.63	9 45 22.11	4 08 05.52
	54†	β Ursæ Minoris	+	74 47	34.5	10.2	25.6	43.0	43.0	14 03 46.27	+ 1 33.75		+	0 02.67	14 02 15.19	9 54 11.13	4 08 04.06

* Instrument reversed between observations 41 and 42.

† Omitted in taking the mean.

III.—A Table of Latitudes and Longitudes Deduced from the foregoing Astronomical Observations, Calculated by Professor Hubbard.

Date.		Latitude.	Longitude.	Locality.
1845.		° ′ ″	° ′ ″	
August	16	38 02 22	103 33 20	Bent's Fort.
	22	38 15 18	104 42 41	Mouth of the Fontaine-qui-Bouit.
	26	38 25 44	105 22 17	Arkansas River, at mouth of the great *cañon*, left bank.
	28	38 43 17	105 39 50	Sheep River, Utah Pass.
	29	38 50 35	105 49 56	Head-water of a tributary to the Arkansas River (heading in the ridge between Platte and Arkansas waters).
	30	38 49 43	106 17 56	Piney Fork of the Arkansas, three miles above its mouth.
September	1	39 05 12	106 30 03	On the Lake Fork of the Arkansas, on the western shore of the upper lake, near the inlet.
	2	39 20 38	106 27 15	Head-waters of the main branch of the Arkansas River.
	4	39 33 48	106 32 03	On Piney River, an affluent of Grand River of the Colorado of the Gulf of California.
	5	39 39 12	106 44 21	Williams's Fishery, Piney River.
	8	39 46 24	107 08 55	Grand River of the Gulf of California.
	12	29 56 54	107 44 57	White River (affluent of Green River of the Colorado), at "*flat prairie.*"
	13	39 57 36	107 47 26	Forks of White River.
	17	39 55 57	108 45 08	Guthrie's Creek (of White River).
	21	40 03 55	109 05 28	" War Eagle Camp," White River.
	25	40 04 00	109 53 43	Green River of the Colorado, left bank, one and a half mile above the mouth of White River.
	27	40 11 40	110 16 35	Lake Fork (of the Uintah), two miles above its mouth.
	29	40 19 38	110 52 05	Duchénes Fork (of the Uintah).
October	1	40 27 42	111 10 49	Morin's Fork.
	2	40 32 05	111 21 31	On a branch of the *Timpana-ozu* or Timpanogos River (of the Utah Lake).
	4	40 28 04	111 39 44	Timpanogos River.
	6	40 13 12	111 54 55	Timpanogos River.
	10	40 09 53	111 47 51	Pimquan Creek, shore of the Utah Lake.
	12	40 33 27	112 02 32	Outlet of Utah Lake, at mouth of Hughes' Creek.
	14	40 45 53	112 06 08	Station Creek, southeastern shore of the Great Salt Lake.
	18	40 58 48	....	Summit of Peak of Antelope Island, in the southern part of Great Salt Lake.
	21	40 42 19	....	Spring Point (extremity of a promontory at south end of Salt Lake, opposite Antelope Island).
	23	40 39 15	112 51 11	Spring in valley, opening on southern shore of the Great Salt Lake.
	25	40 38 17	113 05 09	Valley, near southwestern shore of Salt Lake.
	30	41 00 28	114 11 09	Pilot Peak Creek.
November	1	40 43 49	114 26 22	Spring at head of ravine.
	3	40 42 13	114 55 45	Whitton's Spring.
	8	40 17 16	115 46 00	Crane's Branch (of the south fork of Humboldt River).
	9	39 53 26	115 54 11	Head of south fork of Humboldt River.
	11	39 47 01	116 33 39	Connor's Spring.
	14	39 11 57	117 14 12	Basil's Creek.
	16	38 49 21	117 16 52	Boiling Springs.
	17	38 33 17	117 24 29	Moore's Creek.
	21	38 23 11	118 24 51	Sagundai's Spring, Sheep Mountain.
	24	38 35 11	118 32 19	Eastern shore of Lake Walker.
	26	38 56 36	118 52 54	Walker River, three miles above its mouth in Lake Walker.
	29	39 09 05	119 05 23	Walker River, at its most northern bend.
December	1	39 33 48	119 30 24	Salmon Trout River, above the lower *cañon*.
	2	39 30 51	119 51 52	Salmon Trout River.
	3	39 22 09	120 02 50	Salmon Trout River, at the forks.
	4	39 17 12	120 15 20	Pass in the Sierra Nevada, at head of Salmon Trout River.
	6	39 11 06	120 44 24	On affluent to north fork of the *Rio de los Americanos.*
	7	39 04 11	121 07 48	On Martin's fork (of Sacramento Valley).
	8	38 53 05	121 08 49	On Hamilton's Creek (Sacramento Valley).
	12	38 34 18	121 19 26	*Rio de los Americanos* (opposite Grimes' House).

LATITUDES AND LONGITUDES—*Continued.*

Date.	Latitude.	Longitude.	Locality.
	° ′ ″	° ′ ″	
December 18	37 29 56	120 14 11	Aux-um-ne River (of the San Joaquin).
20	37 07 47	119 28 32	On an affluent to the upper San Joaquin.
1846.			
January 4	36 53 56	119 02 21	On the Tularé Lake Fork (*Rio Reyes*), one mile below the junction of Taplin and Stepp's Forks.
February 18	37 13 32	121 39 08	*The Laguna*, in the valley of *San Jose* (of Francisco Bay).
22	37 09 57	121 54 55	Road from *San Jose* to *Santa Cruz*, on the *Cuesta de los Gatos*.
23	37 08 45	121 52 40	Road from *San Jose* to *Santa Cruz*, near summit of the *Cuesta de los Gatos*.
March 1	36 58 43	121 48 51	*Uva Maron* Creek (Bernardo Castro's), Bay of Monterey.
2	36 54 41	121 34 00	On the Pajaro River (of the Bay of Monterey), one-fourth of a mile below *Anser's* house.
4	36 46 07	121 30 43	Gomez Run, at edge of Salinas Plain.
14	37 25 53	120 35 55	Towalumne River.
22	38 34 18	121 19 26	Rio de los Americanos, opposite Grimes' House.
26	39 07 45	121 30 21	Feather River, mouth of *Yuva* River.
27	39 27 17	121 32 35	Bend of Feather River.
28	39 39 05	121 27 55	Butte Creek (Neal's Rancho).
29	39 52 58	121 52 58	Pine Creek.
April 14	39 56 04	121 56 44	Deer River (opposite Lassen's House), half a mile above its mouth in the Sacramento.
25	40 23 58	122 03 27	Mouth of Nozah River (of the Sacramento).
26	40 38 58	121 57 24	Brant's Creek.
27	40 50 33	121 47 18	Campbell's Creek.
29	40 58 43	121 07 59	Upper Sacramento, above Fall River.
30	41 17 17	121 01 23	Upper Sacramento River, at upper end of Round Valley.
May 1	41 48 49	121 15 24	Eastern shore of Lake Rhett.
4	42 10 52	121 28 53	McCrady River.
6	42 17 56	121 52 45	Denny's Branch (of Tlamath Lake).
7	42 33 13	121 58 51	Ambuscade Creek (of Tlamath Lake).
11	42 36 35	121 58 45	Corral Creek (of Tlamath Lake), observation taken after the fight of the 9th to 10th.
12	42 41 30	121 52 08	Torrey River (of Tlamath Lake, observation taken after the fight at village.
14	42 21 23	121 41 23	We-to-wah Creek (southeastern end of Tlamath Lake).
19	40 53 19	121 05 57	Russels's Branch.
20	40 39 52	121 19 05	Poinsett River (of the Upper Sacramento).
21	40 31 54	121 36 16	Meyers's Branch (Sierra Nevada).
27	39 39 05	121 40 43	Butte Creek.
31	39 12 03	121 38 04	"*Buttes of the Sacramento*" (on a small run at the southeastern base).
June 7	39 14 41	121 33 36	"*Buttes of the Sacramento*" (on a small run or spring at northeastern base).

To all to whom these presents shall come, Greeting:

Know ye that, in consequence of propositions of peace, or cessation of hostilities, being submitted to me, as commandant of the California Battalion of United States forces, which have so far been acceded to by me as to cause me to appoint a board of commissioners to confer with a similar board appointed by the Californians, and it requiring a little time to close the negotiations; it is agreed upon and ordered by me that an entire cessation of hostilities shall take place until to-morrow afternoon (January 13th), and that the said Californians be permitted to bring in their wounded to the mission of San Fernando, where, also, if they choose, they can remove their camp, to facilitate said negotiations.

Given under my hand and seal this twelfth day of January, 1847.

J. C. Frémont,
Lieutenant-Colonel United States Army,
and Military Commandant of California.

Articles of capitulation made and entered into at the rancho of Couenga, this thirteenth day of January, Anno Domini, eighteen hundred and forty-seven, between P. B. Reading, Major; Louis McLane, Jr., Commanding Artillery; Wm. H. Russell, Ordnance Officer, commissioners appointed by J. C. Frémont, Lieutenant-Colonel United States Army and Military Commandant of the Territory of California; and José Antonio Carillo, Commandante de Esquadron, Augustin Olivera, Diputado, Commissioners, appointed by Don Andres Pico, Commander-in-Chief of the California forces under the Mexican flag.

Article 1. The Commissioners on the part of the Californians agree that their entire force shall, on presentation of themselves to Lieutenant-Colonel Frémont, deliver up their artillery and public arms, and they shall return peaceably to their homes, conforming to the laws and regulations of the United States, and not again take up arms during the war between the United States and Mexico, but will assist and aid in placing the country in a state of peace and tranquillity.

Art. 2. The Commissioners on the part of Lieutenant-Colonel Frémont agree and bind themselves on the fulfilment of the first article by the Californians, that they shall be guaranteed protection of life and property whether on parole or otherwise.

Art. 3. That, until a treaty of peace be made and signed between the United States of North America and the Republic of Mexico, no Californian or other Mexican citizen shall be bound to take the oath of allegiance.

Art. 4. That any Californian or other citizen of Mexico desiring, is permitted by this capitulation to leave the country without let or hindrance.

Art. 5. That, in virtue of the aforesaid articles, equal rights and privileges are vouchsafed to every citizen of California, as are enjoyed by the citizens of the United States of North America.

Art. 6. All officers, citizens, foreigners, or others, shall receive the protection guaranteed by the second article.

Art. 7. This capitulation is intended to be no bar in effecting such arrangements as may in future be in justice required by both parties.

P. B. Reading, *Major California Battalion.*

Wm. H. Russell, *Ordnance Officer of California Battalion.*

Louis McLane, Jr., *Commanding Artillery California Battalion.*

José Antonio Carillo, *Commandante de Esquadron.*

Augustin Olivera, *Diputado.*

Approved.

J. C. Frémont, *Lieutenant-Colonel United States Army, and Military Commandant of California.*

Approbado.

Andres Pico, *Commandante de Esquadron y en Gefe de las fuerzas nacionales en California.*

Additional Article.

That the paroles of all officers, citizens, and others of the United States, and of naturalized citizens of Mexico, are by this foregoing capitulation canceled, and every condition of said paroles from and after this date are of no further force and effect, and all prisoners of both parties are hereby released.

P. B. Reading, *Major California Battalion.*

Louis McLane, Jr., *Commanding Artillery California Battalion.*

W. H. Russell, *Ordnance Officer of California Battalion.*

José Antonio Carillo, *Commandante de Esquadron.*

Augustin Olivera, *Diputado.*

Approved.

J. C. Frémont, *Lieutenant-Colonel United States Army, and Military Commandant of California.*

Approbado.

Andres Pico, *Commandante de Esquadron y en Gefe de las fuerzas nacionales en California.*

Ciudad de Los Angeles,
January 16, 1847.

HEADQUARTERS, CIUDAD DE LOS ANGELES,
January 15, 1847.

SIR: Referring to my letter of the 11th, I have the honor to inform you of the arrival of Lieutenant-Colonel Frémont at this place with four hundred men; that some of the insurgents have made their escape to Sonora, and that the rest have surrendered to our arms.

Immediately after the battles of the 8th and 9th they began to disperse; and I am sorry to say that their leader, José M. Flores, made his escape, and that the others have been pardoned by a capitulation agreed upon by Lieutenant-Colonel Frémont.

José M. Flores, the commander of the insurgent forces, two or three days previous to the 8th, sent two commissioners, with a flag of truce, to my camp to make "a treaty of peace." I informed the commissioners that I could not recognize José M. Flores, who had broken his parole, as an honorable man, or as one having any rightful authority, or worthy to be treated with; that he was a rebel in arms, and if I caught him, I would have him shot.

It seemed that, not being able to negotiate with me, and having lost the battles of the 8th and 9th, they met Colonel Frémont on the 12th inst., on his way here, who, not knowing what had occurred, entered into the capitulation with them which I now send to you; and although I refused to do it myself, still I have thought it best to approve of it. I am glad to say that, by the capitulation, we have recovered the gun taken by the insurgents at the sad defeat of General Kearny at San Pasqual.

The territory of California is again tranquil, and the civil government, formed by me, is again in operation in the places where it was interrupted by the insurgents.

Colonel Frémont has five hundred men in his battalion, which will be quite sufficient to preserve the peace of the territory; and I will immediately withdraw my sailors and marines, and sail as soon as possible for the coast of Mexico, where I hope they will give a good account of themselves.

Faithfully, your obedient servant,

R. F. STOCKTON,
Commodore, etc.

TO THE HONORABLE GEORGE BANCROFT,
Secretary of the Navy, Washington, D. C.

UNITED STATES FRIGATE CONGRESS,
HARBOR OF SAN DIEGO, January 22, 1847.

SIR: I have the honor to inform you that the civil government of this Territory is in successful operation, that Colonel Frémont is acting as governor, and Colonel Russell as secretary, and that I am on board of the Congress preparing her for the coast of Mexico.

Lieutenant Gray, who is charged with my despatches, has been my aid-de-camp, and has done his duty with great good conduct and gallantry.

He is the officer whom I sent to relieve General Kearny from his perilous condition after his defeat at San Pasqual, and deserves the consideration of the department.

He will be able to give you the particulars of that unfortunate and disastrous affair.

Faithfully, your obedient servant,

R. F. STOCKTON,
Commodore, etc.

To THE HONORABLE GEORGE BANCROFT,
Secretary of the Navy, Washington, D. C.

OTHER
COOPER SQUARE PRESS
TITLES OF INTEREST

**HISTORY OF THE
CONQUEST OF MEXICO &
HISTORY OF THE
CONQUEST OF PERU**
William H. Prescott
1,330 pp., 2 maps
0-8154-1004-2
$32.00

**WOLFE AT QUEBEC
The Man Who Won the
French and Indian War**
Christopher Hibbert
208 pp., 1 b/w illustration,
4 maps
0-8154-1016-6
$15.95

**THE FINAL INVASION
Plattsburgh, the War of 1812's
Most Decisive Battle**
Colonel David G. Fitz-Ens
320 pp., 50 b/w photos
0-8154-1139-1
$28.95 cloth

THE WAR OF 1812
Henry Adams
New introduction by
Colonel John R. Elting
577 pp., 27 maps & sketches
0-8154-1013-1
$18.95

**ON CAMPAIGN WITH THE ARMY
OF THE POTOMAC
The Civil War Journal of
Theodore Ayrault Dodge**
Edited by Stephan W. Sears
304 pp., 11 b/w illustrations
0-8154-1030-1
$28.95 cloth

**THE CIVIL WAR REMINISCENCES
OF GENERAL BASIL W. DUKE,
C.S.A.**
General Basil W. Duke
New introduction by
James A. Ramage
536 pp., 1 b/w illustration
0-8154-1174-X
$19.95

THE TRAVELS OF MARK TWAIN
Edited by Charles Neider
448 pp., 6 b/w line drawings
0-8154-1039-5
$19.95

**GREAT SHIPWRECKS AND
CASTAWAYS
Firsthand Accounts of
Disasters at Sea**
Edited by Charles Neider
252 pp.
0-8154-1094-8
$16.95

**ANTARCTICA
Firsthand Accounts of
Exploration and Endurance**
Edited by Charles Neider
468 pp.
0-8154-1023-9
$18.95

**CARRYING THE FIRE
An Astronaut's Journeys**
Michael Collins
Foreword by
Charles Lindbergh
512 pp., 35 b/w photos
0-8154-1028-6
$19.95

MAN AGAINST NATURE
Firsthand Accounts of
Adventure and Exploration
Edited by Charles Neider
512 pp.
0-8154-1040-9
$18.95

A NEGRO EXPLORER AT THE
NORTH POLE
Matthew A. Henson
Preface by Booker T. Washington
Foreword by Robert E. Peary
New introduction by
Robert M. Bryce
232 pp., 6 b/w photos
0-8154-1125-1
$15.95

THE VOYAGE OF THE *DISCOVERY*
Scott's First Antarctic Expedition,
1901–1904
Volumes I & II
Captain Robert F. Scott
Preface by Fridtjof Nansen
New introduction by
Ross MacPhee
Volume I
712 pp., 147 b/w illustrations
0-8154-1079-4
$35.00 cloth
Volume II
656 pp., 123 b/w illustrations
0-8154-1151-0
$35.00 cloth

THE DESERT AND THE SOWN
The Syrian Adventures of the
Female Lawrence of Arabia
Gertrude Bell
New introduction by
Rosemary O'Brien
368 pp., 162 b/w photos
0-8154-1135-9
$19.95

THE GREAT WHITE SOUTH
Traveling with Robert F. Scott's
Doomed South Pole Expedition
Herbert G. Ponting
New introduction by
Roland Huntford
440 pp., 175 b/w illustrations,
3 b/w maps & diagrams
0-8154-1161-8
$18.95

THE NORTH POLE
Robert E. Peary
Foreword by
Theodore Roosevelt
New introduction by
Robert M. Bryce
480 pp., 109 b/w illustrations,
1 map
0-8154-1138-3
$22.95

THE SOUTH POLE
An Account of the Norwegian
Antarctic Expedition in the *Fram*,
1910–1912
Captain Roald Amundsen
Foreword by Fridtjof Nansen
New introduction by
Roland Huntford
960 pp., 155 b/w illustrations
0-8154-1127-8
$29.95

EDGE OF THE WORLD:
ROSS ISLAND, ANTARCTICA
A Personal & Historical Narrative
of Exploration, Adventure,
Tragedy, & Survival
Charles Neider
with a new introduction
536 pp., 45 b/w photos,
15 maps
0-8154-1154-5
$19.95